THOMAS MUNRO

The Origins of the Colonial State and His Vision of Empire

THOMAS MUNRO

The Origins of the Colonial State and His Vision of Empire

BURTON STEIN

DELHI
OXFORD UNIVERSITY PRESS
OXFORD NEW YORK
1989

Oxford University Press, Walton Street, Oxford OX2 6DP

New York Toronto
Delhi Bombay Calcutta Madras Karachi
Petaling Jaya Singapore Hong Kong Tokyo
Nairobi Dar es Salaam
Melbourne Auckland

and associates in
Berlin Ibadan

© Oxford University Press 1989

Typeset in Bembo by Spantech Publishers Pvt Ltd
5/58 Old Rajendra Nagar, Shanker Road, Delhi 110060
Printed by Rekha Printers (P.) Ltd, New Delhi 110020
and published by S. K. Mookerjee, Oxford University Press
YMCA Library Building, Jai Singh Road, New Delhi 110001

Contents

Abbreviations

Arbuthnot, *Munro Selections*	A. J. Arbuthnot, *Major General Sir Thomas Munro, Bart., Governor of Madras: Selections of His Minutes and other Official Writings*. London: 1881.
BR	Madras, Madras Record Office, *The Baramahal Records*. Madras: Government Press, 1907–33.
Gleig	G. R. Gleig, *The Life of Major-General Sir Thomas Munro* . . . 3 vols. London: 1830.
H.M.S.	India Office Library and Records. London: *Home Miscellaneous Series*.
IOL	India Office Library and Records, London.
MBOR	Madras [Presidency] Board of Revenue.
MC	IOL. European Manuscripts, *Munro Collection*, F/151.
PSSMSI	B. Stein, *Peasant State and Society in Medieval South India*. Delhi: 1980.
SEIHR	*Selection of Papers from the Records at the East-India House Relating to Revenue, Police, and Civil and Criminal Justice under the Company's Governments in India*. 4 vols. London: 1820–6.
The Fifth Report	*The Fifth Report from the Select Committee of the House of Commons on the Affairs of the East India Company, 28th July 1812*. Ed. W. F. Firminger (1917). Reprint edition, 3 vols. New York: 1969.
Tracts	John Sullivan, *Tracts Upon India, Written in the Years 1779, 1780, and 1788 with Subsequent Observations*. London: 1795.
Wilson, *Glossary*	H. H. Wilson, *A Glossary of Judicial and Revenue Terms . . . Relating to the Adminstration of British India* . . . London: 1855.

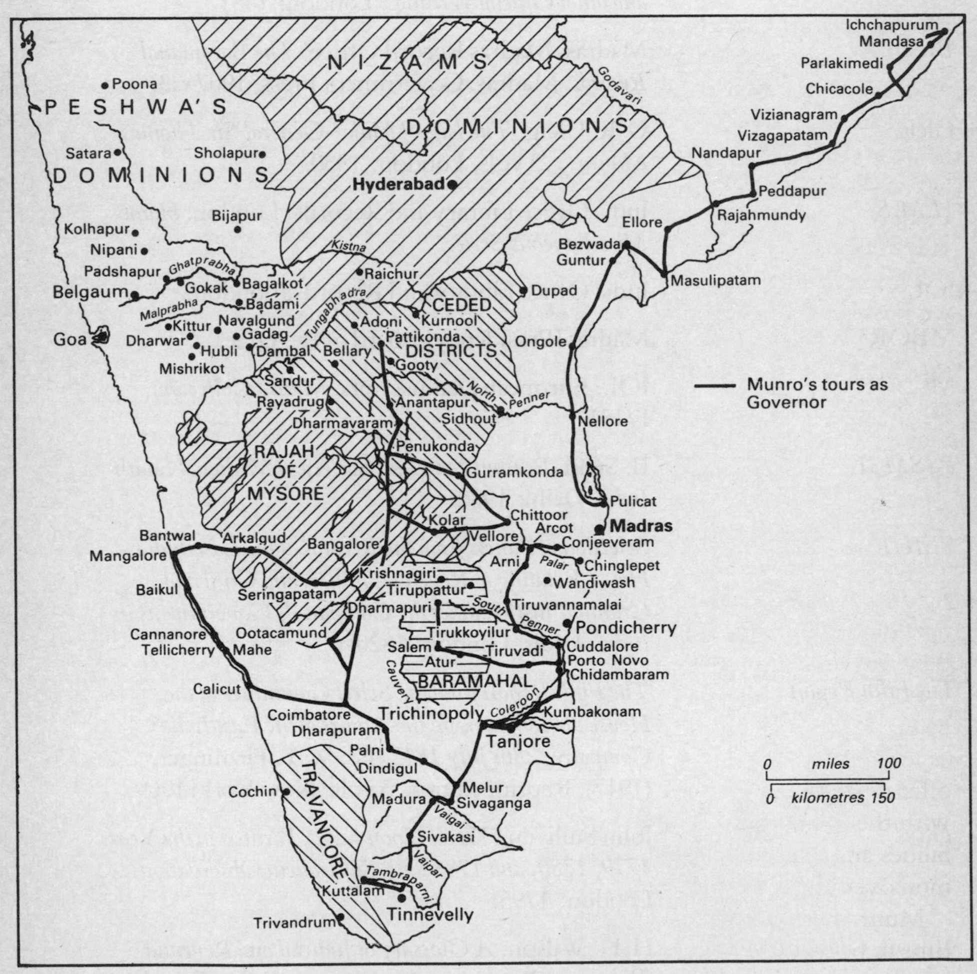

Map 1: General map showing Munro's territory.

Preface

Biographies are expected to entertain in ways that ordinary historical monographs do not, so perhaps no special justification for casting this study of Thomas Munro (1767–1827) in biographical form is required. Nevertheless, partly because Munro revealed little of himself in his correspondence and private papers—which covered almost a half century—and partly because I have not sought to present a psychological view of this major figure of the Indian colonial era, this work needs an explanation that another sort of biographical project might not.

There were several persuasive reasons for a new work on Munro. One is that it is possible for the first time in over 150 years to make use of his private papers.

In 1830, three years after Munro died, George Robert Gleig published a three-volume biography, for which he had had available the personal reminiscences of Munro's family and friends as well as a corpus of letters and papers that now comprise one of the more substantial manuscript collections at the India Office Library and Records, London. The personal recollections which Gleig incorporated into his study give that work an enduring quality that the otherwise obvious criticisms of it cannot diminish; however, the private letters and papers that had been collected by Munro's friends and relations in 1829 for the biography project are more important. When Gleig's work was done and the volumes published, these private papers reverted to Munro's heirs and there they remained until the early 1970s, when they were acquired by the IOL for use by researchers. Between Gleig's time and the present, several accounts of Munro's life were produced, but always without benefit of his personal papers except as these were abstracted by Gleig. Because of the copiousness of Munro's official papers, biographers after Gleig had much to draw upon, but obviously, with the full corpus of private papers available, unscreened by Gleig's sensibilities and interests, the idea of a new work on this 'founder' of British dominion over India became irresistible.

Munro perfected the system of governance destined to bear his name and in time to be adopted in many other parts of India between 1800 and 1807, while he administered the large and potentially dangerous territory called 'the Ceded Districts of Madras'. His system built upon his previous experiences in the

Salem Baramahal, from 1792 to 1799, as well as in the Ceded Districts; its roots were pragmatic and political and could easily have been forgotten along with other experiments being conducted by Company administrators in Madras as they sought to seize control and resources in new territories won in wars that began in the 1750s. Two factors saved and differentiated Munro's experiments, and these are keys to his personal and political development.

One was his ability as a writer to transform essentially pragmatic and political arrangements into a principled system. To accomplish this rhetorical feat required an oppositional 'other' in the form of the legal, administrative and revenue systems installed in Bengal by the much-respected Lord Cornwallis in 1793, the permanent zamindari settlement. By 1807 when Munro left the Ceded Districts, on what was to have been a furlough in Britain for three years, he had set forth his arguments against the adoption in Madras of the Cornwallis system and had laid out the principles of another system of governance phrased in terms of revenue administration and law. Here the second factor entered, the conjunctural London connection.

In 1807 there were others in London who had come to believe that the Cornwallis system was wrong for Bengal and even more wrong for Madras; these critics were also troubled by the sense that the eighteenth-century attacks upon the Company by Adam Smith and Edmund Burke had not been satisfactorily answered by the Cornwallis reforms. For, in Bengal by the early nineteenth century, many of the presumed improving landlords (zamindars) had lost their estates and were replaced by absentee commercial men of Calcutta; an anglicized judicature was proving very costly and too clogged by arrears to provide justice; and tenantry rights presumed to be protected were seen not to be. On Smith's economic grounds and Burke's moral and political grounds the Cornwallis system was found wanting.

But to a Britain transforming itself industrially, and to its politicians—who were changing the Whig constitution of 1688, were in the throes of creating a new world empire, and were resisting a French hegemony in Europe—the plight of Indians and the failures of the East India Company, in any but financial terms, were not vital matters. However, within the Indian establishment in London, especially the Parliamentary Commissioners for Affairs in India, or 'Board of Control' as it was popularly known, Munro's arguments for a new dispensation for India found advocates, and when he arrived in London in 1808 he began relationships with the most active of the Board's members that were to sustain all of his future activities in and about India.

The Board of Control under its first president, Henry Dundas, from 1784 to 1801, and under Lord Buckinghamshire, from 1812 to 1816, steadily eroded and encroached upon the control of Indian policy that had been vested in the owners of East India stock, the Court of Proprietors and their elected executive, the Court of Directors. Munro's programme became a gambit in the struggle between these two parts of what was known as British India's 'Home Government', and as the relationship between Munro and the Board ripened his leave was extended to six years. By the time that he returned to India, the relationship with the Board of Control had become an alliance. Out of this alliance in 1812 had come The Fifth Report of the Parliamentary Select Committee on Indian Affairs upon which the Company charter was renewed in 1813 and a new departure made in the British governance of India. A manifestation of the last was that when Munro did return to India in 1814 it was with a brief defined by The Fifth Report and with a charge to transform the internal administration of Madras Presidency in accordance with his principles. This meant 'ryotwar', or the collection of land revenue directly from peasant producers, eliminating all intermediaries; this also meant the replacement of an anglicized system of judicature by one based on what was called 'native agency', that is on what were thought to be Indian principles and Indian personnel.

As head of a commission empowered to change the internal administration of Madras from 1814 to 1819, Munro enjoyed continued strong support from the Board of Control and the intermittent support of those Directors of the Company who were persuaded that his reforms would save money and ease criticism. By the time his commission ended and Munro had added to his lustre by a brilliant period of military command during the final Maratha war (1817–18), Madras had been so profoundly transformed as to be considered in London a potential alternative form of regime for all of British India. During the seven years he served as Governor of Madras, 1820 to 1827, the potential became substantially realized. The adoption of his system in a Bombay vastly enlarged by the final defeat of the Marathas, and administered by Munro's friend Mountstuart Elphinstone, was a manifestation of this; another was the denial to the zamindari administration of Bengal of the Gangetic conquests from the Marathas, and by the adoption there of a system incorporating Munro's 'native agency' and peasant proprietorship.

By the middle of the nineteenth century other forces overtook his system of administration and his vision of empire. Still, Munro's reputation held and even increased in the late years of the century and during the present century. This was a result of his apotheosis as an imperial hero by whose benevolence towards and sympathy for the people of India the worst horrors of the Company raj were pardoned by an imperial bureaucracy under the Crown. But these were developments that occurred after his death and after his private documents at the IOL had revealed all that they could about Thomas Munro.

Apart from the restoration of this body of primary documents to scholarly use as an impetus for the present work, there were personal, professional interests that decided me upon this Munro project. In the early 1970s, when the Munro collection became accessible at the IOL, I had been working on and was completing a set of studies of early South Indian history begun fifteen years before. When I commenced my work on and in India in 1956, I had in mind a doctoral thesis on the rural development programme then being carried out in Sri Lanka and Tamilnadu (at the time designated Ceylon and Madras). Almost immediately upon embarking on this research in Madras, I found myself plunged into the past of South India, seeking what I hoped to be able, briefly and as background to my contemporary interests, to set out as the development sequence which led to the modernization efforts then in progress with the government and people of Madras. It rapidly became clear that no such brief and easy backgrounding for my project was possible; the historiography and evidence which I naively assumed could be readily recapitulated did not exist. Therefore, first tentatively, then with a clearer conception of the large work to be done, I began to investigate the history of rural social change in the southern peninsula of India. Twenty years were to pass before I had completed that research task on what I now know to be but part of the long, complex transformations through which the societies of the South Indian countryside had passed from the eighth to the seventeenth century.

By the 1970s, also, I had come to understand a good deal about the literature—sources and monographs—on the colonial nineteenth century, and about Munro's central place in that era of British dominance. I also understood, on the basis of my years of research on pre-colonial South India, that the major lines of interpretation of Munro and his works were fundamentally inadequate in one crucial respect. In none was there an historically founded understanding of Munro's system; none previously had a knowledge of the social, political, economic, and cultural pre-colonial foundations upon which Munro and other inventors of the Company raj in the South constructed the colonial regime of the early nineteenth century.

The availability of the Munro collection at the IOL therefore also presented a unique opportunity to bring together my previous research and to say something perhaps new and different about a man and his life that, even now, more than 150 years after his death, are still seen by people throughout South India as synonymous with the British colonial regime in its most winsome guise. I do not refer to the purported 'paternalist', 'romanticist', or Utilitarian orientations of Munro, for these are labels attached, most often wrongly, by scholars. I refer instead to another understanding of Munro that has long been acknowledged and celebrated by educated people in South India, that is as a man of an eighteenth-century world innocent of Victorian arrogance and certainties, who came to India as a young cadet in the Company armies and rose to be a colonial governor over the whole of the South from 1820 to 1827. From this vantage point Munro can be seen as a hinge connecting the long development of South Indian rural political and cultural institutions with the nineteenth-century imperial era, when the foundation of that modernity that I originally came to India to investigate in the middle of the 1950s was formed.

Since I felt that I could show what in Munro's world was an evolutionarily composed stratum, and what he and others brought from eighteenth-century Europe that altered an historic formation, I believed that the moment for another biography of Munro had come, and that I should undertake the work. That was over a decade ago.

The present book is the outcome of that decision. It seeks to answer three principal questions about Munro and his times. The first is, what should be understood as the 'Munro system'; the second is, how and by what hands other than Thomas Munro's was it constructed; and, finally, what has been the legacy of that life and work in the century and a half since Munro died. Death came to him in a tent pitched among a people who had come to look upon him as a rather austere benefactor, one who had invited them into a future that was to be partly of their design. That Thomas Munro could not fulfil the promise of his invitation was not because he lied, or died, but because that future could not be realized in the world then evolving under British capitalism and industrialization. What remained of Munro and his works very shortly after his death was only the dream of a benevolent, historically constructed India. As dream-stuff, Munro has continued to be invoked by the descendants of those who once could see what they and Munro thought was a different reality.

I have accumulated the usual obligations to people and institutions that I must acknowledge. Funds for my several research sojourns in India and Britain to make this book were provided by the American Institute of Indian Studies, the Joint Committee of the Social Science Research Council and the American Council of Learned Societies. To these organizations and to my anonymous colleagues who vetted and approved my several projects, I extend thanks. To the staff of the India Office Library and Records I express my gratitude for their unfailing consideration and efficiency. Finally, my thanks go to David Washbrook and Brian Murton for their readings of portions of this study; the usual responsibility for errors and flawed judgements that remain is mine.

Chapter One

The Beginning in Scotland and India

Thomas Munro was the second son of Alexander Munro, general merchant of Glasgow, whose principal business was with the American colony of Virginia; his mother, Margaret, was the sister of a well-known Glasgow physician and anatomist, William Stark. As children of a well-established merchant, Thomas Munro, his four brothers and two sisters, in other, more peaceful times could have expected to be reared in that style of hardy industriousness and gentility that marked the burghers of late-eighteenth-century Glasgow. But the last quarter of the eighteenth century was not a normal time for those in the Virginia trade, especially if, like Alexander Munro, they were not among the Glasgow 'aristocracy of Virginians'. These were the great firms in the American trade with sufficient resources to withstand the disruption of the trade that attended the revolt of the American colonists.

Though Alexander Munro had inherited his business from his father, Daniel, a second-generation resident of Glasgow, the family firm was neither large nor established enough to place the family in the patriciate of commercial families—the 'Virginians'.[1] Still, a secure status was theirs, and the means were available for each of the seven children of the Munro family to expect the excellent education demanded by substantial citizens of the town for their children. Moreover, if they were excluded from the status of the commercial aristocracy, the Munro family could claim another sort of standing—descent from a fifteenth-century Hugh Munro, Baron of Foulis, whose property was sold in the time of Thomas Munro's great-grandfather in order to pursue business in Glasgow.[2] This aristocratic claim was accepted at the time of the award of Thomas Munro's hereditary baronetcy in 1825.

Munro's first biographer, the Reverend George Gleig, had available for his

[1] *The New Statistical Account of Scotland*, v. 6, 'Lanark' (Edinburgh: W. Blackwood, 1845), p. 232.

[2] *Burke's Geneaologial and Heraldic History of the Peerage; Baronetage and Knightage* (London: Burke's Peerage Ltd., 9th dn., 1949), 'Munro of Lindertis', p. 1453.

task several living witnesses of Thomas Munro's childhood, especially his brother Alexander, an active collaborator in the biography project. The slender knowledge about Thomas Munro before he departed Glasgow for India and commenced a lifetime of correspondence was presented by Gleig, three years after Munro's death.

Along with his brothers, Thomas attended the Grammar School of Glasgow and for three years the college of the University of Glasgow. Mathematics and chemistry were favourite subjects and his teachers in each held out much for his brightness and industry.[3] The quality of his early education is a mark not only of his individual capacity, but of the high standard of education in the Glasgow of his youth. Some of both are revealed in an early letter to his mother in which he spoke of the languages he could use. These included Spanish, which he had taught himself, Italian, Latin and some Greek. His fluency in several of these was tested, he reported, by some of the early friends and benefactors he acquired in Madras, men of science as well as of business; among them was a Baltic German collector of plants and animal specimens and a correspondent with such famous collectors and naturalists as Joseph Banks and Charles Greville. The young Munro reported to his mother that he had translated some of the German naturalist's treatises into English for dispatch to Europe.[4]

Apart from his schooling, Gleig records a severe childhood attack of measles which left Munro's hearing impaired for life; also recorded was his subject's natural physical vigour that was to hold him in good stead throughout an active Indian career. Munro seems to have attained his full height of six feet by the age of sixteen, and this, together with his athletic abilities, made him as popular a companion for those his age as he was a student for his teachers.[5] Not reported by Gleig, but evident enough in the early correspondence, was Munro's often biting sarcasm that may have limited the congruence of admiration and affection in the eyes of his fellows.

Munro had taught himself Spanish at the age of sixteen in order to read Cervantes, and references to the character and adventures of Don Quixote dot his lifelong correspondence. An early instance is found in a letter to his mother in 1783 where he was answering her query about his appearance, after being in India for several years. He was, he said, six feet tall and lank as Don Quixote: 'a person of grave appearance and of a discreet and sober deportment'.[6] Another reference that was to recur in his letters home, especially those to his sister Erskine, was to a place where he and his family spent summers during the family's affluent years. This was on the river Kelvin, some five miles from Glasgow town, where the Munro family rented a house called

[3] Gleig, v. 1, p. 5.

[4] Gleig, v. 3, pp. 4–9, Munro to his father, 30 March 1780.

[5] Gleig, v. 1, pp. 2–3.

[6] Munro Collection, India Office Library and Records, London, hereafter MC, 151/140, Munro to his mother, 21 August 1783.

'Northwoodside'. Here, wood and stream created pleasures that proved more memorable than any of his other recollections of Scotland. The neighbourhood of Kellermont on the Kelvin had been the childhood home of his mother, which added sentiment to the nostaligia of summer holidays there.

At sixteen Thomas Munro was found a place by his father in the Glasgow firm of Somerville & Gordon to begin apprenticeship in the West Indian trade. This was usual for merchant families of Glasgow, for he was to follow his father in business.[7] In 1777 there was no thought that his education, his apprenticeship, and his future as a Glasgow burgher would deviate from a well-established pattern in Glasgow.

The revolt of the American colonies caused that to change, for the dislocation of the American trade upon which Glasgow depended threw Alexander Munro and many other small merchants into bankruptcy. The trade depression of the day was not solely the consequence of political events in America, but was an early manifestation of changing trends in Britain's world trade. By the early decades of the nineteenth century the whole of the British economy entered a downturn which lasted until the close of the century. Glasgow, because of its dependence on the shattered American trade, led the depression in trade that was soon to affect the entire British economy.[8] For many firms in Glasgow the severe depression lasted until around 1795, and Munro's father was therefore compelled to turn his frustrating and humiliating idleness to some account on behalf of his family.[9] With other poor and ambitious Scots he looked to the new colonies in India for the employment of his sons. During the 1780s Thomas and Alexander were found places in the armies of the East India Company in Madras and Bengal; his oldest son Daniel began a commercial career more conventionally in Jamaica, but ultimately he too became a soldier, and later a merchant, in India; and the youngest Munro sons, James and William, were being prepared to become military surgeons with the Company in Madras as well. William died in 1786 before completing his education, but James did serve in India with his brothers as a military surgeon.[10]

These were not the careers that Alexander Munro had planned or wanted for his sons; his inpecuniousness prevented him from providing any better in Glasgow. Nevertheless, there is something perverse in a view that he presented

[7] Gleig, v. 1, p. 11.

[8] Not all firms were so devastated, at least not immediately, according to an address to the throne from the major trading association, Trade Houses of Glasgow of 9 January 1777, which stated: 'We have the pleasure of informing your Majesty that notwithstanding . . . this unnatural rebellion our trade and manufactures in general are in a prosperous state . . .' *The Records of the Trade Houses of Glasgow, A.D. 1713–1777*, ed. H. Lumsden (Glasgow: Trade Houses of Glasgow, 1934), p. 572.

[9] For example, MC, 151/146, father to Munro, 5 August 1784 and MC, 151/148, father to Munro, 23 April 1793, in which the extended business depression is blamed on the government's deflationary measures.

[10] MC, 151/146, 31 January 1786; also MC, 151/147, James Munro to Thomas, 29 January 1790.

to his son Thomas in 1787, as if he and his brothers had somehow disappointed their father: 'I cannot help thinking that there is something singular in my lot, which is, that none of my sons had ever the least inclination to follow business at home, but all must go abroad'.[11] Then, somewhat spitefully, he referred to the better fortune of a family friend: 'How different from Mrs. Brown's sons, they are all careful and plodding fellows, and mind the P Cents'. Among these 'plodding fellows' was George Brown who was to become a wealthy financier in London, the investment agent for many Indian officials, including Thomas Munro, and eventually the partner of Alexander Munro, Thomas's brother.

Relief from grinding and humiliating poverty did not come to the Munro family until the middle 1790s. Then, Erskine thanked Thomas and her other brothers for setting up a £200 fund in London for the use of his parents; she reported the family was now 'diffused in an air of happiness and content which till now I may say we have never known . . . our Mother bustles, lays in her stores, and what *delights* her pays for them in ready money. We assemble round the little bowl every evening and the first glass is a bumper to the lads in India. . . .'[12] The 'lads' by 1796, when this was written, included Daniel in Banaras, Alexander in Calcutta and Thomas in the Baramahal of Madras. By now all were remitting substantial sums to their parents and sisters in order to end the social ostracism of poverty that had blackened their lives for twenty years.

Those decades had been difficult and distressing for the entire family. Alexander Munro's business failed in 1777 because he was unable to collect American business debts of £3500 to set against his obligations in Glasgow of £1780.[13] For the next several years he tried to re-establish his business on a consignment basis, selling coats, beer and ale, but he encountered persistent difficulties with Glasgow tax authorities. More humiliating for him was the reluctance of old business acquaintances to loan him the capital to proceed on a more stable basis.[14] But most humiliating was a judgment won against him by a set of Glasgow creditors for £700 which he could not pay and therefore faced the threat of imprisonment. His American debts were never repaid, and long after hostilities ended and normal diplomatic relations were established with the new United States, Alexander Munro complained to his son in India that American courts denied claims such as his, whereas British courts treated American plaintiffs with the same causes in a sympathetic way.[15] His later business ventures all turned sour, yet he pressed on with them. Munro's mother, writing in 1789, reported the failure of a business of four years' duration using funds that had been sent by their sons in India. She also hoped that her

[11] MC, 151/147, 27 September 1789.

[12] MC, 151/148, Erskine to Munro, n.d., but probably December 1795.

[13] MC, 151/146, father to Munro, 12 May 1782.

[14] Ibid., father to Munro, serial letter, 12 July to 23 November, 1781.

[15] MC, 151/147, father to Munro, 2 June 1788.

'lads in India' would create a fund for Erskine, their sister.[16]

Alexander Munro confided much of his bitterness to Thomas. In a letter of 1783 he criticized the indifference of Daniel to the plight of the family.[17] Moreover Daniel, having been some years in Jamaica and beginning to prosper as the manager of a plantation and merchant, now proposed leaving the West Indies and trying his fortunes in India. The father's resentment towards his son's irresponsibility and exaggerated sense of personal honour, which was causing him to abandon his profitable situation in Jamaica,[18] was reciprocated by Daniel, who complained to his brother that he had taken his position in Jamaica as a result of his father's pressure and against his own wishes.[19]

Their father's ceaseless scheming to advance the fortunes of his sons sprung from humiliation before his neighbours and former business associates in a Glasgow that, he complained, took no other measure of its 40,000 inhabitants than their relative affluence. He complained to Thomas in 1783 and later that he had little contact with old friends; they 'avoid associating with us because we are poor... since the [year] 1777, I have learned that in this country... people are regarded and respected in proportion to the weight of their purses'.[20]

A cruel manifestation of this poverty and ostracism that touched his sons in India, as it did the parents, was the plight of their sister Erskine, whose numerous letters to Munro in India display high intelligence, humour and affection. These qualities are manifested in a fragmentary letter to Thomas in 1788 in which she, now twenty-one years old, reported being attracted to the husband of a friend: 'I must beg you will be on the lookout for a husband to your sister... for to let you into a secret, I am in danger of breaking the tenth commandment for the first time in my life.'[21] To earn money for the family, Erskine was reduced to selling clothing decorations made from leather scraps and drawing patterns for seamstresses of the city. Alexander Munro bitterly observed that Erskine was without a suitor because he could offer no 'tocher' (dowry).[22]

Even in commercial and money-fixated Glasgow, however, family and male honour were not absent. Daniel, having departed from Jamaica, killed a fellow passenger and Scot named McLean on the ship bearing him back to Britain. He alleged self-defence but, to escape the warrant for his arrest for murder, fled to Calais while his defence was organized by the noted Edinburgh attorney, Henry Erskine. The legal fees were generously paid by Daniel's erstwile employer in Jamaica.[23] The notoriety of Daniel's escapade was added

[16] Ibid., mother to Munro, 22 January 1789.

[17] Ibid., father to Munro, 4 May 1789.

[18] MC, 151/146, father to Munro, 1 November 1785, in which Alexander Munro added that it was only during the brief period of Daniel's relative affluence in Jamaica that the family's desperate condition eased a bit.

[19] Ibid., father to Munro, 12 July 1781.

[20] MC, 151/146, 15 August 1783.

[21] MC, 151/147, 29 April 1788.

[22] MC, 151/146, 15 August 1783.

[23] Ibid., father to Munro, 22 November 1784.

to by an affray at the family's Glasgow home caused by members of the McLean 'clan' who broke in searching for Daniel at five one morning. Daniel was acquitted of the murder charge on grounds of self-defence in June 1785, but this did not wholly settle matters since the victim's kinsmen swore vengeance even if he were set free.[24] Hearing all of this, Thomas praised his brother's 'manliness and moderation' in a letter to his distraught mother, though Daniel, with more circumspection than was usual for him, was soon on his way to India to join a regiment of the King's forces there.[25]

More characteristically, family honour in bourgeois Glasgow was gauged by the condition of women, and if Erskine's stitching and drawing lowered status and kept suitors from her door, the question of the youngest daughter's (Margaret's) future was even more fraught. In 1795, as the family's fortunes began to ease, Daniel was proposing that Margaret, then twenty, should join the Calcutta fleet of brides for India, offering to pay £500 for her passage and outfit. However, as he wrote to Thomas from Banaras, his proposal was not well-received by his parents.[26]

This crisis of family honour was averted along with Erskine's lack of courtly attention a few years later. Erskine married in 1798 John Turnbull, a respected Edinburgh advocate and intellectual who was considered for a chair at the University of Glasgow.[27] Turnbull died in 1802 and Erskine was remarried in 1805 to Henry Erskine, the lawyer who had won her brother Daniel's acquittal in 1785 and who was destined for high political office, succeeding Henry Dundas as Lord Advocate of Scotland in 1806.[28] Margaret was to make an equally impressive marriage—to George H. Drummond of a leading Scottish banking family, in 1801.[29] Thus, the young women who for a time caused social distress for Alexander Munro eventually added lustre to his reviving fortunes.

A different source of embarrassment to the Glasgow household of the Munro family were illegitimate offspring of their 'lads in India'. Of their three sons in India, only Daniel was married and his son, John, was to serve as a Madras civilian official when his uncle, Thomas Munro, was governor. Alexander, or 'Sandy' as the family called him, and Thomas remained bachelors until they returned to Britain. Still, Alexander sent a girl-child named Mary back to Scotland in the 1790s as his daughter. The child was received with kindness, but, Margaret Munro wrote, 'she is woefully dark, we do not not give him [Alexander] credit for improving the breed; she is no beauty . . . upon the

[24] Ibid., father to Munro, 3 June 1785. Ibid., father to Munro, 23 January 1785.

[25] MC, 151/140, 16 November 1785; MC, 151/146, father to Munro, 19 March 1786.

[26] MC, 151/148, 22 December 1795, though five years earlier their father was anxious to send Margaret immediately, even scheming to have Erskine paint a portrait of her sister to be shown around by their brothers in Bengal, which Alexander Munro explained was 'a far better mercat than yours' in Madras; MC, 151/147, 18 August 1790.

[27] MC, 151/148, father to Munro, 23 April 1798.

[28] MC, 151/150, father to Munro, 24 March 1806.

[29] MC, 151/149, father to Munro, 23 February 1801.

whole it would have been perhaps better had he left her in the country. . . .'[30]

Then in 1789 an army friend, Lieutenant Macaulay, Persian translator of the Madras government, visited the family in Glasgow and when asked by Mrs Munro whether her son Thomas had ladies in India, said he had a '*black one*'. Startled by this, Munro's mother sought clarification and was reassurred by the Lieutenant that he had said something else—that his friend Tom Munro 'has a *levee* of Indian literati', of which his mother approved.[31] That Mrs Munro had heard right the first time is probable. Her son Thomas did have an illegitimate daughter called Jessie Thompson, whom he later settled in England and for whose care, education, and finally marriage he made himself responsible, and for whom he also made provision in his will.[32]

Of the sons of Alexander and Margaret Munro, only James remained to be launched upon a career by the time that some improvement in their financial condition had occurred in the 1790s.[33] Daniel, Thomas, and Alexander all contributed to James's medical education as well as to his outfitting, stock of medicines and passage to India. James's career there was cut short by illness, and he was compelled to return to Scotland, where he died in March 1798.[34] Daniel's marriage ended in as scandalous a divorce as might have been predicted from his past history. He fought a duel with his wife's lover and was seriously wounded, but recovered to care for his three-year-old son John, who was destined to continue the family connection with India into the next generation.[35] Alexander had managed to maintain a military career in Bengal at consistently higher pay and allowances than his brother Thomas in Madras, while also expanding his Bengal business interests in indigo production and general trading. By 1794 he decided for the latter activity exclusively, resigned from his unpromising military career and joined Daniel in business.[36] Both prospered and sent ever larger remittances back to Glasgow. Daniel died in 1799, leaving his son to be sent back to Scotland, and also a large debt for Alexander to settle.[37] In 1806 Alexander realized a considerable fortune from his Indian business when he sold it and joined his parents and sisters in Edinburgh, to which city the Munro family had removed in 1802. In Edinburgh the parents lived comfortably in a house purchased for them by Thomas at

[30] MC, 151/148, 24 May 1796, father to Munro. Munro's mother wrote on 18 August 1802 that Alexander's child, Mary, was being boarded with a clergyman's family and suggested that the girl's life was an unhappy one, 'of mixt breed', and ignored by her father and by society. Mary married a Glasgow clerk in 1804 according to a letter to Munro from his father of 31 August 1804 in MC, 151/149.

[31] MC, 151/147, 22 January 1789.

[32] This is treated later, in the chapter on Munro's governorship.

[33] MC, 151/146, father to Munro, 31 January 1786.

[34] MC, 151/148, father to Munro, 17 March 1798.

[35] Ibid., father to Munro, 14 March and 7 June 1799.

[36] Ibid., father to Munro, 10 December 1793.

[37] MC, 151/149, Erskine to Munro, 28 February 1800.

the corner of Frederick and Prince's Streets.[38] Margaret Stark Munro was to die in 1807, and Alexander, whose late letters to Thomas display a shakier hand, died in 1809, before Munro reached Scotland on his furlough.

For twenty of the last thirty years of his life, Munro's father strove unstintingly to do well by his son. He desisted only from the late 1790s, when the increased income from India permitted him to live comfortably according to the burgher standards of the time, and thus to cease striving to re-establish himself in business, to the relief of his family. The older Munro always found it difficult to accept how little his sons seemed prepared to do to repay his constant strivings for them, how unwilling they seemed to be to aid him on their behalf. Still, Alexander Munro sought to exercise paternal guidance from afar. Thomas, in Madras for nearly four years, was lectured thus:

> I have seldom had reason to find fault with your conduct; I wish not to do it. But I . . . suspect you have not acquired the graces, nor that you attend the levees of the great so often as you ought . . . humour their foibles and flatter their vanity and self-complacence. . . .[39]

There was some malice in such petty criticisms, especially when one considers the strenuous and inpecunious life that Thomas was following as a soldier in the desperate war against Haidar Ali Khan. In 1782 he expressed the hope to his mother that opportunities would open in America or in the West Indies for his two youngest brothers so that, when they came of age and must leave Glasgow as he did, they would not have to serve in India, particularly as soldiers: 'The life of a soldier in the Carnatic is perhaps more laborious than in any other part of the world. In just a few campaigns a young man has all the appearances of age and a broken constitution. He has no prospects to balance the fatigues he has undergone. . . . He may be a captain in sixteen or seventeen years, and even then he can but barely subsist unless he has an interest to get a command. . . .' But then he soothed his mother: 'all these dismal reflections, however, never give me a moments uneasiness, *for I am a great Castle Builder* and I can't get it out of my head that I shall do something very grand. . . .'[40]

As to courting the powerful, young Munro tasted sufficient humiliation from them to discourage someone with his pride and sense of worth. In his first year in Madras, he wrote to Erskine that the packet of letters of recommendation he had carried to Madras was useless.[41] Ten letters were for Sir Hector Munro, commander of the Madras army: how could the General '*venture to disoblige* so many people who are so concerned for my welfare', he asked. Indeed, 'I was so much convinced that I should have great interest when I arrive, that I could barely avoid telling some of my brother cadets, if they

[38] Ibid., father to Munro, 20 February 1805.
[39] Ibid., 16 May 1784.
[40] MC, 151/140, 9 April 1782.
[41] Ibid., 12 October 1780.

wanted anything in particular to let me *know*, and I would mention it to the Commander in Chief, who would refuse me nothing.' Sir Hector, it appears, received the young man's letters protesting that 'it was not in his power to do anything for me' and broke off his interview with Munro in order to see others with the same sorts of letters and needs, people 'whom he was likewise extremely sorry that he could not serve'.

Later in the decade, with many campaigns under his feet against Haidar Ali, the French and Tipu Sultan, and holding the rank of Lieutenant from 1786, he reported the same sort of frustration with another Madras commander, General Sir Archibald Campbell. The latter had served as Governor of Jamaica during the time that Daniel Munro had worked there and, on the strength of that thin connection, their father gathered up more letters commending his son Thomas to the General: to no avail, for General Campbell, a King's officer, appointed a host of his own relatives in royal regiments to posts usually reserved for East India Company officers like Munro himself. These included such lucrative posts as barrackmasterships, musketmasterships and town major of Madras.[42] Munro predicted accurately that Campbell's appointments, being illegal, would be rejected by the Court of Directors. But that would change nothing in Madras unless the Board of Control also intervened to placate the outraged officer corps of Madras. Campbell was shortly after recalled from Madras for nepotism.[43]

While Alexander Munro continued through the early 1790s to garner influence for his son, and even enjoyed some success, he also tried in other ways to benefit Thomas and himself through enterprise. One ploy for withholding some assets from his Glasgow creditors was to establish a new company—Alexander Munro and Sons—for the finance of which he had obtained a vague promise of a loan from one of the few old acquaintances with whom he had some rapport. Thomas was instructed to write to this man, John Harrison, a printer, thanking him for his prospective support. When this scheme too failed in 1784, Alexander Munro turned to a line which, he explained to Thomas, other former American traders were also trying, namely textile production. For this enterprise Thomas was asked to provide detailed information on the Indian method of dyeing red calicoes. Red dye, his father explained, was the only one which Scottish producers could not fabricate as well as Indian textile producers. With Thomas's fluency in Indian languages, he could make enquiries 'as a thoughtless soldier [and] if you succeed, your fortune is made'.[44]

Many letters on this subject were to follow, including some advice and queries from Thomas Munro's former chemistry teacher, Dr Irvine, on the chemistry of dye-stuffs. However, Munro in India disappointed all by failing to reply to queries about dyes and textile production for four years.[45] When at last

[42] MC, 151/141, abstracts of Munro's letters to his father in 1789.

[43] MC, 151/147, father to Munro, 12 February 1788.

[44] MC, 151/146, father to Munro, 4 August 1784.

[45] MC, 151/147, 2 June 1788.

his answers were received in Glasgow they were deemed wholly inadequate, there being nothing on Indian bleaching methods nor on finishing, and no samples either.[46]

Meanwhile Daniel had established himself at Mirzapur in Banaras, and invited his brother in Madras to join him as a partner in a business involving plantations and trading. Thomas, he pointed out, had been in India for ten years and his monthly pay as lieutenant was a mere thirty pagodas. With his intelligence and knowledge of Indian languages promising possibilities were open, and Daniel urged Thomas to take leave of the army for a year in order to try business. If the plan failed he could always resume his unprepossessing military career.

The advice and example of Daniel were given serious attention by his brother in Madras. A set of his letters to brothers Daniel and Alexander in the North contained detailed questions about production methods and costs,[47] and he and a Baramahal colleague, William Macleod, applied to the Madras authorities to rent some land in Salem district to raise indigo. This was refused, and there the matter of Thomas Munro, entrepreneur, ended.

Ultimately, such schemes for enrichment were abandoned along with the magical preferment that his father continued to seek for him through his somewhat tattered social contacts. That left only two paths to some significant change in his less than brilliant career: prominence through his writing on Indian affairs, and the renewal of war and the chance of rapid advance in rank.

Many of Munro's letters on military and political conditions in South India are of astonishingly high quality for one so young and without actual experience in war or the world. Other letters, more personal, display charm and generous self-ridicule. In London before departing for India, he wrote to Erskine, then nineteen, about being a poor, young stranger in the great metropolis, and of observing in Hyde Park 'the people of quality' in their carriages until, driven off by the crowds and the dust, he sought the quiet of Kensington Gardens. He also related how he was tormented there by a neighbour, a tailor's wife, who plied him with large bowls of soup—'I might as well have swallowed melted tallow'—because she was convinced that he was either consumptive or starving himself.[48]

An early Madras letter to his mother recounted an escapade in which he was the naive dupe of a swindle that left him almost naked and penniless for a considerable time. It began with the young cadet engaging (or being engaged by) a servant—'a grave, decent-looking man . . . [with] a bundle of papers in his hand which he begged me to read . . . certificates from different people of his fidelity and industry'. Congratulating himself on so quickly adapting to his new situation in India, Munro was soon persuaded by his servant that the clothes in his sea chest were quite unsuited to Madras and should be discarded

[46] MC, 151/146, father to Munro, 16 November 1782.

[47] MC, 151/142, Munro to his brother Alexander, 22 August 1794 and 2 May 1795.

[48] Gleig, v. 1, p. 2.

for a new outfit. However, recognizing the cadet's limited finances, the servant offered to sell them for Munro and, with a small additional amount, provide proper furniture for his small quarters. Clothes and money were handed over: 'He went out with . . . six guineas, leaving me with an empty chest, and my head full of new cuts . . . which the tailor was to make in a few days. But all of my schemes were disconcerted by some unfortunate accident befalling my good friend with credentials, for he never returned.'[49]

A year or so later the content of his letters began to reflect the serious matter of warfare as he became involved in the Carnatic campaigns against the French and Haidar Ali. At the behest of his mother he began a journal whose contents he would send to his parents from time to time.

His descriptions of the campaigns in which he took part during the 1780s possess the vividness of a participant, though he scarcely ever, except somewhat mockingly, referred to himself in them. Usually, too, he was more generous to French and Indian opponents of the Company—their bravery and skill—than to the commanders of forces in which he served.[50] Writing to his father on 2 October 1782 he expressed surprise that the latter could be interested in Indian events when his own fortunes were so dangerously tied to developments in America. He said that European impressions of Haidar Ali were quite erroneous; the Mysore ruler and his followers were not 'a parcel of blackamoors' to be routed with ease. Haidar Ali was a soldier and politician of great ability, and his army was both large and brave because the best Indian soldiery had sought service in the Mysore cavalry, or in its excellently trained and provisioned artillery or infantry corps. So fierce was Haidar Ali's challenge to the Company and its allies that most of the civilian population of the Carnatic had fled their homes, fields, shops and towns: 'the only inhabitants are garrisons of the forts, the British and Mysore armies'.[51]

Munro had good reason to respect the military threat posed by Mysore. He was part of the Company forces driven from Kanchipuram after Haidar Ali defeated and humiliated Baille's force in September 1780, and the young cadet was involved in five other defensive actions against Haidar Ali's soldiers in the course of 1782. He was also in the field when victory was narrowly wrested from Mysore at Cuddalore, in South Arcot, on 2 July 1782. This last battle was vividly described for his father later in the same year. After apologizing for the detail and length of this account of Cuddalore, he justified himself by asserting that the battle was a turning point in the struggles for the Carnatic:

> for what could have been a more serious matter, than to engage an enemy so superior in numbers, whose great strength in horse enabled him to take away every advantage, and when there was no alternative between victory and entire ruin? Had we been once broken, it would have been impossible

[49] Gleig, v. 3, pp. 9–13.

[50] Gleig, v. 1, pp. 27ff and v. 3, pp. .13ff.

[51] Gleig, v. 1, p. 30, Munro to his father, 2 October 1782.

> ever to have rallied when surrounded by such a multitude of cavalry. It was known afterward, that when the action began, Hyder issued an order to take no prisoners.[52]

His early military letters covered the second Anglo-Mysore war which concluded in 1784, following the Cuddalore victory. Military letters resumed in 1790–1 during the third Anglo-Mysore war. Between the two periods of active field service he was posted in sepoy regiments on garrison duty at Tanjore, where he was awarded a lieutenancy in 1786, and at the fortress of Vellore until 1788. During these years he persisted in trying for better, more remunerative postings so that he could make larger contributions to his family in Glasgow. Again and again, he found himself frustrated in this as young men with less seniority and ability, but better connections—like members of General Campbell's clan—received the plums of the service.

These were not idle years, however, nor were they years of total despair. He worked hard on Persian and Indian languages in the hope of qualifying for posts carrying higher pay. In 1785 he wrote to his mother that he had especially sought his appointment to Tanjore, shifting regiments to achieve this, in order to study Urdu and Persian with the famous linguist and missionary there, Swartz. His quick intelligence and application made for rapid progress. This is demonstrated in a letter to two intellectual friends in Glasgow, known only as Struthers and Melville, who were provided with what he thought might be a corrective view of the *real* India to set against their bookish understandings. He reported to these friends that he was 'amusing, or rather plaguing, myself with Hindostanee and Persian' and developing fair competence in both. Persian poetry that he had recently read was analysed and condemned as insipid as well as flawed by extravagant imagery. But Persian stories he thought were often quite excellent. Of one, 'the story of Shylock, which I found in a Persian manuscript' under the title of 'the Cazi of Emessa', he provided a translation for his friends. This translation found its way into Edmund Malone's edition of Shakespeare published in 1790, having been sent to Malone by a friend.[53] A copy of Munro's letter to Struthers and Melville, together with his translation of the story of the Syrian Jewish merchant, were sent by Munro to his father and earned a reprimand from him for not sending him equally interesting intellectual letters as he sent to his friends.[54]

This pleasant interlude from warfare ended in 1788. Then, Lieutenant Munro was assigned to the Madras army intelligence force commanded by Captain

[52] MC, 151/140, 6 January 1785.

[53] Gleig, v. 1, pp. 58–67, an undated letter from Munro but received in Glasgow in October 1787. Edmund Malone's Shakespeare variorum of 1793, referring to *The Merchant of Venice*, spoke of 'a Persian manuscript in the possession of Ensign Thomas Munro at Tanjore' in connection with Shylock's negotiation; cited in Horace H. Furness, ed., *A New Variorum Edition of Shakespeare; The Merchant of Venice* (Philadelphia: J. B. Lippincott, 13th dn., 1888), p. 307.

[54] MC, 151/147, father to Munro, 2 June 1788.

Alexander Read, with whom Munro's future was to be joined for a decade. Read was charged with securing the territory of Guntur, recently ceded by the Nizam's goverment of Hyderabad. Following that, Read and his small force were stationed at Ambur, near Vellore on the border with Mysore, to gather intelligence in anticipation of another round of conflict with Mysore, now ruled by Haidar Ali's son, Tipu Sultan. When hostilities actually commenced in November 1790, Munro rejoined the main army and until May the following year was occupied with field duties. He was part of the force that beseiged and seized the fort at Bangalore in March 1791, and he completed his part in that penultimate war with Mysore by commanding the escort that accompanied Tipu Sultan's two sons to Vellore, where they were to serve as hostages against their father's subsequent good behaviour.

The stream of letters that issued from Munro during the eleven years of soldiering in South India show him preoccupied with warfare. These are exemplary pieces, combining broad strategic and diplomatic analyses with descriptions whose vividness can only have come from a participant. Gleig, Munro's first biographer, who was a veteran of the Peninsular campaign under the Duke of Wellington, shared with his biographical subject service under that legendary commander. As an acclaimed writer on military life and history, Gleig's lavish appreciation of and citations from Munro's military letters are high praise. Admiring as he was, however, Gleig discreetly deleted the names of many of the commanders whom Munro castigated for poor field decisions. He also saw fit to delete Munro's complaints as a poor young soldier about pay arrears which he and his brother officers suffered, and their outrage at never being granted the level of extra battle pay (*batta*) that their counterparts—including Munro's brother Alexander—were awarded in the Bengal army.[55]

So severe were his criticisms of military superiors and of civil authorities in Madras that he, like others, often sent letters to Britain by way of visiting comrades in order to avoid censorship by functionaries of the Company at India House, London. One of his letters written from Cuddalore around the time of the battle was carried to Glasgow by the chaplain of the 42nd sepoy regiment because, as Munro explained in the letter, 'many letters are stopped at India House'.[56]

Increasingly, however, letters to his father turned to larger geo-political issues, possibly a reflection of his service with Read between 1788 and 1790, where political, not military, arrangements were salient. An example of this was a letter of January 1790, from Ambur on the flank of Tipu Sultan's Mysore. In it Munro offered an analysis of Mysore's strategic objectives and resources. He began this with an explanation of Tipu Sultan's plans for expansion along the entire western, or Malabar, coast of the peninsula. This would match the Company's control over the eastern, or Coromandel, coast, with the possibility that the port of Mangalore in Kanara would equal or excel that of Madras. It

[55] MC, 151/140, Munro to his mother, 9 April 1782.

[56] Ibid., Munro to his mother, 30 December 1780, and to his father, 30 July 1783.

was explained to his father that the Raja of Travencore, in the far southern portion of the Malabar coast, had come under intimidating political pressure from Tipu Sultan the year before, and this had led the raja to request two sepoy battalions of the Company in his territory whose costs he would meet. The raja's hope, Munro supposed, was not so much that these additional soldiers would deter Tipu Sultan's aggression, but that the Company would feel obliged to become the raja's active ally when the Mysore attack came. Tipu Sultan had now launched his attack, and it remained doubtful that the Madras authorities would engage on the raja's behalf.

Munro set out the principal reason why intervention by the Company was necessary: to construct the broadest possible alliance of powers against Tipu Sultan. Hyderabad feared Tipu Sultan's aggressive designs in the Carnatic and could be relied upon to remain neutral in any conflict between the Company and Mysore, if it did not join with the Company. The Marathas for their part were too preoccupied with their interests around Delhi to act with Tipu Sultan. Thus, Tipu Sultan could be isolated from strong potential allies. This grand diplomatic strategy was supported by potentially subversive forces within the enlarged Mysore state. The Company could count on assistance from many alienated groups, notably the Nayar chiefs of the Malabar coast whose ancient authority had been sharply diminished under Mysore rule.

The major problem was the weakness of British armies; they were as unprepared for a vigorous campaign against Tipu Sultan as they had been against Haidar Ali in 1780, notwithstanding the addition of several regiments from the Royal Army. Munro disparaged these European troops, saying that they were less hardy than sepoys and required far greater logistical support. In short, 'we have therefore made our army more expensive and numerous, though less calculated for the purposes of war, than formerly. . . .'[57] Nor, he complained, had any logistical improvements been made to overcome the glaring deficiencies of the earlier war. There had been no additional depots of stores and provisions established, even though the previous wars with Haidar Ali had devastatingly demonstrated the hazards and delays caused by maintaining all stores in Madras. Magazines ought to have been established where he was in Ambur on the Mysore frontier, for instance, for that was where the great threat would come.

Complaints of nearly the same sort were then being raised to the Governor-General, Lord Cornwallis, by the Madras authorities, but, unlike Munro, they were seeking to avoid or at least delay a dangerous war against Tipu Sultan. When Cornwallis finally determined that there would be war, he decided that he must personally command the forces because of the very hesitancy and unpreparedness of the Madras civil authorities. It was this same suspicion of the Madras civil establishment that persuaded Cornwallis later to turn to the military—to Captain Read and his subaltern officers, including Munro, for

[57] Gleig, v. 1, pp. 81–2.

the governance of the Baramahal after the war with Tipu Sultan brought that territory to the Company.

For the moment, as war against Mysore was being weighed by Cornwallis, Munro was writing to his father on the absolute necessity for war. His letter of January 1790 developed the following astute analysis of the threat posed by Tipu Sultan:

> It has long been admitted as an axiom in politics, by the directors of our affairs, both at home and in this country, that Tippoo ought to be preserved as a barrier between us and the Mahrattas. This notion seems to have been at first adopted without much knowledge of the subject, and to have been followed without much consideration. It is to support a powerful and ambitious enemy, to defend us from a weak one. From the neighbourhood of the one, we have everything to apprehend; from that of the other, nothing. This will be clearly understood, by reflectiing for a moment on the different constitutions of the two governments. The one, [Mysore, has] the most simple and despotic monarchy in the world, in which every department, civil and military, possesses the regularity and system communicated to it by the genius of Hyder, and in which all pretensions derived from high birth being discouraged, all independent chiefs and Zemindars subjected or extirpated, justice severely and impartially administered to every class of people, a numerous and well-disciplined army kept up, and almost every employment of trust or consequence conferred on men raised from obscurity, gives to the government a vigour hitherto unexampled in India. The other, composed of a confederacy of independent chiefs possessing extensive dominions, and numerous armies, now acting in concert, now jealous of each other, and acting only for their own advantage, and at all times liable to be detached from the public cause, by the most distant prospect of private gain, can never be a dangerous enemy to the English. The first is a government of conquest; the last merely of plunder and depredation. The character of vigour has been so strongly impressed on the Mysore government by the abilities of its founders, that it may retain it, even under the reign of a weak prince, or a minor. But the strength of the supreme Mahratta government is continually varying, according to the disposition of its different members, who sometimes strengthen it by union, and sometimes weaken it by defection, or by dividing their territories among their children. That nation likewise maintains no standing army, adopts none of the European modes of discipline, and is impelled by no religious tenets to attempt the extirpation of men of a different belief. But Tippoo supports an army of 110,000 men, a large body of which is composed of slaves, called Chailies, trained on the plan of the Turkish janizaries, and follows with great eagerness every principal of European tactics. He has even gone so far as to publish a book for the use of his officers, a copy of which is now in my possession, containing, besides the evolutions and manoeuvres usually practiced in Europe, some of his own invention, together with directions

for marching, encamping, and fighting, and he is, with all of his extraordinary talents, a furious zealot in a faith which founds eternal happiness on the destruction of other sects.[58]

In this and in another letter of May 1790, Munro, it might have been thought imprudently, attacked higher level civil and military decisions. Gleig, ever poised to censor the censoriousness of his biographical subject, decided not to publish Munro's sentiments on several matters, of which two are important. One was the deletion from Munro's January 1790 letter from which the long citation above comes. Munro had closed with the following jab at the civilian leaders of Madras:

Our operations [against Tipu Sultan] will be . . . impeded by the reference which it [the Madras Government] will, most likely, be judged expedient to make to Bengal, before we proceed on an offensive war. The public look impatiently for the arrival of [here Gleig deleted the name of] General Medows [designated as the new governor and commander-in-chief of Madras] and seem to be sanguine in their expectations of the effects to be derived from the ability and exertion of so distinguished a character.

Experience might have taught them, at least in this country, to build less on great names . . . [and] to prejudice them against any man who should come among them with such credentials.[59]

Or again in December 1790, Munro wrote from Tiruchirapalli ('Trichinopoly') where he was with the main army once again. Now commanded by Medows, Munro was even more explicitly scathing of his military superiors:

Much is looked for from the arrival of Lord Cornwallis . . . [who] has no person to whom he can entrust the management of a separate army. There is not a single military man in the country who conceives that Medows, or [Colonel] Musgrave are such men. Your old officers from Europe are good for nothing. They are seldom in situations which require the exertion of thought . . . and when they are cast ashore in India, or Tippoo [is] in their neighbourhood, they are lost.[60]

The General Medows whose reputation Gleig sought to protect (or was it the reader of his biography that was being protected from Munro's damnation of others?) was not long after dismissed from command of the forces in the field against Tipu Sultan by Cornwallis, who assumed personal command. Another whom Munro condemned in his correspondence relating to Tipu Sultan's attack upon the Raja of Travencore was Edward Hollond of the Madras government. Munro accused Hollond of 'corruption' and of 'greed' in failing

[58] Ibid., pp. 84–5.

[59] Ibid., p. 86; the original letter naming Medows is found in MC, 151/140, ff. 16–20.

[60] MC, 151/141, Munro to his father, 24 December 1790. Gleig tactfully selected these comments. See Gleig, v. 1, p. 107.

to give military support to the Company ally in Travencore until the raja should pay him some money as a douceur. The validity of this charge was confirmed shortly after when Hollond was suspended by the supreme government in Calcutta, a sign of Cornwallis's deepening disgust with the civilian administration of Madras.[61]

Munro's scorn would have meant nothing beyond a revelation of his evaluation of the men and problems of his time if it had been restricted to the privacy of letters to his father and family. Of course, there was also the possibility of having some letter containing critical comment read at India House before being forwarded to Glasgow. This might have incurred the censure of his employers or perhaps their even more stern discipline. But the danger to him was actually far greater because his father regularly made abstracts of his son's letters and sent them to such prominent men of the time as he could approach through intermediaries. As early as 1781, Alexander Munro reported that he sent some of Thomas's letters to the brother of General Stuart of the Madras army and to Sir Adam Ferguson, Glasgow MP and member of the Parliamentary Committee on East India Comany Affairs, chaired by Henry Dundas.[62] Both Stuart and Ferguson commented favourably to Alexander Munro on his son's perceptive reports, as his sister Erskine wrote at the time to tell him. She also added: 'your father . . . is *indefatigable* in spreading you fame . . . all agree *Tom* is a very clever fellow'.[63]

Alexander Munro even sent copies of the Indian letters to Jamaica where his oldest son Daniel was instructed to show them to the governor of the island, General Sir Archibald Campbell. The latter had served in India and would possibly do so again and thus could be in a position to do his son some good turn. The same letter that informed Thomas of his impending fame in another hemisphere also contained the practical suggestion from his father that the private and public portions of his letters ought to be separated to make the copying of the public portions easier![64] By 1784 Munro's Indian letters were being sent to Edmund Burke through one of the faculty of Glasgow University, whose rector Burke had become; this was at the time when Burke was drafting an India Bill for the government of Edward Fox.[65] Munro appeared to be indulgent of all of this activity by his father, and even of his father's proposal that Thomas send a political essay to *The Asiatic Miscellany*, and 'alledge [*sic*] you found it in an old Persian manuscript which accidently [*sic*] fell into your hands'.[66] Clearly, there was no limit to what might be found in old Persian manuscripts!

[61] Munro's reference to Hollond is in a letter to his father, 26 May 1790, MC, 151/140, f. 35.

[62] MC, 151/146, father to Munro on 12 July and 23 November 1781.

[63] Ibid., 1 November 1781.

[64] Ibid., father to Munro, 28 June 1782.

[65] Ibid., father to Munro, 24 January 1784.

[66] MC, 151/147, father to Munro, 27 September 1787.

But remonstrance against his father's promotions did come when he learned that his long letter on Tipu Sultan of January 1790 (cited above) was sent through a series of acquaintances to the editor of the *London Chronicle*. An abstract of this letter appeared in the front page of the 9 September 1790 number and prompted Munro to warn his father that he could easily be identified as the source, beginning as it did with:

> The following is an abstract of a letter from an Officer upon the Madras establishment to his father in Scotland. The letter itself makes one of a series which now has ten years retrospect upon our military operations in India. The writer, though not yet attained to the prime of life, has been in the service of Company since the age of seventeen; and, to the character of an accomplished soldier, joins an ardent love of literature, and a thorough knowledge of the languages of India.[67]

His caution seems to have restrained some of his father's more public venting of letters from India, though he continued to send copies or abstracts to the highest officials of the Company in London. Recipients included Henry Dundas and W. F. Elphinstone, who were reached through intermediaries. The older Munro was proud of his expanding contacts with important men and wrote, crowingly: 'as you must now be convinced of the respectable channel by which I come to Mr. Dundas, you will, I hope, have no hesitation, in future, of conveying to me whatever you may think worth his attention, either with respect to the revenue, or political state of the country.'[68] By the middle of the 1790s the exertions of Alexander Munro to publicize his 'very clever Tom' had become less necessary, for the latter was beginning to enjoy a modest celebrity and growing esteem in Madras and Calcutta. This arose from the circulation of his reports from the Salem Baramahal where Munro was carrying out civil administration under Captain Alexander Read. With the commencement of this new line of activity in 1792 there were fewer reasons or opportunities to write home about military and political affairs, though, interestingly, Thomas Munro asked his brother Alexander to pass to him any political news that came into his hands in Calcutta so that he might offer it to, and thereby impress, Lord Hobart, the Madras governor.[69] He could not have known during the early period of the Baramahal administration that it was to extend over seven years and that, at the end of that period, his reputation would assure for him a much longer career in civil administration than as a young soldier he could have imagined was possible.

[67] British Library, *Burney Collection*, v. 812, *The London Chronicle*, v. 68, 9–11 September 1790, p. 249.

[68] MC, 151/148, father to Munro regarding Henry Dundas, 14 April and 10 December 1793.

[69] MC, 151/142, Munro to his brother Alexander from Salem, 10 January 1795. Letters from 'Sandy' followed with the sort of gossip Munro had requested.

Chapter Two

Baramahal and Kanara

Munro began his second career as a civil administrator when he was a mature twenty-eight years old and an experienced India hand. Though his views on many aspects of Company rule were as yet unformed—as indeed were those of his civilian superiors—on one point he was at one with the Governor-General under whom he served. This was the desirability, if not the inevitability, of the elimination of Tipu Sultan's regime in Mysore. Lord Cornwallis had written in 1788: 'I look upon a rupture with Tipu as a certain and immediate consequence of a war with France, and in that event a vigorous co-operation with the Marathas would certainly be of the utmost importance in this country.'[1]

Military considerations alone cannot explain why Cornwallis placed his reputation at risk and violated commitments he undertook on becoming Governor-General by his determination to destroy Tipu Sultan's regime. Nor can the same determination by Cornwallis' successor, Lord Wellesley, be easily grasped, given the opposition of Henry Dundas' Board of Control and the war fears of the Madras civilian establishment. It is not easily explained even when account is taken of Wellesley's dread of a military alliance between Mysore and the French—which most contemporaries took to be exaggerated. The true reasons appear to be other. Among these were the political and administrative concerns of both Governors-General about the increasingly publicized mismanagement by civil administrators of Madras, and the growing realization that Tipu Sultan's regime constituted a dangerous and viable alternative to Company rule in the South.

SETTING THE TASK

Cornwallis' expressed reason for giving Alexander Read the Baramahal in 1792 was the venality and incompetence of Madras officials, which had become

[1] Cited in T. H. Beaglehole, *Thomas Munro and the Development of Administrative Policy in Madras, 1792–1818; The Origins of the Munro System* (Cambridge: Cambridge University Press, 1966), p. 12.

notorious in the dismal record of territorial governance by Madras over the Northern Circars; in addition, disquieting reports about powerful communal institutions were beginning to be known in the Company's Chingleput 'Jaghire'. Reports on the first tract of twelve years earlier by John Sullivan, and of six years earlier by James Grant, were known to Cornwallis.[2]

Both had observed about the 17,000 square mile Northern Circars, obtained from the Nizam in 1759, that it was not under the control of the Company after seventeen years of possession. An area of ancient and valuable commerce, with a reliable surplus of rice that was annually sent south to the Carnatic, a rich fishery, and a peaceful population, this tract was still under the rule of great and 'refractory' zamindars. Company officials had yet to determine how revenue was assessed on the land and how it was collected by the tax contractors to whom this was entrusted. Sullivan observed these things in 1779 on the basis of several years of residence in Masulipatam.[3] Cornwallis would also have had an explanation for why there was almost total ignorance about such a potentially valuable territory: no officials knew 'any of the country languages' and thus they depended upon 'native interpreters in collusion with zamindars . . . interested in concealing the truth, and of underrating their lands . . .' as both Sullivan and Grant had said.

At this time other disquieting reports were coming from another valuable and strategic possession acquired in 1763, the 2284 square mile 'Jaghire' near Madras. Lionel Place described a form of communal landholding there which not only made penetration by Company regulations and revenue demands difficult, but was, Place insisted, an ancient and viable land system with which it would be dangerous to tinker.[4]

Company authority and control, faced with untamed ancient lordships such as the rajas of Chicacole and Rajamundry in the Northern Circars or the communal unity of *mirasidars* in Chingleput, was not likely to fare better in the extensive, dry interior of Madras. There, in places like Salem, warfare and oppressive government had left an armed population deeply suspicious of all authority, another reason for turning to the soldier Read for the task of its administration.

John Sullivan's published work of 1795 had much to say to Cornwallis and others about the Northern Circars; it was one of two works published in that year that could have been influential with respect to the shape of the emerging

[2] John Sullivan, *Tracts Upon India; Written in the Years 1779, 1780, and 1788 with Subsequent Observations* (London: 1795) where it is stated that the book was prepared with encouragement from Cornwallis. Sullivan included a long 1779 letter to the Court of Directors on Masulipatam; another copy of that letter is found in the IOL, see the note below. Grant on the Northern Circars in *The Fifth Report*, v. 3. pp. 1–118, especially pp. 7, 17, 67.

[3] John Sullivan, 'Observations Respecting the Circar of Mazulipatam in a Letter . . . to the Court of Directors of the East India Company, 1780', IOL, V3226, especially pp. 35–47.

[4] Abstracts of these reports of 1799 in *The Fifth Report*, v. 3, pp. 149–67.

colonial state. The other was Charles Francis Greville's *British India Analyzed.*

There are few observations on South India during the late eighteenth century that match those of Sullivan's *Tracts Upon India*. This work was published six years after he had returned from over twenty years in India, and three years after he entered Parliament.[5] Sullivan had obtained an appointment to the Madras civil service in 1765 through the patronage of his uncle, the influential Company director Laurence Sullivan, and Warren Hastings' sponsorship had assured that his views would be given weight. In the course of his Madras career until 1789, he served in the Presidency city, in Masulipatam and in Tanjore.[6] He was military paymaster and Resident in Tanjore during the 1780s, when Munro was garrisoned there with the 30th and the 1st Sepoy battalions in 1785–6.[7] Though neither spoke of having known each other then, it is probable that they did, and it is also probable that each formed an appreciation for the other that was to endure until Munro's death in 1827. A reading of Sullivan's *Tracts* provides some understanding of the possible origins of some of Munro's later ideas.

Sullivan anticipated several of the major elements of Munro's later policies in the Ceded Districts, including the importance of awarding privileged, low revenue landholdings (*inams*) to win support for the Company among strategic groups in South Indian society; the need and the means for reducing the political dangers from minor warrior chiefs or *poligars* throughout the growing territories of the Company; and the appropriateness of the methods introduced by Read in the Baramahal.

In his *Tracts*, a 1780 letter from Sullivan to Lord North discusses inams. He says that inams should be granted to sepoy officers in order 'to encourage them to the best exertions of their talents, by holding out to them as a recompense... some distinction and emolument amongst their fellow subjects'.[8] Sullivan showed an understanding that seems rare among his fellows that inams were not merely valuable in material terms, but also a form of honour. Such distinctions for sepoys were imperative:

> Our empire in India, however strongly it may appear to be established, must always be considered, as having inseparably connected with it, the disadvantages of a foreign as well as distant dominion. It must be remembered

[5] See Sullivan's obituary in *Gentleman's Magazine*, v. 13 (n.s., April 1840), pp. 428–9.

[6] Mark Wilks provides some information on Sullivan's successful entrepreneurship, beginning with a successful tender, at the age of twenty-two, for construction of a new arsenal and hospital in Madras, before he commenced his service in Masulipatam; while in Tanjore he amassed a fortune as military commissioner of the southern Presidency: *Historical Sketches of the South of India, In an Attempt to Trace the History of Mysoor*... (Mysore: Government Press, original edition 1810, reprinted with notes by Murray Hammick, 1930), v. 2, p. 237.

[7] Gleig, v. 1, p. xv.

[8] *Tracts*, pp. 72–3.

that the army which protects it is principally composed of natives of the country, over which we have fixed our rule, that we differ from them in laws, in religion, in language and in all relations of society; and that under these circumstances, the best constituted government cannot secure permanency to such an empire, without employing an alternative and guarded policy that shall constantly be directed to correct the weakness and defects, which must inevitably grow up in such a state.[9]

To this sense of the precariousness of the Company's colonial regime, expressed by many others later, Sullivan added the following pragmatic and opportunistic solution to the problem of poligars in his letter to North. The Company must diminish the military strength of poligars and bring power to bear upon these local lordships by holding them to a high schedule of tribute, and deposing them when they failed to meet these demands or when any depredations were committed by them.[10] He considered the methods of 'Isoof Cawn' (Muhammad Yusuf Khan) a model for the Company on the control of poligars.[11] However, in neglecting to mention the 'rebellion' of 1763–4 by this distinguished sepoy commander when his request to 'rent' Tinnevelly and Madurai was denied by the Company, Sullivan showed that he had not considered how the contradictory aims of the Company—for a bureaucratically extractive system and the patrimonially oriented one—might have frustrated old regime figures such as Yusuf Khan. Sullivan also opposed the 1792 treaty between the Company and the Nawab of Arcot because it required the Company to recognize the petty sovereignty of poligars subordinated to the Nawab, and thereby jeopardized its military hegemony in the Carnatic.[12]

About zamindars Sullivan was partly pragmatic and partly principled. His view contrasted with Munro's shortly after, but the argument that he put on the matter was congruent with a later position taken by Munro.

Sullivan considered that zamindars should not be eliminated from those Madras tracts where they had been recognized by the Company. He asserted that South Indian zamindars were different from those of Mughal times: in Madras they were politically less independent, and paid their tribute to the Company punctually. The debts of zamindars were, he conceded, disturbingly large, but these could be monitored by the Company so as to manipulate and control zamindar debtors. Where Sullivan adopted a position on zamindars close to that later taken by Munro was in acknowledging that these intermediaries ought to be eliminated eventually so as to permit the restoration of local

[9] Ibid., pp. 77–8.

[10] Ibid., pp. 141–2.

[11] Ibid., pp. 142–3, and also R. Caldwell, *A Political and General History of the Origin of Tinnvelly in the Presidency of Madras* (Madras: Government Press, 1881), pp. 92 and 128, *passim*, and S. C. Hill, *Yusuf Khan, the Rebel Commandant* (London: Longmans, Green, 1914).

[12] *Tracts*, pp. 138–9.

government 'under mild administration of the Hindoos'. This had existed, he believed, before the Muslim incursions into South India.[13] But this course had to be pursued with caution, for refractory and suspicious zamindars had proven dangerous to former Muslim rulers. Bad as zamindar local rule seemed to the British to be, zamindars had long stood between ordinary cultivators and rapacious Muslim regimes, and therefore enjoyed a kind of popular legitimacy. This bond of loyalty to zamindars would pass with time, Sullivan thought, along with bonds based upon family and tribe, if zamindar tenure was made as secure as it had become in Bengal, he said in 1795.[14] The task of setting realistic, even enhanced tributes, or rents, from zamindars was made easy by the existence of 'village registers' of landholding and production which he had seen in the Northern Circars, and which he said were found in the Baramahal as well as in Mysore under Tipu Sultan.[15] Another means of managing the present roles of zamindars, he suggested, was through their judicial functions. Zamindars' judicial courts were essential to local society, and these were capable of being improved by the simple method of appointing 'three or more Bramans as coadjutors in each court, whose opinions should controll [*sic*] them in all matters of law' as long as these 'Braman's' were vigilantly attended.[16]

He also considered the question of money-lenders. The indebtedness of zamindars to 'sowcars' had to be ended, and this could be done by the Company deploying part of the tribute collected from each to a reduction of their debts, and to guarantee that all old debts would be repaid to money-lenders. He insisted that the latter could not ignored, nor their interests neglected: 'public credit' depended upon money-lenders, and the rates they demanded were proportional to risks.[17]

If zamindars were simply abolished, they would have to be replaced by others who might create even greater problems for the Company state in becoming. Sullivan thought Alexander Read in the Baramahal was proceeding in the best way with respect to territorial management in general and zamindars in particular. By using native records and adopting Hindu practices, Sullivan believed that Read had been able to double the revenue of the tract and still secure local magnates to British rule. This success was contrasted with the failures of the Company in Bengal, in the Northern Circars, and among the poligars of the Carnatic.[18]

On a final matter, Sullivan differed sharply with Munro. This pertained to the treatment of Tipu Sultan. Sullivan urged conciliation of Tipu Sultan after the humiliating defeat and treaty of 1792, from which much territory was

[13] Ibid., p. 201.
[14] Ibid., p. 258.
[15] Ibid., p. 209.
[16] Ibid., p. 287.
[17] Ibid., pp. 214–15, 218.
[18] Ibid., pp. 279–86.

acquired by the Company.[19] It was not that Sullivan thought that the defeated Muslim ruler was no threat to the Company, but he believed that his Muslim rule could be undermined from within Mysore itself through aid to the deposed Wodeyar family. To hasten this, Sullivan conducted secret negotiations with agents of the Rani of Mysore while he was in Tanjore.[20] However, he feared the potential threat of the Marathas more, and in this proved himself more prescient than Munro at the time. He was especially fearful of a future alliance between the French and the Marathas when the French recovered from their civil strife and returned to Indian problems in a serious way.

Sullivan's conception of the company state, as its territory was being trebled in the 1790s, implied substantial continuity with the existing regimes of the southern peninsula. On neither economic nor military questions did he see fit to depart from prevailing Indian usage. In this he opposed the general orientation of Cornwallis, and the encouragement which Cornwallis is said by Sullivan to have given to the publication of his *Tracts* reflects credit upon the elder statesman. The purpose of that publication was to describe the ancient revenue system of the Hindus and to persuade the 'Company to engraft upon those established usages, a permanent administration instead of the arbitrary and precarious mode then in use' in Company territories, including the Northern Circars'.[21] In his 1795 notes to the letters he had sent fifteen years earlier to Lord North, Dundas, and the Court of Directors, he cautiously observed that the principles of Cornwallis' Bengal settlement, as he understood them, were in general accord with his own principles; yet he also observed that Shore's opposition to Cornwallis had been too hastily rejected:

> The arguments of Sir John Shore ['recommending a gradual and progressive course for the improvement of our internal system in Bengal, in preference to one that should attempt to embrace the whole at once'] did not prevail, and therefore it is to be presumed that Lord Cornwallis, who held an opposite view, and the Board of Controll [*sic*] with whom the final decision of this question rested were satisfied that the information then before them... was sufficiently full to warrant the immediate establishment of the system in all its extent.[22]

If Shore's cautious approach was thought to be incorrect for Bengal, Sullivan thought it was quite correct for Madras. Existing or past revenue practices, or ideas and principles about them, were a mystery to the British in the Carnatic and in the Northern Circars. Much could be learned about both from extant

[19] Ibid., p. 118.

[20] Wilks, *Sketches*, v. 2, p. 239, on Sullivan's efforts through an agent of the rani. Also, Sullivan to Gilbert Elliot, Bart. (Lord Minto), 17 July 1783 ('My dearest friend. . . .'), Edinburgh, National Library of Scotland, Minto Papers, MS. 11143, f. 12, where Sullivan refers to his Mysore strategy.

[21] *Tracts*, pp. iii–iv.

[22] Ibid., pp. xxv–vi.

records in many places, but these had not been investigated, and certain important lines of investigation were now being closed. Here Sullivan hazarded the dreaded name of Warren Hastings. Saying that he had refrained from any references to Hastings because of 'motives of delicacy' in view of Hastings' impeachment, he added that 'admitted and historic facts' required recognition of Hastings' important contribution to the understanding of governance principles in prior regimes by his support of translations and codifications of Muslim and Hindu legal works. This was a slap at Parliamentary colleagues in England as well as post-Hastings modernizers in Bengal.[23]

British India Analyzed, published in the same year as Sullivan's *Tracts*, was, if anything, a more powerful statement on the advanced character of pre-colonial Indian administrative institutions.[24] The core of this work is a long translation of Tipu Sultan's 1787 administrative regulations for Omalur, in modern Coimbatore.

Like Sullivan, who had served as Under-Secretary of State for War and Colonies from 1801 to 1804, as Parliamentary Commissioner of Trade and as Privy Councillor from 1805, and as Parliamentary Commissioner on the Board of Control for over twenty years, Charles Francis Greville (1749–1809) was a man of standing in the British political establishment. He was the second son of Francis, the first Earl of Warwick, whose older brother's parliamentary seat and place on the Board of Trade he assumed when the latter succeeded to the earldom in 1774. In addition to the Board of Trade, Greville served on the Admiralty Board, as Treasurer of the Household, and as vice-chamberlain from 1794 to 1809. An opponent of Pitt, he was in opposition for much of his political career, from which he retired in 1790.[25] In the introduction of *British India Analyzed* Greville declared his disinterest. He stated that he was never a servant of the East India Company nor a holder of its shares, and he explained that his interest in India arose from the many of friends who served there.[26] An example of his Indian interest, prior to the book, was his placing before colleagues in the House of Commons an early work of James Grant on the Bengal land system. This was apparently a part of Greville's defence of John Macpherson, who attempted to continue the work of Warren Hastings—in opposition to Shore, Francis and others—for a permanent zamindari settle-

[23] Ibid., pp. xxiv–xxx.

[24] The IOL copy of *British India Analyzed* has the name 'Charles F. Greville' pencilled into the title page. Greville is mentioned as the author in catalogues of contemporary publications, though Wilks calls the work anonymous, *Sketches*, v. 2, p. 565n.

[25] Sir Lewis Namier and J. Brooke, *The History of Parliament: The House of Commons, 1754–1790* (London: HMSO, 1964), v. 2, pp. 550–1.

[26] *British India Analyzed*, p. xiii, also has the suggestion that the author did not include his name because of the imperfect nature of the work. However, S. A. Allibone lists the name of Greville, with no Christian name, for the work, which is said to have been published in 1793: *A Critical Dictionary of English Literature and British and American Authors*... (Philadelphia: Childs and Peterson, 1854), v. 1, p. 739.

ment there.[27] He was a friend of Macpherson and believed that the latter had been shabbily treated in being dismissed from the acting governor-generalship to make room for Cornwallis; a section of *British India Analyzed* is devoted to a defence of Macpherson's policies as Governor-General.[28]

The private papers of Greville indicate that he was in regular correspondence with Colonel John Murray, Military Auditor-General of India, and other public officials in Calcutta in the late 1780s, from whom he learned much about a variety of political and administrative matters.[29] He also conducted a wide correspondence with others on topics in which he had an interest, including Asian antiquities, botany, zoology and geology.[30] Alexander Read may have been among his many Indian friends. A file of Greville's papers at the IOL contains Read's will, of which Greville was an executor. Whether Greville knew Read before his Baramahal service is unlikely since Read was a poor young man from Dundee before entering the Company service, someone far in class and geography from Greville. The two could have become acquainted during Read's stay in England after Baramahal and before he took up residence in Malta, where he died. In any case, Read asked Greville to act as executor of his will in 1803.

The declared purpose of the three volumes of *British India Analyzed* is somewhat confused. It is stated to be to confront the recently passed 1793 Charter Act with certain of the realities of Muslim rule in India, as drawn from the *al Sirajiyya* of Tipu Sultan.[31] Few would now, or then, have accepted Greville's claim that by the 1793 Act 'Mr. Dundas has combined in one act of Parliament the interests of *Great Britain* [*sic*] and of the East India Company, and that the prosperity of Great Britain and of British India is attainable by the judicious application of its powers.'[32] The 1793 Act merely extended the powers of the Governor General to his exercise of supreme authority over Madras and Bombay and provided some space for private trade goods on Company

[27] Greville's action is mentioned in *British India Analyzed*, v. 2, p. 383, rather strangely in being the only place in the work that his name appears; this involves an encomium from Philip Francis, against whom Greville's work was explicitly directed, e.g. v. 1, p. iii. On James Grant's opposition to the permanent settlement, see Ranajit Guha, *A Rule of Property for Bengal: An Essay on the Idea of Permanent Settlement* (Paris: Mouton, 1963), pp. 164–5.

[28] Hastings correspondence is mentioned in a letter to Macpherson in 1780 in which Hastings referred to 'your friend, Mr. Greville', *Warren Hastings Letters to Sir John Macpherson*, ed. H. Dodwell (London: Faber and Gwyer, n.d.), pp. 61–3.

[29] British Library, The Hamilton-Greville Papers, Ad. MS. 40716, ff. 9–10, 11–27, 36–7, 50–8, 119–32.

[30] Ibid., Ad. MS. 42071, ff. 84–8, 146. In 1810 Parliament appropriated £13,727 for the purchase of Greville's 20,000 specimens of precious and semiprecious stones and their display cases for the British Museum, *The Annual Register, a View of the History, Politics and Literature of the Year 1810*, pp. 263 and 424.

[31] *British India Analyzed*, v. 1, p. iv.

[32] Ibid., p. i.

vessels. Hence, Greville must have had in mind Cornwallis' land and judicial enactments in Bengal of 1793. This suggestion is supported by another somewhat confused statement in his introduction, where he says that 'the revenue regulations of Tippoo Sultaun appear conclusive both against Mr. Francis and Sir John Shore's revenue plans. . . .'[33] But he does not say that Tipu Sultan's regulations support the Cornwallis scheme! If Greville intended that the confrontation be with Cornwallis' permanent system in Bengal—as Sullivan's work more explicitly is—he was certainly being more circumspect than Sullivan. However, Greville does criticize the Cornwallis plan for having closed off further and needed investigation of existing administrative usage, and for not using the existing resources of knowledge available from local village records.[34] Sullivan saw the Mysore regulations as illustrating his own notion of ancient and still relevant forms of Hindu revenue administration; it is evident that Greville did also, and thus it is possible that his work was intended as a criticism of the new Bengal scheme.

There are differences between Sullivan's *Tracts* and Greville's work. Partly, these arise from approach, and partly from the fact of Sullivan's experience in the several parts of India on which he comments; this contrasts with Greville's dependence upon the descriptions of others. Still, the detailed explanation of administration under Tipu Sultan provides support to the case argued in Sullivan's work, i.e. Indian administrative usages were fully capable of providing the basis for British colonial institutions with some minor modifications.[35]

Sullivan saw Tipu Sultan's regulations as independently corroborating his own views, expressed as early as 1779 to the Court of Directors about the Northern Circars. Sullivan then claimed that Muslim rulers like Tipu Sultan adopted ancient Hindu practices for their own purposes. This notion was shared by another knowledgeable commentator on South India, Mark Wilks, whose *Historical Sketches of the South of India* was published in 1810, after Wilks had served as Resident to the Mysore durbar from 1803 to 1808. Wilks confirmed that Tipu Sultan's regulations, *al Sirajiyya*, had been obtained by Greville's friend Colonel John Murray, then a member of Cornwallis' staff in 1792, and that Murray had passed this Persian text to Burrish Crisp, whose translation was published during the same year in Calcutta.[36] It was Wilks's view that these regulations of Tipu Sultan were in essence the regulations first introduced by the Wodeyar king Chikkadevaraja (d. 1702), adapted by Haidar Ali

[33] Ibid., p. ii.

[34] Ibid., v. 2, pp. 424–5.

[35] *Tracts*, pp. xxix–xxx. It would appear, also, that the two were the merest of acquaintances, judging from the very formal note from Sullivan to Greville in April 1802 thanking him for a paper on Dutch Guiana, in British Library, Hamilton-Greville Papers, Ad. MS. 42071, v. 2, f. 294. 67; *Tracts*, p. xxiv.

[36] B. Crisp, *The Mysorean Regulations, Translated from the Persian* (Calcutta: 1792), cited in Wilks, *Sketches*, v. 1, p. xl. Colonel Murray was also known to Read from the Mysore service they shared, as well as through Greville.

and later used by Tipu Sultan, who falsely claimed they were of his invention.[37] If Wilks could see through this deception, it is difficult to suppose that contemporaries of Tipu Sultan could not. As to Tipu Sultan's commercial regulations, promulgated around the same time, Wilks dismissed these as being the prevailing regulations of the Company at Madras, adopted by the sultan with the intention of 'making the sovereign, if not the sole, the chief merchant of his dominions'.[38] Wilks's unsubstantiated derogations of the originality of Tipu Sultan's administrative and commercial regulations carries the noteworthy implication that these were actually followed in Mysore before the restoration of the Wodeyar kings in 1799, something which was denied by many, including Munro, who knew Mysore far less well than Wilks did.

The regulations called *al Sirajiyya* were ordered to be adopted in Omalur in 1786 or 1788.[39] The comprehensiveness of these regulations would have prompted both Greville and Sullivan to attach importance to them. But more than that, these regulations supported the contentions of each that there existed in India a basis for rule that required no significant modification and certainly no replacement by wholly foreign and new principles such as were introduced in Bengal in 1793. The Omalur regulations cannot, either, be dismissed as formulaic or stereotypic outpourings of Tipu Sultan's grandiose notions, as some British contemporaries chose to label them. Regulations issued by him for the *taluk* of Rayacotta, forty miles from Bangalore and the same distance from Omalur, show variation from the Omalur regulations in style and content.[40]

The main objective of these regulations was to strengthen Tipu Sultan's military by increasing the flow of resources to various sections of his army. To effect this, the civil administration he inherited from Haidar Ali was altered. Revenue was no longer to be raised through tax farmers, but was to be collected by *amildars* appointed by a provincial governor, *asaf*, of which there were eighteen in 1792 and thirty-seven in 1799. Each amildar was to have two subordinate *sheristadars*, and it was to these three officials that the *al Sirajiyya* was addressed. Among the features of the system set forth were: (1) a village settlement made with hereditary headmen who were to be active cultivators of their own fields, with revenue records of each village to be kept by accountants who, because they often were not regular cultivators, were to receive a money salary; (2) assessment was to be based on actual production, with the

[37] Wilks, *Sketches*, v. 1, p. 573.

[38] Ibid., pp. 568 and 570.

[39] *British India Analyzed*, v. 1, p. 94; at the conclusion of the translated regulations there is a statement that the regulations above were to be added to those at Omalur during 'the year of Mahomed, 1215' (1785–6). M. H. Gopal has argued that that, according to Tipu Sultan's calendrical reckoning, the date would be 1788: *Tipu Sultan's Mysore; An Economic Study* (Bombay: Popular Prakashan, 1971), p. 105, n. 37.

[40] These regulations are found in IOL, *H.M.S.*, v. 251, ff. 167–282, 'Translations of Regulations of Tippoo Sultaun for the Management of His Country, Directed to Amuls and Sheristehdars... in the District of Raicottah, Subordinate to the Cutcherry of Bangalore'.

right of officials to inflict corporal punishment upon headmen who failed to maintain full production on village lands; (3) productivity advances and preferential tax rates were to extend production, especially the cultivation of new crops such as sugarcane; (4) tree plantings were to be undertaken by officials for their marketable fruits and for timber suitable for gun carriages; (5) all inam land was to be measured and many types of inams, including those enjoyed by Brahmans and by temples, were to be resumed, and full revenue collected; (6) irrigation works were to be inspected and repairs undertaken under the supervision of state officials, and new irrigation works were to be encouraged by the grant of inams such as *dasavanda* and *kuttukuttage*; (7) cavalry mounts and bullocks for military service were to be maintained by officials; (8) local militias, armed with firelocks and drilled weekly, were to be organized; (9) trade with Madras, or 'Cheenapatam', was prohibited, and encouragement given to trade between the towns of Mysore and the ports of Malabar and Kanara; (10) military industries such as gun foundries and saltpetre factories, and provisioning of all forts and garrisons were to be seen to by officials. In addition, Tipu Sultan changed the official designation of all weights, measures and coins, and adopted a new, Muslim calendar.

A second set of documents contains Tipu Sultan's 'commercial regulations' issued to the 'commercial department' (*mulikut tujar*) of his government.[41] These provide details of a state trade in valuable commodities such as sandalwood, silk, spices, coconut, rice, sulphur, and elephants imported into and exported from Mysore. Trade centres (*kohties*) were established in thirty places in Mysore; in the neighbouring territories under Tipu Sultan's control (e.g. Gurramkonda, Gooty, Dharmavaram and other places later included in the Ceded Districts administered by Munro); in Kanara and other places on the western coast as far north as Kutch; in Madras, Pondicherry, Hyderabad and other 'foreign' places' (despite the ban on trade there, according to the *Sirajiyya*), including Muscat. Provincial governors (*asafs*) were to recruit suitably trained and experienced subordinates to run the trade centres, and each was to be placed under oath according to their respective faiths. Trade capital was to be provided for these trade centres from the revenue collected by state officials, and provision made for accepting deposits of private persons as investments in the state trade with returns fixed at around 35 per cent. Provincial officials (asafs and amildars) were permitted to participate in the trade, but only with their own funds; private traders were also to be allowed to participate in any sales of commodities that were deemed beneficial for the state. Financial records and commercial decisions by those managing each trade centre were to be presented at regular durbars convened by Tipu Sultan for that purpose, and the latter's written permission was to be had before granting large trade advances. In addition, funding for the construction of sea-going

[41] *Select Letters of Tippoo Sultaun to Various Public Functionaries . . . edited by William Kirkpatrick, Colonel, East India Company* (London: 1811), Appendix E, 'Commercial Regulations, dated 25 March 1793 and 2 April 1794'.

merchant and naval vessels was provided from the central treasury. Finally, currency was to be strictly regulated by restricting the minting of coins to five mints in Seringapatam, of which one was exclusively for gold and silver coins.

That Tipu Sultan's agrarian regulations were not fanciful, as alleged, or unique, is supported by regulations of Maratha rajas of Tanjore which provided comprehensive state management of the economy of that territory. They were based upon the usage introduced under the Maratha rajas there and were repromulgated for *tahsildars* (subordinate revenue officials) after the Company annexed Tanjore in 1799. These regulations of 1802 constitute a project of resource control that went beyond merely collecting the revenue to the maintenance of urban as well as export markets; it was an ambitious mercantilist-bureaucratic scheme.

Orders to tahsildars consisting of some 230 paragraphs were circulated throughout Tanjore, under the title 'Public Instructions to Tassildars', by the first collector of the province, Charles Harris. He justified them as an explicit code for the governance of prosperous Tanjore's 420,000 people who had previously been ruled by its provisions under the Marathas without code.[42]

The first part of the 1802 Tanjore Maratha ordinances specified the formal responsibilities and powers of the tahsildar. His 'cutcherrie', or office, was to be set up on a street other than the one where his house was; the office was to be 120 by 40 feet, with shade trees (three kinds were suggested); all business was to be conducted there, never at his home, and 'nothing is to be done in secret or with mystery'. Each month, beginning on the twentieth day, a circuit of his taluk was to be undertaken by each tahsildar and a report submitted as a condition to being paid for the month. Corporal punishment could be inflicted upon any subordinate of the tahsildar and upon others with express permission of the collector. All castes and religious sects were to be treated equally, and from none were presents to be accepted. The rate of interest to be permitted on commercial loans was limited to 1 per cent per month on pain of forfeiture of all interest. The second part of the regulations pertained to a variety of public services to be performed by the incumbent: protection of all from the exactions of mirasidars; enforcement of the maintenance of bridges by mirasidars using non-resident farm labourers ('paragoodies', from the Tamil *parakudi*) for the work; enforcement of household responsibilities for cleaning an area before each house and planting shade trees ('margosa') at a distance of 20 feet from each other and 10 feet from each house; procurement for Europeans and affluent Indians of any bearers that may be required, but for no more than a two-day march if the 'coolies' were working cultivators—in which case non-cultivating labourers, 'town coolies', were to be employed for up to four-day marches.

[42] From Charles Harris to William Petrie, President of the MBOR, *Madras Revenue Proceedings* 26 February 1802, P/286/80, pp. 2183–315. The population estimate is based upon the number of houses reported in the district by Harris in October 1802 (83,753), cited in T. Venkasami Row, *A Manual of the District of Tanjore in the Madras Presidency* (Madras: 1883), p. 321.

Part three of the Tanjore regulations pertained to the tahsildars' exacting supervision of agricultural operations in their taluks. These included: efforts to increase the application of manure to paddy lands; maintenance of riverine irrigation bunds at specified heights and thicknesses, with plantings on all to prevent erosion or crumbling, and protection against damage from rats' nests; storage of a supply of sandbags for use in flood emergencies; seeing that all labour in any village is carried out by resident labourers (*ulkudi*), not 'foreign labourers' ('paragoodies'), except in emergencies; and for no labourers to be employed by the tahsildar or others at a distance exceeding three 'Malabar' miles from their own villages without express permission from the collector. A new provision introduced by the British collector was that Christian labourers were not required to work on Sundays, nor were they required to pull temple cars at 'heathen festivals'. Every male and female 'slave' (*paraiyar*) was to be provided with clothing and no children 'after their tenth year are to be seen uncovered'. Labourers could be beaten for idleness or desertion by tahsildars or their subordinates or by mirasidars, but only with branches of tamarind trees, not rattans. All mirasidars were under obligation to maintain adequate draft animals and labourers, and these were to be regularly inspected by the tahsildar:

> One plough or yoke of strong and healthy bullocks and one man and woman whether paragoodies or slaves are indispensible for every Vayly of land [1 veli=6.6 acres]. The Meerasidar who has less or whose Bullocks are old and sickly is to be reported to the Collector. . . . If the fault is occasioned by the avarice of the Meerasidar and he refuses to complete his establishment the excess of land will be taken away from him.[43]

Part four of the 1802 Tanjore orders deal with the management of labour and the distribution of grain by the tahsildar. Elaborate instructions on harvest procedures specified the supervisory responsibilities of officials as well as the rates of pay and provisions for farm labourers. The government's share of the grain production due as revenue ('mailwauram', or *melvaram*) was to be separated from the cultivators' share ('coodeewauram', or *kudivaram*); it was to be labelled, delivered to the tahsildar, checked for accuracy, and stored by him in such a manner as to prevent damage from moisture or rodents, or else losses were to be made good. When ordered to do so, tahsildars were to send government grain wherever designated, having procured bullocks, carts and, if necessary, rafts for transport. They were to maintain regular contact with government granaries in nearby towns in order to ascertain if supplies were required for consumption or export, as well as to supply government grain to bazaars as needed, and at a price fixed by the collector. Finally, records of all of these various transactions were to be kept and reports periodically filed. This section of the regulations concludes with another provision that was new with the British: 'By encouragement of merchants you are to use your

[43] 'Instructions for Tassildars', para. 41, p. 2235. See, Wilson, *Glossary*, p. 545, for *veli*.

efforts that all bazaars however large or small be supplied with all kinds of not only grain, but [with Company traded goods such as] clothes, threads, silks, utensils, spices and medicines that can find a sale.'[44]

How widely known and discussed the works of Sullivan and Greville might have been in the late 1790s is not possible to ascertain. Both of these books seem considerably at odds with the perceived principled basis of the emergent colonial state and suggest that the Cornwallis scheme for the British colonial state in India was more uneasily set than is now believed. There were mounting doubts about the new beginning made by Cornwallis in his Bengal revenue and judicial arrangements. These doubts extended to the Company's monopolistic control of export production and trade, tightened through the procurement network of the Board of Trade and funded by the now settled and fixed land revenue of rich Bengal. Cornwallis himself was among the doubters, it would seem, for his appointment of Read to the Baramahal, with a few assistants, including Munro, was an open brief in most respects.

Thus, it is quite incorrect to hold that the Cornwallis settlement in Bengal was separated by a generation from the experiments launched by Read and his colleague Munro in the Baramahal, from whence was to come the alternative to the Bengal model of the British colonial state in India. These were simultaneous developments which arose in the closing years of the eighteenth century, when the now mature Lieutenant Munro commenced his long career as colonial administrator.

The 3500 square mile Baramahal and the even more impressive additional territory of 14,000 square miles and over four million people were the gains of the treaty between the Company and Tipu Sultan of 17 March 1792.[45] This must have produced a mixed response from the Madras government. For, set against the relief of a weakened Tipu Sultan and the prospect of additional revenues from the half of his territories seized by the Company was the prospect of governing these diverse territories. If the Madras government felt no trepidation before that prospect, the Governor-General assuredly did. To the profound humiliation of Madras, Cornwallis declared that Madras civilians were incompetent to administer this new territory, and announced this to the Court of Directors in May 1792:

I cannot conceal from you, that from the many circumstances which have

[44] 'Instructions for Tassildars', para, 43, p. 2255.

[45] Madras, Madras Record Office, *The Baramahal Records* [hereafter, BR] (Madras: Government Press, 1907–33), v. 3, pp. ii and vi–vii. There is considerable variation on the area: T. H. Beaglehole, *Thomas Munro and the Development of Administrative Policy in Madras, 1792–1818; The Origins of the Munro System* (Cambridge: Cambridge University Press, 1966), p. 12, speaks of an area 140 miles by 60 miles, or 8400 square miles; Brian Murton, in 'Land and Class: Cultural, Social, and Biophysical Integration in Interior Tamilnadu in the Late Eighteenth Century', in R. E. Frykenberg, (ed.), *Land Tenure and Peasant in South Asia* (New Delhi: Orient Longman, 1977), p. 83, more accurately uses less than half of that, or 3000.

come under my observation, as well as from the present wretched state of the company's Jaghire and of the Northern Circars, that have been so long under the management of the government of Fort St George, I am not without my apprehensions of his [Sir George Oakeley, Governor of Madras] difficulty in finding gentlemen amongst the company's civil servants at this presidency, possessed of all the qualifications that could be wished for discharging properly the duties of collectors and managers of the newly acquired countries . . . unluckily, few of them are acquainted with the country languages, and are obliged, both from habit and necessity, to allow the management of their official, as well as their private business, to fall into the hands of dubashes, a description of people in the Carnatic, who, with very few exceptions, are calculated for being the most cruel instruments of rapine and extortion in the hands of unprincipled masters, and even of rendering . . . the most upright and humane intentions . . . perfectly useless to the interests of the company, and to the unfortunate natives who happen to be within the reach of their power and influence.[46]

To this fear of the manipulation of Company officials by Indian agents—made notorious by Burke—was added the mounting evidence of 'corruption' in Guntur, the Northern Circars generally, the Jaghire and elsewhere.[47] It was for these reasons that Cornwallis determined to place the Baramahal under the control of military officers and to retain personal control over their administration. He chose Captain Alexander Read to supervise the administration because of that officer's brief but creditable administration of Hoskote and Kolar (seized from Mysore early in the war), and because Read was in charge of receiving the actual surrender of the Baramahal from Mysore officials.[48] Cornwallis' decision to place the territory under military rather than civilian officials, and his express reasons for doing so, set into motion a civilian backlash against military administrators which threatened Munro and others like him a decade later.

Read's orders of 31 March 1792 from Cornwallis' adjudant, Lt Colonel Barry Close, repeated the denigration of Madras civilians and assumed that there would not be adequate civilian officials for the Baramahal for at least a year. During that time it was thought that Read's present staff of junior officers, plus another, Lieutenant William Macleod, from the Governor-General's staff, would suffice. These same orders directed Read to refer 'cases of doubt or difficulty' to the Governor-General or to the Madras government.[49] Read's mandate was thus broad and vague: in theory it was to run for a year, after which Madras civilians were to supersede him. In fact it lasted seven years. In theory Read was subject to the Madras Board of Revenue, but in fact he main-

[46] *The Fifth Report*, v. 3, p. 203.

[47] Robert E. Frykenberg, *Guntur District, 1788–1848; A History of Local Influence and Central Authority in South India* (Oxford: Clarendon Press, 1965), chapter 3.

[48] Papers on Read's earlier commission are in BR, Section 21.

[49] *The Fifth Report*, v. 1, pp. 1–2.

tained great freedom to experiment with a framework of administration he considered suited to the conditions of the Baramahal. Because of its perceived provenance as what was to become known as the 'Madras' or 'Munro system' of Indian administration, the late eighteenth century Baramahal has generated an important historiography.

MUNRO IN BARAMAHAL HISTORIOGRAPHY

In Gleig's 1830 biography of Munro, one of the broad lines of interpretation of the Baramahal period was established. This was an imminentist view of the statesman Munro, whose first public profundities were uttered in the 1790s. For Gleig it is 'a new era in his [Munro's] career' and, as appropriate in a biography, Munro occupies centre stage.[50] In one essential respect Gleig's selection of Munro's writing of the Baramahal period and his narrative commentary upon them differs from other, later interpreters. That is, Gleig gives only minor attention to revenue administration and to Munro's contribution to the formulation of the system which was to bear his name after Gleig's time. Few of the letters cited by Gleig mention revenue and little is said of either Munro's differences with Read or of his contributions to and later ultimate acceptance of Read's proposals. In the third volume of his *Munro*, published as a supplement to the original two-volume work, a long letter from Munro to his military friend (and future member of the Court of Directors) Captain Alexander Allan, dated 8 June 1794, is included.[51] This letter explains in some detail Read's idea on settlement and something of the situation then prevailing in the Baramahal. It remained for later Munro students to explore the emergence of what was to be called 'the ryotwari system'. The first of these came some twenty years after the Gleig biography, from James W. B. Dykes, one of Munro's administrative successors in the Salem district, into which the Baramahal had become incorporated.

Dykes' *Salem, An Indian Collectorate* was the first and prototype of the Madras government series of district manuals which were formally ordered in 1862.[52] Like other authors of Madras manuals, Dykes was an official (assistant collector and magistrate) of the district about which he wrote, and his work brimmed with an appreciation of the benefits of British rule in India; unlike others, however, he expressed an irreverent disdain for the revenue-fixated concerns of the Madras government, in Munro's time as well as his own.

This work was also the first to rely upon official documents of the Munro-Read period, documents which, in part, were later to be published as *The Baramahal Records*. On the basis of these, Dykes reconstructed the circums-

[50] Gleig, v. 1, p. 141.

[51] Ibid., v. 3, pp. 91–8. Two other important letters from Munro to Allan of 1793 and 1794 are found in K. N. Venkatasubba Sastri, *The Munro System of British Statesmanship in India* (Mysore: University of Mysore, 1939), pp. 1–6.

[52] Published in London: W. H. Allen for the India Board, 1853.

tances in which a well-intentioned Read sought to devise an appropriate revenue system for the Baramahal, more, it seemed, in opposition to his assistant Munro than to the Madras Board of Revenue. Dykes' large sympathy for Read is manifest in an observation upon the latter's proclamation of 10 December 1796, with respect to which Dykes observes: 'the ryotwarry system was, what Read's mind foresaw it would be, the natural result of a northern sun on tropical vegetation, the growth of village institutions under the British government...[53] but woe betide Major Read if the year's revenue showed a decline.'[54]

According to Dykes, the fully formed idea of ryotwar was contained in this proclamation of December 1796, which was addressed to the people of that part of the Baramahal (Tiruppatur) under Read's personal supervision. Dykes called this proclamation the 'charter' of ryotwar, though he observed that Read in that document and others seemed unable to express the idea very clearly. That was to be Munro's task once he was, as Dykes put it, 'converted'.

> The reasoning powers of... Read were generally as strong and clear as his writings are weak and obscure; he sadly wanted the perspicuity of style which was so essential for an office that he held otherwise so worthily, and which his assistant Munro possessed so eminently. Many will be surprised to learn that the latter was not the originator of the ryotwarry system, still more so that he opposed it at first... it is indeed to be regretted that the powers of language, by which Munro commanded attention to his views, was not given to him who is in reality the author of that policy which so successfully stood the test of time.[55]

Pervading Dykes' *Salem* is the pride of the Madras civil service during the middle of the nineteenth century. Especially his pride in its distinctive and, it was contended, compassionate rural administration. In his time, Dykes was an important proponent and explicator of the Madras system.[56] The statement cited above, as well as others in his works, expressed a confidence and self-satisfaction that were becoming general in British India. They represent the particularistic sentiments of provincial Company officials that were not yet enveloped in the universalistic imperial mystique of later Victorian officialdom. An instance of this provincial pride is Dykes' somewhat invidious contrast between Read's generosity and largeness of view, and Munro's caution. This contrast arose in Dykes' consideration of the question facing Read of whether

[53] Dykes, *Salem*, p. 86.

[54] Ibid., p. 85, under the full title of: 'Proclamation in the Name of Agriculturists, Merchants, and Other Inhabitants of the District of Tripatoor', the full text of which may be found in Dykes, pp. 90–103, and in A. J. Arbuthnot, *Major General Sir Thomas Munro, Bart., Governor of Madras: Selections of His Minutes and other Official Writings* (London: 1881), pp. 587–92.

[55] Dykes, *Salem*, p. 89.

[56] See his *The Ryotwar Tenure: Proposed Manual of General Rules Declaratory and Explanatory of the Ryotwar Tenure 1858*, printed by the Salem District Press and consulted in the Coimbatore District Record Room.

some form of long leaseholds over land (five years) should be established in the Baramahal in order to assure a predictable stream of revenue. This was a view that was being pressed by the MBOR and seconded by Munro. The alternative to this was that the revenue settlement should be an annual one, so that cultivators were free to choose and pay revenue upon those fields they wished to hold for the year. Read himself favoured this alternative. Munro opposed Read's position, as outlined in the proclamation of 10 December 1726, that cultivators were to be free to transfer or give up fields annually. Munro preferred leaseholds for several years, both to assure a predictable level of revenue (important alike to the payer and to the state, he argued), as well as for the inducement that longer tenure would give to developmental investment in agricultural improvements. Chidingly paraphrased by Dykes, Munro is seen to be saying that

> He would [like to] give the soil away outright, because, as he observes, nothing would so effectively induce the outlay of capital. But the revenue!! the revenue to the Government!!! the total amount to be remitted to the Presidency of Fort St George!!! In those days, the subject was regarded by Munro with great awe, and sooner than the Honourable Company should receive less, the ryot's risk must be more.[57]

Enthusiastic advocate of ryotwar that he was, Dykes could only applaud Read's principle of annual settlement and criticize Munro's timid reluctance in early 1797. However, by September of that year Munro had been 'converted' and had placed his full support behind Read's programme at the critical juncture when the MBOR began to exert its supervision over Baramahal affairs. For it was only in 1797, five years after Read's administration there had commenced, as Dykes pointed out, that the Madras government became aware that his policies violated their orders to establish a village lease system, in anticipation of the introduction of a settlement of estates under zamindars, as ordered by Cornwallis.

In his chapter entitled 'Conversion of Munro to the Ryotwarry Faith' Dykes cited two long letters from Munro to Read in 1797, to show how the former had moved from a reluctant yielding on the matter of annual settlements in July to an espousal of that principle in September. Munro concluded the later letter to Read with the following succinctly stated principles and rules that were to apply henceforward in his own central division of the Baramahal:

> The great point in making a settlement is the rate of assessment; all other regulations connected with it are of very inferior importance. It needs no argument to show, that the lower it is, the better for the farmers. I have proposed such an abatement as, when the cheapness of cultivation and the great returns from seed are taken into consideration, will be found to leave

[57] Dykes, *Salem*, pp. 116–17, referring to a letter from Munro to Read of 15 November 1796; emphases in original.

them in possession of as great advantages as any race of husbandmen in the world. It must not, however, from this be inferred that the land will become saleable on a sudden; for the frontier situation of these districts, and other reasons, must long prevent it from attaining that value which it bears in Europe. The plan which, it appears to me, would be best calculated to secure to the people the fruits of their industry, and to the Government a permanent revenue, is comprised under the following heads:

1. A reduction of fifteen per cent to be made on the [present] lease assessment. 2. The country to be rented immediately of Government [i.e. without intermediaries] by small farmers, as at present, everyone receiving just as much land as he demands. 3. Settlements to be annual; that is to say every man to be permitted to give up, or take, whatever land he pleases every year. 4. Every man to have a part, or the whole, of his lands in [long-term] lease, who wishes it; and in order to encourage the application for leases [which Munro took to be explicitly demanded by the MBOR] all lands under annual tenures to be taken from the occupants and given to such other farmers as may demand them in lease, on their paying to Government, as purchase-money, one year's rent for any particular field, or one-half year's rent for the whole farm [i.e. the combined fields that any substantial cultivator habitually farmed]. 5. Villages and districts to be responsible for all individual failures. 6. All lands included in the lease should remain invariably at the rent then fixed, after the proposed reduction of fifteen per cent. 7. All lands not included in the lease should be rented at the average of the village to which they belong. 8. Lands included in the lease, being given up and allowed to be waste [uncultivated] for a number of years, should, when again occupied, pay, for the first year, the full rent as before. 9. All castes, whether natives or aliens, to pay the same rent for all land. 10. No additional rent ever to be demanded for improvements. The farmer who, by digging a well, or building a tank, converts dry land into garden or rice fields, to pay no more than the original rent of the ground. 11. No reduction of the established rent ever to be allowed, except where the cochineal plant, mulberry, &c, are cultivated.[58]

Hence even as late as 1797 Dykes shows that Munro's support for Read's proposals was hedged in one crucial respect, that is he accepted the principle of long-term leases as a permitted, if not a preferred, basis of revenue assessment in the Baramahal; this is stipulated in his rules, numbers 4 to 8.

In this and in the careful attention given to revenue administration, Dykes' view is contrasted with that of Gleig. The former's was a view based upon direct and long experience in the Baramahal as well as an appreciation for the unique colonial administration of mid-nineteenth century Madras. An agnostic with regard to Munro, Dykes gave full credit for ryotwar to Read. Indeed, Dykes seemed almost indifferent to the towering reputation of Munro, suggest-

[58] Arbuthnot, pp. 50–1.

ing that in early Victorian India Munro had not attained that fullness of reputation that he was to possess in the later Victorian age.

Such an assessment of the Baramahal phase of Munro's career is provided in the 1881 work of Sir Alexander J. Arbuthnot, a Madras civil official. Arbuthnot's treatment of the Baramahal Munro is markedly different from that of Dykes. By the late nineteenth century, imperial heroes were wanted; even Warren Hastings was rescued from the moral dustbin into which Burke had stuffed him. Accordingly, Arbuthnot compiled a long (130 page) eulogistic memoir on Munro's life, of which thirteen pages were devoted to the Baramahal period. In it, attention is given to Cornwallis' decision to bypass the Madras civilian administration in 1792. The failures of the revenue administrations of the Northern Circars and the Chingleput Jaghire, the rapacity and corruption of revenue renters, and the complicity of European officials in all this mismanagement are treated dispassionately.[59] This indicated that the injured sensibilities of Madras civilians earlier in the century over the appointment of military collectors had been mollified by an adoption of the soldier Munro as the model Madras civil servant, if not the patron saint of Madras administration. Not for Arbuthnot the carping criticism of Dykes and some of his predecessors of the preceding two generations.

Neither Dykes' irreverence nor his logical coherence was much in evidence in Arbuthnot's treatment of the Baramahal. The ryotwari system is seen to have begun there when the village lease arrangements allegedly 'collapsed', a distorted reading of things. 'Regarding this system', Arbuthnot wrote, 'there has been, and still is, a good deal of misapprehension, even in official quarters.' Obligingly, therefore, he provided an extended and very official explanation of ryotwar drawn from the time of Dykes but not at all attentive to Dykes' criticisms.[60]

For Arbuthnot the Read system in the Baramahal contained the essential features of ryotwar of his own time, except for 'certain serious defects which, contrary to the wise views of the founders [Read and Munro], though strictly in accordance with native ideas, were allowed to hamper its working for many years'. Remarkably, among the 'defects' said to be 'in accordance with native ideas' was the high pitch of revenue demand: 'the rate of assessment constituted an unduly heavy burthen upon the ryots.'[61] So easily was the long, grindingly high revenue demand of Madras during the early colonial phase made a product of pre-colonial history, rather than colonial avarice. Another more accurate 'defect' was that agricultural improvements undertaken by cultivators resulted in higher assessments; still another was that contrary to the principle of revenue demand based exclusively on previously surveyed fields, taxes varied according to the value of crops planted. Munro is alleged

[59] Ibid., pp. xxvii–xxxviii.

[60] Ibid., pp. xxxix–xl, citing the *Administrative Report of the Madras Presidency for 1855–56.*

[61] Arbuthnot, p. xl.

to have opposed these deviations from principle as well as the imposition of joint liability of villages and groups of villages ('districts') for individual revenue defaults. At the same time, Munro is shown, creditably, to have been concerned about losses of public revenue as a result of Read's proposals.

Yet, Arbuthnot cites letters from Munro to Read in 1796 and 1797 with Munro's explicit recommendations for collective liability for revenue shortfalls and reduced assessments for certain cash crops, as noted above.[62] Also noted are other 'defects', such as that increase of revenue demand on lands that had been improved at the expense of cultivators were permitted until the middle of the century, notwithstanding 'the powerful advocacy of Munro' to the contrary. In the end, Arbuthnot's desire was to show a Munro as the apotheosis of a caring Madras colonial administration even during the Baramahal period, but this objective is continually thwarted by the documents which he cites. These contain overwhelming evidence of Munro's career canniness, which repeatedly is expressed as all of the compassion and welfare to the subjects of that administration, consistent with the highest possible revenue!

Two other more modern works on the Baramahal period of 1792–9 present different views of Munro. Nilmani Mukherjee's monograph, published in 1962, evaluated the socioeconomic and administrative consequences of the Madras land-revenue system during the Munro era. In this thorough and balanced study, Read is made the centre of attention of the Baramahal regime, as in Dykes' account.[63]

For Mukherjee the context for evaluating Read's approach to his task was the immediately preceding system of administration of the Baramahal, that of Tipu Sultan. The latter's system is seen to have resulted in low and irregular revenues, despite heavy tax demands, because of defalcations and because of the deep poverty of cultivators. According to Mukherjee it was these conditions, and not the prior (and continuing) failures of British revenue arrangements elsewhere in Madras, to which Read responded in formulating his system.

Isolation from Madras government supervision ended, as Dykes had previously shown, because of the diminishing revenues from the Baramahal in 1796–7.[64]

After this, Mukherjee points out, Read began to be pressed by the MBOR for explanations of these deficits and for why he had, without consultation or permission, abandoned the village-lease system he had been ordered by them to carry out, and which the Board believed that he was carrying out:

> The Board is at a loss of know the reason why Lt.-Col. Read preferred an

[62] Ibid., pp. 1–51.

[63] *The Ryotwari System in Madras, 1792–1827* (Calcutta: Firma K. L. Mukhopadhyay, 1962), pp. 3–17.

[64] Deficits appear moderate: in 1796 revenue collections were about 9 per cent below 1792, and in 1797 deficits were about twice that; Mukherjee, p. 13, and BR, 1, p. 208.

> annual settlement to a lease in the face of opposition from his Assistants. Government have sustained a great fall in revenue and the Board calls for an explanation. Annulment of the lease settlement could be done only by Government and the Board disapproves of his action.... The Board reminds him to send his final report of the Baramahal revenue.[65]

It is Mukherjee's view that under this pressure from Madras, and able neither to explain nor purge the revenue deficiencies, 'Read himself had become less sure about the success of the system which came to be regarded as his brain-child'. Ironically, Mukherjee adds, it was at this very time that Munro's conversion to the ryotwar faith occurred.[66] Resumption of the war against Tipu Sultan in 1799 returned Read and Munro to their military duties, and the 'Baramahal experiment' came to an end.

Mukherjee supposed that Read was disappointed that he could not fulfil his promise to submit a final report on his seven-year administration to the MBOR, a report that was to accompany a compilation of the records of that administration (and was later, in part, to constitute the printed *Baramahal Records*). The Madras government was also disappointed not only with the falling revenues of the Baramahal, which had transformed Read's administration from a success to a failure, but also because the MBOR was certain that any system must be flawed which had to 'depend for its success only on the integrity and ability of collectors and their "native" servants as did Read's system of annual settlements ... [with] 80,000 farmers'.[67] Cornwallis' determination to extend the revenue and judicial regulations of Bengal to Madras closed any further consideration of Read's system, and Mukherjee concludes:

> Thus, the Ryotwari System apparently came to an end in the place of its origin.... At one stage Read was the solitary champion of this sytsem, even his Assistants dissenting from him. No one seems to have taken his experiments seriously. Later on, however, Read's Assistants were converted to the ryotwari faith, but the master himself became doubtful of his system. On the whole the history of the ryotwari system in Baramahal was marked by indecision. But for the extension of this system in modified form to other parts of the Presidency by Read's Assistants, the Baramahal experi-

[65] *Guide to the Records of Salem District*, p. 135. Ironically, at almost the same time, the Madras government was communicating to Read an encomium from the Court of Directors, from a revenue letter to Madras, 4 October 1797, which again illustrates the time warp of the colonial regime: 'we cannot sufficiently applaud his [Read's] conduct in the execution of the trust reposed in him ... we are satisfied that nothing will be wanting, which zeal, ability and integrity can supply for rendering those new acquisitions [taken from Tipu Sultan in 1792] productive and profitable to the Company... we trust that you will profit by the experiment [of Read] and if necessary avail yourselves of the superior talents of Captn. Read and his assistants....'. Cited in BR, 1, p. 220.

[66] Mukherjee, p. 13, citing a letter from Munro to Read of 5 September 1797; the complete letter is found in Arbuthnot, pp. 22–51.

[67] Mukherjee, p. 15.

ment would perhaps have been an inconclusive interlude in the annals of revenue administration of Madras—interesting historically but of no importance.[68]

T. H. Beaglehole's work on Munro of 1966 has a different perspective. It is not upon Read, but upon Munro and 'the Munro system' that Beaglehole focuses, and Munro is made the co-creator of the Baramahal system. This coupling of the two occurs early in the chapter on the Baramahal in which Beaglehole says of Read:

> his distance from Fort St George, as well as his readiness to ignore the Board [of Revenue] when he wished to, meant that for seven years the policy followed was very much his own. In drafting regulations and establishing a method of collecting the revenue Read was much more concerned to persuade Munro and his other assistants of the justice and practicability of his plans than he was to convince and carry with him his superiors on the Board.[69]

While Beaglehole was inclined towards a view of something like joint paternity for what became called the Munro system, in a curious way he uncoupled the Baramahal origin of that system from its future development in the Presidency as a whole, and from any serious consideration with its immediate Mysorean past such as Mukherjee had correctly shown. That is, he tended to see the Baramahal period of 1792–9 as commencing a continuous process which, in the end, produced the Munro system; the process might have begun anywhere in peninsular India, it would seem. The Baramahal period was not an experiment that went wrong, as Mukherjee would have it, but a great beginning. Along with this predetermined unfolding went its underlying driving element: it was the necessary alternative to the Cornwallis system of Bengal. However, this alternative was not based upon different principles of political economy from those of Cornwallis so much as upon what Munro and Read perceived to be the *facts* of South Indian society. It was a confrontation between the abstract theories of Cornwallis and the practical realities perceived by Munro and Read.

Such a formulation is consonant with the terms in which the mythology of the Munro system is expressed, and Beaglehole's is an admiring study of Munro. However, the proposal that the Cornwallis regulations of Bengal shaped the arrangements worked out by Read in the Baramahal until 1797 is not acceptable. Beaglehole concedes too much privilege to the rhetorical stance of Munro and later advocates of ryotwar in supposing that an alien and abstract system of European origin was being opposed by their own, better, understanding of the 'real' social conditions of the South. Similarly, it is a polemical conceit to take Munro or Read as traditionalistically or paternalistically opposed

[68] Ibid., p. 16.
[69] Beaglehole, p. 16.

to the innovations of Cornwallis. The regimes being created in Bengal and in the Baramahal were contemporaneous, for one thing. For another, Read surely looked to Cornwallis as the source of his authority for the Baramahal operations during at least five of his seven years there—even though he (Read) may be accused of stretching his 1791 mandate from the Governor-General by placing his administration completely beyond the knowledge and reach of officials in Madras, and therefore of not considering the lease system then favoured by them.

When in the middle of 1797 the Madras government began to press Read for clear information and compliance to its orders, their intervention was partly a result of Read's proclamation of December 1796, with its explicit commitment to annual settlements with individual tax-paying cultivators, which was thus contrary to the lease system. This added to their concern for the falling revenue from the Baramahal. Until 1797, when Cornwallis began to insist on the zamindari settlement for Madras, there was hardly the basis for the opposition that Beaglehole asserts.

Cornwallis was not Read's adversary, but his protector. At the outset, and for five years after, both were concerned to discover a system that suited the situation in the Baramahal, one that avoided the egregious flaws of extant Madras revenue arrangements. Read's orders from Cornwallis make this conclusion plausible in two ways: there was Cornwallis' expressed lack of confidence in the ability of the Madras government to introduce a viable system in the newly conquered territories, and there was the invitation of Read to address 'cases of doubt or difficulty' to the headquarters [of the Governor-General] *or* to [the Madras] government'.[70] Moreover, while these orders provided that Read's superintendence was only for what remained of the year 1792, neither the Governor-General nor the Madras government sought to end or supervise Read's administration then, or for the next five years.

These criticisms of Beaglehole's interpretation of the evolution of the Munro system pertain to the Baramahal period. There is otherwise much power in his interpretation carried over the course of Munro's subsequent career about which, in the main, Beaglehole is more cautious. He rejects such partisanship as Dykes indulges in when he fulminates against the imposition of the zamindari regulations in Salem after 1802 or when he applauds Munro for ending the miseries caused by that imposition.[71] The ryotwar, or Munro, clique in Madras, more perhaps than Munro himself, justified the Madras system less upon its intrinsic merits than upon its supposed superiority to the Bengal system. Of course, in ideological terms there had to be a Cornwallis system

[70] BR, 1, pp. 201–2. Read clearly attached primacy to the first, as may be judged from the opening sentence of his letter to Haliburton and the MBOR, 24 November 1792, transmitting a copy of his report for the year to Cornwallis: 'The matter contained in these sheets was drawn up for the Governor-General, as the least information he expects from me relative to the Ceded countries', BR, 1, p. 134.

[71] Dykes, *Salem* chapter entitled: 'The Zamindarry System', especially pp. 214–15.

for the Munro system to exist. But, all of this occurred after 'Baramahal' was no longer even in use as territorial designation.

Beaglehole is valuable on the Baramahal period in making Munro a far more active and creative agent in the formulations which were to establish the basis of the later ryotwar system than either Dykes or Mukherjee allow. While Dykes appreciated Munro's role in elaborating the purportedly 'humane' elements of that system, he saw Munro as a reluctant convert to the 'faith' during the Baramahal period. Mukherjee follows the same general tack in making Read the creator of the system which all but expired when he left the Baramahal in 1799, disillusioned with his efforts and, it is implied, happy to withdraw from its thorny problems for the relative clarity of military service.

Moreover, Beaglehole's concise chapter on the Baramahal phase of Munro's career is the most complete of any up to that time in the attention given to the documents of the period. He shows in his analysis of ten major documents, dating from 1 July 1783 to 24 November 1798, that Read again and again altered his formulations to meet Munro's criticisms. There is no mistaking that Munro developed a stake in the Read approach at an early point in their collaboration. Munro's response to a draft of Read's 'fifth report' to Cornwallis, of 1 July 1793 approves the latter's 'infallible rules for regulating a land tax' based on an 'investigation of revenue affairs so minute, so correct, and so original . . . [as was] ever made by any European in India'.[72] However, Munro is anything but reticent about criticizing some of Read's propositions, many of his calculations, and, above all, the opacity of his prose: 'There is hardly a paragraph that I was not obliged to read twice and many of them ten times before I could understand them . . . you forget that everyone was not so well acquainted with the subject as yourself, and you have not attended to perspicuity as you proceed.'[73] This comment of 31 July 1793 by Munro concluded with the following statement which is often, and rightly, cited to demonstrate the mutual respect and confidence that existed between Read and Munro, as well as a hint of Munro's vaunted compassionate disposition towards governance.

> I do not mean any satire, for satire is false, but a truth of which I have had sad experience when I tell you that it will cost any other man as much labour to read and comprehend the book [a reference to the length of Read's report] as it did you to compose it. I have now done with you as a Collector and shall just let fly one volley at you as a politician . . . you say that you will endeavour to ascertain . . . that nothing may be lost to revenue. This is the language of a tax gatherer, not of a politician. Revenue ought not to be all that the subject can pay but only what the necessities of the state require . . . it is neither wise nor just to demand more, the remainder will be more beneficial to the country in the hands of the subject than in the treasury of the Government. The Company have no right to invest a portion of the revenue

[72] Read to Cornwallis, BR, 6, pp. 20–57.

[73] Munro to Read, 31 July 1793, cited in Beaglehole, pp. 19–20, and BR, 6, pp. 58–61.

in trade. The measure can only be justified at present by saying that the profits are employed in paying off debts contracted in defence of the country. Whenever these debts are extinguished, a remission of taxes ought immediately to be made equivalent to the portion of revenue employed in the investment and the company should from that period carry on their trade with their own private funds. But even if... affairs admitted of a remission being made it could never be fairly and equally extended to all the company's possessions until one uniform system of revenue is established, but we are so far from having anything of this kind . . . that our only system is every man collect what he can.[74]

From this and other Munro letters during the early phase of the Baramahal period, Beaglehole's notion of something approaching a joint venture between the two Scots is persuasive. As the junior collaborator, one whose task was to respond to and to help clarify the proposals of his superior, Munro held back his agreement on some matters until September 1797, from when Dykes and Mukherjee date his 'conversion'. In this role as critic, Munro provided the most valuable assistance to Read, but there is perhaps more to it.

THE POLITICS OF EARLY RYOTWAR

Munro had a political sagacity that Read lacked. As we have seen, Dykes chided Munro for his obsessive concern about the revenue, and this caution does come up frequently in Munro's comments on Read's proposals. However, it was more than diminished revenue and Read's indifference to the orders of the MBOR that prompted its intervention in the Baramahal after 1797. Munro perhaps knew this. From his friend Thomas Cockburn of the MBOR and from others in the Madras establishment, Munro would have come to appreciate the powerful advocacy among Madras officials for measures that were being followed in the Chingleput Jaghire neighbouring Madras city. Here, Lionel Place served as collector from 1794 to 1799, and in a series of long reports covering a period nearly as long as Read's in the Baramahal, Place elaborated the basic scheme which, under his skilful rhetoric, became a system called 'meerasee' (from the Arabic *miras*, meaning patrimony, and *mirasi*, meaning hereditary property).[75] Very persuasively, Place outlined an historical process from which this form of hereditary property is supposed to have evolved. This was a sociological and indigenous legal process, in accordance with which the mirasidar or holder of the mirasi right enjoyed great social prominence, rewards and rights; and a political process that conferred local authority upon those

[74] BR, 6, pp. 60–1, and Beaglehole, p. 20. The notion of taxation pitched to the needs of the state rather than to the capacity of subjects to pay was much in the air at this time. Philip Francis, in 1775 and 1776, expressed the same principle in considering the Bengal land revenue, and credited Montesquieu as its promulgator: Ranajit Guha, *A Rule of Property for Bengal*, p. 117.

[75] *The Fifth Report*, v. 3, 'Glossary', p. 30.

mirasidars with the highest standing, called *nattars* or *nattawars*. The culmination of Place's refinement of the institution of mirasi came in his long report of 6 June 1799, his most comprehensive and powerful statement.[76]

Place won the support of the Madras government to his proposals to appoint nattawars to intermediate revenue positions between the village proprietors, whom he called mirasidars, and the European collector. Nattawars were to encourage fellow proprietors to extend cultivation, gather information related to revenue, and help with the annual settlement of revenue. In return, these most powerful of mirasidars were granted a set of privileges that Place argued had long been theirs, namely tax-free ('maniam') lands, tax-reduced ('shortrium') lands, and a higher share ('warum') of the division of produce with those who cultivated their lands than was permitted to other mirasidars. Similar arrangements were initiated by the MBOR in parts of South Arcot. This was at the same time as the Madras authorities were beginning to understand Read's very different revenue administration in the Baramahal. As Read's plans for the Baramahal, where neither intermediaries nor landed proprietors were recognized, began to become clear in Madras, and as the level of revenue begin to diminish, political opposition from Madras stiffened against Read and his junior military colleagues. The Madras civilians were lashing back against the military interlopers within their administrative preserve, and their whip was Place's mirasi system.

In that system, Madras officials had a scheme for revenue administration that had the double virtue of being based on an ancient system of land rights and one that lent itself to the lease system preferred by them. The Burkean critic could only be pleased. Hence, even as the Cornwallis permanent settlement with zamindars was being constructed in Bengal for eventual imposition upon Madras, mirasi was a more immediate and compelling model for revenue administration than that which Read was developing in the Baramahal. While the MBOR was still groping to understand what Read and his juniors were doing in the Baramahal, they had been persuaded that Place's mirasi scheme was the way forward for Madras.

The validity of the mirasi scheme that Place worked out in Chingleput during the 1790s has received recent confirmation in a study by T. Mizushima. Centring his analysis on an ancient institution of local dominance—nattars—he reaches well beyond tenurial questions. His is a complex, historically-conditioned and mutifaceted analysis of powerful local men with whom the British regime of the eighteenth century, no less than prior regimes, had to come to terms.[77]

The title nattar is derived from an ancient territorial unit of the Coromandel plain, *nadu*, whose importance reached back a millennium or more. During the late pre-colonial period of the seventeenth and eighteenth centuries, men

[76] Ibid., v. 3, pp. 149–67.

[77] *Nattar and the Socio-Economic Change in South India in the 18th-19th Centuries* (Tokyo: Institute for the Study of Languages and Cultures of Asia and Africa; Monograph No. 19, 1986).

called nattars or nattawars held crucial intermediate positions in the revenue administration of Tondaimandalam.[78] Nattars were the headmen of caste groups, of villages, and of small territories comprising clusters of villages. They were leaders of the major landholding people of the coast, including Vellalas, Reddis, Nainars, and Brahmans. They were the powerful big-men of any locality, and to them were conceded tasks of revenue assessment and collection under pre-British, state-appointed revenue officials, amildars. In many places nattars were actually small-scale revenue farmers. They therefore added to their status as leaders of landed groups these judicial and police powers that went with tax-farming, and they had major responsibilities for the protection of temples and other religious institutions as well. Nattars were also found in towns throughout the Tamil country and Karnataka, where they dominated the trade and caste organization in urban places as well as rural ones, even when, as Mizushima argues, caste organization may have been becoming weaker and even extinct in the countryside.[79]

Mizushima's assertion that caste organization in the countryside was weak is based on his finding that nattar authority stemmed not so much from their leadership of caste groups as from their control over local tracts called 'magan' and 'turruf', as a sort of minor territorial chiefly stratum. The office of nattar had long before the eighteenth century become hereditary, a form of property which was bought and sold, just as landed property itself was purchasable within these small territories and even across their boundaries. The power of nattars had derived from their local economic hegemony, conferred by landholding and cultivation as well as by livestock rearing. To these, during the seventeenth and eighteenth centuries, was added their major importance in the expanded trade in agricultural commodities.

It was largely in recognition of their local dominance in social, political, and economic relations that the nattars of the Coromandel plain were found useful, if not essential, by pre-colonial regimes there. Without their collaboration in revenue collection, state-appointed amildars could not have fulfilled their tasks to the regimes they served, nor their own independent activities as rural entrepreneurs. Moreover, Mizushima argues that the growth of textile exports through European trading companies, added to the scope of nattars, though that this was a 'new' feature, as he says, is unacceptable. There is evidence that this sort of engagement in extended commodity production occurred much earlier, in the seventeenth century.[80] By the early eighteenth

[78] For a discussion of nattars in ancient times, B. Stein, PSSMSI, chapter on the nadu; N. Karashima and Y. Subbarayalu, *Studies in Socio-Cultural Change in Rural Villages in Tiruchirapalli District, Tamilnadu, India* (Tokyo: Institute for the Study of the Languages and Cultures of Asia and Africa; Monograph No. 1, 1980). For a study of a later period: S. S. Sivakumar, 'Transformation of the Agrarian Economy of Tondaimandalam: 1760–1900', *Social Scientist* (Indian School of Social Science, Trivandrum), no. 70, pp. 18–39. Tondaimandalam was the region around Madras.

[79] Mizushima, pp. 178, 208–9.

[80] Sanjay Subrahmanyam, 'Trade and the Regional Economy of South India, *c.*

century imports of European bullion to finance the trade in textiles had long since stimulated general trade and urbanization. Grain to feed specialist spinner and weaver populations in the towns of the region was principally in the hands of nattars and other local leaders who had the first call upon surplus agrarian production. The lucrative grain trade and the wealth accumulations that resulted from it permitted many nattars to achieve a degree of economic and political independence from the regimes they served. This, together with the disruptive invasions of the Marathas and the succession wars for the nawabship of the Carnatic, undermined the old regimes of which the nattar were part. All of this prepared the condition for eventual domination by the East India Company in the later eighteenth century.

Throughout the 1790s the East India Company experimented with revenue schemes in its Coromandel territories of Chingleput and South Arcot. It sought to set aside the nattars and their privileges as a drain on the tax receipts that the Company hoped to realize and upon the political authority it sought to extend. Repeatedly, the Company had to recognize that, without the active collaboration of nattars, neither the revenue nor the political authority they sought was attainable. As a result, nattar privileges when withdrawn or narrowed were usually restored, as they were in South Arcot in 1785 and Chingleput in 1797.[81] Further experiments in revenue administration during the early nineteenth century resulted in nattars becoming proprietors under the zamindari scheme imposed in 1802, and renters under the village lease scheme introduced by the Madras government after 1808.

In 1797 Munro must have had some understanding that his new-found administrative career might be short-lived, as Read's proposals for the Baramahal began to encounter mounting opposition from the Madras officialdom. Yet the existing corpus of his correspondence suggests little of this.

Available to no writer on Munro, except Gleig, were Munro's private letters during the Baramahal period. These shed an ambiguous light on the question of Munro's participation in the shaping of what came to be known as the ryotwar system, though these letters do tell a good deal about this and other matters pertaining to his relationship with Read, as well as his career concerns at the time. Gleig had had all of these letters, but his biographical method and biases resulted in a distorted selection and editing of them. The letters which Gleig chose to present to his readers were the long political and military analyses which were sent to Munro's father and the charming, intellectual ones to his sister Erskine. Munro was to appear warlike and warm, and many letters were edited by Gleig in a trivial way so as to place Munro in a better light. In actual fact the letters written in the Baramahal period available earlier only to Gleig, who ignored a major part of that correspondence, reveal his notions about many things, including Read.

1550 to 1650', unpublished doctoral thesis, Department of Economics, Delhi School of Economics, 1986.

[81] See Mizushima, pp. 270–1, for a summary of his argument.

Writing to his brother Daniel in Bengal around 1796 in order to accept the latter's offer to put in a good word for him for some military preferment, he denied reports which Daniel had said were circulating in Calcutta that Read's reports were really the work of Thomas Munro.[82] To this supposition by Cornwallis' staff, or the Governor-General himself, which suggests his growing stature, he objected, perhaps less from modesty than to distance himself from Read's reports.

What we are permitted to see of Read in Munro's letters is a man of drudging earnestness and quite admirable congeniality, traits that Munro appreciated and mentioned frequently in his letters. Read, Munro said, would never leave India, 'for he has such a rage for working among accounts... his only happiness is plodding among them... he cares little for society and has no turn for any active amusements unless campaigning can be called such... he will never leave... unless he is driven from it by bad health...'[83] Or again, to his father, on 1 February 1797, after referring to the mismanagement of Company territories on the Malabar and Coromandel coasts, because they are 'in the hands of men totally unqualified for their situations', whereas in the hands of Read, they would be flourishing because he would have determined their worth in two years. He reported in this same letter that he had passed the same opinion to the MBOR, but the latter had rejected his proposal to place even more of Madras under the administration of a soldier as objectionable in 'setting aside civil lines entirely and could not be ventured upon unless authorized by Europe'. Munro cautioned his father, again, that these remarks about the MBOR should not be repeated, something Munro's father chose to ignore. But his biographer, Gleig, obediently deleted it, even though it is an early reference to what was to become a major crisis for his hero when, five years later, military collectors were under attack from the civilian establishment of Madras.[84]

Other issues missed or avoided by Gleig, and therefore by others who have written on Munro's Baramahal years using Gleig, was an appreciation of the superiority of village panchayats over British courts, a centrepiece of Munro's judicial reforms of 1816;[85] another was his early criticism of the near confiscatory pricing policy for procurement of textiles by commercial residents in the

[82] MC, F/151/139, undated.

[83] MC, F/151/142, to his father; this portion was deleted by Gleig, v. 1, p. 186.

[84] MC, F/151/142, 1 February 1797.

[85] MC, F/151/142, to his mother, 5 October 1794 (?). Another of the puffing efforts of Munro's father occurred a year before, that might have caused anxiety. His father wrote on 1 December 1793, enclosing a copy of a letter from Sir William Pulteney which thanked the older Munro for abstracts of his son's letter that had been shown to Henry Dundas, Pulteney's Parliamentary ally in the Pitt ministry. Pulteney favoured greater private trade in India, which put him at variance with Dundas, and he used Munro's letter to discredit the Company's monopoly by his boast that Read's method of revenue administration was far more efficient than the prevailing one in Madras, where Madras civilians were the puppets of 'dubashes'. The letter is found in MC, F/151/148; references to Pulteney are found in Philips, pp. 58 and 114–15.

Baramahal, and an argument which he presented to Thomas Cockburn of the MBOR for terminating the new, extortionate 'investment' programme established by Cornwallis.[86]

Such matters raised in his private letters between 1792 and 1799 afford personal insights at this time. By Munro's reckoning then, his career was not very successful. He had joined Read's service in the Baramahal with reluctance, as already noticed, yet his reasons for reluctance are anything but clear. The ostensible reason for at first rejecting Read's offer for service was that it might impede his progress in the army. But the slowness of his advance there, he had already concluded, was the result of his lack of influence and connection, not a lack of aptitude. In a letter to Erskine of 28 February 1790 we have another, perhaps additional, reason for his hesitation to join Read in the Baramahal: being separated from fellow officers whom he liked in order to serve in the Baramahal with 'a few men and even of these [only] one or two possess qualifications to make their company supportable'. And why? For some additional pay 'enabling me to make a small remittance next year'.[87] This was no unwillingness to remit money to Glasgow to meet his father's debts and to ease his family's financial difficulties, as Munro knew his sister would understand.

His reluctance to serve in the Baramahal sprang from a loneliness he anticipated from the loss of military friends and from his awareness that making friends was not easy for him. The deafness from his childhood disease was an embarrassment to which he referred frequently as a social impediment, and his sarcasm, even with friends, he knew to be a problem for himself as it was for others in his family.[88] We see in this an intimation of Munro's reluctance, later, to serve in Kanara and his efforts, then, to be returned to the Baramahal to which he had formed an attachment by 1799. His confidence and effectiveness in dealing with new and challenging official responsibilities were boundless throughout his career, but new social contexts—such as Madras city society through most of his career and England at the time his furlough approached in 1807—he found stressful and avoided as long as he could.

Still, money, enough money to assist his parents and brothers and sisters in Scotland and to acquire a competence for his own retirement, was much on his mind during the Baramahal years. With the support of Read, Munro joined his other junior colleagues to have their commissions on the revenue that they collected increased, and, along with one of them, William Macleod, sought permission to take up some land for growing indigo.[89] It was also a matter of concern to him that his talented sister Erskine was obliged to work at making textile pattern drawings so as to earn between £50 and £200 a year; and then

[86] MC, F/151/135, ff. 19–24, 10 July 1794.
[87] MC, F/151/141.
[88] MC, F/151/139, to his brother James, 3 May 1790(?).
[89] MC, F/151/135, ff. 28–9, undated.

there were his other siblings to support.[90] To his brother Daniel, then in business in Calcutta, he wrote about their younger sister Margaret who was of a marriageable age. Munro was against his brother's proposal for sending her to India for this, and proposed instead that a small dowry for a suitable marriage in Scotland should be settled upon her, towards which he was willing to make a contribution.[91]

By 1790 his three brothers—Alexander, Daniel and James—were all in India, the first two in indigo business and James a military surgeon in the Madras infantry. Letters to James, who was forced by bad health to quit India in 1793, were full of practical career advice, very much of the sort that he was later to give to his junior assistants in the Ceded Districts. Correspondence with his brothers in Bengal often concerned Munro's money and career preoccupations. In several letters to Alexander in 1794 and 1795 he asked for detailed information about indigo production and spoke of his plan to join Macleod for its cultivation in the Baramahal. That plan never materialized because the MBOR refused to let the land to them.[92] In December 1795 he also asked his brother for advice and help for the remittance and investment of several thousand pagodas in Bengal, which he explained was part of the profits from a trade venture to Malacca that he had entered on with an officer in Tinnevelly; another part of the proceeds from this he invested in the Madras agency house of Colt Baker and Company for a yield of 10 per cent.[93] Other letters of the same time refer to increasingly substantial sums lodged with his brother in the Calcutta agency house of Farlies, in which Alexander had become a partner.[94]

All of this suggests that Munro's military pay and his commissions as a collector had boosted his income considerably, making it unnecessary for him to engage in dubious ventures for money, one of which he described to his mother with robust humour. He told her in 1791 that he had been devising stratagems for adding to his military salary before being appointed in the Baramahal. One of these was an opportunity to head a forage and plunder corps in connection with the campaigns against Mysore in 1791. His task was to seize bullocks for use by the Company's forces, and his description of 'cattle-lifting' is as full of charm, self-ridicule and hyperbole as an episode from *Don Quixote* which he so admired.[95]

[90] MC, F/151/141, to Erskine, 23 January 1793.

[91] MC, F/151/139, undated.

[92] IOL, Board's Collections, F/17/v.752.

[93] MC, F/151/142 for these letters of 22 August 1794 and 2 May 1795, and for other cited letters of the same period.

[94] Munro's monthly income as a captain in 1796 would have been SP76 when in garrison, and SP126 when in the field: W. J. Wilson, *History of the Madras Army* (Madras: 1882), v. 2, p. 378. By contrast, his commissions in the Baramahal for 1793 was SP3000, in addition to which he received about SP30 monthly as military pay. MC, F/151/141, to his father, 17 February 1793 and F/151/142, to his brother, Alexander, 6 July 1795.

[95] MC, F/151/141, 29 June 1972.

But other letters to his family during these Baramahal years were often gloomy and bitter about his career prospects in India. To his father in 1796 he wrote that the Baramahal was bound to be turned over to 'civil successors' soon, and if he could not obtain another collectorship and more money he believed that it would be best either to return to Britain to make a new start in the military or to be content to serve out his time to retirement in India when, by the working of the seniority system, he would have attained the rank of major.[96]

To various members of his family and to friends he wrote with a surprising vehemence against the French Revolution, decrying its excesses and worrying about the spread of its doctrines to Britain. He scolded his sisters for their interest in revolutionary politics instead of in Shakespeare, and especially for Margaret's interest in the 'doctrines of Mrs. Woolstonecraft'. To his mother, earlier in 1796, he wrote of his admiration of Edmund Burke, 'in spite of his declamations and in some places downright nonsense'. In the light of his worries about money and career it is hardly surprising that he bent every effort to win some sort of preferment, some advantage, to offset his lack of 'connection'. He went to the length of asking his brother Alexander in Calcutta discreetly to inquire into political and military affairs involving the Nizam's government or the Marathas from some of his highly placed friends there. This he, Thomas, might purvey to the Madras governor, Lord Hobart, as a means of bettering his standing with the latter whom all believed, erroneously, to be moving to the Governor-Generalship.

Even with the inclusion of Munro's private correspondence, it is difficult to strike an interpretive balance from among existing studies of the Baramahal in the late eighteenth century and Munro's place in it. There are two reasons for this. First, there is the problem of historical perspective. For most students of Munro and the Munro system the sheer weight of the system in its full development bears heavily upon this bit of Indian territory in the late years of the eighteenth century. One must sympathize with Ross Mangles' question, though not his scorn, when, shortly after Munro's death, he asked how the remote, sparsely populated and inhospitable Baramahal could have produced great administrative principles.[97]

Also unanswered, notwithstanding Brian Murton's able reconstruction of the society, economy and culture of the Baramahal in the 1790s, and the work of other modern scholars, is why Read not only defied his orders from the MBOR to establish a village lease system in the Baramahal, but did so in the face of the evidence of his time that there the village was the prevailing base of agrarian and revenue management.[98] Why, by December 1796, was it deter-

[96] MC, F/151/142, 10 May 1796 to his father.

[97] *Edinburgh Review*, v. 55 (April, 1832), 'Sketch of the Ryotwar System. . . .', p. 87: 'The narrow basis of a few facts collected in two or three petty provinces at its [India's] southern extremity. . . .'

[98] Brian Murton: 'Land and Class: Culture, Social, and Biophysical Integration of

mined to make complex and cumbersome revenue engagements with some 80,000 substantial and insubstantial cultivators?

Two answers to these questions are usually offered by those who have worked on the Baramahal, on ryotwar, or on Munro. One is Read's (and Munro's) supposed sympathy for the small Baramahal ryot.[99] The other is that settlement with individual cultivators was seen as a return to the 'traditional' system which rulers like Tipu Sultan had subverted.[100] Some support for both of these propositions, but also their contraries, can be found in some of Read's early reports, especially that to Cornwallis of 15 November 1792, to which Read appended a long historical section.[101]

However, neither sentiment nor compelling historical precedent can account for the system that finally emerged in the Baramahal under Read. Rather, it was political considerations that led to the system of revenue settlements with the host of Baramahal's small and large holders of landed entitlements. The formulation of these political considerations was more the work of Munro than of Read. Fully two and a half years before Read's proclamation to the people of Tiruppattur in December 1796—what Dykes called the 'charter' of ryotwar—Munro set the basic political terms. This was in a report to Read of 31 July 1794, in which he outlined the method he proposed to follow in the central division for which he was responsible. The document is noteworthy in several respects. It established the homogeneous category of 'ryot', which was defined as any cultivator who engaged to 'rent' land from government, however great or small, and who possessed a document ('patta') fixing the

Interior Tamilnadu in the Late Eighteenth Century', in R. E. Frykenberg (ed.), *Land Tenure and Peasant in South Asia* (New Delhi: Orient Longman, 1977), pp. 81–100; 'Territory, Social Structure, and Settlement Dynamics in Tamil Nadu before 1800 A.D.', *Pacific Viewpoint*, v. 17, no. 1 (1976), pp. 3–22; 'Key People in the Countryside: Decision-making in Interior Tamilnadu in the Late Eighteenth Century Countryside', *The Indian Social and Economic History Review*, v. 2, no. 2 (June, 1973), pp. 157–81; 'Mapping the Evidence of Money: Manufacturing, Trade, Markets and Revenue Farming in Salem and the Baramahal in the Eighteenth Century', paper presented to the Annual South Asia Meeting, University of Wisconsin, November 1984.

[99] Beaglehole, p. 21: 'Read . . . had come to the job with a strong sympathy for the ryot. . . .'

[100] Mukherjee and Frykenberg, p. 219, where the Chola term *vellan vagai* used by K. A. Nilakanta Sastri, *The Cola* (Madras: University of Madras, 1955; 2nd ed.), pp. 571–74, is assumed, questionably, to be ryotwari.

[101] Thus, what may in one place seem to be a genuine concern for impoverished and oppressed cultivators, is in another place a pragmatic concern with establishing rules and rates of revenue that could be realized, hence paid, by cultivators. On the restoration of some sort of pre-Tipu Sultan revenue system, Read wrote to the MBOR on 10 May 1792 that he was intent on 'taking the system of this country as my guide in all revenue matters, I . . . follow the established rule for revenue payments . . .', in BR, 1, p. 89. His historical disquisition is also in this volume: 'Sketch of Revenue Management in the Countries North of the Caveri under the Gentu, the Moorish, and the Hon[oura]ble Company's Government', pp. 137ff.

precise holding and the revenue thereon. Simultaneously, Munro outlined and justified a plan to reduce or obliterate the resource command of all superior land-controlling men. These last included not only peasant caste leaders ('head gauds' and 'karaikkars') with authority over localities consisting of many villages, but even those whose dominance was limited to one or two villages ('patels'). In effect, Munro was proposing to strike at the powers and rights of any magnate by whom major decisions about the utilization of men and land were made. The letter reads in part as follows:

> In [1792, *fasli* year] 1202, every village was rented separately in order to extend the benefit of [revenue] farming to all inferior patels and deprive the head gauds of the influence which by holding large tracts of country they had so long enjoyed and generally exercised in the oppression of those under them, but tho' it answered to this end, it was found that great abuses still prevailed by the patels of villages being able to evade payment of their own rents, favour their friends, and make extra collections from the rest of the ryots not only on account of the public revenue but for many private purposes. No way seemed so likely to put an effectual stop to these practices as the descending lower into detail and fixing rent of every individual. This mode was accordingly adopted in... [1793]. The value of the land of every man who paid a single rupee of rent was ascertained as nearly as time would permit, a patta signed by me was given to him individually specifying the quantity and nature of his ground, the rent to be paid, and from the amount of these pattas was formed the assessment of the village for which a [different] patta containing a list of the rents and the names of the ryots was given to the patel but he was expected to act merely as a Collector of the rents for he had no other authority either to raise or diminish them in any instant; a small piece of ground was given to him at low valuation for the trouble of executing the duties of his station. Besides securing all the ryots who paid rent to the... [government] the produce of their labours it was necessary to extend protection to another class who from their poverty being unable to pay monthly rents cultivated lands under the patels and principal farmers for a certain share of the crop. The people frequently complained... that half the produce was sometimes exacted instead of a third and then when grain was dear, payment was taken in kind... to remedy this evil the head-farmers... were ordered to give an account of it to... [Munro's] division cutcherry [office] where pattas were given to each cultivator.... By this means the head-farmers were compelled to adhere to their engagements and prevented from altering them as formerly whenever they found it convenient, for when any dispute arose between the parties respecting the division of the crop, it would be easily adjusted by reference to the patta.... After fixing the rents, the securing the collection of them became the next object; for this purpose in every village all the ryots gave separate bonds for their respective rents and a joint one of the sum total of the village binding themselves to make good any deficiency that might occur from the failure of

any of their number but as it might sometime happen that the loss might be so great as to exceed the capacity of the village to defray it, the joint obligation was extended from the village to five or six . . . to a whole district [taluk]. Tho' this sytem of [collective] obligation would ensure the full collection of the revenue under any circumstance, excepting war or famine, there are such objections carrying it to the utmost extent that it would be better to limit the narrower bounds and to lose the revenue which it would no doubt in consequence sometimes become necessary to remit. It discourages industry because, as no farmer can be supposed to know the exact state of cultivation in a whole district he can never be sure where his payments will end or whether he is working for his own emolument or not it encourages idleness because many men become less anxious to compleat their rents from knowing that whatever deficiencies may be, will be collected from others, it induces the ryots to come forward continually with false statements of losses, it involves the Collector in endless discussions to know whether they are real or pretended and what is worse than all it enables the patels and karnams [village accountants] to collect more from the ryots than the real loss. . . . The end proposed to be obtained by entering so far into detail as to fix individual rents was to give ryots an idea of property to teach them that when they paid their kists [instalments on the revenue due] no person had any further claim upon them and to encourage them to resist extortion . . .[102]

There is nothing of sentiment for the small farmer nor historical precedent here. Munro was proposing nothing less than the completion, by administrative means, of the military conquest of the Baramahal territory. Tipu Sultan, in Munro's mind, remained a real threat to the Company, and it was the perceived task of civil administration in the Baramahal to divest ancient local lordships of any capacity to resist or overturn Company rule. But, more than this, by stripping the ancient *gauds* and *karaikkars* of their locality resource control, and even further by limiting village heads in their command over share-cropping labour and converting them into mere subordinate revenue servants of his own subordinate tahsildars, Munro was introducing a new and very distant authority—ultimately that of London—directly into the South Indian—or any Indian—agrarian system, for the first time. Moreover, in designating the village, and ultimately the taluk, as the unit of joint revenue liability for all patta holders, Munro drove an intrusive wedge into the core of the existing agrarian relations. He had sought to transform a system of political competition of all against all—previously played on a large scale as he and others saw the pre-British condition—to one played out at the level of basic production. In this new political system the Company, or more precisely himself as the Company in place, stood as the protector and guarantor of all.

The question of 'leases', or for how long agreements between any individual 'who paid a single rupee of rent' and the Company were to stand—whether

[102] BR, 1, pp. 220–1.

for several years or annually—was less significant than the principle of the individual patta holder in direct relationship with the Company. Munro was slow to yield to Read on the question of how long the revenue engagements concluded were to stand. Not until September 1797 did he finally capitulate to Read on annual settlements.

Yet his July 1794 report to Read on procedures he had introduced in the central division was revolutionary; it was Munro's most percipient formulation of what later was to be called ryotwar.[103] When Munro, later, was given responsibility for the pacification and settlement of the territories ceded to the Company by the Nizam in 1800, he expanded the provision of granting each patel 'a small piece of ground... for the trouble he had of executing his duties' into authorizing there the alienation of almost half of all cultivated land as inams. Still, his July 1794 report provides a clear idea of Munro's political principle of destroying any and all intermediary authority between the Company and the cultivator as the best assurance of the securing of control by the Company over its new dominions.

Munro's sense of the practical, as well as the acuteness of his political sensibilities over those of Read, are further intimated in his response to a draft of the latter's proclamation of 10 December 1796.

Read's proclamation to the people of Tiruppattur contained twenty-nine rules. Munro commented in detail on six of these as well as on the document in general.[104] He attacked the formulaic complexity of many of Read's provisions, something that he had done in the past and that the MBOR was to do in the near future. Read's penchant for minutely scaling differences and his attempts to frame rules in accordance with such differences were seen as unrealistic and dangerous to real control.[105]

Because there were two matters to which he attributed primary importance—reliable and predictable revenue for the Company and securely tenanted and gradually enriched small farms—Munro disagreed with Read's principle of annual settlements. All lands except those watered by tanks, Munro argued, should be given on leases of five years or longer. He went further to argue that if the existing level of assessment (which he believed to be too high) was

[103] In other ways Munro's procedures differed from those of his colleagues, William Macleod and James Graham. Macleod, in the northern division of the Baramahal, held to a village renting system along with some tax farming, BR, 1, pp. 232–4. Graham in the northern division reported village rentals at the same time, ibid., pp. 222–5, and it was not until 1796 that he became persuaded that the karaikar and others were unreliable agents of revenue collection for the Company, BR, 6, p. 99, Graham to Read, 26 February 1796. It is also obvious that Munro continued to follow the procedure he had outlined in his 1794 report to Read; see BR, 1, pp. 81–2, referring to February 1796.

[104] Munro to Read, 15 November 1796, in Arbuthnot, pp. 3–11; the draft proclamation is also found there, pp. 587–92. The date of Munro's letter confirms that the latter was a draft, and Arbuthnot observes that the proclamation lacked the assent of the MBOR; ibid., p. 3.

[105] See Arbuthnot, p. 6.

reduced by 20 per cent, and the fields presently occupied granted to their peasant cultivators 'in perpetuity', improvements were more likely to be undertaken and the revenue enhanced. Additionally, a powerful lure to migrate to the Baramahal would be exerted upon the peasantry of Tipu Sultan's Mysore and Coimbatore who, it was believed, continued to be subjected to the exactions that had produced the poverty of the Baramahal peasantry. Only long leases, or, better, a permanent alienation of the land to peasant proprietors, could overcome the 'recollection of former times, when new demands always followed close upon the ability of paying them'.[106]

Of course in 1796 Munro was unaware of his grand paternity of ryotwar; he was moved by the clearest of political motives. The Company's revenue, political control and military security were seen as best served by the reduction of all intermediary structures in the political economy of the Baramahal. This meant those vestiges of the post-Vijayanagara and Mysorean polities—poligars, tax-farming amildars, and others; less obviously, it meant also all superior landholders beyond the confines of the villages of the Baramahal. Here, then, was a very different conception of revenue and political administration from that formulated by Lionel Place in the Jaghire and espoused by the Madras establishment. Intermediaries like the nattars of the Jaghire and the karaikars of the Baramahal had no role and were to be purged. The objective was to isolate from older sodalities and power bases the individual peasant and to replace older forms of peasant security with new ones more congenial to the Company.

To achieve this would be slow and difficult, Munro thought, because of the prior experience of the Baramahal peasantry with what he believed to be capricious and rapacious governments. Benevolence and constancy in the Company's government would in time, he believed, create such confidence among the peasantry as to lead to agricultural development and increased and secure revenues:

> collections will be made without difficulty, and will not require much experience to manage them; the farmers will have no temptation to abandon their arable lands to occupy waste, which will render the complicated details of changeably-rated lands in a great measure unnecessary. By degrees, though slowly, lands will become saleable, new settlers will be induced to come from the westward [from Tipu Sultan's Mysore], and cultivation will extend so rapidly, that in ten or fifteen years the amount of revenue will probably be as much as it would have been had no abatement [which he urged] been granted; while the inhabitants, by having within that period the whole of their property at least doubled will then pay with ease what they now pay with difficulty.[107]

Though Munro's arguments in November 1796 appear to have failed to persuade Read, and though Munro a year later came to accept the latter's proposals, the ideas expressed by him in reaction to Read's 'charter' proclamation

[106] Ibid., p. 11.
[107] Ibid.

of 1796 sprang from political convictions of the sort that Cornwallis also harboured at the time. Behind the ideas of both was an imperial conception to which each gave a different expression. This was based in part certainly on what each had experienced in India, and in part obviously on their very different statuses and responsibilities. But it was not, as Mangles contended in 1832, because they were the progenitors of 'two different sects of our Anglo-Indian statesman'.[108] Mangles was correct in recognizing the symbolic significance of the names of Cornwallis and Munro in charter debates of 1832.[109] However, the contrast of the two systems wrongly informs modern views, as manifested in Beaglehole's monograph on Munro.

Placed in their own times—the 1790s—Munro and Cornwallis contrast far less with each other than do their views with the Company traditions and structures with which each worked, and about which they shared a similar sense of inadequacy. Both were Dundas men—Cornwallis directly and explicitly, Munro by implication. They were impatient with the older structure of the Company, with its limited vision, its venal preoccupation with personal wealth and advantage, its unprepossessing and imminent commercialism. Both sought in Company service lofty purposes: Cornwallis because his ripe, aristocratic reputation for statesmanship would admit of no other; Munro, for all of the opposite reasons, because he could afford no other. Both sought some transcendent end, such as to make callings of their careers. This self-conscious purposiveness provided both men with qualities which set them apart from most of their contemporaries and enabled the laying of new foundations.

None of the issues examined above can easily separate the halting, confused measures essayed by Read and Munro in the Baramahal from the ideologized ryotwar system of the later nineteenth century. The burden of origins weighs as heavily upon interpretations of Read's Baramahal, as the burden of heavy assessment weighs upon interpretations of early ryotwar. Yet, apart from a few essentials—annual settlements, direct relations between cultivators and the state, exorbitant revenue demands, and the person of Munro—there is much of the future Madras system absent from the Baramahal. Most important, there was almost total inattention to judicial matters, and this was not seriously taken up until Munro's return to India in 1814. Then, he presided over a commission for the revision of the Madras judiciary and the replacement of many of the legal procedures introduced from Bengal in 1802 by procedures consonant with the re-establishment of ryotwar in Madras. The Baramahal administration of the late eighteenth century did not contain the future. It was not the genetic base seen by Beaglehole, but, as more as Mukherjee's work makes clear, the first, tentative formulation of some of the principles and proce-

[108] *Edinburgh Review*, v. 55, p. 79.

[109] Ibid. Mangles expressed the hope that his discussion 'may be of some use to those engaged in the important enquiries lately instituted by Parliament' regarding the renewal of the charter in 1833.

dures that were ultimately to constitute the Munro system, and a perceived alternative to Cornwallis' system.

When Cornwallis rejected the Madras civilian establishment in favour of the soldier Read, he was choosing more than language competence and knowledge of local customs. He was also choosing a political order biased towards military rather than the commercial ends that the Company's civil servants in Madras were more competent to achieve. Lord Wellesley's choice of Munro for Kanara and later for the Ceded Districts manifested the same priority. Wellesley, more than Cornwallis, was expansionistic and thus impatient with the existing commercial-civil structure of the Company in India. So much was this the case that he seriously proposed to Henry Dundas that the Bombay Presidency be dissolved and all interests in western India be brought under a Madras reshaped by him to imperial purposes.[110]

KANARA

There matters had come to stand in 1799, when Munro was given the Kanara territory. Cornwallis' scheme for Bengal, combining private landed property backed by British legal principles and procedures and a more complete monopoly over export commerce, was drawing criticism. In England this led to a retreat of the directors from their advocacy of Cornwallis' Bengal plan to a more cautious stance previously urged by Sir John Shore, Cornwallis' somewhat reluctant coadjutor. Shore persisted in his opposition to the permanent arrangement first voiced in 1790, insisting that a full ten-year 'period of experiment', if not an even longer time, was necessary to assure that the system was practicable and just.[111]

The impact earlier of Sullivan's and Greville's works upon the directors is impossible to gauge now, but the minimum effect would have been to encourage the caution that Shore continued to express. Taken more seriously, however, Sullivan and Greville could have been seen as repudiating the Cornwallis plan. Both had sought to present the view of an ancient Indian 'civil society', in the meaning Adam Smith had given to the phrase, that constituted a strong base upon which to construct the Company state. To some extent this was a restatement of Warren Hastings' 'orientalist' position, but it was founded upon more solid evidence and experience. Though respectfully presented—because of Cornwallis' heightened and Hastings' diminished stature in the late 1790s—the claims of each (more perhaps Sullivan than Greville) posed caveats to the innovations of Cornwallis. This was despite the fact that both Greville and Sullivan believed that there was an indigenous landlord class deserving protection and security from the arbitrary actions of the Company, as well as from the unregulated practices of money-lenders. The implications

110 Edward Ingram, *Commitment to Empire: Prophesies of the Great Game in Asia, 1797–1800* (Oxford: Clarendon Press, 1981).

111 *The Fifth Report*, v. 2, pp 518–43, for a discussion of Shore's reservations.

of the arguments of both was that there must be substantial scope and opportunity for Indians in the administration of India, something denied or deprecated under Bengal principles. Thus, at virtually the moment of the triumph of Cornwallis' policy for a radically modernized Company state in India, the challenge against that policy also existed—and with that the possibility for its ultimate defeat.

The last Mysore war in 1799 relieved Lieutenant Colonel Alexander Read of further embarrassment over the Baramahal and took him and his junior colleague, Munro, back into the field. For Read it was the last official position he was to hold before retiring from India. For Munro it was the beginning of a transition from being a promising junior soldier–administrator to becoming both an authority on Indian administration and a man with 'connection'.

In May 1799, following the seige of Seringapatam and the death of Tipu Sultan, Munro, along with another rising man, Captain John Malcolm, was appointed as secretary to the commission charged with the partition of the conquered Mysore territory and the establishment of the new, smaller kingdom under its restored Hindu royal family.[112] Senior members of the commission included the Governor-General's two brothers Arthur and Henry Wellesley, and Lieutenant Colonels William Kirkpatrick and Barry Close—the last to serve as Resident to the Mysore court. All were to remain on warm terms with Munro in the years that followed. This fact, taken together with Munro's next two appointments, to Kanara and to the Ceded Districts, suggest that he had attained a superior standing within the highest political and military levels of the conquering British regime in India, if not within the Madras branch of its operation. Upon completion of the commission's work, Munro was named collector of Kanara, a territory gained in the 1799 treaty. Here he served for fifteen months before being appointed to the major position of collector of the Ceded Districts in October 1800.

Kanara proved to be taxing but highly successful for Munro. Sick when he was appointed, he expressed misgivings about what lay before him and about departing from the Baramahal, for which place he had formed an attachment. Having hoped to return there as Read's successor, Munro complained to those whom he thought might help, but he was counselled by several to stick it out in Kanara lest he be thought an ungrateful and fickle man and returned to his slowly-progressing and low-paying military career. Colonel Arthur Wellesley alone spoke differently. He wrote to Munro in October 1799 of being surprised by Munro's complaints and 'much concerned' since both he and his brother, Henry, had supposed 'you desirious of being appointed collector of Canara' and had urged the appointment: 'one word from you would have stopped the arrangement and there is every reason to believe a provision would have been made for you elsewhere. It is perhaps not too late. I have written to my brother

[112] John Williams Kaye, *The Life and Correspondence of Major-General Sir John Malcolm, G. C. B.* (London: Smith Elder and Co., 1856), v. 1, p. 87.

[Lord Mornington, the Governor-General] on the subject; and I hope that he will make an arrangement suitable to your wishes.'[113]

After the peace and order achieved in the Baramahal between 1792 and 1799, Kanara was fraught with difficulty and frustration. A long, narrow tract bounded by the Arabian Sea and the western ghats, its 8300 square miles were divided between an upland tract perched on the edge of the Deccan plateau and a major portion of coastal plain sloping steeply to the sea. It was cut by rivers which, along with the torrential monsoon to which the area was subject, made mobility difficult; its population was scattered in small homestead settlements, with none of the nucleated villages Munro knew from the Baramahal and elsewhere. Thus its people were difficult to assemble for purposes of administration. Revenue administration was in a shambles, its local tax collectors having been replaced by military appointees of Haidar Ali and Tipu Sultan, and, these soldiers having fled after the latter's defeat, Munro's efforts to establish orderly rule were delayed. It was a territory under various lordships—rajas and chiefs—to whom promises of reward, along with arms, had been given by the Company for assistance against Tipu. It was finally a region upon which an able Maratha adventurer had come to prey and against whom a force under Colonel Arthur Wellesley was deployed, the material maintenance of which force was an additional responsibility for Munro.

All of these adversities Munro remarkably overcame, and still found time to submit two long reports to the Madras government. These writings, as much as his political and administrative accomplishments there, boosted his standing to a degree that he was seen to be the man to subdue the even more formidable Ceded Districts territory, a year later. The reports are those of 31 May and 19 November 1800, and by dint of them he had succeeded in writing himself out of Kanara.[114]

The report of May is a notable historical document in at least two senses.[115] It was among the first to insist that individual, private property in land was ancient in India; it was also among the earliest British reports on India to use purportedly historical documents to present findings intended to inform the revenue policy of the Company. This last claim may seem incorrect if one thinks of the contemporary reports of Lionel Place from the Chingleput Jaghire in 1799 and earlier. However, Place was speaking not of private, individual landholding, but of hereditary, corporate landed proprietorship in the hands

[113] Gleig, v. 1, p. 235.

[114] *The Fifth Report*, v. 3, p. 315, wrongly dates this as 9 November. The 31 May 1800 report drew appreciative comment from the MBOR in its 'Revenue Letter', 9 October 1800, paras. 63–70, and the appreciation of the Court of Directors appears in their 'Revenue Despatch' to Madras, dated 24 August 1804, pp. 417ff.

[115] Perhaps three senses, actually: The Madras Governor, Lord Bentinck, in 1806 pronounced himself 'astonished' at the resemblance between the 'actual' state of property according to Munro and the proposed permanency of ryotwar: *The Fifth Report*, v. 3, p. 467, regarding his Minute of 28 November 1806.

of 'meerasidars' whose 'ownership' consisted of fractional shares of income in village production. Moreover, Place's argument for the continuation of this form of ownership was based on analogy with feudal England, as abstracted from Blackstone and fortified by references to unspecified and general 'Gentoo laws'.[116] It was only later, in 1814, that Francis W. Ellis presented historical documentation on *kaniyatchi* and 'mirasi' rights in support of Place's early reports.[117] In contrast with Place, Munro based his claim on 'accounts and traditions' purportedly harking back to the fourteenth century, when the Vijayanagara king Harihara 'made a new assessment of Canara upon principles laid down in the Shastra. . . .'[118]

Six months later, in November 1800, Munro submitted another report on Kanara which was focused less on its history than upon the present vigour of private proprietorial rights among its inhabitants. To emphasize this point he compared Kanara with the Baramahal, where 'a dispute about land scarcely came before me, once in six months... [whereas in Kanara] every other cause of litigation or complaint seems to be lost, in that of land'.[119] His recollection about the Baramahal was more convenient than accurate if we consult his own and others' correspondence about the Baramahal. In 1794 Munro had written from Dharmapuri, in the Baramahal, to his friend Alexander Allan, complaining of being 'engaged at present from morning to night... in debating about rents. . . .'[120] The same preoccupation with disputes about land in the Baramahal is confirmed in the recollections of a younger colleague of his there, that Munro would open his public office at about nine in the morning, at which appeared.'a troop of complainants whose disputes being chiefly land and property. . . .'[121] The differences which Munro alleged between landholding in the Baramahal and Kanara may have been real enough, but these differences appear not to have been reflected in the volume of litigation, as he insisted.

The November report was concerned with how to meet the Madras government's demand for a 'permanent settlement' in Kanara on the lines of the Bengal zamindari settlement. Munro agreed that if there were no private landed estates in existence, 'because the whole is the property of Government', there might be an advantage in creating them. But, in Kanara, he protested, such private estates already existed, together with title deeds whose 'validity has probably stood more trials than all the estates of England.' Thus, the creation of large

[116] *The Fifth Report*, v. 3, pp. 153–6.

[117] 121. C. P. Brown (ed.), *Three Treatises on Mirasi Right by the Late Francis W. Ellis, A.D. 1817* (Madras: Christian Knowledge Society Press, 1852), based on Ellis' replies to government, as abstracted on 2 August 1814.

[118] Arbuthnot, p. 60.

[119] *The Fifth Report*, v. 3, p. 315.

[120] Cited in K. V. N. Sastri, *The Munro System of British Statesmanship in India* (Mysore: University of Mysore, 1939), p. 3.

[121] 'Memorandum Relative to Revenue Servants: Extracts of a Letter from A. Read [then sub-collector in the CD under Munro] to Another Junior Colleague, James Cochrane', IOL, MC, F/151/10, f.95.

estates and 'great proprietors' could not occur in Kanara 'without annihilating all the rights of the present landlords'.[122] That estates in Kanara were small Munro saw as advantageous for several reasons: they were more productive than large estates, notwithstanding the recent experience of agricultural improvers in England, because India was not England; they were more easily administered for revenue purposes; and they were politically less dangerous, for large landholders 'might in time become a kind of petty poligars' of the sort that the Company was then fighting in the southern districts of Madras.[123] To this Munro added another argument: 'small estates may be considered as an arrangement of nature' in the sense that the system of inheritance would assure that large estates, once created, would become smaller unless positive steps were taken to prevent partibility.[124]

If despite his recommendation for a settlement with small estates, which he insisted already existed, the government pressed ahead with the creation of large estates, arguing that these ought to be formed on the basis of existing social or communal territories: 'The most convenient arrangement would be the ancient one of maganies or gramams. . . . To break in upon ancient boundaries and landmarks for the sake of . . . squaring estates, would occasion much trouble . . . because these boundaries serve not only to divide lands, but also particular tribes or families who form distinct communities in their respective villages.'[125] This last is a rare argument for Munro. In all his works, and especially his later writings, he tended to avoid references to rural sodalities, such as those above, on the probable grounds that their existence weakened his claims about ryotwar agreements between the state and individual cultivators. In the case of Kanara this reference to 'distinct communities' and landholding cannot but raise doubts about his major assertion of private, individual, small-landed proprietorship there.

He concluded his November report with the observation that since some parts of Kanara had no private landholdings and 'the land belongs to the 'sirkar', more time would be required to form an estimate of the productive capacity of prospective estates.[126] Therefore, he urged deferring any permanent settlement in Kanara for five years, as well as a substantial reduction in the assessments on all holdings there.

These reports of 1800 won immediate approval from his superiors on the Board of Revenue and from Lord Clive, the Governor of Madras. The latter approvingly noted how Munro's description of Kanara showed the effect of the rapacious Mysorean rule in corrupting the 'wise and liberal institutions of the antient Hindoo government', especially of 'the proprietory rights in the lands of Canara'. Accordingly, Clive urged that the MBOR follow Munro's

[122] Ibid., p. 83.
[123] Ibid., p. 87.
[124] Ibid., p. 84.
[125] Ibid., pp. 86–7.
[126] Ibid., p. 88.

recommendations. He did express puzzlement over one part of Munro's policies in Kanara. This pertained to inams, or revenue-free land, there. Why, the governor asked, when Tipu had resumed inams and when the Company 'having succeeded to rights actually exercised by Tipoo Sultan', were inam rights granted again by Munro? Why, especially, when the value of the inams resumed by Tipu and regranted by Munro reduced the revenue to the Company by more than all the rapacious exactions imposed by Haidar Ali and Tipu and even earlier regimes?[127]

There is no record that these queries about inams in Kanara were ever answered, any more than similar queries from the Court of Directors were when Munro served in the Ceded Districts. With respect to Kanara, though, in 1804—as usual long after the event—the Court of Directors joined in the general approbation of Munro's Kanara reports, expressing their 'great satisfaction' with his 'actual examination of ancient sunnuds and revenue accounts' and what they took as Munro's assurances that 'enough ancient document remain to enable him to furnish a complete abstract of the land rent during a period of more than 400 years'.[128]

At that time, 1804, the Directors did express some surprise that Lionel Place of the MBOR 'should have spoken of these statements [of Munro] as merely hypothetical'.[129] Place had made this accusation at the time that he resigned from the MBOR, in 1802, in protest against the conditions under which the Board operated in Madras. Among his grievances was the privileged position of military collectors like Munro who flaunted the Board's regulations and the fact that, on the basis of the 'hypothetical statements of Major Munro . . . the public revenue of Canara amounts to little more than a tenth of the gross produce' of the province.[130]

Place's objections were well taken. Not only was Kanara's revenue assessment low in relation to other Madras districts, but Munro's justification for that discrepancy—his 'historical' reconstruction of ancient revenue demands—was a mere surmise based on some very vague evidence. What was this evidence?

Munro said in May 1800 that village accountants in Kanara had kept 'black books' of revenue accounts for centuries in order to preserve a record of landholding and transfers as well as to maintain a 'register of the public revenue'.[131] These registers, having been prohibited by the regimes of Haidar and Tipu (for reasons neither offered nor, possibly, sensible), many of these 'books' were lost; but Munro said enough of them remained to permit an abstract of revenue for four centuries, the statement which so forcibly struck the Directors. He also insisted that, according to 'traditions and accounts' from this distant

[127] IOL, *Madras Revenue Consultations*, 19 September 1800, pp. 2239–48.

[128] IOL, *Madras Despatches* 24 August 1804. pp. 417ff.

[129] Ibid., pp. 418–19.

[130] Lionel Place's Minute to 9 October 1802 in: IOL, *Board's Collections* F/4/150; also in MC, F/151/7, ff. 121–41.

[131] Arbuthnot, p. 59.

past, all cultivated lands were privately held and that 'all public documents convincingly testify that sirkar land ['owned' and 'rented' by government] was altogether unknown' except for 'unclaimed waste'. Prior to Harihara of Vijayanagara, Munro asserted, there was no land tax in Kanara; after that ruler's time (*c*. 1334–47), a system was established and was 'still extant', a system which set out the division of land production among landlord, cultivator and the state, as he had described in his May report, and this was taken by him to be the standard rent, or *rekha*, for Kanara.[132]

Other officials, of Munro's time and later, failed to find these ancient documents. Francis Buchanan (Hamilton) visited Kanara shortly after Munro's departure for the Ceded Districts, and he repeated Munro's assertions in the main. Buchanan did not refer to 'black books', but he did speak of a Brahman informant, one whose family had held the hereditary office of accountant of Barakuru town for generations. This man had shown Buchanan Sanskrit books purporting to date from Vijayanagara times and to contain information on revenue administration; the Brahman accountant gave Buchanan an oral summary of that purportedly ancient system.[133]

The alleged transformation of the land-revenue system of Kanara in Vijayanagara times is repeated by Munro's successors there until the present time. None of them was able to substantiate the historicity of these claims, and perhaps none dared to venture upon the iconoclasm of checking on Munro and perhaps finding him wrong. Only one of Munro's successors in Kanara registered disbelief in Munro's claims of 1800. This was John Sturrock, who spent a decade in Kanara as collector during the late nineteenth century. Writing in 1894, Sturrock observed that none of the 'black books' had ever been found even though, according to Munro, those that had existed in his day were called in for deposit in taluk offices, where they were presumably destroyed by insects or fires.[134] Having made this observation, Sturrock somewhat agnostically suggested that there was no way that Munro could have reconstructed Vijayanagara revenue rates, as he had claimed, because to have done so would have required information on acreages and on the money value of grain harvested

[132] Ibid., pp. 60–1. Of 30 measures of output, the government received 5, Brahmans 1.5, temples 1, landlords 7.5, and cultivators 15. 'Rekha' was assumed to be the Vijayanagara revenue term by Munro, and this was repeated by Wilson in his *Glossary*, p. 443. However, it may have been a post-Vijayanagara term, perhaps from the late seventeenth century. Rice speaks of the term used in Karnataka in connection with the Ikkeri nayaka, Sivappa, where it is contrasted with the Vijayanagara 'shist', denominated *varaha; Mysore, A Gazetteer*, v. 2, pp. 349 and 405.

[133] Francis Buchanan (Hamilton), *Journey from Madras through the Countries of Mysore, Canara and Malabar, 1800–01*, v. 3, pp. 110–23.

[134] John Sturrock, *Madras District Manuals, South Canara* (Madras: 1894), v. 1, p. 95. Colin Mackenzie, writing to a nearby Mysore in about 1802, complained of the lack of historical records dealing with older periods of Indian history, IOL, *Catalogue of Manuscripts of Euopean Languages*, v. 1, Mackenzie Collection, part II, 'General', by James Sutherland Cotton, J. Charpentier and E. H. Johnston, p. 29.

during that remote time, neither of which were available.[135]

To probe the validity of Munro's historical claims further than Sturrock could in his time, we may consult the modern historiography of medieval Kanara. Knowledge about landed relations and systems during and after the Vijayanagara kingdom is not great. Two recent monographs dealing with the history of Kanara, or Tuluva country, provide no support for, and to a degree contradict, Munro's contentions.

Like most works dealing with this period of South Indian history, nothing of the detail hypothesized by Munro (to follow Place's denigrating evaluation of Munro's historical arguments) can be discovered. According to both modern historians of Kanara, the extension of Vijayanagara dominance to the coastal province altered little administratively.[136] Governors (*mahapradhanas*) were appointed who were usually, but not always, outsiders and these officials were based in two major trade centres on the coast, each a capital of a part of the country, Managalore and Barakuru.[137] From these towns taxes on the export of rice and spices, often to as distant destinations as the Arabian peninsula, were collected.

Modern scholarship on this time strongly suggests that the scope for major changes in land administration was narrow. During the Vijayanagara occupation of Kanara, its northern portion, especially, remained under ancient chieftainships whose local rule continued unimpaired by the conquest. These chiefs included a number of Jaina families and many who followed matrilineal succession (*aliya santana kattu*); all preserved these heritages as well as their political independence from the Vijayanagara administrative system. Anointment of rajas as of old was continued;[138] large military forces were retained under chiefly control;[139] wars were waged and political agreements made with neither the consent of nor reference to Vijayanagara overlords of even so great a stature as Krishnadevaraya (reign, 1509–29).[140] To this must be added the pervasive evidence of the continuity of village and locality administration under assemblies (e.g. nadu) dominated by martial, peasant communities, impressive evidence of what historians of the medieval period of Karnataka call the persistence of ancient usage (*purva-mariyade*).[141] As to Munro's assertion that state-held lands did not exist in Vijayanagara times or before, scholars of medieval Tuluva refer to such lands, usually designated as *bhandara sthala*, signifying places where state-level taxation was collected.[142]

[135] Sturrock, p. 96.

[136] K. V. Ramesh, *A History of South Kanara, from the Earliest Times to the Fall of Vijayanagara* (Dharwar: Karnataka University, 1970), pp. 258–60; P. Gururaja Bhatt, *Studies in Tuluva History of Culture* (Manipal: 1975), p. 159.

[137] Ramesh, p. 155, and Gururaja, p. 44.

[138] Gururaja, p. 158.

[139] Ramesh, p. 265 and Gururaja, p. 158.

[140] Ramesh, pp. 218–20 and Gururaja, pp. 184–9.

[141] Gururaja, p. 159.

[142] Ramesh, p. 284.

Another of Munro's contentions was that the system of land administration inaugurated by Vijayanagara was modified later by the Bednore regime, otherwise called the Keladi kingdom or the Ikkeri kingdom. Again, modern scholarship on this seventeenth-century lordship—which expanded its control from the upland section of Kanara to the coastal area—provides very little information about land relations, because there is almost no evidence, inscriptional or literary, about the matter. About all that can be said is that the Ikkeri nayakas, like their Vijayanagara predecessors in Kanara, sought control over pepper and other export crops, but did not interfere with land relations or production.[143]

Munro's 'historical' reconstruction of Kanara's land-revenue system was deceptive. It deceived in that Munro constructed a history in order to justify a level of revenue assessment in the province under his charge which could be collected without prompting opposition from its ancient, dominant landholders. On the success of this orderly collection of taxes he—or any appointee of the MBOR then and later—depended for his career. That lesson would have been learnt by Munro as he watched Read's anguish in the late years of the Baramahal administration, when the praise of Madras officials changed to criticisms over revenue shortfalls and misgivings about Read's incipient ryotwar system there.

There were ample grounds for Munro's concern about resistance to Company rule over Kanara in 1800. The coastal tract was in a high state of political chaos when he began his work there. A number of armed local chieftains had re-entrenched themselves in territories from which they had been driven by Haidar Ali Khan and Tipu Sultan, partly with the aid of firearms obtained from the Company.[144] There was also a powerful interloper on the Kanara scene, Dundia Wagh, a military adventurer with forces large enough to require a Company army under Arthur Wellesley to subdue in late 1800.

But above all it was the martial character of the dominant landholding population of Kanara—those private proprietors of small estates about whom he talked—that had to be appeased, in part by a low level of revenue demand. Munro's reports of 1800 do not adequately convey the nature of the political sociology of Kanara, though elsewhere he did draw attention to this and the previous warfare by 'Nairs and Mopillas'. He also spoke of Nayar rajas and their petty chiefly dependants.[145] Most of his small estate holders of Kanara were Banta (Bants or Bunts), a caste of warriors indistinguishable from the Nayars of Malabar, except in language.[146] According to Buchanan's census of Kanara in 1801, Bantas represented about 13 per cent of the population. They

[143] K. D. Swaminathan, *The Nayakas of Ikkeri* (Madras: Varadachary, 1957), and a more recent work by K. N. Chitnis, *Kaladi Polity* (Dharwar: Karnataka University Press, 1974).

[144] Beaglehole, pp. 40–2.

[145] Wellesley Papers, Ad. MS. 13679, Munro to Marquis Wellesley, in Munro's hand, December 1799(?), pp. 2–3.

[146] Buchanan, v. 3, pp. 5–8.

were, matrilineal like Nayars to the south, and enjoyed landed dominance (as *jenmi* or *jenmkar*).[147] They were, as Munro also noted, linked to territorial chieftains, Hindu and Jaina, and through these chiefs to rajas who were anointed rulers, such as the Raja of Nilesvar in the southern portion of Kanara.[148] Munro's historical reasoning on the revenue to be demanded from such potentially troublesome landed groups was intended—without disclosing this to his superiors in Madras and gaining their approval—to win landed magnates over to Company rule. In this he succeeded. Buchanan was told by John G. Ravenshaw, who succeeded to a part of Munro's Kanara as collector, that 'it was impossible for a European to be more respected by Hindus than Major Munro is by those who were lately under his authority'.[149] Just shortly after, in 1802, the MBOR had concluded that Munro's settlement in Kanara was, indeed, highly favourable to Kanara landholders. This we have from a later, well-placed Madras official, Charles F. Chamier, who said: 'the Board became impressed with the strong belief, that the assessment of Canara was lighter than that of any district under the Madras Presidency'.[150] That, of course, was Place's charge in 1802.

None of this diminished the perceived success of Munro's Kanara settlement. A few years later, in 1806, the Governor of Madras, Lord William Bentinck, justified his own enthusiasm for Munro's ryotwar to a doubting council in Madras on the basis of the Kanara reports of 1800:

> Canara . . . became the great landmark by which I hoped to trace out those principles and regulations which might be applicable to the [as yet] unsettled districts. . . . I have reason to believe, though I cannot speak with any positive certainty, that the same tenures as in Canara, existed originally throughout every part of the peninsula. In other parts . . . individual rights have been trodden down by the oppression and avarice of despotic authority; but still there exists almost in every village, the distinction of merasee inhabitants, or hereditary cultivators; now the hereditary right to cultivate certain lands, and to reap the benefits of that cultivation, seems to be nearly one and the same with the right in the land, called property. . . . The information and advice of Lieutenent Colonel Munro, was considered by me essential and indespensible [*sic*]. . . .[151]

That encomium came nearly six years after Munro had left Kanara to take up the principal collectorship of the Ceded Districts, when some of his heightened reputation of that later administration might have coloured Bentinck's state-

[147] *Manual of Madras Administration*, 'Glossary', p. 111.

[148] Buchanan, v. 3, pp. 11–18.

[149] Ibid., p. 33.

[150] *The Land Assessment and Landed Tenures of Canara* (Mangalore: German Mission Press, 1853). The Preface of the British Library volume is signed 'C.F.C.' and identified in the British Library catalogue as Chamier.

[151] *The Fifth Report*, v. 3, pp. 467–8.

ment. In 1800 Munro, reaching towards that fuller stature, was being considered for substantially greater responsibility and authority by Richard Wellesley. One possibility was filling the Residency either at Poona or Mysore. Wellesley sought the advice of Josiah Webbe, his informant upon and instrument of Madras policies, and Webbe, having himself declined the Poona posting and having eliminated a number of military officers who might have been thought suitable, finally proposed that Captains John Malcolm and Thomas Munro were probably best suited. He thought that Malcolm would be excellent in either posting, and that Munro would be better at Mysore than at Poona. However, it was Webbe's view that Munro was, above all, best placed in the Ceded Districts, where there were great challenges and problems.[152]

[152] Wellesley Papers, Ad. MS. 3780, Webbe to Wellesley, 12 December 1800.

Chapter Three

Collector: The Ceded Districts

The districts ceded to the Company by the Nizam's government in October 1800 were for the purpose of defraying the costs of an 'augmented subsidiary force' in Hyderabad.[1] These 'ceded districts' (hereafter CD) could hardly have been more different from the Kanara which Munro was leaving, though the tract was in many ways like the Baramahal for which Munro had ultimately formed a strong attachment. Extending over 26,600 square miles, about half the size of England, and over three and a half times larger than Kanara, the CD differed from Kanara also as an environment and a place with a known or knowable past. But, like Kanara when Munro assumed its administration, the CD was in political turmoil, a condition which favoured his choice for appointment there. And again like Kanara, the CD shared a frontier with the potentially troublesome states of the Marathas and Mysore as well as with Hyderabad. Kanara and the CD together present the range of contrasts of which the Madras Presidency of the early nineteenth century consisted: two almost antipodal situations. And yet these were to be encompassed by Munro's ryotwar administration, with Kanara representing to him—and to others like Bentinck—what the CD was to become in time.

The CD occupied an elevated plain, a tableland suspended between the high, dense western ghats and the low, scattered eastern ghats.[2] From its western border in Bellary to its eastern border in Cuddapah, the territory extended over 200 miles, and from the Tungabhadra river on the north of the CD to Arcot in the south about 150 miles. The largely monotonous and treeless CD plain, sloping from west to east, and ranging between 3000 and 1000 feet above sea level, was cut by several river systems. These were the Tungabhadra in the

[1] *The Fifth Report*, v. 3, xxviii.

[2] Walter Hamilton, *The East Indian Gazeteer; Containing Particular Descriptions of the Empires, Principalities . . . of Hindostan and the Adjacent Countries . . .* (London: 1815), p. 67, where it is designated as a tableland, 'balaghat', or 'above the plain', in contrast to 'payenghat', in the plain proper.

north and west, the Pennaru and Cheyyaru systems in the east; but only the Pennaru opens to a basin of any size, in Cuddapah. Dry as well as high, the CD lay within the low rainfall zone which stretches from Maharashtra to Cape Comorin, defined by an annual minimum of fifteen inches and a maximum of thirty-two inches. It was therefore an area with a high risk of drought. During Munro's nearly eight years in the CD, this potential for disaster was realized frequently, while floods struck in late 1804, following upon drought.[3] The same dreary hazards are recorded throughout the remainder of the nineteenth century.

The landscape of the CD presents a daunting though often beautiful appearance now, as it did at the time of Munro. At Hampi on the western edge of the tract, as elsewhere in the CD, abrupt outcrops of granitic rocks are stunning in their texture and in their light effects. Hampi's massive boulders and rocky hillocks are surmounted by structures, usually temples or ascetics' retreats. Elsewhere in the CD these same formations characteristically are crowned by fortresses. Winding through the great rocky masses at Hampi is the Tungabhadra, and from it channels were long ago cut to water an extensive arable area within the twelve-square-mile city site of Vijayanagara, the eponymous capital of the great kingdom in South India from the fourteenth to the late sixteenth centuries. At Uravakonda, half-way between the two *qasbah* towns of Bellary and Anantapur, a 200-foot rock extrudes from the plain and hovers over a small market town and its surrounding fields. These form a patchwork of red and black soils, cropped with minute differences to the advantages of each of the soil types, and dotted with gneissic rocks everywhere. The horizon here is short, for hill-like outcrops of granite limit the gaze. On many of these hills, bluntly etched against the sky, are fortifications, most of which go back to the Vijayanagara age. Or again, south of Anantapur, on the Dharmavaram road, such hills several hundred feet high run on for miles, and on their rocky spines a thin grass cover gives the impression of a felt glove over short fingers which seem to grasp the walls of forts. Hardly a coventional kind of beauty, but this was a landscape that Munro came to appreciate in the later years of his stay.

Topographically and physically varied, the CD resembles the Maharashtrian Deccan and the Mysore upland, between which the CD is perched. The high Mysore plateau intrudes into the western part of the CD to its northern border on the Tungabhadra. That river wraps around the northwestern portion of the CD and defines a frontier with the Mysore kingdom to the north and west, and with the Maratha state to the north. At Bellary a wide plain opens to the east. That high plain (average elevation of about 1500 feet) extends to the central portion of modern Kurnool, which was then included in the CD. Here, in Kurnool, the plain encounters a double set of hills running from north to south. These are the Nallamalai and Lankamalai hills, separated by a narrow valley from the Veligonda hills, and they run to the southern edge of the CD

[3] IOL, *MBOR Proceedings*, 14 June 1804, p. 4825, of 11 May 1807, p. 3954, and of 1 August 1805, p. 57.

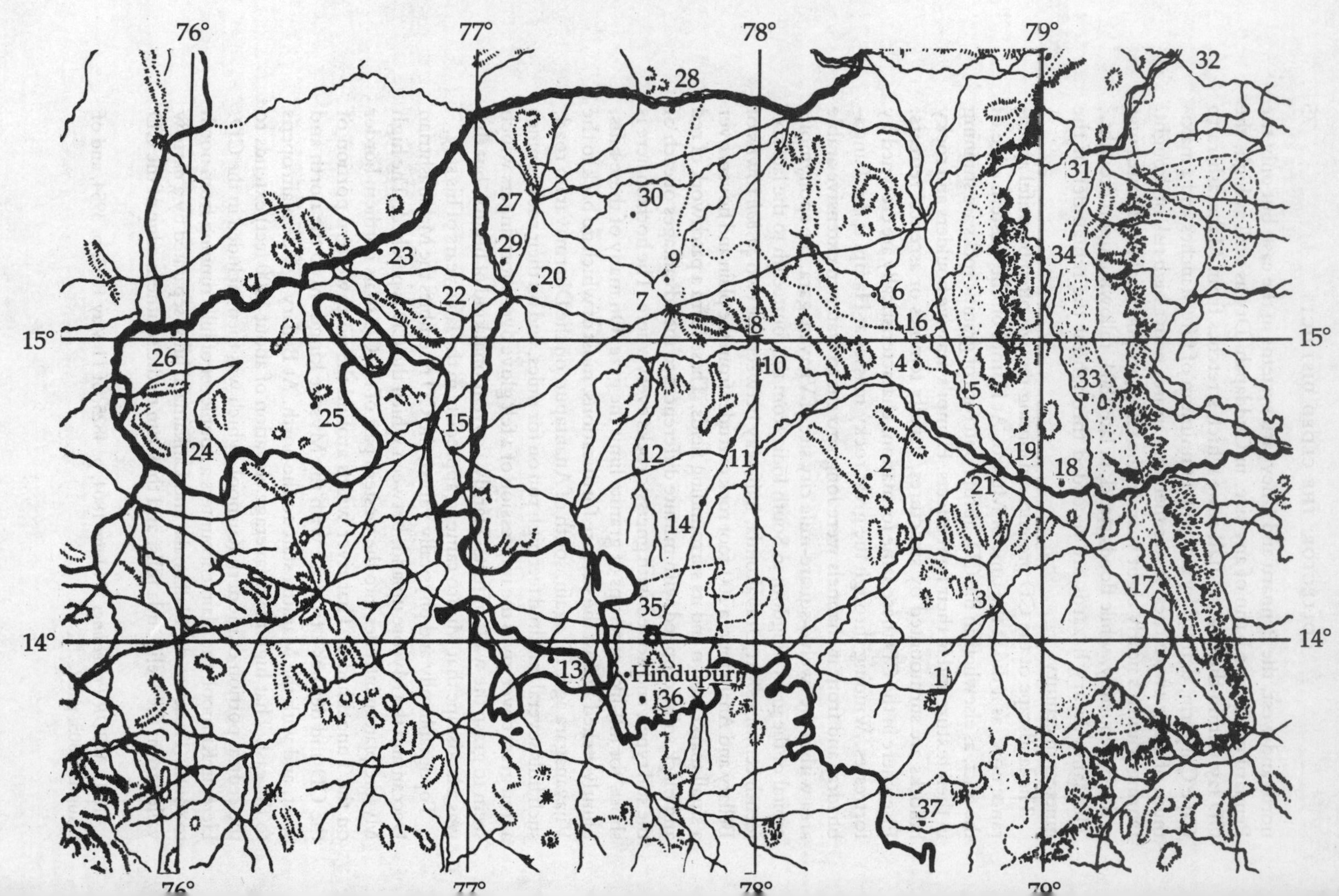
76°
77°
78°
79°
15°
14°
Hindupur
1
2
3
4
5
6
7
8
9
10
11
12
13
14
15
16
17
18
19
20
21
22
23
24
25
26
27
28
29
30
31
32
33
34
35
36
37

Map 2: PLACE CODE OF THE 37 TALUKS OF THE CEDED DISTRICTS, 1805.

The heavy black line on map outlines the Ceded Districts on three sides; the eastern side is demarcated by a hill running northwards from Tirupati ('Terpetty') to Cumbun ('Cummum') on the right side of the map. Numbers indicate the 37 taluka headquarters. These are:

1. Gurramkonda
2. Pulivendla
3. Rayachoti
4. Jammalamadugu
5. Duvvuru
6. Koilkuntla
7. Gooty
8. Yadiki
9. Chennampalle
10. Tadpatri
11. Tadimarri
12. Anantapur
13. Madakasira
14. Dharamavaram
15. Rayadrug
16. Nossam
17. Chitvel
18. Siddhavatam
19. Chennuru
20. Chintakunta
21. Kamalapuram
22. Bellary
23. Kampili
24. Harpanahalli
25. Kudligi
26. Huvinhadgalli
27. Adoni
28. Nagaladinne
29. Gulyam
30. Pattikonda
31. Cumbun
32. Dupadu
33. Badvel
34. Giddaluru
35. Penukonda
36. Kodikonda
37. Punganur

in the east, near Tirupati. Overall, the proportion of hill to plain in the CD is about 1:5, varying from 1:2 in the forested hill taluk of Siddhavattam in the east to 1:20 in Bellary.[4] The natural vegetation of the CD, except for its open-forested hills, is low, scattered shrubs. This, together with outcrops of the granitic geological base of the territory, gives much of the CD its bleak and harsh appearance. Shown on early colonial maps, and still to be found thirty years ago, were scattered forested zones, such as the one of 600 square miles between the Tungabhadra and Bellary town in the west, another north of Anantapur, and of course in the eastern hills marking the frontier on the east with Nellore and North Arcot.

Agriculture in this harsh environment was defensive. In 1800, paddy and irrigated millets were cultivated in the eastern valleys and, to a more limited extent, in the western portion of the CD along the Tungabhadra. Over most of what was to be called 'the Ceded Districts of Madras' the major field crops were millets, cotton, and pulses, with the great millet, jowar, dominant. The limitation of human adaptation to this environment was adequate moisture for agriculture. In 1950, no more than 10 per cent of cultivation in the erstwhile CD was under irrigation, about the same proportion as in 1800.[5] Riverine irrigation was found along the Tungabhadra and in parts of the higher valleys in the east; tank irrigation predominated in the lower reaches of the eastern valleys. For the rest, cultivation was limited by its meagre rainfall that resulted in from five to eight dry months each year.

During Munro's collectorship in the CD and for long after, grinding poverty, punctuated by famine, was the lot of its people. Famines were reported in Bellary in 1792–3, 1803, 1833, 1851–4, 1866 and 1876–7; in Cuddapah in 1800–2, 1803, 1818, 1820, 1851, 1866 and 1876–7; and in Kurnool in 1804, 1810, 1824, 1833, 1854, 1866 and 1876.[6] In the late nineteenth century, when population statistics became somewhat reliable, they revealed that the risk of survival for the people of the CD was greater than anywhere in Madras. Inter-census losses in population between 1871 and 1891 for the districts comprising the CD were 21 per cent, while the overall Madras decline in those famine decades was 1.5 per cent. The nearest comparable losses were found in Salem with 19 per cent, and Nẹllore with 17 per cent.[7]

As Munro journeyed from Kanara to the CD in late 1800, he well understood

[4] The data for this discussion has been based upon an excellent set of maps of the CD at the IOL, prepared between 1809 and 1820, at the scale of two inches to the mile: *Atlas of the Company's Ceded Districts under the Presidency of Fort St George, Office of the Surveyor-General, Colin Mackenzie, 1 January 1820*, IOL Map Collection, no. W-IX-2. I have also found the following map sheets of great value: *International Map of Vegetation and of Environmental Condition* by H. Gaussen, P. Legris and M. Viart, of the French Institute of Pondicherry, scale 1:5 million: 'Madras', 1962 and 'Mysore', 1965 (New Delhi: Indian Council of Agricultural Research), with 'Notes on the Sheet(s)'.

[5] *The Fifth Report*, v. 3, p. 516.

[6] *Madras Manual of Administration*, v. 2, pp. 470–1.

[7] S. Srinavasa Raghavaiyangar, *Memorandum of the Progress of the Madras Presidency*

the political and military difficulties he was to confront, but he had little idea of the poverty of his new charge. Even now, this can only be assessed crudely. One may compare the CD with other territories added to the Presidency in the late eighteenth and early nineteenth centuries, according to the schedule of revenues set by the several treaties of acquisition. This is attempted in Table 4.1, where the revenue of the CD is seen to be among the lowest. Comparisons among the several parts of the Madras Presidency in the early nineteenth century must be so hedged about with qualifications that they often have little utility. There are, however, a few within-Madras comparisons that should be considered as a means of grasping the degree of backwardness of the CD at the time. One pertains to the modest resource base upon which subsistence in that environment may be assessed. A relative measure of this can be gained from Table 4.2, which compares some of the Madras territories in terms of revenue and population. Its great size—18 per cent of the area of the entire Presidency—made the CD by far the largest administrative unit as well as the most populous. Yet the per capita revenue demand was lower than all other districts being compared, save only Salem and Coorg. The proportion of the land revenue to total revenue in the CD was slightly higher than the average for the districts enumerated in Table 4.2. Apart from Kanara, with its extensive mountainous zone, the CD had the lowest population density of any of the new territories added to Madras. Another comparative measure of relative poverty is in the proportion of the land of the CD under irrigation. Figures from the middle of the nineteenth century show that 93 per cent of the cultivated acreage of the CD was dry-cropped, i.e. totally dependent upon rainfall. No district of Madras exceeded this degree of reliance upon rainfall, except the west coast districts, which enjoyed a great monsoon.[8]

Another comparison involves the quantity of inam, or revenue-reduced lands in the Presidency. By the middle of the nineteenth century the CD had about 38 per cent of all of the holders of inam lands, or inamdars, of the Presidency; here was also found 35 per cent of all inam land, whose inamdars paid about 12 per cent of the total quit-rents levied upon inam lands in the Presidency.[9] It quickly became Munro's belief that without the inducement of copious, virtually revenue-free lands, there was little to hold those cultivators with the capital and labour to produce taxable surpluses—what Munro called the 'better sort' of CD cultivators.

during the Last Forty Years of British Administration (Madras: Government Press, 1893), pp. xci and c–ciii.

[8] Given in *Reports of the Nature of of the Food of the Inhabitants of the Madras Presidency on the Dietaries of Prisoners in Zillah Jails* compiled by W. R. Cornish (Madras: 1863), IOL, 23/937.

[9] IOL, *Selections of Records of the Madras Goverment, New (Revenue) Series, Number 1*, 'A Collection of Papers Relative to the Inam Settlement in the Madras Presidency' (1906), Appendix 'C', Table 10, p. 346, and *A Brief Report on the Entire Operations of the Inam Commission from Its Commencement, 30 October 1869*, W. T. Blair, IOL, V/26/312/7, Table 7, p. 35, and Appendix 'B', p. 368.

TABLE 4.1: TERRITORIES CEDED TO THE COMPANY IN MADRAS, 1792–1803: AREA AND REVENUE

Date	*Territory*	*Ceded by*	*Area (miles²) [square miles]*	*Land revenue[a] (rupees 000)*	*Rs/Land revenue/Area*
1792	Malabar Dindigal Coimbatore[b] Salem	Tipu Sultan	13,789	4,406	314
1799	Kanara Coimbatore[b] Nilgiris	Tipu Sultan	13,000	4,200	323
1799	Tanjore	Raja of Tanjore	3,513	4,141	1,183
1800	Ceded Districts	Nizam of Hyderabad	26,592	5,750	213
1801	Tondaimandalam Trichinopoly Madura Tinnevelly	Nawab of Arcot	35,732	14,550	404
1803	Coorg	Raja of Mysore	1,715	192	113

SOURCES: *The Fifth Report*, v. 3, pp. xxvi–xxix, and Madras *Manual of Administration*, v. 2, Appendix 2.

[a] According to the treaty schedule.

[b] Part of Coimbatore was ceded in two different treaties.

TABLE 4.2: AREA, POPULATION AND REVENUE : SELECTED DISTRICTS, *c.* 1800*

District	*Area*[a] *(miles²)* [*square miles*]	*Revenue*[b] *(000 rupees)*	*Population*[c] *(000)*	*Revenue/Capita (rupees)*	*Per cent land revenue of total revenue*	*Population density (miles²)* [*square miles*]
Ceded Districts	26,592	6,100	1,900	3.21	87	71
Chingelput	2,842	1,500	271	5.50	75	97
Salem	7,483	1,900	613	3.10	93	81
Trichinopoly	3,561	1,800	459	3.92	90	128
Tinnevelly	5,381	2,000	571	3.50	85	106
Malabar	5,765	2,300	466	4.93	73	80
Kanara	7,720[d]	2,400	397	6.04	68	52

* Selected for their relatively reliable population estimates for *c.* 1800.

[a] Data from the *Madras Manual of Administration*, v. 2, Appendix XI. *The Imperial Gazetteer of India; The Indian Empire*, v. 1 (New Delhi: Today & Tomorrow's Printers, reprint ed.), p. 490.

[b] From IOLR, European Manuscripts, Munro Collection, F/151/106, for the year 1817.

[c] From Dharma Kumar, *Land and Caste in South India* (Cambridge: Cambridge University Press, 1965), p. 120.

[d] This is alternatively given as 8360 square miles, from which could be subtracted 2744 square miles for that portion of Kanara consisting of the western ghats, yielding an area of 5883 square miles and a density of 67/miles²: Arbuthnot, p.52, where Munro's collections for 1800 is given £186,059 or SP465,148, equal to Rs 1,628,018; p.54.

In 1805 Munro reported that ryots of the CD were divisible into three classes. a 'better sort' comprising about 20 per cent of landholding, revenue-paying cultivators (*pattadars*) who paid about 35 per cent of the land revenue; a 'middling sort' of about 45 per cent of pattadars who paid an equal proportion of the land revenue; and a 'poorer sort', the remaining 35 per cent, who paid 20 per cent of the total land revenue. Munro also noted that the share of net production (i.e. deducting the cost of production as well as accounting for various local customary payments, or 'merah') to the first sort of farmers was 52 per cent, to the second sort 47 per cent, and to the last 38 per cent; the reciprocals of these proportions are what was collected as land tax by the Company.

Testifying before the House of Lords' Select Committee on East Indian Affairs on 7 April 1813, he added to the threefold division he had spoken of in 1805 by providing information about income and consumption for the entire population. Rich and higher castes, he said, consisted of about 400,000 people, 20 per cent of the CD population. Their per capita consumption was about two-thirds greater than a middle group made up of cultivators and artisans of the CD (his estimate was 40 shillings versus 27 shillings per person), and over twice as much as the lowest of the three groups, labourers whom he estimated as about 20 per cent of the CD population (reckoned to spend 18 shillings per person). This was based upon a survey he had conducted in 1806 to form an estimate of the effects of an increase in the house tax on different classes in the CD. At the time, Munro discovered that for the approximately 54 per cent of the population engaged in agriculture expenditures on food and non-food articles purchased in the market varied in an interesting way. This 54 per cent was differentiated, on the one hand, from the 25 per cent of the population belonging to 'principal castes' of Brahmans, Muslims and large merchants ('wurtucks'), and on the other from labourers, about 20 per cent of the total population. The agricultural castes went to the market for one-fourth as much as the highest social group and for one-half again as much as labourers. Almost all of the food and about one-half of the cloth requirements of agricultural castes were found to be met through self-production or through barter.[10]

There is no comparable evidence on social stratification from the pre-British period, but it is doubtful that Mysorean or Hyderabadi regimes prior to the British either sought or expected the level of revenue which the British did from 1800. Munro and others came to accept that only with great inam privileges could a regular and large revenue be collected from the CD; and this system was maintained to the end of British rule.

POLITICS AND POLIGARS

At the outset, Munro must have found the political conditions of the CD a fitting reflection of this hard land. An indication of the difficulties posed by this territory may be gained from the fact that it had been ceded to the Nizam

[10] IOL, MC, F/151/10, to Petrie and the MBOR, 25 August 1805, especially ff. 84–5,

by Tipu Sultan in 1792 as part of the spoils won by the Nizam, who was an ally of the Company in its penultimate conflict with Tipu Sultan. The tract had proven difficult for him, but he was able to pass it off as more valuable in revenue than it actually was when he was forced to cede it, as Munro was to discover shortly after taking over its administration. Another indication of the potential difficulties of the CD was that Colonel Arthur Wellesley was sent with British troops to occupy it and to establish order prior to Munro's civil administration. Military occupation was announced as completed by January 1801.

When the CD was about to be occupied by the Company, there was a general concern about the level of military expenditures that might be required. In informing Colonel Arthur Wellesley of Munro's appointment as 'the sole collector' of the newly acquired CD in October 1800, Josiah Webbe, Chief Secretary of Madras and Lord Wellesley's principal agent there, also conveyed the Governor-General's orders to his brother to rendezvous with Munro so that they might enter the CD together. He also commented on the high costs of the occupation force: 'This is expensive, I acknowledge, but if you are determined to conquer all India at the same moment, you must pay for it.'[11] Nor was the matter one of cost alone. Lord Wellesley had solicited the views of his military advisors and of Lord Clive, Governor of Madras, about the force to be sent to the CD for its pacification and occupation, and he was told that forces were dangerously low in the Presidency. Troops involved in the final assault against Tipu Sultan at Seringapatam were considered in poor condition for what might prove a difficult service in the CD. This meant that soldiers would have to be drawn from elsewhere in the Carnatic and Northern Circars, reducing garrisons there to a critical level. The Governor-General was warned that when troops had been drawn off from the Northern Circars to comprise part of the Mysore invasion force, rebellion had broken out. Reducing Company garrisons in the Carnatic was seen as an invitation for a general poligar uprising there. The defeat of Tipu Sultan had certainly reduced 'serious danger from a foreign [!] enemy in India', but the dangers of rebellions were thought present in Malabar, Dindigal, Ganjam, and Masulipatam.[12] The perceived precariousness of Munro's entry into the CD, with its 'unsubdued' and armed inhabitants, conveys a good deal about the confidence which the Governor-General and his advisors were prepared to vest in him.

Munro was charged to 'introduce regular government into a province hitherto unsubdued . . . [and] to suppress the evils arising from the weakness of the . . . [Nizam's] government. . . .[13] To accomplish this daunting task meant

---

and IOL, *Charters and Treaties, Minutes of Evidence taken before the House of Lords . . . as relates to the Charter of the East India Company* (London: Directors of the E.I.C., 1813), p. 78.

[11] British Library, Hardwicke Papers, Ad. MS. 29239, dated 10 October 1800.

[12] IOL, *Home Miscellaneous Series*, v. 462, Clive to Wellesley, 18 September 1800.

[13] Wellesley Papers, Ad. MS. 37280, dated 12 December 1800.

that he must cope with some 30,000 armed retainers of poligars who roamed the countryside.[14] Almost everywhere these local chiefs or poligars had constituted such government—local and provincial—as there had been. Of their military capacities Munro spoke early and consistently with disdain. However, he was wary of the esteem and local political influence of such chiefs, as he had earlier encountered them in the Baramahal, and accordingly he saw them as potential dangers to his rule in the CD. The methods he devised for dealing with these dangers held dangers of their own for his career as a civilian administrator.

The care with which he proceeded against poligars in the CD is illustrated in his first instructions to William Thackeray, one of the subordinate collectors assigned to him, in December 1800. In Adoni division, where Thackeray was to serve, 'a state of anarchy' had long existed. The inhabitants there, he told Thackeray, had been 'plundered not only by revenue officers and zamindars, but by every person who chose to pay a nazzernamah [gift to the ruler] for the privilege of exacting money from them... and the heads of villages having on the same terms been permitted to carry on a continual predatory warfare against one another.' Still, Munro reassured him, all powerful poligars of Adoni had been driven off, and there was therefore no actual danger of organized opposition, even though rumours of this always circulated.[15] More immediately a source of civil disorder were former soldiers of the Nizam's forces in the CD who were seeking to collect arrears of their wages on drafts ('tunkhas') against the revenue collections of many villages, for this is how they had been paid by the Nizam's officials.[16] But by far the most serious menace to order were the poligars, and towards these local lordships Munro devised early and stern measures for their extirpation, which brought him into conflict with higher authorities.

Poligars, according to the thinking of his superiors in Madras and Calcutta, were to be divested of their political and military capabilities, but were to be considered as candidates for landed enfranchisement under the settlement principles of Bengal that were to be extended to Madras. 'Enaums', lands alienated to privileged holders subject to payment of a small quit-rent (*jodi*), were to be validated, not by the collector, but by 'courts of law', again in accordance with Bengal regulations. Inams were to be resumed by the Company if found invalid, as it was expected many were. Under Munro poligars were eliminated in a manner so ruthless and devious that rare criticism of him occurred. Inams, on the other hand, were never subjected to judicial review in Munro's time, nor diminished, but rather were used by him to win the allegiance of powerful local interests, beneath the level of the poligars, in what Frykenberg aptly calls the 'silent settlement'.[17]

[14] Srinivasa Raghavaiyangar, *Memorandum*, p. xxiv.

[15] MC, F/151/10, ff. 1–5.

[16] 'Tunkha', *Madras Manual of Administration*, 'Glossary', p. 933; MC, F/151/135, ff. 147–48.

[17] R. E. Frykenberg, 'The Silent Settlement in South India, 1793–1853: An Analysis

The anglicized poligar is *palegadu* in Telugu, *paleyagararu* in Kannada, and *palaiyakkarar* in Tamil. The word means one who holds a village or group of villages on condition of rendering military service to some superior.[18] The history of this institution in South India, generally, is unsatisfactory. It offers little correction to the views held by Munro and those of his generation. According to the medieval historian T. V. Mahalingam, the authority of the poligars derived from *padikaval*, a right to income in return for the provision of protection over a village, or in some cases over a locality during the Vijayanagara period.[19] Income could be realized in various ways: as a privileged rate of land tax—usually a quit-rent and sometimes land held without any payment whatever; as a low cess in kind upon every plough or upon the proportion of seed sown; as a low money payment levied upon ploughs, shops, or looms; as customs charges; as charges for markets and fairs held within the jurisdiction of the poligar.[20]

This view of poligars as minor police officials reflects a falsely bureaucratic conception of this Vijayanagara institution. It merely accepts a convenient view of administrators like Munro, that poligars could be replaced by a superior form of police service. Actually, as Munro admitted at times, poligars had the status of locality lords whose credentials were derived from prebendal entitlements granted from the time of the Vijayanagara king Krishnadevaraya (reign 1509–29). The latter sought to establish a form of local war-chief to oppose existing chiefly households, particularly in the heartland of the Vijayanagara kingdom that was later to be called the Ceded Districts. By so doing he hoped to check powerful coalitions of chiefs opposing Vijayanagara royal authority. Newly-created poligar chieftaincies were intended as competitive sovereignties, little kingdoms whose authority, it was hoped, would remain dependent upon the great kings of Vijayanagara rather than upon the local constituencies of dominant cultivating groups that supported older chiefly houses.[21]

The new British rulers of South India in the late eighteenth century knew little of this history. In the various territories which they took under their control they merely saw powerful, armed, local authorities who stood in the way of their own political objectives. All such opponents were lumped together

---

of the Role of Inams in the Rise of the Indian Imperial System', in R. E. Frykenberg (ed.), *Land Tenure and Peasant in South Asia* (New Delhi: Orient Longman, 1977), pp. 37–54.

[18] *Tamil Lexicon*, v. 5, p. 2638.

[19] T. V. Mahalingam, *South Indian Polity* (Madras: University of Madras, 1967), pp. 247–9.

[20] Mahalingam, *South Indian Polity*, p. 249.

[21] A more general discussion of this earlier formation and its subsequent history may be found in B. Stein, *Vijayanagara* (Cambridge: Cambridge University Press), forthcoming, and Nicholas B. Dirks, *The Hollow Crown* (Cambridge: Cambridge University Press, 1987).

and treated according to their willingness to accept without violence the often violent deprivation of their local authority.

Well before Munro assumed control of the CD, the Company's position with respect to these authorities or poligars had become set. Annihilation was to be the fate of most, certainly all who opposed the British.[22] The high costs of the various ensuing campaigns against poligars in the far south during the late eighteenth century, culminating in the widespread uprising of 1800–1, produced some circumspection within the Madras government by the time that Munro was instructed about his tasks in the CD. The Court of Directors and the MBOR had come to favour more leniency towards poligars. In addition to this prudent reconsideration of policy, the Madras government had been instructed by the Governor-General, Lord Wellesley, late in 1799, that the Bengal regulations of Cornwallis were to be established in Madras, in 'poligar countries' and elsewhere.[23] This meant that on lands under poligars the latter were to be 'confirmed in them, in the most full and solemn manner'.[24] For, if there were to be zamindars in Madras, they would have to be created mainly from the local lordships of poligars.

As prospective candidates for zamindari enfranchisement under the Madras regulation of 1802, the poligars of the CD were plausible enough. According to a survey conducted by Munro and his staff during the first two years of his administration of the CD, there were some eighty families of these local authorities who, a hundred or fifty years before had controlled two thousand villages, nearly one-sixth of the villages of the CD.[25] They claimed to have exercised authority in their 'palems' (*paliyam*) from the seventeenth century, and some at least could provide convincing evidence of this from temple inscriptions of that earlier time, evidence which is extant still.

About this time there were other voices that conceived poligars to have an appropriate position within an emerging civil society in Madras. Lionel Place, collector of the Company's Jaghire in Chingleput, stated this view in 1795 when writing about one 'Pap Rauze', poligar of Covelong:

> The conduct of this old man who has attained the age of 90 affords an example of probity which is rarely met . . . [especially in relations between Indians and agents of the European companies in Madras] and the uprightness of his character has established an almost unprecedented reverence from the Natives who on many occasions refer their disputes to him . . . for the justice of whose decisions appeal has never been made to me.[26]

[22] K. Rajayyan, *South Indian Rebellion* (Mysore: Rao and Raghavan, 1968), pp. 35–42.

[23] Wellesley Papers, Ad. MS. 13655.

[24] *The Fifth Report*, v. 3, p. 336, 'Report of the Southern Poligar Peshcush', 29 December 1800.

[25] *The Fifth Report*, v. 3, pp. 350–82, 'Memorandums of the Poligars of the Ceded Districts', 20 March 1802, Tables, pp. 383–92.

[26] Tamilnadu Archives, Madras, *Proceedings of the Board of Revenue* 'Settlement', 'Mr. Place's Report on the Jaghire', 6 October 1795, p. 29.

Place's was one of the few voices in Madras that had any good to say of poligars. Therefore the MBOR could hardly have been enthusiastic about Wellesley's instructions that these chiefs were to be vested with permanent rights in their lands unless there were strong and particular reasons against. There remained considerable consternation in Madras about the treaty of 1792 between the Company and the Nawab of Arcot stipulating that the Company was to assure that poligars observed all older 'customary ceremonies' honouring the Nawab.[27] To the MBOR, Munro's truculent opposition to poligars must have seemed reasonable and may account for the considerable indulgence which he enjoyed in pursuing his tough policies towards these awkward chiefs.

Immediately after arriving in the CD, Munro had outlined to Webbe how he intended to grasp the nettle of poligar authority. Where poligars had been driven off and had not been permitted to return, Munro wrote: 'we had best go quietly to work, establish ourselves firmly in the country and conciliate the inhabitants a little before we begin with them. . . .' Elsewhere, where poligars were present, 'It is my intention to examine the revenue of the districts of all poligars as I go along without dispossessing them, but giving them however to understand that any opposition on their part will be deemed rebellion.'[28]

Two months later, on 31 December 1800, he expressed exasperation to Webbe that he might not be able to reduce poligars in the manner he preferred because of a desire among military officers in the CD to act with force against them. This he thought wrong and unnecessary. Fears of a rising of poligars in the CD were alarmist, he wrote. Most poligars had been expelled from the CD by Haidar Ali's brother-in-law, Mir Ali Riza Sahib, and 'John Company Bahadur is at least as strong as Mir Saheb ever was. . . .'[29] Besides, he wrote to Webbe a few days later, Company forces, being mostly cavalry in the CD, were wrong for the task and would only rally the presently divided and discordant poligar forces.[30] For the moment, Munro thought, it was best to proceed slowly, and

> it would be decorous before we begin with them to have some reasons to produce such as might be worked up into a manifesto after the fashion of modern Europe. As the whole gang of them was expelled by Hyder and Tippoo though restored by the Nizamites I am for turning every last soul of them adrift again. . . . But tho' this is what I would do if there were no one to call me to account for oppressing fallen royalty, I see many obstacles in the way at present.[31]

Munro's ironies ('the fashion of modern Europe' and 'fallen royalty') tell us

[27] IOL, *Board's Collections*, F/4/40–41, 'Court's Political Letter to Fort St. George', 10 June 1795, para. 63.

[28] Wellesley Papers, Ad, MS. 13629, f. 153.

[29] Ibid., f. 166.

[30] Ibid., f. 168.

[31] Ibid.

something about the confidence obtaining between the two men, and the congeniality that Munro had for the aggressive policies of Lord Wellesley which Webbe was pressing in Madras. But these remarks, and others of the early months of 1801, also demonstrate Munro's sensitivity to the shoals in the political waters he was attempting to navigate in this new and difficult posting. This applied most seriously to his actions against poligars. In purging the CD of poligars he knew that he had to appear to be following procedures which satisfied a growing sentiment in official Madras that a Bengal-type of settlement, which had been ordered by Wellesley, was correct and could be made with poligars. This was also a procedure which would make it appear to Munro's employers in London, still smarting under Burke's lashes, that justice was being done in India. As to the actual reduction of poligar authority, which Munro saw to be in competition with his own authority, he suggested the following bold line to Webbe:

> contrive some means of giving me the military command [of the CD], weed out the useless military dogs above, raise some reg[imen]ts to make me a Lt Col and then Majors might be easily got to work under me. I am certainly a better general now than I shall be in twenty years. My civil situation gives me the means of procuring information that no military man can have, and I am also more interested in bringing matters to a speedy decision than many another military man.[32]

Did this mean that Munro, like his military colleagues (of whom he seemed not to think much), sought a military solution to the problem of poligar authority? It would seem not, at least at this time, for the actual policy which Munro was proposing was not a military but a political one. However, he feared that the independent Company military in the CD could well spoil his plan. This was to permit the eighty or so poligars to remain in their territories and not directly challenge their authority. Instead, he proposed to increase the level of tribute (*peshkash*) demanded from each to a theoretical maximum previously demanded but never collected by Haidar and by the Nizam's regime. At this high pitch of demand, Munro reasoned to Webbe (as previously John Sullivan had reasoned to Lord North), poligars could not pay their troops and maintain their military capacity and also pay the tribute to the Company. When, as he expected, they defaulted on the latter, they could be deposed and expelled legally. He concluded this proposal to Webbe with: 'I am convinced that it is possible to expel them all and to hang the great part of them.'[33]

So smitten was Munro by this approach—and he might have been encouraged in this by Webbe—that he wrote to his friend later in the same month, April 1801, with an even more audacious proposal, explicitly military now, and one that would clear the entire Presidency of poligars. This involved the same tactic of increasing the tribute demanded from all poligars, but also being

[32] Ibid.
[33] Ibid.

prepared with an adequate force when their joint resistance exploded. This force, Munro specified, should consist of nine regiments of cavalry and thirty-two of infantry, one-third of which was to be European. To the demurer that he could reasonably expect from Webbe, Munro added: 'I am afraid you will say that this army is rather intended for conquest than defence, but if you are attacked by a Native Power you can only oppose him . . . by invasion.'[34]

Not surprisingly, to Munro's superiors in London his poligar policy appeared cynical and aggressive, and he found himself in danger of being returned to military duty in disgrace. He was attacked for his treatment of the poligar of 'Vimlah' (Vemulakota village and locality in the Pulivendla taluk of Cuddapah). Munro had deprived this poligar of his territory after ordering that the poligar's fort be forcibly seized by Company troops in May 1801. His reasons for this action were that the poligar was an old, blind man who had been set in place as a puppet by the head of the armed retainers of the poligari family, and he was prevented from attending Munro's office as he had been ordered repeatedly to do. A second reason for Munro's action was that relations between him and the poligars of the CD were stalemated and, according to Munro, required a demonstration by the Company that its authority would be established. His violent action against a pathetic old man became the focus for widespread criticism of his poligar policy as a whole.

The Madras Governor, Lord Clive, had given full and explicit approval to Munro.[35] He accepted Munro's concern that if he made no move to reduce some of the more intransigent poligars in the CD, the commander of the Company army there, Dugald Campbell, would have launched an action against all poligars, something which Munro believed could only exacerbate conditions.[36] Josiah Webbe, chief secretary of Madras, had written in November 1801 approving Munro's move against the 'Vimlah' poligar, an approval which put him in opposition to some in Madras. As usual, Webbe's tone was heavily ironic:

> the refractory spirit of the rebellious polygars will yield . . . to a gentle care of the native prejudices, timidity, and ignorance of European maxims: the halcyon times will return when jamabundies shall be settled through the more natural channel of the native dubashi, conversant with native manners; the crooked sword into a scythe shall bend. . . . In sober truth I fear that all our plans for a vigorous government within [the] conquered country are frustrated. . . .[37]

Another friend and counsellor, Mark Wilks, was not supportive, but fearful of the consequences of Munro's ruthlessness. He advised his friend to go slowly, for he feared that the uprisings of poligars in the southern part of the Presidency

[34] Ibid., ff. 185–9, 10 April 1801.
[35] MC, 151/18, extract of a letter from Lord Clive to the MBOR, 19 January 1803.
[36] See, MC, 151/5, letters from Campbell and Mackay, 4 and 7 January 1801.
[37] MC, 151/5, Webbe to Munro, 9 November 1801.

against Company authority could become more general; there was, he said, 'a last struggle for savage independence'; the effects of Company policy had 'made mortal enemies of every Mussulman in the Peninsula, and now we are proceeding to the same point with the Hindoos'.[38]

A judgement yet more harsh and dangerous came from the Court of Directors:

> it is our positive injunction, that force be never resorted to against the Poligars... unless in case of actual rebellion, until every lenient and conciliatory measure has been tried without proper effect... It is our anxious wish to owe the obedience of Poligars and others of our Tributaries to their confidence in our justice rather than to the dread of our power.[39]

The Directors found Munro's actions objectionable, and they absolutely opposed 'so disengenuous and indirect a means' as to set the tribute demand so high that poligars must default and thus lose their lands: 'that such a principle of conduct should have suggested itself to Major Munro's mind, is to us a matter of surprize and regret... [for] it is our wish to uphold and preserve the poligars in their rights and enjoyment in the soil whilst we gradually aim at the reduction of their military power and wean them from... feudal habits.'[40] The Madras government was declared to be at fault for giving its approval to Munro's deceitful poligar policy, and Munro himself, they said, should be removed from his office and never again 'employed in any Revenue Post in future which the violent and mistaken principles of his conduct seem to render him unqualified to fill'.[41]

Against these harsh recriminations Munro's defence was prompt and creditable. His instructions and support from Lord Clive had been unambiguous and sustained with respect to poligars. So much was this true that he did not seek nor expect special instructions with regard to the 'Vimlah' poligar. That action was justified by the circumstances and proved to be salutary, for, from the time of the deposition of that chief, not only did the CD poligars come into line with Company authority in the CD, but Munro successfully negotiated the surrender of rebellious poligars in Arcot (Chittoor).[42] He also applied to Clive's successor, Bentinck, for intervention against influential members of the Madras establishment who opposed his poligar policies.[43] The strictures of the Directors against Munro and their call for his dismissal were not pressed, though the odour of that affair lingered in Madras among many who viewed the 'Vimlah' incident as part of a larger problem involving military collectors, an issue which also came to a head in 1802.

[38] MC, 151/5, Wilks to Munro, 11 May and 2 July 1801.
[39] Cited in Beaglehole, p. 65.
[40] IOL, *Madras Despatches*, E/4?892, para. 19, pp. 364–8.
[41] Beaglehole, p. 65.
[42] Ibid., pp. 65–7.
[43] Bentinck Papers, PwJb, 659/1, 1805.

ADMINISTRATOR AND TEACHER

Even the harshest critics of Munro's pacification policies in the CD had to concede that he had made an almost instant success of his task of creating order and a reliable revenue from a turbulent and large territory, and therefore established himself as a first class political manager. This was done in close co-operation with Josiah Webbe, his vigorous sponsor in Madras. While Munro must have known that his proposal for a grand army to liberate the peninsula south of the Kistna from poligar authority (with himself at its head?) could only be rejected by Webbe, he had hoped for a freer hand to conduct things than Webbe was ready to allow.

As when Alexander Read had been installed in the Baramahal by the then Governor-General and had been invited to consult with Lord Cornwallis on problems he might encounter, so too Munro received his initial appointment and instructions from the Governor-General, Lord Wellesley, through Webbe. Webbe's advice to Wellesley had been to appoint four subordinate European collectors under Munro, who was to be Principal Collector, and Munro's opinions about candidates were accordingly sought. His response to this on 24 November 1800 was typical; it was to negotiate the order. Four subordinate collectors, he told Webbe, were too many; three would be better since there were three constituent parts of the CD: Bellary (which included Anantapur then); Cuddapah; and Kurnool. Moreover, Munro wanted to directly administer one of the districts of the CD himself, which could have reduced the usefulness of subordinates even further. But he did see the point of Webbe's suggestion about assistants: 'Your desire is I conceive to train up a number of young [European] collectors, and is actually one that should be pursued where it does not lead to serious inconvenience.'

Munro suggested that the best plan for the administration of the CD would have been 'to have left the whole of the country to me the first year'. That was bound to be the most difficult time, given the poligar problem, 'and would be easier to get over myself with the help of amildars [Indian revenue officers] than by leaving any part of the business to young collectors'. Another reason for having sole responsibility during the first year, he argued to Webbe, was that there were too few Indians with proper training to serve as staff for novice European collectors. His 'veterans', he said, had been left in Kanara for his two successors, and it would require a year in the CD to train others: 'just now I am obliged to trust my supposed skill in decerning what they [his newly recruited Indian revenue officials] were made of by catichising them on revenue and lanaterising their physiognomies'. Whether this last meant instilling the beards of wisdom or pulling the wool over their eyes is not clear. Care was needed to avoid the appointment of Indian subordinates who might 'intrigue with poligars'.[44] Perhaps, Munro suggested, in the second year he could be given two European collectors to train, and if necessary a third could be added in the next year.

[44] Wellesley Papers, Ad. MS. 13629, f. 155. Spellings as in the original.

Webbe compromised. Munro was assigned three subordinate collectors (William Thackeray, James Cochrane, and Alexander Stodart), and this first group of young Europeans commenced their training under him at the onset of his administration of the CD.[45] In the course of his sojourn there Munro was to train a number of young men who, after a few years, went on to more responsible postings. In later years these men constituted a Munro claque within the Madras administration, a group on which he could depend to support his revenue and judicial reforms.

The progress of his juniors in their acquisition of languages—Kannada, Telugu, Marathi—was watched carefully and approbation given for competence. The demanding report forms of the MBOR were carefully explained to each and he insisted that these be followed. He reminded Peter Bruce, who joined his staff in 1803, that the Board expected to receive a monthly diary from every collector, 'whether... sick or well, in camp or the cutchery [office]', so Bruce was ordered to complete his for the previous month from memory if necessary.[46] Another time, Munro informed his young colleague of an error in his accounts of one pagoda, which he had corrected.[47] When Bruce worried that complaints from cultivators and headmen about the high level of revenue demand might bring him under criticism, Munro reassuringly observed that this was common enough 'when rents are too high'; this was not to be taken too seriously until resort to 'kootums' was had. The last referred to a means of resistance to State demands by large protest assemblies threatening to withhold revenue payments and even to abandon villages and take refuge in jungles. Even then, Munro stressed, 'patience and gentleness are always preferred to punishments'.[48]

But Munro was not always soothing. In 1806 he upbraided Bruce for his conduct towards an amildar from Mysore, near his Bellary boundary with that kingdom. Bruce was scolded for failing to show proper respect to an Indian official who, among other things, was held in high esteem by General Arthur Wellesley. In the month of August 1806 alone Munro sent Bruce ten letters on one or another aspect of administration, showing the degree of supervision he was prepared to exercise over those in his charge.[49]

The patient if sometimes stern nurturing of his assistants was matched by his generous support of their careers. Unfailingly, he gave advice about career strategies and warmly recommended them for promotions and new postings. When Bruce asked his advice about writing to the Governor, Bentinck, about a promotion from his present rank as assistant collector to that of sub-collector, Munro thought it could do no harm, provided the letter was not too long.

[45] Beaglehole p. 55, mistakenly adds a fourth, John G. Ravenshaw, who actually was posted in Kanara on Cochrane's transfer to the CD.

[46] MC, 151/11, 4 June 1803.

[47] MC, 151/11, 11 September 1803.

[48] MC, 151/12, 1 July 1806. In Tamil, *kuṭṭam*.

[49] MC, 151/12, 17 November 1806.

He then supplied Bruce with a detailed draft which his protege had but to sign and post. When in 1807 the Madras government decided to reduce the commissions enjoyed by collectors, including junior ones, and retrenched the salaries of Bruce and another junior in the CD, Frederick Gahagen, Munro threw his support behind his juniors. Their petition for a restoration of the retrenched salaries was favourably received by the MBOR, and the Board said that a major reason for this was the strong support which it had from Munro for 'particular indulgence' to be shown.[50]

Munro's increasing stature as an administrator won him respect among the Madras establishment as the years passed in the CD. He was also an instant favourite of Bentinck when the latter assumed the governorship of Madras in August 1803. Munro's high standing with Bentinck may have accounted for a good deal of his influence. In 1804 Bentinck wrote to Munro that his old Baramahal colleague William Macleod was too ill to continue as collector of South Arcot. He asked for Munro's evaluation of two of the latter's assistants as possible replacements. The two were Cochrane and Henry Graeme, and Bentinck spoke highly of both in his letter, adding:

> They have the additional recommendation of having been educated under your immediate inspection and in that system of management which has the reputation of being the most perfect in India. What are their comparative merits[?]... the extensive districts which you have had continuously under your charge for so many years will have given you frequent opportunity of observing the qualifications of the younger civilians. . . .[51]

Administrative success was slow to confer career security, however. At almost the outset of his administration of the CD in 1802, it appeared that his career might be a short one as a crisis broke around his head and those of other 'military collectors'. Intimations of the latter threat to Munro's budding civilian career came from his sardonic friend Webbe, who was himself deeply implicated in the attack upon military collectors and among the first victims of it.

Webbe became the chief agent of Governor-General Wellesley in Madras from 1800, when he was appointed chief secretary, and after he had adopted Wellesley's aggressive policy against Tipu Sultan's Mysore. Earlier he had opposed war with Mysore on the grounds that the Company was neither prepared militarily nor financially for it. As Wellesley's trusted agent in Madras, Webbe was supposed to lead the hesitant Lord Clive to a recasting of Madras Presidency policies along lines dictated by the Governor-General.

However, in October 1801 Webbe was dismissed from his pivotal post by the Court of Directors, and he warned Wellesley that this was but the first step in the reversal of the latter's plans for a new Madras. He had some forewarning of his dismissal, as he wrote to Wellesley, when an important member of the Directorate, David Scott, informed him of dissatisfaction among the Directors

[50] IOL, *MBOR Proceedings*, 1807, P/288/63, 27 August 1807, pp. 6697–9.
[51] MC, 151/7, Bentinck to Munro, 29 April 1804.

with Madras policies. Webbe interpreted this to the Governor-General as a determination of Scott's enemies among the Directors 'to frustrate the present mode of conducting affairs of Fort St. George' by replacing some members of the Governor's council and by removing him.[52] His surmise proved correct, for shortly after he was dismissed Webbe outlined a larger picture of intrigue of which the Governor-General was certainly aware: 'the intention of the Court of Directors appears to be adverse to the principles, on which the affairs of India are now administered; and [we may look for] direct intervention on the part of the Court of Directors in the local government of India.'[53] To this presumed violation of the constitutional principles formulated by Cornwallis, resistance was essential. Webbe thought that Clive should resign in protest, and that he, Webbe, should do likewise. Clive did submit his resignation on 2 November 1801, but was requested by Wellesley to stay on at Madras to await the orders of the Directors, and Webbe, the Governor-General decided, was to serve as Clive's private secretary.[54] Munro learnt of these events from Webbe within the month. Webbe would leave India with regret because of old friends like Munro. However he was not alone in the victimization, for Thomas Cochrane of the MBOR was also being deprived of office to be replaced by others who 'will probably drive you and your organization into a fit of despair or into a battalion of Sepoys'. What 'your organization' meant is not clear to one reading these documents now. What Munro may have understood by the phrase is equally uncertain, since there is some evidence that there was something happening in connection with Webbe's dismissal that he did not grasp, but that, perhaps, his friend John Malcolm did.

In December 1801 Munro in the remote CD had either heard enough or surmised enough of the implications of Webbe's dismissal to write to John Malcolm of his concerns. One pertained to the dismissal of another long-time friend and supporter, Thomas Cochrane, from the MBOR and his replacement by Thomas Oakes and Lionel Place: 'I lament these changes not only from private regard but from a full conviction that the two men who have been superceded [Webbe and Cochrane] are precisely the two men of the whole establishment who are the most capable of filling the situations from which they have been so shamefully removed'.[55] Referring to a previous letter from Malcolm, Munro said he did not understand what was meant by '"intended changes at Madras"', for had not the changes now taken place? Nor, he confessed, did he understand what Malcolm meant in expressing confidence '"of yet defeating the agents of weakness and wickedness"': 'you talk like a French minister of Police who has discovered that we are standing upon a Volcano, and that a grand explosion must ensue unless it is counteracted . . . ' What,

[52] Wellesley Papers, Ad. MS. 37280, Webbe to Wellesley, 10 October 1801.

[53] Ibid., Webbe to Wellesley, 13 and 28 October 1801.

[54] Ibid., Lord Clive to the Court of Directors, 1 February 1802.

[55] IOL, Positive Microfilm, no. 4218, 'Cleveland Public Library', Munro to Malcolm, 9 December 1801.

Munro wondered, could be worse than the 'Dubashical counter-revolution' that has occurred? The answer to this he appeared not to learn for another year, and again from Webbe.

From Madras, where he continued to be under Wellesley's protection as the private secretary of the resigned but not replaced Lord Clive, Webbe told Munro about the determination of the Directors to be rid of military collectors. The military officers first appointed to the Baramahal by Lord Cornwallis (for the express reason that Madras had no adequately trained civilians for the tasks there) were later confirmed and even boosted by Wellesley. This must have been the 'your organization' to which Webbe had earlier referred, and the attack upon them the 'intended changes' to which Malcolm referred. 'Military collectors' had become as much of a shibboleth for the anti-Wellesley faction of the Directorate and of the Madras establishment as 'dubashi' was for their opponents. These were pejorative labels for two contrasting systems of administration.[56]

In 1802 the fight between the two began. It was fought in London and in Madras, and was almost as profound an imperial crisis as that involving Warren Hastings two decades before. The central issue was the political control by the centre over the parts; how closely London was to control the Governor-General and thus the policies of the Company in India; and how closely the collegiate bodies of Madras and Bombay (the Governors in Council, the Boards of Revenue) were to control collectors in the burgeoning territories of each.

Webbe provided Munro with a partial (i.e. one-sided and incomplete) explanation of what was happening:

> The Directors think that nothing can go well unless the old school is revived; ministers and government abroad have endeavoured to root out that notion, to adopt permanent measures and promote meritorious men. . . . The supporters of the new school ['that which you invented in the Baramahal'] are irresistible in fair, open argument; in the field the Directors cannot stand; they have therefore acted on private information... they have opened their arms wide to receive all the discontented, ignorant, and unprincipled people who have lately been compelled to return home. This opens a grand theatre: calumny advances to the front of the stage and as the old [view] . . . cannot... maintain its footing in a free country, the Directors seek to obtain through their instruments the implausible reasons to be subsequently assigned for a conduct previously determined.[57]

[56] In the days after Burke's fustians against 'dubashis', the term continued to bear the pejorative signification of the dualistic structure of Company authority, its indigenous forms of relations and English-speaking officials, both linked metaphorically and actually by the so-called 'dubashi', meaning user of 'two languages', able to operate in the languages (idioms/codes) of the two parts of the dualistic structure of Company authority.

[57] MC, F/151/2, Webbe to Munro, 24 November 1802.

In their resolve to oppose and reverse the system of Lord Wellesley, the Directors hit upon Place and Oakes as their 'intruments'. Of these two men, Webbe said: 'When Tipoo fell, Oakes wished to be president of the commission to supervise the new country [ceded to the Company, including the CD]. Place having exhausted the Jagheer [in Chingleput, where he served as collector during the 1790s] wept like Alexander for other worlds.'[58]

These two disappointed men fell in with the plans of the Directors while they were on furlough in England, Webbe said, and Place provided them with 'a deposition on his management [of the Jaghire] of which they did not understand a syllable'. Included in that 'deposition' was a condemnation of military collectors such as Munro, James G. Graham and William Macleod, all of whom had served under Colonel Alexander Read in the Baramahal and were, under Wellesley and Webbe, raised to high positions in the revenue administration of the Presidency. Webbe concluded with the observation that the campaign against military collectors had begun with the dismissal of Graham from South Arcot, he being the most vulnerable owing to failures in his administration there, but it would extend to others: 'By all of this you will observe that you stand in danger'. He added some cautionary advice to Munro: send the MBOR the most complete and detailed settlement information ('with 450 columns showing the quantity of arable land cultivated . . . the proportions in the 16ths . . .'); stop using historical precedents ('because to read of past times is vulgar and nobody in Leadenhall' Street does it'); and do not cite for comparison the Baramahal, Salem, Coimbatore, or Kanara ('because all of these districts were managed by military men'). Webbe's prediction was soon after realized with the resignation of Lionel Place from the MBOR, and his fustian launched against Presidency policies of the recent past, including the favour shown to military collectors.

Place, as we have seen, was returned to Madras to replace Thomas Cochrane and to effect changes in Madras administration, specifically to reverse the measures which Wellesley, through Lord Clive and Josiah Webbe, had introduced there. The choice of the Directors proved unfortunate, for almost exactly a year later Place resigned from the MBOR in a blaze of criticism of it.[59] This was contained in a letter addressed to the MBOR with the request that it be passed to the Court of Directors.

Place provided valuable and alarming insights into the managerial difficulties confronting the MBOR with its massive responsibilities. He claimed that a 'crisis' in the operation of the Board prevented him from performing any useful work. The Board, he said, was incapable of supervising the revenue proceedings of the Presidency. There had been too few meetings to scrutinize important and regular requests from collectors for guidance; the Board's president, William Petrie reportedly came to only some of the meetings because of his

[58] Ibid.

[59] The text of Place's letter, covering forty foolscap pages, may be found in MC, F/151/7, ff. 121–41 and IOL, *Board's Collection*, F/4/150; it is dated 9 October 1802.

other responsibilities; and there was no adequate link of revenue decisions with those of other major departments of the government. Secondly, there was insufficient staff to handle the large business of the Board with the result that some 470 pieces of settlement proceedings for the year 1802 remained unexamined in the late part of that year. Thirdly, the Board's records were not adequately kept and the quarters occupied by the Board in Fort St George were too small. To these accusations of inefficiency and inadequacy, Place added others. One was the appointment of the Special Commission for a Permanent Settlement of Madras Revenues with a broad mandate to consider the principles of settlement to be followed in Madras. Place complained that the Commission was guided solely by abstract theories and neglected practical experience and considerations, and complained further that while the Commission was supposed to have worked co-ordinately with the MBOR, it did not. Rather, it drew some of the personnel and thus added to the difficulties of the BOR. Among the 'principle[s] subverted' and the 'plan[s] overthrown that... [were] judged and proved by experience', the Commission consistently deprived 'hereditary proprietors of the land' of their rightful interests as discovered by him while collector of the Jaghire.

Most pernicious, according to Place, were the appointments to collectorships in recent years. He singled out Alexander Read and John G. Ravenshaw, who were appointed to succeed Munro in Kanara in 1800. These men were too young, he insisted, for such responsibilities, having served for a mere five years prior to being given their own collectorates. Moreover, in their concern to economize, the Board had made some of the collectorates too large to be managed by a single man, however competent. Tanjore and South Arcot were examples. The former territory, though very large, was well managed by Mr Harris, Place admitted, but South Arcot was badly managed under Captain James Graham. A recent inqury revealed this, along with evidence of revenue defalcation on a great scale. He continued: 'I am not prepared to say that the conduct of the other military collectors has been equally culpable, for indeed the records of this Board afford little insight.... Both with regard to Major Macleod and Major Munro it may be said that on the nature of their revenue, the principles which determine it . . . is in vain sought for.'

With respect to Munro in particular, Place charged that native revenue servants carried out tasks in violation of the regulations; indeed, he said they exercised the powers of Munro. These Indian officials were remunerated at a scale higher than those elsewhere and, again, in violation of regulations. Native officials could only work well with European supervision, but Munro's European assistants are given no scope for this. The result: in the CD the revenue had not reached more than two-thirds of the scheduled revenue according to the treaty of cession to the Company. Place supposed that the same criticisms applied to Macleod:

> It is in vain that the Board attempts to correct the improprieties that they see in the military collectors, they have all along felt the insufficiency of

their control over them. By courtesy or prescription, these gentlemen are allowed to be or make themselves exempt from the regulations and restraints which are observed by Civil Collectors. Their communications are so superficial, and so infrequent as to leave the Board in ignorance of the affairs in their districts. . . . For political reasons privilege is allowed to them in corresponding with Government and they thus avail themselves of the pretext to communicate upon matters purely of a revenue nature, which other collectors would be and have been required to refer through the channels of their immediate superiors.

Because Place was aware of no 'transcendent merit... found in the military which eclipsed that of the civilian collector and entitled them to preeminence' he claimed that the regulations which secured to civilian appointees of the Company 'all offices, places, and employments of a civil nature' were being violated.

Webbe, still in Madras, understood the seriousness of Place's attack as if that was necessary. Noting the severe drought conditions in the CD, he warned Munro that his principles against the granting of remissions, which one of his assistant collectors was urging, should be eased. Munro's troubles with the MBOR could increase as a result of petitions against him from the CD. 'Your principles are fundamentally awry, so expedients should be permitted to supercede principles; as you have the unprecedented audacity to reject the advice and example of your assistant who is a civil servant, you cannot expect that the Revenue Board will support a system of tyranny and oppression under a military collector'.[60] He confirmed to Munro that Graham had been dismissed from South Arcot 'for not exacting enough [revenue] and Macleod has driven Malabar into rebellion by exacting too much' and has also been removed.

Munro weathered the condemnation of his poligar policy and the attack upon military collectors for two reasons. One was that there continued to be too few collectors with adequate linguistic skills and revenue experience, even though ten years had passed since Cornwallis had spurned the Madras civil establishment by appointing Read and his military juniors to the Baramahal. This was recognized by the Court of Directors when, in 1802, they confirmed Munro's appointment to the CD on the basis of his work in Kanara and noted, too, that they had no evidence that civilians were being trained to supersede military collectors, especially in language competence.[61] The second reason was the esteem in which Munro was held by General Arthur Wellesley, commander of the forces operating against the Marathas from 1802, and the General's appreciation of the critical role of the CD in provisioning the army during the early phase of the war in central and southern Maratha country. Both permitted him to formulate and then publicize his ryotwar revenue administration.

[60] MC, 151/7, Webbe to Munro, 2 April 1803.

[61] *Board's Collection*, F/4/147, 'Extract of a Political Letter to Fort St. George', 12 March 1802, para. 47.

RYOTWAR COLLECTOR

Having pacified the CD and survived the criticisms of his means and the attack upon military collectors, two complex and taxing processes mainly occupied Munro from 1800 to late 1807. These were, first, the establishment of the ryotwar system of revenue administration there and polemicizing for its adoption elsewhere, and, second, the provisioning of Arthur Wellesley's army in the war against the Marathas from late 1802 to early 1805. While it was the first of these, together with his later judicial reforms, that earned for Munro much of his enduring fame as the humane and just face of British imperialism, it was the latter that won for him the support of the British imperial establishment and deepened his friendships with many important people, not least with Arthur Wellesley, the future Duke of Wellington. The irony of this is that the usual focus upon ryotwar and its administrative implications, and its tunnel-like view of the future Munro system, often neglects to notice that, shortly after Munro's departure from India in late 1807, the system that he had laboured so hard to create was dismantled and replaced by the village lease system. Only when village leases proved a failure was Munro's system restored by a reluctant Madras establishment, at the insistence of London. However, his contribution to this war against the Marathas—a major turning point in early British imperialism in India—is scarcely noticed in the official or scholarly discussion of Munro in the CD. Yet the victory over the Marathas in 1805, to which bullocks and grain from the CD contributed so much, made the British the supreme power in the subcontinent, and most importantly in the Delhi heartland of Mughal authority.

For Munro, concerns about empire and administration were absolutely linked, as we know from his earliest letters to his father from India. Thus, it is not difficult to see why a system of revenue administration based upon a mass of small peasant holders, under the close administrative scrutiny of a large body of revenue officers and tightly controlled by British officials, would have commended itself to him and other Company officials—like Josiah Webbe—in the Madras of 1800. Even if he were not already won over to this sort of scheme, as Munro had been in the Baramahal by 1797, the objective conditions of the CD might have urged something like ryotwar upon him. The CD's eighty poligars, their 30,000 or so armed followers, villages fortified and armed, and a history of at least thirty years of marauding armies coursing over the tract—all counselled an arrangement like that which had been evolved in the Baramahal ten years earlier.

That plan, as rephrased by Munro in September 1797, contained the essential elements of ryotwar. These were: an annual settlement with small farmers who were permitted to add to or freely reduce their holdings of the previous year; villages and taluks ('districts') jointly liable for revenue failures of individuals; and no additional taxes to be demanded for improvements carried out by farmers. The rules he had introduced into the central division of the Baramahal in 1797 did differ in some respects from later formulations of ryotwar. Several of the 1797 rules pertained to provisions for cultivators to take up lands on lease for longer than a year, as then favoured by the MBOR. Another stipulation was that all were to pay the same revenue for the same land, a provision substantially altered by the inam settlement in the CD and elsewhere. A third prohibited remission except for the cultivation of commercial crops such as cochineal and mulberry.[62] Munro's underlying political concerns about the central division of the Baramahal, even before he fell into line with Read about annual settlements, were evident in the middle of 1794, when he declared his intention to exclude any possible role or influence for 'head gauds [leaders of peasant castes, also called karaikar] and small cultivators from pre-exisiting political and economic networks.'[63]

Thus, when he was appointed to Kanara, Munro had in mind a method and an approach, if not a wholly operational administrative system, and he perceived no difficulty in assimilating what he found in Kanara to his conception. This was remarkable, for almost everything about landholding and the social and environmental conditions of agriculture in Kanara were different from those of the Baramahal of his past and the CD of his future. Nevertheless, after fifteen months in Kanara he brought away the conviction that landed property existed there in the form of the small estate, and a notion that the Kanara jenmi was the same as the small farmer of the Baramahal. This last conceit formed the basis of his persuasive and successful reports of May and November 1800. But the central contribution of his Kanara experience to his view thereafter was that small landed property was ancient in India and could become common again, provided the large intermediate landholders of the Bengal scheme were not installed in Kanara and the revenue demand was moderate. This conception he incorporated into his Kanara reports and carried with him to the CD in October 1800, from whence, in the following several years, the complete Munro version of ryotwar issued.

Historical writing on the development of the ryotwari system is too voluminous to recapitulate here. The existence of two major works on the evolution of Munro's programme makes such a task unnecessary, and our purpose is to draw attention to aspects of this evolution under Munro's hands between 1800 and 1807 which appear not to be adequately noticed by Nilmani Mukherjee or T. H. Beaglehole, or by official commentators upon the subject.[64]

A question at the beginning is whether in the distant past the state settled its revenue demands upon individual, small cultivators as Munro claimed. Beaglehole avoids this question and seems to accept, with most official commentators, that Munro's claim was valid, even though Munro himself almost always added that evidence on the point is absent.[65] On the other hand, many of

[62] Arbuthnot, pp. 50–1; Munro to Read, 5 September 1797.

[63] *The Baramahal Records*, Section 1, 'Management', p. 220.

[64] Mukherjee, *Ryotwar System*, chapter 2, pp. 17–40; Beaglehole, chapter 3, pp. 55–87.

[65] Noted in the case of 'black books' of Kanara revenue records; for the CD see the Cuddapah volume of the *Madras District Gazatteers* by C.F. Brackenbury, with respect to the 'kamil' accounts of Golconda-period revenue settlement there.

Munro's contemporaries—men with as much experience and ability such as John Hodgson and Lionel Place—and some modern scholars who have studied the question, have been persuaded that the base from which the revenue was passed, from the point of production to whatever stood for 'state authority', was more likely to be a village or a set of villages (later called a 'mootah').[66] Munro's critics in the early nineteenth century had only a slim basis in inscriptional evidence to refute his claims about the historicity of ryotwar as a system of direct relations between state officials and cultivators. But where this was cited, as by Ellis in his reports on 'mirasi', the effect was telling and might have been devastating upon Munro's position had not the major decision been made for ryotwar by the time that Ellis' work was published, in 1818.[67] Moreover, Munro's critics, such as Hodgson, made skilful metaphoric use of Munro's elegiac 'village republic'.

In the 1808 report of the MBOR, of which John Hodgson was the most influential member (and the most often cited in the document), the decisive argument to the Madras Governor, Sir George Barlow, for replacing ryotwar with village leases began with the following proposition:

> The country is divided into villages. A village, geographically, is a tract of country comprizing [*sic*] some hundreds or thousands acres of arable or waste land; a village politically, is a little republic, or rather corporation, having within itself, municipal officers and corporate artificers; its boundaries are seldom altered; and though sometimes injured, or even devastated by war, famine, and epidemical disorders, the same name, boundaries, interests, and even families, continue for ages.[68]

Mimicry of Munro becomes plagiarism in later sections of the report when the following phrases ring forth: 'The village (Mozawar) system is, at least as old, as the age of Menu.... Every village with its twelve *ayagandees*... is a petty commonwealth... and India is a great assemblage of such commonwealths.'[69] Nor should it be forgotten that Munro himself, in his late reports on the CD, acknowledged that more than a third of the villages of the CD had a corporate form of organization similar to mirasi in Chingleput and Tanjore,

[66] The writings of Place and Hodgson are conveniently found in *The Fifth Report*, v. 3; for the view of Mukherjee and Frykenberg, their joint essay, 'The Ryotwari System and Social Organization in the Madras Presidency', in Frykenberg, *Land Control and Social Structure*, p. 219, referring to the period immediately preceding Company rule; for the longer historical period, Mukherjee believed that both ryotwar and village systems had long existed in South India, his *Ryotwar System*, p. 75. Murton's views are found in two of his previously cited works: 'Key People in the Countryside', pp. 168–9, and 'Territory, Social Structure . . .'.

[67] F. W. Ellis, *Replies to Seventeen Questions Proposed by the Madras Government of Fort St. George Relative to the Mirasi Right, with Two Appendices* (Madras: 1818).

[68] *The Fifth Report*, v. 3, report of 25 April 1808, p. 431.

[69] Ibid., p. 435; note Hodgson's recommendation for the village lease system, para. 31, p. 434.

'in which they settle among themselves the exact proportion of the whole rent that each individual is to pay'. This was the 'veespuddi' (*visabadi*) system which presupposes a group of persons entitled to enjoy the major benefits of landed income and to stand jointly responsible for a tax placed upon the village as a whole.[70] It must be granted that Munro's reiteration of the historic character of ryotwar was never the principal argument for ryotwar; hence, it should not be given exaggerated significance by those who wish to understand that historical context. However, Munro's 'history' should be appreciated for the rhetorical contribution that it made at the time, when he was confronted with engaging with over 200,000 individual cultivators of the CD to pay their annual land revenue, ranging, as he wrote later, from Rs 10 to 10;000.[71]

As compared with the Baramahal, and certainly with Kanara, the CD presented Munro with problems of scale that were daunting. Where in the Baramahal an annual settlement involved 80,000 pattadars, that is farmers who engaged to cultivate particular fields for the year and at a fixed revenue rate, in the CD the number was about 209,000 in 1804.[72] And where in Kanara heavy monsoon rains mired the few roads, swelled rivers that traversed that territory, and made ascents to upland villages difficult, the 26,000 square miles of the CD obliged an administrator of the diligence of Munro to move about incessantly. During the administrative year 1805–6 (fasly 1215), Munro's correspondence provides evidence of the following itinerary: late March 1805, Chitvel; late May, Anantapur; early October to early November, Rayadrug; middle November, Hampi, Bellary and two smaller places; early December, Adoni; early January 1806, Harapanahalli; late February, Rayachoti; and late May, Anantapur. There is no reason to suppose that this was an extraordinary year for him.[73]

But there are two elements in the revenue administration of the CD that go to the central conception of ryotwar, elements quite different from earlier ideas about it. These were inams and judicial problems.

That almost half of the cultivation of the CD then and for the next 150 years was under privileged revenue demand is at least anomalous, given the principles of ryotwar first articulated by Munro in 1797; that the average revenue demanded for inam holdings was 7 per cent of that for the same land on full revenue mocks the expressed principles of ryotwar, though the reasons for this are clear enough. It was well recognized by Munro and his colleagues that a condition of collecting the stipulated revenue from the CD was the provision of a vast reserve of lowly taxed, prime agricultural land at the disposal of the wealthy peasantry. It was also recognized that access to inam holdings at very reduced revenue for inamdars was a means of fixing at least part of the CD peasantry in its villages. This meant reducing their migrations, with the stock

[70] *The Fifth Report*, v. 3, p. 204, Munro to the MBOR, 5 January 1807.

[71] MC, 151/92, f. 39, Munro to Charles Wynn, President of the Board of Control, 14 June 1823.

[72] Mukherjee, *Ryotwar System*, p. 24.

[73] MC, F/151/12.

and skills they possessed, to the nearby non-British territories of Mysore and Hyderabad, or, just as alarming from the viewpoint of any collector, to neighbouring districts under the Company. Where went the wealthy peasantry went the revenue, and it was by the revenue that careers were made and unmade in Madras. The inam element in the ryotwar of Munro's CD meant that this system was a settlement with and for wealthy cultivators, those whom Munro called 'the better sort of rayets' (the top 20 per cent of farmers). This was not the egalitarian system it may have begun to be under Read in the Baramahal and was claimed by Munro to be throughout his career, even as he also claimed that under ryotwar gradations of ranks in society were preserved. Inams made Munro's ryotwar work, it seems clear, but inams also raised fundamental problems about the extant judicial system.

The new order being created by Munro depended on the recognition by established peasant communities that their welfare was best vested in the securities provided by the tall, hard soldier who represented the Company in the CD, rather than in those of the fierce old fighters who had previously ruled the countryside. Munro's inam policy was meant to make such a decision inevitable, for the respectable peasant communities of the CD were the major beneficiaries of the inam policy.

The word *in'am* is Arabic; it designated a gift, usually of landed income, as an honour or mark of distinction from a ruling authority, and it was often accompanied by a document, *sanad-in'am*. This Arabic word entered South Indian usage, ironically, from the Marathas in their seventeenth-century expansion over the southern peninsula.[74] Adopted by the British, the term underwent a change, being extended in meaning in one sense, and contracted in another. Inam came to encompass all extant alienations of land revenue. In this the British took a single technical term of previous administrative usage and applied it to all cases of revenue privileges which they additionally asserted were conditional, not permanent. The usefulness of such an adoption should not be minimized. As a gloss for a variety of entitlements which in the various Dravidian languages implied a moral component, inam as a technical term was contracted in meaning by the denial of moral content and by the view of a wide range of prior grants as contingent, utilitarian, and service-connected alienations which could be resumed at the discretion of the state. For the Madras establishment, the example of Tipu Sultan was a precedent. His official policy of disallowing various prior alienations of landed income, including those for support of Hindu shrines and religious persons, while extending those to Muslim institutions and persons, was inspired by his consciousness of being a Muslim sovereign—as were his nomenclature changes in calendar, titles, and currency.[75]

[74] Wilson, *Glossary*, pp. 217–18.

[75] B. Stein, 'Idiom and Ideology in Early Nineteenth Century South India', in *Rural India: Land, Power and Society under British Rule*, ed. by Peter Robb (London: Curzon Press, 1983), pp. 23–59, and Nicholas B. Dirks, 'Terminology and Taxonomy; Discourse and Domination: From Old Regime to Colonial Regime in South India', in

Somehow, Munro's superiors in Madras or in London appear not to have noticed the cognative disorder of, on the one hand, justifying the wars against the Muslim Mysore state on the basis of its religious oppression, while, on (or with) the other hand, seizing all of the privileges of sovereignty that Tipu Sultan had possessed.

Munro collected a mass of information about inams in the CD, and regularly sent it to Madras. Among his first instructions to tahsildars in the Adoni taluk, in anticipation of his young assistant Thackeray's assuming charge of it, was for all inams to be carefully examined and information about them sent to Munro's office.[76] However, neither he nor his superiors in Madras ever undertook to consider the entire matter of inams, nor seriously to question or justify their continuation at a level which was seen as massive in his most complete statement about them in 1806.[77]

Inams then comprised 44 per cent of all of the cultivated acres in the CD and, though less clear, paid a mere 7 per cent of the assessed revenue for fields under inam holders (inamdars). Moreover, Munro had reported in 1801 that the potential revenue from inam lands in the CD constituted 54 per cent of the total land revenue actually collected.[78]. So glaring a fact could not have been missed by the MBOR nor, eventually, by the Court of Directors in London. The latter called for explanations in 1804, and they repeated the call in 1811, suggesting that their earlier queries had gone unanswered.[79] Even then, little of anything official was undertaken on the inam question in the CD, and this was quite desultory considering the singularity of the concern for revenue by the Company, then and later. In fact, no reductions in inam holdings (nor even serious questions about their appropriateness) were entertained until quite late in the nineteenth century, by the Inam Commission. Even so, by the end of the century about half of the revenue-yielding lands of the Madras and Bombay Presidencies was under privileged revenue demand, and the inam category was not wholly abolished until after independence, in 1950.[80]

Some judicial regulations and procedures impinged deleteriously upon the operations of ryotwar and the resumption of 'unauthorized' inams, according to Munro. He claimed that most litigations arose from these two causes and also

---

Studies of South India, eds. Robert E. Frykenberg and Pauline Kolenda (Madras: New Era Publications, 1985), pp. 127–51.

[76] MC, F/151/10, 'Instructions to Tehsildars, Adwanee Division, December', 1800, paras 7–8.

[77] MC, F/151/106, ff. 57–70.

[78] Munro to Petrie and the MBOR, 23 June 1801, from Anantapur, para. 2; reprinted in Madras Presidency, *Selections from the Records of the District of Cuddapah, No. 1* (Cuddapah: Collectorate Press, 1870), pp. 25–7.

[79] IOL, *Madras Despatches*, E/4/892, 'Revenue Letter to Madras, 10 April 1804, para. 23, pp. 377–8.

[80] Bruce L. Robert, 'Agrarian Organization and Resource Distribution in South India: Bellary District, 1800–1979', Ph.D. thesis, Department of History, University of Wisconsin, 1982.

that the courts were hopelessly unprepared to deal with cases arising under both. Partly, this was because revenue regulations in Madras had been set in anticipation of a permanent, zamindari settlement, with respect to which annual settlements with individual cultivators were antagonistic; and partly it was because the court system, which was established with the same anticipation, lacked the expert knowledge and experience to deal with problems involving either the revenue or inams. At the same time, he was to carry on a debate, through official and unofficial channels, with his superiors in Madras on the same matters. This was with William Petrie, President of the MBOR from 1800, who was respectful of but not wholly persuaded by Munro's ryotwar arguments. The second person with whom Munro debated was Bentinck, Governor of the Presidency, who, while convinced by Munro on ryotwar, was too much the politician to attack a judicial system promulgated by the great Cornwallis and impatiently pressed by the Governor-General, Richard Wellesley.

When zamindari revenue regulations were extended to Madras in 1802, it was provided that the land revenues of as yet unsettled districts of Madras should be made permanent as zamindar estates; or, if that was not possible, under leasehold estates; or, failing that, under an annual ryotwar settlement until a permanent system could be established. These were the provisions of modified zamindari worked out for those parts of Awadh which had been ceded to the Company in 1800.[81] To Petrie, Munro protested against the too hasty construction of revenue estates in Madras as yet insufficiently known to predict whether or how they would work: 'It is really an extraordinary method of proceeding—first to deprive yourself of the means of acquiring information, and then to sit gravely down to pursue your research'.[82] Bentinck needed no convincing about the inappropriateness of the Bengal–Awadh revenue scheme for Madras and had determined in June 1805 to see Wellesley in Calcutta to protest against its introduction in Madras. But, on the matter of the Bengal judicial system he opposed Munro and the MBOR, both of whom protested that these judicial arrangements precluded investigations into the best revenue scheme for Madras. Bentinck, perhaps rightly, believed that Calcutta was quite fixed on these judicial arrangements as being best for Madras. Accordingly, the courts were introduced in all of the districts of Madras in 1806, even in territories like the CD which were not fully surveyed for revenue purposes.

Nevertheless, Munro continued his opposition to a judicial system which he was convinced was in conflict with an equitable and constructive revenue administration, for him the central pillar of British rule in India and one best realized through ryotwar. He continued this struggle for another eight years before his views prevailed. The reasons for this obsessive opposition were of two sorts. One line of reasoning was public and turned on practical as well as

[81] Roberts, *Historical Geography*, part 1, pp. 248–9; the tract transferred comprised about half of Awadh.

[82] Beaglehole, pp. 76–7.

principled difficulties of a judicial system whose procedures were considered by him as inimical to indigenous custom and social realities. On this most conceded that Munro was correct. His arguments were advanced in reports beginning in 1807. The other reasons arose from his realistic apperception of the politics of policy determination in British India. This was knowledge that he did not possess ten years before in the Baramahal, when he adopted ryotwar and gave to that mode of revenue administration a voice that it had not previously had. The second reason was, in many ways, the guiding one for his long and successful opposition to the Company judiciary.

After the first few years of the CD administration, Munro had come to understand that the single, great requirement for enduring British rule over India was the construction of a unified conception of sovereignty derived from and therefore appropriate for India. This understanding was not nearly so perfect as it was to become by 1824, when it received eloquent expression in his Minute of 31 December, but the kernel of that understanding was planted by 1806. Believing as he did that British rule rested on land-revenue administration, and believing further that the principles of ryotwar were best calculated to establish that foundation, he had become convinced that the usual reason for rejecting ryotwar—that it was at odds with established principles of jurisprudence as derived from British law and experience—must be attacked at the highest political level. His opposition here was formidable: the arrogant confidence that British institutions provided the essential means for ruling India according to the still hallowed Cornwallis. His attack upon the Bengal system was unrelenting—against its zamindari revenue regime and its Awadhi modifications, as well as its deeper Anglicized commitment of which law was the centrepiece. Munro launched this attack upon all levels of the system of Company policy determination, and the centre of his attack was against the existing legal system, with respect to which ryotwar could never be made to fit. Ryotwar in Munro's hands would not change; the law must.

More immediately, however, in the few years that remained to him in the CD and India, Munro pressed his argument on the incompatibility of the court system with normal administration because it not only ignored but also contradicted many Indian customs and realities. An example of this line of argument is found in his letter to the MBOR on 15 May 1807.[83] There, he began in an interesting way by denying the relevance of some of the reigning historical authorities, 'Menu' (Manu) and Abul Fazl, on a matter where they had previously served him. In attempting to determine the proportion of the gross produce which actually went to the cultivator and that which was taken by the state, the Company was hampered in two ways. First, there was no private property in land, except in Malabar and Kanara, upon which to base real shares of production; and, secondly, such authorities as 'Menu' and Abul Fazl were not convincing. These two venerables spoke of the state receiving a low one-

[83] MC, F/151/135, f. 136–48, reproduced, with deletions in *The Fifth Report*, v. 3, pp. 501–14.

third to one-sixth as its share of gross production, and yet it was necessary for Manu to require that any landholder who failed to cultivate his land should have it taken and given to another. Munro asked why, if the share to the state was as low as claimed, a landholder would not quite happily cultivate his land, and concluded that the assessment in ancient times was not low but high.[84] Still, practical experience of the Company's officials everywhere in Madras, except on the Malabar coast, was that one-third of gross production was all that a cultivator could pay to the state and still realize a sufficient profit from farming to make land a valuable asset. The benefits of a moderate revenue demand in increasing land values and private property in land would be greatest under a ryotwar mode of settlement than under either a 'zemindarry' or 'mootadarry' (village lease) settlement.

Regardless of the mode of settlement, however, the existing judicial system was a barrier to progress. There were then, and there would continue to be, long delays in actions involving property owing to the formal procedures of the courts as then constituted.[85] It was vexatious for cultivators to attend often distant zillah courts, for this interfered with cultivation.[86] He argued that bribery, the concomitant of delays in suits brought under the extant regulations, and the concentration of judicial functions in the small number of judicial officers of the Company—both would increase from the present intolerable level. Bad decisions would inevitably continue to issue from courts which lacked knowledge and experience about rural conditions and customs known to experienced revenue officials, and even better known by native panchayats in which most ordinary people vested their trust.[87] Munro cautioned that unless a responsive judicial system was devised for the collection of debts, creditors would soon withhold loan funds and cause grievous dislocations in the economy. He drew attention finally to the inequity of the present court system which insisted on enforcing the collection of drafts ('tungkhas') issued on village revenues by the late Nizam's government as a means of paying their soldiers' wages; he warned that this could seriously threaten the level of revenue there as well as continuing the extortions of Hyderabadi adventurers.[88]

Another complaint lodged by Munro against the extension of the court system to Madras districts in 1806 pertained to the diminished ability of collectors to investigate and punish revenue servants charged with corruption and illegal exactions from cultivators. This would apply to any mode of settlement, but had special consequences for ryotwar. Munro pointed out that powers expressly vested in collectors in 1803 (regulation 2, section 37) to appoint and dismiss subordinate revenue officials, and to hear complaints arising from the people against such servants in the collection of the revenue, had been with-

[84] MC, F/151/135, f. 136.
[85] Ibid., f. 145.
[86] Ibid.
[87] Ibid.
[88] Ibid., ff. 146–8.

drawn in 1806. This same regulation made mandatory a court hearing on such allegations. Munro's comment:

> To restrain the Collector from examining the charges . . . [against] the revenue servants is to proclaim to these servants that they may exercise any species of exaction with impunity and to the rayets that they must submit in silence to this evil. To tell them that the law will do them justice is a mere mockery. The rayets know that it cannot, and they will commit more acts of extortion in a week than all the law in all the courts will redress in seven years. . . .

Some exactions may amount to no more than two rupees ('about 1/2 pagoda on each rayet's rent'):

> But who will go to the law for this sum, not one in fifty, and against him who does go the chances of success are at least ten to one. Who are his witnesses. If he summons the potail and curnam [headman and accountant], they are in league against him for as Rev[enue] officers of the village they have received their share of the [illicit] collection. If he summons 2 or 3 rayets of the village, the money taken from them will be returned and the promises or threats of the revenue servants will induce them to conceal the truth.[89]

Munro's critical observations on the courts at this time were not much different from those of other collectors. In the short run, the effect of these criticisms was to induce the Madras and London authorities to abandon ryotwar in 1808. They saw it as a system whose workings seemed to depend on a large body of scheming and corrupt Indian revenue officials held in check only by a British collector of great industry and diligence, someone like Munro. It was moreover a system which seemed to require abandoning the judicial system installed by the great Cornwallis. In the long run, Munro's criticisms then laid the ground for the restructuring of the entire judicial process that he won in England while he was there on furlough from 1808 to 1814.

But for the moment Munro devised another method for blunting the disruptive effects of introducing the new courts and code into the CD in 1806: the appointment of judicial officials to the CD courts who would be sympathetic to his programme there. In this he had the support of Bentinck and willing instruments in his long-time protege and Scottish friend Peter Bruce (who had served under him for five years), and another younger colleague and friend, William Thackeray.

In May 1806 the Governor had written to Munro asking for a 'character' for Bruce in connection with a possible appointment to a zillah (district) judgeship in the CD. Bentinck expressed his regret that he could not make Thackeray

[89] MC, F/151/125, 'Memo on Mr. Ravenshaw's Paper on Ryotwar', n.d., but possibly Ravenshaw's instructors to his sub-collectors in South Arcot, included in his report to the MBOR, 1 July 1806, abstracted in *The Fifth Report*, v. 3, pp. 215–19.

the only judge in the CD, for the jurisdiction was very large, and he added: 'I hope . . . that the persons appointed there are such as will not interfere with you or give unnecessary trouble' [90] Bruce was duly appointed to a post in the CD and received congratulations from Munro, though a minor reservation attended his felicitation: revenue officers, Munro wrote, were 'more useful to the Publick and Inhabitants than . . . any Judge can possibly be. . . .'[91] Then, in late 1807, on the eve of his departure for Europe, Munro delivered a farewell exhortation to Bruce on the subject of the relations between revenue and judicial officials. He reminded Bruce that the existing regulations were not well adapted to a permanent settlement of the revenue, and 'still less for a Rayetwar one', for they led inevitably to a clash between both kinds of officers and therefore required the prudence and good temper of both. Bruce was urged never 'to impede the Collector' and to act towards his revenue successors in the CD 'as you would have them act to you if they were judge'. If differences arose, Bruce was to work them out with his revenue colleagues, 'for Government dislikes being troubled with petty disputes' and forms bad opinions of those involved.[92]

Though grateful to have the sympathetic Bruce, whom he warmly recommended, Munro had made efforts to avert any appointment or court in the CD. When Bentinck had written to him in April 1806 for advice about where the new zillah court should be located in the CD, Munro had responded that no place in the CD recommended itself. Cuddapah, the most central place, was also the hottest in the CD, and Rayachoti, another proposed site, was rejected as unhealthy. Munro suggested that Nellore might be a better place for the CD court! Though this would place the court some seventy miles outside the CD, that was not a problem: 'The people of the CD are a more hardy and travelling race than those on the coast'; in any case, the major consideration in locating the court should be the convenience of the judge, not the Indian litigant! This might have been viewed as disingenuous in the light of Munro's criticisms of the court system as taking cultivators from their fields for the treks to and long absences at distant courts.[93] In any case, the Nellore suggestion was rejected, and the court was set up in the CD under the compliant Bruce, leaving Munro free to refine ryotwar practice through the training of others.

William Thackeray was one of the first, and he remained devoted to Munro's interests on the whole throughout his very long career. In 1806, now an experienced ryotwar collector, Bentinck was considering Thackeray for a judgeship in CD. However, he was instead appointed the judge of Masulipatam, but remained available to Munro as a spokesman on matters of judicial-revenue relations and on ryotwar in general from 1806. At that time, Bentinck

[90] MC, F/151/9, Bentinck to Munro, 23 May 1806.

[91] MC, F/151/12, Munro to Bruce, 1 December 1806.

[92] MC, F/151/12, 21 October 1807.

[93] Bentinck Papers, PwJb 25, p. 309, Munro to Bentinck, 13 April 1806; regarding Bruce, p. 324, 29 May 1806, where Munro says that Bruce is not a genius, but a man of great abilities and correct principles.

designated Thackeray as his expert companion for a projected tour of the Presidency to determine, finally, whether ryotwar should be adopted. Though Bentinck later decided that he could not undertake the tour, he set Thackeray that task. Immediately, Thackeray applied to his mentor, Munro, for guidance on how he should proceed and what questions had to be seriously considered. The results of this will be examined below, but it is worth noting that Thackeray appears to have fully shared Munro's antipathy to the intrusion of the courts in 1806. He wrote to Munro in May 1806, thanking the latter for his advice on how to proceed with the tour and passing the news that three more judges were to be appointed within the month, 'so Lord have mercy on the poor people'. However, one of the three new appointees was to be James Cochrane, another of Munro's proteges from the CD and thus another ally.[94]

In all, a good number of young Britons in the civil service of Madras passed through Munro's hands while he was in the CD, and many of them in their turn became collectors who trained another cohort of men dedicated to the Munro system. The awe in which Munro was held by his juniors was obvious and earned by Munro's experience, confidence, and ability. That there was also affection is attested by the correspondence that exists. We have seen that Munro was reluctant to have junior men assigned to him in the CD because, as he argued, it would not ease his administrative tasks and it might inhibit his political ones. But once there, Munro proved a patient teacher and a supportive superior. This may best be judged from the full correspondence with Peter Bruce which has survived, but it is found with respect to his other tutees as well, and on a great variety of topics.[95]

Ryotwar and its operation was the obvious topic of importance. His instructions to Thackeray when the latter assumed responsibility for the Adoni division in 1800 comprise among the clearest exposition on ryotwar that Munro ever constructed.[96] Thackeray was told that the 'potails' were answerable for the revenue of their villages and jointly with other headmen for the districts in which their villages were. They would settle with 'inferior rayets' partly in grain, but mostly in money, and any surplus over what the headman contracted to pay to Thackeray's revenue officials was to be retained by the headmen, since they were collectively liable for revenue deficiencies. On the last, Munro cautioned not to be harsh on the collection of deficits from village headmen; they were not to be weakened 'materially'.

Munro provided Thackeray and his other assistants with their initial staff of Indian subordinates, and any changes in their staffs were to be made by each of them after having interviewed candidates carefully. He told Thackeray that the inhabitants of Adoni were to understand that he, not Munro, would 'manage the country'. One way to assure the last was for Thackeray to maintain

[94] MC, F/151/9, Thackeray to Munro, 12 May 1806; Cochrane was appointed a judge in North Kanara in 1806.

[95] MC, F/151/10–12, principally, but also F/151/9 and 20 and elsewhere in MC.

[96] MC, F/151/10, ff. 1–5, 31 December 1800.

a double office staff: one 'cutcherry' made up of Marathi speakers, and the other of Kannada speakers. This, he said, would stimulate competition and minimize cabals against him, and it would ensure that there was open communication regarding government business.

> It is by general and unreserved communication not merely with your own cutcherry, but with such of your tahsildars or inferior servants as appear to be men of capacity, and by receiving all opinions, and being guided explicitly by none, that you can restrain every person in office within the line of his duty, guard the rayets from oppression, and the publick revenue from defalcation, and preserve in your own hands a perfect control of the country.[97]

The great expanse of waste—uncultivated, but cultivable land—and the CD were to be treated as a special problem by Thackeray. The policy of granting such lands on lower revenue through issuance of a 'cowle' (*kaul*) to expand cultivation in the country was to be carried out with caution.[98] Thackeray must recognize that the prime objective of the ryot was to maximize his money income, and this was necessarily in conflict with the collector's objective of maximizing the revenue. While the government wanted to increase the cultivation of waste land for added food and industrial raw material, not to speak of revenue, it was from the lands presently and regularly cultivated that increased revenue was most likely to come.[99] Similar care had to be taken with the grant of production loans from the revenue, or 'taccavi', to be repaid at the time of harvest. Munro warned that unless care was exercised, these production loans were used by amildars, sheristadars and other revenue officials to improve their own lands while being shown in their records as loans to others. Munro's method in both matters was to insist that accurate records be kept, to constantly query cultivators about cowles and taccavi, and to frequently inspect their proper application in person. Tank repairs was another matter on which fraud could occur, especially for funds for such repairs be accompanied by detailed surveys. As to the construction of new tanks to replace badly silted ones, Munro was discouraging: 'scarcely any place where a tank can be made to advantage... has not already been applied to this purpose....'[100]

Other matters on which Munro instructed all of his assistants had to do with inams, poligars and trade. Some attention has already been given to the first two. On inams Munro usually answered queries from his assistants by relating how he dealt with particular kinds of inams, and essentially by counselling the renewal of inams where there was some proof that these had existed

[97] MC, F/151/10, f. 5.

[98] Wilson, *Glossary*, p. 270; an agreement between a cultivator and revenue official setting the terms of landholding.

[99] MC, F/151/10, Thackeray to Munro, 25 May 1801.

[100] MC, F/151/10, ff. 16–21; most of this is abstracted in *The Fifth Report*, v. 3, pp. 204ff.

for a considerable time.[101] On poligars, once he had completed his draconian measures against them, he advised that these chiefs should be supported. When Bruce informed him that the allowance of the poligar of Chitvel, Rs 600, had been stopped owing to an action by the poligar's *vakil* (agent) in Madras, it was Munro's view that the allowance should be resumed and the vakil investigated for swindling the poligar and punished.[102] On the Company's trade in the CD and the operation of the Madras Board of Trade's commercial residents in the CD, Munro became increasingly critical of their interference with free commerce and their exploitation of CD merchants and artisans. Still, he maintained a scrupulously correct position in instructions to his juniors. In 1804 he sent them a circular about an impending visit to the CD of the commercial resident, J. Greenhill. He said it was their responsibility to ascertain that all engagements entered by weavers were voluntary, but once made they must be enforced. No sales of cloth by weavers was to be permitted until contracts with the Company had been fulfilled. However, coercion by head weavers, often using Company peons and even soldiers, was discouraged.[103] On the other hand, however, Munro was quite prepared to interfere with market arrangements if necessary. Accordingly, he sent a circular to his assistants in 1804 with the instruction that because of the grain scarcity of that year of drought and flood crop damage, and with large procurements to meet the needs of Wellesley's army in Maharashtra, all sales of CD grain outside the territory, notably in Raichur north of the Tungabhadra, were to be curtailed.[104]

Many of his instructions and much of his supervision pertained to matters involving Indian subordinate officials. Their large number—which Munro took to be a strength of ryotwar and his critics its weakness—occupied much of his time. Munro often stripped his own staff of its best people to supply the initial staff of his new assistants. In effect, he was conducting a double training process during most of his time in the CD, that of young British civilians and Indians. His consistent instructions to the former was that they must depend upon and support their Indian subordinates.

Being acutely consciousness of his own dependence upon Indian subordinates, Munro was aware of how much greater that of his assistants had to be. The balance between encouraging his European subordinates to carry out their responsibilities in an independent manner—to be seen to be managing affairs in their jurisdictions—and interfering with his own superior experience was a delicate one which Munro managed admirably. This is brought out in an exchange with Bruce in 1806 when the latter complained about an exchange of letters between his sheristadar, Hanumantha Rao, and Munro. Munro hastened to sooth: 'sorry that my correspondence with your servants should

[101] MC, F/151/10, Munro to Thackeray, 31 December 1800, where uninterrupted occupancy of forty years is suggested.

[102] MC, F/151/12, Munro to Bruce, 12 June 1806.

[103] MC, F/151/10, circular dated 1 April 1804.

[104] MC, F/151/10, 7 August 1804.

have given you so much uneasiness, and that you should have supposed that my writing to them proceeded from any want in confidence in you'. There was no assistant with whom he was more pleased than Bruce, he said, and the correspondence with Hanumantha Rao had arisen over some matters in Munro's division of the CD, not about Bellary.[105] The delicate sensibilities of all involved was very much in Munro's mind and in his instructions. To Bruce, in 1804, he had written that Hanumantha Rao was to be in charge of settling the revenues with the ryots and that Bruce should inspect such arrangements and determine that all increases or decreases in revenue were justifiable: 'But you should take care not to do away [i.e. alter] in the presence of rayets what he has settled, because this would lessen his influence so much that he would not be able to make anything of them. You should hear the complaints or objections of the rayets against the settlement, but never make any alteration unless on the fullest conviction that it is right.'[106] The vulnerability of European officials to their trusted Indian subordinates was widely recognized. The young Alexander Read, who had served under Munro briefly in the Baramahal and had succeeded him in Kanara (along with another Munro protege, John G. Ravenshaw), refers to this in a letter to his younger colleague James Cochrane before the latter joined Munro in the CD. Read wrote that when taking up a new posting in a district not yet permanently settled it was accepted practice for the collector-designate to bring 'as many of his own people fit to serve as amildar as possible'. He should also bring an able 'peshkar, or head [office] man, a good seerishtadar and one or two clever gomasthas'. These were to replace 'corrupt' officials that were found in the new post and persuade the people of the district of the 'fairness' of the new regime.'[107] The worst scandal that could beset a ryotwar collector was the loss of control of his district to a cabal of revenue servants. The wreckage of careers of Company collectors strewed the revenue history of Madras from this cause, and, as Munro knew, it was one of the persistent reasons for the resistance of governments in India and London to ryotwar.[108]

There were other hazards of which Munro sought to make his European juniors aware and to have enter into their executive calculations as collectors. One of these Munro had given thought and expression to early in his CD

[105] MC, F/151/12, 21 June 1806, f. 113.

[106] MC, F/151/11, Munro to Bruce, 7 November 1804. To Thackeray, a few years before, he had expressed similar cautions about his Indian staff, especially their dismissals: 'The common revenue peon ought never to be dismissed without the fullest proof of his misbehaviour, for though he is not strictly speaking an hereditary servant, he is generally so and this consideration renders him . . . trustworthy'. This is cited in MC, F/151/12, Munro to Thackeray, 31 December 1800.

[107] MC, F/151/10, f. 95 ff.

[108] An example: IOL, *Madras Despatches*, 1809, E/4/903, pp. 704–5, regarding Munro's settlement for 1805, where the Court of Directors condemn the reliance of Munro on 'native agents' and say that the temptations of corruption 'constitute strong objections to the [Munro] system'.

administration: the proper level of revenue to be demanded of cultivators. In September 1802 he wrote to Thomas Cockburn, an old friend and senior official of the MBOR from 1793, on his perceptions of the pressures that affected the level of revenue demanded.

> The desire that men at the head of affairs usually have of seeing the country, or at least the public income, flourishing under their auspices, will most probably compel me to proceed too rapidly, and bring revenue to a standard four or five lacs below the point to which it ought to have reached. If I am ever left entirely to my own judgement it is possible enough that I may have sufficient resolution to follow the wisest course. I may get nervous as I get older, and become afraid of censure. If I leave room for my successor to raise the revenue, it would be said that I allowed the inhabitants to defraud Government. If I raise all that the country can pay, and he could raise no more, it would be said that I had oppressed the people for the sake of exhibiting a high settlement. However . . . I shall, for the sake of assisting the public want of money, press the rayets rather more than I ought to do.[109]

Other matters touching revenue and the welfare of cultivators were not within the power of the collector to totally control in a place as poor as the CD, but still efforts were to be made to minimize revenue losses. Thus, he wrote to his assistants in 1802 that there was a period in most years, from early in April to the middle of July (the lunar months of 'Chyter' or Cheitram, to 'Jaisht' or Jyestham) when poor peasants desert their villages and even their taluks, looking for easier terms of landholding. This was called the 'kalawedi' season (Tamil: *kalavadi*, meaning sweepings from the threshing floor).[110] Then, village headmen sought to lure poor farmers from elsewhere by offering low revenue demands, and this encouraged the 'spirit of emigration . . . [and] hinders the improvement of land', warned Munro. Therefore, each assistant was advised to instruct village headmen and accountants that no cowles were to be granted to non-resident cultivators at rates lower than standard, even if the migrant cultivators were indigent, or in a condition of what was called 'nadar'.[111] Vigilance for the Company's revenue and concern for career must override other considerations.

In the light of this, Munro's warnings to his assistants were unceasing. To Bruce, again, regarding reportedly large loans made by the shroff or money-changer attached to the latter's office, Munro wrote that 'if the shroff is much involved in debt I should not think him a safe man, for he will be endeavouring to speculate on the coins of the kist [revenue instalments paid into the collector's treasury]'.[112] To all of his sub-collectors he had written in 1802 that he had taken the precaution of cancelling the outstanding debts of tahsildars because

[109] Gleig, v, 1, pp. 334–5.
[110] Wilson, *Glossary*, p. 250.
[111] Possibly an Arabic word, Wilson, *Glossary*, p. 361.
[112] MC, F/151/11, Munro to Bruce, 7 May 1804.

many were found to be the result of bribes for their appointments then. He urged his assistants to do likewise so that they and other Indian officials were under no obligations which might suborn them. He also advised that they guard against future debts and presents involving such officials for the same reasons of the corrupting consequences of such practices.[113] To his orders that each assistant was to have a dual staff of servants using Marathi or Kannada or Telugu, he added to exercise care in the appointment of 'crakoons' (*karkun*), subordinate registrars and writers. They were often, he said, appointed at the recommendation of amildars from among their kinsmen, but should be independent men who might be 'useful as spies'.[114] In view of Munro's later strong advocacy of a 'native agency', i.e. major administrative responsibilities for Indians, such suspicions and minute scrutiny of Indian subordinate officials who were so essential for the operation of his method may seem contradictory. However, then and later Munro insisted that the venality of Indian officials was inversely proportional to their rewards in money and honours, and he urged that the Company increase both. In any case, the embarrassment of a scandal involving his Indian subordinates never happened to Munro during the fifteen or so years that he served as a collector, and one reason for this was the close supervision he exercised.

It is difficult to think that Munro's plans could have progressed as far as they did during most of his time in the CD without Lord Bentinck's warm support as a balance against a usually hostile Board of Revenue. Perhaps it was with an eye to bolstering Munro's reputation in London as well as his own strong confidence in Munro and his methods that Bentinck arranged for the son of the then President of the Board of Control, Lord Minto, to serve as assistant under Munro in the CD. Writing to Munro in 1806, Bentinck had reported that his old friend Minto had suggested that his son serve the Company in Madras city, but the Governor urged instead that the young man, whom he described to Munro as 'energetic and intelligent', should learn about India, and the best means for this was to work with Munro. Minto agreed that his son should become 'an able revenue servant', but the plan was scrapped when Minto was appointed Governor-General late in 1806.[115] In these arrangements involving Minto's son, William Thackeray may have had an influential role, for in 1806 Bentinck had come to depend upon him and to see him, perhaps, as a Munro surrogate.

Thackeray had been singled out to be Bentinck's special advisor on the permanent settlement of Madras revenues and to accompany him on a tour of the Presidency to determine, finally, which mode of settlement was to be adopted. Thackeray had then been in Company service for thirteen years and had sound knowledge of the Company's commercial operations. This he

[113] MC, F/151/10, 26 July 1802.

[114] MC, F/151/10, circular dated 28 May 1802.

[115] MC, F/151/9, Bentinck to Munro 5 October and 9 November 1806;, Thackeray to Munro 16 September 1806.

gained in the Northern Circars before joining Munro in the CD in 1800, and subsequently when, following his three years there was a revenue assistant of Munro's, he was for three additional years judge of the zillah court in Masulipatam. Regarding the tour Thackeray wrote to Munro: 'I shall have an opportunity of discussing revenue matters, and it is a good thing to know the best system'; then, plaintively for so seasoned an official:

> I therefore beg of you to write me your ideas of the best way of settling the country permanently as they call it. You used to write to me a great deal... I wish that you would again . . . and write me an Indian utopia, or a scheme for managing a country in India. . . . If you could do this, it may do much good, and I may have an opportunity of explaining your principles of govt and expatiating on their benefit in such a way as to produce good.[116]

Three months later, as plans for the tour matured, Thackeray again wrote requesting some queries by which to inform himself on the relative merits of permanent zamindari and ryotwar systems. He said that there were doubts expressed in Madras about the appropriateness of ryotwar and again pleaded: 'if you desert me now, I shall look foolish'.[117] During the ensuing months of 1806 Thackeray wrote frequently and with growing assurance about the tour. He thanked Munro for the suggestions the latter had sent. Out of these Thackeray said he had 'Compiled a pretty dissertation on permanent Ryotwar settlement which is not worth sending to you though the B[oar]d [of Revenue] are engaged in refuting my principles.'[118] Thackeray's notes on ryotwar had been passed to the MBOR by Bentinck, for their comment—'bones for the B[oard] of Revenue and Bengalees [i.e. those in Madras who favoured a zamindari settlement there] to gnaw at . . . it is all your sentiments and most likely your words in many places.'[119]

Objectors to Munro's ideas as reformulated by Thackeray were led by John Hodgson of the MBOR. According to Thackeray's report there were two major objections to ryotwar. One was its failure to attend Regulation XXX of 1802 which specified the protection to tenants by zamindars. To this Thackeray remarked: 'Neither I nor any other . . . judges nor the natives here [in Masulipatam] can make out exactly what the devil said regulation means. . .'. The other objection was its presumed social levelling. Proponents of a zamindari settlement insist that 'we must have a nobility in the country and a regular gradation of society . . . ryots composing the base, the zamindars above them all like the apex of the pyramids'. Thackeray concluded with the news that he intended to propose a public debate, with himself supporting ryotwar and Hodgson taking the zamindari position.[120]

[116] MC, F/151/9, Thackeray to Munro, 30 January 1806.
[117] MC, F/151/9, 10 April 1806.
[118] MC, F/151/9, 5 May 1806.
[119] MC, F/151/9, 16 June 1806.
[120] Ibid.

Shortly after this, he was raised to the MBOR by Bentinck. Thackeray wrote that Bentinck actually favoured Munro for this appointment to the MBOR, as its president, but that appointment 'would have brought down a terrible storm, and you are certainly needed in the Ceded Districts'. Bentinck, he assured Munro, 'is very strenuous for ryotwar, however not another soul here supports it' though 'the Court of Directors . . . seem to have some idea of its utility' [121] In the end, Thackeray undertook the tour of the Presidency without Bentinck, who had become engulfed in the aftermath of the Vellore Mutiny of July 1806, an event which ended, for the time, his Indian ambitions. Thackeray's report of 4 August 1807 with its support for a permanent ryotwar settlement is preserved in *The Fifth Report*, as the final words of its lengthy appendixes, a fitting place for perhaps the most eminent of Munro's apprentices in the CD.[122]

THE LOGISTICS OF WAR

The middle years of his collectorship in the CD, from 1802 to 1805, were preoccupied with provisioning Arthur Wellesley's army in Maharashtra, a task that made his duties extremely arduous. Personal relations between the two men went back to 1799 at least, when both served on the Mysore Commission following the defeat of Tipu Sultan. We are reminded of this friendship in a letter from the then Colonel Wellesley to Munro in 1799 in answer to Munro's complaint about being appointed to Kanara, one of the many letters sent by Munro at the time. Wellesley then wrote of his surprise and dismay at Munro's disappointment, because, as he put it, 'I had some hand in sending you to Canara'. He said that Munro's appointment had been suggested by another military member of the Mysore Commission at the time, Captain J. A. Kirkpatrick, Resident at Hyderabad, and it may have been that Wellesley's influence on Munro's behalf was motivated by the perceived usefulness of a reliable soldier in charge of Kanara, given its strategic importance in any warfare against the Marathas.[123] When war did break out in 1802, Wellesley's armies were indeed provisioned at crucial times from Kanara as well as from the CD, and from Hyderabad through Kirkpatrick.

With his usual foresight, Munro had perceived a large role for the CD and for himself in the war against the Marathas. Late in 1802, relations among the Marathas had become confused and disunited as Jaswant Rao Holkar succeeded in defeating both Daulat Rao Sindhia and the Peshwa, Baji Rao II. Such a situation would have comforted any potential enemy of the Marathas. However, instead of leaving 'the Maratha rulers to settle their own disputes', Lord Wellesley decided that the time was opportune for a blow against the most powerful of the Marathas by allying the Company with the Peshwa.[124]

[121] MC, F/151/9, 16 September 1806.

[122] *The Fifth Report*, v. 3, pp. 562ff.

[123] Gleig, v. 1, p. 235.

[124] Roberts, *Historical Geography*, part 1, pp. 254–5.

This Wellesley achieved by the treaty of Bassein of 31 December 1802. It was this sort of adventurism that Dundas had come to fear in Wellesley, of course, but it was a policy which Munro strongly favoured.

In fact, he wrote to the Governor-General prior to the alliance treaty with the Peshwa with some strategic observation.[125] He proposed that the southern Maratha country be seized immediately so as to cut the Marathas off from any possible assistance from the French through the Kanara ports via Dharwar, or being provisioned from the latter place. This pre-emptive seizure, Munro suggested, could be accomplished by an invasion from the CD, with logistical support principally from Gurramkonda and Penukonda in the CD, as well as from Kolar in Mysore. The conquest could be easily achieved with the armed peons of the CD and Mysore, under their own chiefs. Such forces were adequate militarily against the peasant chiefs of the southern Maratha country and would serve to win the latters' confidence more readily than a large British army. Following the conquest, regular forces of the Company could be deployed in garrisons and would gradually help bring the southern Maratha country under Company rule. Not stated, but obvious enough, was the idea that such an invading force would be led by Munro. In a subsequent letter to the Governor-General's brother Arthur, in 1803, he explicitly proposed himself for the role. Neither of these offers were taken up then, but his explicit offer to command such a force was accepted later, during the final Anglo-Maratha war, and he was brilliantly successful. In his 1803 letter to Colonel (soon to be General) Wellesley, offering himself as the leader of an invasion force, he said that he must insist on retaining his position as principal collector of the CD lest, with the coming of peace, he be simply another army major without a command.[126]

Though Arthur Wellesley had a high opinion of Munro's military abilities, his offers for a command were not accepted. Munro participated in the Maratha war of 1802–5 adjunctively. The CD was a major staging area for the Company forces operating in the southern Maratha country. Partly, this was owing to the substantial garrison force stationed in the CD from September 1801, after the CD was declared secure from all internal sources of organized resistance to the Company. Cavalry, infantry and artillery regiments were garrisoned at Bellary, Gooty, Kamalapuram, Gurramkonda, Chitvel, Siddhavatam, Cumbun, Dharmavaram and several smaller places.[127] These forces were under the command of Major General Dugald Campbell during the occupation of the CD. Later during the Maratha War his successor Archibald Campbell had moved most of these forces north, across the Tungabhadra, to Mudgal in the Raichur Doab, where they could secure that area and also protect the frontier of Hyderabad from possible Maratha incursions which were regularly threatened. This left Munro little military support for his regime in the CD. It also

[125] Gleig, v. 3, pp. 170–4.

[126] Ibid., pp. 174–5, Munro to Colonel Arthur Wellesley, 28 August 1803.

[127] W. J. Wilson, *History of the Madras Army* (Madras: Government Press, 1883), v. 3, p. 26.

required that Campbell's forces be provisioned from the CD. As if provisioning the Company's armies was not enough, Munro was regularly called upon to deal with its soldiers, who were moving from Vellore and other garrisons in the Carnatic into the active theatre of war in Maharashtra through the CD. The transit of these armies was often a trial for Munro, as it must have been for other collectors through whose territories Company soldiers passed.

An example of this occurred in 1805. Then European soldiers of the 34th Regiment entered the houses of a village in the CD, took pots, milk and grain without payment, and also bayoneted some men attempting to protect their village. In reporting this affray to the private secretary of the Governor, Lord Bentinck, Munro said that the thefts and damages would be made good from CD revenue, and offered as an explanation of the soldiers' actions the inadequacy of their route provisions and the failure to assure that native troops accompany Europeans. This implied that the latter could have negotiated the demands of their European colleagues without resort to violence.[128]

Munro was also called upon to provide grain, bullocks, and even basket-boats for the troops under General Wellesley in southern and central Maharashtra. Grain for fodder and for consumption by soldiers was acquired in Kanara, Hyderabad, and the CD. It was purchased for the army with bills of exchange drawn upon the Company against the treasure sent from India for trade purposes, to Dundas' chagrin, and from revenues raised in adjacent government territories, including the CD. Munro was charged with maintaining a regular movement of thousands of bullocks carrying provisions to Wellesley's army, which meant continuous negotiations with bullock contractors, the payment for hire of the animals and for losses. He also negotiated with itinerant grain haulers—'brinjarrys' (*banjara*)—who collected grain from places to the south and east of the CD and carried it into the war area to be purchased by the British or their enemies. In one letter from General Wellesley to the Resident at Poona, Barry Close, the former referred to a train of 14,000 bullocks bearing provisions for his forces and those of Colonel Stevenson.[129] A field officer in Wellesley's army operating in Maharashtra in 1803 recorded that a train of between two and three thousand bullocks turned up in the vicinity of a British camp, which was short of grain. Its banjara leader, having loaded his bullocks with grain either in the CD or in Hyderabad with the intention of selling it to the Marathas, was quite prepared to sell it to the British, and did so. This officer, Jasper Niccolls, spoke about the ways that Wellesley sought to win and hold the favour to these itinerant suppliers by his prompt payment of the going prices, the presentation of gifts, and his personal and flattering attention to these banjara leaders.[130] Munro can have been no less attentive to banjara traders, though he considered them to be less reliable for supplying the army than the

128 IOL, *Madras Military Proceedings*, P/155/59, pp. 8061–7.

129 IOL, *The Dispatches of Field Marshall The Duke of Wellington During His Various Campaigns in India . . . 1799 to 1818*, v. 1, p. 478, dated 31 October 1803.

130 *Dispatches of Wellington*, v. 1, pp. 420–1.

direct hire of animals which were loaded with grain held or purchased by the Company. A considerable part of his time between 1802 and 1805 was spent in direct military procurement in the CD and in the reshipment of provisions acquired in Kanara and in Hyderabad for Wellesley's forces.

A major portion of the Munro papers at the IOL are devoted to this wartime activity by Munro and his assistants in the CD. The full record of correspondence with Bruce is a fair indicator of how preoccupying the war was. Munro wrote to Bentinck in 1805 that since 1802 he had spent as much time on the supply of Wellesley's army as upon revenue concerns in the CD. Seldom, he reported, were there fewer than 8000 bullocks employed in transferring grain to the army, and at times there were as many as 30,000. The relative efficiency of military supply through the CD Munro attributed to the fact that the CD was a major cattle area. He also believed that his own knowledge of banjaras and his good relations with them were important.[131]

In addition to grain for the military encampments in Maharashtra, Munro was regularly called upon to supply fodder grasses for the cavalry operating under Wellesley, to recruit and provide transport for 'dooly' bearers required by the army, and even to construct a flotilla of basket boats, twenty in all, to be added to some being constructed under the supervision of Alexander Read in Kanara and in Mysore under the dewan, Purnaiya.[132] Besides the boats, skilled boatmen were needed for crossings of the Kistna and Malaprabha rivers in the southern Maratha country.[133] These boatmen were to be paid by Munro at a rate determined by General Wellesley, and Munro was to be recompensed for the wages and the cost of the transport of the boatmen by Wellesley.[134]

The large and prolonged logistical responsibility upon Munro obviously strained his managerial tasks in the CD, as he complained to Bentinck, and they severely taxed the resources of the CD. Munro had to mollify Bruce's injured feelings at being scolded by General Archibald Campbell for some delay in the provision of grain by pointing out that such irritations were a part of 'publick life'. More serious than ruffled feelings were the consequences of supplying the army when drought struck the CD in 1803, causing Munro, reluctantly, to curtail the commercial sales of grain for export from the CD, though not military shipments. In addition, the great demand for bullocks and the high mortality of these animals limited the extension of cultivation in the CD.[135] Munro reported this to Bentinck early in 1805 in a general letter outlining the operation of ryotwar in the CD. He said, then, that until draft animals of the CD were increased by a third at least, there could be no additions to the cultivation of the enormous area of waste.[136]

[131] Bentinck Papers, PwJb 28, p. 358, dated 3 May 1805.

[132] MC, F/151/12, Munro to Bruce, 9 June 1805; MC, F/151/12, 12 June 1805.

[133] Gleig, v. 1, pp. 341–2.

[134] *Dispatches of Wellington*, v. 1, pp. 162–3, A. Wellesley to Munro, 14 May 1803.

[135] *Dispatches of Wellington*, v. 1, pp. 186–7.

[136] Bentinck Papers, PwJb 28, Munro to Bentinck, 10 June 1805.

On the other hand, the Maratha War did provide some in the CD with profit and advantage. Banjara traders found lively trade, not always with the Company military but also with its enemies. Those who traded in grain and other commodities consumed by the army must also have done well, as did the rich peasants of the CD who were principal holders of surplus grain which they regularly traded. The ease with which Wellesley's drafts in payment for supplies circulated at the time was noted by Jasper Niccolls. He commented on the activities of Indian shroffs and bankers attached to General Wellesley's army who promptly negotiated all of his bills.[137] Apparently there was no shortage of money for the conduct of the war, thanks to the largesse of the Governor-General, brother of the commander. Apparently, too, Munro's dedicated service during the war blunted any lingering notion of denying him his office in the CD as a result of his invidious poligar policy or on account of the criticism of military collectors, though references to both matters continued to turn up in official correspondence from 1803 to 1806.

Freed from this career threat, and from the arduous logistical tasks of the war, Munro was able to devote himself to the promulgation of a set of papers on ryotwar between 1805 and 1807. These were intended to meet objections of critics of what was increasingly seen as the Munro system.

RYOTWAR: THE PAPERS

The corpus of Munro papers setting out the principled arguments for ryotwar have been commented upon with care in the monographs of N. Mukherjee and T. H. Beaglehole. Most have also been available, incompletely in *The Fifth Report*, for over 170 years. Hence, detailed treatment of these papers will not be undertaken here. Rather, an effort will be made to penetrate Munro's purposes and concerns at the time that these papers were in preparation. This will be based upon the collection of private Munro documents presently lodged at the India Office, but not available to Mukherjee and Beaglehole, nor to others who have studied Munro's system since the Gleig biography over 180 years ago.

Richard Wellesley had decreed that the Bengal system be established in Madras in 1798. He was supported in this by Henry Dundas, President of the Board of Control. The Court of Directors, however, opposed this plan for several reasons. They were unconvinced that there existed everywhere in South India a class of men who might be called 'zamindars' and in whom might be vested the proprietary rights conferred in Bengal by Cornwallis. They also held that no permanent revenue should be established without better knowledge of existing systems of tenure in the new territories of Madras. At base, the Directors distrusted Wellesley's ambition and their ability to control affairs which they deemed their responsibility, including the principles of land tenure

[137] *Dispatches of Wellington*, v. 1, pp. 450–1.

and revenue to be established.[138] In the end, Dundas prevailed over the directorate, or so it appeared; actually, the Directors did not insist that Madras impose the Bengal rules and persisted in their agnosticism about several other Wellesley measures. This is evident in a revenue letter to Madras commenting upon Munro's 1805 settlement in the CD, in which they reiterated their opposition of a year before to a permanent settlement of the CD without more deliberation on the matter and without their expressed sanction.[139]

The breathing space afforded by this opposition from the directorate had less to do with the specific issues of revenue and more with their control over Indian policy against their officials in India. Here, Wellesley's power was great and proximate, and when the vigorous young Bentinck assumed the Madras governorship in August 1803, he was quickly importuned by the Governor-General to enact the Bengal rules. Bentinck wrote to Lord Castlereagh, President of the Board of Control, a year later, that he was completely persuaded that a reform of the Madras judicial system along the lines of Bengal was imperative. Shortly thereafter, in December 1804, Bentinck ordered the MBOR to institute a settlement in Madras along the modified lines that had been recently adopted for parts of Avadh ('Oude') that had been ceded as a result of the military success against the Marathas. These rules specified that a rent on land was to be fixed for several years and estates established either under zamindars or, if they did not exist, under leaseholders by auction, and if that was impossible a ryotwar settlement should be arranged.[140]

Though Munro knew of the reluctance of the Directors to extend a permanent zamindari settlement beyond those parts of Madras already under that system, and though he also knew from Thackeray that Bentinck had become increasingly sympathetic towards ryotwar, the forces pressing for the full imposition of Wellesley's preferred system certainly created a need to respond, and respond Munro did. Delicacy was required in this. While the Directors appeared to be unwilling to approve a zamindari solution for Madras, they had, only a few years before, in the affair involving Webbe and their changes in the composition of the MBOR, acted to support those who favoured mirasi tenure and their daemonic 'dubashical' proclivities. The discredit which Place brought upon himself by his refusal to carry out his duties on the MBOR, and his intemperate resignation letter of October 1802, weakened the position of the mirasi camp in Madras, but they could still call upon the support of John Hodgson in the MBOR. In rejecting a zamindari settlement, therefore, Munro had to be careful not to strengthen the position of mirasi proponents who were as antithetical to ryotwar as Munro was to their scheme.

In his relationship with Bentinck, Munro, in 1805, was on firmer ground. Since Bentinck's arrival on the scene, Munro had formed a close and forthright relationship on which he was prepared to draw support. Just three years before,

[138] Beaglehole, pp. 6–7.

[139] IOL, *Madras Despatches* E/4/903, 30 August 1809, para. 22, p. 459.

[140] Beaglehole, p. 74–6.

Munro had written to his father that while he had enjoyed the support of the present regime in Madras—Webbe and Lord Clive—he said that Bentinck was expected shortly and 'may think it necessary to pursue different measures'.[141] Bentinck turned out to be a supportive superior in regard to Munro's poligar policies, on which there was a copious and cordial correspondence from late in 1803 to the middle of 1805.[142] In the same period, Bentinck had sought Munro's advice on younger civil servants, and Munro had advanced the careers of Bruce, F. Gahagen, H. Graeme, and of course Thackeray.[143] In less than a year—between December 1804 and May 1805—Munro was able to change Bentinck's position on ryotwar. An important step in this conversion was Munro's long letter to Bentinck, possibly in July 1804.[144]

What Munro sought to show was that the Bengal regulations would engender uncertainty in the minds of Indians over the enjoyment of real property, would diminish the capacity of collectors to discover enough about existing tenures and practices to make a proper permanent settlement, and would delay the resumption of the '500 to 1000 surreptitious Enams' by making each the subject of a separate judicial action. Since 'a permanent rent [arrived at by autonomous collectors] would go further in one year in promoting the improvement of the country and comfort of the Inhabitants than Courts of Justice in Twenty', the Bengal rules were obstructive and dangerous.

On successive days in May 1805, Bentinck wrote to Munro that he had changed his thinking about the Avadh settlement regulations. His letter of 26 May announced that he was proposing to the Governor-General that on all lands in Madras not then permanently settled—'to confirm the Ryots in possession of their lands in perpetuity upon a fixed rent without any intermediate agent between the Government and the Ryot'. On 27 May he asked Munro for his 'private' thoughts about 'making ryotwar permanent' and the effect of this upon Munro's arrangements in the CD. The Governor particularly asked about the relationship of an 'individual settlement' and the 'principle of collective responsibility' for revenue shortfalls of individuals. He wondered whether the latter provision might no longer be required or if it should be continued for the first years of the new scheme.[145] Finally, on 28 July 1805, Bentinck informed Munro that a Minute he had prepared against the imposition of the

141 MC, F/151/143, 18 May 1802.

142 Bentinck Papers, PwJb 28.

143 Ibid., pp. 37, 295, 467, 471.

144 Wellesley Papers, Ad. MS. 13679, ff. 73–6.

145 MC, F/151/8, 26–27 May 1805, and IOL, *Home Miscellaneous Series* v. 530, no. 17, pp. 291–340, 'Permanent Settlement and Ryotwar at Madras by a Madras Government Covenanted Servant...', by James Cumming, chief clerk for the Revenue and Judicial Department of the Board of Control, who appended a note to this document saying that it was by William Thackeray, p. 340, and this identification is confirmed by a reference within the document to the author's report on Malabar, Canara, and the Ceded Districts, 4 August 1807, p. 298; this last report is found in *The Fifth Report*, v. 3, pp. 565ff.

Avadh revenue arrangements into Madras had been accepted by the Governor-General and approval was given to proceed with a ryotwar survey leading to permanent ryotwar. The judicial aspects of this scheme were to remain in force, however, though this was softened by Bentinck's decision to assign Munro's protégé, Thackeray, to establish the Court of Justice in the CD.

Wellesley himself appeared to have recognized Munro's influence over Bentinck, for in May 1805 he ordered that a set of queries pertaining to the 'Oude regulations of 1803' be sent to Munro for his comments.[146] The draft notes of Munro's reply to Wellesley exist as well as a letter incorporating some of Munro's reservations about the Avadh rules for Madras (especially those touching upon the salary of collectors) to William Petrie, President of the MBOR, on 29 May 1805.[147] Thus, in the middle of 1805, there was a readiness by both Wellesley and Bentinck to move towards closure on the question of the permanent settlement of Madras revenues. This launched the most important debate on Madras for many years and spurred Munro to some of his most clear and forceful writing on any public question.

While throwing open the question of what kind of revenue settlement was to be followed by Madras, Bentinck made it clear that the decision on judicial arrangements was final: the Bengal regulations would be imposed. Munro thus shifted the ground of his previous arguments to the principles which should inform revenue alone, leaving for another day the fight over judicial reforms.

His first major statement on ryotwar came soon after Bentinck's success with Wellesley for delaying the final revenue decisions until surveys had been completed, and expressing his own preference for ryotwar. In August 1805 Munro sent a long letter to William Petrie and the MBOR setting forth the principles and practical as well as programmatic implications of ryotwar. Subsequent papers by Munro were variations upon and extensions of this letter.[148]

Referring to a previous communication to the Board in May, when he claimed that it was 'impracticable to form a settlement of the Ceded Districts by estates', he was now prepared to give reasons for this view. He began with a sweeping characterization of the conditions governing all questions of British rule in India:

> When a country falls under the dominion of a foreign power it is usually found to be the wisest plan to leave it in the possession of its own laws and customs, and to endeavour rather to ameliorate than to abolish them and to substitute others in their room, and the more ancient and civilized the subject nation is the more requisite it is to pursue this course, for institu-

[146] MC, F/151/8, Benjamin Sydenham, aide to Lord Wellesley, to Munro, 'private', 19 May 1805.

[147] Wellesley Papers, Ad. MS., 13679, ff. 84–6.

[148] IOL, *MBOR Proceedings*, 1805, P/288/25, pp. 6875–969; a copy of this letter is in MC, F/151/125(1), from Anantapur, dated 25 August 1805.

tions of such people are not only in themselves perhaps better adapted than any to that they could receive from strangers to their own circumstances and habits, but they have also over their minds of the strong influence which is derived from antiquity. If the system of landed property and tenures which has always prevailed in India be examined it will appear that the sovereign has at all times been regarded as the sole landlord, that the country has been divided into an immense number of small farms held immediately of him by their respective cultivators, that this great mass of tenants were all tenants at will, that there was no description of land holders similar to the owners of estates whom it is now proposed to raise up, that the numerous class of enamdars who might be mistaken for landlords were in fact landed pensioners whose lands were resumable at pleasure and that private property in land was altogether unknown.

Under this landlord state all offices, from those denominated 'zemindar' down to the lowly village watchman or 'tallari', were remunerated by inam holdings and, for some, a percentage of the revenue collected. Even the greatest of these offices differed in no way from village offices such as those of 'Potails and Curnams'—except that the latter held hereditary inam lands and the others did not. The sovereignty of the landlord state was based on military power and, when that weakened, subordinate authorities in their territories—'Rajahs and Poligars'—seized sovereign authority. Any of them could replace that authority, and with that—except in Malabar and Kanara—'compleat ownership of the soil'.[149] This authority, Munro emphasized, was not landlordship but sovereignty, and could be granted and resumed at the pleasure of a ruler. Revenue was collected from cultivators by 'the Potail or head cultivator of each village'. Any settlement by large estates would therefore be 'a new system . . . hitherto unknown to the inhabitants'. He continues:

> The compleat abolition of an ancient revenue system can never be advisable until it has been fully proved that [that] which is intended to supplant it is better. In order to decide whether the new is preferable to the old, it should first be ascertained whether it is practicable, whether it will be liked by the inhabitants, and whether it will ultimately augment the wealth of the Country and the resources of the Government.

The criteria for a satisfactory replacement of the 'ancient revenue system' are then shown to be fully satisfied by ryotwar: practicable, because it is in actual operation; liked by the inhabitants as evidenced by the peace and order in the CD; and capable, 'ultimately', of increasing the revenue of the country and the revenue of the state. Munro then reminds the MBOR of the extreme

[149] This statement of historical processes is similar to that of one of the best informed epigraphist-historians of medieval India, D. C. Sircar, who described the same process, only Sircar labelled a point in the process as 'landlordism' which he preferred to 'feudalism', *Landlordism and Tenancy in Ancient and Medieval India as Revealed by Epigraphical Records* (Lucknow: University of Lucknow, 1969).

difficulties of the CD: its sparse and impoverished population; its armed villagers; its absence of older local authorities; its enormous number of cultivators (about 200,000) paying on average a small annual land revenue, equal to about £1, but nevertheless showing considerable differentiation between the most wealthy and the most poor cultivators. These difficulties imply to Munro that if ryotwar could succeed in the CD, it could succeed anywhere.

The 25 August 1805 letter to Petrie and the MBOR continues by observing that the prospects for establishing large estates, as envisaged under a Bengal type of settlement, were nugatory, for whatever might be established would only last for a short time as a result of sales and patterns of inheritance, and would revert to ever smaller estates until they approximated those of Kanara. The estates of Kanara, Munro asserted, were

> on an average nearly as small as the farms of the Rayets . . . in the Ceded Districts . . . and . . . the head farmer or Potail of the village is in reality now what the owner will then be, for he has usually Enam lands yielding Thirty Pagodas or more and his income being therefore as great as that of the landowner he is as well qualified to be responsible for the public revenue.[150]

It may be confusing to anyone seeking deeper understanding of Munro's principles of ryotwar that the basic holding of many ryotwar pattadars—perhaps all of his 'better sort' and many 'middling sort'—was a small farm, a consolidated holding of fields. This idea of Munro did confuse even such contemporaries as Thackeray and Ravenshaw, not only at early points in their careers but later as well. Thus, Ravenshaw, when he was Director of the East India Company in 1821, wrote to the then Governor Sir Thomas Munro asking whether 'putkut' (Telugu: *pattukattu*) in ryotwar was similar to estates in Kanara (where Ravenshaw served as collector following Munro's tenure there). Munro agreed that they were indeed similar, and the 'putkut' meant ' "lands which a man possesses, the fields which every old rayet usually cultivates are called his putkut" '.[151] He also admitted then that the 'putkut' farmholding had constituted the revenue unit by Read in the Baramahal as well as in the CD during his own time. Both Thackeray and Ravenshaw appeared to be troubled by the notion that consolidated farmsteads seemed more a kind of mirasi or zamindari tenure than ryotwar, as indeed John Hodgson had suggested in his reports on Dindigul in 1808.[152] But Munro dismissed such questions, in his early as well as his later expositions on ryotwar, which did nothing to rid ryotwar of conceptual ambiguousness, in 1805 and later.

To Petrie in August 1805 Munro conceded that if large estates could be managed as they were in Britain, that would be an excellent system from all points of view—revenue, welfare of most inhabitants, productivity, and socially

[150] MC, 151/125(1), Munro to Petrie and the MBOR, 25 August 1805, para. 5.

[151] IOL, *Carfrae Collection*, E/225, Munro to Ravenshaw at East India House, 30 September 1821 and Wilson, *Glossary*, p. 412.

[152] *The Fifth Report*, v. 3, pp. 345 and 555 for Hogdson's papers.

in maintaining 'a just gradation of ranks'. But, however desirable, large estates could not endure in the CD. 'Potails', the most prominent people in the CD and those most likely to become estate owners, 'have never heard of private landed property or of any Landlord' but the government. Many years would be required for them to become 'persuaded of the stability of their tenure', and in the meantime their demands upon subordinate ryots for greater profits would have increased. To restrict this increase in income from the holding of land would be to deny Indian landowners the rights which are enjoyed by landowners elsewhere and retard the development of landed property. Yet, a too-rapid transformation of village headmen into Bengal-styled zamindars would be injurious to the welfare of subordinate ryots, accustomed to seek redress from injustice in the village from the headman, or in the taluk from the 'district Manager' (*nattavar*?), both likely to become landowners under a Bengal-type of settlement.

As to the purported advantages of creating or maintaining a social hierarchy:

> The want to a due gradation of ranks in Society in this country is more imaginary than real for what is effected in establishing such a gradation by property in other parts of the world is accomplished here by the distinction of casts [*sic*] and the Manners of the people. The lower, the middle and the higher classes of inhabitants preserve mutually as just degree of respect and Subordination as the different orders in England.

So the only major advantage of a settlement of large estates would be the reduction of revenue collection charges, but this saving might be no greater than the losses of revenue which the Company would have derived from 'small farms or Estates as at present'.[153]

Against this are the advantages of a settlement with cultivators, 'the system which has always been followed'. First, the revenue demand is not fixed, but variable with the season, and thus may be adjusted to blunt the effect of bad seasons. Instead of whole large estates failing, some individual smallholders might, and most of these would save once again to replace the stock lost and retrieve their standing as independent cultivators. Secondly, more revenue and more production would result from the combined efforts of many independent smallholders with small debts, as against the failure of large landholders with large debts and outstanding balances on the purchase of their large estates. Third, an equivalent reduction of revenue demand would increase the wealth and security of smallholders more, would result in immediate productive investment in land improvements, and would hasten the time when land acquired a saleable value. Small estates being less risky as investments would have a more ready market than large estates. Summarizing:

> As I have endeavoured to show that the system of great farms will raise less produce from the soil than that of small farms, that it is more liable to failures,

[153] MC, 151/125(1), Munro to Petrie and the MBOR, 25 August 1805, para. 7.

and affords less security to the revenue, that it will be less agreeable to the inhabitants because they would rather hold their lands under Government than under private individuals, and that it cannot be permanent because their laws and customs continually urge on the rapid division of landed property—I am therefore induced to recommend the Ryotwar system of settlement with the cultivators not only as a temporary but as a permanent arrangement in the Ceded Districts.[154]

Caste is made a principal factor in certain of the arguments presented by Munro in this August 1805 letter to the MBOR. Caste jealousy and competition act as a check upon fraudulent claims of poverty by a cultivator seeking excuse from part or all of his revenue obligation. Since persons of other castes become responsible for a portion of revenue defaults, they would remonstrate against the false claims of others. Caste pride served to cause cultivating castes, 'coonbis', to resist falling into the status of labourers who, in the CD, were composed not of 'coonbis' but almost entirely of low castes ('Dhers and Bhoys').

This long letter concluded by reiterating the claim that ryotwar was the system best calculated to help poor farmers—more than one-third of cultivating families in the CD—to bootstrap upwards into the position of 'middling' farmers. As for the existing 'better and middling' farmers, ryotwar afforded them the means to 'convert their farms into little estates like those on the Malabar coast . . . [and to] renounce their wandering habits and become stationary on their respective lands. . . .'[155] Being pressed by the MBOR to introduce a lease settlement in the CD, he thought it necessary to give his reasons for continuing the system of annual ryotwar settlements against the proposed creation of large estates to be leased for a series of years, 'which would be an inversion of the established order of things'.

A second major document on ryotwar by Munro is dated 20 June 1806. Its form is different, being answers to a set of queries ostensibly emanating from Bentinck on the feasibility of introducing a permanent settlement of revenues in Madras, and as a necessary background for the latter's planned tour of the 'new' territories of the Presidency to determine the mode of settlement to be installed there. The form of the document—fifteen brief questions and their answers—is something of a charade since it is obvious that the questions were devised by Thackeray from those originally drawn by Munro.[156] The set of queries of the 20 June 1806 document was originally contrived by Munro in response to letters written him by Thackeray, and possibly some of his answers to these questions were already in the hands of Thackeray, who was constructing his expertise for Bentinck. Quite possibly, they were in the hands of Bentinck himself, who apparently passed the questions to the MBOR as his own. The Governor, it appears, had assumed a conspiratorial role!

[154] Ibid., para. 11.

[155] Ibid., para. 36.

[156] Text of the queries and Munro's answers are found in K.N.V. Sastri, pp. 22–46, and taken by him from a volume of *Selections from the Records of Bellary District*.

Munro's answers to his own questions on 20 June 1806 were addressed to Archibald Obins, private secretary to Bentinck, suggesting that the MBOR had not circulated them to the collectors of the Presidency, but that Bentinck had through his secretary in May. The order in which subjects are treated was considered important by Thackeray, who had specifically requested that Munro number them. The first matter taken up pertained to a 'permanent settlement with each individual'. Permanent ryotwar was not practicable, Munro answered, until lands became saleable, for the hazards of agriculture in the CD and the poverty of most of its cultivators required a system in which land for cultivation could be taken up and thrown off by each cultivator annually, depending upon his resources. To compensate for the fluctuations in individual holdings, the revenue should be fixed for each village and each taluk. Hence, while the revenue demand upon each cultivator would vary, the demand from villages and taluks ('districts') would be fixed within a range of 10 per cent, taking into account seasonal variations. The advantages of a ryotwar 'permanent settlement', whenever it could occur (and Munro here supposed that lands would not have become saleable for perhaps twenty years), were the several he had previously enumerated.[157] It was the 'accustomed system' and preferred by ryots because it 'would render them independent as proprietors', and because 'they would enjoy more freedom in the management of their lands than the mootadar [village renter] would, since the latter is restrained from demanding a higher rent than what would have been fixed by survey'. It would 'diffuse more widely than any other system the benefit of private property in land' while adapting to the 'narrow circumstances of the ryots' by permitting expansion and contraction of holdings. It would encourage greater production and generate more revenue by passing the advantages of remissions directly to producers and by distributing the risks of failure among a mass of smallholders. It would engender greater order and obedience to governmental authority since there would be no, or fewer, wealthy landowners capable of maintaining armed followers.

The disadvantages of ryotwar were acknowledged by Munro to be several, but for each that he specified there was contrived some compensatory advantage as well. Thus: the administrative charges of ryotwar are high as a result of the large number of subordinate officials required to survey lands, to assess and collect revenue upon them, and to assure that cultivation occurs. But once lands are saleable, these officials and their interference would cease. Detailed accounts are indeed required under ryotwar, but this laborious task affords 'a view of the state of the cultivation and of the resources of the country'. Major tank repairs are difficult for smallholders to carry out, but this can be remedied by continuing 'Dasbandam' inams which provide monetary advantages to substantial ryots for maintaining tanks in good repair. The need for taccavi (production advances) remains, but these are small loans and repayable in a

[157] K.N.V. Sastri, p. 34.

year. And finally, under ryotwar the revenue fluctuates from year to year, but not by more than about 10 per cent.

Next, Munro considered the relative advantages and disadvantages of a settlement with 'zemindars and Mootadars' but curiously he discussed only the latter and presented a strong case for it. He assumed that the village renter ('mootadar') would be its present 'Potail', headman or 'head farmer'. This would ensure a greater interest in the promotion of production and improvements than would be the case under a revenue official, and would ensure that the renter himself was an experienced agriculturist and farm manager who knew the subordinate cultivators intimately. He would be interested in their welfare if only because the discontent of the latter would lead to their departing to another village, causing a loss of labour for the mootadar's own enterprise. A 'mootadar' settlement would instantly establish private ownership of land, 'for every Mootadar understands at once that the village or villages composing his estate are his own property'. It would also relieve government of both tank repairs and taccavi advances, for these would pass under the interest of the mootadar and his profit. This and other aspects of the mootadari settlement would immediately reduce the number and cost of subordinate revenue officials.

The main disadvantage of the mootadari or village-lease settlement was that it changed 'the established order of things'. Munro seems not to have noticed that this 'order of things' included an almost total ignorance of private landed property according to his long letter to Petrie of a year before. Now, it seemed, 'every Mootadar understands at once' the nature of private property. What Munro meant by the 'established order' was a statement which has shaped the discourse about not only Indian land systems from this point forward, but also the most fundamental conceptions of the relationship among property, the state, and social structure for writers like Henry Maine and Karl Marx: 'Every village is a kind of little republic under the management of the Potail or head farmer, assisted by the Curnam or Register, the Taliari or watchman etc.'[158] In this 'accustomed order of things':

> The Potail superintends cultivation, collects rents, and settles all petty disputes, and he enjoys an Inam land [modern spellings for Munro's 'Enam' or 'Enaum'] usually equal to about 5% of the rent of the village. By possessing this Inam he is a hereditary land-owner, but with regard to other land, he has no advantage or right, which every common ryot has not equally in the land, which he occupies. If therefore the Potail become the Mootadar, the right, which was common to all ryots, becomes exclusively his. . . .[159]

[158] Ibid., pp. 31–2; this is the earliest reference I have found to this famous metaphor, which is cited by Mark Wilks in somewhat different form as dating from 15 May 1806, a month earlier than the above instance; Wilks, *Historical Sketches*, v. 1, p. 139n.

[159] K.N.V. Sastri, p. 32.

Should any but the potail become the mootadar, the violation of customary rights then includes those of the potail himself. Moreover, even the dispersed form of property enfranchisement of the mootadari settlement would concentrate private property in land to a considerable degree. It would also make more difficult the advance of the great mass of cultivators, as well as the political security of the state as a result of potential collusion among village-lessees.

Other queries deal with the impact of different levels of reductions in revenue demand on ryots; the share of gross production which was taken by the government among different segments of the cultivating population; the place of joint liability for revenue charges from the cultivation and sale of grain; a record of taccavi advances in the CD over the previous five years, which classes of ryots received them, and how such productivity advances would be arranged under a permanent settlement; the level of revenue arrears over the previous ten years in the CD with a detailed examination of the causes for arrears in five selected villages over the ten-year period.[160] The document ends with questions and answers about the quantity of waste land brought into cultivation and tank repairs. Munro's answers to all of these are much the same as he had previously written in the Petrie letter of the previous August.

Even though it was explicitly requested in the questions of his devising, it is curious that Munro did not address the zamindari alternative to ryotwar in his submission of June 1806. That he did not might be explained by his perception that the zamindari alternative for Madras had already been foreclosed by the Governor-General. This was evident in the framing of the 'Oude' regulations of 1803, which admitted the possibility that there might not be persons found to be appropriately denominated as zamindars, as also by the concession wrung by Bentinck from Wellesley the year before to delay any decision until a survey had been completed in the CD and elsewhere in the newly-acquired territories of Madras. Then, too, there was Thackeray's long memorandum to Bentinck, that of April 1806, which argued against a zamindari settlement and for permanent ryotwar. Thackeray had already asked for Munro's views on the question, and cited Munro's views in the memorandum. Therefore, Thackeray's expressed objections to 'Permanent Zemindarry' can be supposed to have incorporated Munro's arguments against a zamindari settlement.

Thackeray's paper of April 1806 was passed by Bentinck, who commissioned it and to whom it was addressed, to the MBOR on 29 April 1806, along with his sentiment that as good as the Bengal settlement may be in that Province, 'Here . . . [in Madras] the same circumstances do not exist. . . .'[161] He asked that members of the BOR reflect upon Thackeray's paper and that each record an opinion about its content. Bentinck's council agreed and, transmitting Thackeray's paper and Bentinck's comment upon it to the MBOR,

[160] This potentially valuable detailed village evidence is not cited by Sastri, nor is it available in the extant records of the IOL.

[161] *The Fifth Report*, v. 3, pp. 455–65.

also agreed that it 'contained the principal objections to the establishment of large zemindarries, and arguments in favour of making the ryotwar system permanent.' The transmittal letter to the MBOR added that, the question being of the greatest importance, it should be fully and speedily discussed. The response from the most talented member of the Board, John Hodgson, was not long in coming; his memoir commands the most serious attention.

Hodgson's long (fifty-one paragraphs, twenty-eight printed pages) memoir of 1806 is a defence of a zamindari settlement for Madras.[162] At the time it was written Hodgson was second member of the MBOR, having served on that body from 1803. Before that he had been Lionel Place's assistant in the Jaghire and had succeeded Place there in 1799. Relations between Place and Hodgson appear to have become strained by Hodgson's secretaryship on the Special Commission for the Permanent Settlement of 1802. This was a body that had drawn Place's excoriation for having usurped the authority of the MBOR and for having diverted its resources and staff to a crippling extent. Mark Wilks had hinted to Munro at about that time that Hodgson seemed susceptible to some sort of rapprochement, perhaps a reconciliation over unspecified past differences at that time.[163]

Hodgson's argument against ryotwar in 1806 commands attention for several reasons. As a senior member of the MBOR, with impressive experience and a career of major responsibilities in Madras revenue matters, his judgements carried weight. Of all of Munro's opponents in the Madras government, Hodgson was the most able to formulate arguments at the same level as Munro and to make as good rhetorical use of learned authority as Munro made of Indian historical precedent. Also, in the following two years, Hodgson was to undertake detailed investigations of several major provinces in Madras—Coimbatore, Tinnevelly and Dindigul—and would submit reports on them which increased his stature as an experienced revenue official and one, in addition, with a broad, comparative perspective on the Presidency as a whole.[164] Apart from Munro and his surrogate Thackeray, Hodgson occupied the most serious place in *The Fifth Report*, constructed by boosters of Munro and his school. It is therefore clear why Munro, as his personal papers repeatedly show, paid very close attention to Hodgson's public papers and took the time to refute them when *The Fifth Report* was being prepared in 1812–13. Clear too was Hodgson's careful reading of Munro and the perceptiveness he showed in going for the heart of his opposition—Munro himself—rather than a limb such as Thackeray.

For now, 1806–7, however, it is necessary to consider one other paper of Munro's, one that is addressed to the general comparison of permanent ryotwar and zamindari settlements. Beaglehole rightly considered this paper of 15 August 1807 of equal weight with the paper of August 1805, though his

[162] Ibid., pp. 470–98.

[163] Wilks to Munro, 14 January 1803, MC, F/151/6.

[164] *The Fifth Report*, v.3, pp. 526–80.

general interpretive comment on the two papers is questionable.[165]

The field survey of the CD took five years. Its completion was the ostensible cause for raising the question of the mode of permanent settlement anew in this paper of 15 August 1807.[166] Admitting that he had nothing to offer on the various methods of permanent revenue systems beyond what he had previously said, he undertook to review these positions. Where in 1806 he neglected entirely the subject of zamindari and concentrated on a comparison of the ryotwari and mootadari systems, he now devoted a brief two paragraphs to the zamindari settlement. In comparing the zamindari and mootadari systems, he found the latter better with respect to the welfare of the ryots and the peace and order of society, but in the end, he argued, mootadari tenure dissolved into ryotwar.

Ryotwar, again, is presented as the ancient system and 'no other can be permanent' because of the operation of inheritance rules. It also is a more 'simple' system than the mootadari in that it did not interpose 'artificial constraints contrary to custom'. Ryotwar was as fully capable of maintaining social gradations as other revenue systems and had other advantages: it more readily increased production, added more proprietors and independent farmers and reduced common labourers. Ryotwar also ensured that the benefits of remissions went to primary producers, who were most keen to increase their production and wealth and were the principal payers of revenues to the state. These independent farmers, with greater wealth and food production, would add to the sparse population of the CD. Other benefits are specified. One is that with the principle of variable taxation under the ryotwari system, the great number of revenue payers would assure that failures of individual farmers would not effect the income of the state. A second is that as the general wealth of ryots increased, their cultivation would become restricted to irrigated lands, assuring fewer revenue failures and increased well being. Finally, under ryotwar government retained possession of all waste and thus, as wealth and population increased, so would revenue proceeds without adding to the burdens of ordinary cultivators.

Given these benefits and advantages of ryotwar over both of the alternative systems, Munro outlined how a permanent ryotwar settlement in the CD could be conducted, one that yielded an average revenue as great as that under zamindars and one that is more beneficial to the 'great body of inhabitants'. There follows a set of thirteen principles, several of which repeat those principles Munro had formulated almost a decade before—in July and September 1797—in

[165] Beaglehole, p. 79: 'The two reports amount to more than a plan for a system of revenue settlement: they reflect Munro's experience and his conservatism in the emphasis that the social habits and political institutions existing in the districts should form the basis of any revenue settlement or judicial system. It was not conservatism, however, of stubborn ignorance or of self-satisfied vested interest, but of informed sympathy, of a paternalism both autocratic and Romantic.'

[166] *The Fifth Report*, v. 3, pp. 501–14.

the Baramahal.[167] The settlement was to be with small farmers and annually; there was an initial substantial reduction of revenue which in 1797 was to be 15 per cent and in 1807 was to be 25 per cent; there was joint liability for individual revenue failures; and unoccupied waste would belong to the government. Differences between the two sets of principles are that there was no provision in 1807, as there was in 1797, for leaseholds of several years' duration which Read and the MBOR sought in the Baramahal; that a differential rate of assessment should apply to the lands of Brahmans, Muslims and inamdars according to the 1807 principles, while ten years before such distinctions were expressly prohibited: that in 1797 no increase in assessment was to be made on lands which cultivators had improved (with a tank or well), while the 1807 statement was silent on this; that taccavi advances were gradually to be discontinued under the 1807 provisions; that no reduction in assessment was to be allowed in 1807 for commercially valuable crops such as cochineal and mulberry, though a further 8 per cent beyond the 25 per cent reduction proposed was to be allowed for those who maintained their tanks and wells without the assistance of the government—a change from a partially crop-based system of assessment to a wholly field-based system; that in 1807 no addition to his income will be allowed to a pattadar who uses a field for houses or shops instead of cultivation; and, finally, in 1807 Munro stated that, in cases of destraint for debt, government should have privilege over private creditors.

At the base of all considerations about revenue administration, he said, is the nature of Indian rural culture and society, and no system which failed to take account of this can succeed. The nature is classically peasant: 'The ryot of India unites in his own person the character of labourer, farmer, and landlord: he receives the wages of the labourer, the profit of the farmer on his stock, and a small surplus from one to twenty per cent of the gross produce as rent, but on average, not more than 5 or 6 per cent.'[168] So long as uncultivated waste existed, as it did abundantly in the CD and in most other parts of India, there was no pressure for a cultivator to become the tenant of another, and thus little for the creation of a landlord class of any size. The latter development is further retarded by custom:

> The tendency of the Indian system of casts [*sic*] and laws of inheritance, always has been, and must be, to keep land divided into small portions among the ryots, and to make the same person labourer, farmer, and landlord. Why, then, attempt to subvert an antient system, which places the great body of ryots above want, renders them industrious, frugal, and comfortable, and preserves the simplicity of their manners, and their respect for public authority; but it can be said that there can be no proper subordination, without just gradations of rank in society; and that zemindars are

[167] Compare the principles stated in *The Fifth Report* v.3, pp. 505–6 and those of 1797 in Beaglehole, p. 29.

[168] *The Fifth Report*, v. 3, p. 511.

required, in Indian society, to accomplish this desirable end: but this opinion is contradicted by experience; for there is no people on earth among whom there is a greater subordination, than among Hindoos, who never saw proprietary zemindars, until they were created by the Company's government.[169]

Two final matters are discussed by Munro: first, the introduction of an income tax on labourers, artisans and merchants; second, the modification of the joint liability of villages and of taluks for revenue deficiencies caused by individual defaults. Munro took the view that the existing house tax was really a tax upon income for the most part, and was viewed as that by the people of the CD. A tax on the income of artisans could easily be contrived by placing a tax upon productive implements—say, the looms of weavers or, for merchants, the house, which is also a shop. He observed that merchants were scarcely ever taxed by native governments, but this was because it was expected that they would supply clothes and other commodities on demand to native officials or provide goods for public use (e.g. military) at a low price. Since the Company had abolished this form of forced appropriation, a mercantile tax could be contrived by estimating the aggregate income of merchants in a taluk from such things as custom accounts, population, estimates of production and consumption of commodities, and a 15 per cent tax levied upon total mercantile transactions within a taluk. This levy would then be distributed among the merchants themselves, those in the best position to know best the liabilities of each. Such a scheme had in fact been tried in one of the taluks of the CD—Rayadrug—and worked to bring under tax liability wealthy merchants who, in justice, should contribute to the tax burdens of the province.

Justice also dictated that in the event of individual failures and revenue defaults by cultivators, a major source of compensation to the state should come from the inams of headmen and village accountants, but this should not exceed 10 per cent of the deficiency in revenue. Since the inams held by powerful headmen and accountants were on the whole unauthorized, a major portion of this greatly privileged landholding should be applied to revenue shortfalls. Only afterwards should the balance of 10 per cent of revenue deficiencies be met by a generalized levy among ryots of a village or a taluk, as previously provided.[170]

CONCLUSION

These several Munro papers of 1805 to 1807 are the chief exigetical texts on ryotwar. It is to these that all subsequent principled statements on ryotwar return for authority until the time of independence, in 1947. None of the intervening events of the next 150 years—the ryotwari resettlement of the middle of the later nineteenth century, the famines of the late nineteenth cen-

[169] Ibid.
[170] Ibid., pp. 512–13.

tury, the Royal Commission on Indian Agriculture of the 1920s, and the great Depression of the 1930s—appear to have altered the formulations of these two years.[171] Munro was subsequently to produce a few specialized papers on aspects of ryotwar, especially during his furlough in England, when he became deeply involved with James Cumming and Samuel Davis in the preparation of *The Fifth Report*, but these merely restated the principles first and most elaborately stated in the last years of his stay in the CD.[172]

Munro's last two years in the CD, which saw the crowning achievement of his ryotwar papers, were relatively unstressful, almost leisurely as compared with the first five years. Under the sheltering patronage of Bentinck the earlier threats to his civil career—over poligars and over the issue of military collectors—receded, though both of these issues continued to manifest a ghostly presence in the lagging correspondence from London.

Apart from his continued, strenuous administration of the CD in these two years, the completion of the field survey, and the preparation of the papers discussed above, one other matter occupied Munro's attention in the final two years in the CD. This was a dispute over his salary, and that remained unresolved until some time after his return to Britain. Involved was the large sum of over 11,000 Star Pagodas (equal to about £4500), which London claimed was an overpayment to Munro of his revenue commissions for the years 1805 and 1806. This was an 'overpayment' in the sense that Munro's salary exceeded by that amount the statutory ceiling on collectors' salaries set in June 1805. Having been paid this, Munro was compelled to lodge an equivalent amount in the Madras treasury as security while he pursued redress by petition of the Court of Directors. His appeal was strongly supported by a letter from Petrie, President of the MBOR in 1807, but rejected by the Directors for several years until they granted Munro a money 'gift' of equivalent amount in recognition of his services.[173] His correspondence with the Court of Directors on this matter offers an interesting view of his conception of his role as collector.

The draft notes of his 4 May 1808 memorial to the Court of Directors are found in his private papers at the IOL, and these notes suggest that they might have been prepared in 1806 or 1807, before leaving India. In them he puts two reasons for why his full commissions for the years 1805 and 1806 ought to be paid to him, even though they exceeded the limits of what collectors could be paid. One was that the rate of commission established for him in the CD was based upon that allowed to Alexander Read in the Baramahal by Lord Cornwallis, partly as a reward for past services and partly in anticipation of the difficulties of the Baramahal. Munro claimed eligibility to the same considerations. Alone in Kanara, he had restored that chaotic province to order and to

171 See B. S. Baliga, 'Land Tenures in Ryotwari Areas', in *Studies in Madras Administration* (Madras, India Press, 1960), v. 2, pp. 117–53.

172 For these later ryotwar papes: Arbuthnot, pp. 106–18.

173 IOL, *Madras Despatches*, 'General Letter to England in the Revenue Department', 27 October 1807, paras. 201–3, a copy of this is in MC, F/151/135, ff. 153–6.

a high and easily collected revenue, as compared to the melancholy record of neighbouring and similar Malabar: 'Let the Honourable Court reflect on the blood that has been shed during the last fifteen years in Malabar and the heavy expences of maintaining an army at all times in the province . . . [this gives] you some conception of the evils which have been avoided by my having been selected for the organization of Kanara. I have done the same with regard to the Ceded Districts.' Not only were there no military expenses in controlling the CD, but Munro was able to make positive contributions to the Company's military during the Maratha war: 'I enabled the army . . . by regular supplies of grain and baggage cattle to keep the field when it must otherwise have fallen back. . . .' He concluded: 'I think that when your Honourable Court has considered these services it will reckon them sufficient grounds for granting me either the commission retrenched from me or a percentage on the supplies provided by me for the army.'[174]

Two letters composed by Munro after his return to Britain may also be cited here in connection with his pleadings for the full allowances that were being withheld from 1805–6. Both shed light on Munro's conception of—or at least his claims about—his role in Madras over the previous decade. He wrote to Edward Parry, Chairman of the Court of Directors, in June 1808 to add to his formal memorial of 4 May of the same year. His situation in the CD was not that of a

> common collector . . . that it was so extraordinary as not be likely to recur again . . . that the Madras Government were so perfectly convinced that these provinces [the CD] could be successfully settled only by me . . . that had these districts not been placed at first under my charge there is the strongest ground for believing that like Malabar and several other provinces under the Madras Government they would have continued in a state of confusion and proved a source rather of heavy expence than of revenue to the Company. . . .[175]

To Charles Grant, a year later, when the latter was Chairman of the Court of Directors, he wrote that he had not claimed any commission for supplying the army, as he was entitled to do, because he considered his salary with the commission on the revenue collected in the CD to be adequate for all that he did. Moreover, Munro said, his duties in the CD were not simply revenue collection, but political and military as well. Proof of this was his role in negotiating with the 'western poligars' of Chittoor in Arcot in 1804–5, when they were in rebellion against the Company's authority. These poligars had insisted upon Munro to mediate their quarrel with the Company as a condition of disarming: 'these poligars though under the authority of the collector of Arcot would surrender only to me. . . .' Munro told Grant that he raised this case of

[174] MC, F/151/135, ff. 116–17.

[175] IOL, *Board's Collections*, F/4/261, no. 5826, 'Services of Lieut. Colonel Munro and His Claims for Remuneration for Services', dated 6 June 1808.

the Arcot poligars both to show the true scope of his official responsibilities and to counter 'an unfavourable impression in this country [England, regarding]... the supposed bad treatment of the Vemlah Polligar'. After defending his action against that poligar, Munro concluded with the following: 'I never was considered by Government as an ordinary collector; I acted rather as a kind of Lieut. Governor.'[176]

Claims such as these by Munro reflect a confidence in their acceptability, suggesting that he had some reasons, which are anything but obvious, about the climate of opinion in the London to which he was shortly to return or to which he had just arrived. That is entirely likely, for on the eve of his return to Britain after twenty-seven years in India, the Company was prepared to make decisions on a variety of issues upon which he had in the previous several years pronounced with increasing effectiveness. The acute moral crisis of a generation before—the time of Burke's attack—had passed. Now the stage was set for a celebratory recapitulation of progress and a launching of future programme, in the design of which Munro was to have a major place—whether or not he knew this when he departed Madras.

[176] *Board's Collections*, F/4/261, no. 5826, letter dated 25 May 1809.

Chapter Four

England

Munro's stay in Britain was to have been for three years, until 1811. He did not return to India until 1814, thus extending his time in Britain to almost the same duration as his service in the Baramahal (April 1792 to March 1799) and in the CD (November 1800 to October 1807). At first, extensions of his furlough were requested by him; later they were offered by his superiors, grateful for his contributions to preparation of *The Fifth Report* and to the debates on the 1813 charter. When he did return to India, it was with a reputation and standing more heightened than he could have hoped, for it was as an official with responsibility for revising the entire civil administration of Madras, with the rank and perquisites of a Resident to a princely durbar, and with the opportunity and the determination to institute those policies—'to turn everything upside down', as a young colleague hoped—upon which he had devoted much thought and ingenuity for a decade or more.[1]

The stellar role he was to attain in the late part of his long stay in Britain—principally in London—could not have been anticipated by him or by any of his most sanguine well-wishers when his ship reached Deal in Kent, from which place he had departed for India twenty-eight years before. His prospects were not promising. To his sister he had written two months before departing the CD:

> I shall leave India with great regret, for I shall carry with me only a moderate competency, which remaining four of five years longer, I should double my fortune; this, however, is of little consequence, as I am not expensive. But what I am chiefly anxious about is, what am I to do when I go home. I have no rank in the army there and could not be employed upon an expedition to the Continent, or any other quarter; and as I am a stranger to the generous natives of your isle, I shall be excluded from every other line as well. . . . I

[1] MC, F/151/22, Gahagan to Munro, 17 September 1814.

much fear that I shall soon get tired of an idle life and be obliged to return to this country for employment.[2]

His fortune was modest for one whose mind, interests and experience disposed him to some sort of public life in Britain, and though he said that he was 'not expensive', he had had before him for almost a decade advice such as that of his friend Mark Wilks:

> England is a good place enough for a man who has an abundance of guineas; and . . . I can tell you . . . that I advise no man from India to go thither with the boyish cant of content on a little; rural felicity . . . the cottage and the balderdash. We have all attained habits that are at direct variance with those doctrines, and there is nothing which disgusts me so much as the littleness, which is absolutely necessary, if you desire to keep out of gaol. I therefore desire most earnestly to keep in feather in this country [India], until my plans are well grown.[3]

Munro's private papers afford considerable detail about his financial condition going back to 1787, when he placed SP1000 (about £440) with the Madras merchant Andrew Ross, an early benefactor, and shortly after arranged with another Madras firm, Colt and Company, to remit £200 each year to his father. By 1805 he had re-established relations with a friend from his youth, George Brown, now a rising London man of business, who became his advisor on the best means to remit and invest his funds in Britain. He told Brown that he preferred the safety of mortgages in land and public funds. The fund which he put under Brown's management in 1806 was between £30,000 and £40,000.[4] Bills in these amounts were sent to Brown from Madras along with an instruction that they should be invested as the latter, in consultation with Munro's brother-in-law Henry Erskine, 'think advisable'.[5] Other remittances of around £10,000 from his Madras bankers were made on Munro's account in 1808, and with the settlement of his outstanding salary dispute another SP 10,000 (£4700) was deposited in his favour.[6] The last was decided in Munro's favour by an enactment of the Directors. After refusing several of his petitions for release of the SP 11,211 retrenched from his salary as a payment in excess of the limit set for collectors' salaries, the Directors made a donation to him in recognition of his services.[7] So, though he was not a wealthy man when he

[2] Gleig, v. 1, p. 371, dated 5 August 1807.

[3] Gleig, v. 3, pp. 155–6.

[4] MC, F/151/151, Munro to Brown, dated Anantapur, 29 August 1805. According to a memo in Munro's hand of that time, his holdings with the Madras bankers, Harrington and Company, was SP74,500, and with Colt and Company over SP26,000. In addition to this he held balances in the Madras treasury of SP3500; against these assets he listed SP8770 in debts; conversions to sterling are provided in MC, F/151/18: SP2.25=£1.

[5] MC, F/151/165, ff. 2, 53, 94, 114, 156.

[6] IOL, *Personal Record*, O/6/1, p. 393, August 1809.

[7] MC, F/151/155, William Ramsey for the Court of Directors to Munro, 3 August 1809.

returned to Europe in 1808, he was financially comfortable, and he had the assurance of an additional two and a half years of salary while on furlough.

He spent the first year of his furlough as most men of his age and rank in Company service would. Still, these were special times and he was a special sort of man, and what contented others did not content him for long. A continental military campaign engaged his interest and almost his participation, and the unfolding of the East India Company charter renewal process brought him into public life in England, first somewhat obscurely—as what his biographer Gleig called 'a scene shifter'—and later openly, in his own right.[8]

As for others of his generation, the return to Britain after long years in India was not easy. To his old friend and protege Peter Bruce, still in the CD, Munro wrote from Edinburgh, where he had chosen to live after a brief, nostalgic stay in Glasgow, that he had seen their mutual friend James Cochrane, and the latter was determined to return to India soon: 'he is right for India is a much pleasanter country than this. It is our native land, but after long residence in India appears so cold and dark and wet and dirty that to one who likes to ride or walk the fields, no fortunte I think can make it comfortable.'[9]

In Edinburgh he had the companionship of his sister Erskine and her husband Henry Erskine. The latter had risen to the Dundas family office of Lord Advocate of Scotland. There too he found intellectual engagements, including a resumption of his interest in chemistry, on which subject he attended lectures.[10] However, his parents were now, in 1809, dead, and apart from his brother Alexander and the Erskines there was little to hold him in Scotland. After old friends and family had been visited and the responsibility for visiting the families of friends still in India, such as Bruce's family in Dundee, had been acquitted, there were no other strong ties. Moreover, during his first months of return and frequently thereafter, he was deeply troubled by an intensification of his deafness. As he touchingly revealed to his sister shortly after reaching Glasgow in 1808:

> I must I believe stay at home until I recover my hearing; for I am now deafer than ever I was in my life, owing to a cold which I caught, or rather caught me, a day or two before I left Edinburgh. I have been little more than a dumb spectator of all the gaiety which you talk of, for I can hardly hear a word that is said. I never was so impatient under deafness as at present, when I meet every moment in my native city old acquaintances, asking fifty questions which they are obliged to repeat four or five times before they can make me comprehend them. Some of them stare at me, and think no doubt, that I am come home because I am deranged. I am so entirely incapable of taking part in conversation, that I have no pleasure in company, and go into it merely to save appearances. A solitary walk is almost the only thing in which I have enjoyment.[11]

[8] Glieg, v. 1, p. 376.

[9] MC, F/151/12, 6 January 1809.

[10] Gleig, v. 1, p. 379.

[11] Ibid., p. 378, Glasgow, 25 October 1808.

Inevitably, he was drawn south to London. There, he had many friends from India, military and civilian colleagues, and even older friends from his youth who now lived in south-east England, such as George Brown his financial advisor, and Graham Moore a naval officer. There too he found others like himself who were seeking wives to accompany them on their new duties in India when furloughs were ended, men with rank and standing and some wealth, acquired, as Munro had, over many years of service. One colleague, Colonel Thomas Marriott of the Madras army, confided the joys of his marriage to his old friend Tom Munro. His wife, he said, was of 'sweet disposition, delicately pure and clean of person, a fine set of nice teeth . . . with a very good figure and bone enough to throw a fine child if she should be inclined that way'.[12]

In London, too, he was in a position to try to promote something useful for himself through his connections with Arthur and Richard Wellesley. Gleig suggested this along with the notion that Munro was a part of the Welcheren, or Scheldt, expedition of late 1809, an enterprise whose bad planning was exceeded only by its bad luck, and thus was a humiliating military failure.[13] Munro was not, in fact, part of the expedition. He wrote to his brother Alexander on 29 July 1809 that he had been to Ramsgate and Deal in Kent to see the departure of the expeditionary force and was sorry that he could not accompany it. Munro said that he had been advised to remain in London by Sir Francis Baring, a director of the Company, in order to discuss some aspects of Company business.[14] This business concluded only in August, when Munro informed Erskine that he would be returning to Scotland after a brief tour of England.[15] The Scheldt expedition was evacuated early in September.

What Baring's business was we do not know, but London was where Munro would have wanted to be in order to be closer to the news and activities of the East India Company at a time when its future was again being seriously considered in charter deliberations. There was little determination in Leadenhall Street or in the Whitehall offices of the Board of Control to change much about governance in India, as Beaglehole has rightly said. The presumed principled basis of that governance was Cornwallis' Bengal legislation, and this was swaddled in a reverence heightened by Cornwallis' death in 1805. True, there had begun to be murmurs that even these fine principles may have been badly applied in India. Recalling those days of innocence and confidence, Samuel Davis, a director and co-author of *The Fifth Report*, said in 1817 that 'there was

[12] MC, F/151/153, 28 January 1811.

[13] Gleig, v. 1, p. 381n. On the Walcheren expedition: J. W. Fortesque, *A History of the British Army* (London: Macmillan Co., 1910–30), v. 7, pp. 60–9 and Great Britain, Parliamentary Papers, *House of Commons, Session 1810*, vols. 6 and 7, 'Papers Relating to the Expedition to the Sheldt', paper 34, 'Journal of the Proceedings of the Army . . .', 13 February 1810, in v. 7.

[14] MC, F/151/143.

[15] MC, F/151/143, letters to Erskine of 4, 5 and 12 August.

a ready belief on insufficient grounds, that everything was going right until irresistible evidence forced itself forward to show that almost everything had been wrong'.[16] Davis was one of those who marshalled the 'irresistible evidence' against the Cornwallis system: his companion in this was James Cumming, clerk of the Board of Control. The instrument of their work was *The Fifth Report* and the spirit of it was, or became, Munro's.

There is little doubt that the series of Parliamentary reports emanating from the Select Committee on the Affairs of the East India Company had prepared the way for a reconsideration of the foundations of the Company's governance of India, nor that, as Beaglehole showed, Samuel Davis and James Cumming brought these investigations to a high climax in their fifth report of July 1812. However, there are other aspects of the situation to take into account. One was the disarray within the Company during the years from 1810 to 1813, particularly about affairs in Madras. This was set forth clearly by C. H. Philips in his *The East India Company, 1784–1834*.[17] Secondly, British governments were too continuously distracted by the war against France, on the continent and elsewhere, to take up Indian problems very seriously.

Robert Dundas, President of the Board of Control, following his father Henry, the first Lord Melville, sought vainly to bring renewal of the Company charter to the agendas of both the ministry which he served and the directorate in 1808. But, it was not until 1811 that the directors agreed, privately, to meet the demands of 'agency house' merchants in London for opening the export trade with India to them. Then, discussions in Parliament could proceed.[18] While this concession to London merchants broke one of the barriers to a full debate on the renewal of the charter, it opened another.

This was the demand by merchants elsewhere in Britain to be included in the Indian trade, partly, it was argued, to compensate them for their diminished trade in other places caused by disruptions of the war. Towards this end Liverpool merchants, especially disadvantaged by the curtailment of trade with the United States, which eventuated in warfare in 1812, led others of the 'outports' to press for an end to the London monopoly over the Indian trade. This pressure came in the form of pamphlets and petitions to Parliament. The first were skilfully answered by the Company, mostly written by Charles Grant. Nevertheless, the Company was placed in a defensive position on this 'outport' question, as upon other questions before it at the time.

These other questions before the Company tended to divide rather than unify the directors at this time. Two were paramount; both originated in Madras and were embarrassing as well as potentially dangerous because they concerned the military. One was the Vellore mutiny and the issue of missionaries in India; the other was the so-called 'white mutiny', a rising of Company military officers against the Madras government. Charles Grant took a leading part in the debates

[16] Beaglehole, p. 87.
[17] Pp. 168ff.
[18] Philips, p. 181.

on both issues, as was to be expected from the most powerful of the directors in the first decade of the nineteenth century.[19]

In July 1806 sepoy troops of the Vellore garrison rose against their European officers, killing or wounding some 200 of the complement of 370 there. On learning of the mutiny and its alleged cause—the proselytizing activities of Company military officers—the directors immediately split into pro- and anti-missionary factions, bringing into the open a division which had smouldered for two years after Grant and his ally Edward Parry had begun to send evangelical clergymen to fill chaplaincies in India. This move had been opposed by fellow directors who prophesied resentment and fear from the Company's Indian soldiers. Vellore seemed to validate the last concern because it was widely held that the cause of the mutiny was change in military regulations touching on dress and physical appearance which had been introduced by Sir John Cradock, commander of the Madras army, and supposedly construed by sepoys as an attack upon caste privileges within the army (signified by regulation dress differences) and pressure to convert them to Christianity. Adroitly, Grant and Parry managed to shift the blame for the mutiny from the evangelical enthusiasms of Cradock to a purported conspiracy led by members of the family of Tipu Sultan under exile at Vellore.[20]

Grant and his friends succeeded in making the then governor of Madras, Lord William Bentinck, along with Cradock, responsible for the mutiny, for failing to heed warnings of the conspiracy they insisted to be its cause. Robert Dundas at the Board of Control was persuaded to agree to recall both from Madras. To replace Bentinck at Madras was Sir George Barlow, an old Bengal hand, inclined to support Grant's leadership and his conspiratorial theory, which was essentially an attack upon the policies that Wellesley had instituted in Madras.[21] Munro's policies were anonymously implicated in this attack.

In letters to Robert Dundas at this time, Grant and Parry argued that far from being missionary influence, the immediate cause of the mutiny was the work of Tipu Sultan's family and their adherents in the Carnatic. But this, they said, masked a deeper cause for Indian discontent with Company rule in Madras. Grant and Parry argued along lines suggested by Munro in his 25 August 1807 letter to William Petrie where he spoke about the frustration of Indians 'under the dominion of a foreign power'.[22] For Munro this had been a charter for the annihilation of poligars so as to free India's ancient civil institutions from oppressive intermediate authority. For Grant and Parry, however,

[19] Grant was elected to one of the two chairs of the Court of Directors five times between 1804 and 1809 and commanded a block of 1500 votes in the Court of Proprietors, Philips, p. 154.

[20] Philips, pp. 159ff; for Grant's explanations in letters to Bentinck, 17 April 1807, to Barlow 18 April and 1 June 1807, see: Henry Morris, *The Life of Charles Grant* (London: Murray, 1904), pp. 298–9; and Ainslie T. Embree, *Charles Grant and British Rule in India* (New York: Columbia University Press, 1962), pp. 233–4.

[21] Embree, pp. 242–5.

[22] IOL, MBOR *Proceedings*, P/288/25, pp. 6875ff.

the intention was precisely to condemn policies such as those pursued by Munro. This is elaborated in their lengthy explanation of the Vellore mutiny as the manifestation of generalized discontent among Indians in Madras.

> The general causes that indispose the Indians to us may be briefly stated thus: We are foreigners, comparatively few in number, who from trading Factories and the humble character of Merchants, have risen to the possession of Kingdoms and the rank of Sovereigns. . . . We are every way dissimilar to the people over whom we rule, in origin, in language, in religion, in manners, so that there is no common principles or bond of union between them and us. Our interest is thought to be in several respects opposed to their's [*sic*]. The public tribute which we derive as Sovereigns, the private wealth Individuals among us acquire, is transferred from India, whereby the growth which that Country naturally so productive, would have been in prosperity, is prevented. We engross all the important stations of the Government Civil, Military and Political, with their emoluments and honours. From that which is common stimulus to exertion and hope in most Countries, our Native subjects are cut off. They are excluded from rising to political power or distinction. We occupy the principal channels of Commerce also—more energetic, adventurous and intelligent, we outstrip the Indians in commercial activity and enterprise. In short it is a general conception among them that they do not possess the rank and importance they ought to hold in . . . their own Country. And this sentiment is the more dangerous because the evil seems to grow out of the nature of our Character and Government—it is therefore one of which they must deem vain to complain to us, and from which under our rule they see no prospect of relief. Evils which admit not of complaint are the most dangerous kind, as directly leading people to look for a remedy in Revolution. We hold, and think it not difficult to prove, that with all these disadvantages the subjects of British India may, and, in our old possession, do enjoy greater means of happiness than they did or perhaps can, under their Native Governments, but we are now describing their opinions, not our's. We need not wonder if with general impressions of the nature above described, our new subjects in the Peninsula should not be disposed to regard favourably, the rigid style of Collection or the System of Judicial Administration introduced there, or even the permanent Settlement of the Lands, all measures, for which they required to be prepared by previous confidence. . . .

From this condemnation, that reaches back to Adam Smith and anticipates many of Munro's later ones, Grant and Parry turn to issues of immediate danger to Munro:

> The late revolution in the Carnatic passed before the eyes of our own Subjects, those who were then or have since become such; it came home to their feelings, the circumstances on which the Family of Wallajah, our earliest ally, was divested of its possessions, were not understood by the common

> people; they commiserated the fallen Family and disapproved of the annihilation of its power. . . . All the Mahomedans in India justly consider us as the subverters of their power through the whole of that Continent. They are our inveterate enemies, disposed to do us internally all the mischief they safely can, and to join any standard lifted up against us. . . . It were to be wished that the Mahomedans were the only class of people inimical to us from the personal feelings of apprehended injury. But by much greater provocation, a large class of Hindoos, the whole of the body of Southern Poligars and their adherents as far as they yet survive, are made our determined enemies. We have carried on a Species of Warfare and a system of severity against them, of which it is hoped our Transactions in the east furnish no other example. A high spirit warlike race of men accustomed to a certain degree of independence, have been by sudden process, before perhaps their grievances were sufficiently heard, attacked, broken down, some banished, some imprisoned, some proscribed, and not a few executed, some even without the forms of Trial. Whatever defence may be made by the Fort St George Government for this violent, severe procedure (and some at least of the Transactions it will be very difficult to vindicate) neither the sufferers nor the people of the Country were convinced of the justice of it, and a sentiment of Sympathy for the unfortunate must be generally prevalent.[23]

Much later, at the time of his minute of 31 December 1824, Munro saw fit to incorporate many of the same sentiments about the causes of discontent among Indians and the virtues of 'native agency' as a means of reducing the alienation which fed this discontent. However, as it was the approach of Grant and Parry to shift the blame for the Vellore mutiny from the alleged subversive effects of Christian evangelicalism within the Indian army, they found it convenient to deepen their attack upon the Wellesley system as the major cause of that discontent. The resonances of their attack could not but implicate Munro, and therefore add to his discomfiture in England and his hopes of finding a place in the coming debates about the Company. It appeared that, for such powerful men as Grant, Munro was a part of the problem, not the solution to the Company's civil problems in India as these were being perceived at the time—a time made the more hazardous by the other Madras event which focused concerns then. This was the mutiny of the Company's military officers in Madras in 1809.

In the same 1807 letter, Grant and Parry expressed serious concern about the frustrations and dangerous alienation of European officers in the Company forces. They suggested there that one factor in the sepoy mutiny at Vellore was the degradation of the authority of European Company commanders in the eyes of their Indian troops. This allegedly resulted from the preference

[23] IOL, *Political and Secret Department*, L/P&S/3/3, Charles Grant and Edward Parry to Robert Dundas, 18 May 1807, para. 6.

shown to officers with King's commissions, officers of 'His Majesty's Regiments there' in respect of military command and perquisites. Grant complained that Company officers with long careers in India, with knowledge of the languages and customs of their soldiers, upon which trust and discipline had long been based, were regularly passed over for the most important commands. This included the post of Commander-in-Chief of the Madras army. Company officers were also now to be deprived of commissariat responsibilities which had given them patronage: 'In a word the officers of the Company, tho' a highly meritorious set of Gentlemen yielding in Military Character to none of any Nation, instead of being cherished and conciliated by Governors and Commanders in Chief, have in late years been notoriously overlooked and depressed.'[24]

Added to these complaints raised by Grant and Parry, there were other grievances that agitated officers of the Madras military. The first was the decision by the Court of Directors not to appoint Lieutenant General Hay Macdowall, commander of the Madras army after the recall of Cradock, to the Governor's council—as had been the usage previously. Their reason for refusing this was that Cradock had made errors in judgement that were held to have caused the Vellore mutiny. Macdowall appealed that decision, claiming that it was a slight upon the entire Madras army. As the directors deliberated that appeal, another perceived insult was made upon the honour of Madras officers. This was seen as the work of Sir George Barlow, who had replaced Bentinck in the aftermath of the Vellore affair.

Seeking to reduce military spending in response to London's demand for that, Barlow ended a financial perquisite of commanders of field units of the Madras army. This was the so-called 'tent contract', a monthly allowance given to every such commander for equiping their sepoy soldiers. Barlow's order was seen as a further slur by suggesting a possible conflict between the private advantages which might accrue to each officer and their public duty. Macdowall, already angry over his exclusion from the Madras council, was prevailed upon by brother officers to arrest and court martial the army Quartermaster-General for carrying out Barlow's order. Barlow countermanded that action by releasing that officer. This, along with word from London that the directors refused to alter their ban to his membership in the Madras council, caused Macdowall to resign his position and precipitately to leave Madras. However, just before his departure, from aboard the ship that was to carry him away, he issued a general order to the Madras army which he asked two of his aides to circulate. There he said that his departure alone prevented him from opposing the Governor and rearresting the Quartermaster-General for contempt of military authority. Barlow lashed back by suspending the two junior officers who had acted, lawfully under Macdowall's orders,

[24] IOL, *Political and Secret Department*, L/P&S/3/3, Charles Grant and E. Parry, 18 May 1807, para. 5.

and then Barlow rashly suspended a group of Madras officers who petitioned him for the release of the two Macdowall aides.

Soon after, Company officers mutinied at Masulipatam, Hyderabad, Seringapatam and other garrisons. A planned unified march upon Madras from these garrisons was probably averted by the bravery and persuasiveness of two respected Madras officers. One was Barry Close who sped from his post as Resident in Poona to Hyderabad to check the plans of the Company officers of that garrison (and allegedly organized the opposition of sepoy troops against their own officers); the other was John Malcolm, recently returned from his diplomatic mission to Persia, who tried to defuse matters at Masulipatam.[25]

Both mutinies in the Madras army—that of sepoys at Vellore in 1806 and that of the officers at several places in 1809—were rightly seen as dangerous. They were also events which added to the deep divisions among the directors of the Company in the years leading to the charter renewal debates. In addition to shifting the blame for Vellore from evangelical chaplains to the inherently bad policies of the previous Madras governments, which 'indiposed Indians to us', Grant and a majority of directors who voted with him forced full support of Barlow and his actions against the Madras officers and dismissed William Petrie from the Madras council for opposing the latter's handling of the officers' mutiny. When shortly after, in 1810, Grant and several others left the Court of Directors, having completed their triennial terms, an anti-Barlow majority of the directors was able to bring about his recall from Madras in 1812.[26] However, this reversal was dearly purchased, for the divisive factionalism and recrimination among the directors weakened that body in relation to the Board of Control on the very eve of the great charter debates in 1813.

Munro had been drawn into the Vellore affair in 1806 by Bentinck. When the latter had expressed his fears that the notorious poligari elements of Gurramkonda might rise in support of the sepoys at Vellore, Munro calmly answered that when he heard about the uprising at Vellore he had ordered his staff to closely monitor 'the principal people of Gurramkonda', anticipating some attempts against the Company. His reason for that concern, he told Bentinck, was that many of Haidar Ali's and Tipu Sultan's soldiers had taken up residence in that prosperous part of the CD. However, Munro told Bentinck that it was unlikely that any poligars in the CD would risk support to the cause of Tipu Sultan's family; those that might have Munro had already imprisoned or expelled. Moreover, Munro doubted that a restoration of Tipu Sultan's house was behind the mutiny of the sepoys at Vellore since Hindu soldiers

[25] IOL, *A Letter from an Officer in Madras ['Captain John Malcolm, later Sir John'] to a Friend in that Service, Now in England . . . [on] the Late. . . . Insurrection in the Indian Army* (London: Murray, 3rd edn., 1810) and SOAS Library, *Observations in Lt. Col. Malcolm's Publication Relative to the Disturbances in the Madras Army; Containing a Refutation of the Opinions of that Officer* (London: Black, Parry and Co., Booksellers to the Honourable East India Company, 1812).

[26] Embree, p. 254.

who comprised the mass of the sepoy regiments had no interest in that. Munro thought that the cause of the Vellore mutiny was resentment and fear among the sepoys about their 'religious ceremonies': 'there is nothing so absurd but that they will believe when made a question of religion'.[27] Munro hinted vaguely that 'artful leaders [acted] to inflame the minds of the ignorant . . .' sepoys that their religious practices were at risk, but implicitly he seemed to be blaming the mischief upon Cradock's regulations, and therefore upon Bentinck's assent to these regulations.

Being absent from India when his brother officers rose in 1809, Munro was not called upon to take sides, and on that set of events his correspondence is silent. His sentiments may well have been those of his friend Malcolm, though they were never so freely expressed. Malcolm, having taken an active and courageous part in the suppression of the officers' mutiny, published a book of almost 300 pages which sought to explain and thus partly excuse his brother officers' distress and provocation, though he condemned the resort to armed opposition to Company civilian authority. In this book Malcolm spoke of the grave injustice of Barlow's suspension of two Macdowall subordinates and also of the unresponsiveness of the Governor-General, Lord Minto, to the Madras officers' petitions, which led to their despair and to their condemnable acts of mutiny.[28] While Munro aided some of the officers involved, notably Lieutenant Colonel Thomas Boles, with money and considerable moral support for the many years during which Boles sought to be reinstated in rank, he seems not to have made any public statements about the matter, at the time or later.[29] Certainly, he avoided anything as rash as Malcolm's book, and therefore the opprobrium of an answering pamphlet defending Barlow's actions—presumably composed by an ally of Charles Grant.[30] But it is not unlikely that his sympathetic views on the officers' mutiny were made known to some of those directors who supported the restoration of Boles and others suspended by Barlow, and who ultimately combined to bring Barlow back in disgrace.[31]

The disarray of the Company in the years preceding the charter renewal debates of 1813 justified C. H. Philips' chapter title on the period, 'The India House Divided Against Itself, 1806–12'. Dissensions among the directors, plus the continuing European war, delayed formal consideration of the charter

[27] Gleig, v. 1, p. 362, Bentinck to Munro, 2 August 1806, and p. 364, Munro to Bentinck, 11 August 1806.

[28] Malcolm, *A Letter. . . .*

[29] Several letters from India at the time from military and civilian friends of Munro refer to the mutiny and Macdowall's General Order of 28 January 1809, and condemn Barlow: MC, F/151/20, *passim*. Thomas Boles was an old friend of Munro and a sometime partner in commercial ventures by which both sought to increase their captaincy salaries, using Boles' posting at Pondicherry for this; MC, F/151/163, f. 57, Boles to Munro, 21 October 1796.

[30] *Observations on Lt. Col. Malcolm's Publication. . . .*

[31] Philips, pp. 173–4.

by Parliament until the early months of 1813. Prudently, however, the select committees sitting to consider East India affairs had previously set about gathering information for presentation to the House of Commons and to the House of Lords, their *Fifth Report*. Munro was made a part of that endeavour, in spirit at first, and then later as an immediately personal force in the making of that document.

The main influence upon the makers of *The Fifth Report* was the Board of Control. It could not have been otherwise, given the factionally riven Court of Directors. And, the main subject of debate when the charter was before Parliament was not the territorial governance of India, but two other matters: the Company's monopoly in Britain and the question of missionaries in India.[32] These two issues were vigorously argued in pamphlets and petitions before and while being considered by Parliament. More than thirty pamphlets were prepared by opponents of the continuation of the Company monopoly in 1812–13; these were co-ordinated by a lobby called 'the Outport Deputation'. Each such pamphlet was answered by one from the Company, many written by Grant. Over 800 petitions assailed Parliament in 1813 on the question of missions in India while evidence was being given on that question. At the same time, witnesses were being examined on the internal governance of British India, but here there was neither vigorous debate, nor much interest among members of Parliament.[33] The governing text for most of these discussions was *The Fifth Report*, which became available to Parliament in July 1812. However, interested participants like Munro received sections of the *Report* in the form of printers' proofs from James Cumming and Samuel Davis, the makers of the work.[34]

Davis went to India first as a military officer and surveyor, participating in a mission to Tibet in 1784. He subsequently served in various civilian capacities in Bengal: as a district judge and as agent of the Governor-General in Banaras.[35] He was elected to the Court of Directors in 1810 with the help of Robert Dundas, President of the Board of Control (now Lord Melville and attempting to emulate his distinguished father's successful interventions in elections in the Directorate).[36]

Davis served as a director until his death in 1819. During much of that time he was a critic of the Cornwallis scheme in Bengal, and he was moved by a reformer's zeal to prevent its extension to other parts of the subcontinent. Apart from this passion, he was an independent member of the directorate, sometimes opposing the dominant force of Grant, at other times voting with

[32] Embree treats these matters very well, pp. 261–76.
[33] Philips, pp. 182–90.
[34] Kenneth Ballhatchet, 'The Authors of the Fifth Report of 1812', *Notes and Queries*, v. 202 (November 1957), p. 477.
[35] *The Fifth Report*, Note by W. F. Firminger, 'Authorship of the Fifth Report', v. 1, p. 1, where it is supposed that Davis was the sole author.
[36] Philips, p. 175.

him. In an early vote as a director Davis opposed the dismissal of Petrie, which was being pressed by Grant in connection with his defence of Barlow in Madras; and he voted against Grant and for the restoration of Lieutenant Colonel Thomas Boles to his rank in the Madras army. On the other hand Davis voted with Grant and a minority of directors against the appointment of Lord Buckinghamshire to the presidency of the Board of Control on the grounds of the latter's antagonism to the directorate and his irascibility.[37]

Recalling his early opposition to the expansion of the Cornwallis system in an 1818 letter to Mountstuart Elphinstone, Davis said that it had been his desire 'to unmask the effects of Lord Cornwallis' Code of 1793'. He also told Elphinstone that he had been encouraged to pursue this purpose as a co-author of *The Fifth Report* by Lord Melville and by Sir J. Anstruther, a former chief justice in Bengal and an MP.[38] But even before this letter to Elphinstone, Davis had put his reasons for opposing the Cornwallis scheme to his fellow directors when he said, in a dissenting minute, that he and other directors had supported Munro's proposals in order to bring '*relief to our suffering subjects*' in India and to oppose the system introduced 'under the auspices of a Nobleman [Cornwallis] distinguished less for the solidity of his understanding than by the purity and benevolence of his motives'.[39]

Davis' views of the Bengal system were apparently shared by the chairman of the Select Committee on East Indian affairs in the House of Commons, Thomas Wallace; he called upon Davis for assistance in an enquiry into the condition of the 'suffering subjects of India'.[40] Davis was instructed to obtain relevant evidence from James Cumming, clerk of the Board of Control department of revenue and judicial records, and he found in Cumming a man of talent, knowledge and a zeal to match his own. The two soon decided to share the drafting of the report of the enquiry sought by Wallace, which became *The Fifth Report*, Davis to prepare the Bengal section and Cumming the Madras portion.

Cumming had joined the office staff of the Board of Control in 1792 and served that organization for thirty-one years, sixteen as head of the revenue and judicial records department.[41] Beginning in 1801, he began to devote his free time to an investigation of the conditions of people in Company territories. It is doubtful that any in London had ever before undertaken such a study of the vast corpus of records that were accumulating in the Board's quarters in Cannon Row, Whitehall, or at least that was the opinion of the long-time

[37] Philips, p. 172n and p. 184n.

[38] Cited in Ballhatchet, 'The Authors of *The Fifth Report*', p. 478.

[39] IOL, *Appendixes to Court Minutes; Copies of Dissents*, B/329, 9 August 1817, emphasis of the original.

[40] Beaglehole, p. 87.

[41] IOL, *Brief Notice of the Services of Mr. Cumming, Late Head of the Revenue and Judicial Departments, in the Office of the Right Honourable Board of Commissioners of the Affairs in India. July 20, 1824* (London: 1824).

secretary of the Board, Thomas P. Courtnay.[42] Cumming later revealed that no Parliamentary commissioner of the Board had ever approached him to make use of the knowledge he was assiduously acquiring until Wallace, a member of the Board and chairman of the Commons Select Committee, did in 1811.[43]

Wallace was responsible for bringing together the two authors of *The Fifth Report* and thereby launched the Board of Control upon a period of dominance equal to that enjoyed by Henry Dundas and more productive of significant change than any achieved under the senior Dundas. The division of labour between Davis and Cumming was presented to the Select Committee by Wallace and that body of parliamentarians approved the collaboration.

Cumming reported that while writing the Madras portion of the *Report* he 'had full and frequent communications . . . with some of the best informed and most enlightened men then in England, who had been carrying on the affairs of Civil Government in the Peninsula.'[44] Few could have been more active than Munro, though it is difficult to be certain when his participation began. None of Munro's surviving letters from 1809 mention Cumming, and it is clear from his letters of that year and the preceding half year that he had had no sustained contact with any involved in Company policy, except in connection with his salary dispute.

Shortly after his debarcation at Deal in 1808, Munro had begun his attempts to persuade the directors to restore the equivalent £4000 which remained lodged in the Madras treasury against the overpayment of his salary in 1805. He complained to his father, whom he was not to see alive again, that he was wasting a good deal of time during the late months of 1808 waiting upon various directors to solicit their support on his behalf. He had met many influential people in London then, some through his sister Margaret's banker husband George H. Drummond. Among these were Henry Dundas, the great benefactor of Scottish servants of the Company.[45] However, he found them all too absorbed in the 'sale' of writerships and cadetships, in discussions of the Vellore mutiny, and in the election of the chairman to succeed Grant, to give any attention to his case. He had submitted his petition for restoration of his retrenched 1805 salary in May 1809, and learned that he would be awarded a donation of nearly that amount in late August. His informant among the directors, John Bannerman, formerly of the Madras army, told him that Grant had supported Munro's petition, and Munro speculated to his brother that Grant's support had probably been mobilized on his behalf by his other influential brother-in-law, Henry Erskine.[46] These were signs of Munro's growing network of connections.

42 Beaglehole, p. 88 and footnote 3, p. 159.
43 *Brief Notice* . . ., p. 65n; see *D.N.B.* v. 20, pp. 562–3, for Wallace.
44 *Brief Notice* . . ., p. 67n.
45 MC, F/151/143, Munro to his father, 17 August 1808.
46 Ibid., 9 July 1809.

When it was that Cumming became impressed with Munro's writing is not clear. He seems not to have known of Munro's long paper of 10 April 1806 submitted to the Madras Committee on Police while preparing what might have been his first paper on Madras affairs, 'Notes by James Cumming Respecting the Police under the Madras Presidency, 23 August 1808'.[47] Apart from a brief reference to a Bellary magistrate's report, there is mention of neither the CD nor Munro. By late 1810, however, Cumming had definitely discovered Munro. His next substantial paper composed from the records in his department of the Board, was 'An Historical Account of the Administration of the Land Revenues in the Territories under the Presidency of Fort St George,' dated 30 November 1810.[48] This was the first of a series of Cumming papers on ryotwar that soon became a dossier marking Munro's brilliant new career as an Indian statesman, though one, for a time at least, who worked through others.

'SCENE-SHIFTER' AND SUITOR

Cumming's 1810 paper on ryotwar surveyed reports from nineteen Madras districts. The section dealing with the CD exceeds by about four times the length of any other district, and Cumming took without reservation Munro's claims that his revenue proposals were based on historical documentation going back to the early seventeenth century for most of Cuddapah. He also accepted Munro's prejudices and policies against poligars in the CD and Munro's claims that the revenue demand under his administration was more moderate than that of earlier regimes in the CD. But most important, Cumming provided a sympathetic presentation of the 'ryotwar or kulwar' principle of settlement and gave Munro an impressive advocacy voice by liberal citation of the latter's report of 30 November 1806. At the close of his paper, Cumming prudently observed that the directors were concerned that 'too much was left to the agency of native servants' under ryotwar, but he also repeated Munro's defence against that criticism.

During 1811 Cumming continued to produce papers on Madras revenue and judicial questions in which Munro's writings figured prominently. One completed in March 1811 was entitled 'Memoir of the Revisions of the Judicial System under the Government of Fort St George with a View to the Reduction of Expenses and the More Expeditious and Efficient Administration of Justice'.[49] Munro's opinions shaped this document on such matters as the judicial role of village headmen and panchayats. At this same time, as Cumming was defining the argument of the Madras portion of *The Fifth Report*, he was also collecting and abstracting the various papers that came to comprise its

[47] *HMS*, v. 528, pp. 131–85.

[48] Ibid., v. 526, pp. 337–468; this paper is signed by Cumming.

[49] A copy of this may be found in MC, F/151/24, pp. 68–118; also in *HMS* vols. 693 and 694. Munro was cited on pp. 77–8, 82, 86 and 99–101.

extended appendix. Correspondence of the period from 1810 to the middle of 1812 does not permit a certain answer to the question of whether Munro was in personal contact with Cumming at this time. Munro did spend a good deal of time in and around London, but he also spent long months in Scotland in 1810, in Edinburgh, or at the country houses of his brother Alexander or his sister and their families, and elsewhere.[50]

Munro's travel about Britain was incessant in 1810 and 1811, and traces of it are found principally in letters to his brother and sister. His brother Alexander now shared responsibility with George Brown for Munro's finances, the two having formed a partnership in 1810.[51] Munro found no pleasure in his peregrinations; the charm of seeing old Indian friends was dulled by his occasional bouts of deafness following upon colds he contracted. This inhibited social relations with new acquaintances and frustrated his quest for a wife. On the last, his letters to Erskine, especially, speak of meeting many presentable young women, but none whose intellectual companionship he found satisfactory. A more general discontent was probably not very different from that of many Indian hands on their furloughs. To his sister he wrote in 1810:

> A man might spend a winter as pleasantly in a cave in Lapland as in England with his vision bounded on every side by a thick wet mist through which men and horses sail past as dimly as if they were ghosts. How different all of this from India where at this moment it is the middle of harvest, the sky is without a cloud, the day just warm enough to make the coolness of the evening agreeable. The field resounding with the busy voices of the peasantry and this prospect bounded only by the other horizon.[52]

Late in 1811 references appear to a Miss Campbell, his future wife. He either met her or renewed her acquaintance at a party of the Thackeray family in Scotland. William Thackeray was then chief secretary to the Madras government and still a regular correspondent. He was to return to England in 1813 and would remain there until after Munro's departure for India in 1814. However, his family was in Britain prior to his return. Reporting the pleasure of being with them in October 1811, he told Erskine that Miss Campbell would 'make a good wife for most men'.[53] More frequent reports about Miss Campbell followed in the coming months, though still as late as June 1812 he had made no choice. Writing to his brother then he said that the petition that he had presented to the directors in April for an extension of his furlough had been granted, but that he could not be detained in Britain beyond December 'unless some lady comes in the way with whom I wish to get acquainted, at present I am . . . far from anything of this kind . . . for . . . [London] is not a place of men little known to see much of female society'.[54]

[50] MC, F/151/144, Munro to Alexander Munro, 20 October 1810.

[51] Letters are found in MC, F/151/143 for 1809 and F/151/144 for 1810–12.

[52] MC, F/151/144, Munro to Erskine from Wakefield, 20 January 1810.

[53] Ibid., Munro to Erskine, 15 October 1811.

[54] Munro to Alexander, 5 June 1812.

Thus, even as late as June 1812, Munro had found neither wife nor much favour in the eyes of those who could advance his career. In an 1812 letter to Alexander about his petition to remain longer in the country he commented despairingly that extending his furlough would have been no problem had Lord Melville, Robert Dundas, still held office at the Board of Control; but, Lord Buckinghamshire, Melville's successor, 'will not detain me or say that my presence is in any way necessary'.[55] Nor had preferment to high office in India come from his connection through his brother-in-law, Henry Erskine. The latter, as a friend of Lord Moira (Francis Rawdon, Marquis of Hastings), a prospective Governor-General, Munro hoped might have led him to an important diplomatic or staff assignment.[56] All of these frustrations found expression in a letter to Erskine in September 1812, in apparent response to a perhaps irritated query from her about the difficulty of knowing where to post his mail because of his rapid moves about Britain. He wrote to his sister with rare exasperation: 'Can you think I have any pleasure in running about from place to place or that I should do so without some object. I have no enjoyment in such a life. I think there is something disgraceful in it, and I am ashamed of myself when I reflect that I have been above four years in England as an idler, and frequently wish that I had never left India.'[57] In this same letter Munro said that there was no other purpose in remaining in Britain except to find a wife, 'some woman for whom I could form an attachment'. But, there were so many 'obstacles in my way': long absent from his home, a member of no recognized society of the country, a man with friends principally like himself—bachelor officers or men with young families—hence few opportunities to meet young women. Moroever, he complained, a man of his age drew attention by speaking too long or frequently to any young woman. As to Miss Campbell, whom Erskine had mentioned, Munro was not sure what to think since he had spoken with her so infrequently. Even so, 'it was reported in Glasgow that he was to be married to Miss C...': 'I am not very fastidious about a wife; I want neither fortune nor family. All I want is a good sense and temper with a moderate share of good looks. But I should be sorry to fall into the hands of a mere amiable creature whose society would be a burden to me.' It is not always quite clear from the numerous references to Miss Campbell whether this was Jane Campbell, daughter of Richard Campbell of Cragie, County Ayr, whom he did marry in 1814.[58] In other letters of this time several Miss Campbells are mentioned and even joked about. 'Miss Campbell' became a cognomen for any marriagable young woman in the same way that 'Lt. Campbell' had served,

[55] Ibid., Munro to Alexander, 22 April 1812.

[56] Ibid., Munro to Erskine, 22 July 1811. Moira, or Lord Hastings, was offered the Governor-Generalship by the Prince Regent in January 1812, but he refused; he accepted the position later in the year: Philips, pp. 177–8.

[57] MC, F/151/144, Munro to Erskine, 17 September 1812.

[58] *Burke's Genealogical and Heraldic History of the Peerage; Baronetage and Knightage* (London Burke's Peerage, Ltd., 9th edn., 1949), p. 1453.

when he was a young, unimportant Madras cadet, to designate any other young Scot who advanced by being a kinsman of the General Campbell commanding Madras forces. Marriage, in any case, lay eighteen months off, and his disappointing marital quest was soon to be interrupted by a time of intense activity on the renewal of the Company's charter.

Also unclear was Munro's movement to centre stage in the debates on charter renewal. His biographer, Gleig, speaks of his role as a 'scene-shifter', the anonymous hand behind many of the articles on Indian questions in reviews of the time and in pamphlets.[59] This may have been correct and could have been based upon information provided to Gleig by John G. Ravenshaw, a long-time friend to Munro and Madras colleague who was on home leave during the time of the charter debates. Ravenshaw became a director of the Company and personally compiled Munro's private and public papers at the latter's death in order to do a biography of Munro; all of this was turned over to Gleig for completion.

Some documentary evidence now exists bearing upon the question of Munro's involvement in the debates. Letters to Munro in1812 show that he was in regular contact with the highest echelons of the Company and Board on matters pertaining to revenue and judicial procedures in Madras and elsewhere. In January of the year William M'Cullock, assistant to the examiner of East India records in Leadenhall Street and successor to the office in 1817, sought a memorandum from Munro on 'land rents' in the CD as well as revenue arrangements under native governments. This was at the request of the deputy chairman Hugh Inglis, and for the eventual eyes of the Governor-General, the Earl of Minto.[60] From the Board, James Cumming wrote on 2 March that the president, Lord Melville, hoped that Munro would be in London before Parliament rose, anticipating the debate on the charter, and the director, John Bannerman, wrote in the same month in similar vein, 'as I have heard you express the wish to be in the way when the Company charter comes under discussion'. Another director and old Madras Army friend, Alexander Allan, also wrote then to say that Munro should be in contact with the chairman of the Company about the evidence he would present to Parliament, and with Lord Buckinghamshire, who was designated to replace Lord Meville at the Board of Control. Two questions were important, Allan thought: the opening of private trade in India and the incorporation of military forces under the Crown.[61]

Munro did work for some time in 1812 on a paper dealing with the opening of Indian trade to merchants from ports other than London, the so-called 'outports'. This work, he told his brother in May of the year, left him no time for anything else, and it pertained to a conflict in which, he reported, 'I can do no good to either party'. He appeared to mean that he would please neither

[59] Gleig, v. 1, pp. 376 and 399.
[60] MC, F/151/21, 6 January 1812.
[61] Ibid., Allan to Munro, 14 March 1812.

the Company, wishing to preserve its monopoly intact, nor the 'delegates' from the outports, who sought to end the London monopoly of the Company's trade with India and China. The product of this labour is preserved in a long, fifteen-page paper reproduced in Gleig's biography.[62]

In still other letters of early 1812 Alexander Allan revealed other evidence of Munro's rising esteem in Company councils. Allan advised Munro not to be hasty about accepting the governorship of St Helena which he said Inglis was proposing for him, but to wait for a more suitable high office in India. Allan also spoke of John Sullivan's high regard and the prudence of cultivating a relationship with Sullivan, who was appointed to the Board along with Buckinghamshire. He expressed regret in this letter that Munro was determined to depart for India late in the year, but he agreed that even though his friend was becoming a familiar among the most powerful men of Indian affairs, in the Company as well as at the Board, Allan could see no prospects for any spectacular change in Munro's career prospects.[63]

As the year drew to a close, still without the parliamentary debate, now scheduled for early 1813, Munro's departure was delayed again. This time, however, it was at the bidding of the Board of Control, probably particularly by John Sullivan and James Cumming. As the time for the Parliamentary committee hearings on Indian affairs finally approached, the last months of 1812 became increasingly occupied with advising on many issues which the Company and Board of Control anticipated would be raised in the hearings. It was a period in which Munro prepared himself as a witness and probably participated, anonymously, with others, in the preparation of public articles on these questions, as Gleig suggests. William Empson, a critic of Company policies, reviewing Gleig's biography later in the *Edinburgh Review*, expressed doubt that Munro was thought to be a very impressive witness in the committee hearings on the charter in 1813. He based this judgement on his discussions with the counsel for the Company at the time who reported that Munro's extraordinary abilities were never revealed to him or he would have made greater use of Munro as a witness.[64] This later view accords with Munro's letters of 1812 and earlier, reflecting his frustration at not being recognized, of being an 'idler' with little to show for his considerable and increasing labours in the charter renewal cause.

James Cumming seems to have been crucial in the transformation of Munro's position in 1813. He was the bridge between the Munro of the CD, as represen-

[62] Gleig, v. 1, pp. 384–99. Munro posthumously drew considerable hostility at the time of the charter renewal of 1830–3 for his views on the outport question in this paper. This matter is touched upon in a review of Gleig's biography in the *Quarterly Review*, v. 43, pp. 81–112, possibly written by Gleig himself—according to W. E. Houghton, *The Wellesley Index to Victorian Periodicals* (London: Routledge and Kegan Paul, 1966), v. 1, p. 710.

[63] MC, F/151/21, 19 July 1812.

[64] Vol. 51, pp. 267–8.

ted his papers of 1805 to 1807, the Munro whose testimony before Parliament was finally deemed so impressive, and the Munro who, in 1814, was given charge of a commission empowered to re-establish ryotwar in Madras and to reconstruct the judicial administration in the Presidency.

Cumming had become a regular correspondent of Munro by the middle of 1813. Letters of his from November and December referred to papers sent to Munro for comment, and thanked Munro for answering questions involving revenue and police.[65] Sullivan, too, had become a friend and consumer of Munro's knowledge and experience, judging from other Cumming letters of the time mentioning Munro's visits to Sullivan's home in Richings Park, Buckinghamshire.[66] Cumming also expressed his pleasure that Munro was to remain longer in England, 'for there is no saying in what different ways, your presence may be useful'. More extravagantly, he continued: 'I am perfectly convinced that no two men of ordinary understanding and unbiased minds who have examined attentively the revenue records of the old governments[?] abroad can entertain the least doubt that the ryotwar principle of *government* (for I will [not] use the words revenue administration which is of so limited signification) is far, very far superior in its good effects to any other.'[67] Thus, while John Sullivan was important in this incorporation of Munro's approach at the highest levels of Indian policy determination as time passed, the real 'discovery' of Munro appears to have been Cumming's.

MAKING THE FIFTH REPORT

The Madras section of *The Fifth Report* is now known to have been the work of Cumming, and it appears that Munro's conceptions had seized Cumming's attention and his advocacy by 1811. The decisive imprint of Munro's views is manifest in the *Report* proper, but even more in the large number of Munro's papers that fill the long appendix of the work.

Still, it is uncertain from extant evidence to what degree Munro was personally involved in the selection and editing of the documents comprising the Madras appendix, or in the formation of the argument posed in the *Report* itself. The probability that Munro was involved in both is suggested in a letter to Alexander, two months before publication of the *Report* in which he spoke of being at work on Indian papers. This might have been on the outport question, which formed the basis for much of his testimony before parliamentary committees, and not the content of the *Report* itself.[68] However, another letter from Cumming shortly after his completion of the Madras portion of *The Fifth*

[65] MC, F/151/21, Cumming to Munro, n.d., October (?), f. 73, and 17 November 1813.

[66] Munro also refers to visits at Sullivan's Buckinghamshire house, MC, F/151/144, Munro to Alexander Munro, 20 August 1812.

[67] MC, F/151/21, Cumming to Munro, October 1812, f. 73.

[68] MC, F/151/144, Munro to Alexander Munro, 5 May 1812.

Report asks Munro to meet with Stephen Rumbold Lushington, a Madras civil servant (and the successor of Munro in the Madras governorship), in order to resolve certain differences in their views about 'Talliars', or village 'police', to be treated in the Madras appendixes. Again, in late 1812, Cumming spoke of plans to publish *The Fifth Report* as soon as it was printed for presentation to Parliament, and asking Munro for his opinion of that plan, the suggestion there being that Munro had seen all of the work and thus could make a judgement about the potential popular demand for it.[69] On the other hand, there is a letter from Cumming in November 1812, telling Munro that Lord Buckinghamshire had begun reading the *Report* and that Cumming was looking forward to Munro's return to London even though, he said, 'I am perfectly prepared for many defects, inaccuracies, and incompletions which you will be able to point out in the *Report* when it comes under your perusal. . . .'[70] This last makes it appear not only that Lord Buckinghamshire, Cumming's superior at the Board and the major framer of Indian policy, had not seen *The Fifth Report* before its printing and presentation to Parliament, but that Munro had not seen it until late 1812, though he still could have had a hand in the selection and editing of documents of the appendix. In fact, copies of the printed work appear to have been difficult to obtain even for its authors, for we find Samuel Davis writing to Thomas Wallace, at the Board of Control, asking, as a favour and in recognition of 'the part I had in preparing the Fifth Report, for half a dozen copies of the Report . . . for the use of myself and some Indian friends.'[71]

C. H. Philips attributes major influence to Cumming as the initiator of the Board's adoption of Munro's positions on Madras revenue and judicial policies. He also says that John Sullivan was Cumming's ally in this strategic shift against the Bengal system.[72] It is not difficult to understand the influence that Sullivan was able to exert, for he had long experience in Madras, had written an important book on policy (*Tracts Upon India*) in 1795, was the nephew of the powerful East India Company director Laurence Sullivan,[73] was brother-in-law of Lord Buckinghamshire, President of the Board from 1812 and, formerly, as Lord Hobart, governor of Madras. Moreover, he was a Parliamentary commissioner (constituency: Old Sarum) on the Board from 1806.[74] His career was very successful.

He joined the service in Madras in 1765,[75] and in 1780 won the profitable

[69] MC, F/151/21, Cumming to Munro, 10 August (?)1812.

[70] Ibid., Cumming to Munro, 12 November 1812, the date is supplied in Munro's hand; the emphasis is mine.

[71] Newcastle, Northumberland Record Office, *Letters of Thomas Wallace*, ZMI, S.76/2/17, Samuel Davis to Wallace, 17 September 1812.

[72] Philips, pp. 203, 204, 211.

[73] Ibid., p. 102n.

[74] L. Melville (ed.), *The Huskisson Papers* (London: Constable, 1931), Biographical Appendix, pp. 343–4 and Sutherland, *East India Company*, p. 59.

[75] Sutherland, *East India Company*, p. 59. On one of his journeys to India he travelled

appointment of Resident and paymaster of the Tanjore Company garrison with the patronage of Warren Hastings.[76] During part of that time he also conducted secret negotiations with the Rani of Mysore against Haidar Ali,[77] and one of his sons, John, a coadjutor of Munro after 1816 as a member of the Madras civil service, took up the cause of 'India's princes' in the middle of the nineteenth century.[78] In *Tracts* Sullivan gave a favourable report on the work of Read in the Baramahal, though he was somewhat mistaken about the latter's views on poligars.[79] Contact with India continued after leaving the Company service through his relationship with Lord Hobart, whose daughter he had married in 1798 and whose agent he was in England while Hobart was in Madras.[80] Sullivan became under-secretary of state for war and colonies in 1801, under the sponsorship of Henry Dundas; he also served as commissioner on the Board of Control in 1806, and then for an extended period from 1812 to 1837. He was a strong supporter of Lord Wellesley in Parliament when charges were brought in 1806, and this seems to have been his only active participation in the House of Commons over his long tenure there.[81] Sullivan remained intellectually active and capable until his death at the age of ninety, and was a valuable resource to be called upon and reckoned with as late as 1832, when he presented a vigorous statement on revenue systems in India before the House of Commons committee hearing evidence on the charter renewal of 1833.[82]

Distinction and money were possibly the movers for Sullivan as they were for Cumming, but it is impossible not to also credit the curiosity and intellectual

---

the Tigris River by raft and his account of this exploit is cited by Thomas Love Peacock in his advocacy of a later project to use the Tigris as a steam link with India in 1834: Felix Felton, *Thomas Love Peacock* (London: George Allen and Unwin, 1913), p. 233.

[76] British Library, Private Correspondence of Lord Macartney, Ad. MS. 22455, Macartney to John Sullivan, 5 January 1782.

[77] *HMS*, v. 174, 557–60 and 605–18; ibid., v. 179, pp. 449–654; and ibid., v. 788, pp. 248ff. Also G. Liscomb, *The History and Antiquities of the Country of Buckinghamshire* (London: Robins, 1847), p. 519.

[78] IOL, 'Tracts, No. 549', *Are We Bound by Our Treaties; A Plea for the Princes of India, 1853.*

[79] Sullivan, *Tracts Upon India*, pp. 278ff.

[80] Aylesbury Record Office, *Abstract Papers*, D/MH/ India/K. The cover on this bundle of letters notes that Sullivan was Hobart's agent and from 1794 kept Hobart informed on political developments relating to India. Many of these letters were from Richings Park, Iver, Buckinghamshire, which Sullivan bought in 1786, according to William Page (ed.), *The Victorian History of the Countries of England; Buckinghamshire.* (London St Catherine Press, 1925), v. 3, p. 290.

[81] British Library, Wellesley Papers, Ad. MS. 37309, Lord Buckinghamshire to Wellesley, 16 June 1806.

[82] Great Britain, Parliamentary Papers, *1831–32, Reports from Committees*, v. 2, *East India Company Affairs*, part 3, 'Revenue Minutes of Evidence', Appendix no. 8, pp. 49ff.

mastery of both men regarding the complexity of governance problems facing the Company in India at the turn of the nineteenth century. These were motives for Munro and for many of his colleagues in India, as well as for a handful of men in England. Preparations for the difficult charter debates in 1813 provided the spur and the opportunity for men of very different experience, but of similar class and social standing as Munro, Sullivan and Cumming, to advance themselves by their wit and energies. These qualities in each became evident in early 1813. Then, the task was not merely to present cogent reasons for the continuation of the Company charter with as little change as possible, but also to frame a different basis for the governance of India. The first of these objectives is well explored in standard historical works of that period; not so the second.

The major point of attack upon the Company in 1813 was launched against its monopoly. This was well organized through petitions submitted to Parliament in 1812 and 1813.[83] It was some of these petitions from delegations of major ports outside London that Munro had begun to examine in 1812, and with respect to which he drafted his long memorandum against the opening of Indian trade to British outports. This was also the basis of much of his testimony before the committees of the Commons and Lords.[84]

In his evidence before the Select Committee of the House of Lords on 7 April 1813, with Lord Buckinghamshire in the chair, Munro spoke of the dangers of the unrestricted access of European merchants to the interior of India. The most serious danger was that such men, without knowledge of the customs and the sensibilities of Indians, would jeopardize 'the high respect that the natives feel for the European character . . . one of the main pillars of our government'.[85] Further, unless European goods became much cheaper, only a small increase in the demand for them was conceivable and that only as a result of the natural increase of population, not from any change in Indian tastes. This was the position he had worked out in his memorandum on trade and the outports. On police, he extolled the 'ancient' system of local police and condemned the late development of a professional police force under the supervision of the courts. In these committee sessions Munro reiterated his notions about a rural class structure of three broad income groups; the secure conditions of Muslims and women in the society of the CD; the need to maintain European officers over sepoy forces in the armies of the Company and to

[83] *Journals of the House of Commons*, v. 67–8, Session of 1812–13.

[84] IOL, *East India Company Charters, Minutes of Evidence taken before the Right Honourable the House of Lords* [and Commons meeting as a Committee of the Whole and the Select Committee of Commons] *on the East India Company's Affairs* (London: Court of Directors of the East India Company, 1813, V/26/220/1). Munro's testimony, pp. 69–83, 105–22. 140–49; also found in Great Britain, Parliamentary Papers, *House of Commons, Session 1812–13*, v. 7, Munro's testimony: 12–15 April, pp. 121–57 and 167–75.

[85] *East India Company Charters*, p. 72.

encourage sepoys to believe that they were part of a European force; and the need, too, to gratify ambitions and aspirations of European officers in Company armies in relation to Crown officers in India (an oblique reference to the 'white mutiny' of 1809).[86]

Asked by a committee chairman, S. R. Lushington, whether Indian civilization was likely to be improved by an opening of trade with Europe, Munro offered a strong anti-Orientalist view that would have pleased one of the members of the committee, Charles Grant, in some ways, but disturbed him and other evengelicals in others.

> I do not exactly understand what is meant by the civilization of Hindoos; in the higher branches of science, in the knowledge of the theory and practice of good government, and in education, which by banishing prejudice and superstition, opens the mind to receive instruction of every kind, from every quarter, they are inferior to Europeans; but if a good system of agriculture, unrivalled manufacturing skill, a capacity to produce whatever can contribute to convenience or luxury, schools established in every village, for teaching reading, writing and arithmetic; the general practice of hospitality and charity among each other, and above all a treatment of the female sex, full of confidence, respect and delicacy, are among the signs which denote civilized people, then the Hindoos are not inferior to the nations of Europe; and if civilization is to become an article of trade between the two countries, I am convinced that this country will gain by the import cargo.[87]

Again, when he was asked by Lushington whether European traders would cause a disturbance in the interior, Munro responded that only one private trader had ever come to the CD during his many years there. That man was temporarily provided with a house that had been vacated by one who had gone on a pilgrimage. When the pilgrim returned, the European refused to vacate until Munro ordered him off. Munro concluded his anecdote with: 'it was fortunate that he [the private trader] was a Dane, had he been an Englishman he would most probably have kicked out the owner, for presuming to molest an Englishman in his castle and it would have required a suit of law to eject him.'[88]

John Sullivan presided over another session before which Munro gave evidence. Under the cover of a set of questions on the relation of inheritance rules to capital accumulation, Munro was encouraged to comment upon differences among zamindari, ryotwari and mootadari revenue systems, and the superiority of ryotwari over the others. Sullivan's questions also permitted Munro to provide a creditable review of much of his CD administration, emphasizing the success of his system and the basis of his experience and competence to comment upon all administrative systems.

[86] Ibid., pp. 77–8; 204; 208–10; 211; 213.

[87] Testimony, House of Commons, 12 and 14 April 1813, pp. 199–257 and *Charters of the East India Company*, p. 217.

[88] *Charters of the East India Company*, pp. 227–8.

Sullivan's evocation of Munro's authoritativeness should be seen as a public exercise of what was being privately pursued within the Board of Control, again on Sullivan's initiative, and at East India House in 1813 and 1814, a process which led to Munro's appointment as head of a commission to reconstruct the Madras administration. Throughout 1813 Munro worked to provide expert arguments for Lord Buckinghamshire and the Board to use in support of the Board's bid to seize control over Indian policy formation and to initiate great changes in the governance of India. The new charter of 1813 was to become the charter for an entire recasting of the British government in India as far as the Board was concerned.

Evidence of these labours in 1813 are contained in one large file of the Munro papers at the IOL, along with some of his correspondence of the time.[89] Most of the papers are undated notes for his own use. However, most must have been composed in 1813, and several were probably composed in close consultation with John Ravenshaw, as well as with Cumming and Sullivan. Ravenshaw had returned to England from Madras on furlough in 1813 after serving as principal collector of South Arcot from 1805. In England he had not only proved a highly competent ally for Munro, one dedicated to ryotwar and regarded as among the most competent civilians in Madras, but he also carried with him a long report which he had submitted to the Madras Board of Revenue in October 1812, on the question of ryotwar in relation to extant judicial procedures. Munro commented in great detail on that report and used it as independent evidence against positions he was attacking.[90]

Several of Munro's memoranda of around 1813 comment interestingly on his own earlier papers. Among the latter so treated was his report to the MBOR of 25 August 1805. His 1813 notes on this document were intended to underline contrasts between ryotwar and zamindari arrangements present in the 1805 report, as well as to raise some points not in the original, early argument. Among the last were the standing of 'potails' (village headmen) as a local gentry and thus a manifestation of gradations in society under ryotwar, and the appropriateness of Kanara as a model for other parts of Madras in establishing the average size of private estates that might be expected elsewhere. He also admitted the possibility that a more certain and swift realization of

[89] Papers are in MC, F/151/125; correspondence is in MC, F/151/144 and 145 covering the years 1810–24.

[90] Ravenshaw summarized his career in 1814, in connection with an appeal to the Court of Directors for a restoration of his 1805 salary retrenched at the same time as Munro's. Interestingly, Ravenshaw built his argument on the same basis as Munro had—the special difficulties of the situations which he was called to administer. One was Kanara, as one of Munro's two successors there in 1800, on which he wrote: 'your memorialist found the Province by no means in a settled state [as Munro had proclaimed that it was!], either in regard to internal peace or revenue. . . .' He made the same kind of argument about South Arcot, to which district he followed two of Munro's Baramahal colleagues, Macleod and Graham, and spoke of their failures. See, MC, F/151/27 for a copy of Ravenshaw's printed submission to the directorate in 1814.

private landed proprietorship and profitability would occur under a village lease system, but insisted that ryotwar was superior in the long term because 'waste', the vast uncultivated, cultivable land remained in the hands of the state for future revenue appropriation.

His report of 15 August 1807 received similar treatment, along with a copy of William Thackeray's report of 15 May 1806 to Lord Bentinck favouring permanent ryotwari settlements.[91] All contain marginal notes intended to emphasize or extend some point previously made. Among these are that 'potails' have more influence with ordinary ryots then either a zamindar or a poligar, and that this influence could be used by the government because the inams of headmen were resumable by government; or, 'we ought also to maintain ryotwari in order to raise up active, energetic and intelligent [European] *collectors*'.[92]

This evidence from 1813 is disappointing in one way, i.e. on account of Munro's derisive rather than incisive remarks on the papers of John Hodgson, his most trenchent Madras critic. Comments on Hodgson are found throughout the file of his papers on ryotwar, though most are concentrated in a set of his notes entitled 'Notes on the 5th Report', twelve folio pages. Some of these comments and criticisms of Hodgson are merely carping quibbles, or they are sarcastic; they are not serious refutations of Hodgson's argument. An example is his comment on the Hodgson-authored MBOR's report of 11 July 1808, opposing any continuation of ryotwar and favouring a village-lease system. In that report there is a banal statement quoting the Tanjore Commission of 1807, also headed by Hodgson, that 'a combination of circumstances' makes accuracy difficult in the calculation of capital accumulation by farmers in Tanjore. Munro seized on this with the comment: 'This is indeed a combination, but it is a combination of the Committee['s] own making—a person of less knowledge than these gentlemen would suppose that rent might be fixed by the average produce and that this average would be pretty well known in the village. They talk as if the earth had just been created and the seasons began for the first time to fluctuate. . . .' He notes Hodgson's concession in the latter's report on Tinnevelly of 24 September 1807 that ryotwar seems to work in predominantly dry-cropped districts and observes: 'It appears that Mr Hodgson admits that a Rayetwar rent may be established in a District consisting chiefly of dry land, but with the exception of Bengal, Tanjore and some other Districts the greater part of India is this description and derives its revenue *more from dry than from wet cultivation*. . . .' Then Munro comments: 'Mr Ravenshaw's rayetwar settlements in the Carnatic [i.e. South Arcot] show that there is no incompatibility of rayetwar and mirasi tenure as Hodgson claimed.'[93]

[91] 'Memorandum on Ryotwar and Zamindar from the Report of 25 August 1805', paras, 7, 19, 4; and *The Fifth Report*, v. 3, pp. 455–65.

[92] MC, F/151/125, on Thackeray, 15 May 1806, f. 3, 114, and notes on his own report of 15 August 1807, ff. 3–4, emphasis in original.

[93] MC, F/151/125, in a bundle of Munro papers entitled by Ravenshaw, 'Papers on Ryotwar System', 27 pp., of which the portion quoted is from p. 23, emphasis in original.

As already noted, Hodgson's papers form a substantial portion of *The Fifth Report*. These papers advocated a village system of revenue settlement on the grounds that this was the historical system of South India, thus presenting a counter-historical case to that proposed by Munro. In addition, Hodgson's papers cast reasonable and persistent doubt upon the practicability of vesting all executive powers in the single person of the collector. Finally, Hodgson argued, again with persuasive clarity, that the village system would bring immediate benefits to cultivators and would raise a stratum of local men—village headmen who were prospective village renters—to the status of a substantial and dispersed class of landowners. He conceded that such a class might also emerge under ryotwar, but only doubtfully, and after a very long time. On both these points Munro agreed.

Cumming went to considerable lengths to discredit Hodgson's views. This suggests that Hodgson stood well within the London counsels of the Company, and therefore required continuous denigration. While there is no direct evidence on the matter, it may have been that Hodgson had made an impact upon some of the directors and others within the Company during his furlough there from 1808 to 1810. He was in England during the meetings of the Select Committee of the House of Commons then, but he does not appear among the witnesses called to give evidence. Perhaps this was because the brief of that committee, formed in March 1808, was to investigate the increasing Indian debt of the Company and the failure of remittances from India to liquidate the debt owing to the continued high costs of warfare in India.[94] In any case, Hodgson had returned to Madras before Cumming's composition of the Madras section of *The Fifth Report*, though even if Hodgson had been permitted to remain longer in England, as Munro was, he might have been able to do little to blunt Cumming's artful attacks on his views in the *Report*.

Hodgson, perhaps rightly, was made to bear the brunt of growing criticisms of the village-lease system that had been substituted for ryotwar in the CD and in some other districts of Madras in 1808. As the most able and knowledgeable of the revenue officials in Madras who opposed Munro, Hodgson's writings had to be included in the appendix of *The Fifth Report*. These, either in his name or that of the MBOR—which body for some years he dominated—occupy a significant place in that work. The rescision of ryotwar in the CD and elsewhere followed upon a letter to Sir George Barlow, Bentinck's successors, from the MBOR, two of whose three members were Hodgson and Thackeray. The latter had presumably come to accept Hodgson's arguments on revenue problems in Coimbatore and Tinnevelly and also his reservations about Munro's report of 15 August 1807. The MBOR letter of 1808 proceeded to offer arguments against Munro's position, and finally it was declared in paragraph 31 that 'the transition from ryotwar to village rents, as suggested by Mr Hodgson, appears to us best adopted to secure the revenue of the state and the prosperity of the country.[95]

[94] Philips, pp. 178–9.

[95] *The Fifth Report*, v. 3, pp. 431–7, wrongly dated on p. 437 as 1801 rather than 1808.

The MBOR report of 1808 observed that it had previously, in 1806, opposed a zamindari settlement for Madras and had agreed that a ryotwar settlement was to be preferred in newly acquired territories as a means of 'remedying the inveterate abuses of the Mahomedan government'. However, the Report continued, under ryotwar there was the 'difficulty, if not the impossibility of one collector being able to attend to all of the legal formalities'. The expense of ryotwar as a system and its other problems were 'found insurmountable embarrassments to a ryotwar mode of administration'.[96] Hence, the village system ('mozawar') was recommended to government in 1806. This mode of revenue settlement was commended as the ancient system of the country, as one based upon the village, 'a petty commonwealth', and as one which would guard against overassessment because of the interests of the village renter, who was the 'head inhabitant' of exisiting villages. The appropriation of some of Munro's key phrases to make an opposing argument in this and other of Hodgson's papers of the time is evident. Several of the latter are included in the appendix of *The Fifth Report*, but the strategic final place in the entire Madras appendix is given to Thackeray's long paper of August 1807, written prior to the latter's apostasy to the village scheme.[97] Thackeray was set to answer many of the Hodgson objections to ryotwar, and he ended his paper by recommending to Bentinck that a permanent ryotwar system be established in Madras. This recommendation was made the final word and assessment of *The Fifth Report*.

That conclusion of the Madras documentary appendix and the last portions of the Madras section of *The Fifth Report* uncover the line of argument informing the whole: the inherent superiority of ryotwar. Noting that over the years the 'zemindarry principle' was at various times questioned by Madras officers, it was not until Munro's report of 15 August 1807 that a 'specific and detailed plan' for a real alternative was tabled, that of permanent ryotwar. This plan was considered by the MBOR and hastily—without proper consultation either with experienced collectors in India or the Court of Directors—rejected in favour of triennial village leases. This proposal for village leases and the rejection of ryotwar was supported by an erring Madras government, notwithstanding the previous endorsement of ryotwar by Bentinck and by 'persons serving under the Government, in the revenue department, whose local knowledge and experience entitled their opinions to much attention; they [the Select Committee] consider, that the House [of Commons] would desire to be made acquainted with what has passed on the subject'.[98] Bentinck's report of 29 April 1806, recommending permanent ryotwar. Thackeray's report and Bentinck's endorsing minute had won the approbation of the Court of Directors in their letter to Madras of 30 August 1809, the *Report* continued, and Bentinck, meanwhile, had also charged Hodgson with the preparation of

[96] Ibid., para. 33, p. 434 and para. 36, p. 435.
[97] Ibid., pp. 437–47; 470–98; 526–60; 561–2.
[98] Ibid., v. 1, p. 307.

a memoir on the entire question which 'production may be considered a reply to the remarks of Mr Thackeray'. Curiously, however, Thackeray's report, to which Hodgson's memoir is considered a reply, is given the final argumentative place in the Madras section of *The Fifth Report*, as it has in the Madras appendix of that work. Equally curiously, Kanara took a leading place in the Select Committee s argument for ryotwar in the same way that it had in Munro's papers after 1805.[99]

TOWARDS NEW POWER

It is ironic that Thackeray should have occupied the anchoring place in Cumming's argument for ryotwar in *The Fifth Report* since it had become clear to many, including Munro, that Thackeray had ceased to be an advocate of Munro's system and had become persuaded by Hodgson's arguments for a village-lease system. His conversion is attested in the MBOR report of 1808 with its advocacy of the latter system, to which Thackeray was a signatory, and became yet more clear in a letter of his to Munro in England. Thackeray wrote in January 1810: 'The village rent which has been almost generally introduced is not so good as your [not *our*] ryotwari managed by you, but it is better than ryotwari managed indifferently under a controlin' power such as we exercise . . . you were the ablest revenue man we ever had and had unbounded authority. . . .'[100] And in July he wrote: 'your system is the best abstractly. It is the best as far as regards the country itself; it is not with respect to our gov[ernmen]t'.[101] From Fredrick Gahagan, an old protege and successor in the CD, Munro had a letter in 1813 confirming this desertion by Thackeray. Gahagan asked Munro whether he had seen Thackeray, then in England on furlough, and said that Thackeray had become 'a terrible [village]-lease-monger', a judgement he apparently sought to soften with: 'he never was of the same opinion for six months. . . .'[102]

Thackeray was not nearly as fickle as Gahagan charged; he had a view about the overall political and administrative structure of Madras that was different and possibly very realistic. This he expressed to Munro with considerable percipience and wit in 1810:

> Our gov[ernmen]t is one of form, private interest, of rise by seniority, a corporation gov[ernmen]t of senior merchants, junior merchants and factors who must be employed . . . [and] a right to be moderately stupid by act of Parl[iament]. How the gov[ernment] is to find men among them to be Collectors, upon the old footing [as enjoyed by Munro], with unbounded authority, that is to be Legislators, Judges, Financiers, Princes of large provinces to unite in their own persons all the authority, duties, and functions

[99] Ibid., pp. 310–12.
[100] MC, F/151/20, Thackeray to Munro, 19 January 1810.
[101] Ibid., 16 July 1810.
[102] MC, F/151/22, Gahagan to Munro, 17 September 1814.

of Civil Gov[ernmen]t I cannot imagine. I know them all pretty well . . . a great many well-meaning, honest, moderately industrious and moderately well-informed young gentlemen. Many who will be in a few years capable to fill the office of Zillah judges, several who are now quite capable of that of collector on its present footing, but hardly one fit to be the prince which the collector was formerly. This is the real cause of changes in the system, the others that are assigned in the public writings were pretenses. We must not therefore attack the Bengallees upon other grounds. Having now been three years in some measure behind the curtain at Madras, I have seen how the puppets are played, and I own that I am disposed to think very differently than I did before I was initiated. The Gov[ernmen]t must consider the relation in which they stand to the laws and Gov[ernmen]t at home as well as to this country—they must consider the Europeans they have to manage, as well as the Hindoos they have to govern. It is the most difficult task to manage these Europeans properly.[103]

Letters such as these from Munro's men in Madras, their pessimism and mounting cynicism, stand in contrast to the vigorous and possible naive optimism of men like Cumming and even Sullivan in London. If supporters of his ideas were becoming shaky, those in London, especially those connected with the Board of Control, were becoming Munro-men and, by 1813, they were pressing for an entire recasting of Madras administration under Munro's leadership. The Presidency of the Board of Control had now passed into the active, not to say impetuous, hands of the Earl of Buckinghamshire. With Sullivan as his coadjutor, this assured powerful backing from that quarter. The Directorate from 1812 to 1814 was chaired by three men—Hugh Inglis, Robert Thornton, and W. F. Elphinstone—chosen by the divided directors for their seniority and conciliatory ways and thus not likely to block Buckinghamshire's purposes.[104]

With the charter renewed for another twenty years and with far less lost by the Company than was feared, except, perhaps, for the failure to prevent the evangelical alliance of directors and MPs from opening British India to missionaries, Buckinghamshire was pleased. He considered the passage of the 1813 charter act as a personal triumph and could anticipate no serious opposition to his plans to alter things in India. On this he boasted in the draft of an early dispatch to be sent to India, explaining the new act. There he stated that the 1813 act established the Board as ascendant to the Court of Directors, and this immediately brought a coalescense among directors of such strength as to deny some of his fondest wishes.[105]

Among these was the appointment of his friend, Thomas Wallace, to the governorship of Madras. Wallace, like Sullivan, was a paid Parliamentary commissioner on the Board. Buckinghamshire was forced to yield on Wallace

[103] Ibid., Thackeray to Munro, 19 January 1810.
[104] Philips, p. 183.
[105] Ibid., pp. 18–91.

and to accept the appointment of Hugh Elliot, a brother of the Governor-General, Lord Minto, and an uncle of Buckinghamshire's wife, as a compromise candidate.[106]

Though in frequent, often violent, disagreement with the directorate during the first years of his presidency of the Board of Control, Buckinghamshire actually shared the outlook of the majority about the administration of the Company's territories in India. In particular, he shared with most the undesirability of any proliferation of the Bengal system, and thus he placed himself against Wellesley and in support of Bentinck on Madras. With the encouragement of Sullivan and the support of Cumming, Buckinghamshire decided that reform should be pursued, and he was prepared to follow Cumming in the establishment of 'the system advocated by Munro', as Philips put it, in all Company territories except Bengal.[107]

This radical approach was resisted by most directors who favoured a slower schedule of reform, beginning with the appointment of a 'special committee' of Directors in 1812 to frame reform proposals. This special committee eventually drafted a revision of the Madras judicial system, proposing a special commission in 1814 empowered to frame revenue and judicial changes in Madras with Munro at its head.[108]

Munro's appointment as 'Principal Commissioner for the Revision of the Internal Administration of the Madras Territories' in May 1814 culminated a political process lasting nearly two years within and about the Company's affairs in India.[109] As a result of Cumming's publicity of Munro's writings on revenue, justice, and the police in Madras, there was a growing interest about the same things within the directorate. The 'special committee on revenue, judicial and political affairs' in Madras, as one hostile director labelled it, was set up in 1812.[110] Even before that, it seems that some directors had become aware of Munro's work and curious about his views. Early in 1812 William M'Cullock, assistant to the Company's examiner of Indian correspondence, sent a 'treatise' to Munro for his comments at the behest of (now Sir) Hugh Inglis, the deputy chairman of the Court of Directors and chairman after April 1812. This dealt with land revenue, and M'Cullock reminded Munro of his earlier conversation with Inglis on CD rents. The 'treatise' was intended to form the basis for a dispatch destined for the Governor-General, and Munro was asked to provide a draft for the portion dealing with land revenues under native governments, and the principles as well as the details of his arrangements in the CD from 1800 to 1807. He was also asked for any other papers he might have, especially on sources of revenue other than from the land.[111] Munro

[106] Ibid., pp. 195–6.

[107] Ibid., p. 203.

[108] Ibid.

[109] This is Munro's version of the title, taken from his summary of his services, cited in Gleig, v. 1, p. xix.

[110] IOL, *Appendixes of Court Minutes, Copies of Dissents*, v. 3, B/239, 1 April 1814.

[111] MC, F/151/21, 16 January 1812.

seems not only to have supplied the papers sought, but also his comments upon the papers of others on the same subjects.

In fact, almost none of the papers comprising the Madras appendix of *The Fifth Report* appears to have escaped Munro's comment for Inglis and others who sought his views in 1813–14. The major portion of a file in the Munro collection at the IOL is devoted to comment upon Hodgson's papers. These seem to have been prepared while Munro was still in England, probably in late 1813 and early 1814.[112] It is also probable that his copious notes and comments were intended for the use of Cumming and Sullivan, at the Board, as well as for some directors. This last is indicated by M'Cullock's letter already referred to as well as by the bitter denounciation of the 'special committee' of directors by another director, John Hudleston, in 1814.

Hudleston, an MP, a former Madras civil servant and a director of the Company from 1803 to 1826, had objected twice, in formal dissents, to the judicial dispatch which was prepared for Madras in 1814 and was meant to serve as Munro's brief as judicial commissioner.[113] In a forty-page dissent against the approval of the majority of the directors of the proposed dispatch, recomended by the 'special committee' of directors, Hudleston charged that Munro's system was nothing more than what he did in the remote and unimportant CD. Moreover, Munro's notions had, or should have had, no greater standing than those of other Madras officials who argued otherwise and supported the existing judicial system of Madras.[114] In a later dissent to the same judicial dispatch, Hudleston also objected to the usurpatious extension of the Board of Control's authority over the directors to issue instructions to its servants in India, and particularly to the Board's substitution of a draft judicial dispatch, which he claimed was already objectionable on practical as well as on principled grounds, with an even worse one conferring enormous judicial powers upon the office of Collector. All of this violated the wisdom of Cornwallis and British constitutional practice, he argued.

Hudleston also objected to recommendations from the special committee for creating a commission 'which vests in Lieutenant Colonel Munro the efficient power both in the Revenue and Judicial Departments' of Madras. This commission that Munro was the head was 'wholly unnecessary', but even if it were necessary, why go to the army for its president, Hudleston asked.

[112] MC, F/151/125, 'Papers on Ryotwar System' contained the following comments of Munro: on Lionel Place's Chingleput report of 6 June 1799 (App. 16) of *The Fifth Report*, v. 3; MBOR, 'Instructions to Collectors', 15 October 1799 (App. 18); John Wallace's report on Tanjore and Trichy, 15 June 1806 and 8 September 1805 (App. 20 and 26); H. S. Graeme on North Arcot, 18 October 1806 (App. 20); George Harris, on Tanjore, 9 May 1804 (App. 25); 'Report of the Tanjore Committee', 22 February 1807 (App. 31); John Hodgson on Tinnevelly, 24 September 1807, on Dindigal, 28 March 1807, on Coimbatore, 18 September 1807, on Peddapore, 23 November 1805 (App. 25 and 31).

[113] IOL, *Court* [of Directors] *Minutes, 1814* B/159, pp. 104–11, 'Secret Court of 11 May 1814'.

[114] IOL, *Appendixes to Court Minutes, Copies of Dissents*, B/239, 1 April 1814.

Recalling Lionel Place's condemnation of a decade earlier, Hudleston charged that Munro's selection denigrated the character and abilities of Madras civil officials who, with qualifications equal to Munro's had the misfortune of being unknown in England. Among these, Hudleston named John Hodgson and George Stratton, and asked why they 'should be passed by or required to serve in their own Departments under a military officer'.[115] Stratton did serve on Munro's commission, and Hodgson was a member of the MBOR during Munro's governorship.

Correspondence of the year 1814 confirmed Hudleston's assessment of the strong position which Munro had attained. His letters of this time are a remarkable contrast to lamenting ones to his sister in 1812, when he spoke of his disgust of his life as an 'idler'. By then, however, he had had M'Cullock's letter of January 1812, relating Inglis' request for a draft dispatch for India, an inquiry that hinted at Munro's entry into the highest levels of policy determination in the Company.[116] This draft is not among extant Munro papers, though it is frequently mentioned.

Munro was also involved with Robert Dundas during the latter's final months in the presidency of the Board of Control. They discussed Munro's testimony before the Select Committees.[117] Another person with whom he was involved then was John Bannerman, a director and former Madras soldier of poligar war fame, who had become a booster of Munro as a potentially valuable witness.[118] Yet another old Madras military colleague who had risen to the office of director as well as being an MP, Alexander Allan, was scheduling Munro for testimony on several matters, including trade and the army, and also arranging meetings with Chairs of the Court of Directors and with Lord Buckinghamshire—who was soon to succeed Dundas at the Board. Allan was also in close contact with Munro on the proposal then abroad to offer him the governorship of St Helena, on which Allan agreed with John Sullivan that Munro should reject that offer and await something higher in India.[119]

The arrangements of his testimony, the St Helena appointment, and other matters that brought involvement with the great names involved with India at this time prompted his old Baramahal colleague, James G. Graham, to ask Munro to use some influence to secure Graham a regiment to command: 'as you appear to have powerful *friends* both in the Direction and the Board. . . .'[120] But mere influence on policy was not Munro's chief objective between 1812

[115] Ibid.

[116] Other letters of the time indicate more and regular contact with Inglis, e.g., Mark Wilks to Munro 16 May 1812 saying that Inglis had asked whether Munro had read some papers he had sent, MC, F/151/21.

[117] MC, F/151/21, Cumming to Munro, 2 March 1812, regarding Dundas, now Lord Melville.

[118] MC, F/151/21, Bannerman to Munro, 2 March 1812.

[119] Ibid., 14 March 1812 and 19 July 1812.

[120] Ibid., 18 December 1812.

and 1814. It was attainment of a distinguished appointment in India. The culmination of that striving was his appointment as head of the commission appointed in 1814. Before that, however, there were other possibilities and other signs of his high favour with those who ruled India from England. As 1812 drew to a close and the long deferred Parliamentary debates on the charter neared, the tempo of correspondence and contact with the powerful intensified. From his sister Erskine in Edinburgh he learned of a conversation which she and her husband, Henry Erskine, had with William Fullerton Elphinstone, and the latters' reassurance that Munro's interests would be attended by the chairman Hugh Inglis. Elphinstone promised to write to the Governor-General on Munro's behalf and encouraged Henry Erskine, also a friend of Lord Moira, to do the same.[121]

Early in 1813 Munro was meeting Lord Buckinghamshire and others, including John Sullivan, in anticipation of Buckinghamshire's assumption of the presidency of the Board of Control. Among the matters discussed was a plan to oppose the decision by the Madras government, on 29 January 1812, to extend village leases from three to ten years, according to a report years later by the elder Sullivan.[122] Cumming wrote then, in February 1813, about Buckinghamshire's esteem and praise for Munro which the latter had expressed to a ministerial colleague. Cumming also extended Buckinghamshire's invitation to Munro for a meeting in Whitehall in order to discuss the introduction of ryotwar into the 'Ceded and Conquered' Gangetic territories.[123]

During his appearances before the Parliamentary hearing on the charter, Munro's expertise on many aspects of India brought invitations for discussions at India House. One extended by the Company's Committee of Warehouses was to discuss Indian cotton production; another pertained to the Madras army, and an appeal from his friend Thomas Dallas to use his influence with the directors for increasing allowances to officers in Madras in order to reduce the dangerous demoralization in the army. A similar request on behalf of the Company's Madras officers came from Alexander Allan, himself a director, who asked Munro to use his apparently superior influence at the Board of Control on behalf of army colleagues.[124]

In August 1813 Munro was asked by Thomas Wallace, an active candidate for the Madras governorship, whether he would accept a post in his government should he receive that appointment:[125] Wallace offered any post except that of

[121] MC, F/151/150, Erskine to Munro, 11 November 1812.

[122] Great Britain, Parliamentary Papers, *House of Commons, Session 1831–32*, v. 2, 'Reports from the Committee on East India Company Affairs', part 3, 'Revenue Minutes of Evidence', Appendix 8, pp. 49ff, 'Observations on the Revenue Systems of India, by the Right Honourable John Sullivan, Richings Lodge,' 28 April 1832, p. 64.

[123] MC, F/151/21, 2 February 1813.

[124] Ibid., William Simons to Munro, 28 April 1813; Dallas to Munro, 5 and 26 July 1813; Allan to Munro, 23 February 1813.

[125] See the Wallace letter to Lord Liverpool, Prime Minister, 19 July 1813, and Liverpool to Wallace, 23 July 1813: British Library, Liverpool Papers, Ad. MS. 38410.

private secretary because Stephen R. Lushington, an ex-Madras civilian official and MP, had already spoken for that.[126] A week or so after this Munro wrote to John Sullivan about a meeting with Wallace and expressed chagrin that Wallace had offered him the town mayorship of Madras, which he spurned as a post appropriate for an officer of low rank, while he merited command of a corps. He did assure Sullivan that 'he would be happy with any position in a Wallace government'. Sullivan's answer to this was interesting in marking Munro's status then. He said that Wallace was very pleased at Munro's willingness to serve him in Madras because he thought that Munro's support was a way of countering Charles Grant's efforts (successful in the end) to block Wallace's appointment of the Madras government.[127] The Wallace appointment was supported by Lord Buckinghamshire, as already noted, and Cumming told Munro in October 1813 that, whether or not that appointment was approved by the directorate, there was a general feeling that Munro should return to India in a high station. He added another bit of information that presaged the sort of 'high station' in which Munro did return to India a year later: this was the convening of a special committee of directors to deal with judicial and political affairs in India. Cumming added that this committee would include John Hudleston.[128]

Minutes of the Court of Directors of 22 September 1813 record the decision to establish four 'special committees' to consider the financial implications of the recently renewed charter of the Company.[129] One of these was to be a committee on revenue, judicial, and political affairs, and its membership first included Hudleston, as Cumming reported. However, a series of complicated and perhaps rancorous moves excluded Hudleston (and James Pattison) from the six originally named. This committee did, however, include Charles Grant and Edward Parry, two stalwart defenders of the Bengal system.[130] It was the report of this committee, which Hudleston charged was biased in favour of Munro's views, that led to the commission and Munro's very 'high station' in India from 1814 to 1817. The committee did not include such directors as Elphinstone and Inglis—the former was chairman that year and the latter was now dead—who had supported Munro before, while it did include Grant and his friend Parry along with a sometime ally of Grant, George Smith, as potential spoilers of any majority for Munro.[131]

Grant had not changed his mind about the superiority of the Cornwallis judicial system of Bengal. In October 1813 he was reading Munro's papers and wrote to Munro:

[126] MC, F/151/21, Wallace to Munro, 7 August 1813.
[127] Northumberland Record Office, *Letters of Thomas Wallace*, S.76/10/1, Munro to Sullivan from Edinburgh, 16 August 1813, and Sullivan to Munro, 22 August 1813.
[128] MC, F/151/21, Cumming to Munro, n.d., October, 1813.
[129] Philips wrongly dated this decision as 1812, p. 203.
[130] IOL, *Court Book, September 1813–April 1814*, B/158, pp. 700–1 and 702–3.
[131] Embree, p. 234.

I see in them, many things which as coming from a well informed and discerning mind cannot fail to make an impression; but still I frankly own the remedies you propose do not equally recommend themselves to me. The question of a judicial system for our vast Indian population taken in connection with the nature of our general administration there and that principle of progressively improving the state of the people . . . seems to me a very deep one.[132]

Though not converted by Munro, Grant was obviously reading and listening. He was also aware of how persuasive other directors and, of course, those of the Board of Control, were finding Munro's proposals for reducing the costs as well as increasing the efficiency of the judicial system in India.

Cumming reported to Munro the enthusiasm with which his papers were being received, especially those on the relationship between revenue, judicial and police administration: 'Ryotwar is after all, the only system of revenue management compatable with the close administration of judicial, of fiscal, and of police affairs. . . . I am happy to tell you that your report on police which you prepared at Anantapur was received by the last ship; it arrived very opportunely.'[133] This letter of October 1813 ended with the surmise that Munro would certainly be called by the directors' special committee. Almost simultaneously, the deputy chairman of the Company, W. F. Elphinstone, did invite Munro's views for the benefit of the special committee on judicial affairs on how to reduce the costs of the judiciary.[134]

In those late months of 1813 Munro was engaged in the solicitation of votes for two friends in the coming April elections to the Court of Directors. He wrote to his sister and brother in Edinburgh for their help in electing Alexander Allan and Captain Hugh Lindsay-Bulcarry, the election of whom would be 'helpful to me and to [their nephew] John Munro hereafter'.[135] He told them that 'I have a strong friend in Mr Elphinstone, but I want more and Allan is a young man'.[136] Both Allan and Lindsay entered the directorate in April 1814,

The year 1813 closed with a letter from Lord Buckinghamshire thanking him for some papers and making an appointment for a meeting. This letter has a label in Munro's hand: 'To check about going [to India] with Mr E[lliot]. As there is nothing in the letter about that, it must have come up during their personal meeting later, for, indeed, the time was approaching when Munro must return to India. However, by year's end, what he would be doing there was not yet determined. Nor was it yet certain whether he would be living there with a wife, let alone who that might be.

Both matters were resolved in March and April 1814. Of his marriage to Jane Campbell, Munro told his brother in early March that he had formed a

[132] MC, F/151/21, Grant to Munro, 5 October 1813.
[133] Ibid., n.d., October 1813, Cumming to Munro.
[134] MC, F/151/21, W. F. Elphinstone to Munro, 5 October 1813.
[135] MC, F/151/145, Munro to Erskine, 24 November 1813.
[136] Ibid., Munro to Alexander Munro, 1 December 1813.

strong attachment to her and hoped to persuade her to accompany him to India when he departed in May, in the company of Hugh Elliot, the governor-designate of Madras.[137] By the end of that month he was wed; a marriage contract was filed on 29 March and the ceremony took place the next day.[138] The marriage contract recognized the differences in their ages—Munro was 53 years old—by making provisions for a settlement on his wife should she become widowed and choose to remarry, and also by providing for her transport back to Britain should Munro die outside the country. The trustees named to execute the contract were his brother, his long-time friend and financial counsellor George Brown, and Munro's brother-in-law (through his sister Margaret) George Drummond.

His appointment to head the commission for the revision of the internal affairs of Madras seems to have been as slow to be consummated as his courtship, and the final outcome was not certain until early May, in the month he was to depart.

Intimations of the formation of the judicial commission under his presidency came to Munro in February 1814, when Bannerman wrote to tell him that a 'committee to revise the judicial establishments in India' had been approved with Munro at its head, and also communicated some thoughts about keeping Munro in Madras after the expiry of the commission.[139]

At this time the brief for any such 'committee' or 'commission' was vague, and not surprisingly since there remained deep divisions among the directors about the entire matter. Cumming wrote to Munro in Scotland in February 1814 with the news that the directors had been informed by Lord Buckinghamshire that the Board was preparing a draft judicial dispatch for Madras.[140] There would be some delays in its finalization because it was deemed wise to await the return to England of Lord Minto and Sir George Barlow, the retired Governor-General and the recalled and humiliated governor of Madras, so that they too might be consulted. Cumming claimed that the chairmen , Robert Thornton and W. F. Elphinstone, were in favour of a judicial dispatch emanating from the Board, but that Grant and Parry were opposed to that as a usurpation of the directors' prerogative to frame Indian policy.

Cumming also reported to Munro that answers to queries which the Special Committee of the Court of Directors had circulated in India about judicial matters were coming back, and some twenty were in hand, mostly from Bengal servants.[141] Respondents had added nothing to the facts and opinions already known, but Cumming said that Lieutenant-Colonel Alexander Walker of the Madras army and Resident at Baroda, had offered the best suggestions and these were in accordance with Munro's argument about panchayats, or 'native

[137] Ibid., Munro to Alexander Munro, 3 March 1814.
[138] MC, F/151/154, marriage contract.
[139] MC, F/151/22, Bannerman to Munro, 17 February 1814.
[140] MC, F/151/33, Cumming to Munro, 11 February 1814.
[141] These queries and their responses are in *SEIHR*, v. 2.

juries'.[142] This February letter closed with Cumming's intelligence that Elliot, prospective governor of Madras, had been reading *The Fifth Report* in the Whitehall offices of the Board, at the suggestion of Cumming, and that since he and Elliot were to sail to Madras together, John Sullivan had offered to introduce them to each other. Finally on 4 May Alexander Allan reported that he and his colleagues on the directorate had passed the resolution for Munro to head the judicial commission for two years, with his salary and expenses to be set by the chairs and Buckinghamshire.[143] The latter subsequently fixed Munro's salary at SP10,000 plus expenses, based upon the salary and perquisites of a Resident, and they also offered as justification—for departing from the rule of not appointing soldiers to civil office—Munro's unique experience and qualifications.[144]

Grant had said that the question of an Indian judiciary, taken in relation to the general administration of British India, was a very deep one, and he had implied that he disagreed with Munro's answers. Yet he was also either unable or unwilling to block the advance of Munro's answers. Nor could he block his advance to the orienting centre of policy formation on this 'deep question'. Percipient man that he was, Grant was aware that a fundamental shift in that centre was occurring, or might have occurred by 1814. Officers of the Crown and Members of Parliament were now moving to the forefront of decision-making, replacing the heretofore almost unchallenged position of the self-selected and self-perpetuating Court of Directors. Grant had long been a master of that earlier system by dint of his clear purposes, his intelligence, and his abilities in speech and writing. These same qualities must also have persuaded him that there were at work simultaneous and fundamental changes in the governance of India, and by whom decisions about that were to be made. The Crown and established political forces in England were moving inexorably into control over Indian policy, not in the manner of Fox in 1784, which was fixated upon London with its powers and patronage perquisites, but in another way which recognized, as never before, the seriousness and complexity of the tasks of ruling India. There was abroad in the England of 1814 a sense that Munro, and people like him, could show the way to achieving a more secure British imperium. This was but a sense, however; much depended upon what Munro would do in India with his vague yet powerful brief.

When Munro embarked on the Indiaman *Prince Regent* in May 1814, with a new wife and in the company of Hugh Elliot, he had achieved all that he could have hoped for from this extended stay in Britain. He had married a woman with whom he was to enjoy a companionable and affectionate relationship for the rest of his life. He had found the distinguished situation that he yearned for,

[142] Walker was a sometime correspondent of Munro after 1817; he had served in the Madras army during the wars against Haidar Ali and Tipu Sultan, and from 1822 served as governor of St Helena: *DNB*, v. 20, pp. 499–500.

[143] MC, F/151/22, Allan to Munro, 4 May 1814.

[144] IOL, *Personal Records*, O/6/8, p. 632 and O/6/17, pp. 685–711.

to which friends like Sullivan had committed their help late in December 1812—when neither wife nor distinctive rank seemed within his reach. To Alexander, his brother, on the eye of his departure from Portsmouth, he passed some late news on the patronage which had been found for their nephew John Munro, who had a writership thanks to W. F. Elphinstone. He also reported that there had been great opposition to his appointment to the very last among many directors; that it had been carried because of the ability of Samuel Davis to persuade fellow directors, and because of the sympathetic intervention of Hugh Elliot on Munro's behalf.[145] This last bode well for the confrontation which he must expect from his old revenue and judicial opponents in Madras, when he appeared there with but a vague brief for overturning the administration of the Presidency.

145 MC, F/151/145, Munro to Alexander Munro, 9 May 1814.

Chapter Five

Judicial Commissioner

Munro returned to Madras in the middle of September 1814, accompanied by Jane Campbell Munro, a new wife, and Hugh Elliot, a new governor of the Presidency. He seemed optimistic about his official, if daunting, task of transforming the governance of Madras, beginning with revisions of legal and police procedures and extending to the broad and vaguely defined internal administration of Madras, including the restoration of ryotwar. He was armed with the directors' judicial letter to Madras of the previous April and with orders from the directors, going back to December 1812, for the restoration of ryotwar because village leases were thought to be responsible for a reduction of revenue and for oppression of cultivators by renters.[1]

His high expectations might have been thought rash. After all, his appointment as judicial commissioner came at the last hour before he was to depart England. Was this not a hint, perhaps, of the opposition among some of the directors to Munro himself, which John Hudleston, for one, took no pains to disguise, or to his reform brief? In addition, since 1805, he had known the hostility of the powerful senior officialdom of Madras; this must occasionally have raised qualms, for it was they that overthrew his ryotwar in 1808 and proved—as if that were necessary—that the entrenchment of those whom he had taught Cumming to call 'regulation men' was formidable.

Despite all this, his sanguinity was not unreasonable. Having spent seven years in England he was impressed as never before with the structure of Company rule which conferred upon the Court of Directors, and now Buckinghamshire's Board of Control, absolute executive authority to command its Indian officials. This authority was not merely constitutional, a delegation of sovereignty confirmed by the recent Charter; it was the power held as employers to dismiss any of its 'servants' in India. True, as an old India hand now, with thirty-four years of service in India under his 'Honourable masters', he was aware of how easy it was for the Company's senior servants

[1] Mukherjee, *Ryotwar System*, p. 95.

to seize mastery of local affairs by denying the imperatives of London if in no other way than by delay. Against this inerita and resistance in India, however, Munro had great confidence in Hugh Elliot, whom he had come to know in England and whom he had continued to instruct over the five-month voyage to Madras in 1814. More than that, there was the energetic and committed support of the Board of Control under Lord Buckinghamshire and his two friends James Cumming and John Sullivan at the Board's offices in Whitehall. On balance, the promise of great changes did not seem excessive.

However, it was to take two long years for the judicial and police changes directed by the board and accepted by the directors merely to be promulgated; yet more time was to be required for their establishment in practice. Still, when the magnitude of his tasks are measured and their underlying objectives appreciated, the struggle in which he was to be engaged was neither longer nor more strenuous and frustrating than required, for his was an attack upon the core institutions and values of the Madras civilian establishment.

The Madras judicature established in 1802 was to be modified by transferring police and general magisterial responsibilities from judges of district courts to collectors and by greatly enlarging the role of Indians in the adjudication of minor judicial causes. It was not intended by Munro or anyone else that these changes would displace the powerful judicial officialdom of the Presidency, represented most authoritatively by the judges of the Sadr Adalat ('Sudder Adawlut') court, nor would these changes diminish the power of the keepers of the sacred revenue of the Presidency, the Board of Revenue. These two pillars of the Madras colonial regime continued to bear all of the weight and authority they had always had, under even the broadest construction of Munro's brief in 1814. But beneath the manifest purposes of the judicial and police reforms lurked deeper questions implicitly posed to the custodians of the Madras regime, both in India and in England.

One was how a system of law—principles of procedure and of property—developed in capitalist and self-governing Britain could be made to work any better among a subject Indian people, powerless to affect the arbitrariness and extractive demands of the Company state, than it was working in Britain itself. It must be remembered that the later eighteenth century opened an extended 'age of riots' in Britain.[2] At the turn of the nineteenth century, when the colonial state was being constructed in India, the trustees over the British polity were more deeply worried about the spread of revolutionary doctrines from France than about French soldiers. Munro expressed this fear in respect of his sister at about the same time that Edmund Burke proclaimed it for Britain. Burke was then also formulating his solution to the dilemma that was being simultaneously faced in India: how to frame a law of procedure and property suited to a people without the political means to counter or to influence an arbitrary and increasingly extractive state. George III's realm was not less about the creation of a

[2] John Stevenson, *Popular Disturbances in England, 1700–1870* (London: Longman, 1979), chapter 2, 'The Age of Riots.'

modern, capitalist polity than India under Cornwallis, Wellesley, Minto and Moira was about the creation of a colonial polity.[3]

A second question lying behind the changes in law, police and revenue administration that Munro was charged by the directors to bring to pass pertained to the relationship between the metropolitan state in England and the colonial regime (or regimes) in India. The 1813 Charter insured that the Company would continue to provide the formal government of India; at the same time, however, the Board of Control, under the energetic Lord Buckinghamshire, had shifted the balance of power in decision-making for India from the Court of Directors to the ruling British ministry, an adjunct of which the board was. Great distance prevented the board from being any more immediately and effectively directive of affairs in India than the men of India House had been, but certainly, before the death of Buckinghamshire in February 1816, Munro could expect, and did receive, support for his approach to law and police changes from the Board of Control. This is documented in the stream of letters which he received from James Cumming and John Sullivan in London. Those from the latter were transmitted through Sullivan's son, John, now a confidant and colleague of Munro in Madras. Notwithstanding this shift in the basic relationship between the Company's Indian territories and superior authority in England, those in a position to influence the shape of the colonial regimes of India—whether in India or from England—could hardly seek a direction very different from anything understood and valued in British politics. Nonetheless, Munro had a degree of freedom and support denied to many of his predecessors in India, and this he exploited to the full during the first two years as judicial commissioner.

The broad objectives of reform for which he laboured from September 1814 to September 1816 were outlined in the judicial letter of 29 April 1814 from the directors. The tone and much of the content of this document were vague. As Munro knew, this reflected the limited enthusiasm for reform among several members of the special committee of directors by whom the judicial letter was drafted, including Charles Grant. Vagueness also reflected the principle, still conceded by most directors of the Company, that officials in India must have the freedom to exercise judgements about how policies contrived in London were to be implemented. This last was questioned by the Board of Control under Buckinghamshire and became a rancorous issue between the two London bodies.

The long judicial letter of 29 April was primarily concerned with the civil judicature of Madras (seventy paragraphs) and secondarily with police administration. The directors declared to the Madras government that they were motivated by a 'careful examination of your official records' and by a determination to reduce judicial and police charges; they also spoke of having been

[3] Asa Briggs, *The Age of Improvement, 1783–1867* (London: Longman, 1978), p. 1: 'The period from 1783 to 1867 was one of formative changes in the structure of the English economy, the shape of English society and the framework of government.'

guided in their considerations by Company servants from Madras then in England.[4]

The Madras judiciary was considered as much a failure as that of Bengal, and the remedies proposed in the directors' April letter were not thought to be 'departures from an ancient and long established order of things [with] the mischiefs that too often result from innovations'. They insisted that their recommendations were based upon extant and old practices for which Munro was their most frequently cited authority.

Near the beginning of the judicial letter, Munro's 15 August 1807 report to the MBOR was endorsingly cited, as other portions of this report had been in *The Fifth Report*.[5] Here Munro had made an argument for the use of Indians and of Indian institutions as the sole means to 'penetrate' that 'strange mixture of fraud and honesty in the natives of India'.[6] The directors agreed with Munro and with similar observations from John Ravenshaw, of 1808 and 1809, dealing with South Arcot. Ravenshaw was at one with Munro that 'the superior tribunals of England' were an inappropriate model for zillah (district) courts of Madras. Munro again was cited on the great inconvenience caused by the 'cumbersome formalities' of judicial procedures that compelled village headmen to neglect their local duties in order to attend upon British judges at often distant courts. To these the directors added other deficiencies in existing judicial practice: the outrageous backlog of unsettled cases, the ease of appeals that contributed to such gluts by extending litigations, the role of the Indian lawyer, or vakil, in promoting frivolous litigations, and the vast records required by existing procedural rules.

To remedy these defects Munro's prescriptions were invoked. These were from his famous statement of 15 May 1806: 'every village, with its twelve Ayangandeas [village servants] is a kind of little republic. . . .'[7] 'Native juries' or 'punchayets' had been recommended by Alexander Read in 1794, by Munro in 1807, and by Mark Wilks and John Malcolm, the directors noted, and they also observed that it was 'remarkable that this institution should have been passed over without notice' by Madras officials. The latter had also failed to appreciate the judicial role of village headmen who, together with 'native juries', the directors thought, composed the basis for a coherent judicial system for most people and their petty causes. The directors concluded the portion of their letter devoted to the judiciary accordingly:

> By reverting to the established practice, under the native governments, of employing the heads of villages, the punchayets assembled within [villages] . . . [and] the introduction of district punchayets . . . we are persuaded that we shall confer the most solid benefits upon our native subjects,

[4] *SEIHR*, v. 2, pp. 236.

[5] *The Fifth Report*, v. 3, pp. 501–14.

[6] *SEIHR*, v. 2, p. 239, also Arbuthnot, pp. 275–8.

[7] Ibid., pp. 240–4.

and relieve the European Judges in a very considerable degree. . .[8]

On the native police, Munro's *Fifth Report* views about the hereditary village-watch constituting an adequate as well as acceptable form of local policing were appreciatively noted and formed a similar basis for their proposals to Madras.

While this judicial letter focused substantially upon Munro and his criticisms of judicial practices in Madras—as Hudleston had complained in his dissent to the report of the special directors' committee—the tone of the letter to Madras was recommending rather than peremptory. It was also a little confusing in places. Thus, when the point about 'mischiefs that too often result from innovations' is made, it is not clear whether this was a reference to Munro's proposals or to the prevailing practices established *de novo* in 1802!

The seemingly permissive tone of the 29 April letter was repeated in a subsequent judicial letter to Madras, written by the directors before Munro left for Madras. This letter of 4 May 1814 instructed Madras upon the establishment of a commission which was to be the instrument for changing judicial and police practices. Somewhat defensively, the directors reminded all of the senior officials of Madras (except, of course, the governor, who was en route to India with Munro) that in a revenue dispatch of ten years before (!) they had suggested the usefulness of convening 'committees of your servants to examine into the State and condition of the Provinces under your Government'. They now considered it wise to create such a body to consider 'modifications in the present system of administration' as discussed in their 29 April letter, and, further, they proposed that Munro should be appointed head of it with a salary of SP 10,000, plus expenses and allowances equal to that of a political resident.[9] While this was to be a commission to investigate and recommend the best way of implementing their instructions to the Madras government, it was singular that, for what was intended as an official Madras body, all of Munro's reports as judicial commissioner were ordered to be sent immediately to the directors. This was an arrangement which suggested something of the dual authority under which Read had been charged by Cornwallis in 1792 and suggested, too, the desire for closer monitoring of the implementation of their policies than was customary for the directors.

Notwithstanding this authority from and supervision by the Court of Directors, it was not until 13 September 1816, an exasperating two years after returning to Madras, that the six regulations implementing the 29 April judicial letter drawn by Munro and his colleague commissioner, George Stratton, were finally promulgated as law by the governor, Hugh Elliot.[10] These regulations provided, first, for the transfer of police and magisterial duties from zillah court judges to collectors, something that Munro considered the most critical,

[8] Ibid., pp. 249–50.
[9] Ibid., p. 257.
[10] Ibid., pp. 421, 460, 467; Minute in Council, p. 468.

for upon it all others pivoted. The other regulations provided for the appointment of 'village moonsiffs' from among village headmen to hear minor cases and, where required, to convene village panchayats; the appointment of native district judges (district 'moonsiffs') to hear more serious minor cases and convene district panchayats; and the authority of the collector to enforce sub-tenants' rights and limit the distraint of the property of these tenants by zemindars and other landholders as well as to settle disputes involving boundaries of villages.[11] Simple as these regulations of 1816 appear, they were excruciatingly wrung from the concerted opposition of the high court of Madras (Sadr Adalat) and the MBOR, even after the Court of Directors intervened vigorously to force the changes sought by Munro in December 1815 and these same authorities were embarrassed by the revenue scandal in Coimbatore. Enacting the regulations had finally to be done by Elliot on his own authority and against his council. In the two years it took for this apparently modest achievement, Munro battered the Madras mandarins into only a resentful capitulation, one from which, a decade later, after his death, they were to lash back.

Operations in Madras began with deceptive ease late in 1814 when Munro drafted the orders creating his own commission. This is revealed in a file of his personal papers at the IOL of which one paper, entitled by him 'Instructions to the Commission', began with the words: 'A Govt order may be published to the following effect. . . .' These instructions were heeded verbatim, except for one paragraph, which was deleted from the published orders establishing the commission on 23 September 1814. This paragraph, interestingly, instructed Munro to report directly to the governor.[12] This document not only demonstrates Munro's confident and confidential relationship with Elliot, who passed the commission order, but also his efforts to avoid having his commission subordinated to either the high court or the MBOR. This buoyant confidence still existed in December of the year when Munro wrote to his old colleague Peter Bruce, still in the CD, saying that he was hard at work trying to 'get the late orders from home carried into effect'. He said that he was anxious by the next month to get a short regulation on 'the most important part of this . . . which directs the Police to be placed under the Collector and the heads of villages and punchayets to hear and decide cases'.[13] At the same time, he outlined the scope of his proposed regulations to David Hill, chief secretary to the Madras government. He confidently divided the subject into two categories: one consisting of measures which the Madras government, in consultation with leading judges, could accept, modify or reject; the other pertaining to 'all those [matters] on which the order [of 29 April] . . . is imperative, and no discretion is left with Government'.[14]

[11] Beaglehole, p. 103 and pp. 104–5.

[12] MC, F/151/114, ff. 22–9. The order appears in *SEIHR*, v. 2, p. 291.

[13] MC, F/151/12, Munro to Bruce, 15 December 1814, f. 258.

[14] Gleig, v. 1, pp. 417–18, dated 24 December 1814. Nevertheless, Munro circulated a set of private queries on his reform proposals to his trusted protégés Peter Bruce,

Within a month this imperious confidence had begun to wilt. As much in despondence as in anger, he wrote to John Sullivan at the Board of Control that the commission seemed to be stalled owing to a weakening of Hugh Elliot's resolve. The latter, Munro said, had become convinced by senior Madras civilians that many of the suggestions in the directors' judicial letter

> had, in fact, been anticipated; that more could hardly be done without danger; that great improvements had taken place since I left India; and that were I now to visit the districts, I would abandon all my former opinions, and acknowledge that the collector could not be entrusted with magisterial and police duties, without injury to the country.[15]

These revelations to Sullivan were the beginning of his mobilization of counter force from England against the Madras judicial establishment. His chosen instruments were Sullivan and James Cumming at the Board of Control. To Cumming he wrote in January 1815 that, having carefully read all of the police reports prepared during the years of his absence, he was convinced that 'nothing has been done which was not known in England' when the 29 April letter was dispatched to Madras. 'You are aware,' he told Cumming, 'that most of the men in office about the Presidency are Regulation-men, stickling for every part of the present system, and opposing every reform of it from home'.[16]

This was Munro's call to action by the Board of Control, a test of Lord Buckinghamshire's will to enforce the board's pretension to dominate Indian policy, not merely with respect to the directors but with respect to Indian governments as well. The last problem was clearly the more difficult, for, apart from the great distance and time that separated Whitehall from Madras, there lingered the caution about London's management of detailed policies in India. It was Munro's intention in January 1815 to invoke Buckinghamshire's presumptions of authority over precisely those policies.

He tutored Cumming well for the coming struggle. At the outset he insisted that judicial changes were essential for the restoration of ryotwar in Madras on the understanding that in Cumming he had the most passionate adherent to ryotwar in England. Cumming was therefore treated to vicarious outrage by being told how Munro had sent a respected, eighty-year-old ryot from the Baramahal to be interviewed by his old friend and former protégé, James Cochrane, now a member of the Board of Revenue, Munro's only ally there. The purpose was to show Cochrane and his revenue colleagues how false was the claim that courts provided any protection from illegal exactions. This old man, Munro explained, had always paid his revenues in full and punctiliously, and now sought protection from extra demands of revenue officials. He had

---

Alexander Read, Frederick Gahagan, William Chaplin, and Charles Ross: MC, F/151/118, dated December, 1814.

[15] Gleig, v. 1, p. 424, Munro to Sullivan, 20 January 1815.

[16] Ibid., p. 425, Munro to Cumming, 12 January 1815.

paid substantial court fees and had made many time-consuming appearances before the zillah court, but still there was no remedy forthcoming. 'Under a collector-magistrate, the injury could not have happened', Munro charged.

This point was elaborated in a subsequent letter to Cumming in which he complained of the growing difficulties of gaining assent for the measures of the directors from those 'adverse to the proposed changes'. This now included the governor, Elliot, his council and its secretaries, as well as the Sadr Adalat judges and their secretary, and 'every member of the Board of Revenue, excepting Cochrane, [who] are hostile to everything in the shape of the rayetwar system.'[17] If such resistance to the directors' express command and the Board of Control's implicit wishes was to be overcome, it was essential that the home government be more directive in dealing with Madras:

> I think it necessary to caution you, that if it is expected that instructions are to be obeyed, the strongest and plainest words must be used: for instance, the expressions, 'It is our wish'; 'It is our intention'; "We propose'; do not, it is maintained here, convey orders, but merely recommendations. Unless the words, 'We direct', 'We order', are employed, the measures to which they relate will be regarded as optional.

Cumming was also cautioned about Madras claims that suits being brought before courts were declining and that therefore reforms to reduce judicial backlogs were not required. Fewer civil suits were not the result of growing confidence in the courts as the protectors of the rights of ryots, and thus greater wariness by would-be oppressors—official and private—of being apprehended and punished. Rather, the opposite. Because justice was delayed by backlogs or perverted by the influence of wealthy renters under the village-lease system in most of the Presidency, ordinary ryots despaired of receiving justice in courts and were loath, therefore, to pay the fees necessary to have their just complaints ignored. Positive action was needed:

> In order to protect rayets, it is not enough to wait for their complaints, we must go around and seek for them. This is the practice of every vigilant collector; he assembled the ryots of each village on his circuit, inquired about what extra collections had been made, and caused them to be refunded. . . . It will require a long course of years, perhaps ages, before . . . [ordinary ryots] acquire sufficient courage and independence to resist [illegal exactions]; and until this change is effected, our present courts cannot protect them. We must adapt our institutions to their character; they can be protected only by giving the collector authority to investigate extra collections and cause them to be refunded.[18]

Cumming was bidden to influence Lord Buckinghamshire 'to take up this subject', and to issue clear and strong orders for conferring magisterial powers

[17] Ibid., p. 426, Munro to Cumming, 1 March 1815.
[18] Ibid., p. 428.

upon collectors. Munro also said that he required explicit orders from London about the Commission's competence to investigate revenue matters. John Sullivan of the board had recently written to his son, John, in Madras that he assumed that the Commission already had that power, but Munro admitted to Cumming that, 'The dispatch [of 29 April] certainly gives no authority of this kind', nothing beyond 'examining how far the courts protect the rayets.'

In other letters to Cumming through 1815 Munro developed many of these points, which he had reason to believe were being used by his London friend to encourage a more active, interventionist role by the Board of Control. These letters also expressed increasing frustration with opposition in Madras. He did admit that the Commission had been strengthened by Elliot's appointment of another member, George Stratton, on Munro's recommendation. The latter was additionally to serve as a judge on the Sadr Adalat, again on Munro's suggestion.[19] Stratton had revenue as well as judicial experience and proved valuable to Munro throughout the Commission. He ably prepared its final report to the Madras government when Munro was engaged in military duties in Dharwar.

Stratton's appointment was explained to Cumming in the following way in June 1815:

> You already know that the Commission is composed only of Stratton and myself. It is quite enough; for the more members, the less is done. I wished... to have been the sole Commissioner; but I see now, that nothing can be done without a member of the Sudder Adawlut in the Commission; for, unless Stratton were in that court, there would be not a single man there, or in the Government, to support the proposed changes.[20]

It exaggerated his isolation to say that there were none save him and Stratton who sought judicial reforms. James Cochrane, on the MBOR, and General Thomas Hislop in Elliot's council, were among those who sought to mediate the intensive, often personal, hostility of senior Madras civil servants to Munro, and, at a lesser level, there was John Sullivan, the younger son of the Parliamentary Commissioner in London.

The latter was a collector with a decade of experience in Madras then, and he willingly served as a conduit to his influential father, reporting his father's views and news to Munro, and vice versa. In 1815 he joined Munro to investigate a revenue scandal in Coimbatore, a case that was to weaken the basis of

[19] Ibid., p. 431, Munro to Cumming, 14 March 1815. Dodwell and Miles: George Stratton: writer 1793, assistant to MBOR 1796–9, collector Western Poligars' Peshkush 1800–3, judge Chingleput zillah 1803–6, judge Tinnevelly 1806–10; at home 1810–15 at the same time as Munro; 1815 second Judicial Commissioner and third judge of the Sadr Adalat. Apart from his letters Munro committed many comments to paper in notes on the MBOR reports of 29 June 1815 to 27 December 1817, as well as on the Coimbatore investigation in MC, F/151/117.

[20] Gleig, v. 1, p. 435, Munro to Cumming, 20 June 1815.

the resistance in Madras to Munro's judicial reforms. The younger Sullivan had been furloughed in England at the same time as Munro and must have come to know him then. It was possibly on the strength of this personal relationship that the young collector wrote to Munro early in 1815, requesting advice on problems he was encountering in the Chingleput district where he had been appointed the year before, and imploring Munro to meet him.[21]

Through the younger Sullivan, Munro was told of his father's confidence that Elliot, about whose failing support Munro was now widely complaining, would in the end act as Munro's protector. If for no other reason, Elliot would do this to please Buckinghamshire and Sullivan to whom he owed his appointment.[22] By March 1815, however, the younger Sullivan was writing to Munro that from a conversation he had had with Elliot he feared that the governor would go along with Robert Fullerton and other Madras mandarins who opposed the directors' orders of 29 April. Sullivan reported the chilling news that Elliot had said 'that he did not view anything in the judicial letter in the light of orders but merely as points thrown out for his consideration . . . and particularly pointed out the absurdity of trusting information on judicial subjects to four *colonels: yourself, Malcolm, Wilks, and Leith*.[23] The privileges of the soldier-administrator still rankled Company civilians.

In this same distressing March letter it was mentioned that Elliot intended to appoint Sullivan to the Coimbatore collectorate with the anticipated resignation of the long-serving William Garrow there; he implied that this was a promotion made possible by Elliot's desire to appoint someone whom he wished to advance in the service through an appointment to Chingleput, where Sullivan was then serving. Then, shortly after taking up his new post in Coimbatore, Sullivan wrote to Munro that within hours of his arrival he was presented with proof of an enormous scandal involving the collectorate treasury clerk, 'Caussy Chetty' (Kasi Setti), who was 'exercising all the powers of the Collector in the district' and had influence far beyond Coimbatore itself. He reported telling Elliot that a commission was immediately required to investigate affairs there, and he implored Munro to send some Indian subordinates from his own staff so that investigations could begin. It was clear that Sullivan had assumed a role with Munro like that of younger colleagues in the Ceded Districts, expecting Munro to provide Indian officials trained and trusted by him to aid them in carrying out their work.[24]

At the close of 1815 the elder John Sullivan in London departed from his usual disclosures of information for Munro through letters to his son in Madras by

[21] MC, F/151/28, Sullivan to Munro, 19 January 1815.

[22] Ibid., Sullivan to Munro, 28 February 1815.

[23] Colonel James Leith, 5th Native Infantry and Judge Advocate General, Madras. His answers to the queries of the Special Committee of the Directors are found in *SEIHR*, v. 2, pp. 95–105.

[24] MC, F/151/28, Sullivan to Munro, 13 September 1815, plus other letters in this file to the end of 1815.

enclosing a long and sobering letter for Munro. In it he reported on what support could be expected from London. Not much, it would seem. Sullivan regretted that the Madras civil establishment should be resisting the judicial orders from the directors of eighteen months before, but he observed that the Board of Control was meeting similar resistance from powerful elements within East India House as well. Even now, Sullivan reported, the directors seemed unsure of how imperative they intended their letter to Madras to have been. There was a strong sentiment among many directors that local governments in India should have discretion to alter certain details of their instructions. Thus, there were many who felt that the Madras Sadr Adalat was correct in demanding that, where possible, there should be concurrent magistracy by the zillah judge and the collector. Sullivan also reminded Munro of the ingrained prejudices of the directors against rapid changes of any sort, and he spoke of serious division amongst them about whether or not to extend the Bengal regulations to the Gangetic territories won to the Company some years before, or whether to adopt Read's and Munro's methods of revenue administration there. The directors, Sullivan reminded Munro, had a tendency to want a great body of facts over the broadest of questions and to be satisfied of low administrative costs before approving any changes.[25]

In the light of this pessimism it is surprising to read the judicial letter to Madras, signed by Charles Grant, and dated a day after Sullivan's letter to Munro.[26] That dispatch considered the measures that had been taken in Madras for 'carrying into effect the instructions which were conveyed in our Judicial dispatches of 29 April and 4th May 1814.' The directors approved of the instructions to Munro 'on his appointment to the office of First Commissioner of internal administration of the Madras Provinces', Munro's own drafted definition of its tasks. Stratton's appointment, again on Munro's suggestion, was also approved, along with his generous salary and secondment to the Sadr Adalat, by which 'the objects of the Commission will be facilitated.' Finally, approval was given to the 'latitude' of Munro's Commission: 'we much approve that you have directed his enquiries to the Revenue, as well as to the Judicial branch of administration, and we have no doubt that you [Elliot] will . . . attend to his suggestions for the improvement of the one and the other.' These preliminaries done, the directors' letter of 20 December 1815 turned to substantive consideration of the principal objections by Madras authorities to the Commission's recommendations.

Commencing with a major difference between Munro's understanding of the directors' 1814 letter and that of the Madras government, they sided with Munro. This pertained to the question of whether complete magisterial functions should be transferred from judges to collectors, or only those related to supervision of the police. The directors insisted that they meant 'the whole duties of Magistrate', Munro's interpretation. However, as Sullivan had already

[25] Ibid., Munro, 19 December 1815.
[26] *SEIHR*, v. 2, p. 313.

intimated, the directors were 'not averse' to a sharing of magisterial functions, provided there was no clash between the two officials. Explicitly, however, the contention of the Madras government that it was unnecessary for collectors to hold complete magisterial powers was rejected. The Madras government was also reminded that they had failed to heed the command to frame a regulation empowering collectors to deal with boundary disputes between villages and to hear disputes arising between zamindars and other landlords and their tenants.

Against the Madras claim that the 'conduct' of the Commission would, 'to use your [Court of Directors'] own language, "unsettle the minds of the people with regard to the established system of internal administration and destroy their confidence in their permanence". . . we entirely agree with the Commissioners. . . .' Specifically, the directors agreed with Munro that there should have been no delays in making the reforms—all of the reforms—immediately known to the people.

This letter of December 1815 closed with a reiteration of the 'unison' of sentiments that existed between themselves and the Commission: 'we cannot too strongly express our satisfaction at the additional evidence [the latest attack by Madras upon Munro and the Commission, dated 5 July 1815] affords of their [the Commission's] peculiar fitness for the discharge of the important trust that has been commissioned to them.'

The last—to have had his condemnation used by the directors to commend Munro and the Commission—was a bitter draught for Elliot, who had cringingly passed along the hostility of his advisors. But more was to follow. The directors' letter accused Elliot of disobedience for his decision—strongly urged by his council—to refer the Commission's recommendations to the Governor-General in Calcutta before considering to act upon them. This ploy was obviously intended to delay the enactment of the Commission's regulations and possibly even to enlist Lord Hastings in Calcutta against the directors and the Commission in Madras.[27] Elliot was scolded not only for pusillanimously yielding to the delaying tactics of his advisors but for having seriously breached constitutional principles since the matter he had referred to Calcutta was one on which 'authorities at home had pronounced a deliberate opinion and prescribed a course of proceeding'.

The older Sullivan's uncertainty about the degree of support which Munro's Commission might expect from the directorate, his apparent ignorance about the strongly endorsing judicial letter which they did send late in 1815, is difficult to explain. One explanation is personal to Sullivan. It seems that he had been considering resigning from the Board of Control about that time and had possibly ceased to be active there. The reasons for this may have been the rancorous relations between the board and the directors, stemming from the arrogant claims of his friend, Lord Buckinghamshire, about the supremacy of the board in policy determination. There was also the possibility that

[27] Beaglehole, p. 105.

Buckinghamshire had left to Sullivan negotiations with Grant and other directors over the Commission and other matters after he himself had poisoned relations with them. All of this is suggested in letters sent to his son in Madras, as reported to Munro in January and July 1816.[28]

Beyond the personal, however, it is clear that there was a greater willingness of the 'Bengalees' among the directors, led by Grant, to see changes in the Bengal system and to recognize the need for changing the costly judiciary as new territories were added to the Company. Reflecting this change was Sullivan's letter to Elliot complaining that the latter's opposition to the Commission was deplored in London; Sullivan hoped that the orders sent to Madras in December 1815 would prompt Elliot to put the directors' orders into immediate effect. Elliot was even chided for lagging behind Bengal on judicial reforms, and instructed to 'keep your Govt on a level; *at least*, with the other Presidencies where... public functionaries have already brought the principles [of the April 1814 judicial letter] into action.' Lord Buckinghamshire's letter to Elliot made the same exhortations.[29]

In the same month as these letters were made known to Munro through his colleague Sullivan, the news of Buckinghamshire's death arrived. Once again, the older Sullivan considered resignation from the Board, now because of differences with Canning over party politics.[30] By this time, though, the need for vigorous intervention in Madras had passed. Major opposition to the Commission had been weakened by revelations of scandal in Coimbatore. More importantly, opposition to the Commission and reform had been decisively weakened when the directors' judicial letter of December 1815, with its backing of Munro, arrived in May 1816. This document, over Grant's signature and thus bearing the support of those whom he influenced in London—whether they were supporters of the Bengal system or not—was a signal to all that the notion of 'regulation-man' had to be redefined.

BREAKING THE MANDARINS

This change was not so precipitous as is sometimes assumed in the conventions of imperial historiography, where Cornwallis and Munro are pitted against each other as the makers of opposed models of colonial governance. Actually, the idea of ryotwar was recognized by Cornwallis' colleague, John Shore, as early as 1789, as readers of *The Fifth Report* would have known. Shore spoke

[28] MC, F/151/28, Sullivan to Munro, 6 January and 6 July 1816.

[29] Ibid., Sullivan to Munro, 3 June 1816; emphasis in original.

[30] Ibid., Sullivan to Munro, 26 June 1816. Buckinghamshire had died in February 1816, and Canning was appointed to the Board of Control in order to bring him into Liverpool's cabinet. Others who sat or served on the board then were: Liverpool, Castelreagh, Bathhurst, Sidmouth, Teigmouth, Lowther, John Sullivan, Viscount Apsley (son of Bathurst) and 'two Canningites', Sturges-Bourne and Lord Binning—according to Peter Dixon, *Canning; Politician and Statesman* (London: Wiedenfeld and Nicolson, 1976), pp. 185–6.

of two basic forms of tenure, of which, in one, revenue was charged upon surveyed and classified lands and paid by 'the ryots'. In the Bengal portion of *The Fifth Report* of 1812 its author Samuel Davis had also observed that when the revenue administration of the territories ceded to the Company in Oude in the Gangetic plain, by the treaty with the Nawab of 20 November 1801, was being considered, Lord Wellesley was at first opposed to extending the Bengal regulations there. He sought instead to frame a revenue regime 'more on the model of native governments', according to Davis.[31] Though the Bengal regulations were introduced there in 1803, Wellesley at least continued to be interested in further experimentation. This is evident from a request to Munro by Wellesley's aide Benjamin Sydenham, in 1805, to comment upon those 1803 regulations in the light of his system in the CD.[32] The directors, too, continued to give intermittent attention to altering revenue arrangements in Gangetic territories gained during the second Maratha war, and especially changing the disastrous tax-farming schemes in Etawah and Aligarh, though they hesitated to act. As late as January 1813, in their revenue letter to Bengal, they worried that the 'local circumstances of the two countries [North and South India] differ very materially' and doubted that Munro's claims about ryotwar for all of India, notwithstanding his authority and experience, overrode the contrary views of Edward Colebrook and others of Bengal. At all points, the directors' suggestions about ryotwar in the Gangetic plain were rebuffed by the Bengal government. Still, the policy makers at India House persisted in considering ryotwar for some parts of Bengal as late as 1819, when they proposed to order that government to introduce it on some estates under government (*amani*) revenue collections, but failed to win the assent of George Canning, then President of the Board of Control.[33]

The ryotwar being considered for the Gangetic territories and even for some parts of Bengal was increasingly seen in London as a system which eliminated tax farming and oppressive village renters and placed direct power and authority in British hands, as the Cornwallis scheme never had nor could. In addition, many in London had become convinced that Munro's judicial reforms would lower costs in Bengal as well as in Madras. Thus, for those who believed in the zamindari system of Cornwallis, judicial reform was a plausible defence against those who argued that the *entire* Cornwallis system was to be condemned for its inability to deal with judicial pressures upon it without spending vastly greater sums on the judicature. All of the directors were resolute in their determination to reduce expenditures.[34]

[31] *The Fifth Report*, v. 2, pp. 53–4, and v. 1, pp. 89–90.

[32] MC, F/151/8 Sydenham to Munro, 19 May 1805. Drafts by Munro in 1803 on this question are found in the Wellesley Papers, Ad. MS. 13679, 88ff.

[33] See Cumming's 1820s(?) discussion of this correspondence in IOL, *Home Miscellaneous Series*, v. 530, pp. 253–89. Apparently, Canning deleted this paragraph of the directors' letter on the grounds that further consideration was required to make a final decision, p. 286.

[34] General discussion of these issues in Philips, pp. 202–4.

But, even as the judicial letter of December 1815 was being signed and readied for transmittal to Madras, the last substantial attack by the Madras authorities upon the Commission was before Governor Hugh Elliot. This was a report to Elliot and his council from the MBOR which had become the major focus of resistance to the Commission. That the Presidency's revenue officials should have displaced the judges of the high court of Madras, who had logically carried the early fight against judicial reforms, is not surprising.

Objections of the judicial officials to the Commission could be trivialized or dismissed by Munro on a variety of grounds. Against their claim that European, especially British, judicial principles were superior to all others stood the counter-claims of Warren Hastings, and later Munro and others, who argued that such principles were both inappropriate and too costly for India. This was a position taken also by Wellesley and increasingly by the directors. Other objections of judges to the Commission's proposed regulations were said by Munro to stem from various motives.[35] These included a reluctance to change any system, whatever it may be; a fear that greater 'native agency' was politically dangerous; and the concern that Indian litigants would prefer adjudication of their disputes by 'heads of villages and punchayets . . . [and] leave little business to zillah courts . . . [and thus] that many of these will be reduced'.

Munro had disparaged the views of the high court judges on matters of internal administration as being too ignorant about any local institutions to offer relevant counsel. Of none of this could the revenue officials of the MBOR be accused: men like John Hodgson, James Cochrane (a Munro colleague from the CD] and Robert Alexander (who had been in the Madras service for twenty-five years and a member of the MBOR for seven of them).[36] Moreover, as custodians of the Madras revenue their views of the possibly disruptive effects of Munro's reforms upon the level of revenue would command attention not to be accorded to judicial officials. The MBOR report of 18 December 1815 was an attack upon the Commission's objectives, launched from both a revenue and a judicial perspective, and it skilfully drew upon the opinions of eighteen of the most experienced collectors in the Presidency, among whom were several 'Munro men'.

Though signed by three of the four members of the MBOR, it bore all of the signs of being written by Hodgson, a member of the Board since 1803 and

[35] Munro's discussion of these matters in a letter to Cumming, 1 September 1815, Gleig, v. 1, p. 439.

[36] Dodwell and Miles, pp. 4–5 and 302–3. Robert Alexander: writer 1790, assistant collector in Vizagapatam and Viziangaram 1791–96, assistant collector Vizagapatam 1797 and 1800–3, collector Vizagapatam 1803–6, judge zillah of Vizagapatam 1806–8, collector Ganjam 1808–14, Member, MBOR 1814 and President of Council. William Wayte alone lacked this: writer 1797, assistant to the secretary to the military, political and secret department 1800–2, assistant secretary to the MBOR 1802–6, secretary MBOR 1806–10, member MBOR 1810–19.

Munro's ancient nemesis. The other signatories included Cochrane, an ally and old friend of Munro, who, like Thackeray, when the latter was a member of the MBOR that recommended village leases in 1808, was either carried along by Hodgson's argument or could not oppose or alter it. The Hodgson touch is evident in the range and adroitness of the argument, the balance of detailed evidence and large generalization, the use of evidence and witnesses from the side of his adversary—in this case seasoned collectors, some of whom had served under Munro in the CD and were posted there still.

This MBOR report was addressed to the governor of Madras and his council.[37] It had been ordered by Hugh Elliot in the previous March. The council's most important members were Robert Fullerton, a defender of the Bengal system, and Robert Alexander, then President of the MBOR and an official whose major experience was in the zamindar-settled Northern Circars of Madras. The report began with an anticipation of criticism from the directors about the failure of Madras to provide a regulation requiring the issuance of pattas, or contractual engagements, by all Madras zamindars and other landlords to their under-tenants and cultivators. Their hesitation, the board said, arose from an unwillingness to use compulsion in what they claimed was a 'private agreement between individuals' and, especially, that compulsory pattas might prove more oppressive than beneficial to cultivators. Hodgson and his colleagues also pointed out that under ryotwar, where pattas were issued by government to cultivators, these were seldom issued before the cropping season, as was required under ryotwar regulations, but often only when seasons were 'very far advanced, and the actual state, not only of the *cultivation* but of the *crop*, had been ascertained.'

Having thus placed its barb against the ryotwar advocates of reform, the report turned to the evidence on the Commission's reforms from precisely those officials that ryotwar and reform arguments based themselves on: the experienced revenue officials of the Presidency. Eighteen collectors were cited, of whom four were either protégés of Munro or his friends: Chaplin, Sullivan, Graeme and Alexander Read. Among the very few Madras collectors whose views were not mentioned in the report was William Garrow, formerly of Coimbatore, around whose head scandal was about to break. However, in evaluating the purported advantages of the Commission's reform proposals the MBOR anticipated a specific issue raised by the Coimbatore 'abuses', as they were beginning to be called. This was the Commission's proposed method for reducing expenses of the police by allocating police duties to subordinate revenue officers involved in the collection of land revenue, land customs, and the salt and tobacco monopolies. Hodgson and his colleagues could subtly suggest that it was precisely from such revenue officials of Company monopolies that the head of the Coimbatore cabal of 'corruption', Kasi Setti, drew many of his co-conspirators! Another of the purported advantages of reforms advocated by the Commission was that judges of the Company's courts, in

[37] *SEIHR*, v. 2, pp. 389–414.

being relieved of magisterial duties, would have more time for the reduction of the mass of civil suits 'supposed to be much in arrears', but, the MBOR seemed to be suggesting, actually were not. A final purported advantage of Munro's reforms was that of bringing all local officials under a single authority, that of the collector.

These 'advantages' were summarily dismissed. They violated the constitutional principle of separating executive and judicial authority, and it was absurd to assume that revenue officers—British or Indian—could cope with the tasks of magistracy without neglecting either revenue or judicial tasks.

Hodgson then justified intervention by the Presidency's highest revenue officials in judicial questions owing to the conjoined character of the two, a point upon which Munro had also insisted. As a general consideration, the report asserted, the establishment of civil courts in 1802 had brought order to portions of the Presidency—notably the Northern Circars—that had been under Company rule for three decades, but not under its control owing to lawlessness. Suppression of this had been a major drain upon the treasury of the Presidency. Having brought order to turbulent tracts such as these, the courts that replaced the army as maintainers of the peace should have been evaluated not only in terms of their expenses but in terms of what they saved in military costs and disruptions to production. A second argument of a similar sort was made about police expenses. It was the ostensible purpose of the Commission to reduce these. The MBOR report argued that police, as well as judicial expenditures or 'charges', usually failed to account for the revenues which both police and courts produced as fees and fines; if properly accounted, these would show that, far from being an expense, they produced a surplus over the charges of their maintenance!

Other reservations to the Commissions' proposals were jurisprudential, but here the MBOR argued less a principled than a pragmatic line. Doubtlessly, the writers of the MBOR report possessed the knowledge (probably from Hodgson's London friend, John Hudleston) that most directors were not merely inclined to an idea of a sharing of magisterial responsibilities between zillah judges and collectors, as the older Sullivan had written to Munro at the same time, but may have preferred this. Thus armed, the report permits words of the several collectors to carry the major point. This was that any notion of sharing magisterial authority was impossible, and thus, according to the MBOR, there should be no changes in the locus of judicial authority. Charles Ross, collector of Cuddapah, in the CD, is quoted as insisting that magisterial duties had to fall either to judges or to collectors, not to both. William Chaplin, another of Munro's old juniors from the CD, reported from Bellary that 'the change must be complete' or not at all.

Shrewdly, the first of the collectors whose views were cited from consultations conducted between May and September 1815, were Munro-men, Alexander Read in Kanara and William Chaplin in Bellary.[38] The former

[38] Ibid., pp. 390–408. Chaplin and Graeme both prepared long private responses to Munro's queries in August 1817, MC, F/151/36.

thought that, in Kanara, merely coping with criminal matters of magistracy would fully occupy any revenue officer, leaving no time for the revenue. Chaplin agreed and also argued that it was difficult to see how officers such as amildars and village headmen, being responsible for revenue and to the collector of the revenue for their careers, could be expected to carry out police duties justly. Nor did he see how the necessarily peripatetic collector could supervise the police. James Hepburn, the collector of Tanjore, also saw the last as a problem, but one not nearly so serious as others. In a district like Tanjore, he said, the demands of revenue supervision were enormous and the collector could not undertake the arduous work of magistracy without endangering the revenue. Also, if it were thought that some sharing of magisterial duties between judges and collectors would help by leaving supervision of the police to judges, he denied that this could work: if the collector was to have any magisterial responsibility he must also have power over the police. And so it went, from collector to collector: undertaking full magistracy, as the Commission was proposing, would overtax already pressed collectors. Yet less than full magisterial powers, as the directors seemed inclined towards, was unworkable.

Testimony of experienced collectors was also brought to bear on another aspect of the Commission's proposals, that of empowering village headmen—'potails'—to act as village judges of small causes (less than Rs 10).

> The Board [of Revenue] are aware that in the Ceded Districts of 1792 [Baramahal] now denominated. . . . Salem, as well as in the Ceded Districts of 1800, now . . . Bellary and Cuddapah, and in Coimbatore, the practice has been established for the Collector to select one or more of the inhabitants of each village to be officiating Potail or Potails, and to pay him or them from the revenue of certain lands assigned by the native government in enam tenure to be heads of villages collectively. Whether . . . an innovation or not is perhaps now difficult to determine; but the Board believe it to be a matter of fact, that from Ganjam [at the northern boundary of the Presidency] to Cape Camorin, east of the ghauts, the word 'Potail' is not known, and that office, as vested by authority exclusively in one person, does not exist.[39]

That the office of headman did not exist in many parts of the Presidency was a serious criticism of Munro's judicial proposals. This was especially significant in places with the greatest populations, the most productive agriculture and hence the most reliable revenue from the land. It was also here that mirasi tenure flourished.

Based on an Arabic word, the Hindustani mirasi referred to land (occasionally to office) held hereditarily either as a joint coparcenary right, for example the right to a share of produce from fields cultivated in common or individually (either permanently or periodically rotated), or as a single landed estate under the mirasidar. In places such as Chingleput and North and South Arcot the

[39] *SEIHR*, v. 2, p. 410.

mirasi right also included privileged rates of assessement as well as labour services and money dues from subordinate cultivators. The cognate Tamil word for mirasi was ***kani***; the terms kaniyatchi and kaniyatchikaran had the same meaning as mirasi and mirasidar. Arabic terms were introduced into parts of what was to become the Madras Presidency during the eighteenth century dominance of the Arcot nawabs;[40] the kani right, which mirasi superseded terminologically, was much older, being found in inscriptions of the thirteenth century.[41]

Not surprisingly, the views of collectors from those districts of Madras in which communal mirasi tenure existed were invoked in order to substantiate Hodgson's disparagement of ryotwar; among those was John Sullivan, then still collector of Chingleput district. Pressing on this line, the MBOR pointed out that in non-mirasi districts such as Coimbatore the office of potail, far from being a symbol of primordial corporateness as alleged by Munro and other ryotwar advocates, was 'actually purchased'. Also, reports of his friend John Ravenshaw from South Arcot were cited to cast yet deeper doubts on Munro's claim that villages were moral and political unities ('republics'). Ravenshaw had reported widespread oppression by 'head inhabitants' of inferior ones and the abuse of their offices and powers for 'purposes of fraud, injustice, and private gain'.[42]

This 18 December 1815 report was among the last of a series of oppositionary moves against Munro and the Commission, a set of rearguard actions which, according to Munro, and later Hugh Elliot, were mischievously intended to delay implementation of the 29 April 1814 letter from the directors.[43] Delay, it may have been hoped, would permit a correction of the directors' mistaken notion that Madras required reform of either its judicial or its revenue administration.[44] Delay was also calculated to woo Elliot from his advocacy of reform, and the governor was enlisted as an agent of delay, as Munro saw it. He had written to John Sullivan in London that by early 1815 Elliot was convinced by his 'council that there were many objections to the Commission's proposed regulations and that the opinions of all of the collectors should be solicited before the regulations were enacted'.

Elliot's council also persuaded him that a detailed survey was necessary to ascertain that there were 'potails' in all villages capable of serving as village judges, or munsifs, and that the inams that they held were adequate for their remuneration. The governor acceded to this in an order of 1 March 1815, six months after Munro had returned to Madras! Munro objected to all of this to

[40] Wilson, *Glossary*, p. 342 and pp. 257–8. Also S. Sundaraja Iyengar, *Land Tenures in the Madras Presidency* (Madras: Commercial Press, 1921, 2nd edn.), pp. 43–4.

[41] N. Karashima, *South Indian History and Society: Studies from Inscriptions, A.D. 850–1800* (Delhi: Oxford University Press, 1984), pp. 15–18.

[42] *SEIHR*, v. 2, p. 411–13.

[43] MC, F/151/115, Munro to Cumning in which these matters are discussed.

[44] Beaglehole, pp. 163–4.

Lord Buckinghamshire, whose death in February was not known in Madras, complaining that Elliot had not even consulted him about his orders of March.[45] He also reported with considerable acuteness that Elliot had become very defensive with him, and more so after the directors' letter of December 1815 supporting Munro and the Commission. Munro said that only General Thomas Hislop, commander of the Madras Army and thereby a member of the council, supported the Commission; others on the council opposed it. He said that John Hodgson of the MBOR 'controlled' both Robert Alexander, President of the MBOR and also a member of the council, and Edward Greenway of the Sadr Adalat. Confronted with this powerful opposition it had become clear, Munro said, that Elliot would not support the Commission 'until he was satisfied by experience that his advisors were mistaken'. The issue must now be forced in order to prevent longer delays, hence this letter ended with an appeal to Buckinghamshire, as President of the Board of Control, to write to Elliot exhorting his co-operation with Munro.

Elliot, for his part, later in 1816, reported events in a similar way to W. F. Elphinstone, under whom, as chairman of the directorate, the 29 April letter had been dispatched to Madras.

The governor acknowledged his gratitude to the director 'for the pleasantest and most important public situation I have ever filled and [which] in the long run, if you let me have *a long run* [*sic*], I shall not discredit your selection. . . .' Obviously stung by the criticisms of his complicity in the delays of the judicial reforms in Madras, Elliot sought to exculpate himself. He warned Elphinstone that sudden changes such as those proposed by the Commission were dangerous. 'The natives are all children of habits and prejudices which must be respected . . . until they die away of themselves in the growing intercourse . . . with Europeans.' He also put forward another of the arguments of the opponents of the Commission, saying that long before the Company's European officials became fluent in Indian languages, Indians would be able to conduct all official business, including judicial, in English. Notwithstanding all of this, Elliot protested to Elphinstone, he had promulgated the rules set down by the Commission, responsive 'to the great stress laid by Lord Buckinghamshire and his friends . . . [for] a new code of justice more conformable to the inclinations and understandings of the natives', and this against the strenuous wishes and opposition of 'the matadors of our Civil Service here . . . [to] what they call Colonel Munro's system'.[46] The latter opposed both Munro and his system, Elliot said: 'The circumstances of his wearing a red coat and being a soldier created great jealousy among the civilians who thought themselves

[45] University of Manchester, John Rylands Library, Munro to Buckinghamshire, 30 May 1816, and to Sullivan 28 April 1816; these letters are included with a batch of *Melville Papers* which have not been assigned manuscript numbers. Elliot's order is reprinted in *SEIHR*, v. 2, p. 296.

[46] IOL, W. F. Elphinstone Papers, F/89, box 2, Elliot to Elphinstone, 25 September 1816.

competent to fill a place in the Commission and who were by no means averse to having shared in its emoluments.' One of the 'matadors', Robert Fullerton, 'who cannot divest himself of certain local prejudices', was opposed to Munro on personal grounds, Elliot continued, and this was true of others as a result of former feuds that left a residue of 'hatred and personal animosity' within the high civil service. All of this had made Elliot's efforts to carry out the mandated changes of the directors, 'with perfect impartiality' very difficult.

Munro had, of course, long known of the personal, careerist and principled oppositions to his judicial and ryotwar proposals within the high officialdom of Madras. Opposition from experienced collectors was something different. Though he had dismissed the likely responses of collectors to the MBOR solicitations of 1 March 1815 as vague and useless, he devoted a good deal of care to preparing counters to them. Letters to James Cumming and John Sullivan show to what uses Munro put these labours.[47] This was to prepare the Board of Control and through them sympathetic members of the Court of Directors for the detailed criticisms of the Commission's proposals that were finally formulated, probably by John Hodgson, at the MBOR, in December 1815. Any real hopes by him and other opponents of Munro for a change of mind in London were about to be dashed by the 20 December 1815 judicial letter from the directors supporting Munro and the Commission. This reached India in May 1816.

Even before the directors' strongly supportive letter arrived in Madras, however, it had become clear to some that far from reversing their position the directors had stiffened their resolve to see economizing changes in the judiciaries of all of British India. Hodgson, at least, seemed to be aware of this by the beginning of 1816, for James Cochrane, Munro's ally on the MBOR, reported that the influential Hodgson was now saying publicly that the Court of Directors could not make him change his views about Munro and the Commission, but 'as they pay him a thousand pagodas a month, for carrying their orders into effect, he will gladly do so, whether this may be for the introduction of Ryotwar, or any other system.'[48] In this same letter to Munro, Cochrane reported that Elliot was to order Munro to join John Sullivan in the investigation of corruption in Coimbatore, a case that was to become a major rebuke to the Madras establishment following revelations of how senior Madras officials were attempting to suppress knowledge of 'abuses' there. The 'Casi Chetty' scandal was about to break upon Madras, and with that the sweeping away of all remaining opposition to the promulgation of the Commission's regulations.

This case was more than merely another of the large number of 'corruption'

[47] MC, F/151/115, for revenue papers, and especially ff. 23–39, entitled by Munro as 'Statements of 8 June 1815' with his comments on the responses of collectors to MBOR survey; F/151/34 for personal papers; see also Gleig, v. 1, pp. 426–48, and the Munro papers at the Rylands Library in Manchester.

[48] MC, F/151/35, Cochrane to Munro, 24 January 1816.

scandals that embarrassed Madras from the late eighteenth century. It was perhaps the most interesting of these in revealing how what the British were calling 'corruption' and 'abuses' was best understood as the continuation of normal fiscal arrangements from pre-colonial times thought by some of the Company—by no means all—to be serious breaches of rules and trust owed by Indian revenue servants of the Company.

Documentation on this case is too voluminous to be dealt with here.[49] In essence, the situation was about what Sullivan had described to Munro in September 1815, when he had assumed responsibility for the collectorate of Coimbatore from his long-serving predecessor William Garrow. A lowly district official, 'Caussy Chitty . . . was exercising all of the powers of the Collector' and the staff and treasury of the district were employed in the private business of this Kasi Setti and his friends. Allegations that something like this was occurring were raised as early as 1810 when Garrow was informed about certain malversations by an enemy of Kasi Setti, one 'Arunchellan Moodely', a writer in the collectorate office.[50] This led to an investigation of the clerk for embezzlement which was inconclusive, apparently because Garrow failed to press it. That all was not well in Coimbatore continued to be thought by many. For example, some months before learning from Sullivan about Kasi Setti, Munro had reported to James Cumming that one of the useful effects of the Commission was the widely held supposition among Indians that its purpose was to investigate 'abuses in the revenue line . . . [and] I do not undeceive them; for the belief . . . deters the native head-servants from peculating to so great an amount as formerly . . .', and even led to corrections such as in Coimbatore where lands previously cultivated, but returned as waste, were being charged the full revenue.[51] That was in March 1815; by September, when Sullivan took charge of the district, he called upon Munro for help to investigate Kasi Setti's labyrinthine influence and power. He pleaded for Munro to send some of his Indian staff, saying there was some idea in Madras of sending one of their European assistants. Sullivan dismissed that: 'We want no secretary, young or old, but lots of Brahmins, *Ferretts and blood hounds*.'[52]

Cochrane's letter of January 1816, relating Hodgson's presumed capitulation to the Commission, also referred to Elliot's determination to force a genuine investigation of Coimbatore past his reluctant council. Cochrane suggested that the governor was piqued by the unwillingness of his chief councillors, Robert Fullerton and Robert Alexander, to co-operate with him in initiating such an investigation. He also hinted that both the councillors and Elliot feared a revenue scandal might tarnish their reputations. Nonetheless, Cochrane reported, Elliot was ordering Munro to prepare a report on Coimbatore for the earliest dispatch to England, and he was doing this against the expressed,

49 Much is found in *SEIHR*, v. 1, pp. 710–91.
50 MC, F/151/28, Sullivan to Munro, 13 September 1815.
51 Gleig, v. 1, p. 429, Munro to Cumming, 3 March 1815.
52 MC, F/151/28, Sullivan to Munro, 23 September and 2 October, 1815.

minuted advice of Fullerton and Alexander. Elliot was now angry, particularly with the Sadr Adalat and the Board of Revenue, 'meaning by the last Hodgson and Alexander', Cochrane explained.[53]

The Coimbatore scandal broke the hold which the senior, prestigious civilians of Madras had gained over Elliot soon after his arrival. Their adamant refusal now to see a full investigation, especially by Munro and John Sullivan, confronted Elliot with the spectre of being dragged down with those defending their own reputations in the Coimbatore 'corruptions', the first scent of which had reached Madras in 1810, before Elliot's term. The governor was prepared to revert to being the compliant ally of Munro he had been in his first months in office in Madras in 1814: he had learned, as Munro thought he must, 'that his [other!] advisors were mistaken', and that Munro could be relied upon to help him have the '*long run*' he wanted as governor of Madras.

Elliot confirmed all of this a few days later, on 29 January 1816. He wanted Munro to join Sullivan to report 'ascertained *facts*' about the situation in Coimbatore in order to counter the 'minutes of my colleagues [Fullerton and Alexander]'; he wanted this to be done quickly so as to be sent by the late February fleet sailing from Madras. In return, he promised to include a report to the Directors on the Commission's draft regulations.[54]

The Coimbatore report was speedily prepared by 26 February 1816. It is one of the major sources on the 'corruptions' of Kasi Setti.[55] The latter, it appears, began his career as a treasury assistant in the Coimbatore district office in 1806. By 1810 he had reportedly gained such influence as to make appointments to the staff and to discharge those who did not co-operate with him and his schemes. He had also become the renter, in his own name or that of others, of ninety-six villages in the district. Kasi Setti's power was built upon collusion with the tehsildars of the collectorate to extort illegal payments from cultivators and to use these funds, as well as regular revenue payments, held back for a time, for investments in and control of trade in the district. Together with over forty tehsildars, a network of commerce and influence was established by and centred upon him. Still, Munro and Sullivan found themselves frustrated in attempting to use the purportedly general knowledge of 'corruption' in the district to make a definite case against this powerful man. For example: 'The profits derived by Casi Shitty from his extensive trade, tho they cannot exactly be classed either as embezzlements of revenue or exactions from the Ryots, had in fact the same operation as these would have had, both upon the revenue and the Ryots. . . .' In fact, few could be found by Munro and Sullivan and their Brahman 'ferrets' willing to give concrete evidence against Kasi Setti and his powerful associates. Much of their report was therefore surmise, but

[53] MC, F/151/135, Cochrane to Munro, 24 January 1816.

[54] 29 January 1816; Elliot conceded that the Commision's draft regulations 'have in my opinion been detained by the Sudder Adawlut 5 [*sic*] months longer than they might have been'.

[55] *SEIHR*, v. 1, pp. 715–54.

this did not prevent the case from being useful to Munro in his condemnation of the judicial system.

Munro and Sullivan charged that it was difficult to bring forward a provable case of what all took to be a flagrant violation of revenue administration because of the formal demands of the court system. 'Proper' revenue administration, it seemed, allowed only the Company to monopolize commerce by using the land revenue for commercial investment, and only it could demand a massive proportion of production and personal wealth as revenue! The feeble case made out against Kasi Setti also demonstrated what Munro claimed was the encrusted, remote and uninformed nature of the higher institutions of civil governance in Madras. The MBOR had refused, both before and after the investigation by Munro and Sullivan, to indict Kasi Setti, even though, as the Board members admitted, as the renter of almost one hundred villages in the district and as an active merchant Kasi Setti's profitable operations might have been thought incompatible with his public employment.[56] There may also have been reluctance on the part of the MBOR to acknowledge that William Garrow, long-time collector of Coimbatore and one of those most highly esteemed by Hodgson, might have been guilty of not only negligence in Coimbatore but personal gain at public expense.[57]

Still, the Board of Revenue could hardly disguise, nor dismiss, the massive power this one man in Coimbatore had created and maintained under one of the most experienced of its collectors. Here was a condition which deserved to be judged as harshly as Burke had judged, and had taught his countrymen to condemn. It was the dubashi system at its worst, and a profound discredit to the Madras civilian establishment.

The Kasi Setti scandal helped to persuade Elliot to take decisive action against 'his advisors' and to heed the stinging criticisms of the directors in their December 1815 letter to him. Elliot was further encouraged in this by letters from Lord Buckinghamshire and John Sullivan exhorting him to promulgate Munro's regulations without further delay. Nevertheless, another six months were required for that to occur, and in the end Elliot had to promulgate the six regulations on his own authority and against the expressed and minuted opposition of his council.

During the same period, repeated efforts to bring Kasi Setti to book failed. The younger Sullivan wrote to Munro in September 1816 that a week after having been acquitted of corruption by a court of circuit, Kasi Setti had lodged a suit against Sullivan himself.[58] To the latter's chagrin, the Board of Revenue

[56] Ibid., p. 781.

[57] Garrow was named by the MBOR to succeed the dismissed and disgraced George Graham in 1802. Garrow added substantially to the level of revenue and, in the view of Garrow's successor, Ravenshaw, nearly ruined the province. Ravenshaw referred to Garrow later as an 'idol of the Board [of Revenue]: MC, F/151/8, Ravenshaw to Munro, 6 June 1805.

[58] MC, F/151/28, Sullivan to Munro, 22 September 1816.

was insisting that Sullivan had to answer Kasi Setti's charges![59] Clearly, the MBOR, having lost on the Commission's regulations, was not repentant, but quite prepared to give further battle as Munro moved from the task of enactment of the judicial regulations to the next tasks of seeing to their installation throughout the Presidency and to the re-establishment of the ryotwar revenue system, which the judicial reforms were intended to facilitate.

In 1816 Munro had at last achieved the objective which Bentinck had blocked in 1805. Then, Bentinck, though completely converted to ryotwar, had decreed that the Madras judicial structure established under Wellesley in 1802 was inviolate and could not be changed to conform with the principles and procedures of ryotwar. Now, with judicial and revenue principles reconciled in accordance with Munro's ideas, it remained for the principles to be made to work, on the one level in administrative practice, and on another level to constitute the foundation of a political order—a state regime—whose coherence would ensure permanent British control and whose structure would afford scope for the statesmanship that Munro had long sought in his career.

Hodgson, in his usually clear way, had seen this next step when, as reported by Cochrane in early 1816, he said that he must accept the Directors' commands—however much his own disagreed with them—even including the introduction of ryotwar in all of Madras. The system of ten-year leases which he had persuaded the Madras governor, Sir George Barlow, to establish in 1808 in all of the non-permanently settled parts of the Presidency, was doomed. Mostly this was because of the failure of the system to maintain the previous level of revenue collections, but also it was because there were substantial parts of the non-permanently settled areas of Madras where renters of villages could not be found. There, collections had had to revert to a system in which the government assumed the role of landlord (amani). as under ryotwar, except that this was a share-cropping arrangement of such complexity as to require the same large revenue staff as ryotwar and the same detailed management.

Village leases had been condemned by the Court of Directors in their revenue dispatches beginning in 1812 because of the alleged oppression perpetrated by renters upon cultivators. The Kasi Setti case merely added to the ubiquitous evidence of this. Not only had Kasi Setti allegedly extorted illegal payments from cultivators, he also used his villages and their production as a part of his system of 'revenue frauds'.[60] The most permissive of the Company's officials

[59] Ibid., 1 October 1816.

[60] According to the report on Coimbatore compiled by Munro and Sullivan, 26 February 1816, and reprinted in *SEIHR*, v. 1, Kasi Setty held leases on four villages in 1808–9 and, by 1813–14, he held ninety-six, most under false names (p. 737). Tank repairs in Coimbatore afforded an example of how he used these villages to 'defraud'. He paid workers who carried out that work a small part of their contract wages in cash, the balance he paid in products from his villages (e.g. grain) and from his trade goods (e.g. tobacco and salt) at commutated prices said to be advantageous to himself

on matters of enterprise and profit-seeking could not condone the use of power and influence derived from public office for this. Nor could they answer the charges levelled by Munro and others that under the village leases oppression could more easily be practised since collectors were prevented from being as active, informed, and interventionist as under ryotwar. Nor, finally, could the Company's judiciary be vigorously defended as a curb to oppression owing to the delays and backlogs and to the great inequalities between poor plaintiffs and wealthy, officially-connected defendants.

Continued mockery of the courts by Kasi Setti underscored this last point. During John Sullivan's humiliating trial in 1817 on a suit brought by the Coimbatore magnate, the MBOR, having seen fit to permit Sullivan to be tried, now prejudiced the outcome against Sullivan. It published some of its proceedings on Coimbatore in an effort to defend itself and Garrow from the accusation of inadequate supervision of Coimbatore affairs, thus appearing to exonerate Kasi Setti and his co-conspirators in the district. As a result, Sullivan publicly complained that many potential witnesses against Kasi Setti withdrew their testimony, assuming that the Board supported Kasi Setti against Sullivan![61] As late as 1821 the ex-treasury clerk remained free on a security bond of around Rs 30,000 contributed by ninety-three men from all over the Presidency and from every discernible status: former high Indian officials, Coromandel and Malabar merchants, village headmen, with the largest contributor (Rs 11,000) a Coimbatore merchant.[62]

RESTORING RYOTWAR

Doomed though the village-lease system was, there was still opposition to the expansion of ryotwar, even though this had been decreed by the directors. At stake for those like Hodgson, who continued to oppose ryotwar and Munro's vision of the colonial state, were two-thirds of the districts of the Presidency not then considered 'permanently settled'.[63] The MBOR report

(p. 718). Relevant London letters against village leases are found in *SEIHR*, v. 1, pp. 525ff., for the revenue letter to Madras; the revenue letter to Bengal of 29 January 1813 is found on pp. 75–84; revenue letters to Madras of 6 June 1814, pp. 536ff., especially pp. 543–5, of 12 April 1815, pp. 634ff., especially pp. 634–6, 650–1; for 3 September 1817, pp. 706ff. Notes on these Madras letters are found in Munro's papers, MC, F/151/112, ff. 15–20.

[61] IOL, MBOR *Proceedings*, 2 March 1819, pp. 804ff., reprinted in *SEIHR*, v. 1, pp. 706ff. Sullivan's charge against the MBOR is found in *SEIHR*, v. 1, p. 809.

[62] IOL, MBOR, *Proceedings* 1821 (P/293/74), pp. 649–54.

[63] *SEIHR*, v. 2, p. 393. In the six districts deemed permanently settled (Ganjam, Vizagapatam, Rajahmundry, Guntur, Chingleput, Salem-Baramahal) the gross revenue collected in 1814–15 was SP3.4 million (or £1.4 million), against which the charges were SP325,000 (£130,000) about 10 per cent; gross revenue in twelve districts not permanently settled was reckoned by Hodgson at SP12.6 million (£5 million), against which charges for collection were set at SP1.9 million (£800,000), about 15 per cent.

of 18 December 1815 had been at pains to show that the board and the individual collectors which it supervised, having had Munro's judicial reforms foisted on them, could now hardly manage the responsibilities entailed by ryotwar. It was with ryotwar in mind, the board now argued, that they had opposed any increase in duties that would attend the transfer of magistracy.

Hodgson and his anti-ryotwar colleagues now sought to limit the damage of having lost on the judicial reforms. They argued that most of those parts of the Presidency not yet permanently settled were inappropriate for a ryotwar settlement because there land was held on the communal mirasi tenure. Neither headmen ('potails') assumed in the new judicial regulations of September 1816, nor individual landholding as assumed under ryotwar, existed in large parts of all the Madras territories below the interior upland of the Presidency where mirasi tenure was found. It was against this claim of communal property, and the corporate village polities upon which communal tenure was presumably based, that Munro had now to contend—having at all costs to avoid a trap of his creation—the notion that every village was a little republic!

He pitched himself into the struggle with more than his usual energy because he knew better than others how formidable and entrenched his Madras enemies still were. Particularly, he knew why, for over three years, most senior officials of the Madras government had opposed his judicial reforms: these were the necessary precondition for a viable ryotwar, as Munro had insisted since 1805. Simultaneously, the MBOR was constructing defences against the return of ryotwar proper, to which the Court of Directors had vaguely committed themselves as early as December 1812.

Shortly after Lord Buckinghamshire had taken up the presidency of the Board of Control and under the advice of ryotwar advocates James Cumming and John Sullivan, it was made known that the board favoured Munro's system everywhere in India. To blunt this impetuous enthusiasm, the directors countered with the proposal that the ryotwar system should be given a further trial in Madras and instructed the government to commence that task in its revenue letter of 16 December 1812. Despite subsequent reminders to Madras of the directors' wish to see ryotwar restored, it was to take another six years for resistance of its opponents in Madras to be overcome and ryotwar re-established. This hiatus can be attributed to the skill and persistence of John Hodgson, a member of the MBOR from 1803. That even in 1819 he had not capitulated on the issue of ryotwar is evidenced by his long, valedictory revenue minute of that year, shortly before his departure from Madras and retirement from the Company.

Hodgson's 1819 minute, to be treated at the close of this chapter, is carefully analysed by Nilmani Mukherjee as part of his summary of the struggle for the restoration and expansion of ryotwar from the time of Munro's return to Madras in 1814 to his death in 1827.[64] The quality of Mukherjee's discussion

[64] Mukherjee, *Ryotwari System*, chapter 5, pp. 97ff.

is enhanced by its critical objectivity towards ryotwar, something absent from most discussions of even the quite recent past.

When the Court of Directors had pronounced itself in favour of restoring ryotwar in Madras in 1812, it was partly to forestall the Board of Control's hasty, and for many directors dangerous, commitment to ryotwar for all of British India. It was also partly the result of the directors' growing concern about the ten-year village leases that had been established in half of the districts of Madras. Hence, in 1812, the MBOR was compelled to abandon its village-lease programme in several places (Coimbatore, the Palnad section of Guntur, Trichinopoly, Tinnevelly, Madura, Dindigul and Salem), and in these places collectors were ordered to revert to ryotwar at the expiration of current leases. In late 1815 and early 1816 the MBOR undertook to make ryotwar settlements in any village anywhere in Madras (except Tanjore), where the lease system was deemed to have failed as a result of arrears by renters or an inability to find reliable renters of villages. To facilitate this shift to ryotwar, all collectors in the Presidency were instructed to consult earlier revenue records for information which might be used for making ryotwar settlements in these places. Tanjore, again, was exempted from this because the powerfully entrenched mirasidars there defied any alteration of their privileges. One of Munro's first tasks, after Elliot ordered the judicial regulations and after the completion of the report on Kasi Setti's 'corruption' in Coimbatore, was to investigate the tenurial conditions in Tanjore and to recommend how ryotwar might be introduced there.

A major further step in the restoration of ryotwar demanded by London was Elliot's decision to waive a precondition long supposed as essential for any ryotwar settlement, that is, a land survey and field assessment. He decided, apparently with the tacit approval of Munro, once again his revenue advisor, that, instead of surveys, reliance could be placed upon village records of what had previously been paid as revenue and by whom. In May 1817, concerned that the pace of restoration of ryotwar was too slow, the MBOR was instructed to report its general progress. The MBOR's report of 29 May 1817 disclosed that in most parts of the old 'circars' on the Andhra coast and in parts of Chingleput, where many permanently-settled estates had been resumed by the government as a result of failures, ryotwar had been established to the extent the expiry of village leases permitted. In other districts, where village-lease agreements were not due to expire until 1820 or 1822, collectors were to encourage renters to give up their leases so that ryotwar could be introduced, or reintroduced. This same report of 29 May 1817 contained draft ryotwar regulations to be followed by all collectors, most based upon Munro's methods in the CD and enshrined in *The Fifth Report* by Cumming. Munro, being consulted about these draft ryotwar regulations, suggested that they should not be enacted without further consideration by experienced ryotwar collectors, suggesting some suspicion of the MBOR's version of his system but no essential disagreement.

By 1817 Munro was prepared to accept certain fundamental modifications in ryotwar. This included setting aside its whole survey and assessment procedure—long deemed essential—and also the idea of individual fields as the unit of assessment. Substituted for the last was an assessment unit consisting of all fields held by a ryot in a single village assessed according to productive capacity and their location in relation to village residence sites, roads and markets. This total holding, or 'farm' ('putkut' from the Telugu *pattukattu*) of each cultivator, consisted of any mix of wet and dry fields. 'Putkut', Munro had latterly decided, was usual in ryotwar settlements everywhere in South India. He now recalled that 'putkut' was recognized by his mentor Read in the Baramahal and after Read's time in the CD, as well as in Coimbatore.[65] Munro never deigned to challenge Hodgson's version of 'puttookut' ryots. Hodgson had said that, in Dindigul and elsewhere, these ryots were the same as 'nautamcars and gours' (district headmen whom Read and Munro had divested of powers in the Baramahal over twenty years before) in possessing private property in their lands. Nor did Munro challenge Hodgson's claim that ryotwar violated the ownership principle by its claim that the state owned all land.

What Nilmani Mukherjee's summary account of 1814 to 1820 does not consider is how Munro affected the process of restoration of ryotwar against the resistance of the MBOR, and especially Hodgson, its powerful spokesman, and why the Court of Directors maintained steady pressure upon Governor Hugh Elliot for that restoration. Because Munro's private papers were not available to Mukherjee, he could not have known how strong the current remained against ryotwar among the most seasoned collectors—including some of Munro's closest colleagues.

In a manner reminiscent of his detailed 1812 comments for Cumming on his opponents to ryotwar, Munro again sought to discredit the view that ryotwar was incompatible with the established rights of mirasidars and others with ancient privileges. Among those whose views he subjected to examination, and not a little scorn, were his old allies and friends, Ravenshaw and Thackeray. Ravenshaw had prepared an analysis of F. W. Ellis' mirasi papers probably at the request of some directors, whose number he was to join in 1819.[66]

Munro argued against some of his friends' assumptions about the history of mirasi rights. He disputed Ravenshaw's surmise that while mirasi rights

[65] IOL, *Carfrae Collection*, E/225, Munro to Ravenshaw, then a director, 30 September 1821. 'Putkut' he defined as 'lands which a man possesses; the fields which every old rayet in a village cultivates are called his putkut. . . .'

[66] Published as *Replies to Seventeen Questions Proposed by the Government of Fort St George Relative to Mirasi Right, with Two Appendices* (Madras: Government Gazette, 1818). Other later discussions by Ellis are: *Papers on Mirasi Right; Selected from the Records of Government and Published by Permission* (Madras: 1862, compiled by W. H. Bayley of the MBOR) and *Three Treatises on Mirasi Right by . . . Francis W. Ellis, Lt. Colonel Blackburne, Sir Thomas Munro*, ed. by C. P. Brown, Madras Civil Service (Madras: 1852).

were becoming increasingly assimilated to ryotwar by recognizing certain individualistic rights, the two were originally different, especially in their corporate emphasis. Ignoring the impressive inscriptional evidence marshalled by Ellis, Munro asked how Ravenshaw or anyone else could know what original mirasi rights were and thus how it was asserted that they were changing: 'Was it [mirasi] not always nearly as now?' He particularly attacked Ravenshaw's agreement with Ellis that originally 'all land was vested in the occupants'. Where was the proof of that, Munro asked? On one point, though, he emphatically agreed with Ravenshaw, that is where the latter stated that mirasi led to the enslavement of many: 'This is just'![67]

Thackeray was diparaged for a similarly easy accommodation to Ellis and, more culpably, to Lionel Place. This was when Thackeray differentiated the genuine hereditary ownership of mirasidars from the mere '"symbol of proprietary right of the service inams of Potail and Reddy Maniyam [tax free holdings] held in Telugoo and Canarese countries"'. To this Munro, who refused to acknowledge such a difference between the security of tenure of his 'Potail and Reddy' inamdars and mirasidars, jibed: 'This seems to be utopian jargon about symbols. . . . The simple act of granting an allowance in land in place of money for service is *called a symbol*'.[68]

Greater attention is given to the Ellis paper itself, an appreciation of the seriousness which Munro attached to the latter's reservations about the prospective or retrospective universality of ryotwar in Madras.[69] He cast doubts upon Ellis' historical contentions that 'Caniyatchi' or hereditary ownership, the Tamil term for mirasi, was ever conferred by ancient kings upon whole 'tribes' such as the 'Tuluwa Velals' (Tuluva Vellalars), as Ellis deduced. Instead, in Munro's understanding, these were an award to single individuals in each village or, perhaps, 'an allowance for managing the affairs of the village'; or that 'caniyatchi' meant 'free and hereditary property', not merely occupancy rights, which Munro thought a more correct formulation as long as it was understood to preclude waste land; or that all revenue was in kind and that money demand was new, which Munro conceded, but insisted that this was slowly changing in order to encourage production. Finally, Munro dismissed an entire set of distinctions which Place and after him Ellis claimed on the basis of ancient inscriptions as well as from current usage.[70]

Munro's attacks upon mirasi in 1817 were not made publicly until 1824, when a major section of his general review minute of 31 December was devoted to discrediting it, though then he was prepared to concede the antiquity of

[67] MC, F/151/135, ff. 200–1.

[68] Ibid., f. 201.

[69] Ibid., 'Notes on Mr. Ellis' Answers on Mirasi', ff. 202–9. Munro also had a long and detailed paper on the difficulties of adapting ryotwar to conditions in Chingleput from A.D. Campbell, then secretary to the MBOR, which shaped his arguments on that, for him, troublesome area: MC, F/151/36, dated 8 September 1814.

[70] MC F/151/135 f. 203.

communal landholding. In 1817 his notes and comments were probably for Hugh Elliot's instruction on how to defend the ryotwar decision against continued opposition. In more public terms, his manner of dealing with critics of his judicial and revenue reforms is indicated in his report on Tanjore in early 1817.

He went there stung by the MBOR's implicit challenge to transform the district's irrascible mirasidars, with their strongly corporate tenurial and political organization, into pliable 'ryots'. In his report to the chief secretary in Madras on 8 February he complained that the collector there, James Hepburn, a consistent critic of both judicial and revenue reforms, had reported that of the 6000 villages of Tanjore, in only 4000 or so were there 'potails' who might undertake the duties of village judges.[71] To ascertain this and perhaps to persuade others to come forward, Munro arranged to meet with mirasidars of Mayavaram taluk. In a frustrated letter Munro reported to the chief secretary that he had met for many hours with the Mayavaram men. They had he said:

> brought forward every argument they could devise against their being required to act as *Potails or Heads of Villages*. It was evident, from the whole of their arguments and from each individual concurring without the slightest variation in every point with the two or three principal speakers, and from all asserting what they knew to be unfounded—namely that no mirasidar has superior authority to another—that they had all preconcerted their answers and that they acted under the influence of some of their number, or some leading men of the country who directed them. . . . I thought it advisable to have no more meetings with bodies of principal inhabitants.[72]

Having freed himself from contradiction to his certain knowledge from those in whom he had always before vested great confidence—assemblies of local inhabitants—he now accused collectors like Hepburn of having failed to identify the village headmen. These, it turned out, were discovered by Munro to be supralocal authorities called 'nattamkars', the sort of extra-village local authorities (e.g. 'head gauds') he had taken special efforts to eradicate in the Baramahal and in the CD. Now, however, he told the chief secretary, 'It is a bad principle to have no intermediate authority between the tehsildar of the district and his officers . . . there should be in each principal or community of smaller villages one of the body of rayets empowered by government to act as head of the village, to settle petty disputes and direct its affairs.' If Tanjore mirasidars did not see fit to recognize this cherished Indian usage and convenience to British authority, then other candidates for the office should be found to serve.

[71] Ibid., a long letter, ff. 213–18.

[72] Ibid., f. 214, See Charles C. Prinsep, *Record of Services of the Honourable East India Company's Civil Servants in the Madras Presidency from 1741 to 1858* (London: 1885), p. 73, for James Hepburn's career; he served along with John Hodgson as an assistant collector in the Jaghire from 1798 to 1801. Letters pertaining to Hepburn's opposition to Munro and to ryotwar follow Hodgson's criticisms: see those of 3 February, 13 March, and 22 April 1817 in MC, F/151/36.

During the summer of 1817 he extended his survey of judicial and revenue arrangements to other southern districts of the Presidency; most of his old stamping-ground in the north of the Presidency was considered to require none of his attention. Trichinopoly, Madura, Dindigul, Coimbatore, Malabar and Kanara were all visited. The ostensible purpose for all of this was to determine whether there existed 'heads of villages' everywhere, as he believed, and, if not, how these officials could be provided to serve as village judges. He also asked whether, if there were none ready to assume the office, this was because of Company regulations in the past which had denigrated or eliminated them. Incidentally, he also sought to discover whether the 'new system' of judicial procedures was acceptable to the people. The latent purpose of this extensive tour seems to have been otherwise. It was to persuade collectors in the various districts that his new arrangements were workable and that the basis for a ryotwar tenure actually existed.

He sent a steady stream of letters to the chief secretary for Elliot's attention, reports meant to counter what he saw as the resistance and delays of the MBOR. Collectors who offered opposition to his proposals and his reasoning were treated to scorn in his letters. They were either toadies of Hodgson at the MBOR or, more damning, were being manipulated by powerful local interests, such as mirasidars seeking to preserve their oppressive privileges. Other collectors whose opposition yielded to his persuasion or to the persistent support he seemed to enjoy from Elliot and from the directorate in London earned his approval. Thus, he sent heavy praise to Elliot for the Trichinopoly collector, Charles Lushington, who, having disapproved of the judicial reform of 1816 and having argued vigorously against it, 'on being told that notwithstanding these objections it was to be carried into effect, he began immediately and zealously and soon completed the arrangement.'[73] Lushington, it seems, had pointed to the 'radical differences' between land tenure in his Trichinopoly and that of the CD, as described by Munro, where each field was supposedly held by a single cultivator. In his district Lushington said, no less than five owners occasionally held a field, though 'a field' there might be as large as seven acres. Lushington had based his arguments on a detailed survey of a single village using Munro's method of ryotwar settlement of the CD according to Munro's instructions.[74]

In June 1817, during the course of his tour of the southern Presidency, he asked for and obtained the extraordinary inquisitorial power of commanding any collector to dismiss subordinate Indian revenue officials 'whom I may, on examination deem guilty of bribery, embezzlement of revenue, or undue exactions'. Claiming that often he was given information on such malversations by people he knew, the implication of this power was to threaten to bring

[73] MC, F/151/135, Munro to the chief secretary, 26 May 1817, ff. 219–26, reporting on Trichinopoly, Dindigal, Coimbatore.

[74] *SEIHR*, v. 3, Minute to the MBOR, 26 November 1818, extract on pp. 515–20 from MBOR consultation of 6 November 1817.

into question the supervisory competence of any collector whom he thought uncooperative or insufficiently enthusiastic about ryotwar or his judicial proposals.[75]

Two months later Munro was in Dharwar, far away in the southern Maratha country, beginning a new phase of his career. He was appointed to serve as civil administrator and field commander in the army operating against the 'Pindaries' and ultimately against the Marathas in the final Anglo-Maratha war. Specificially, he was ordered to receive the Dharwar territory on behalf of the Company after it had been ceded by the Peshwa Baja Rao II in the treaty of 13 June 1817. While in Dharwar he continued the activities upon which he had been embarked in the far south of Madras during that summer, that is investigating revenue arrangements and establishing an orderly administration before joining the army of Lieutenant-General Sir Thomas Hislop, as commander of its reserve force.[76] In September he reported to the MBOR on the steps he had taken to purge the Dharwar administration of corrupt revenue officials who had been responsible for exactions and misappropriations amounting to SP219,000.[77] The transition in 1817 from peripatetic civil inquisitor, salesman of judicial and reforms, and fixer of revenue and judicial procedures to that of brilliant field commander was as smooth as he had argued it would be when he solicited a military command from the Governor-General, Lord Hastings, early in 1817.[78]

Before taking up this next remarkable phase of Munro's career, it is necessary to close the discussion with the struggle by the Madras civilian establishment against the restoration and expansion of ryotwar. Even during his arduous field campaigns in the southern Maratha country, he maintained a regular correspondence with Elliot, through the chief secretary of Madras, in opposition to the dogged resistance and the delays of Hodgson at the MBOR.

The difficulties of fitting powerful and entrenched communal landholding arrangements in the most valuable parts of the Presidency to ryotwar were treated to elaborate analysis by the MBOR in its important minute to government of 5 January 1818. This was another of Hodgson's works, showing that Cochrane's report of his capitulation two years earlier was incorrect. Hodgson was no more disposed to accept ryotwar in 1818 then he ever was, nor did his promotion in February 1817 to Elliot's council as provisional member quell his opposition, as John Sullivan and Samuel Davis in London hoped it might. Rather the contrary, it seems, for the younger Sullivan admitted to Munro

[75] MC, F/151/135, draft letter to government from a Shivaganga, 30 June 1817. Other letters of the time indicate that a scandal like that in Coimbatore was emerging in Salem, thus Munro was able to keep the MBOR on the defensive; see letters to him from Hugh Elliot on 23 June 1817, from D. Hill, chief secretary, on 5 July 1817, and from W. Wayte of the MBOR on 2 August 1817 in MC, F/151/36.

[76] Gleig, v. 1, p. xix, Munro's memoir of service prepared in 1819.

[77] MC, F/151/135, draft letter, Munro to Wayte, 11 September 1817, from Dharwar.

[78] MC, F/151/135, Munro to Hastings, ff. 260–1.

that Hodgson's appointment to the council by the directors was seen by many senior Madras officials as a sign that London authorities were having doubts about the Commission's recommendations and 'that the scale is turned at the India House'.[79]

Mukherjee rightly gives considerable attention to this document of early 1818 because of its skilful presentation of the various and formidable difficulties posed by the directors' orders, beginning in 1812, for the establishment of ryotwar throughout Madras. It was to be the last collective effort by the MBOR to resist ryotwar, and the basis of this resistance was, as before, partly pragmatic and partly principled.

Practical difficulties with ryotwar included finding forms in all parts of the Presidency that were equivalent to those fabricated by Munro in the CD and persuading cultivators in these non-permanently settled places to co-operate. The MBOR—Hodgson once again—found the last impossible to achieve for a set of stated reasons. Among these were: high and unequal assessments under ryotwar; the violation of long-standing, private rights in land; the oppressive joint liability for individual revenue arrears; the compulsion that was worked upon cultivators to take up fields and pay revenue, often in excess of their wishes or their resources. The MBOR concluded that ryotwar was '"revolting to justice and to all sound principles of civil government"';[80] it was a system said to have as its only justification that it garnered the highest revenue.

Going further, the board charged that the oppressive, arbitrary, and unjust characteristics of ryotwar had gradually been checked in Madras thanks to the imposition of the 1802 court system, based on British principles. Deprived of its arbitrary powers as a result of the courts, by 1808 the ryotwar system had totally failed. It had failed because under the judicial protections of 1802 the oppressions upon which its successful working depended were eliminated. The MBOR was compelled to launch the village-lease scheme because of the failure of ryotwar, and this latter system, the board complained, was never given the opportunity to resolve some of its admitted problems before the directors determined on the restoration of ryotwar.

The MBOR mockingly observed that the ryotwar being considered now was different: it was '"the New Ryotwari System". New because the MBOR had succeeded in rectifying the shortcoming of Munro's ryotwar of the CD by eliminating coercion and joint revenue liability, by recognizing private property and ancient rights, and by a determined avoidance of overassessment.

[79] The letters of the younger Sullivan of 12 September 1817 reporting his father's view, MC, F/151/28, and of 17 February 1818, MC, F/151/37; Davis on 4 March 1817 to Munro, in which he said: 'I do not know what the provisional appointment of Mr Hodgson may portend to your regulations, but I am given to understand that he is a great admirer of Lord Cornwallis' system, and that he is opposed to your code.', MC, F/151/36.

[80] Mukherjee, *Ryotwari System*, p. 108.

The cumbersomeness of Munro's scheme was also mitigated by eliminating field surveys.

Evident throughout this 1818 MBOR minute, as Mukherjee observed, was its preference for either a zamindari or a village-lease settlement for Madras. So blatant was this preference, in fact, that Elliot reprimanded the board of misrepresenting ryotwar and for actually praising the two competing forms of revenue administration under the guise of criticizing them. Elliot ordered that the board expunge these offending sections prior to circulating the minute among collectors of the Presidency.[81] The MBOR was also scolded for its sarcastic references to a proposal from Munro for an extra-assessment of ten per cent to make up any revenue deficiencies caused by the establishment of ryotwar. As if to underscore his reprimand, Elliot ordered that copies of Munro's reports on ryotwar accompany the board's draft regulations for ryotwar administration to its collectors. Thus, humiliatingly, the resistance of the MBOR seemed formally broken.

Still, a year later, Hodgson launched a final personal attack upon ryotwar in a minute to government of 8 December 1819.[82] He was no longer under the corporate cover of the MBOR, from which he had for over fifteen years directed the revenue concerns of Madras and exercised very great influence over all aspects of policy and from which position he was to thwart the expressed wishes of the directorate and their agent, Munro. This fustian of December 1819 was all his own. It was the testimony of the most senior and perhaps the most capable of the old Madras civilians, its most able and committed 'regulation man'.

Ostensibly his minute to the Madras government was prompted by the difficulties of bringing Tanjore under ryotwar. This had been admitted in a recent government order permitting village leases to be retained there. But, it was also prompted by Hodgson's impending departure from Madras and Company service.[83]

His decision to retire from the service was arrived at in some haste, causing Hodgson to apologize for the incompleteness of his paper. However, after a quarter of a century in Madras, he said that he had a duty to record his observations on the changes contemplated in the mode of revenue administration. The change to 'individual assessment, technically termed Ryotwar, by the author of it... was too variously interpreted to convey any definite and precise idea', therefore a need remained, after all the time that had passed, to clarify the intentions of the directors, beginning in 1812, to restore and expand

[81] Ibid., p. 109, regarding the letter from government of 29 December 1818.

[82] IOL, MBOR *Proceedings*, 15 November 1819, pp. 13713–92, entitled: 'A Minute to Accompany the Proceedings of the Board of Revenue under date 15 November on the Subject of the Renewal of Village Leases in Tanjore'. Mukherjee' summary of this is found on pp. 112–14.

[83] Hodgson enjoyed an extended retirement; he died in 1857 at Chigwell, Essex, aged eighty-two years. Unfortunately, none of his papers survive.

ryotwar. He intended no attack upon Colonels Read and Munro 'with idle declamation', but rather sought to make a last attempt to present a system of administration which, while securing 'a fair and regular revenue to the State will defend the resources of the people from violent impairment'. He admitted though, that on the eve of retirement after a long career, his views would not be without 'the prejudices of early education'.

His attack took the form of a set of deft queries. Was any system under which a cultivator paid his revenue to a village headman who was a 'stipendary revenue officer' or under which a patta for a specific money tax was granted ryotwar? Was this the case with even such corporately-held villages as those under visabadi tenure in the CD or mirasi elsewhere—simply because Munro had said that each sharer of rights knew his own contribution? As to the claim that '*a permanent field assessment in money* is a sine qua non of ryotwar' and 'quite necessary', why, Hodgson asked, should it matter whether the agent collecting the money tax is a holder of an estate consisting of numerous villages ('zamindar'), a renter of a single village ('mootadar'), or why, he asked, did both Read and Munro insist on taking into account the particular crop and its market price when setting 'the fixed' ryotwar assessment?[84] Hodgson was able to show that the ryotwar which was presumed to exist in many places—Nellore, Trichinopoly—was nominal and could not be otherwise because in those places wet cultivation was extensive and there was a system of state procurement, carried out under a mass of revenue servants (e.g. over 5000 in Tanjore). Under these circumstances there was no specified money demand for the revenue; collections were in kind and from the village as a whole, not from individual cultivators. Was this too ryotwar?

With five-year village leases in Tanjore about to expire, Hodgson asked what the prospect was of establishing ryotwar given the compromises that ryotwar had undergone in other places where there were substantial wet lands? When 50,000 garce of paddy (about seven million bushels) were collected from cultivators by the state and stored and then sold retail by Tanjore district officials, how was the ryotwar assessment for a Tanjore mirasidar to be assessed? Was it to be according to the value of his crop at current prices? Should the total revenue be divided among mirasidars? In what proportions? Should the cultivated land there be measured and assessed following Munro's techniques in the CD? Should mirasidars themselves assess fields in their own villages and apportion the tax liability of the village among each according to their holdings? And, how were any of these methods to be determined?[85]

He attacked the arbitrariness of the current ryotwar system. For example, the commutation of previous collections in kind to money collections could not be challenged by cultivators, even though Munro had spoken of co-operation between cultivators and revenue officials in the setting of commutation rates.

[84] MBOR *Proceedings*, 15 November 1819, para. 6; general discussion of ryotwar paras 6–29, pp. 13716–52; quotations are from para 12, pp. 13727–28.

[85] MBOR *Proceedings*, 15 November 1819, p. 13729: 139.5 bushels equal one garce.

There were no such formal provisions for negotiations in any MBOR 'rules' (though, it was followed in practice in many places). The solace taken by directors that revenue engagements (pattas) were enforceable by courts was chimerical, Hodgson charged, and would be as long as the government was one party to these 'contracts'. In the absence of court enforceable protections for ryots, these 'free' agreements with government made ryotwar a 'compulsory change' from a system of collections in kind to that in money. Ryotwar was therefore oppressive and destructive of existing property rights and of the 'spirit of productive industry'.

Munro's historical precedents were denied. In no native government was revenue collected in money from each cultivator by its officers, he asserted. Rather, revenue collections were assigned to petty rajas, zamindars, poligars, jagirdars and village renters. He also correctly asserted that it had been a village system of assessment and collection that Read found in the Baramahal. This Read modified (cosmetically, Hodgson implied) and called 'ryotwar'. In the Baramahal, 'an underhand village rent' was the foundation of ryotwar—'the rent was paid by the inhabitants *collectively* and not by each individual'. He admitted in some places where dry grain cultivation predominated (i.e. the CD, Coimbatore, Salem, and portions of Tinnevelly, Trichinopoly, Madura, Nellore, North and South Arcot, and Chingleput) 'ryotwar existed *practically* and the revenue collected . . . on a *fixed permanent field assessment* in money'. But, contrarily, revenue settlements in wet parts of many of these same districts, what were 'theoretically' ryotwar settlements were 'practically' annual village settlements and had so to be.[86]

In view of these deceptions and inconsistencies, Hodgson insisted that local investigations were called for in order to ascertain the following: Was ostensible ryotwar actually based upon fixed field assessments in money collected from individual cultivators? Were pattas issued by collectors to individual cultivators '*before* or *after*' ryotwar revenue was collected, that is, was the patta merely a receipt for revenue paid or was it a contract? What do ryots actually think of ryotwar, and do they want it? Unless answers to these queries were obtained, and the relative merits of ryotwar over zamindari or mootadari arrangements was established, the present ryotwar 'rules' merely imposed the practices of one part of Madras—its backward dry zone—over the rest of the Presidency.

Now Hodgson returned to the theme of innovation and to what he regarded as the massive flaw of ryotwar, that is the demand for a money revenue. This was the major attack of his minute. He cited the experience in Tanjore where commutation of crop shares to a money demand resulted in the justified resistance of mirasidars because, in the course of three years, the prices they received for their rice fell drastically owing to falling international prices. This led to widespread revenue defaults and land sales. Tanjore mirasidars therefore demanded a return to the amani system in which land revenue was taken by government as a share of production and thus shared uncertainties with

[86] Ibid., p. 13748.

landlords. He drew attention to conditions that compounded the difficulties of converting to a money-revenue demand, including a deficient supply of currency and the effect of that upon prices (a problem that was soon to affect all of the Presidency), the consequences of peace and diminished military and court expenditures by Indian princelings, and the adverse impact upon the prices of Tanjore's exports of rice from Bengal imports. Was not this compulsory imposition of a money revenue under ryotwar a violation of existing and ancient revenue practices of the Presidency, more even than the imposition of a zamindari settlement which had drawn the castigations of the directors in 1812 and later?

Hodgson finally turned to the dangers posed to public order and to equity by the all-powerful ryotwar collector. The records of the Board of Revenue, he said, were replete with evidence of the compulsion exercised by collectors seeking to meet the schedule to money revenues for which they were responsible and upon which their performance was evaluated; the MBOR, he claimed, had always opposed any system 'that permitted a Collector . . . to fix without appeal' the money-revenue demand for entire provinces. Collectors were loath to adjust their collections downwards from considerations of their careers 'so as to produce what ought to be understood by the word "moderate"'. Hence, the MBOR had been reluctant to accede to Munro's insistence upon 'rules' over 'regulations' and his argument that 'it would be impolitic to fetter the Collector with a Regulation'.[87] The directors were wrong if they thought that ryotwar was either favoured by the people or that it worked; the contrary was true, and it was therefore urgent to pause to reconsider whether that system should be imposed upon the whole of Madras. Accordingly, Hodgson urged that the money demand of ryotwar should be dropped and a revenue demand in kind set at no more than one-third of production: 'It is by moderation we want to repair the mischief already done by over-assessment. . . . Private wealth [will thus increase and] will ultimately produce public riches'.[88]

This Mandevillean coda—private advantage leading to public good—is perhaps a fitting close to Hodgson's final critique of ryotwar and his Madras career. It is also a fitting expression of the ultimate faith of the 'regulation man' in early colonial India. There is the confidence that an explicit and ordered code, based upon European principles of property and governance—including a state whose executive authority was circumscribed—would create in India what it was thought to have created in England. It was this lack of a plausible alternative to Munro's politically inspired ryotwar and its promised economies that defeated Hodgson.

In the case of no other actor who shared the stage with Munro is the absence of personal papers—the historian's eternal lament—so much to be regretted as in that of John Hodgson. None save Hodgson occupied the role of alter-ego, as the Other whose political principles and rhetorical artiface consistently shaped

[87] Ibid., para. 52, p. 13777.

[88] Ibid., p. 13786.

Munro's discursus on the colonial state in becoming, and few could equal Hodgson's potential for matching Munro's success at lobbying authorities in London or his ability to instruct and sway the most senior officials of Madras over the two decades that the two men contended for the enunciatory prize of setting and stating Madras policies. Both also proved adept manipulators of the collegial system of decision-making there—the several boards, the judicial officialdom, the governor's council, all of whose members were appointed in London as a fruitless means of frustrating peripheral autonomy within the Company's world organization. Both proved capable of converting that set of competing and balancing particularisms into an unified executive at once able to thwart directives from London as well as to still, if not to persuasively incorporate, those such as Munro's friends William Thackeray and James Cochrane—who might have divided and weakened that unity.

Behind Hodgson's large corpus of official papers one glimpses the same web of allies and supporters as the corpus of documentation showed that Munro had in Madras and in London. What one lacks with Hodgson is the same record of private reflections about problems and policies, the same gropings for solutions and for those efficacious and persuasive locutions about problems and policies that enrich our understanding of Munro over the same long period. Because all that we have of his work are official papers, Hodgson is reduced to a single dimension, to a flatness that is even more distorting than the Munro presented to the historian between Gleig's time and nearly a century and a half later, when Munro's personal papers were again available. For Munro's public utterances were infused by a morally-toned, Indian-centred and visionary quality that Hodgson's more bureaucratic and philosophically abstract perspective could not achieve, much less sustain.

It is perhaps not surprising that Hodgson's view harboured serious contradictions which, when set against Munro's views at the same time, generate a set of paradoxes.

Hodgson's cogent attack upon the money-based revenue system and the technical and political difficulties of commuting payments in kind in the most populous and prosperous parts of the Presidency carried the serious contradiction of supposing that a European-like political economy could survive under the constraint of a night-watchman state with limited authority and power while its principal revenue was derived through some sort of direct or indirect state procurement from producers, as in Tanjore. Also, it is evident that Hodgson presented a more reasoned and correct idea than Munro of how fundamental was the change in the social relations of production when a money demand for state revenue represented a massive proportion of total agrarian productivity and when the state, possessing neither strong fiscal nor monetary controls, was committed to a drain of resources through its commodity procurement for export. Moreover, though it was not explicit in his 1819 minute, Hodgson still favoured the village-lease system, a form which, whatever else it might have meant, limited the profits and benefits of rural property to fewer people and assumed the continuity, in some manner, of many communal forms.[89] This was surely at variance with prevailing English ('European') notions of private, individual property whose tangible advantages were to be realized through an all-pervasive market.

Munro's notion of a powerful, local executive authority—the collector—unfettered by regulations, and his notion of a wholly monetized rural economy based upon a multitude of small properties was potentially more appealing and more correct from the viewpoint of the Court of Directors than Hodgson's proposals. Yet, again, the contradictions. Munro's ryotwar purportedly based upon historical praxis and thus presumably free of innovations and disruptions was a powerful force for extended monetization and individuation of wealth through society! There was also the contradiction of a Presidency-wide ryotwar that could not be made to fit—even with the most imaginative contortions—the conditions extant in many places, and especially in the most wealthy and productive parts of the Presidency, such as Tanjore.

The general paradox is unavoidable. There is Hodgson, the consummate 'regulation man' with his devotion to European principles and practices, urging solutions which intensified communal and non-monetary economic relations; in this, he was anticipating by a generation Madras policies that systematically limited the scope of market-governed economic behaviour and restricted inheritance rules, probably, as D. A. Washbrook has argued, in order to avoid the political alienation and resistance of conservative elements in the Madras society of the later nineteenth century.[90] As to Munro, he was the alleged 'paternalist' or 'conservative' struggling from 1805 to 1816 to install communalist judicial and political processes, but, at the same time, restoring and expanding a ryotwar based upon market and money-mediated processes.

Possibly some of the paradoxes and contradictions are soluble, at least where Munro is concerned. For him the task of ryotwar, as for the colonial regime then generally in formation, was not to replicate a European capitalism and state—as Hodgson seemed to desire—but to create the conditions for a durable colonial state within a capitalist empire. This was a distinction that Munro never permitted to be lost in his own thinking nor, when he could affect them, the thoughts of others in Madras and in London. During the final decade of his life, from 1817 to 1827, he was to attain the standing to which his career had long pointed: that of a great soldier and that of an even greater statesman. These personal ends were to be public means for making manifest the imperial state that had long been forming in his imagination.

89 Mukherjee, *Ryotwari System*, p. 114.

90 D. A. Washbrook, 'Law, State and Agrarian Society in Colonial India', *Modern Asian Studies*, v. 15 (1981), pp. 676ff.

Chapter Six

Warrior

The portrait of Munro by Sir M. A. Shee is that of a warrior; it was judged by those who knew him to be 'strikingly correct' except that the torso appeared 'too stout'.[1] The face is fierce, determined and strong, and his chest was adorned with three medals: the star of the Companion of the Order of Bath awarded in October 1818, the grand cross of Knight Commander of Bath awarded in November 1819, and the medal struck for those who participated in the seige of Seringapatam in 1799.[2] Munro had taken only a minor role in the field operations that concluded the final war with Mysore with the capture of Seringapatam on 5 May 1799; he was not involved in the actual seige and seizure of Tipu Sultan's fortified capital. But, from October 1817 to August 1818, he gloried in a field command that finally brought him the recognition as a soldier that he appears to have sought throughout his long civilian career. He had been denied a command in the penultimate Anglo-Maratha war because Josiah Webbe and Lord William Bentinck in Madras considered his potential contribution to the war in the strategic CD in 1802 exceeded any he could make as a soldier, and that contribution was indeed a critical one.

Now, in 1818, though he was in his late fifties, had had no serious military experience for almost twenty years, suffered from his old deafness to which was now added increasing difficulty with his sight, he campaigned in what was called 'the southern Maratha country' with the energy and abandon of a subaltern. His force was, by his own humorous observation, little larger than that of a subaltern's, and yet, in the course of a campaign of less than a year, he not only won the military honours he craved but astonished even such old admirers as John Malcolm with his exploits.

In February 1818 Malcolm wrote to his influential friend John Adam, secretary to the Governor-General, Lord Hastings, commenting on a letter from Munro to the commander of the Company's Madras forces operating against the Peshwa.

[1] IOL, *The Asiatic Journal, 1831*, p. 27.
[2] Gleig, v. 1, p. xxiii, 'Memoir of Service'.

I send you a copy of a public letter from *Tom Munro Saheb*, written for the information of [General Sir Thomas Hislop]. If this letter makes the same impression upon you that it did on me, we shall all recede, as this extraordinary man comes forward. We use common vulgar means, and go on zealously, and actively, and courageously enough; but how different is his part in the drama! Insulated in an enemy's country, with no military means whatever (five disposable companies of sepoys were nothing,) he forms a plan of subduing this country, expelling the army by which it is occupied, and collecting the revenues that are due to the enemy, through the means of the inhabitants themselves, aided and supported by a few irregular infantry, whom he invites from the neighbouring provinces for that purpose. His plan, which is at once simple and great, is successful in a degree, that a mind like his alone could have anticipated. The country comes into his hands by the most legitimate of all modes, the zealous and spirited efforts of the natives, to place themselves under his rule, and to enjoy the benefits of a Government which, when administered by a man like him, is one of the best in the world. Munro, they say, has been aided in this great work by his local reputation—but *that* adds to his title to praise. His popularity, in the quarter where he is placed, is the result of long experience of his talents and virtues, and rests exactly upon that basis of which an able and good man may be proud. Confess, after reading the inclosed, that I have a right to exult in the eagerness with which I pressed upon you the necessity of bringing forward this *master-workman*.[3]

There is only a little hyperbole in Malcolm's extravagance and certainly none about his consistent support of Munro's ambitions. Yet, obtaining a military command was difficult for 'this *master-workman*'. Munro had importuned Lord Hastings for a military appointment in January 1817, when the prospect of war with the Marathas was not only seen as a possible outcome of the campaign to suppress 'pindari' marauders in the Deccan, but was a planned opportunity to rid the peninsula of the last vestiges of Maratha rule. To this end Hastings was assembling a vast military force, one in the north of India, the other in Madras, and men of Munro's age and rank lobbied for the best postings.

Munro claimed a command on the basis of his seniority in rank over his brother Madras officers: 'I have seen as much service as any officer in the Madras army, having, with exception of Lord Wellington's short campaign of 1803, been in every service in the army since June 1780 when Hyder Ally invaded the Carnatic'.[4] Buttressing his claim, he outlined an aggressive strategy for seizing the Maratha districts on the northern side of the Tungabhadra. It was this plan that Malcolm outlined to Adams.

Munro had put the same sort of argument to Lord Wellesley fifteen years

[3] Ibid., p. 503, 17 February 1818.
[4] Ibid., p. 546.

before, only to have his request for a command that would permit him to carry the plan forward rejected because of his important role in the CD as provisioner of Arthur Wellesley's forces and as the major political anchor on the exposed flank of the Company's forces operating north of the Tungabhadra. In 1817 he feared he was being fated for the same political role, of being placed in charge of Dharwar, really an extension of the CD for purposes of the war. Impatience for military honours combined with his sense of having accomplished all that he could, or needed to, with respect to the Madras 'revisions' impelled this renewed application to Calcutta for a field command.

At this time the highest military honour open to Munro and others in India was the Order of Bath, established by George I in 1725 and extended in 1815. No officers in East India Company service were raised to the Order in the first round of selections under the redefinition of 1815, and this caused widespread consternation, as Malcolm observed to Munro in January of that year.[5] Malcolm did report that this omission would be rectified in the next selection when it was expected that fifteen Company officers would be made Knight Commanders of Bath, and that he would soon be addressing Munro as 'Sir Thomas'! It was to be the other way around, in fact; included among the twelve generals and colonels from the Company forces chosen in negotiations between Lord Buckinghamshire and the Duke of York in 1815 was 'SirMalcolm'.[6] Munro's candidacy failed because of the provision that no military service before 1803 would be considered; hence for him it was service now in Maharashtra and a likely knighthood or the denial of that sort of distinction for all time.

Moreover, as he wrote to the senior John Sullivan in London, he had achieved all that he thought he could with respect to the judicial commission. Admitting that he was not altogether content with the regulations passed by Elliot in the previous September:

> I was very glad to get them passed in any way. I thought it better to do this, than to run the risk of something happening to prevent their being carried into effect at all, while we were wasting time in unprofitable debates. I was satisfied that the main object was to get them established anyhow; that when this was accomplished, they would maintain themselves, and that whatever corrections might be found requisite, could easily be made hereafter.[7]

For now, Munro instructed Sullivan, the task was for London to appoint the right men to senior posts in Madras:

> I must still repeat what I have said in every letter, that the only chance of rendering either the present or any other system efficient, is to employ men who are not hostile, but friendly to it; and that as opportunities offer, men of this description ought to be placed in [the Governor's] council in the Sudder Adawlut and the Board of Revenue.

[5] MC, F/151/34, Malcolm to Munro, 10 January 1815.
[6] IOL, *Board of Control, Letter Book, 1811–1815* F/2/3, pp. 245–7.
[7] Gleig, v. 1, pp. 452–3, 17 March 1817.

Sullivan and other London authorities must therefore continue to support Munro's programme with their appointments. As he elaborated to Sullivan in July 1817, 'Three or four years more will work a great change . . . here. It cannot be expected that men who have been accustomed to regard the [Cornwallis] system of 1793 as perfect will easily give it up. . . .'[8] This correspondence suggests that Munro was leaving the difficult revisions of the Madras revenue and judicial systems in something of the same degree of fragility and incompleteness as Read had left the Baramahal in 1799: relieved to have an opportunity to return to the unambiguousness and, ironically, less conflictful arena of war rather than to attempt to complete and to secure all that had been accomplished over several years. Like Read, too, he did not prepare the final report of this work. This was done by Stratton, though there is no question, as there was with Read, that Munro could have produced an able and convincing summation of the Commission's programme to the Madras government. His relations with Elliot were now very close; the latter's dependence upon Munro had become very great. There even appears to have been a move, jointly pressed by Elliot and by Sullivan in London, to extend the Commission beyond its three-year term, due to end in the middle of 1817. This would allow Munro the consolidate his labours, but, more important, enable him to be in Madras to inherit the governorship when Elliot himself should leave. They also believed that Munro would be in line for a knighthood. However, this last won little support from ministers of the Liverpool ministry when Sullivan sounded it in August 1817, as he later reported to his son in Coimbatore.[9] So Munro, with his commission about to expire, refused merely to extend it without some greatly enhanced rank; therefore, he had nothing but to bid for military command and its likely honours, or to return home an esteemed and wealthy gentleman, if not something more august.

His second appeal to Lord Hastings for a command came at this time. In his earlier application, in January 1817, he asked to command a force being assembled from the subsidiary garrisons in Hyderabad and Nagpur to operate against pindaris in the Khandesh area of Maharashtra. Once again he claimed this as a right of military seniority, but he added the audacious condition that he was only interested in a command involving a vigorous offensive campaign. He declared that 'without offensive operations, I have no wish for the present to join the army'.

> Against native armies, in general, defensive measures are always ineffectual, but more especially against Pindarries . . . who move without bazars [supply contingents] and enter the country merely for plunder. . . . They can only be put down by seizing the districts in which they assemble, and either keeping them, or placing them under a native government, which can keep them under complete subjugation.[10]

[8] Ibid., p. 453.

[9] MC, F/151/28, Sullivan to Munro, 8 April 1818, regarding a letter from his father in London, dated 31 August 1817.

[10] Gleig, v. 3, pp. 220–1.

Now in August he again put his case. The southern Maratha districts where he was, having been ceded to the Company by the Peshwa in accordance with the subsidiary treaty of June 1817, were under the occupation of a small sepoy force commanded by a British officer. Munro was charged with the administration of the tract. After reporting on administrative matters he reiterated his plea for a command:

> With regard to what more immediately concerns myself, though I cannot but regret deeply to feel, for the first time, the army in advance shut against me, and that your Lordship's plans do not admit of my being employed with the forces of the Deccan, I am sensible that those plans ought not to give way to the views of individuals. I have accepted the command offered to me by the Madras Government, of the troops destined for the occupation of the Peishwah's cessions in Dharwar. . . . Had I been certain that it would have led to nothing else, I would have declined it; but I indulge the hope that, in the event of hostilities, and of any vacancy occurring among the brigadiers in the Deccan, it may possibly lead to my being employed in that quarter.[11]

In mid paragraph this somewhat rueful tone changes, as does the content of the remainder of this Hastings' letter of 12 August 1817. For Munro here launches on an analysis of the Indian political system which ranged over an enlarging compass until he reaches the most general level of 'our Indian Empire'.

He began by asserting that the 'Native states' and their chiefs were too weak to carry a dangerous war against the Company. In this he disagreed with Sir John Malcolm's 'able observations on the subject' which Munro thought exaggerated the military power of Scindhia and Holkar. Both were too weak even to suppress the pindari ravages in their territories and thus too weak and too distant from Company territories to be menacing. The military balance had changed to such an extent during the previous twenty years, owing to the improvement of cavalry forces in the Company's armies, that not only was there no military danger from the most powerful of 'Native governments', but there was no longer a need for the system of subsidiary alliances initiated by Lord Wellesley.

This last shift of subject and of the range of his discursus also comes in mid paragraph and masks the startling character of what Munro continues to argue to Hastings.

Subsidiary alliances were jusitifed when the military power of Mysore and the Marathas was vigorous, 'but that time is now past', and practical advantage had now given way to principled disadvantage:

> There are many weighty objections to the employment of a subsidiary force. It has a natural tendency to render the government of every country in which it exists, weak and oppressive; to extinguish all honourable spirit among the higher classes of society, and to degrade and impoverish the

[11] Gleig, v. 1, pp. 460–7.

> whole people. The usual remedy for bad government in India is a quiet revolution in the palace, or a violent one by rebellion, or foreign conquests. But the presence of a British force cuts off every change of remedy, by supporting the prince on the throne against every foreign and domestic enemy. It renders him indolent, by teaching him to trust to strangers for his security; and cruel and avaricious, by showing him that he has nothing to fear from the hatred of his subjects. Whenever the subsidiary system is introduced, unless the reigning prince be a man of great abilities, the country will soon bear the marks of it in decaying villages and decreasing population. This has long been observed in the dominions of the Peishwah and the Nizam, and now is beginning to be seen in Mysore.

The recent history of Mysore showed that the able dewan Purnaiya,[12] minister of Haidar Ali Khan and Tipu Sultan before being appointed by the patron Company to serve the boy Wodeyar ruler of Mysore, Krishnaraja III (r.d. 1799–1831), 'had saved that country from the usual effects of the [subsidiary] system'. Unfortunately, in 1810, the young raja had dismissed his Brahman dewan and began a tyrannical and profligate personal rule that squandered the goodwill of his subjects and the treasury built up by the minister. The lesson of Mysore in its growing chaos (which led to the assumption of direct administration by the Company in 1831 following a recommendation from Munro when governor of Madras) was that an able dewan, appointed by the British and discreetly supported by a British resident, was a far better means of protecting both the interests of the British and of the subjects of native rulers than the presence of a subsidiary force under British officers. Such a force had the 'inevitable tendency to bring every native state into which it was introduced, sooner or later, under the exclusive dominion of the British government.'

Munro had now entered upon a set of questions which were to dominate policy deliberation between the time of Bentinck's and Dalhousie's governor-generalships, several decades in the future. The fate of the nawabs of the Carnatic awaited every Indian state under British rule, for, Munro insisted, none could keep to the terms of the subsidiary alliance 'as long as there remains in the country any high-minded independence, which seeks to throw off the control of strangers'. Munro said, 'I have a better opinion of the natives of India than to think that this spirit will ever be completely extinguished; and I can therefore have no doubt that the subsidiary system must everywhere run its

[12] Personal information is sparse about this famous minister, whose name is usually spelled 'Purneah' in records of the time. He seems to have been a Tamil Madhava Brahman from Coimbatore, and in the course of his career won recognition and other rewards from Haidar Ali, Tipu Sultan, and a host of British officials besides Munro, who was certainly very lavish in his praises. Perhaps the best available account of his measures in Mysore is that of M. H. Gopal, *The Finances of the Mysore State, 1799–1831* (Calcutta: Orient Longman, 1960).

full course, and destroy every government which it undertakes to protect.'

An India without native states—entirely British—Munro was suggesting was within grasp, but it was not, he thought, desirable:

> One effect of such a conquest would be, that the Indian army, having no longer any warlike neighbours to combat, would gradually lose its military habits and discipline, and that the native troops would have leisure to feel their own strength, and, for want of other employment, to turn against their European masters. But even if we could be secured against every internal convulsion, and could retain the country quietly in subjection, I doubt much if the condition of the people would be better than under their Native princes. The strength of the British Government enables it to put down every rebellion, to repel every foreign invasion, and to give to its subjects a degree of protection which those of no Native power enjoy. Its laws and institutions also afford them a security from domestic oppression, unknown in those states; but these advantages are dearly bought. They are purchased by the sacrifice of independence—of national character—and whatever renders a people respectable. The natives of the British provinces may, without fear pursue their different occupations, as traders, meerasidars, or husbandmen, enjoying the fruits of their labour in tranquillity; but none of them can aspire to anything beyond this mere animal state of thriving in peace—none of them can look forward to any share in the legislation, or civil or military government of their country. It is from men who either hold, or are eligible to public office, that natives take their character: where no such men exist, there can be no energy in any other class of the community. The effect of this state of things is observable in all the British provinces, whose inhabitants are certainly the most abject race in India. No elevation of character can be expected among men who, in the military line, cannot attain to any rank above that of subahdar, where they are as much below an ensign as an ensign is below the commander-in-chief, and who, in the civil line, can hope for nothing beyond some petty, judicial, or revenue office, in which they may, by corrupt means, make up for their slender salary. The consequence, therefore, of the conquest of India by British arms would be, in place of raising, to debase the whole people. There is perhaps no example of any conquest in which the natives have been so completely excluded from all share of the government of their country as in British India.

The line of moral and political reasoning of this August 1817 letter to Hastings was one to which Munro was to return at what he believed was the end of his governorship of Madras in 1824. But, in a letter soliciting a military post, the discussion is surely remarkable. It is possible that Munro was hoping with this letter not merely to impress Hastings with his neglected merit as a soldier, but, even more, his potential merit an an imperial advisor to the Governor-General himself.

He exercised a somewhat less lofty statesmanship to Malcolm later in the same month as he wrote to Hastings. His friend had reported on the treaty of

13 June that Elphinstone had forced upon the Peshwa. Munro's opinion was that the money and the troops which were promised by the latter were good enough, but the territory around Dharwar and Belgaum yielded to Madras (and in which he was illustriously to serve very soon) was disappointing: 'a little corner of country . . . for better or worse as a man gets his wife' and lacking easy access to Mysore and the CD. He expressed the hope that this was not final and that Madras would get more territory.[13]

COMMAND

Command and rank did come before the year was out. In early November, on the same day that Lord Hastings' powerful field force of 113,000 men and 300 guns intimidated Scindhia into capitulation,[14] the Peshwa rose against his British protectors, burnt Elphinstone's residency in Pune and launched the war for which Munro had waited. Two weeks before this, as the crisis mounted in western India under the moves of the provocatively massive British force, Lord Hastings took the precaution of strengthening his army of the Deccan by promoting Munro to the rank of Brigadier-General. Munro was informed of this by his new superior and sometime ally in Elliot's council during the recent revenue and judicial debates, Sir Thomas Hislop. The latter commanded an army consisting of five divisions of which one, the reserve, Munro was to command. He was to have the pay and allowances he had enjoyed as first commissioner which Hislop told him was the equal of Malcolm's.[15]

Ironically, Munro learned of all this when he was already in the field on a service *for* the Peshwa, Baji Rao II. He was leading a small sepoy force to wrest a fortress from a Maratha chief at Sundur, about 130 miles north of Dharwar, and to hand it over to officials of the Peshwa. This chief, Siva Rao, had refused to surrender his fort to the Peshwa, and the latter, in accordance with the treaty of June 1817, called upon his British protectors. Munro managed to receive possession of the fortress without opposition and had returned to Dharwar to resume his administrative duties when the war with the Peshwa broke out in November.

In Dharwar, Munro found himself separated by soldiers loyal to the Peshwa

[13] MC, F/151/120 Munro from Dharwar to Malcolm, 30 August 1817.

[14] P. E. Roberts, *A Historical Geography of the British Dependencies*, v. 7, 'Part 1, History to the End of the East India Company' (Oxford: Clarendon Press, 1916), p. 283.

[15] MC, F/151/33, Hislop to Munro, 20 October 1817. Munro had previously been told by Hislop that authorization for his promotion had been granted while discussing other division commanders serving under him. Among the latter was Colonel Theophilus Pritzler, who was to prove a valuable subordinate to Munro throughout the southern Maratha campaign. Pritzler served in the King's 22nd Dragoons: MC, F/151/38. Other references to Pritzler in the Munro Papers are frequent, e.g. in F/151/40, dated 4 April 1818, and especially regarding the dispute raised by Brigadier-General Lionel Smith over whether it was he or Munro who commanded Pritzler, in which Munro gave strong support to his subordinate; MC, F/151/39.

from the division he commanded which was now north of the Kistna under the charge of Brigadier-General Theophilus Pritzler. Thus, isolated from his command, Munro determined, as he put it 'to subdue the neighbouring districts, by the influence of a party among the leading inhabitants, and by the aid of a detachment from the garrison at Dharwar, assisted by a body of irregulars collected from the country.' With this ragtail force, as Malcolm appreciatively noted, Munro spent the next five months campaigning in a territory extending some 120 miles in a broad arc north of Dharwar, taking the surrender of some twenty-five forts. At times his curious force was augmented by a small artillery unit from the Bellary garrison, but for the most part he was able to win possession of the hill forts around Dharwar, and between Belgaum in the west and Badami in the east, without much fighting. Some fortified places taken by him did offer resistance and were formidable. One was the hill fortress at Badami, whose ramparts even now present a strenuous and dangerous ascent; another was Belgaum, where the fighting was sharp and bloody after a seige of three weeks.

Late in April 1818 Munro rejoined the main reserve division and marched it to Sholapur, 170 miles north of Dharwar, to engage and defeat a main force of the Peshwa's infantry on 10 May and take its fortress after an attack on 15 May. From here Munro marched part of his reserve division another 140 miles to the west to Nipani ('Nepauni'), in modern Belgaum district, near Kohlapur, to force a yielding of the Peshwa's major forts there, and then to the fortress of Paurghur, north of Kohlapur, to seize the last of the fortified places held by the Peshwa in his southern districts. When he resigned his commission on 8 August 1818 he had, in his own words, 'in the course of the campaign, reduced all of the Peishwah's territories between the Toombuddra and Kistna; from the Kistna northward to Akloss [Akolkot, Sholapur district], on the Neemah, and eastward to the Nizam's frontier'.[16]

This outline account of Munro's part in the final Anglo-Maratha war, from October 1817 to August 1818, is taken from the memoir that he prepared as part of his application for the Bath award. Behind its bareness is the remarkable achievement of having wrenched a 3000-square-mile tract from Maratha control, of denying resources of money and men to the Peshwa at a time of great need, and of opening a broad path to Pune from the south. All of this was done with a force of some 600 sepoys and the occasional support of seige guns from the Company's regular forces. His success, as Malcolm noted to Adam, was partly a result of knowing a good deal about local political and social conditions in the Dharwar–Belgaum area, where he had been active as an administrator from the previous August. But, as Malcolm also noted, this knowledge and Munro's use of it hardly diminished his achievement.

A year earlier, in August 1817, Munro left behind the frustrations of imposing his judicial and revenue procedures in the southern Presidency to take up the administration of Dharwar. He did so with a sense of liberation. His route to

[16] Gleig, v. 1, pp. xx–xxi, 'Memoir of Service'.

Dharwar took him to the familiar haunts of the Ceded Districts, pleasing after the heat, humidity, and perverse resistance of Tamil country mirasidars of that summer. Nearing Dharwar on 4 August he wrote to his wife, whom he had left as a guest in the home of his friend Colonel Thomas Marriott in Bangalore, to report his progress northward: 'I began my journey my dear Jane by losing my road 2 miles beyond Bangalore. I did not sleep all night, next day and night. I had the most troublesome headache. I however got to Chittledroog [about 130 miles from Bangalore] on the second, about 10 o'clock when I got a good breakfeast and a walk among the rocks which restored my health.'[17] But soon Dharwar began to pall as well, and he complained of having 'to waste time with Mahratta vakeels', the Peshwa's agents, arranging the cession of lands around Dharwar that were demanded from the Peshwa as the price of the subsidiary force to which the latter had agreed in the June treaty negotiated by Elphinstone.[18] Boredom and frustration with these duties found expression in his August letter to Lord Hastings requesting a military command and arguing against the subsidiary system; now again, in early November, he wrote to Hastings in a more confident tone, for he had just returned from a successful mission against the Maratha chief, Siva Rao, deep in the Maratha country. He complained to the Governor-General about the vagueness of his orders for the occupation of the area around Dharwar. However, that very imprecision had permitted Munro to formulate his own plan of action in the light of his own sense of things. Hence, he explained to Hastings why he had decided to undertake the expedition to Sundur with what Elphinstone worried was a very small force, considering he was to traverse a dangerous tract far from his Dharwar base. Munro rejected the alternative of treating with the able Sundur chief at a distance through vakils, believing that a direct and rapid action would permit him to accomplish more. 'Sheo Row', confronted by Munro, complied with his demand for a release of the fortress; in return for the co-operation of the chief, Munro had granted him a jagir in the value of Rs 12,000 'and some little provision for his principal servants'.[19] In this way a strategically placed chief in the heart of the Peshwa's country was possibly neutralized in the coming struggle. However, it is important to notice that this chief, Siva Rao, was already in rebellion against the Peshwa, and it was because of this that the latter prevailed upon the resident Elphinstone to have a British force sent to punish the recalcitrant chief and to bring the Sundur stronghold under a *killadar* (fortress commander) of his own.

Early in November 1817 Munro was conveying to Hastings a strategy for the pacification of much of the Dharwar–Belgaum area. One method he proposed was to assume the role of protector and guarantor of chiefs who sought protection from the demands of the Peshwa or merely a bit of buffering against the time when, if war broke out between the Peshwa and the Company, they

[17] MC, F/151/183, dated 4 August 1817.
[18] MC, F/151/135, Munro's draft letter to Lord Hastings, 9 November 1817.
[19] Ibid., Munro to Hastings, 9 November 1817.

might make the right choice. Munro urged even that tentative neutrality could be gained at a price that was negligible to the Company. He also told Hastings that the threat of the pindaris in the Dharwar country had been exaggerated. There were not, as believed, some 30,000 in these plundering bands, but probably half that number, and they could be checked by an aggressive campaign. He closed with the hope that he would not be ordered to return to the tedium of the 'Mahratta vakeels', but permitted to remain with Brigadier Pritzler's force now operating against pindaris north of the Kistna, or, even better, to join the staff of General Hislop.

This letter to Hastings was sent from Dummul, a fortified town north of the Tungabhadra as Munro made his way back to Dharwar from Sundur. Dummul was to be taken by him and his small force in January 1818. However, in late 1817, when he returned to Dharwar, he found his commission to serve on Hislop's staff, as a brigadier over the reserve division, and that the war with the Peshwa had begun. But as his way to the reserve division was blocked by the Peshwa's soldiers and a great territory of potential supporters of the Peshwa, he devised a dangerous alternative. In letters of 26 and 28 November he proposed 'expelling the Mahrattas from . . . [around] Dawar . . . [with] this subaltern command I deem more useful at the present moment than that of any division south of the Toombuddra'. This was the plan described to Adam by Malcolm. It was set by early December and launched later in that month when he led his small force out of Dharwar against Maratha horsemen around Navalgund ('Nawlgoond'), north of Dharwar.[20]

Brave indeed! Perhaps foolhardy. But Munro explained to Hastings why, at this juncture, what he proposed was reasonable. From 'my present situation in the middle of the southern Mahrattas. . . . I have an opportunity of seeing a good deal of their civil and military government'. He asserted that the Peshwa's regime should be overthrown by the main force of the Madras army without difficulty because that regime lacked any credibility:

> All other Hindoo states took a pride in the improvement of the country, and in the construction of pagodas, tanks, canals, and other public works. The Mahrattas have done nothing of this kind; their work has been chiefly desolation. They do not seek their revenue in the improvement of the country but in the exactions of the established chout from their neighbours, and in predatory incursions to levy more. . . . A government so hostile in its principles . . . ought, if possible, to be completely overthrown . . . [it] is little better than a horde of imperial thieves.

To its lack of legitimacy as a 'Hindoo' state, Munro added other reasons for the vulnerability of the Peshwa's overlordship. The territory between the

[20] Gleig, v. 1, pp. 470–1 and pp. 480–2, Munro to the Adjudant-General of the Army, 24 December 1817. The following work is useful in locating many of the places mentioned: Irfan Habib, *An Atlas of the Mughal Empire* (Delhi: Oxford University Press, 1982), plate 16A.

Wardha and Kistna rivers was 'not properly Mahratta', he said. Its people were a mixture of Maratha and 'Canarese', and the latter 'form the great body of the people. . . . Mahratta jageerdars and their principal servants are therefore considered, in some measure, as strangers and conquerors'. This diminished the capability of the Peshwa to defend against a determined military operation by the Company. He pointed out that while the Peshwa's cavalry consisted of Marathas who were loyal to their chiefs, the infantry garrisons in the numerous forts of the western Deccan and local militias who protected villages 'are mostly Canarese, and ready to join any power that will pay them'.[21]

Further weakening this polity, and dividing the civil society from the government of the Marathas in Pune, was the hostility of merchants and of the most powerful and respected agriculturists of Maratha rule: 'All trading classes are anxious for the expulsion of the Mahrattas, because they interrupt their trade by arbitrary exactions, and often plunder them of their whole property'.

For all of these reasons, Munro argued, the prospect for undermining the Peshwa's forces around Dharwar were good. He added for his approach that it had been used successfully 'by Hyder Ally in this very country'. The latter had garrisoned forts and villages with armed 'peons' brought with him from Mysore and the CD, just as Munro had done. Adoption of this strategy would relieve Hislop's main divisions from the responsibilities for garrisoning, and therefore increase the troops available for pursuit and destruction of the Peshwa. At the same time, as Haidar Ali Khan had shown, if a cavalry force such as that of the Marathas were denied access to towns and villages for supply, they could not hold together as large formations, and thus, having lost their military capability, they would become dispirited and disperse. Finally, this method being proposed by Munro would create the conditions in the southern Maratha country for the most rapid, full, and permanent civil control by the Company.

Whether Hastings was persuaded by these adroit arguments or even understood them is not clear. Nor was it very material, for by late November the Peshwa decided to commit his army against the Madras army north of the Kistna, and also in the southern districts that he had been persuaded to cede to the Company five months before. Maratha cavalry and infantry under Kasi Rao Gokhale moved into the doab of the Kistna and Tungabhadra, and Hastings promptly issued his orders to Munro. His first task must be to defend Company territory in the CD against Maratha incursions; secondly, he was to protect the frontiers of the Company's client states of Mysore and Hyderabad; and finally, he was to attempt to consolidate the Company's position around Dharwar. With the contemptible forces at his disposal, these were formidable tasks, and they were set by a Governor-General who, as commander of the northern Company forces operating against the Marathas, had neither the time nor the knowledge to appreciate Munro's analysis and strategy.

However, Munro was fortunate in being instructed by Hastings to co-ordinate his actions with Mountstuart Elphinstone, Hastings' agent at Pune

[21] Gleig, v. 1, p. 472.

for dealing with the central Maratha territory. Elphinstone was already prepared by his knowledge of the Marathas and his respect for Munro's reputation to support the latter's politically reasoned plan for carrying the attack aggressively to the Marathas instead of attempting a defence with such forces as he had.

In late 1817 Munro reported his actions around Navalgund to Hislop. This had involved engaging Kasi Rao Gokhale's horsemen who sought to take forts from small groups of armed revenue servants under which they had been left during Munro's strike against Sundur the previous October.

He justified his rapid and dangerous march to Navalgund not only as a means of protecting the 'peons' who he had previously left, but, more importantly, as a means of tying down Gokhale's forces there and deflecting incursions into Company territories whose protection had been made his first responsibility. Because the Maratha commander, Gokhale, had jagirs around Dharwar, he was well positioned to endanger the CD and Mysore unless Munro could frustrate this by denying Gokhale his base: 'The most likely way of preventing [Gokhale's attack upon the CD] . . . was to find the enemy employment in the defence of his own possessions, but as there was no disposable regular force present, I determined at once to avail myself of the aid of the inhabitants in accomplishing this object.'[22] This was neither an obvious nor an easy task. What Munro did and why it might have been successful require explanation.

The *what* is at once straightforward and mystifying. He informed Hislop that after driving off Kasi Rao Gokhale's troopers from around Navalgund, he immediately set about appointing 'military amildars', i.e. heavily armed civil administrators, throughout the large tract north of Dharwar to the Malprabha River, forty miles away. These men were for the most part recruited in Mysore and authorised by Munro to raise armed contingents ('peons') from among local Kannadiga people, and to assume the administration over all of these places. The armed peasants recruited by his amildars came to number between 7000 and 10,000 during the course of the year.

One of Munro's amildars was Rama Rao, a Kannada Brahman, perhaps originally from these districts of the Peshwa's domain, as many Mysore administrators were then and later. Munro appointed Rama Rao to the Navalgund area, and, with 500 armed 'peons' that he had quickly gathered, he attacked the town then held by Kasi Rao Gokhale's son, Govind Rao. He drove the latter's horsemen from Navalgund, capturing horses along with the town and its fort. When Kasi Rao heard this he marched to Navalgund where he encountered, and prudently withdrew from, Rama Rao's small force, to which had been added a small unit of sepoys under a British officer serving under Munro.

This, like most of the engagements at the time, did not involve large formations, nor the use of artillery. The successes were political rather than military—they depended upon the rapid mobilization of local people for resistance to the Marathas. Munro's letters to Elphinstone in Pune from December 1817 to

[22] Ibid., p. 481.

the following August reveal much of this. In December he told Elphinstone that he was conducting negotiations with all the jagirdars around Dharwar except Gokhale, and that one important jagirdar, Appa Desai of Kittur (about twenty miles north of Dharwar) was a promising potential collaborator with the British.[23] Munro then boasted that 'nine-tenths' of such chiefs 'are in our favour' and that the whole of the area south of the Malprabha should fall to him soon, largely 'by the help of the armed inhabitants'. He reported that he had issued proclamations throughout this area instructing village headmen not to pay revenue instalments (kists) to officials either of the Peshwa or Gokhale, and soliciting their co-operation in expelling the Marathas. He also told Elphinstone that among the defenders of the numerous fortified places around Dharwar 'I have partisans . . . who, with the help of the inhabitants, will gradually expell . . . men from the countries north of the Kistnah'.[24] He shrewdly expected that the more substantial village people would be alienated from Maratha rule when, as a result of being denied revenue, the Peshwa and Gokhale began to plunder villages to pay their soldiers.[25] The success of all this, he warned, was contingent upon the failure of the Peshwa to commit large forces to the Dharwar–Nelgaum districts in support of Kasi Rao Gokhale; such moves would have to be countered by the main force of the Madras army.

THE POLITICS OF CONQUEST

This was the approach in early 1818 and letters of this period go to prove its effectiveness. Why? One answer is that Munro had, long before, grasped a central principle of Maratha political organization. This he understood in the late 1790s, before the final war with Tipu Sultan, and he understood it before many others did.

It is recalled that in Munro's letters of that time on the politics of the peninsula he set a higher importance upon Tipu Sultan and Mysore than upon the Marathas as potentially dangerous enemies of the Company.[26] That this view was not based upon any experience of Marathas does not diminish its perspicacity. An astute observer of Indian politics, Munro knew enough of the Marathas to discern fundamental differences between their polity and that of Tipu Sultan, and he knew enough to realize that the latter represented the most dangerous future for the Company's dominion in the peninsula, and in India as a whole. That future was precisely the same for European conquerors of the subcontinent: the creation of a unified political power through military modernization supported by a bureaucratic fiscal structure. The technology of both were

[23] See a file in the Munro Collection on Kittur, F/151/126.

[24] Gleig, v. 1, pp. 222–3, 18 December 1817, and p. 224, Munro to Elphinstone, 20 December 1817.

[25] Gleig, v. 1, pp. 225–6, Munro to Major-General Lang, commander in the Ceded Districts, 2 January 1818.

[26] Gleig, v. 1, pp. 102–4, Munro to his father, 30 September 1796.

within the grasp of Indians, as the performance of the Company's sepoys had demonstrated and as Tipu Sultan's state-building was threatening in the 1790s. Munro's understanding of the Maratha political potential was therefore based on a reasoned comparative sense of the significant systemic differences between the Marathas, a typical Indian old regime polity, and a newer sort of regime which was incipient in some places in India, but especially in Tipu Sultan's Mysore.

An additional and more immediate source of his sense about the southern Maratha situation was his experience in the Ceded Districts. There, his 'silent settlement' with poligars proved a means of pacifying the intractables in the huge territory in which he suddenly found himself thrust in 1800. His policy had been to reassure this stratum of petty territorial magnates, who Munro insisted were more like princelings than the landlords sought under the programme of establishing a zamindari regime in Madras. His policy had worked to prevent any concerted opposition by them to the pacification of the Ceded Districts and the inauguration there of a civil administration. By 1802, when he found himself strong enough, he launched an attack upon the eighty or so major poligars and succeeded—by keeping them divided and uncertain of his determination to uproot them all—in eliminating them.

But this was not the method he seemed now to favour, and he was stung by Malcolm's jocular accusation in June 1818 that Munro was 'sukht [harsh] toward Maharajahs'. Malcolm had reported his own generous treatment of some of the high Marathas he had captured in the northern theatre of the war and anticipated Munro's criticism. Correctly supposing that Malcolm was referring to his policy in the Ceded Districts, Munro protested that those whom he had driven from authority or punished were not the same as the Maratha grandees. These Ceded Districts chiefs, Munro sneered,

> were a set of fellows whose ancestors had been expelled forty of fifty years before. Some of them were serving as common Peons, when they were discovered by some adventurer of a Karkern [*karkun*? from the Persian, a financial agent], who borrowed a hundred rupees in the bazar, rigged out the new Rajah with a turban and a mantle as fine as Timour the Tartar. . . . On these fellows I certainly had little compassion. . . . But for fallen monarchs I have great respect. . . .[27]

Of course, the southern Maratha country in 1818 was not the Ceded Districts in 1802. The Dharwar–Belgaum area had for a century been part of a Maratha state when it had been *the* great state of the subcontinent. By contrast, the Ceded Districts was turbulent and dangerous precisely because, for more than two centuries, it had been a border land between the kingdoms of Mysore and Hyderabad after the demise of the great Vijayanagara kingdom. Munro, of course, gave no credence to the greatness of the Maratha state, and he even denied that the southern portions of the Peshwa's state were actually part of a

[27] Gleig, v. 1, p. 261, Munro to Malcolm, 19 June 1818, and Wilson, *Glossary*, p. 261.

Maratha polity at all. Far from the Maratha heartland of Pune, it was peopled by Kannadigas who regarded Marathas, especially Maratha jagirdars and the Peshwa's officials, not as compatriots but as oppressors.

Munro, of course, would immediately have identified local magnates around Dharwar, who often used the title of *palegar*, as men with whom accommodations and considerable manipulation were possible. Therefore, his letters to Elphinstone in the middle of 1818 supported the latter's soft and conciliatory line. This was not merely respect for his new friend's cautious and conservative approach nor was it a temporary expedient to be changed, as it was in the Ceded Districts, when the dangers of war had passed and normal production and trade had resumed somewhat in southern Maharashtra. The Munro of 1818 was no longer one who would raze the royal abodes of Dharwar jagirdars and poligars as he had hung, imprisoned, and banished similar men in the Ceded Districts. He thus agreed that most jagirdars should be left in possession of their small territories and urged Elphinstone to attempt no more than inducing them to be neutral in the fighting between the Company and the Peshwa. That is, to persuade them to withdraw their dependants from the Peshwa's army and refrain from paying their tribute.[28] More than this, Munro believed, was impossible to hope for: 'their pride and their fears will deter them from deserting the Peshwa while there is any chance of his continuing to be their master because of 'the disgrace they would sustain from the charge of rebellion and ingratitude, were they to abandon him.'[29]

One letter to Elphinstone, in April 1818, suggested how much he had changed since the early Ceded Districts days. It is a remarkable letter in a number of ways, a position at which reads:

> The Jageerdars have now, I believe, no expectation of seeing Bajee Row, or any of his relations, at the head of a state; but their zeal for the continuance of the office of Peshwah, even though divested of real power, is as strong as ever. They retain their possessions, and feel, therefore, in a much smaller degree the dissolution of the substance of the Mahratta empire than that of the forms. [But] They derive whatever they possess from those forms; they have for generations been accustomed to respect and serve [the Peshwas]... and they regard it as disgraceful to abandon them for others. The easiest way of subduing these prejudices, and of rendering them useful feudatories, would be for the Company to take upon itself the office of Peshwah, and to issue all public acts as coming from the Pundit Purdhan [*pradhan*: Peshwa's minister], as under the late Government investiture might be received, according to custom, from the Rajah of Sattarah. The Company, acting as the Pundit Purdhan, would hold an office, which, as in the case of that of

[28] Gleig, v. 3, p. 245, Munro to Elphinstone, 23 April 1818. This and other letters cited for convenience in Gleig, v. 3, principally, are found in the Munro Papers at the IOL, F/151/37–40.

[29] Gleig, v. 3, pp. 227, Munro to Elphinstone, 9 January 1818, and pp. 237–8, 29 March 1818.

the Dewanee in Bengal, would take from it none of its sovereign powers; and its governing the country under this ancient title, would, I believe, reconcile the Jageerdars to the change of masters, and induce them to employ their troops willingly at the call of the British Government.[30]

This proposal to assume the chief ministerial office in the Maratha state, as had been done in Clive's Bengal, is surprising in view of the opprobrium that measure had released in Warren Hastings' impeachment. It is the more surprising in the light of Munro's advice earlier to Lord Hastings about the management of 'Native governments' through the appointment and control of a dewan; for here, the Company was to stand as dewan! But, also noteworthy in this proposal to Elphinstone, is its basis in a theory about how the Maratha polity worked.

Munro seemed to base his proposal on a theory recently analysed by Andre Wink—that for the Marathas sovereignty was a shared quality between a king (or his *pradhan*) and the vatandars (hereditary landholding households), *samasthaniks* (minor ruling houses) and zamindars (local chiefs). This theoretical position is actually elaborated in a seventeenth-century Marathi text entitled *Ajnapatra*, attributed by Wink, ambiguously, to a time in the 'wake of the Mughal invasions', but more accurately probably the work of a minister of Shivaji.[31] A legal work by a Brahman sastric scholar presumably, this text is given an important place in Wink's explanations of eighteenth-century Maharashtra for its realism, and for its refusal to join most works on polity of the time which 'pass over' the subject of the crucial position of the locally powerful because of the bias of these 'highly schematic centralist accounts'.

Thus, the text, as cited by Wink, says:

The vatandars in the kingdom, the desmukhs and deskulkarnis [district headmen and accountants], the patils et cetera, they may be called 'office-holder,' but this is only a term of convention. They are in fact very small but self-sufficient chiefs. They are not strong on their own, but they succeed in keeping up their power by allying themselves with the 'lord of the land', the *sarvabhaum* [sovereign]. Yet it must not be thought that their interests coincide with that of the latter. These people are in reality the *co-sharers* (*dayada*) of the kingdom.[32]

This seventeenth century Marathi text also observes that vatandars were habitually dissatisfied with their possessions and always sought more, and that

[30] Gleig, v. 3, pp. 247–8, 23 April 1818.

[31] A. Wink, 'Land and Sovereignty in India under the Eighteenth-Century Maratha Svarajya', doctoral thesis, University of Leiden, 1984, p. 212. This monograph was published by Cambridge University Press in 1986. However, citations here are to the thesis kindly provided by Dr Wink. The *Ajnapatra* is analysed and partially translated in two numbers of *The Journal of Indian History*, v. 8 (1929), pp. 83–105, 207–33 and v. 29 (1951), by V. D. Rao, pp. 63–89.

[32] Wink, p. 86.

they never intended loyalty 'to the lord of all the land, the raja'. Still, the *Ajnapatra* recommended that the raja use moderation with them, neither to force an abrupt end to the aggrandizing schemes to these small chiefs nor to give them free reign: rather, something between 'friendship and suppression'. According to this view the 'self-sufficient chiefs' were not seen as corrupt, disloyal office-holders acting seditiously against the ruler, but as 'his partners, his co-sharers'.[33]

Munro's understanding of these principles of Maratha polity is impressive. In his dealings with the jagirdars of the southern districts he exploited both the weak and the opportunistic links between the Peshwa and the autonomous samasthaniks and poligars of Dharwar and Belgaum. He exploited the susceptibility of local lordships distant from the Maratha centre to disengage from commitments not seen to be advantageous as long as dishonour or fear did not exact too high a price. This was what the Maratha rulers called sedition, or *fitna*. Munro also understood the notion in the *Ajnapatra* that authority in this polity was not exclusively hierarchical and centralized, but especially in those parts of the realm that had not been brought under the direct rule of the Peshwa's officials on a permanent basis, where *makta*, or tax farming and tribute payments obtained, political authority was a shared thing, dayada between an authoritative centre and each of the numerous peripheral and autonomous lordships.[34] An instance of this understanding was Munro's recognition that Kasi Rao Gokhale's military actions around Dharwar were not essentially that of agency on behalf of the Peshwas, but protection of family properties—jagir lands—there. Understanding all this, Munro told Elphinstone that he was negotiating with all jagirdars except 'Goklah'.[35] This same apperception was conveyed to General Hislop, commander of the Deccan army, when Munro justified his bold mix of diplomacy and threats of military action north of Dharwar. He said that 'the Southern Jageerdars, who form a considerable part of the Peishwah's force, can be under no necessity to abandon his cause while their own districts are untouched'.[36] And his proposal to Elphinstone in April 1818, that the dewani of the Peshwa's domains should be assumed by the Company, intended to substitute the Company for the Peshwa as the co-sharing other in the relations of dayada that bound the numerous small chiefs into a polity there.

He outlined to Elphinstone his civil programme for the Maratha tract south of the Malprabha in January 1818.[37] A negative aspect of this programme was ironically sketched for his wife, a short time before, when he characterized his tasks then as 'a new line of business . . . encouraging plots against constituted authorities of the ancient government and hearing the accounts of success or

[33] Wink, pp. 247–9.
[34] Wink, p. 551, 'Glossary'.
[35] Gleig, v. 1, p. 305, 18 December 1817.
[36] Gleig, v. 3, p. 300, 5 December 1817.
[37] Ibid., pp. 230–1, 25 January.

discomfiture of my friends the conspirators.'[38] More seriously, and presumably in response to an inquiry from Elphinstone, he disagreed that it was feasible to attempt to achieve full civil administration over the Dharwar tract while warfare against the Peshwa continued. The authority of such an administration was bound to be weak as long as any part of the tract was subject to attack from the Peshwa's soldiers. Instead, he preferred to continue to govern through his military amildars, Kannada-speaking revenue officials that he had brought with him from Mysore the previous summer.

This would assure military possession, the first requirement for the area. Revenue was secondary, and this should be collected through the tahsildars already there whom village headman knew and from whom the revenue could then be gathered by his amildars: 'there should be no innovation, at least during the war'. Nor should revenue be set at a high pitch 'or the inhabitants will have no motive to join us'. In any case, the object was not a great revenue but the denial of any revenue to the Peshwa or his supporters. Munro added that he was finding revenue administration fatiguing owing to his failing eyesight, and he asked Elphinstone to appoint a military officer to assist him, proposing the names of two that he thought had adequate experience and knowledge. He concluded by announcing to Elphinstone his intention to introduce the judicial provisions which had been adopted in Madras during the previous September.

A further expression of Munro's expectations for the numerous Maratha lordships of the southern districts is gained in a letter to Elphinstone in early February 1818.[39] Asked by the latter for his opinion about the Governor-General's proposals for the post-war political system of Maharashtra, Munro said one advantage of the new, smaller Peshwa state being contemplated with its centre at Pune was that the soldiers and officials of the defeated Peshwa would find employment and would therefore not contribute to disorder or be a political danger. But, he continued, this same sensible end could be achieved without such a new state, i.e. if the British assumed control of the Peshwa's territory. Then, both soldiers and civil officials of the former regime could be employed by the British to the extent that the disbanded soldiers and dismissed officials could not be employed in the service of jagirdars! Munro seemed to be thinking then of a continuation of the rights and powers of the Maratha jagirdars, including their substantial employment of soldiers, within a territory ruled by the Company. This is a quite novel suggestion, surely, indicating again a fundamental change from his Ceded Districts policies. Then, fifteen years earlier, he had seen local lordships such as jagirdars and poligars as being inimical to Company rule, if not to political order itself.

Later in the same month he answered other questions put by Elphinstone. These pertained to military strategy against the Peshwa. Munro had been kept in close touch with general military matters from the time of his eleva-

[38] Gleig, v. 1, p. 512, 28 December 1817.
[39] Gleig, v. 3, p. 234, 5 February 1818.

tion to the staff of General Hislop, and it was clear that Elphinstone valued his opinions on military questions. Among the suggestions which Munro offered to the latter was for an assault upon Satara, 170 miles north of Dharwar. This place, he observed, was not particularly strong, and its seizure would have the important political consequence of further inducing major jagirdars everywhere, and especially those in the south, such as Appa Desai of Kittur, whose breach with the Peshwa Munro had been cultivating. Most of the southern jagirdars would then quickly follow suit, 'for they adhere to him only because none of them would like to incur the reproach of being the first to desert him'.[40] As a result, Munro said, he had adopted an inducement in his negotiations with jagirdars, offering a substantial increase in the jagirs of the first among them to desert the Peshwa.

TOWARDS ANOTHER DEPARTURE

By May 1818 the massive British force operating against the Peshwa achieved the result that Lord Hastings had planned, of hammering the Maratha confederacy into submission. In that face of the imminent collapse of the Peshwa's resistance and authority, Munro found himself facing some impatience from Elphinstone about the slow pace at which the jagirdars in the south were coming forward as allies of the Company. Among the longest to fend off the pressures of Munro was one upon whom he had lavished the most assiduous attention. This was the chief of Kittur who held the heavily fortified Nipani. He had paid no tribute to the Company and had not desisted from occasionally firing upon parties of Munro's amildars in the neighbourhood of his holdings. Still, Munro asked for more time, and also for whatever records from the Peshwa's 'Duftus' that might help in his negotiations with the jagirdar of Kittur and the others.[41]

Despite these delays, plans could now progress to the installation of the civil administration that was to succeed Munro in the southern Maratha districts. He desired no place for himself in these plans and sought to discourage Malcolm for his efforts to persuade John Adam and Lord Hastings in Calcutta to give him the administration of southern Maharashtra. Munro thought that Elphinstone was well suited for governing the whole of the Peshwa's dominion. All that he lacked, Munro said to Malcolm, was confidence, and Munro said that he was trying to bolster that in Elphinstone. The main task with respect to the southern part of the Peshwa's domain, Munro insisted somewhat startlingly, was 'to keep the new territory out of the hands of the Madras Government for some time' by establishing an administration under Elphinstone with responsibility to Calcutta, not Madras. The reason for this anti-Madras stance, especially when a year before he had complained to Malcolm about Elphinstone's treaty

[40] Ibid., pp. 308–13, 21 February 1818.

[41] Ibid., pp. 266–71, 6 July and 8 July. The Hindustani *daftar* refers to official records and accounts; Wilson, *Glossary*, p. 117.

with the Peshwa as having failed to yield substantially to the territory of Madras, will be discussed below. But, part of Munro's concern to keep Madras at a distance was reminiscent of Cornwallis' reasons for appointing Read and Munro to the Baramahal twenty-six years earlier. It was essential, Munro told Malcolm, that Elphinstone should be permitted to establish his own administration in Maharashtra; he must be free to choose as subordinates those 'who will act zealously with him; not fellows sent from a [Madras] presidency who have been all their lives in a state of lethargy', and he should have a powerful and mobile military force at his disposal. For himself, Munro said, his eyes prevented further active service and he looked forward to returning to their Scotland to pass 'the evening of life [quietly, rather] than going about the country here in my military boots and brigadiers enormous hat and feathers, frightening every cow and buffalo. . . .'[42]

Having removed himself, he urged Elphinstone to recommend the appointment of William Chaplin to head the civil administration of southern Maharashtra following his departure. Chaplin was then serving as collector of Bellary, and Munro spoke of him as 'the fittest person in the Madras Civil Service'. He also performed the role of the conscientious patron by proposing an ample salary for his long-time younger colleague, one thousand pagodas per month, which he justified on the grounds of the arduous tasks attending 'first settlements of a country'.[43] If Madras was reluctant to free Chaplin from his important responsibilities in the Ceded Districts, then Munro proposed William Thackeray, his even older protege who was then serving as a replacement in Coimbatore for the ill Sullivan.

Elphinstone accepted Chaplin, and Munro expressed his satisfaction by saying that the latter had deep experience and sympathy with Indians and their institutions, a quality which he insisted was vastly superior to 'all of the regulations and codes of Calcutta and Madras together':

> It is too much regulation that ruins everything; Englishmen are as great fanatics in politics as Mohamedans in religion. They suppose that no country can be saved without English institutions. The natives of this country have enough of their own to answer every useful object of internal administration, and if we maintain and protect them, our work will be easy. If not disturbed by innovation, the country will in a few months settle itself.[44]

There were at this time other concerns that Munro expressed to his old friend, John Malcolm, to his new one, Elphinstone, and to others. These were his failing sight and his chagrin with Madras over another pay dispute, and, more importantly, the lack of support and appreciation by Madras of his military achievements.

Deterioration of his eyesight appears to have begun during the middle of

[42] Gleig, v. 3, pp. 258–9, 10 June 1818.
[43] Ibid., p. 250.
[44] Ibid., pp. 252–3.

1817 when he was touring the southern Madras country seeking to install his judicial and ryotwar reforms. Since coming into the field early in 1818, his sight problems had sharply increased; reading and writing became more difficult. He wrote to his sister Erskine in March that he was now unable to do either by candlelight.[45] Even before this, he had been encountering difficulty, as he wrote to his friend and financial advisor George Brown in London, the previous October. He told Brown that because of his failing eyesight and because 'I am now on my way with a military force to subdue the petty Mahratta chief of Soondoor' Brown would be receiving fewer letters.[46]

Adding to this impairment, his distance vision was also failing. He told Elphinstone that during the seige of Belgaum, between 21 March and 10 April, 'I was day after day straining my sight to observe the effect of our artillery, that I could not pronounce positively, as I could have done some months ago, whether the breach was practical or not'. He continued:

> But I am not obliged to look at a breach everyday. It is in civil affairs, which require writing every day, that the decline of sight becomes a most serious evil. There are many days when I cannot write at all, in consequence of a painful straining of my eyes. There is no day in which I can write without pain, or for more than a few minutes at a time. . . . A man who wishes to enter into the details of civil and political arrangements, among Jageerdars and Zemindars, must examine himself every person who can give him information, take down in writing what each person says, and compare their different reports. This is the course I have always followed, but I cannot continue it now. I should not get through in a month what was formerly the work of a few days. I must not, therefore, disgrace myself by holding high employments, the duties of which the decay of my sight will prevent me from discharging with efficiency.[47]

His friends caught Munro's growing alarm about his sight. Malcolm advised him to get away from India as soon as he could, to take the rest his exertions had earned and his eyes demanded. For himself, Malcolm said, if he failed to win high office, i.e. the Bombay governorship, he too would leave India in a year.[48]

His friend Malcolm was also involved on his behalf in a dispute over his military salary. Malcolm had intervened through John Adam to press Hastings to instruct Elliot in Madras to end a looming wrangle over Munro's pay. According to Munro, as stated in a letter to Malcolm thanking him for his support, Elliot had apparently decided, early in 1818, that the unlimited expenses that were allowed while serving as judicial commissioner were now to be held to a fixed and low amount as long as he was on military duty. Munro

[45] Gleig, v. 1, p. 516.
[46] Ibid., p. 508, 15 October 1817.
[47] Gleig, v. 3, p. 249, 26 April 1818.
[48] Ibid., pp. 272–3, 10 July 1818.

reminded Malcolm that both had been in Lord Buckinghamshire's Whitehall office when Munro was promised Star Pagodas 10,000 a year as salary and 'all my expenses'. This, Malcolm had then observed, was nearly the same as the remuneration to Residents, and therefore should be made the same. Munro went on: 'I never thought of taking a Muchulka [Hindustani: *muchchilika*, a written bond] from Lord Buckinghamshire'. Nor had he expected the abrupt termination of his commissioner office and its liberal expenses: 'that Mr. Elliot would have taken me by the neck and pushed me out of the appointment the very day of which the three years recommended by the Directors expired, though they authorized the term to be prolonged if deemed advisable'.[49]

Elliot's renewed coolness towards Munro seems to have developed as the latter's military role and prestige had grown. Elliot, it seems, was fearful that, having promulgated the judicial reforms in opposition to his councillors during the previous September and without Munro at his side now, he would face difficulty in justifying that action. Sullivan said that Elliot was considering the appointment of James Cochrane to continue the work of the commission, having taken a dislike to Munro's fellow commissioner, George Stratton. The latter's final report of the commission Elliot thought was inadequate, and he had rejected it. Stratton was told that Elliot wanted 'something in which general principles are more dwelt upon, in short a systematic defence of the new system against the different attacks which have been made upon it'.[50]

This dispute over pay and Elliot's apparent panic and treatment of George Stratton may explain why Munro had changed his view about the territorial interests of Madras in the war, and why he now favoured a plan for the whole of the Peshwa's territory to be placed under Elphinstone, who would report to the Governor-General, not to Madras. Yet another bit of rancour with Madras arose early in the difficult campaign against the southern Maratha jagirdars and Kasi Rao Gokhale. Then, the Madras government had demanded the return of a small squadron of the Company's native cavalry, which Munro had persuaded the military commander in the Ceded Districts to release to him. Munro had ignored this—to him crippling—order to reduce his force on the grounds that a detachment of European cavalry which had been allotted to Munro by Hastings had been detained elsewhere.[51] Munro saw this as

[49] Ibid., pp. 257–8, 10 June 1818. Support for Munro's position in this controversy is found in several authorizing letters and orders: Hislop to Munro, 20 October 1817, and from Lord Hastings to Munro, 11 May 1818, MC, F/151/39 and 12 May 1818 in MC, F/151/37.

[50] MC, F/151/28, 29 April 1818.

[51] Gleig, v. 1, p. 486. The official history of the Madras army recounts this issue and condemns the Madras government by citing Munro's angry words: 'The only notice the Madras Government took of me, or my letters to them, was in a strong censure about the three troops of Native Cavalry, which, had I been permitted to carry to Sholapoor, not a man of the Peshwa's infantry would have escaped', in Wilson, *History of the Madras Army*, v. 4, p. 101. Another criticism of the lack of Madras support of his military needs is Munro's earlier letter to the Chief Secretary, David Hill, suggesting

another indication of Elliot's resentment and, as adding to his eye problems, another reason for quitting India.[52]

Two other tasks remained to be done before that, however. These were important letters to Mountstuart Elphinstone and Lord Hastings. Before leaving his civil and military responsibilities in Dharwar, Munro sent Elphinstone a long final report on the conditions he was leaving for Chaplin and other successors. This was posted from Bangalore, where he had rejoined his wife and was enjoying a rest.

His intention, he said, was to give an estimate of the disposition of 'every class of people' towards British rule in the Dharwar area, and to suggest the means 'to ensure future tranquillity'.[53] Militarily there would be no danger, providing that a force of sufficient strength and mobility were maintained for some years to check any organized opposition from the great jagirdars and the smaller chiefs in the Maratha tract he had subdued. The danger of opposition was greatest from small chiefs, but the threat that they posed was not serious: their resistance would be that of 'banditti, rather than of rebels'. They would be easily defeated by the mobile force he proposed. He cautioned Elphinstone against too hastily destroying minor fortifications that could not at that time be garrisoned by the Company. These were important for the defence of local inhabitants against pillaging horsemen and were of potential use to the British, who still relied heavily upon their infantry, in contrast to the irregular horse troops of potential enemies. This last advice was in line with that earlier offered to Elphinstone about restricting the possession of arms among the inhabitants. Munro had argued that there should be no bar on individual travellers and merchants and 'higher class of inhabitants' carrying arms or engaging small bodies of armed escorts when going about. Issuing passes for this was a bad idea because these would be a vexatious source of bribery for legitimate travellers who should be able to defend themselves against robbers and plunderers.[54]

A final advice on military matters was the employment of all regular professional soldiers by the Company or by jagirdars, and the disbanding of all irregular Maratha soldiers so that they could return to their villages and to agricultural occupations. Irregular horsemen had constituted half of the Maratha field forces, Munro reckoned, and they often were wealthy village people, frequently village and district officers, and always from among the 'most substantial rayets'. Under the Peshwa, and especially during times of war, these

that the large garrisons of Company soldiers in the Northern Circars would be better employed under him in an aggressive campaign than in static defence; MC, F/151/40, 10 December 1817.

[52] Gleig, v. 3, p. 308, 22 January 1818.

[53] Gleig, v. 2, pp. 66–81. Elphinstone was not the only high official he was then instructing. The newly appointed civil administrator at Nagpur, R. Jenkins, sought Munro's advice on principles and procedures to follow in establishing Company rule there, MC, F/151/37, 27 April 1818.

[54] Gleig, v. 3, pp. 264–5, 6 July 1818.

men bred horses for sale to the army and often also sent their dependants—'their own domestics and labourers'—to serve as soldiers as an investment in plunder operations. With an end to the war, these substantial rural families should now be encouraged to deploy their resources 'in some other branch of trade'.

What this might be Munro had indicated in a letter to Kirkman Finlay, a fellow Glaswegian with business interests in Bombay. Munro wrote to Finlay with a promise to instruct his successor, Chaplin, to assist Finlay's business partner when the latter visited Dharwar to explore commercial potentials there. Munro spoke approvingly of the intention 'of showing the Rayets how much better customers free merchants were than a Company of monopolists' and also about the advantages of Dharwar: 'a great deal of fine cotton is grown in the provinces which have fallen into our hands'.[55]

To Elphinstone once again, on 28 August 1818, Munro was reassuring about the political situation in the Dharwar–Belgaum area. It was stable and would remain so if the promises he had made to all of the major jagirdars (except Gokhale, whose lands were seized) and to many of the minor chiefs were kept, and if no startling changes were introduced. He recapitulated the commitments he had made and the reasoning for them, for why he had rewarded some jagirdars and chiefs and punished others. He also provided his assessments of some who might prove particularly helpful, or troublesome, to the British: Appa Desai of Kittur was distrusted and despised by the people of his jagir for his cruelty and extortions and by Munro for the latter's numerous defiances. On the other hand, the Brahman Patwardhan jagirdari family of Sangli (modern Kolhapur district on the Yerla river) enjoyed popularity in their tract, were peaceful, and were grateful to Munro for his award of additional jagir lands. All such magnates should have their cavalry forces reduced to a quarter of the contingents they had previously. This would limit their military capabilities and also encourage deployment of their resources on agriculture and stock breeding.

He had left the political foundation of the Dharwar–Belgaum tract pretty much as he found it, Munro said, and recommended to Elphinstone that nothing should be done to weaken the 'gentry' formation there, a recommendation with which Elphinstone had much sympathy.

Munro's 28 August letter to Elphinstone closed with a consideration of the civil administration of the Dharwar–Belgaum tract. He admitted that his military duties had prevented consistent attention to civil matters which had been made most difficult by the flight of the Peshwa's collectors and accountants with the onset of war. Several months would be required to form an estimate of the revenue collections during the past decade, but Munro was confident that a large and consistent revenue could be gathered. It was, he observed, a fertile country, but its cultivators were both few and poor. Hence the greatest encouragement should be given to increasing cultivation by a low revenue demand, by permitting village headmen to collect from ryots as

[55] Ibid., p. 275, 11 September 1818.

a means of reassurring the former of their older privileges and authority, and to encourage them, as the most resourceful of cultivators, to make investments in agricultural production. A land survey should be delayed for several years so as to minimize fears among village heads and wealthy ryots that this would result in increased revenue demands or a change in their extensive inam rights. District and village headmen, as well as accountants, held 'considerable enaums'. These should be left undisturbed 'as it establishes a respectable class of landholders and gradations of society' and fortifies the authority of district and village officers upon whom the British must depend. All inams had been guaranteed by Munro, but he told Elphinstone that many had been granted on no authority higher than district or village headmen; and these should be treated as resumable by government under certain circumstances.[56] Given Munro's cautions about not proceeding with haste, he was in effect recommending that the settlement of inam lands in the southern, former Maratha, districts be left intact, as they had been left by him in the Ceded Districts.

Minting, trade cesses, and other prerogatives of jagirdars that inhibited trade should be abolished, but compensations should be paid 'for the sacrifices of these rights'. The Madras judicial reforms should be established here except that there should be no zillah court for some years. This was to permit Chaplin, as principal collector, and his European assistants, to gain 'more weight in the eyes of the natives'.

Munro closed this long instruction to Elphinstone with the reminder that his revenue policy had been to collect as much as he could without incurring the opposition of chiefs and village headmen to British rule. This was to deny resources to the Peshwa and weaken his military. Following that policy, he had been able to pay the salaries of his twenty-five military amildars and their nearly 10,000 armed peons by whom most of the territory had actually been held against the Peshwa. Yet he had left a surplus in the Dharwar treasury: so 'the campaign in the Carnatic [as he and others were calling the tract] may be said to have been carried on without any expense of Government'![57]

It is scarcely to be wondered at, then, that Munro won the plaudits of all for his remarkable year in Dharwar: his courage and political astuteness had not only contributed to the final defeat of the Marathas but also smoothed the way for the civil incorporation of a large tract with a prospectively large revenue from its excellent cotton soils—all at virtually no cost!

The balance of 1818 was spent in repose, with his family, and basking in the laurels being heaped on him in India and England. Among those from whom

[56] Gleig, v. 2, pp. 266–81. The circumstances specified for resumption were if they were granted after 1792, when part of the country fell to Tipu Sultan, or, in other parts, if they were granted after 1796 when the Maratha minister, Nana Fadnavis, was removed from power by Baji Rao II.

[57] This claim of a self-financed military campaign in the southern districts of Maharashtra was acknowledged in Calcutta as Hastings writing, through John Adam, to Munro attested on 7 November 1818, MC, F/151/37.

commendations came was Lord Hastings, and in November 1818 Munro wrote to the Governor-General thanking him for his praises. He told Hastings that he had resigned his Dharwar office only because of his poor health, and on the same grounds he had to reject Elliot's offer to remain for a longer time in Madras to complete the work of the Commission. Civilian tasks would be no easier for him to perform, given the difficulties with his sight. All of this Munro said he regretted because it was his greatest wish to 'give what assistance I could in carrying into effect the orders of the Court of Directors, for employing the natives more extensively in the internal administration of the country'.[58]

He continued this last communication with Hastings in that tone of high statesmanship that he had previously effected. The reliance upon Europeans for the administration of India was excoriated: 'such agency is too expensive; and even if it was not, it ought rather to be abridged than enlarged, because it is . . . much less efficient than that of the natives'. Nowhere was this more true than in the judiciary. As to the supposed corruptibility of Indians, are not the lessons of England and of Bengal that corruption could be reduced by increasing the pay and standing of civil servants? This was as true for Indians as for others. Finally, Munro said that as long as the British hold upon India depended upon 'our military power' alone, it will be fragile. Only when trust and confidence are vested in Indians, and their employment in the administration of the country expanded and properly rewarded, would British rule become secure. Here in outline is another portion of the argument later to be developed in his 31 December 1824 valedictory minute on the state of the country and the condition of the people.

He had received the honour of Companion in the Order of Bath order in November, shortly before this letter to Hastings. From August 1818 to that time Munro and his wife were guests of his old friend, James Cochrane, in Bangalore, a place which was fast becoming a favourite resort for Madras officials. Then the journey to Madras was made for their departure from India. However, his passage from India was delayed, until late in January 1819, by storm damage to the ship they were to have boarded.

The voyage to Britain was marked by two memorable events for Munro. One was the opportunity to visit the Napoleonic haunt of St Helena, something to which he had long looked forward; the other was the birth of a son, Thomas, aboard the ship *Warren Hastings*, near the Azores, on 30 May. One month later the Munros were in Scotland. There Jane Munro and her infant son stayed in Ayr with her father, while Munro undertook a tour of the Highlands.

[58] Gleig, v. 1, pp. 517–20, 12 November 1818. Munro also turned down Elliot's offer to take command of the Madras division operating in northern Maharashtra under Sir A. Floyer. He anticipated Munro's rejection of the offer on account of his eyesight by saying that he had learned from George Stratton that Munro merely needed the correct spectacles! MC, F/151/37, Elliot to Munro, 5 August 1818.

But he knew that his stay in Britain was likely to be brief, for there had been talk, even while his ship stood off Deal in Kent, that he was among the preferred candidates to succeed Hugh Elliot in Madras. That appointment was made, along with the award of the Knight Commander of Bath, in November 1819, the last such award made by the aged king George III.

Chapter Seven

Governor

Major-General Sir Thomas Munro, K.C.B., returned to Madras after the briefest of stays in Britain. In fact the time of the return voyage of Munro and Lady Munro exceeded their home sojourn, and he was destined to see neither Britain nor the infant son he left there again.

In December 1819, once again at Deal awaiting a favourable wind to carry him to India, he wrote to his sister Erskine of his sense, now, of being as much tied to Britain as to India:

> I had no wish to ever leave . . . [Britain] again, but as I must return to India, I am impatient to be there. My attachment to both countries is so nearly equal, that a very little turns the scale. I like the Indian climate and country much better than our own; and had we all our friends there, I would hardly think of coming home; but this country is the country of all our relations and of early life, and of all the association connected with it. It is also the country of all the arts—of peace, and war, and of all the interesting struggles among statesmen for political power, and among radicals for the same object. It is near France and Italy, and all the countries of the Continent, which I have earnestly wished to visit since I first read about them. The only objection I feel to going to India is my age. I might now, perhaps, find employment in this country, and I have health enough to travel over Europe, and visit whatever is remarkable for having been the scene of actions in ancient times; but when I return from India, it will be too late to attempt to enter upon a new career in this country; and my eyes will probably be too old, if I am not so in other respects, to permit me to derive any pleasure from visiting the countries of the Continent. I may deceive myself, and fancy, like many other old Indians, that I am still fit for what may be beyond my power. There is no help for it now; I must make the experiment of the effects of another visit to India upon my constitution and mind. I hope that you visit Cragie sometimes, and see that my son is not spoiled, but brought up hardily as we were in Glasgow.[1]

[1] Gleig, v. 2, pp. 8–9, dated 12 December 1819.

Included among 'our relations' were Erskine and his other sister, Margaret, and their husbands, his only surviving brother Alexander, and the kinsmen of his wife, Jane, including her father at Cragie, with whom his son had been left. There was one other person at least, Munro's illegitimate daughter.

She was called Jessie Thompson and had been placed with a Captain Samuel Ward of the Shrewsbury Yeoman Cavalry in 1816. This was arranged by a military friend of Munro, Colonel William Cunningham. The latter had written Munro in India then that 'your child' would require about £50 a year for her clothes, schooling, and lodgings with the Wards, and Alexander Munro had confirmed these arrangements at about the same time.[2] Munro visited his daughter in the company of another old army friend, Major-General Charles Dallas, late in November 1819, and his will provided her with an annuity of £100.[3] Other correspondence suggests that Munro behaved with consideration towards this, perhaps miscegenous, child, as did many other Britons in Madras then.[4]

Munro's child by an unknown, perhaps Indian, mother was one of the many-stranded bonds that so nearly balanced the pull of his divided attachments to Great Britain and India. Two others were the young men of his family and that of his wife. The first was John Munro, son of Munro's brother Daniel, who had died in 1799.[5] Care for this orphaned nephew in his youth was the major responsibility of Erskine, though Alexander also maintained a continuous avuncular interest and kept his brother Thomas informed about their nephew's progress. The other young kinsman, William Campbell, was a brother of Jane Munro. His Indian career and destiny were totally different from that of Munro's nephew, John, who served and died in India as a Company official. During Munro's tenure as judicial commissioner he (Munro) was informed by the collector of Kanara, with some embarrassment to Jane Munro, that his assistant, Campbell, had fallen into a wretched state under the influence of drink and an evil Muslim butler.[6] Munro noted on this 1817 letter that Campbell's debts amounted to 21,000 pagodas, which he undertook to pay. Campbell was shortly afterwards suspended from the Company service.[7]

[2] MC, F/151/35, letters to Munro in March and on 15 April 1816.

[3] MC, F/151/198, General Dallas then witnessed Munro's declaration that Jessie was his daughter and that Munro afterwards sent her a Bible. Munro's will of 12 December 1819, in MC, F/151/154, specified that Jessie should receive £70 each year; this appears to have been increased to £100.

[4] Attested in letters of Mary Symonds, sister-in-law of Sir Henry Gwillim, a judge of the Madras Supreme Court, IOL, European Manuscripts, Symonds Collection, C240/2a, f. 124, in a letter dated 6 June 1803.

[5] MC, f/151/149, in a letter from Erskine of 28 February 1800. The date of Daniel's death in Bengal was April 1799.

[6] MC, F/151/36, M. T. Harris to Munro, received on 30 May 1817.

[7] MC, F/151/168, ff. 26–9, and letter of 24 January 1818. Also, F/151/174, George Brown to Munro, 20 October 1818, referring to Lady Munro's brother William Campbell, on whose account Munro paid S.P. 11,053 into the treasury of Fort St George.

Sir Thomas and Lady Jane Munro reached India again in May 1820, touching at Bombay, where they enjoyed an affectionate visit with Governor Mountstuart Elphinstone before re-embarking for Madras. He assumed the governorship from Hugh Elliot on 10 June 1820.

Before taking the ship that was to convey him from Bombay to Madras, Munro wrote privately to George Canning, President of the Board of Control. He appears to have been executing a commission from Canning to assess conditions in Bombay, a mark of confidence in Munro's judgement and discretion. Canning had been influential in Munro's appointment to Madras, possibly along with the Duke of Wellington, and Canning's was among the most generous of the tributes when Munro was feted in London prior to his departure for India.[8] Munro reassured him that all was quiet in India, and that Bombay was under Elphinstone's able management, thanks in part to the skilful administrative collaboration of Munro's protégé Chaplin, 'who, of all of Madras Civil servants, is the best qualified for the purpose'.[9]

He warned Canning that John Malcolm would surely leave India for good at the end of the year unless some high office was offered to him. Malcolm, he felt, should be kept in Malwa and made responsible for what was soon to be called 'Central India'. For some years, he said, someone of Malcolm's abilities and experience would be needed to deal with the turbulent conditions of that newly conquered area. He did not say to Canning what he was obviously thinking—that after a few years in Malwa Malcolm could succeed to the governorship of Bombay. Bombay is what Malcolm had told Munro he wanted and deserved and was, indeed, to receive in 1827 when Elphinstone returned from India. Munro's boosting of Malcolm was a repayment for the latter's many interventions on behalf of his career.

But, ironically, even as he was building Malcolm's case for Bombay, he sought to reduce Bombay to a much smaller province than it was under Elphinstone. Some months after assuming his duties as governor, Munro put it to Canning that the security of British rule in India required that the present condition of peace be used to fortify that rule.

> The first step for this purpose should be to assign limits to the different Presidencies within which they are respectively to exercise immediate authority, leaving to Bengal the general control of the whole. The limits that I would recommend for Madras are the Mahanuddy [in Orissa] and the Nerbuddah [on the border of Malwa] to the north; to the west, the boundary between the Nizam's and the Peishwah's country, as it stood in 1792; and to the north-west a line drawn from the Kistna to the Ghauts, including within it the southern Mahratta states.[10]

He followed this suggestion with some arguments that delineated the respective

[8] Such encomiums are cited by Gleig, v. 2, p. 6.
[9] Munro to Canning, 15 May 1820, in Gleig, v. 2, pp. 50–1.
[10] Munro to Canning, 14 October 1820, in Gleig, v. 2, p. 52.

interests of Madras and Bengal while ignoring altogether any interests that Bombay might be thought to have. It is notable too that by 1820 Munro had dropped his earlier reluctance to see the southern Maratha country under Madras, and for that matter a substantial additional portion of the Indian peninsula as well. The office and interests of Madras had settled swiftly upon Governor Sir Thomas Munro!

If Bombay was to be weakened, even partitioned, according to Munro's suggestions, Bengal was viewed with many of the old suspicions. He knew little of the capital of British India, and what he did know renders doubtful his sincerity about 'leaving to Bengal the general control of the whole' of British India, even though, statutorily, Calcutta was the seat of the 'supreme government' and Governor-General. His suspicions about Bengal sprang from several old and some new prejudices. His Madras enemies—Hodgson and Fullerton, and Petrie before them—were men whose authority in Madras stemmed from their expressed commitments to the Cornwallis system. That system had the support of all Governors-General from Wellesley on, and of a dominant section of the courts of directors from 1800. To all, the prescription for British rule in India had been set by Cornwallis, 'a name', as Grant had written to Petrie in 1808, 'never to be mentioned without regret [at his death] . . . when acts of peace are truely cultivated'.[11] And it was Bengal, after all, that had dissuaded Bentinck in 1804–5 from supporting Munro's judicial changes. These changes, in Munro's estimation, could have made ryotwar a workable administrative strategy then, and perhaps raised it to the preferred form of imperial administration for the Company's growing dominions.

More recently, Munro was presented with a view of the bankruptcy of Calcutta as a source of imperial leadership by his old friend and colleague Colin Mackenzie. This view was proferred before Munro began his governorship. In January 1819 Mackenzie wrote of his disappointment that Munro and his wife would not have time to visit him in Calcutta, from whence they could have embarked for England. Pleasant as that visit would have been, however, he doubted that Munro would have learned much 'in the opulent Capital of British oriental Government'. Calcutta's byzantine 'establishments' would not have yielded their secrets during a stay of a few months, even to so acute an enquirer as Munro. For 'the Prime Movers in the scene for 40 years back have now all passed away and I am sorry to observe we have little to expect from the *Dandies* of the present day.' He excepted from this condemnation two members of the Governor-General's council, James Stuart and George Dowdeswell, who, alone among officials of the supreme government, eschewed the 'universal objects . . . to live as comfortably and economically as possible to save a fixed income to retire on, while all cares of the welfare of the Public is out of sight'. Less jaundicedly, Mackenzie continued with a confusingly stated argument of the sort that Munro had put elegantly to Lord

[11] Morris, *Life of Charles Grant*, p. 306, citing a letter from Grant to Petrie ot 16 September 1808.

Hastings, the Governor-General, some time before. Mackenzie wrote:

> To retain India a downright Military Force . . . seems to be looked to, with the Army of course this doctrine will be ever prevalent; as I consider it impossible that all India can ever be governed without a share in its administration is left to some portion of the natives [for] as we find it impossible to administer justice promptly to that portion (40 million perhaps) that were already under our jurisdiction what are we to do with all India? . . . undoubtedly with the progressive reduction of India from its Native States to Alliances, supported by a Subsidiary Force, which ultimately ends in a provisional assumption of the territories first of our enemies, then of our Allies, until at last it culminates in the direct cession of the Provinces . . . there is no doubt but that a British Government affords more security of property and to the freedom of the subject than an Indian one; but that Government must be permanent on fixed principles . . . .[12]

Mackenzie apologized here: 'the subject has carried me away my friend', and proceeded to speak with unguarded bitterness about the peremptory way in which his antiquarian activities in Madras had been terminated by the Court of Directors on the word of 'one man' in Madras who never valued all that Mackenzie had done and sacrificed for his 'Literary, Historical Researches'.[13] Still, he hoped to be able to continue his acquisition of orientalia from his Calcutta office as surveyor-general, through such mutual friends as William Chaplin in Dharwar, from whom he had sought historical materials on the Vijayanagara kingdom and its 'Carnatic Empire and all Inscriptions'. He closed his long 1819 letter with the hope that Munro would continue their correspondence after his retirement in England and would look to him in Calcutta for information about India; in this way their friendship, which, dated from 'when we first met in Nellore in 1787', would continue.

Old friendships and enmities were much in Munro's mind when he arrived in Madras on 10 June 1820, a year and a half after Mackenzie's Calcutta letter. His first order consisted in stating his commission of 6 December 1819 from the Court of Directors, appointing him to the governorship of the Presidency of Fort St George and its dependencies and naming his council. The latter consisted of his old comrade in arms, General Thomas Hislop, his former judicial co-commissioner George Stratton, and his old adversary John Hodgson. In a separate commission for the directors, Munro was empowered

[12] MC, F/151/39, Mackenzie to Munro, 1 January 1819.

[13] Mackenzie had complained to others in the same vein, e.g. to Sir Alexander Johnstone, some four years before, when he wrote that in his new post in Calcutta he would find 'more consideration than I have hitherto found in the current administration of Madras', suggesting that the 'one man' might have been the Governor, Hugh Elliot, towards whom Munro then nurtured a similar distaste, W. C. Mackenzie, *Colin Mackenzie: The First Surveyor-General of India* (Edinburgh: W. and R. Chambers, 1952), p. 180.

to command the garrison of Fort St George and the town of Madras; it also stated that John Hodgson was to return to England and be replaced on the council by William Thackeray.[14]

John Ravenshaw, now a director, wrote at that time that in addition to Thackeray in his council it was thought to also appoint Henry S. Graeme, another old friend: 'this will secure you from all factious opposition during the whole of your reign'.[15] In addition to all these allies, James Cochrane assumed the presidency of the Board of Revenue. Felicitous appointments such as these cannot but have cheered Munro, as must the departure within a month of Hugh Elliot and John Hodgson. The business of governing could now commence.

And so it did. Between June 1820 and January 1825 Munro dedicated himself to the consolidation of the programme of revenue and judicial reforms he had to suspend in 1817. He did this by exercising his executive powers as governor to place men who actively supported his ideas, or were, at least, open to them, into positions of responsibility and to get rid of men who opposed him. He also advanced his programmes through his writings, as he had done since at least 1805. In the first four years of his governorship he drafted a large number of minutes for presentation to his council on political, administrative, judicial and military matters. Ostensibly, these were matters that arose from the normal conduct of governmental business—his solutions to specific problems. Often, however, he seized upon exigent, often minor, problems in order to reiterate—and sometimes to modify—the principles of governance he sought to set permanently in Madras. These various arguments were masterfully pulled together as a grand statement of principle and purpose in his minute 'on the state of the country and the condition of the people' of 31 December 1824.[16] The latter document was to have been a valedictory summation of his vision for British India prior to his retirement from Madras and the Company.

That he yearned for retirement by then is clear from a September 1823 memorial to the Court of Directors asking to be replaced in his office at Madras following the usual term in the office. This request was somewhat unusually dispatched for London by four different ships to assure its timely receipt by the directors and his early relief after four years in office.[17] The reasons for leaving India in 1824 or 1825 were numerous. His deafness had become greater, and his sight had also deteriorated, notwithstanding improved spectacles. Then, too, he was concerned that he and his wife and their second son, Campbell, born in 1823, should be reunited with their first-born, Thomas, left as a four-month-old to be reared by Lady Munro's father in Scotland. The health of his wife and their infant was worrisome. Lady Munro had injured an eye in a fall from a horse in 1821 and this had been slow to heal, while the infant Campbell's health, never robust, became so serious a concern that Jane Munro was induced

[14] *Madras Government Gazette*, 10 June 1820.
[15] MC, F/151/73, Ravenshaw to Munro, 13 July 1820.
[16] IOL, *East India Registry and Directory* (1820, 2nd edn).
[17] Gleig, v. 2, p. 89.

to depart from India in 1826. By then, Munro's departure had been long delayed by the onset of the Burma war. The logistical provisioning (and a considerable part of the strategy) for this war had come to be Munro's. Finally, by 1824 Munro could at last count himself a wealthy man. Thanks to his salary in Madras of £16,000 he now felt himself affluent enough to purchase a substantial landed property and retire comfortably as a statesman of renown whose experience might be called upon for great public tasks. One such public task discussed even before he could depart from India was his appointment to the Governor-Generalship.[18]

CONSOLIDATING THE PAST, DRAFTING THE FUTURE

In the middle of 1820 all of that lay ahead; more immediately before him were some tasks dropped in January of the previous year when he left for England, doubtful of whether he would ever return, and some tasks that were then beyond his competence as judicial commissioner. Among the latter were problems involving the Madras Presidency in relation to the rest of British India, a whole range of problems involving the army and military questions, and finally the diplomatics of Madras and Indian principalities in the peninsula. On most of these matters he had had definite views, but had lacked the authority to bring them to effect as he could now do as governor. Between 1820 and 1824 Munro wrote over two hundred minutes of which almost two-thirds were on the military; the remainder were for the most part prompted by specific questions brought by one of the Madras departments for policy from the governor-in-council. These policy documents form a major part of the Munro corpus. They were read eagerly by his contemporaries in Madras (and elsewhere) to whom they were circulated, often on request. Elphinstone, for example, constantly importuned Munro for minutes that were to be studied assiduously by his successors and, later, by historians.

Most of Munro's minutes were composed before the end of 1824 as essential instruments for shaping and justifying the colonial regime he sought to create before his term as governor came to an end. While it is true that the issues which urged preparation of his minutes were, in some degree, adventitious, the assembled corpus of these documents, whether they deal with revenue or politics or the military refract a unified character and purpose, one that became evident in his minute of 31 December 1824.

The underlying unity and purpose of these influential writings is reinforced by the content of Munro's copious correspondence in those years. The public correspondence between him and his council and the Committee of Correspondence of the directors at India House—the most senior of the directors—has

[18] MC, F/151/62, 1820–2, letters of Malcolm and Ravenshaw, referring to Lady Munro's poor health. Munro's salary is mentioned in Philips, p. 252, and the estimate of Munro's assets is provided in George Brown's letters to Munro, MC, F/151/170, ff. 6–7.

long been available to Munro scholars, together with other public documents of the time. But, as noticed before, his private correspondence did not become available again until 150 years after Gleig made the selection used for his Munro biography. Not surprisingly, private correspondence during the period of the governorship is far greater than for any previous time of Munro's career. He maintained a regular and frequent exchange with Canning at the Board of Control from 1816 to his retirement from that office in 1821. With Canning's successors, Charles Bathurst and Charles W. W. Wynn, the correspondence was less frequent and less interesting than letters between Munro and the seniormost of the directors. The last reflected the importance of patronage that accompanied the office of governor. Munro had benefits to confer upon British soldiers and civilians on his own authority and, since his recommendations were given weight in London, for the highest posts in Madras as well. For his part Munro was under an obligation to privilege requests from the directors because their goodwill remained important for sustaining a sympathetic reception for his proposals about Madras, and India more generally.

Some of the directors had worried that Munro would in fact lavish his patronage over civilian posts in Madras upon his military friends. So at least Ravenshaw reported to him during his first year as a director, along with a warning that Munro must guard against such preferment.[19] As for the directors, their chairman, George Robinson, assured Munro that his colleagues would rarely 'add to the embarrassments of your situation' by patronage requests, and then that Munro must 'satisfy your own mind that those recommended have claims'.[20] The more senior and powerful the people seeking Munro's patronage, the more specific the request—as when Campbell Marjoribanks, chairman of the directorate, in 1819 and 1824 sought an appointment for the son of a peer who was a neighbour and friend as Munro's aide-de-camp.[21] From another long-serving director, Joseph Cotton, Munro had a letter asking that his son John, in the Madras service, be appointed to the MBOR. The senior Cotton conceded that the death of his son's wife in India and the care of their eight children might impair his efficiency on the Board, but he did need the additional salary![22] It took some years for Munro to accommodate the Cottons, and when he did propose a place on the Board he was told by John Cotton that being appointed as third member of the MBOR under a second member with less seniority than him 'was not doing justice to myself or giving any satisfaction to my friends at home'!

George Brown channelled occasional patronage requests to Munro from London. One came from James Mill, 'the writer upon India and political economy at India House who sought to make the name of a young Madras cadet known to Governor Sir Thomas Munro'; Brown 'could not well refuse

[19] MC, F/151/73, Ravenshaw to Munro, 6 December 1819.

[20] MC, F/151/73, Robinson to Munro, 10 February 1820.

[21] MC, F/151/73, 10 March 1822.

[22] MC, F/151/73, 24 December 1821, Cotton to Munro.

him' since Mill and his superior at India House, William M'Cullock, 'are so attentive to us upon all occasions'.[23]

Other calls upon Munro's patronage largesse came from Munro's old Indian friends. Some had to be refused, of course, and this could put a strain upon old friendships, as when Malcolm sought a position in Madras for one of his Malwa military proteges who Munro chose not to help, perhaps mindful of Ravenshaw's warning. His refusal momentarily threatened a breach with Malcolm, as will be noticed below. Munro's letter books, with abstracts of his letters between 1822 and 1823, show that most were about civil and military patronage. In these Munro often said that he would consider the request, but in a few cases he rejected the request on the basis of knowledge he had of the candidate.[24]

Patronage sometimes opened unexpected communications, intercourse that for other reasons might have been closed. An example is a series of letters from John Hudleston, a director from 1803 to 1823, and Munro's vigorous opponent among directors when Munro's judicial commission was being established by the Special Committee of Directors in 1814. In November 1821 Hudleston wrote to thank Munro for the kind report on the careers of two of his sons in Madras, and to say that another son was on the way to serve there.[25] Hudleston continued with a discussion of the determination in London to retrench upon costs in India. He supposed, with regret, that military costs would continue to be high, 'a millstone about the neck of the Company' as a result of Wellesley's adventurism and the 'abandonment of the system and opinions of *Lord Cornwallis*'. The director concluded that if military costs could not be reduced, London expected that other costs would be lowered by Munro's government.[26]

Hudleston's seniority as a director made him very important, and his previous opposition to Munro made him potentially dangerous. Still other directors were too junior to do more for Munro than to advise on the prevailing moods and currents among their seniors. One of these was Munro's old army friend Alexander Allan, whom Munro had known as long as had known Colin Mackenzie; another was John G. Ravenshaw, whose friendship dated from a decade later.

Allan was elected to the directorate in 1814 with the active canvassing of Munro, then in Britain, and of Munro's brother-in-law Henry Erskine. Sadly for Munro, Allan died in 1820 before he could be of much help,[27] but a mark

[23] MC, F/151/175, 2 March 1824.

[24] MC, F/151/93, letter book of that year written by Munro's private secretary, John W. Russell.

[25] *Madras Government Gazette*, 5 February 1824, reported the promotion of Josiah Andrew Hudleston to head assistant registrar to the Sadr Adalat.

[26] MC, F/151/73, Hudleston to Munro, 29 November 1821.

[27] MC, F/151/174, George Brown to Munro, 30 June 1821, with information of Allan's death.

of the dearness with which Munro held him is that the original portrait of him done by M. A. Shee was given to Allan, after whose death it was sent to Lady Munro's family for safekeeping until the Munros should return from India.[28] John Ravenshaw became a director about the time that Allan died, and he rose to the dignity and power of a Chair in 1831–2. His correspondence with Munro during the early years of the governorship were of first importance, as the collection of Munro's private correspondence demonstrates.

Ravenshaw kept Munro informed about affairs at India House and about relations between the directors and the Board of Control. He also, and perhaps more importantly, supplied his friend in Madras with copies of his substantive papers that circulated among fellow directors, such as the one on mirasi-right that he composed while Munro was en route to India in 1820. Munro made good use of this paper by drawing upon Ravenshaw's arguments to split the positions of F. W. Ellis and John Hodgson, both opponents of ryotwar, using Ellis to cast historical doubts upon Hodgson's position.[29] Another place where Ravenshaw was helpful was when Munro's judicial arrangements of 1816 were criticized; Ravenshaw was able to answer these criticisms from his deep knowledge of and long experience in South Arcot. However, most of Ravenshaw's letters to Munro reported high-level political gossip.

One subject of this was George Canning and his political future. From the time that he assumed the presidency of the Board of Control in 1816, Canning was a strong supporter of Munro's judicial and revenue reforms in Madras and was even open to their application in other parts of British India.[30] Munro also thought of Canning as an ally in his efforts to expand his Madras to the northern edges of the peninsula, virtually expunging Bombay.[31] He must therefore have been pleased to learn from Ravenshaw that Canning would consider the governor-generalship, providing that Lord Hastings, who was then being vilified in London for the costs of the last Maratha war, resigned or was recalled.[32] This pleasing prospect appeared threatened when Canning wrote to him a year later that he was contemplating leaving the Board of Control. Munro responded that such a resignation was a source of sorrow and concern, 'both on public and private grounds . . . I always dread changes at the head of the India Board, for I fear that some downright Englishman may at last get there, who will insist on making Anglo-Saxons of the Hindoos'.[33] When in 1821, after Canning had left the Board of Control, Ravenshaw, though still

[28] MC, F/151/169, ff. 86–9, Brown to Munro, 24 February 1820.

[29] MC, F/151/73, Ravenshaw to Munro, 1 March 1820. Ellis' findings are here made to conform to Ravenshaw's views on the conditional character of property rights of mirasidars and against Hodgson's claim of unconditionality, i.e. regardless of whether land is cultivated or not.

[30] Dixon, *Canning*, p. 187.

[31] Munro to Canning, 14 October 1820, in Gleig, v. 2, p. 51.

[32] MC, F/151/73, Ravenshaw to Munro, 13 July 1820.

[33] Munro to Canning, 30 June 1821, in Gleig, v. 2, p. 57.

being considered for Calcutta, wrote that though his fellow directors were keen to see Canning appointed to India and the King, George IV, had agreed somewhat reluctantly, there was still a formidable barrier to this owing to the resistance of Lord Hastings. The Governor-General held Canning responsible for the letters criticizing his government that had been sent to India from London.

When Hastings finally yielded Calcutta in 1823, he was succeeded not by Canning but, temporarily, by John Adam, influential councillor and chief secretary of the supreme government, and then permanently by Lord Amherst. Amherst was the reluctant choice of a small majority of the directors, Ravenshaw reported to Munro early in 1823; he also spoke admiringly of Munro's minute against Lord Hastings' proposal for a 'free press' in India and suggested an invidious comparison with Amherst in stating that India now needed 'a man of more nerve and judgement'.[34]

Ravenshaw clarified this last in another letter in January 1824. Then, he was anticipating resumption of his place on the directorate. The self-selecting directorate maintained a practice in which one quarter of their number rotated every year at the end of four-year terms. Ravenshaw had gone 'out of rotation' in April 1823, and was about to rejoin in April 1824, by 'election',[35] and he aired a whole set of problems that faced him when he resumed his place. Principally, he wanted to exhort his fellows 'to encourage all you governors . . . to benefit the great body of the people by *relaxation of the tax burthen* imposed on them . . . it will be too bad if the whole advantage of our present prosperity are to be distributed to everyone but those for whose benefit in the first instance we are solemnly bound to govern and from whose labours all of our affluence proceeds.'[36] A major problem to be addressed, Ravenshaw thought, was the consequence for Indian finance of ending the Company monopoly of the China trade. It was questionable whether, without its trade profits from China, the Company could govern India. He continued:

> At present the revenues of India are more than equal to all the expenses there and those incurred on account of [British Indian] territory, but will the surpluses last? And if it does will it be sufficient in addition to all present charges to provide the dividend here, the Home Charges, etc. I cannot help thinking that if India was governed well, that is to say, if the great body of the people felt the advantages of our government, not in a trifling but in such a degree as to induce them to support it for interest and not from fear that our military establishment might be reduced, and I am quite sure the civil might be [reduced also] by bringing the natives more into play. Something of the sort must be done if we are to govern India without the aid of the China trade.

[34] MC, F/151/78, 3 January 1823, and Philips on Amherst, p. 255.
[35] Philips explains this, p. 335.
[36] MC, F/151/79, Ravenshaw to Munro, 27 June 1824.

Ravenshaw closed this January 1824 letter with the warning: 'Keep a lookout after the missionaries in India and do not let us have a religious war there.'

The warning about missionaries was unnecessary, for Munro had long and consistently warned of the dangers of a replication of the bigotry that had brought on the Vellore mutiny and the terrible threat to British rule from a disaffected Indian soldiery. He also acted sternly in 1822 to demand the dismissal of a subordinate collector in Bellary whom he accused of publicly denigrating Hindu theology and ritual, of seeking the conversion of Hindus and Muslims to Christianity, and thereby of raising the spectre of civil disaffection as well.[37] However, the war, when it came, was not over religion, but over Burma, and it broke even before Munro had received Ravenshaw's warning letter.

On 8 March 1824 Lord Amherst, after much hesitation, declared war against the kingdom of Ava. All his diplomatic efforts had failed to remove the encroachments of Burmese forces upon the Company's jungle-bound eastern border. On 23 March Munro placed a notice in the *Madras Government Gazette* requesting the company of the military forces of His Majesty's forces and those of the Honourable Company, along with civilian officials, to a ball and supper marking the declaration of war. This was to be held at the sumptuous banqueting hall adjoining his official residence in the Government Garden along the Cooum river, adjacent to the teeming Triplicane quarter of Madras city.

LOGISTICS OF ANOTHER WAR

The Burma War divides Munro's governorship almost exactly in half and burdened him once again, as in the Ceded Districts, with enormous additional responsibilities.[38] Before the onset of the war, the three years and ten months after his return to Madras in June 1820 were devoted to the framing of a wide range of measures that were the subject of minutes to his council. The three years and eight months after the declaration of war and before his death were taken up with the management of that war and, latterly, with impatient plans for a return to Britain that became ever more pressing after the departure from Madras of Lady Munro and his young son Campbell in 1826.

That over half of Munro's minutes pertained to military matters reflects the war in Burma,[39] for which he bore major responsibility, and one other factor,

[37] 'Interference of European Officials in the Conversion of Natives', 15 November 1822, in A. J. Arbuthnot (ed.), *Sir Thomas Munro: Selections from His Minutes and Other Official Writings* (London: C. K. Paul, 1881), pp. 548–54. Hereafter cited as 'Arbuthnot, *Munro Selections*'.

[38] See Philips for a brief discussion of the causes of the war, p. 254.

[39] Apart from the selection in Arbuthnot, *Munro Selections*, a selection of his minutes is found in IOL, European Manuscripts, 'Papers of John, 13th Lord Elphinstone, F/87, to which should be added three of Munro's minutes on the commercial department of

namely Munro's own sense of competence on military questions, evident in his earliest letters to his father when a young soldier. His letters then and later often turned quite professionally upon logisitics, organization and strategy, as is evident in his correspondence with Richard and Arthur Wellesley during the second Maratha war and with Lord Hastings during the final Maratha war.[40] Beyond this interest in and sense of competence about military matters, recently burnished by his campaigning in the southern Maratha country, he was ever alive to the political aspects of military questions.

This manifested itself before the Burma War in several of his military minutes prompted by differences with the commander of the Madras army. The commander was Archibald Campbell, a member of his council by constitutional rule, a friend, and, as the father-in-law of his dear friend Malcolm, a person deserving special consideration.[41] In a minute of 1822 Munro entered into a controversy over the new cantonment that was being constructed at St Thomas Mount, near Madras. Campbell had argued that Munro's commission as commander-in-chief of Company forces was restricted to Fort St George and Madras city, the same as the jurisdiction of the Supreme Court. Munro rejected this as too restrictive a scope for the head of the Presidency, and he insisted on the authority to command the forces to be garrisoned at St Thomas Mount as well as those within the city.[42] He also opposed another of Campbell's suggestions, that the number of European officers attached to units of sepoy infantry should be increased. No evidence that this would increase the efficiency of Indian soldiers existed, Munro said, whereas it would increase the underemployment and idleness of European officers.[43]

On the other hand, Munro supported Campbell's proposal that sepoy regiments should be regularly rotated in such a way that soldiers spent some of the time in the districts from which they had been recruited. This was to strengthen the double character of the Company's sepoy regiments as partly a standing army subject to duty anywhere within Company territory and partly a militia attached to its locality and their families. The danger, Munro thought, was that sepoys could be turned into a 'body of mercenaries, finding homes

Madras pertaining to the Board of Trade, in the British Library, European Manuscripts, Peel Papers. The British Library European Manuscripts collection also contains a set of the minutes in Ad. Mss. 22071–22080, Wellesley Papers; this consists of a total of 1816 folios with minutes by the following categories: military 164, secret/political 17, foreign/political 26, public 37, judicial 31, revenue 53.

40 E.g. in Arbuthnot, *Munro Selections*, pp. 363 ff., on the use of black soldiers from the West Indies in India, dated 11 June 1805, and his observations on the abolition of European regiments and the reliance on sepoys under European officers presented to the Select Committee of the House of Commons, 12 April 1813, in Arbuthnot, *Munro Selections*, pp. 372ff.

41 M.C., F/151/73, Ravenshaw to Munro, 26 December 1820.

42 Dated 28 May 1822, this arrangement obtained until 1859, when the Governor was relieved of military power. Arbuthnot, *Munro Selections*, pp. 402 and 403n.

43 Arbuthnot, *Munro Selections*, p. 376, dated 21 January 1821.

and families wherever they went, ready to join in any disturbance and dangerous to the State'.[44] He also strongly advocated the logistical advantages of 'pioneer', or construction, units integrated into the field corps of the army and of efficient 'bazaars', or commissariat contractors, also being attached to field units. The lack of an efficient commissariat, he argued, had greatly diminished the effectiveness of the army of Sir Eyre Coote in the Carnatic campaign against Haidar Ali, where Munro had seen his first service from 1780 to 1783, and in the Mysore war prosecuted by Lord Cornwallis in 1792, in which he had also served. Moreover, he argued that military supplies be exempted from custom duties within the presidency, and between it and the territory of the Nizam, so as to reduce the costs of military 'bazaars' and make them less subject to fraud by revenue officials.[45]

When Rangoon fell to British forces in June 1824 in the opening phase of the Burma War, Munro was quick to minute his council with an appreciation of the reliability and bravery of Madras sepoys in a campaign made difficult by the need to provision by sea, by disease, and by the unanticipated resistance of the Burmese. He spoke proudly of how Madras sepoys on leave when the war began made strenuous efforts to join their comrades' departure for Burma, and how some pioneers from around Hyderabad marched twenty-four miles a day for two weeks to join the expedition. He did not say what any reader of his minute then would have known, that this devotion by ordinary sepoys contrasted with the refusal of many Bengal sepoys to undertake service in Burma, thus placing major responsibility upon Madras and upon Munro for conducting that war.[46] As the war in Burma dragged on through 1824, Munro's military minutes acquired a more sombre and less celebratory tone. He acknowledged the potential dangers to order within his Presidency, with its best soldiers engaged overseas in a difficult campaign. Revealing a good deal of his sense about how India had been and was being conquered, he wrote then:

> In the present war there are difficulties of a nature which we have never experienced before; not from the military skills of the . . . [Burmans] for that is far below what we have met with in India, but from our ignorance of the country and the people, the obstacles opposed to an invasion by land, by mountains, rivers, and unhealthy jungles, and the hindrance caused to operations of every kind by the long continuance of the rainy season. In all our Indian wars we had the advantage of a long previous establishment in the country, and a perfect knowledge of the people. We had a station that was our own from whence to extend ourselves, and we acted in alliance with some native chief, and by supporting his title and authority we secured the submission of the people and obtained aid as we advanced, from the resources of the country. The people were not hostile to us, but as willing

[44] Ibid., p. 375; dated 19 December 1820.

[45] Ibid., p. 379; dated 23 February 1821; also pp. 387 and 419, 27 July 1824.

[46] Ibid., p. 432, 18 June 1824; also see Wilson, *History of the Madras Army*, v. 4, p. 293.

to be the subjects of our Government, or of our ally, as of their former princes. In Ava we have none of these advantages. We land at once, as an enemy, in a country to which we are strangers, where we have no ally, and where the whole nation is hostile to us, and where, having no fort, arsenal, or granary, we are dependent for everything on our shipping. In India, and still more in Europe, the occupation of the principal town or fortress secures the submission of the adjacent country. But in Ava this will not be the case. The people will abandon the towns as our army approaches, because they know that we do not mean to fix ourselves permanently in the country, and because they know that if we were to remain, they would be punished by their own Government. In most countries the defeat of the enemy's armies in the field, and the capture of his principal places, and above all of the capital, usually compell him to make peace; but even if we were to reduce Amarapura, it does not follow that the Burmans will submit to our terms. They might abandon their capital, avoid our main army, and carry on a harassing war against our supplies. The great extent of the country would, of itself, be a powerful ally in promoting the success of such a plan; and though our army might march through the country, it could not subdue it while the people are hostile. . . .[47]

The war in Burma was to continue to drain Madras of soldiers, material, and Munro's energies for an additional fifteen months after this minute of December 1824. Indicative of this preoccupation is that half of his numerous military minutes came in 1825–6, the final phase of that war.

However, by 1825 Munro appears to have done as much as he thought he could to use his governorship to fortify what historians were to call 'the Munro system'. During the final phase of the war he expected to be relieved of his responsibilities, but so vital was he seen to be for the war, and so difficult was the choice of a successor owing to politics in London,[48] that he was persuaded to remain in Madras even after Lady Jane departed with their ailing son. Shortly after her departure, Munro was awarded an hereditary baronetcy for his contributions to the war, an ironic comment upon a career whose historical reputation was to be set by his consolidation of the Madras colonial system. The final reasoned statements about that system were contained in his minutes of 1820 to 1824.

THE MINUTES

Political and administrative matters dominate these minutes. Following these subjects were revenue questions; only minor attention was given to judicial, economic, or fiscal matters. Among the political subjects which his minutes explored were the conditions of great zamindar families and of client princes.

[47] Arbuthnot, *Munro Selections*, pp. 442–3, 24 December 1824.

[48] The politics of choosing Munro's successor is discussed by Philips, pp. 252–3.

He saw in these matters profound dangers to the stability of the political order of Madras (and of British India), and he blamed this potential destabilization on the Company's bureaucracy and its courts.

In September 1820, a few months after his return, he drew the attention of his council to how revenue procedures in the Presidency were undermining the status of different classes of zamindars and of other major landholders.[49] The impetus for his alarm seems to have come from William Thackeray, who had replaced Hodgson on his council. Thackeray had prepared and sent to Munro his notes on several matters, including entail and the prevention of corruption by 'native revenue servants', saying that he was prepared to draft his own reports for discussion by the MBOR, or that Munro himself could use the notes to initiate discussion of the issues with his council. Munro took the second course,[50] and he opened his minute on entail by deploring 'our code of regulations' which has 'already ruined many ancient families'. The reason for this, he contended, was that 'needy adventurers' induce members of zamindari families to apply to the courts for the division of estates. Because most such families were ignorant alike of business and of law, expensive suits led to indebtedness and, often, through corruption of law officials, the dissolution of joint landed properties. His fear was that 'if the whole of the zemindars were swept away . . . by the operations of our present institutions, we should have nothing of native rank left in the country'. Then:

> All rank and power would be vested in a few Europeans. Such a state of things could not but be dangerous to the stability of our Government,[51] because the natives could not fail to make the comparison between the high situations of their foreign rulers and their own abject condition; in the event of any discontent rising, it would be more likely to spread when they are reduced to one level. . . . They have no common sympathy with us, and but little attachment to our Government . . . and nothing tends more effectively to shake what they have, than to behold the destruction of every ancient family, and its domains passing into the hands of a set of low retainers of the Courts and other dependents of Europeans.[52]

The same concern was extended to other 'ancient' notables such as village headmen and accountants whose landholdings, unless similarly protected from partition by the courts, would sink to those of 'a common cultivator'.

[49] 'On the Expediency of Introducing Entail Regulations in Zemindaries, and of Entrusting some of the Zemindars with Police Authority', 19 September 1820, Arbuthnot, *Munro Selections*, pp. 118–22. Succeeding notes will identify the official label and date as well as a source for reference.

[50] MC, F/151/75, Thackeray to Munro, n.d., probably September 1820, and in Munro's draft of the regulation, MC, F/151/128, he acknowledges Thackeray's initiative.

[51] In his draft of this Munro used the phrase 'your empire' instead of 'our Government', MC, F/151/128, f. 44.

[52] Arbuthnot, *Munro Selections*, p. 419.

An entail regulation preventing the partition of estates would check the ruin of 'a class of native nobility and gentry [presumably headmen and accountants] and preserve those gradations in society through which alone it can be improved in its condition'. The dignity of such a superior class would be further enhanced by permitting zamindars to hold police authority, thereby sparing them the humiliation of having police officials operating in their estates.

Two years later Munro again minuted his council on this regulation, taking notice of criticisms which had been lodged against his earlier proposal and delayed its promulgation. The major criticism was that removing land from debt liability prevented zamindars from contracting loans to meet their revenue obligations during poor crop seasons. Hence, zamindars would come into the danger of losing their estates for failing to meet their revenue. In his concern about rank as an incentive for responsible civil participation by Indians of wealth, Munro seemed to be ignoring one of the colonial imperatives of which he had always been mindful: the punctilious and complete collection of the revenue; and on this he was bound to yield. It also appeared that many of his 'nobility and gentry' were loath to assume police functions because in their eyes to do so lowered them to the degraded status of policemen.

He undertook to meet these and other objections from his usually friendly and compliant council. First, he agreed to make the entail regulation optional, to be used or not as estate holders saw fit. To another criticism that the regulation would increase, not diminish, government supervision of zamindari estates, he argued that such supervision, however undesirable, was to be preferred to dealing with disputed successions. Even these compromises failed to still the objections to his entail proposal, and it was not enacted. Instead, entail came to be achieved through the intercession of judicial interpretations protecting 'ancient zemindars, jagirs, and polliams',[53] a paradoxical outcome for a regulation by which Munro intended to remove courts and their manipulative vakils and corrupt officials from zamindari affairs.

Judicial officials and procedures were the target of another of Munro's attacks launched in a minute to his council in February 1822. This was on the subject of 'altamgha inams', and it qualified in an important way how Munro believed preservation of the Indian 'nobility and gentry' should be achieved.[54] The case involved the greatest of all nobles in Madras, the Nawab of Arcot, who granted a jagir to his dewan as a royal grant, or gift (inam) in 1789. The Turkish term *altamgha*,[55] Munro conceded, signified an entitlement to be enjoyed by the grantee and his descendants 'forever, from generation to generation'. However, he insisted that such permanence and unconditionality 'are mere forms of expression'. In reality, he argued, such grants were annually renewable and thus subject to revocation. For one purportedly concerned with the nobility of Madras, Munro's position may seem contradictory, especially

[53] Ibid., p. 124n.
[54] 'Altamgha Inams', 1 February 1822, Arbuthnot, *Munro Selections*, pp. 135–63.
[55] Wilson, *Glossary*, p. 19, where it is deemed hereditary and transferable property.

when courts insisted that such inams were permanent and heritable properties. What this case actually clarifies is that Munro's notions about 'nobility and gentry' were not based upon the British model of great and protected proprietors, but on something of a Russian model of a nobility dependent upon and completely subordinate to the state.

In contrast to his stand on the protection of hereditary entitlements by an entail act, Munro on altamgha inams insisted that hereditary rights were conditional upon the discretion of the Company. This, Munro argued, was the same principle as that operating under the nawab who made the grant originally and could, he insisted, resume it at will. According to Munro, this was a political decision, and therefore the Madras Supreme Court had erred in allowing the suit by the sons of the original grantee for a sharing of the income from the estate as their personal properties.

The court had also rejected the Madras government political and historical claims about such grants, and this exceeded its competence, especially when a matter touched the public revenue. Munro charged that the courts' decision was an unconstitutional intervention into the domain of politics and administration. Moreover, by consenting to the sharing of the income of the several villages comprising the estate, the court had violated the residual rights of cultivators since what had been alienated in the jagir grant in the first place was the government's share of the revenue due from these villages. This share Munro estimated to be no more than 40 per cent of gross production, and therefore such property as might be conceded to the heirs of the original grantee could be no more than that; the remainder was the property of the cultivators of the several villages.

All of this was common knowledge to revenue officials, Munro asserted, 'but . . . the Chief Justice certainly never understood clearly' that the grants by the nawab and by the Company 'were of a political nature', stipulated in the treaty of 1801 between the two.[56]

In admitting the case and finding for the plaintiffs, the Supreme Court not only denied the sovereignty of the Company but had done so on a flawed English analogy that such grants were an alienation of 'crown land'. Munro denied that there were crown lands in India; there were only lands from which the state was entitled to receive revenue. Hence, all grants of land bearing this revenue liability were conditional upon the needs of the state, formerly and under the Company. This stricture applied to minor inams as well as to major jagirs, but the former, being small holdings, were characteristically treated as charities and allowed to pass hereditarily. Confirmation of this practice long extant in Madras was had from Maharashtra, Munro said, on the basis of evidence provided by William Chaplin, commissioner of the Peshwa's erstwhile territories. Munro had solicited this from Chaplin some months before.[57]

He concluded this 'altamgha' minute by insisting that the jurisdiction of

[56] Arbuthnot, *Munro Selections*, pp. 141–2.

[57] MC, F/151/176, Munro to Chaplin, 28 October 1821.

the Supreme Court must henceforward be limited. It should no longer be permitted to intrude upon explicitly political enactments of the government and the court's spatial jurisdiction, which had been fixed long ago 'without much consideration',[58] should be limited to Madras city (excluding Chepauk, where the nawab's palace stood, and neighbouring Triplicane, where a large proportion of the Muslim population lived).

Another cause for Munro to rail against the courts arose as a result of a bloody caste riot in Masulipatam in May 1820.[59] His minuted intervention was prompted by the course of action, proposed by the Collector of Masulipatam, which Munro claimed would not diminish, but only exacerbate the conditions that produced these affrays in the towns of the Presidency. Specifically, he rejected the view that courts should be left with the powers to determine how, where, and what public caste ceremonies—especially processions in public ways—should be conducted on the basis of 'natural right'. Munro objected that magistrates could neither determine the principles of 'natural right' pertaining to these public ceremonies that often led to riot in the streets of Presidency towns, nor the correctness of custom in a society where there was vast variation in custom. He also derided the substitution of sepoys for local police in quelling riots on the grounds that police were often partisan in such disputes. Employment of troops to restore civil order was in every case dangerous, for it could lead to the loss of the 'fidelity' of Indian soldiers upon which British power rested.[60] Munro advised—somewhat rigidly and impractically—against permitting *any* changes in the established ways in which public ceremonies were conducted in particular places and, having frozen existing usage, punishing any who breached the rules.

Late in 1822 he embarked upon a three-month tour of the northern coastal region of the Presidency in something like the same way he had toured while a collector and, later, while judicial commissioner. Now, however, he said that he was not interested in details of administration, but in becoming known to civil leaders of society—'zemindars and principal inhabitants'—and in ascertaining the general condition of people in what was called 'the Northern Circars'.

About Ganjam, the northern-most district of the Presidency, he minuted his council with the observation that zamindar rule was deplorable. This was largely because of the adoption there in 1800 of the Bengal settlement principles under Wellesley's insistence. He found most of the numerous small zamindars mediocre men and the people totally cut off from the Company's government of Madras, his government: 'No village people ever came near me either to solicit favour or seek redress'.[61] Some of the larger zamindars of the region

[58] Arbuthnot, *Munro Selections*, p. 157.

[59] 'The Prevention of Riots in Connection with Caste Disputes', 3 July 1820, Arbuthnot, *Munro Selections*, p. 287.

[60] Munro returned to this perceived danger in another minute of 15 March 1825, Arbuthnot, *Munro Selections*, p. 304.

[61] 'Tour of the Northern Sirkars and Nellore', 7 January 1823, Arbuthnot, *Munro Selections*, p. 184.

drew his appreciation. The rajas of Bobili and Vizianagram were able, he thought, and appeared to be good managers of their estates. The Raja of Vizianagram, 'regarded as the first among the northern zemindars', manifested his quality by agreeing with Munro's entail proposal and agreeing with Munro that those opposed to entail were either self-interested moneylenders or servants of zamindars seeking some private advantage.

But even the Vizianagram rulers' administration was poor as compared to most of the Presidency where British rule was direct. Conditions in the Circars were the most poorly understood in the whole of the Presidency, though these were among the oldest of the Company's territories in India, an echo of John Sullivan's observations of the 1770s. Early decisions about the revenue administration had been wrong not only in the matter of the permanent settlement but also in supposing that the Hindu mode of revenue collection had always been in kind. 'We are certain that the Hindoos had no one uniform system....',[62] and he was equally certain that the collection of revenue in kind was 'clumsy' though possibly more fair than an immoderate money demand. These are somewhat startling admissions from the maker of ryotwar as *the* ancient system of revenue. Munro added a view that he had come to adopt in the southern Maratha country, if not well before, that the British decision to enfranchize a few great magnates with full landed property had been a mistake. This policy had led to the degradation of the historical landed rights and interests of many old, small zamindar families of the Northern Circars, and of independent cultivators. Instead of using its military hegemony to create new, large proprietors on lands seized from the great zamindars over the previous fifty years, the Company should have taken such forfeited lands under its direct management. This would have yielded a larger revenue, and would also have presented a way of controlling those 'military classes' who otherwise maintained themselves by serving turbulent zamindars, by granting warrior families small, privileged landholdings (i.e. inams). Direct management by the Company would also have encouraged 'the better class of traders and cultivators' in the coastal hills as well as the plains to pursue orderly production and commerce. This middle group of traders and cultivators provided the sort of 'gradation of society' that was most likely to assure the longevity of Company rule.

Another political matter to which his minutes of 1820 to 1824 were devoted and solutions proposed pertained to relations with princely dependants of the Madras government. Arbuthnot's notes on the Munro minutes show that these suggestions were not always heeded during his own time or later. One of 1821 involved the succession to the nawabship of Kurnool, a portion of his old CD which had remained outside his management under a Pathan chieftain. In this minute he attacked Alexander D. Campbell,[63] collector of Bellary, a part of whose responsibilities included the conduct of relations between that minor ruler and the Company. Campbell was criticized for suggesting that

[62] Arbuthnot, *Munro Selections*, p. 199.

[63] Ibid., pp. 329–33, 'On the Subject of Interfering in the Succession of Native Princes', 27 April 1821.

the ailing, incumbent nawab should be deposed and replaced by a relative then in detention in Kurnool. In opposing this Munro reminded his council that during recent years two expensive military campaigns had had to be mounted in Kurnool to secure the present occupant of the *masnad*, or throne, and to follow Campbell's advice would assure disorders and another campaign. The realities of succession in India, the unreliability of assuming some sort of uncomplicated hereditary succession given the ubiquity of factional disputes within ruling families, Munro said, dictated only one practical method. That was to support the choice of reigning rulers and that of the 'leading men of the country'. In Kurnool there was an agreed heir, and any deviation by the British would lead to disorder and the need, again, for military repression: 'It is of no importance to us whether he or any other person of the family ascend the masnad: whoever does, will always be punctual in the discharge of his duties to the British Government', for they could not do otherwise. It is only in the final sentence of this minute that it becomes clear that the candidate favoured by Campbell was also favoured by the Governor-General, Lord Hastings, so that Munro's heavy criticism of Campbell's proposed solution was actually aimed at the interference, as Munro saw it, of the Bengal government into a matter that he claimed belonged to Madras.

Campbell was a special target for Munro for another reason: he was one of the two collectors appointed during the regime of John Hodgson at the MBOR to districts formerly under Munro's unified collectorship of the CD. When ryotwar was replaced by village leases there Campbell and his colleague in Cuddapah, John Hanbury, having served under Hodgson at the MBOR, were appointed by the latter to the CD. It is not therefore surprising that both should have felt the sting of Munro's authority now that Hodgson had removed himself from India by retirement.[64]

The Kurnool succession dispute touched the sub-imperial interests of Madras, something—from his earliest days as Governor—Munro sought to strengthen and extend. He considered that Indian princelings in most of the peninsula, from the Narbada southward, should be subject to his control; thus his covert attack upon Hastings in his Kurnool minute of April 1821. Munro had outlined his programme for a territorially enlarged Madras to Alexander Allan in October 1821 (unaware the Allan had died the previous month). 'You are the only person in the Direction that knows anything of Madras', he wrote, ignoring Ravenshaw's recent election, and therefore Allan should explain the diplomatic and military situation of Madras to his colleagues. Munro's view of the situation was that a substantial portion of the Madras army—he suggested half—was garrisoned outside the Presidency and under the control and patronage of the Governor-General or of residents appointed by Lord Hastings. This led to a weakening of control over that portion of the Madras army and therefore of its discipline, far from its home command. Hence, a new arrangement should be made with respect to the 'foreign states[!],

[64] Munro's draft comments on Campbell in MC, F/151/128, f. 33.

tributaries and allies' in India. Bengal should control those various kinds of polities 'within its own limits', including Holkar, the Rajputs, Delhi, Lucknow', and so on, 'but Nagpoor, Hyderabad and all petty states south of the Nerbuddah should be under the authority of Madras'.[65]

It was not military control and discipline alone that dictated the hegemonic position of Madras in these latter places. Cultural affinities were important. Munro offered Berar as an example of a principality that should be 'a province of this Presidency . . . people of Berar are the same as those of our provinces in language and manners and we are better acquainted with them and therefore better qualified to lead them gradually to the change which must take place than the Bengal Government.'[66] At the same time, Munro was writing to Lord Hastings in Calcutta and, as already noticed, George Canning in London, asking for control by Madras over 'native states' in the northern Deccan as well as those of Travancore, Mysore, and the southern Maratha jagirdars. He excused himself for raising the matter with Canning by saying that as such questions were not likely to be raised in London by Lord Hastings and the Supreme Government in Calcutta (concerned not to diminish Bengal's sway), therefore he must raise them.[67]

Given these sub-imperial conflicts, it is scarcely surprising that several of Munro's minutes before 1824 should have turned on relations between British India and princely states. The question of the Kurnool succession was minor on the canvas of all of British India (though useful for Munro's needling of Hastings and against what he thought were Hodgson's creatures in the CD). A major question was raised by the growing administrative and fiscal chaos in Mysore. Madras had depended on this princely state in two Maratha wars, and its ruling family had been installed by a Company treaty, in the drafting of which Munro had taken a small part in 1799.

Munro made a state visit to Mysore in July 1821 and subsequently queried the practice of elaborate exchanges of presents with Indian rulers. Some had suggested that these exchanges should be curtailed; he disagreed. His experience in Mysore convinced him that prestations were an important 'attribute of sovereignty' among Indian rulers; 'the loss of much of their real power makes them more anxious to preserve forms that yet remain of royalty'. In Mysore, as elsewhere in India, these forms should be observed while taking care to note the value of all gifts and to provide equal value of return gifts.[68]

The same sensitivity to the reduced royal power of Mysore kings was

[65] IOL, European Manuscripts, Carfrae Mss, E/225, Munro to Allan, 14 October 1820.

[66] Ibid., E/225/, Munro to Hastings.

[67] Ibid., E/184, where Munro reiterated the same thing to the Governor-General, Lord Amherst, in a private letter of 1 June 1826.

[68] 'On the Complimentary Exchange of Presents on the Occasion of an Interview Between the Governor and a Native Prince', 24 July 1821, Arbuthnot, *Munro Selections*, p. 350.

tested a few years later when Munro felt compelled to press the Raja, Krishnaraja Wodeyar III, to reform the administration of his state. As a client placed on the throne by the British after the defeat of Tipu Sultan in 1799, a special relationship was understood to exist between the Mysore raja and Mysore. Munro's interests in Mysore were more close than most, not only because he served on the commission that restored the ruling family but for other reasons as well. From 1800 to 1808 his Bellary district of the CD shared a frontier with Mysore, across which there was a high level of commercial activity and considerable movement of people owing to existence of families on both sides of the border. Moreover, during his career as judicial commissioner Munro and his wife, along with other senior Madras officials, enjoyed residence in salubrious Bangalore, the seat of the British resident to Mysore. Also, with others of the Madras establishment, Munro had much praise and admiration for the dewan of the state, Purnaiya, under whose supervision the kingdom was administered from the time of restoration under the five-year-old Raja to the time that the latter attained maturity.

A Brahman whose family originally migrated to Mysore from the southern Maratha districts, Purnaiya had served both Haidar Ali and Tipu Sultan before being selected by the British as virtual regent. He was forced to retire from office in 1811 when the raja assumed direct rule of his kingdom, and for the British this signalled a dangerous change expressed in the usual manner of Britons of the time: diminished state revenue and high expenditures that could lead to financial collapse. The treaty of 24 June 1799 restoring the Wodeyar family to the throne under British protection had exacted a heavy cost. More than half (58 per cent) of the estimated revenue of the state was to be paid to the Company as a subsidy for its protection. Except for an underestimate of the state's revenues, this obligation would have ruined Mysore in very short order. As it happened, Mysore's revenue exceeded estimates and that, together with Purnaiya's prudence, yielded a consistent and appreciable surplus for the royal treasury, the surest sign to the British of Purnaiya's good governance. The raja, having freed himself of Purnaiya's tutelage and restraint in 1811, ran through the accumulated reserves, raising alarm in Madras about the time Munro assumed the governorship.

One source of this alarm was the danger of a mutiny owing to the arrears in soldiers' pay, including the 4000 horsemen—the so-called 'Silladar Horse'—that the 1799 treaty required the raja to keep available for service by the Company. This cavalry force proved valuable to Munro and other commanders during the final Maratha war. Another was the more frequent resort by the raja to revenue farmers whom he permitted to increase the pitch of revenue collections, thus threatening many parts of the kingdom with poverty and unrest.

The principal cause for the increased expenditures of Krishnaraja was royal largesse, the granting of money and land to those deemed worthy of royal patronage and prestation. As a proportion of gross revenue collections in Mysore between 1799 and 1823, royal grants nearly doubled from 7 per cent in the last year of Purnaiya's administration to 13.5 per cent in 1823.[69] At this point Munro's attention was seized. His minute of August 1825 recapitulated his earlier concerns about Mysore's finances and his determination to personally persuade the raja to set matters right. Munro recalled that his advice to the Mysore resident, A. H. Cole, in 1822, when the latter had made his own concern known, was to do nothing that might cause alarm in the raja about British intentions. Cole was actually discouraged from hearing and reporting complaints of subjects and discouraged also from directly pressing for reforms, nor in general to create any anxiety that the Company contemplated invoking those articles of the 1799 treaty which permitted the Company to assume management of the administration of the state, or part of it, in the event of maladministration. For this indulgence of a client state Munro was to be criticized by his successor, Stephen R. Lushington, in 1831.[70]

Munro's approach, as stated in the 1825 minute, had been to reassure and encourage rather than threaten the raja. To this end he made an official visit there in September 1825. There, he had delivered a stern lecture to the Mysore ruler on retrenching his extravagances lest the discontent among his subjects, and especially his soldiers, boil into outright rebellion. Munro justified his forebearance with the raja on the grounds that if the dignity of the ruler was lowered by him, it could not be easily restored, and further decline of this 'British ally' would inevitably follow—and with that the assumption of the territory by the British. All of these hazards of the subsidiary alliance system he had warned Hastings about years before, and his certainty, as well as his prescience, was undiminshed in 1825. He closed the minute with an almost nostalgic, if not rhapsodic, reference to the great work of the old minister, Purnaiya. Now, he feared, the raja's maladministration had reached a point which even a Purnaiya could not reverse; the prospects for the state were very unfavourable. This last was prophetic since in 1830 Mysore was convulsed by a rebellion against the raja, his Maratha Brahman administrators and rapacious tax farmers, and the expulsion of the royal family was only averted by the introduction of Company troops. This was followed by the assumption by the Company of Mysore's administration in 1831 for the next fifty years.[71]

A related though less serious native state problem involved Travancore, and it constituted one of the numerous points of contention between Munro and the commander of the Madras army, Archibald Campbell.[72] In February 1823

[69] M. Gopal, *The Finances of the Mysore State, 1799–1831* (Calcutta: Orient Longmans, 1960), pp. 191 and 206–8.

[70] 'Maladministration in Mysore', 23 August 1825, Arbuthnot, *Munro Selections*, p. 339.

[71] B. Stein, 'Notes on "Peasant Insurgency" in Colonial Mysore', *South Asia Research* (School of Oriental and African Studies, London), v. 5 (May 1985), pp. 11–27. Care must be taken with an error in pagination beginning on p. 20 of this essay as printed.

[72] 'On the Question Whether it is Necessary to have European Corps with Every

he informed his council of a difference with Campbell over the relief of European troops garrisoned at Quilon and their replacement by sepoys. Campbell thought the reduction of European troops there dangerous and lodged a formal dissent in council based upon the following considerations. Travancore, Campbell said, was in a disturbed state as evidenced by a threatened rebellion a decade earlier when a plot had been hatched to incite Company sepoys to revolt. European troops were necessary to check the subversion of 'treacherous' elements as well as to serve as a model of disciplined service for the Company's Indian soldiers. Munro answered these objections. In many places along the west coast—such as Kanara—there was a history of turbulence, and sepoy garrisons maintained good public order and discipline. The rebellion in Travancore had occurred twelve years before, and the causes for it had all been eliminated, principally by removing the diwan who had sought to suborn the loyalty of some sepoys in 1812. As to the 'treacherous' Travancore people, Munro thought they were no different from, but very like, other people of the Malabar coast who, though potentially irrascible, were mostly peaceful. Finally, he thought that maintaining large European forces excited suspicions about British intentions and therefore delayed the full acceptance of British overlordship.

Minutes dealing with revenue and administration were less frequent than either military or political ones. Still, more than fifty revenue minutes were presented to Munro's council, and of these a number of the earliest dealt with ryotwar, as do a large proportion of his private letters of the time. So much was ryotwar an early concern that John Sullivan complained from Coimbatore in 1823:

> I am sorry to hear that it is still thought necessary that something should be written in favour of Ryotwarri. The tale has been so often and so well told, so many striking facts have been adduced to shew the good effects of the system, that it is vain to expect the conversion of those who oppose it. There is one argument however which perhaps has not been sufficiently dealt upon and that is, that every object, which either Lord Cornwallis, or Hodgson or any of their followers had in view in advocating different modes of settling the Revenue can, and most of them are, actually attained under Ryotwarri and that system has many striking advantages peculiar to itself.[73]

Sullivan promised that when an opportunity arose for advancing this last point he would seize it, and he fulfilled this promise with his 1831 pamphlet, *Sketch of the Ryotwar System* for English readers and a tract prepared for Madras colleagues.[74] In the latter he referred to a private letter from Munro, dated 25 June

Large Body of Native Troops', 18 February 1823, Arbuthnot, *Munro Selections*, pp. 410–13.

[73] MC, F/151/89, Sullivan to Munro, 5 July 1823.

[74] Published in London while Sullivan was on furlough between 1830 and 1835 before returning to serve as senior member of the MBOR.

1825, which seems to have prompted Sullivan's words quoted above, namely Munro's somewhat exasperated insistence that 'ryotwar is no new system, but the usual one in the best of times under all Indian governments'.[75]

Another who stimulated Munro's thoughts about revenue policy was Ravenshaw, his advocate in London. Ravenshaw described his own efforts to attack the privileged position that was being accorded to mirasi right as a result of the skilful writing of Francis W. Ellis and John Hodgson in the magisterial MBOR minute of 5 January 1818. He thought that he had succeeded in using Ellis' evidence to discredit Hodgson's claim that mirasidars had unconditional ownership of their lands, that they could cultivate it or not and only be obliged to pay revenue when they did, and that mirasi right superseded all other landholding rights. These claims of Hodgson were 'quite monstrous . . . such a right never could have existed' Ravenshaw asserted.[76] He also reported that the violence of the most recently received Hodgson minutes from the MBOR had shocked many in London. ('I pity the man who has such a temper and cannot control it'.)

Other gossip Ravenshaw reported from London included the antagonism among the directors to the appointment of Sir Archibald Campbell to succeed Hislop as Madras commander-in-chief, ostensibly because of Campbell's advanced age but actually and secretly because he was the father-in-law of John Malcolm, whom some opposed. Many at India House were also convinced that Hodgson planned to enter the Direction in two years time and had begun to garner support for the move.[77]

When Ravenshaw wrote to say that Munro's term of governor was extended for a year in 1824 because of the divisions among directors and between them and the Board of Control about a successor, he urged Munro to use the additional time to prepare a comprehensive report on the results of all of his measures and minutes for use in London, especially against 'Bengalee' directors.[78] That request for a report was more than fulfilled in Munro's great minute of 31 December 1824.

Munro was also attentive to catechizing, as he would have called it, other important men in England on ryotwar. These included the presidents of the Board of Control of which there were three following the death of Buckinghamshire in 1816: George Canning, who served for five years, to 1821; Charles B. Bathurst, who served briefly after Canning; and Charles W. W. Wynn, who served from 1822 until after Munro's death.

Canning had suggested that Munro write to Bathurst in September 1821, to establish communication with one whom he hoped would be as sympathetic to Munro's programmes as Canning had been. A sketch of conditions in Madras

[75] *Report on the Ryotwari Settlement of the Coimbatore District* (Coimbatore: District Press, 1886), consulted at the Tamilnadu State Archives, ASO (D), v. 97.

[76] MC, F/151/73, Ravenshaw to Munro, 1 March 1820.

[77] Ibid., 26 December 1820.

[78] Ibid., 6 December 1824.

was duly provided for Bathurst in which Munro was reassuring about the general tranquillity of India. However, he went on to complain that relatively poor Madras had been saddled by rich Bengal with military responsibilities that prevented any lowering of its high revenue demand. He complained, too, of the slighting of the revenue line of administration in favour of the judicial. He then launched into an explanation and justification of ryotwar. The designation 'collector', he said, 'is an unfortunate one, and it ought to be changed', for he was no 'mere tax-gatherer'. The whole of the administration of a territory as large as a province is his, and the collector should therefore be as richly rewarded as judges. Instead, able men with revenue experience switched from the revenue service to the judicial and often left less capable men to serve in revenue administration. This would not be so serious if the revenue demand were low, but the pitch of revenue demand in Madras was very high, and thus 'ignorance or misconduct' could easily injure the people of the country. Moreover, 'skilful collectors . . . we find from experience . . . are only to be formed in districts where the rayetwar prevails'.[79]

Bathurst was then treated to Munro's harangue on Madras sub-imperialism. All would of course be made easier if the revenue available for Madras could be increased by assigning to Madras those territories it deserved to hold because of its sacrifices in obtaining them for the Company. Madras soldiers and treasure had been vital in the victories over the Marathas in 1803–4 and 1817–18, but from that sacrifice Madras 'has not acquired a single acre of territory'; all of the gains had gone to Bengal and to Bombay. Thus, fairness and fiscal efficiency combined with powerful cultural reasons to urge that the southern Maratha districts of Belgaum and Dharwar should be given to Madras.[80]

Charles Wynn was provided a brief primer on ryotwar in June 1823.

> The land revenue under this Presidency is what is called Rayetwar. This term, simple in itself, has been much misunderstood and has caused unnecessary discussion. It means nothing more than . . . a settlement with each proprietor individually whether the public assessment on his land is ten Rupees or ten thousand. It is a settlement with each proprietor or occupant of land instead of one with zemindars or farmers of revenue. It is the settlement usually made under Native Governments in their best times. Such a proprietor if applied to England would include every proprietor whether his rental were £10 or £50,000 and the richest and poorest would alike be termed Rayets. This settlement, so natural to all countries is undoubtedly best adapted to the prosperity of this. It is also that which is best adapted to our security, because it brings us into communication with every class of inhabitants.[81]

[79] Gleig, v. 2, pp. 59–65.

[80] Munro devoted several minutes to this: IOL, Elphinstone Papers, F/87, box 1B, 'Minutes of Munro', pp. 264–78.

[81] MC, F/151/92, Munro to Wynn, 14 June 1823.

Wynn was given to understand that after long being disdained as a system by officials in India and England, whom Munro always regarded as ignorant of Indian conditions, ryotwar was now gaining adherents in India and at home. On the strength of this Wynn was asked to support the appointment of men who knew his system to the highest offices of the Presidency. These included James Cochrane, William Chaplin and John Sullivan—whose father continued to be a regular recipient of Munro's letters and suggestions for the Board of Control.[82]

RYOTWAR FORTIFIED

In Madras, where he could do more than suggest and recommend, Munro took strong steps to place ryotwar on a firm and permanent base. A file of his papers reveals that in June 1819, even before his appointment to the governorship, though perhaps anticipating it, he drafted a review of 'modes of settlement' in Madras and obtained, for the purpose, a map from Colin Mackenzie's surveyor-general department showing when each district of the Presidency was surveyed.[83] A note of his in this 1819 file listed the papers of the Madras government he had consulted. These included papers on the village lease system (which, strangely, he equated with 'putkut') and on the ryotwar system 'to be adopted on its [village lease] termination'. He exempted from this proposed replacement by ryotwar only those villages, as in Tanjore, where all 'consent to be parties to the collective village settlements [i.e. mirasidars] [there]... settlements should be renewed for a further ten years'. If agreements among villagers could not be concluded, then 'annual field assessments, with modifications as needed [should be] reverted to'.

His determination to carry this plan forward was heralded early in his governorship by an attack upon Alexander D. Campbell, Hodgson's appointee to Bellary in 1820. His attack was presented to his council on 31 August 1820.[84]

This was in the form of responses to a set of reasoned queries received by the MBOR from the new Bellary collector, Campbell, and passed from them to Munro. Campbell asked (a) whether inam land cultivation should be restricted in order to increase acreages under fully taxed government land; (b) how a proposed 25 per cent reduction of revenue demand in Bellary was to be accomplished, particularly in the light of the several reductions already made there before Campbell assumed charge of Bellary; and (c) whether cultivation of waste was to be encouraged or discouraged. These queries were based on Campbell's careful reading and citing of Thackeray's reports on Bellary during the latter's brief tenure as collector there.

[82] Gleig, v. 2, dated 12 October 1820 and, for example, Munro to Sullivan, 24 June 1821 in MC, F/151/92. Henry Graeme was appointed as provisional member of Munro's council in July 1820, and James Cochrane was appointed to the MBOR.

[83] MC, F/151/98, f. 3, map and 'Summary Modes of Settlement...', ff. 8–9 and memo from Campbell dated 3 July 1820, ff. 18–21.

[84] 'The Ryotwar Settlement of Ballari', Arbuthnot, *Munro Selections*, pp. 110–17.

Munro commenced his attack with the observation that once prosperous Bellary had been reduced to misery during the years since he departed from there in 1807. This decline was documented by reference to Thackeray's report of 1807, the last of the documents comprising James Cumming's voluminous appendix on Madras in *The Fifth Report*. Munro also cited correspondence between Chaplin, a successor in Bellary, and the MBOR which consistently ignored warnings of great damage to the welfare of the Bellary cultivators. Thackeray, it was found, had urged a reduction in the revenue demand of 25 per cent in 1807 following Munro's recommendation. Easing the condition of Bellary farmers became a vital necessity when the village lease system was introduced with revenue demand set at the highest level of collections ever achieved in Bellary, that by Munro in 1807. Munro showed that Chaplin tried and failed to persuade the MBOR to reduce this pitch of demand, by even 10 per cent. Hence, debt and misery mounted until 1819, when it was decreed that Bellary should revert to ryotwar, and the MBOR at last ordered a full 25 per cent reduction. At that point, Chaplin was placed in charge of the southern Maratha districts vacated by Munro, and Bellary was passed to Thackeray, who immediately reduced the assessment in two taluks of the district and prepared a report detailing further reductions elsewhere. Then, Thackeray left Bellary to take a seat on the MBOR and was replaced by Campbell. There the matter stood when Munro returned to Madras in June 1820.

Impatient with Campbell's cautious queries, Munro insisted that the staged approach advocated by Thackeray had now to be replaced by an instant reduction of revenue demand throughout Bellary. This was dictated by conditions. Owing to the high pitch of this demand, renters of about three quarters of villages (1800 of 2644 villages) had become insolvent and their villages were now under government collections. Cultivators in many of its taluks had migrated to other places, including Mysore. In Rayadrug taluk this involved half of all cultivator families. Most headmen were now impoverished and many had been jailed for debt.

Three years later Munro returned to problems in his old CD and more attacks upon Campbell, in Bellary, and upon the collector of Cuddapah, John Hanbury, demanding the dismissal of both.[85] He was writing from Bellary while on another tour of the Presidency, and he saw fit to minute his council even before completion of the tour because of what he discovered in Bellary. He reiterated the long-term causes of decline of the former Ceded Districts: the village-lease scheme imposed by Hodgson's BOR, the high rate of assessment set at the time, the inexperience of several of the collectors appointed to the districts carved from his CD, and, in part as a result of the last, the practice of Indian revenue subordinates 'endeavouring to make up the loss of revenue

[85] 'State of the Southern Ceded Districts' Arbuthnot, *Munro Selections*, pp. 211–20, and on 20 April 1824, 'On the Depressed Condition of the Ballari District, Consequent on the Triennial and Decennial Leases', pp. 221–7.

of the deteriorated villages . . . by forcing upon the ryots more land than they could cultivate'.[86]

He noted that in 1820 the MBOR obediently acted on his August minute and had ordered a reduction of 25 per cent to take effect in the following year (fasli 1230). This order was not carried out by Campbell, the collector, but, instead, those cultivators in Bellary not completely impoverished were forced to take up waste land (cultivable, but not cultivated ryotwar fields). Munro said that he had been disappointed to read Campbell's settlement report of 1821, but he had hoped that the collector would 'remedy this error' in the succeeding crop year. That did not happen, as Munro came to learn when he visited Bellary in his current tour. Ryots told him that there had been no reduction of assessment and tahsildars were demanding that they cultivate more waste. Campbell had also committed two settlement errors, one of supposing that field assessments could be dispensed with and the other that a 'putkutt' settlement was a satisfactory alternative to a ryotwar settlement.

Munro's objection here is somewhat contrary and vindictive, for he had already conceded to critics of ryotwar that field assessments *based on survey* were not essential and had also said that 'pukut', or the system of assessing the total farm (consisting of several fields) of a cultivator, was 'only another name for ryotwar'. Now, however, he was charging Campbell with the same fatal error that had marred the work of his mentor John Hodgson: 'that everything must be right in proportion as it is assimilated to the practice of England . . . [and] The collector looks upon the ryot as a mere tenant, and hence he infers that the occupation of the land in India may be regulated as in England'.[87]

Those ryots whom Munro reportedly spoke with in Bellary had assumed that Campbell's measures were approved by the government and did not therefore complain; Campbell himself seemed to have no idea of how serious the whole problem was. To Munro, Campbell's failure was evident on the examination of revenue collections for the previous several years: the level of collections did not show the reductions that should have been there. Munro said that his encounter with complaining ryots was deeply disturbing because they 'rather resembled a mob than an ordinary party of complainants'. This had convinced Munro of Campbell's indifference or malicious intent.

There remained a question of what to do about the successive years of overcharging on the revenue. Because it was 'a breach of public faith', the forced collection of some three lakhs of rupees should be returned to those from whom it had been exacted. But as this number exceeded 10,000 ryots, perhaps as many as 20,000, Munro judged that too large a number to repay. But, Campbell must be removed: 'We cannot commit the character of Government by allowing the people to suppose that we are not dissatisfied with his conduct. There will

[86] Arbuthnot, *Munro Selections*, p. 214.

[87] Ibid., pp. 224–5.

never be any ordinary cordiality between him and them.'[88]

The collector of neighbouring Cuddapah, John Hanbury, was, like Campbell, a Hodgson protégé.[89] Munro found ryots there marginally better off than those in Bellary in 1824 because the terms of the village leases executed there had been less onerous than in Bellary, and cultivators had been granted more generous remissions because, Munro opined, Cuddapah ryots were 'too substantial and independent to submit to extra assessments' by subordinate revenue officials, a possible consequence of the numerous powerful poligars Munro had found there in 1802. Hanbury was found also to have failed to introduce the 25 per cent reduction ordered by the MBOR, and while he did not impose waste land on cultivators, or to so great an extent as Campbell, he was charged, like Campbell, with having lost control of his Indian subordinates: 'His tahsildars have been too long accustomed to a total relaxation of authority to pay any attention to it, and he was too indolent to enforce it.' There followed a catalogue of Hanbury's offences: his indifference to orders from the MBOR since 1817 when he was appointed to Cuddapah; his arbitrary dismissal of subordinate officials and failure to replace them so that in 1821–2 as many as five tahsildar posts were vacant; accounts and records of the collectorate were in disarray as a result of insufficient staff as well as the poor supervision of Hanbury. For all these reasons he should be dismissed from his office.[90]

Apart from these actions to remove resistance to a restored and successful ryotwar in Madras, he took other steps to improve the revenue administration of the Presidency. In 1822 a minute of his launched a proposal to 'attach a native cutcherry', or office, to the MBOR in order to provide that department with the same direct knowledge and experience of senior Indian revenue officials that collectors had in their own districts. 'There is no Collector, however long his experience may have been, who does not find himself obliged to make constant reference to his cutcherry, for their advice on revenue affairs; and the Members of the Revenue Board, though they do not, like a Collector, enter into the executive details of revenue, enter into the executive details of revenue, must often . . . stand as much in need as he does of the assistance of a cutcherry.'[91]

Considering his often harsh past criticisms of the ignorance of members of the BOR about actual conditions affecting the revenue in Madras, his proposal was quite restrained. This may have reflected the composition of the board in his own time when men devoted to his policies dominated. In his proposal he could not, however, resist a slap at the judiciary. He pointed out that the Sadr

[88] Ibid., p. 217.

[89] From 1811 to 1820, during which time he was also secretary of the College Board. Like Bellary with its 17,000 square miles, Cuddapah was very large, nearly 13,000 square miles.

[90] Arbuthnot, *Munro Selections*, pp. 218–20.

[91] 'Proposal for Attaching a Native Establishment to the Board of Revenue', 9 April 1822, Arbuthnot, *Munro Selections*, pp. 131 and 131n; this office lasted through most of the British period.

Adalat had long had a native staff and its business was not as important as the revenue administration.

The 'native cutcherry' of the MBOR would add a group of seasoned revenue officials to the overworked secretariat of the board and also constitute a staff for any touring members of the BOR or other officials and thereby obviate the necessity of drawing upon the busy staffs of collectors in whose districts these touring officials might be. Records of the proposed office should be in Marathi ('Hinduwi') since that was the language used in most revenue accounts of Madras, and its records should reach to the village level of every Madras district. He specified the number of members, their ranks and functions, and pay.

On another question, the proposed farming of the land customs of the Presidency, he recorded another, surprising minute.[92] This was to support the recommendation of A. D. Campbell and the MBOR to rent, or farm, the collection of inland customs. Surprising in this was Munro's agreement that the dangers of fraud from Indian revenue officials was too great to leave collections in their hands! Unlike the land revenue where the European collector supervised all phases of assessment and collection, the collection of land customs was too diffused to be managed by European collectors, especially in a place like Bellary, the largest district in the Presidency—with a 300-mile frontier shared by Mysore, the southern Maratha country, and Hyderabad. Renters of land customs would be merchants with every incentive to see trade flourish; they would do nothing to discourage transits through their territories by excessive and unlawful demands, but might even lower (i.e. subsidize) customs charges to facilitate trade. Moreover, in Bellary and in other districts of the Presidency, frontiers were easily crossed at so many points that a large corps of officials was required. Unsupervised by European officials, little of what was collected would ever reach the government, whereas under merchant renters supervision would fall on them and probably more revenue would actually be realized by government. This decision is interesting in revealing his strongly held notions about free trade in India.

In another report to his council in the same year, 1821, he drew attention to the depressed state of trade in Salem town through which he passed en route to Bangalore to join his wife for a brief holiday. Salem he found depressed owing to two factors: illegal exactions from merchants by revenue officials, causing many to leave the town, and restrictions placed by courts upon revenue and police officials which led to increased theft and robbery of merchants. The solutions he proposed to restore the trade of Salem was the granting of permission to local people, especially merchants, to arm themselves against robbers and the supervision of the police by revenue officials. The last was essential to prevent the tahsildar becoming 'a cypher in his District compared

[92] 'On the Farming of Land Customs', 28 December 1820, Arbuthnot, *Munro Selections*, p. 125.

to the Darogah [police official]'.[93] Elsewhere in his cursive notes of the time Munro invidiously compared local police and revenue officials: the 'Daroga—a law man; no talent, but activity, a mere accomplished *thief catcher*. . . . Tahsil[dars are] well educated, interested in welfare and justice of the country.'[94]

These views on trade are consistent with those he had long held. Long before in the Baramahal and later in the CD he had expressed misgivings about the monopolies of the Company and its procurement of export commodities by using land revenue receipts. As governor, Munro was to press for the earliest abolition of these monopolistic export enterprises under the Madras Board of Trade and its network of commercial residents, and he was swift to end that system of the Cornwallis era when London agreed that could be done.

A last focus of Munro's minutes before 1825 pertained to a variety of administrative practices which, if they were not corrected, could undermine the operations of ryotwar and his judicial reforms of 1816. Munro steadfastly pressed the principle that good administration meant the appointment of able men to responsible and powerful offices, whether a governorship or a collectorate. He expressed this in his letter to John Sullivan at the Board of Control after the promulgation of his judicial reforms: London must now promote able men to Madras posts or the reforms failed. Munro was not alone in holding that it was not formal, bureaucratic procedures, but virtuous, powerful men who knew India and its people that assured a proper administration for the country; desk-bound careerists, who knew nothing of India, dangerously applied inappropriate British models.

Malcolm was one who shared this view.[95] This was revealed early in Munro's governorship when he found on his arrival in Madras a bitter letter from his old friend. Partly, Malcolm's bitterness was personal, and directed at Munro for his 'hesitation' to take up the patronage request channelled to Munro Malcolm's wife on behalf of his protégé, Captain A. Macdonald. This apparent neglect had 'annoyed' Malcolm until he recalled their 'long friendship' and Munro's 'Glasgow prejudice against Kelts [Irish?]'.[96] In more detail, Malcolm spoke bitterly of his own career and his determination to leave India unless offered a 'permanent situation of high rank' such as lieutenent-governor and military commander of Malwa and Bhopal. He complained that his career had consisted of a series of 'mere *stop gaps*. . . . I tumble from one expedient to another as necessity called'. Better to return to Britain with his competence of £50,000, 'which will give at least porridge and butter to me and the weanies. I will not stay except for an object of ambition such . . . as I told [Bengal councillor, John]

[93] MC, F/151/101, ff. 120–6, 'Revenue Minute of 23 November 1821; this is not in Arbuthnot's selections.

[94] MC, F/151/128, f. 50.

[95] Copies of the series of letters by Malcolm to John Adam, in February and March 1821, are found in MC, F/151/62, ff. 135–42, but especially Malcolm's letter of 29 March 1821, referring to the political system and his 'school'.

[96] MC, F/151/62, Malcolm to Munro, 28 May 1820.

Adam [as] the introduction of that new system . . . by which B[ritish] India on its present scale can be preserved. Let me be a *Subah* in rank, name and power and I am their man . . .'[97]

What Malcolm may have meant by a 'new system' was that outlined in his report to Lord Hastings on Bhopal and Malwa and later elaborated in his *A Memoir of Central India, Including Malwa and Adjoining Provinces* . . . published in 1823.[98] It was a view of political relations very like that presented by Munro to Lord Hastings prior to his departure for India in 1819.

For Munro, then and before, 'new system' meant something else as well, something about the administration of British India. Constant attention to the choice of men for the superior posts reserved for Europeans was essential. This involved about 200 Europeans in Madras during Munro's governorship and, according to a memorandum found in his private papers, the annual salaries of these men ranged from 50,000 pagodas, of which there were five, to 6000, of which there were twenty-nine.[99] Munro's salary as governor exceeded any by a wide margin. Though not princely, the salaries of these 200 Company civil officials were adequate to attract able men to Company service and to provide to those who survived long careers in India a sufficiency on which to retire—to buy 'porridge and butter' for themselves and their families in Britain. Still, adequate salaries were not enough to produce a high-level civil administration for India—though it might reduce the fraudulence and self-interest of the Madras civil service of less than a century before. Another major impediment to quality were the seniority rules for Company officials in India.

Seniority and security of tenure in offices were guaranteed by the charters of the Company according to provisions that threatened to terminate Munro's civilian career at its outset. How was it possible, then, to assure that the most important offices of the Presidency were held by the most capable officials?

Munro's able chief-secretary of Madras, David Hill, proposed one answer to this question in a memorandum on seniority in 1822.[100] Hill proposed that all superior offices in the Presidency should be treated as temporary and assigned on the basis of merit among the best men then in service. This was the method used for appointing members to the governor's council, each being appointed by the court of directors for a fixed number of years, without security in the office. At present, Hill pointed out, offices in the civil service were guaranteed to an incumbent until they were moved to a vacant superior office, were suspended from the service, or retired. The result was that many important offices were

[97] MC, F/151/62, Malcolm to Munro, 11 June (?) 1820, received by Munro on 24 June.

[98] Published in London in two volumes, the first being a history and the second Malcolm's ideas of the sort of regime to be established and why he should head it, v. 2, pp. 264–81.

[99] MC, F/151/128, ff. 64–73 showing the number of officers in Madras and their salaries; Munro's salary was £16,000, about 15 per cent of the combined total of the 164 other officers enumerated.

[100] MC, F/151/77, dated 8 July 1822.

occupied by incompetent men. In England, where 'public opinion' was a check, inadequacies could become known and corrected. In India, where it was not permitted to exist, 'The only substitute which can be found for public opinion . . . is the opinion of the Government by which alone the public is in any sense represented'. In the several cases where Munro acted to advance able men to high presidency offices, such as the MBOR, he incurred the wrath of civil servants with greater seniority than those whom he appointed and, as already noticed, sometimes their supporters in the directorate who grumbled about the present, arbitrary 'government of Fort St George'.[101]

If the purportedly arbitrary authority assumed by Munro's government of Fort St George was thought to place it at variance with other governments, which sought a unified system for all of British India, Munro had a defence: administrative variety was healthy. In a draft memorandum labelled by him as '"gen[eral]-gov[ernment]-Internal"', he wrote:

> Let each presidency pursue the course best calculated to promote improvement in its own territories. Do not suppose the one way will answer for all and that Madras, Calcutta and Bombay—placed a thousand miles from each other—must be in everything so alike as to require exactly the same rules of internal administration. . . . Let each Presidency act for itself. By this means a spirit of emulation will be kept alive and each may borrow from the other every improvement which might be suited to the circumstances of its own provinces.[102]

Appointments to superior offices and the privileges of seniority for civil servants were matters to be decided by London, of course. The first was a prerogative of the directorate to be defended from the engrossing purview of the Board of Control and the ministry of the day; the second was a matter of statutory right under the Company charters. Hence, neither were subjects of Munro's minutes however they may have figured in private correspondence within India, and between himself and others in England. But there were other administrative issues that he could and did pronounce on to his council. These were consistent with his understanding of 'new system', that is of an administration to match the 'new system' of politics that Malcolm was concerned to create.

Among these subordinate administrative subjects was that of the relationship between principal collectors of districts and European sub-collectors serving

[101] Munro's appointment of McDonell to the MBOR in 1821 prompted protests from the latter's senior in the civil service; see letters from Clarke, 30 January 1822, from Lushington, 2 February 1822, from Cotton, 5 February 1822, and from Ravenshaw in London, 18 September 1822, in MC, F/151/77.

[102] MC, F/151/127, f. 2, drafted in 1822 or 1824 for inclusion in his minute of 31 December 1824. Interestingly, the final sentence quoted, 'By this means . . .' had a large 'X' placed over it and Ravenshaw's initials, another example the latter's first editorial work on the Munro papers.

under them. Munro had long defended the system of principal collectorships in Madras, of which his regime in the CD was one of the first and certainly among the most famous. To Munro this meant a powerful local executive over a substantial territory and population, a responsibility that approximated that of a lieutenant-governorship, as he had said. Though he had attempted to resist having European assistants in the CD, he finally acceded to Josiah Webbe's plan to provide proper and supervised training in local administration for junior European revenue officials. Indeed, Munro soon went further than Webbe and argued that all Company civil servants, even those in the judicial and commercial lines, should so begin their service. However, the relationship between the principal collector and his European juniors was inherently ambiguous, for the latter, not less than the former, were selected and supervised by the MBOR, who determined, in the end, the careers of all. Munro sought to remove some of this ambiguity in a minute of 1822.[103] He insisted that a sub-collector and magistrate, as these juniors were then called, must be totally under the authority of the principal collector: 'It is his duty to obey, not to discuss the orders of his superior'. And certainly, 'The Sub-Collector can never be permitted to enter into controversy with his Principal, or to seek to put him in the wrong [with the BOR]'.

No less important was the relationship of Indian subordinates to the European collector, as the many scandals involving 'abuses' of authority that plagued Madras from the late eighteenth century on made obvious. One that broke in Salem was but another of those apparently insoluble instances of collectors losing control of their district administrations to combinations among Indian staff.[104] The Salem scandal was one of that serious sort that extended over a very long period and was the more difficult because the frauds alleged to a Salem sharistadar, one Narasa Iyer, 'Narsiah', were for a long time unprovable.

Narasa Iyer served collector E. R. Hargrave from the time the latter assumed control of Salem in 1808 to when he was dismissed from office during Munro's governorship. In his minute on the case Munro observed that Narasa Iyer retained the 'unlimited confidence' of Hargrave to the end as a result of his great caution and of his having assiduously covered his abuses. Munro contended that the Kasi Shetty scandal in neighbouring Coimbatore, which he had investigated on behalf of the MBOR, had at once alerted Narasa Iyer to the danger of being discovered and reassured him, and all other malefactors, that judicial procedures were not to be feared.[105] Hargrave's culpability in Narasa Iyer's crimes was obvious to Munro, though he thought that Hargrave gained nothing personal from them. This and similar cases inevitably were

[103] 'On the Relations of the Sub-Collectors to the Collectors of Districts', 13 December 1822, Arbuthnot, *Munro Selections*, p. 183.

[104] 'On Certain Alleged Embezzlements of Public Money in the Salem District', 23 March 1823, Arbuthnot, *Munro Selections*, p. 208.

[105] Munro observed this in the margins of a Thackeray memorandum on the recovery of exactions and embezzlements, n.d., MC, F/151/128, f. 57.

serious for Munro and his system, in which collectors were to possess enormous powers. It was a weakness that Hodgson and others had already used against ryotwar and the heavy supervisory responsibilities of the collector. To answer the problem Munro proposed a new regulation for enactment by which collectors were empowered to punish Indian revenue servants for their abuses, and courts were denied jurisdiction in such matters.[106]

Munro had to concede, however, that if a collector 'abandoned himself blindly to the guidance of a native servant, no regulation whatever could have been of the smallest use'. Where neither regulations nor judicial processes could protect the public and the Company from negligence by its European officials, increasing the supervisory authority of the MBOR must have seemed a weak solution and one that Munro rejected.

Presumably, however, it was in recognition of the inadequacy of the board's supervision of its collectors and Indian officials—something about which he had long complained—that he proposed his 'native cutcherry' in 1822. This was one of his most enduring innovations, for this office long remained a part of the MBOR. Yet its establishment drew criticisms almost immediately from London, as Ravenshaw reported in late 1822.[107] Also, of course, the dismissals of Alexander Campbell from Bellary and John Hanbury from Cuddapah for failing to carry out the reduction of ryotwar assessments was a reminder, if one were needed, of how difficult was the control over collectors whom Munro seemed determined to make ever more powerful, and how difficult it was to construct an administration that was at once responsive to central directives from Madras, as Munro expected Campbell to be, and, at the same time, responsive to the specific conditions of local administration. For the most part, Munro contented himself with resisting all possible incursions by non-revenue departments of the Madras government upon the executive authority of the collector and his subordinate tahsildars; each, in a sense that was never defined clearly by him, was seen to command a discrete domain of administration.

Accordingly, he opposed the appointment of Indians trained in Muslim and Hindu law at the Fort St George college to the positions of district munsifs. His scheme of 1816 provided that these offices were to be filled by local and district headmen who had demonstrated their knowledge and trust to the appointing collector under whom they would serve.[108] The training in the formal legal procedures of Muslim and Hindu law was intended to provide subordinate Indian officials for the courts, but owing to Munro's severe retrenchment of the district courts in Madras such placements became rare. Still Munro disapproved the appointment of such 'graduates' to munsif positions on the formalistic grounds of unseemly bureaucratic competition: 'It is the nature of every public body, when not vigilantly watched, to endeavour

106 Madras Regulation IX of 1822, cited in Arbuthnot, *Munro Selections*, p. 210n.

107 MC, F/151/77, Ravenshaw to Munro, 10 October 1822.

108 'On the Appointment of Mahomedan and Hindu Law Students at the College to the Post of District Munsif', 4 January 1825, Arbuthnot, *Munro Selections*, p. 302.

to extend its authority and influence; and the college would gradually... acquire the whole of the native judicial patronage.[109] Knowledge of the law he did not consider a superior qualification to prove good character and knowledge of 'local habits and customs'. Therefore, too, he had recommended that the powers of tahsildars should be increased within their jurisdictions by the appointment in all of the districts of 'karkuns', agents of tahsildars charged with overseeing cultivation, revenue collections and police matters in the several villages under the authority of tahsildars.[110]

Most of the issues on which Munro was moved to minute his council between the middle of 1820 and the beginning of 1825 were discursively embedded in his minute of 31 December 1824. However, even before finalizing that masterful political statement, he had anticipated it with his minute of opposition to Lord Hastings' proposals to liberalize the press of British India. This argument 'on the dangers and the mischief' of a free press was dated 12 April 1822,[111] and, as was usual, it saw Munro's council (General Archibald Campbell, George Stratton and William Thackeray), 'concurring most fully in the sentiments submitted... and deeming the question therein considered to be of the highest importance', resolved to forward it to the Court of Directors.

Rigorous restrictions on newspaper publication in India were somewhat peevishly imposed by Lord Wellesley in May 1799, as a result of criticisms of his policies by English editors in Calcutta. His press regulation stipulated pre-publication censorship by the chief-secretary to government, or his agent, and threatened banishment from India of any offending editor.[112] In August 1818 the Governor-General, Lord Hastings, abolished censorship while maintaining certain restrictions introduced previously by Lord Minto upon press discussion of governmental policies and of Indian religion and custom. Hastings' relaxation of the previously draconian censorship control of the press was inspired by his belief and that of others in India (including many members of the Madras civil service in 1822) that public discussion of governmental policies would mobilize support from the European community for these policies.

Hastings' measures were opposed by the Court of Directors, whose draft dispatch stated:

> Under a free government the press is at once the organ of expressing and

[109] Between February 1821 and March 1823 a number of zillah, or district, courts were abolished by Munro. This brought criticism from the directorate for not having been consulted prior to such abolition. Munro responded to this in a long minute of 1827 entitled 'Reduction of Zillah Courts', 20 January 1827, Arbuthnot, *Munro Selections*, pp. 306–22.

[110] 'State of the Southern Ceded Districts', 5 March 1824, Arbuthnot, *Munro Selections*, p. 213, and an unpublished minute of 23 November 1821, found in MC, F/151/101, ff. 120–6.

[111] Arbuthnot, *Munro Selections*, pp. 538–47. The phrase 'danger and mischief' is from the version of this minute in the *Madras Secret Proceedings*, 1825, v. 103, pp. 305–408.

[112] Malcolm, *Political History of India*, v. 2, pp. 292–5.

> the instrument of influencing public opinion. But in India public opinion cannot be said to exist. . . . How can a Government devote its individual energies to the greater interests of the state when it permits itself to be daily harassed and irritated by attacks of journalists, and how can it preserve unity and vigour of action when the press becomes at once its rival and opponent?[113]

Inasmuch as the press whose freedom was being debated was an English language one under English editors, and there being no Indian language press to speak of (the Bengali *Samachar Darpan* having come into existence in Serampore in 1818), justifications for censorship had seldom risen much above the pique of Wellesley or John Adam, who, as acting Governor-General in 1823, restored Wellesley's restrictions and sent off offending James Silk Buckingham of the *Calcutta Journal*. Peevishly or not, the discussion of press limitations went on for another ten years, engaging the wisdom, or at least the comment, of many of the fraternity of the early-nineteenth-century procounsuls, including John Malcolm and Munro.

Malcolm's contribution to the debate is found in his *The Political History of India* of 1826 including, in an appendix, his speech on the question before the Court of Proprietors of the Company defending his friend Adam.[114] His long argument in favour of press censorship turns on several points: the ignorance of most Britons of the true character of British rule in India, the generally low and scurrilous tone of the English press in India, the political dangers (primarily from 'half-castes' and secondarily from Indian soldiers of the Company), the ease with which constructive journalism could be carried out under the censorship regulation, and the good character of Adam and those responsible for the administration of the press regulations.

Munro's treatment of the question is revealingly more interesting; it is—not surpisingly for those who have read both Malcolm and Munro—less prolix and more subtle and penetrating.[115]

While addressed to his council, this statement on the press of 12 April 1822 was immediately sent on to London, as already mentioned. It was known that George Canning, before leaving the Board of Control, had agreed with the directors and others that Hastings' action to remove censorship was unwise. However Canning, along with his prime minister, Lord Liverpool, was loath to reverse Hastings, partly in the belief that to do so would cause difficulties for the government in Parliament. Canning advised leaving the matter at rest and desisted from acting in concert with the directorate against Hastings' liberalization. The matter stood there after Canning was replaced by Bathurst, and Munro seemed to be acting to break this stand-off between the directors and the board by presenting the former with a higher and more principled

[113] Philips, pp. 223–4.
[114] Malcolm, *Political History of India*, v. 2, p. 292ff and appendix, ccxxxiii–ccxlviii.
[115] Arbuthnot, *Munro Selections*, pp. 287–97.

argument than had been offered before. He was encouraged in this course by letters from Charles Wynn, John Sullivan and James Cumming of the Board of Control.[116]

It began with the proposition that liberties, like those of the press, are neither the basis of British rule in India nor are they consistent with it. However laudable a free press for the British people and political system, in India it was exceedingly dangerous and would lead to 'insubordination, insurrection, and anarchy'. Those who advocate an unfettered press in India considered only the entertainment and commercial benefit to a small British population. Considered more seriously and with regard to Indian sensibilities, 'A free press and the domination of strangers are things which are incompatible, and cannot long exist together'.

This was principle not to be ignored: the first purpose of a free press among those ruled by strangers is freedom. Moreover, a free press, once permitted to Englishmen in India, would inevitably lead to the same right for Indians; no existing law could prevent that. And, though a free native press might at the outset devote its attentions to constructive causes, such as moral and religious instruction, these and other public constructive interests must be overtaken by the first concern of a conquered people, their freedom.

The contribution of a free press to the genuine improvement of the government or the people in India is illusory, continued Munro. British rule 'should be prolonged to the remotest possible period' and, when it is relinquished, it must leave the natives so changed as to assure 'a free, or at least a regular government'. Towards this necessary duration of British tutelage the two objectives of proprietors of newspapers make a dubious contribution. These objectives are to guide and instruct the public, which is good, and to make a profit, which is potentially mischievous. Since India has no public as known in England, the second end must dominate. Most Britons in India are civil or military officers, the remaining small number are mostly merchants. All have access to the press of Europe and need none in India. Hence, proprietors of newspapers in India will scurrilously criticize India's governors in order to profit themselves, for, 'nothing in a newspaper excites so much interest as strictures on the conduct of the government or its officers, but this is more particularly the case in India where... almost all of the individuals composing.... ['European society'] are known to each other, [and where] almost every European may be said to be a public officer.' The more censure and attacks upon government and its officers, the more the sales. This must eventually discredit the government with the people of India and 'stimulate them to expel the strangers who rule over them and to establish a national government'.

Serious as all of the above is, Munro spoke of a yet more grave threat arising from a free press: its effect upon the 'native army'. Under an extended British rule the spirit of freedom among the general population would grow slowly,

[116] MC, F/151/72/, Wynn to Munro, dated 11 January 1823 and from Sullivan 25 February 1823.

a 'quiet and uniform' progress of education and knowledge such as finally to constitute a 'silent and tranquil revolution... in the character and the opinions of the people'. Permitted to run that long course, the Indian people would be able to check any danger of uprising in the 'native army'. But a free press now, immediately, would engender a spirit of unrest and freedom among Indian soldiers who would 'hasten to execute their own measures for the overthrow of the Government and the recovery of their national independence, which they will soon learn from the press it is their duty to accomplish'.

The special danger of the 'native army' arises from its strategic place in British rule. Close contact with European soldiers in camp and garrison facilitated the spread of potentially subversive ideas, and sharpened grievances of Indian soldiers: discontent with their pay and privileges relative to those enjoyed by European soldiers with whom they regularly consort; bitterness over the lack of opportunity to attain high rank; and the favourable climate for the spread of rebellious ideas afforded by garrison life.

Munro joined Malcolm in believing that military revolt was a real danger. It could not be averted through additional European troops. The last would be expensive and ultimately useless if there were support from the people of India for the mutineers. True, many Indians, such as merchants who had benefited from their rule, would remain passive in a military rising against the British; but others would actively support the sepoys. These included the displaced nobility, for whose interests Munro had become a vocal spokesman, and officials of conquered states and the heads of villages from whom ancient perquisites had been denied by British administration and courts. Though the danger of a massive military rising may seem distant, Munro asserted that it would be the certain outcome of a free press permitted to exist along with foreign domination.

To avert the danger the gradual improvement of the Indian people under British rule must proceed, unhampered by press scurrility. The best of its policies must be strengthened: mild government, low revenue demand, support of Indian religions and schools, and, especially, conferring responsible administrative posts and honours upon Indians. Under these policies India would develop a public able to resist a rebellious army. But, should Indians lose respect for English character upon which its rule now depended, an uprising of the sepoys and the people was a certainty. A free press would help to produce this last: 'We are trying an experiment never yet tried in the world—maintaining a foreign domination by means of a native army, and teaching that army, through a free press, that it ought to expel us and deliver their country.'

For effect, Munro attached to this minute to his council, and later the directors, a letter he received from an Indian soldier expressing deep discontent, and begging Munro—'the sepoys' friend'—to improve conditions of service.

Few of those who contributed to the discussions about limiting the press in India between 1799 and 1834 (that fills eight large volumes in the *Home Miscellaneous Series*[117]) expressed either the urgency or the deeper significance

[117] *Home Miscellaneous Series*, vols. 532–9.

of that matter than Munro did. The Vellore Mutiny was behind the British then and adequate provisions against any repetition seemingly in place; but the sepoy uprising at Barrackpore and the Great Mutiny lay ahead to astonish and horrify the British in India and at home. In this sense Murno can be, and has been, seen as the prophet of these later events. Indeed the dangers that he perceived from this source can be traced to his earliest writings during the Mysore wars of the 1790s, a preoccupation that sheds light on Munro's larger and later (1824) views of the British empire in India.

For Munro, as for the more authoritarian of the utilitarians of the later nineteenth century, the largely unquestioned right of British rule over India derived from conquest. But, unlike Strachey or Fitzjames-Stephens, Munro never forgot that it was a conquest carried out by Indian soldiers upon whom, moreover, British rule continued to depend. But British rule also rested upon the efficacy of what was seen to be the superiority of 'British character', the perceived foundation of its rule. Any serious criticism of this superior character—as by public attacks upon Company policies or its leaders—left as the sole basis for its rule the naked might of its armies, and this, to Munro, must awaken in sepoys their own latent nationalism. The latency of nationalism for him—the inexorable desire of a subjugated people for their freedom—undergirds his argument about the press. That, and a concomitant, belief that if British rule continued long enough—'to the remotest possible period' as he wrote—a government would have been created in which Indians themselves would prevent the seizure of power by Indian soldiers. Along with justifying a controlled press in India, Munro was also setting forth the moral basis for an indefinitely long imperium in India: an extended custodianship over a forming Indian nation and the inevitable establishment of a free Indian state.

THE GREAT MINUTE

All of this was a prelude to Munro's longer and more elaborate 'Minute Reviewing the Condition of the Country and People, Stating His Sentiments as to How It May be Improved, 31 December 1824'.[118] This later statement was, like the press minute, not a policy statement to guide his council with respect to some Madras business, but a reflective and general statement from one accustomed to being listened to and heeded. Like his press minute, too, it was for the eyes and minds of London authorities, following Ravenshaw's suggestion, perhaps. However, some parts of the minute and even some of its phrases were first composed as notes before Munro's tenure as governor began;[119] and this minute endures as the classic enunciation of Munro's statesmanship.

Lengthy and carefully argued, the minute occupies seventy printed pages

[118] This title is from the official version in the *Madras Secret Proceedings*, 25 August 1825, v. 103, 305–408; also a version of MC, F/151/127.

[119] Evidenced by a set of Munro's notes entitled, 'Alterations Required at Madras', MC, F/151/127.

in Gleig's biography and forty-four long paragraphs in the original manuscript version; it defies an easy summary.

There are two preambles. Only one is usually cited in the various published versions, and that begins: 'We are now masters of a very extensive empire, and we should endeavour to secure and improve it by good internal administration'.[120] However, in Munro's notes for the minute and in the official version preserved in the *Madras Secret Proceedings* there is a prior assertion of his entitlement to pronounce upon the subject and its London audience: 'After having long been employed in publick affairs in this country it is natural that I should be desirous of expressing my sentiments upon the system by which they are conducted. I have accordingly often wished to have given some account of the principal branches of our internal administration and to have pointed out as far as I was able their defects and the means by which they might be remedied.' Lacking the leisure to do this, Munro proposes instead 'to explain in general terms what is the present condition of the people and how it may be improved'.

The topics taken up by him and the attention accorded to each deserve notice considering that this was intended as his last public, official, and summary pronouncement when the last cited preamble was first composed in 1823. Interestingly, he did not prepare another general statement though he served as governor for more than two years longer.

Landed property and revenue occupy more than half of the pages of the minute. This may occasion no surprise for those who consider his major achievement to have been the formulation of ryotwar, the heart of the 'Munro System'. However, his review of tenurial forms, especially of mirasi tenure, and his insistence that ryotwar encompassed all other systems as well as predating most is unexpected. After all, his appointment to Madras in 1819 was in part a recognition of the triumph of his administrative principles, and his governorship, predictably, secured these even more strongly. Other topics treated by him are: the pragmatic and moral foundations for a greater role for Indians in the internal administration of the country, the compelling need for 'native agency'; judicial and police administration in the light of his 1816 reforms, and eight paragraphs bearing directly upon the nature and purpose of British rule in India.

Comprehensive as this document is, not all of the subjects that might have been considered appear. There is no discussion of military affairs, though there was a war with Burma in which he played a major role, and no discussion of trade, though at this time the monopolistic structure of Company trade based on the 'investment' of Indian revenue was being dismantled. Such other matters as the press are also ignored, perhaps because he had already pronounced on them.

Rhetorical analysis requires that the minute be taken as a whole. That it was a carefully formulated, much revised and worked, statement urges this

[120] Gleig, v. 3, p. 319.

approach. His notes on the minute contained in a file of the Munro papers at the IOL makes this careful design obvious.

Munro followed his two preambles with a point he had made so often before in his writings that it is almost a rhetorical signature:

> We proceed in a country, of which we know little or nothing, as if we know everything, and as if everything must be done now. . . . We must not be led away by fanciful theories founded on European models. . . . We must not hastily declare any rights permanent. . . . We must proceed patiently, and as our knowledge of the manners and customs of the people and the nature and resources of the country increases, frame gradually from the existing institutions such a system as may advance the prosperity of the country, and be satisfactory to the people. The knowledge most necessary for this end is that of the landed property and its assessment, for the land is not only the great source of public revenue, but on its fair and moderate assessment depend, the comfort and happiness of the people.[121]

All may be seen to proceed from this materialist beginning.

The long land-tenure section is intended not merely to show, once again, that the ryotwar system was superior. Of the nineteen paragraphs (out of the total forty-four paragraphs of the minute) dealing with land, a major critique of mirasi tenure occupies the core. It is noteworthy that the zamindari, or Bengal, system against which Munro had long inveighed is given almost no attention. The reason for this concentration upon mirasi is evident in the argument of the minute: mirasi tenure was conceded to be native to peninsular India and hence that form of landholding could claim an historical standing equal to that claimed for ryotwar. Mirasi was not one of those 'fanciful theories founded on European models' which, like the zamindari system of Bengal, 'inevitably end in disappointment'; it was a customary form of tenure in the peninsula with, if anything—thanks to Ellis' researches, and those of others like Chaplin in Maharashtra—better historical qualifications than ryotwar. Moreover, mirasi tenure had recently been defended for some of the richest parts of Madras in a Hodgson MBOR minute of 1819,[122] and Hodgson, Munro knew from Ravenshaw, had become a candidate for the directorate.

Munro's argument against this and other forms of communal land tenure in Madras was that they were vestigial, mere manifestations of an ancient land system which history had repudiated and had so altered that they were genuinely communal no longer. Land held by the 'meerasidar' was no different from that held under ryotwar, 'a great body of petty owners'. What had long ago been communal and joint tenure had devolved into separate tenures, not as a result of government fiat but as the preference of erstwhile joint holders 'in the nature of things . . . because no man labours with the same spirit to

[121] Ibid., p. 320; all subsequent citations are from Gleig, v. 3, pp. 319–90.
[122] *Home Miscellaneous Series*, v. 528.

improve what he is to share with another. . . .' Native governments had acceded to this change from communal to severality tenure because the residual rights claimed by communal holders limited the revenue which could be realized from improvements such as irrigation. Here, Munro repeated his erroneous understanding that irrigation was a state investment under pre-colonial regimes. Another reason for the preference of pre-colonial regimes was that increased production and therefore revenue was more likely under individual than under collective tenures.

The great advantage of ryotwar is its foundation upon numerous small holders under the strongest 'natural' inducement to increase productivity and the absence of any non-cultivating intermediaries, such as a mirasidar, between the primary (and for Munro enterprising) cultivator and the tax collecting state. But there was yet another consideration besides those of historical precedence and custom, popular preference and greater revenue to the state, i.e. justice: there is greater justice in retaining current, individual land rights, than in overturning such rights by forms that merely have precedence. Finally, the fixity of demand under ryotwar encouraged the fullest planning for improvement by cultivators, and the detailed management by state officials required by ryotwar provided the government with accurate knowledge, thus control, over conditions in agriculture and in rural life.

The incontrovertible superiority of ryotwar over communal tenure, and certainly over the disastrous zamindari tenure which had been imposed over about one-third of the Presidency, established the foundation for the next stage of his larger argument having to do with 'native agency'.

Only Indians could manage the complexities of their historical land systems. The only question was whether they were to be various kinds of intermediaries, such as zamindars or renters, or whether they were to be servants of the British working under their immediate supervision. Ryotwar requires the last and, in addition to the highest quality of management, provides a pathway for Indians to honourable and rewarding employment under the British to whom they thus become ever more attached. Utility and justice combine to make native agency crucial for British rule. In this discourse whose moral tone has helped to earn Munro a place among British statesmen and a high place among enlightened imperial proconsuls, one surprisingly finds the pragmatic, or even cunning, proposal that: 'If we are to have corruption, it is better that it should be among the natives than ourselves, because the native will throw the blame of evil upon their countrymen, they will retain their high opinion of our superior integrity, and our character, which is one of the strongest supports of our power. . . .' But more typical was his insistence on the honours and rewards of high office for Indians:

> With what grace can we talk of our paternal government, if we exclude them from every important office and say, as we did until lately, that in a country containing fifteen million of inhabitants, no man but a European shall be entrusted with so much authority as to order a single stroke of the rattan.

Or:

> Our books alone will do little or nothing, dry simple literature will never improve the character of a nation. To produce this effect, it must be open to the road of wealth, and honour, and public employment. Without the prospect of such reward, no attainments in science will ever raise the character of the people. This is true of every nation as well as of India; it is true of our own. . . . Even if we could suppose that it were practicable without the aid of a single native, to conduct the whole affairs of the country . . . by means of Europeans, it ought not to be done, because it would be both politically and morally wrong.

The involvement of qualified Indian officials was substantially advanced by the 'native cutcherry' attached to the MBOR, Munro said. Henceforward, senior Indian revenue officers would contribute to the highest level of policy decisions without, he promised, diminishing British control of that important department of government. Even with the most complete 'native agency', British officials, experienced in all phases of administration, will always be necessary.

The next stage of his argument was nicely contrived. It deals with judicial and police matters, and Munro's opening statement startles: 'it may be said that we have perhaps been more successful in our judicial than our revenue institutions'! For over a decade prior to his becoming governor, no Madras official was more consistently critical of the existing judicial and police administrations of the Presidency nor had worked as diligently to change them. As judicial commissioner he succeeded very substantially in achieving those changes, not simply in the belated promulgation of his reforms by Elliot in 1816, but by his subsequent year of pressing for the acceptance and installation of these reforms among his Madras colleagues. In applauding the judicial and police administration of the Presidency he was not merely congratulating himself, however. For him the 1816 reforms and their apparent successes vindicated the principle of 'native agency', that is Indian personnel and institutions such as village and district munsifs and panchayats. It only required a recognition of that success to proceed to the full realization of the benefits of granting a major share of administrative responsibility and office to Indians in all other departments of the government.

Munro then returns to one of the first premises of his argument: that it is the 'rayet' upon whom the welfare of all of the people and the government alike depends. The judicial and police reforms of 1816 directly served 'the peculiar character and conditions of the Rayets . . .' and, if these measures seemed strange to Englishmen, Munro reminds them that, 'Our institutions here, not resting on the same foundations as those of a free country, cannot be made to act in the same way'. This begins the transition to the last part of his argument, its coda.

Two transitional elements—warnings—bridge to the final portion of the argument. On concluding his discussion of judicial administration Munro cautions:

> we must endeavour to protect ['the Rayets'] by laws, which would be unnecessary in England, or in almost any country not under foreign domination; and we must, for this salutary purpose, invest the [European] Collector and Magistrate, the person most interested in their welfare, with power to secure them from exaction. . . .

Then he repeats:

> Our great error in this country . . . has been too much precipitation in attempting to better the conditions of the people, with hardly any knowledge of the means by which it was to be accomplished. . . . It is a dangerous system of government in a country, of which our knowledge is very imperfect, to be constantly urged by the desire of settling everything permanently. . . . The ruling vice of our Government is innovation; and its innovation has been so little guided by a knowledge of the people, that [it] . . . must seem to them little better than caprice . . . our anxiety to make everything as English as possible in a country which resembles England in nothing. . . .

The transition is completed with a brief, summary paragraph setting the balance of 'advantage' and 'disadvantage' of British rule for Indians. The advantages were security from external and internal violence against persons and security of property from the evils of arbitrary government and rapacious taxation; against these purported advantages were: the exclusion of Indians from legislation entirely, and from most administrative positions of trust; the humiliation of being 'regarded as an inferior race' and rather as 'servants than as the ancient masters of the country.'

The conclusion consists of six brief paragraphs of purpose; they constitute Munro's charter for British imperialism, the moral base upon which alone British rule can exist. Laws and protection by themselves, he says, are a necessary but insufficient foundation for that rule. Foreign domination, even one as benevolent as that of the British, destroys public character:

> It is an old observation, that he who loses his liberty loses half his virtue. This is true of nations as well as of individuals. . . . . The enslaved nation loses the privilege of a nation as the slave does those of a freeman . . . the privilege of taxing itself, of making its own laws, of having any share in their administration, or in the general government of the country. British India has none of these privileges; it has not even that of being ruled by a despot of its own; for to a nation that has lost its liberty, it is still a privilege to have its countryman and not a foreigner as its ruler . . . It is not the arbitrary power of a national sovereign, but subjugation to a foreign one, that destroys national character and extinguishes national spirit.

Among the changes most destructive to the national character of Indians has been the reduction of the erstwhile 'higher ranks of society'. British erosion of 'gradations of society' by the elimination of 'jageerdars and enamders and of all higher civil and military officers' and many 'principal merchants and Rayets is without precedence'. Previously, men had risen and fallen with the fortunes of the times', but social ranks remained; now Indians were without hope of achieving wealth and standing: 'Are we to be satisfied with merely securing our power and protecting the inhabitants, leaving them to sink in character lower than at present, or are we to endeavour to raise their character, and to render them worthy of filling higher stations in the management of their country, and of devising plans for its improvement?' That is the 'one great question to which we should look in all our arrangements'.

Reconstruction of Indian national character required time and patience. 'Liberal treatment' was essential as was proper perspective; it must be remembered 'how slow the progress of improvement has been among nations of Europe and through what a long course of barbarous ages they had to pass before they attained their present state'. How long would it take the British in India, Munro asks: how long did it take England? 'When we compare other countries with England, we usually speak of England as she is now, we scarcely ever think of going back beyond the Reformation'.
Therefore:

> We should look upon India not as a temporary possession, but as one which is to be maintained permanently, until the natives shall in some future age have abandoned most of their superstitions and prejudices and become sufficiently enlightened to form a regular Government for themselves, and to conduct and preserve it. Whenever such time shall arrive it will probably be best for both countries that the British control over India should be gradually withdrawn.

The task of reconstructing Indian national character must be undertaken for two reasons. First, Indians deserve it, for, while public character may be deficient, the individual character of Indians was as good (or as bad) as that of Englishmen and others. Culture, not nature, made civil societies good or bad.

> Those who speak of the natives as men utterly unworthy of trust, who are not influenced by ambitions or by the law of honourable distinction, and who have no other passion but that of gain, describe a race of men that no where exists, and which, if it did, would scarcely deserve to be protected. . . . We cannot easily bring ourselves to take an interest in what we despise . . .

A second compelling reason for seeking the reconstruction of Indian national character is that 'our national character and the future good government of the country [Britain]' demands such sentiments and purposes.

In this minute Munro leads his reader through a subtle and persuasive discourse. His manifest intention was to provide an understanding—his understanding—of the nature of British imperialism and its improvement during the early nineteenth century. A latent purpose was to provide a justification for not only an enduring imperium, but one that took its shape and direction from India and not from Britain.

This December 1824 minute may be looked at in a different way. An Indian empire of long duration may have been viewed by Munro less as the outcome of reasoning from the material basis of an historically derived land system and appropriate land revenue administration—ryotwar—than as a moral imperative—a good in its own, absolute right. Ambient moral concerns were a fixture of Munro's writing on India from an early point in his public career. In this he may have been one of the most percipient of the Company's servants in the early nineteenth century. Edmund Burke's imprimatur is important here.

Peter Marshall, whose research combines Indian imperial history and Burke studies, is only the most recent scholar to have made the point that the last fifteen years of Burke's life were preoccupied with India. Burke became 'convinced that the growth of a British Empire in India was raising political, constitutional, and above all moral issues of the utmost importance for the future of Britain itself...'[123] In Munro's argument the moral imperative of India cut in two directions. One pertained to Britain and Britons. His castigation of 'English models' as 'disasterous' for India was intended not simply to exclude proposals lacking in recent and relevant Indian experience from policy consideration, nor simply that Indian policy and a future Indian polity could only be forged by those in India with sympathetic knowledge of Indian institutions and traditions, namely by resident administrators like himself and John Malcolm. These were important considerations, of course. Their experience and linguistic knowledge permitted them, and them alone, to choose, adapt, and nurture Indian institutions that would shape the transformation of an Indian nation into an Indian state.

More darkly, Munro hinted at the destructive consequences for Britain if the sole guide and measure of Indian policy were to be the narrow interest of Britain and its emergent dominance as the major European trading power in the East. It was inconceivable to him that the meanness of trade profits could long sustain British power in India. A loftier purpose had to be discovered, not merely in which to wrap British self-interest but upon which to establish a moral foundation for transforming British rule in India—of setting British rule upon a new and noble path, one infused with transcendent purpose.

To Britons like himself and Malcolm, prepared to devote their entire lives to this noble task, the restrictive status they held as servants of the East India Company and its directors was galling. British servants of the Company in India at best possessed a delegated authority which could be revoked by those in London with inferior knowledge of India and no commitment to any sort of grand enterprise. Malcolm, in his outspoken way, made this point vigorously in the chapter on Company administration in his *The Political History of India*, written at the same time as Munro wrote his 1824 minute.

As for Munro, he had before spoken of his powers as a collector being those of an independent agent, a lieutenant-governor, or even a 'prince', and this was

[123] *The Writings and Speeches of Edmund Burke* (Oxford: Clarendon Press, 1980), v. 5, p. viii.

the authority he thought the highest officials in India must possess. Along with Malcolm, though less publicly and vehemently, he was ever more impatient with his 'Honourable employers', the directors, and inclined to regard his credentials and writ as derived from the Crown. Honours which both men received for the Crown—Orders of Bath and baronetcies—fortified such pretensions. An India ruled by autonomous proconsuls of the Crown, trained by a lifetime of service in India, knowledgeable of and sympathetic towards its cultures, languages, and peoples: this was the empire that Munro envisioned in his later writings.

Moreover, his great minute of 1824 provided the arguments for why such a vision and moral mission was conceivable: nothing either in India nor in Britain blocked its pursuit. With the Company's trade monopoly at an end, most of its commercial operations of forty years' standing being closed down after having become subordinate to the China trade (itself being transformed by free trade pressure), and with the prospect of the continuation of its charter always at risk, prudent statesmanship required that the relationship between Britain and India be reconsidered.

As for India and the Indians, the prospects for a fundamental change were even more promising from Munro's point of view. Indian society had lost most of its ancient communal features, partly because Indians themselves preferred them gone, and because ancient Indian ruling groups—which sprang from communal forms and protected them—had been destroyed or badly weakened by the British. India was rapidly becoming a society of individuals, as Munro saw it, freed from communal constraints and from older corporate loyalties, therefore ripe and ready for being constituted anew. And, by whom other, or better, than men like himself?

Munro appears to be claiming that a reconstruction of Indian civil society was morally necessary and practically achievable because, among other reasons, ascriptive communal social forms had become too weak to sustain the ancient civil society. This reconstruction would be mediated by men like himself and Malcolm who, precisely because of their humble births, were denied access to positions of high authority and trust in Britain. Munro's acute sense of irony could scarcely have missed this, and it may account for some of his persistent denial of a place for 'European models' in Indian policy. Better than most men of his time, because he had scaled the heights of the Indian power system without the advantage of social connection, Munro understood that his own British society was based upon a very qualified individualism.

As a young student in Glasgow he may have heard the lectures of a well-known Glaswegian professor of law and social critic of the day, John Millar, and he may have read Millar's book, *Observations Concerning Distinctions of Rank in Society*,[124] with its argument on imperfectly individualized societies, including Britain. Millar based his argument upon what was to become the most com-

[124] Published in London, 1773. Millar was professor of law in Glasgow from 1761. A sketch of his life is contained in his *The Origin of the Distinction of Ranks*. . . . (Edinburgh: 1806).

pelling of nineteenth century conceptual frameworks, that of historical stages. Something like a Millar view informed his comment in the 1824 minute about how comparisons between British and other societies were often flawed by not considering pre-modern British society, or of not comparing like stages in national development. But whether or not he knew Millar's work on the stages through which a society evolved from 'tribes' to a ranked and 'extensive society' based on agriculture, he had long assumed just such a development in South India.[125]

From his earliest days in the Baramahal, during the 1790s, sodalities such as caste, sect, and even village were seen as vestigial and epiphenomenal.[126] Such institutions are rarely discussed or even mentioned by him. Instead, he spoke of headmen, his 'potail', and 'respectable' or 'leading' men whose leadership, whether as heads of panchayats or spokesmen for dominant agricultural groups, were not ascribed but achieved statuses as public individuals. As seen in his position on the Kurnool succession, he believed that hereditary succession was not practised in India; men were raised to a 'masnad' on the basis of their abilities as perceived by others. He lamented the destruction of such achievers as well as others who were formerly rewarded for their public endeavours ('enamdars'). The decay of these gradations of achieved rank could be arrested and greater scope for their flowering established under the tutelage of men like Munro himself.

Munro's rhetoric defies easy labelling. Few of the voluminous writings of his long administrative career are without persuasive intent—even the most mundane reports on revenue or judicial matters. His basic orientation was Burkean. Munro spoke more admiringly of Burke than of any public figure of his day, though he was even with respect to Burke spare in his admiration. Yet the latter's influence on Munro's ideology and rhetoric is apparent. Ideologically he shared with Burke a veneration of tradition and a loathing for theoretically inspired social change. With post-Burkeans of his day, he was deeply conscious of the power of nationalism and of what he called 'national character' as expressing the highest order of public values. With these latter-day Burkeans he also shared an appreciation of hierarchy, but especially one

[125] Millar, *Observations*, pp. 173ff and 191ff.

[126] Since the notion of the village as a 'little republic' is attributed to Munro by Mark Wilks in 1810 (in his *Historical Sketches of the South of India*, v. 1, p. 139n), this may seem a strange assertion. However, Munro's discussion of revenue in 1801 and later, both with his assistants and with the MBOR, make it clear that it was from individuals that revenue was to be collected ('the individual supercedes both village and district settlements', he wrote to the Governor-General, Richard Wellesley, in July 1802, according to Beaglehole, p. 71); the village was seen by him to consist of a collectivity of individual inhabitants, not, as Marx supposed, some sort of primordial corporation, nor as Hodgson (writing in opposition to ryotwar in 1808—*MBOR Proceedings*, 25 April 1808) supposed, some sort of proprietary, corporate right of mirasidars stemming from an ancient colonization of a village; again, Beaglehole, p. 84.

based, like Coleridge's, on a meritocracy of public leadership by men of talent and probity.[127]

We may even see Burke's public career and his ideas as models of (though not for) those of Munro. Like the young, poor Irishman who came to establish himself among the political and rhetorical giants of his day, Munro, the impoverished young Scot, did the same on the more distant stage of India. Both appreciated the opportunities which their respective public arenas provided for public careers and both contributed greatly to these arenas.

When Munro is called a 'romantic' by Beaglehole,[128] it must be taken to mean what Coleridge meant by that term as shown by Cobban in his study of Burke and his successors—and not the vague sense of sympathy for pre-industrial society, the simple rustic life of the crofter or ryot, and a love of natural beauty. It is the same when Beaglehole and others apply the term 'paternalist' to Munro. All but the most crass imperialists have sought to ennoble their enterprises with expressed concern for those subjugated to their rule and for whose benefit (however violently for the intended presumed beneficiaries) that rule was carried out. Since Munro vehemently denied that English models were appropriate for India, and since no other model was postulated, it is doubtful that he could be called a paternalist in any ordinary sense. There is little doubt, however, that Munro believed that there was a legitimating Indian constituency—the individuals comprising the 'respectable classes'—of whom he spoke frequently, to whose interests as he saw them he was devoted, and whom he saw as the foundation of a reconstructed Indian polity. Empire for him was the special preserve of civil and military careerists whose immediate benefits were as certain and clear as the vision of a reconstructed polity for those whom they ruled was vague and distant.

A final observation about Munro's argument in 1824 is that the vision it adumbrated is processual in nature, a state in becoming rather than in being. The 'free, or at least regular government' of Indians at the end of a long period of British rule is too unspecified to be taken as an end. What is important in Munro's formulation is the scope or freedom of Britons like himself to lead Indians to a discovery of their 'national character' and a polity which expresses and preserves that character. For this, British proconsuls in India had to be free in two senses: free from the constraints of British models imposed from London and free to knowledgeably choose and adapt Indian institutions to the governance of the country. In essence Munro demanded an 'Indian agency' of imperial control to parallel the 'native agency' of imperial administration. The reconstructed polity, when at length it should appear, would be based

[127] Arthur Cobban, *Edmund Burke and the Revolt Against the Eighteenth Century* (London: George Allen and Unwin, 2nd edn, 1962). According to Munro's remarkably detailed records on books purchased, he acquired the 12-volume set of Burke's writings from John Murray, the bookseller and publisher, on 8 March 1814 during his England furlough: MC, F/151/158, f. 3.

[128] Beaglehole, p. 131.

upon indigenous institutions and ever greater Indian participation. Benevolent consuls like Munro would know when British rule should be withdrawn, leaving a viable, new Indian polity.

This process of discovery of the appropriate basis for the reconstruction of an Indian polity was hardly a new idea for Munro in 1824. It was prefigured in Read's administration of the Baramahal in the sense that, to their subjectivity, the system they were seeking was only a modified version of what Read and Munro found in Salem then. When the Baramahal land system, later to be polished and called 'ryotwar', was abolished in 1802, ostensibly because it was found to be incompatible with Cornwallis' legal code, Munro determined to change that judicial system and promote one which, like the land system as he saw it, was based upon Indian usage. His judicial measures triumphed in 1816 and, along with these, the idea of 'native agency'. In short, therefore, the 1824 minute, with its principled argument for a reconstructed Indian public character and permanent empire, can be viewed as a reasoned defence of a correct Madras governance since the 1790s, to which Munro had made the most significant contributions. It also suggests that Munro's conception of British rule in India may have been formed quite early in his career, by 1800. The next twenty years were devoted to its realization.

Chapter Eight

End and After

Thomas Munro died in a manner fitting his contemporary dominance as an Indian statesman and his future stature as an imperial hero. Death came in a tent near Gooty, in the Ceded Districts, from whence his reputation had been launched. He was there in the summer of 1827 in order, partly, to escape the heat of Madras and partly to bid farewell 'to his old Indian friends'. Early in the morning of 6 July, at Pattikonda in modern Kurnool district, Munro succumbed to cholera which had struck his small camp several days before. Then, several sepoys of his military escort were afflicted and died very suddenly. Still, Munro maintained his schedule of visits and interviews around Gooty. On the night of 4 July he complained of indisposition which brought the attentions of the doctor in his company who diagnosed cholera and commenced medication.

Notwithstanding considerable and growing discomfort, Munro spent the next morning at business, and only when his symptoms became very distressing did he suspend that and ordered all from his tent so as to prevent further contagion. By nightfall he worsened and died.[1]

His contemporary biographer, Gleig, could not refrain from the dramatic suggestion that Munro's death was the cruel consequence of wholly avoidable delays by London authorities in appointing a successor. For, it had been long before, on the day that Madras learned of the signing of the treaty ending the Burmese war—28 May 1826—that Munro had written to the directors of his strong desire to be relieved. What Gleig could not have known in detail when he was writing the biography in 1829 was that the delay in naming a successor to the Madras governorship was the result of divisions within Lord Liverpool's cabinet and between the government and the Company. Some, including the Prime Minister, favoured the appointment of Stephen Rumbold Lushington, a former Madras civil servant then serving as Secretary of the Treasury, as a reward for the latter's services to the Tory party; others, like Canning, formerly president of the Board of Control and now the foreign minister, and the Duke of

[1] Gleig, v. 2, pp. 200–5.

Wellington, favoured Sir John Malcolm to succeed to Madras.[2]

When this division in the Liverpool cabinet became known to the Directors of the Company, their chairman, William Wigram, decided to challenge the government. He demanded restoration to the Company of what he and others at India House held to be an usurpation by ministries of the time, namely control over appointments to the superior posts in India. The matter became more complicated when Malcolm began a campaign for the Bombay governorship. He was in England when it was learned that Mountstuart Elphinstone requested to be considered for Madras when Munro left. The directors saw Malcolm as another weapon with which to challenge the Government and adopted Malcolm's candidacy for Bombay. Negotiations over these several candidates between the Company and the government reached such acrimony that the King was finally brought into it to reject the directors' choices.[3] The rancour of these differences confirmed in the minds of many—including the president of the Board of Control Charles Wynn, that the influence of the Company's directors must in future be curtailed, a change that was to be effected in the 1833 Charter.

None of this made staying on in Madras any more acceptable to Munro. His agreement to remain in office for the duration of the Burma war had eased the crisis of his succession until early 1826, when the Burmese king accepted the harsh terms being imposed and when Elphinstone expressed his desire to be relieved from Bombay, either to take up the Madras governorship or to return to Britain. This hiatus had permitted the conflict between the government and the Company to be compromised by giving Bombay to Malcolm and Madras to Lushington. But by now it was early 1827, and too late for Lushington to arrive in Madras in time for Munro to avoid the unfavourable sailings of the monsoon period along the Coromandel coast. Disconsolately, therefore, Munro decided on a final tour, not merely to escape the heat of the city but also to ease his longing for his wife and small son, now separated from him for almost a year.

Considering the whole of Munro's forty years of correspondence from India, his last letters to his wife Jane are the most warm and personal. Lady Jane Munro had left Madras in March 1826, with their ailing son Campbell, then two and a half years old. The child's health had been a problem since his birth in September 1823,[4] and by early 1826 had become so worrying as to overcome Lady Munro's reluctance to depart before her husband. A short time after his wife's departure Munro visited their spacious house at the edge of Madras, in Gindy on the Adyar river, and wrote poignantly to her of how he and his secretary Colonel Carfrae arrived at the now darkened house:

> we passed through the garden without finding you . . . the garden where I

[2] Philips, p. 251.

[3] Ibid., p. 252.

[4] When informed of the birth by a note from an aide, Munro laconically labelled the note, '7th Sept. 1823, rcd 9th, Capt. Watson, Lady has got a son'. MC, F/151/78.

always found you and Kamen [their name for the child] trotting before you, except where he stayed behind to examine some ant-hole. How delightful it was to see him walking, or running, or stopping, to endeavour to explain something with his hands to help his language. The causes which occasioned the desertion of this house give everything a melancholy appearance. I dislike to enter Kamen's room. I never pass it without thinking of that sad night when I saw him lying... with leeches on his head, the tears streaming down his face, crying with fear and pain, and his life uncertain. His image, in that situation, is always with me whenever I think of this house. How easy, and artless, and beautiful, are all the motions of a child . . . I have lost his society just at the time when it is most interesting. It was his tottering walk, his helplessness, and unconsciousness, that I liked. By the time I see him again he will have lost all those qualities.[5]

This plaintiveness was not only about a longing for his wife and youngest son, but also for their eldest son, Thomas, whom they had left with her parents in Scotland as an infant of a few months. The manifest delight Munro took in Campbell is a measure of what had been sacrificed in order to serve the Company for those additional years. Another aspect of this career cost was registered in a letter to his wife two months after the one above. In it, he once again pined for the sight of Campbell: 'I cannot tell you how much I long to see him playing again'; then, he asked for 'a full account of Tom, and all the points he is like or unlike his brother'.[6] Also expressed here was anxiety about the future. He drew attention to the shakiness of his writing: 'a sign that I have been long enough in a warm climate'. What then of the future? 'I am quite at a loss to know what I am to do when I go home. Where are we to live? in town or country? or both?'

During the late months of 1826 he sent several additional letters to await his wife's arrival in Britain. In them he described a tour he had undertaken of the southern districts of the Presidency: Tanjore, Trichinopoly, Madura, and from there to Coimbatore to visit John Sullivan, his old friend and the long-serving collector there. From Coimbatore he and Sullivan climbed to the high Niligiris plateau at Ootacamund. In September he wrote from there of the beauty and crisp salubriousness of the place. He spoke too of Sullivan's houses and of his improvements, including the formation of a small lake amidst rolling downs. The coolness he found a relief from Madras, but complained of the cold nights; nevertheless he reported favourably upon Sullivan's suggestion that Ootacamund should be made a sanatorium for British soldiers then returning from the arduous campaigning in Burma.[7]

There was another issue that turned on his health as well as being prompted by a conflict in his mind between his public opportunities and responsibilities,

[5] Gleig, v. 2, pp. 179–80; Munro to Lady Munro, 2 April 1826.

[6] Ibid., 182–3; Munro to Lady Munro, 11 June 1826.

[7] Ibid., pp. 190–2; also, Munro's minute in the Public Department of 28 May 1826, *Madras Public Proceedings*, 1 June 1826, IOL, P/245/74.

and his personal wishes. This was the prospect of being appointed Governor-General of India. Some of his ambivalence was expressed in a series of letters to John Ravenshaw, now for several years a director of the Company. In March 1825 Ravenshaw had written of the deep concerns at India House about the mutiny of the Bengal army in November 1824 over service in Burma, and about the general conduct of the Burma war by the Governor-General, Lord Amherst: 'There are some who would send *you* to the City of Palaces [Calcutta] with a *carte blanche*. . . .'[8] Answering, Munro defended Amherst as having done all that any with his limited experience could on the Burma war, though 'Some of the military arrangements are not exactly what I approve of—but what of that?'[9] When, a year later, the subject of the governor-generalship was again raised by Ravenshaw, Munro turned it aside by again defending Amherst to his friend, saying, 'You cannot have a Lord Cornwallis or Wellesley or Hastings every day, and must take such men as there are to be found.' On more personal grounds, he sought to end Ravenshaw's importunings with the following:

> I should have been delighted with it ten or fifteen yeas ago, or even when Lord Hastings resigned; but it is now too late. You forget that it is above forty-six years since I arrived in India, and that I have always been in laborious situations. I ought according to all ordinary rules, to have been dead seven years ago and nothing but a strong constitution and great temperance have saved me. My constitution may be expected to break every day; for I fancy that I see some symptoms. My hand shakes in writing . . . which it did not do till lately; and I lost from a cold more than one-half of my bad hearing. I am like an overworked horse, and require a little rest. . . . Were I to go to Bengal, I could hardly hold out for two years, certainly no more; and this period is too short to do any good.[10]

Deafness, a quivering hand, fatigue from years of anxious and demanding persecution of the Burma war made administrative tasks in Madras obnoxious; the heat of the city added to his impairments, and the melancholy of once delightful and distracting Gindy all combined in Munro's decision to tour the Presidency in 1826 and 1827. His zest for camping in beautiful places and seeing old friends—European and Indian alike—remained undiminished, as his letters attest. Moreover, he had placed the ordinary task of Madras administration into the hands of trusted and experienced Madras officials. This had freed him to deal with the war and to concentrate on drafting his last minutes on all aspects of Presidency affairs. He intended to leave an administration in Madras that was set in its principles and led by men devoted to them when he at last laid down his responsibility and departed India.

[8] MC, F/151/80, John Ravenshaw to Munro, 12 March 1825.
[9] Gleig, v. 2, p. 175, Munro to Ravenshaw, 18 July 1825.
[10] Ibid., pp. 176–7, 17 May 1826.

THE TROUBLED IMMEDIATE AFTERMATH

It might therefore have been supposed that his sad, swift death in the Ceded Districts would smooth the transition to a successor regime in Madras that assured the continuity of Munro's system and the principles on which it was founded. But, almost immediately, there were signs that this might not be.

Munro's body was removed from Pattikonda to Gooty where it was interred. Immediately thereafter the honouring of Munro—his person and his legacy—commenced. The Extraordinary Madras Government Gazette of 9 July reported his death and spoke of how his 'attainments as an Oriental scholar' combined with his 'intimate acquaintance' with ordinary Indians—soldiers and civilians—to create the most popular government that Madras had ever known. There was great sorrow expressed at Munro's passing from everywhere in the Presidency, it went on to say, but especially in the Ceded Districts where he had breathed his last and had 'long been known by the appellation of *Father* of the people'.[11] In the same month a general meeting in Madras—'Native as well as European'—resolved to raise a public subscription in order to erect a statue in Munro's memory. Contributions to this were quickly oversubscribed and a group of Munro's friends in London were instructed to undertake a commission for the work. This was done equally quickly in London where a sculptor, F. Chantry, was engaged to do a work in bronze at a cost of £8,000.[12]

Still within the month of his death, there arose the first signs of a struggle over how and by whom the symbol of Munro's name was to be controlled and enunciated. The cause of this was the grief that was shown by Indians in Gooty, according to the reports of the collector there, F. W. Robertson. At the place where Munro's body had been buried Rs 30,000 was raised to erect a 'choultry' or travellers' rest house, where a tomb, it was suggested, should be constructed by the government. At Pattikonda, where Munro actually died, it was proposed to raise a fund to build a garden in his memory.[13]

Henry S. Graeme, who assumed the office of Acting Governor as the senior member of the Madras Council, rejected Robertson's proposal for a charitable memorial to Munro in Gooty. He proposed instead that the Madras government should, from its own funds, construct the choultry in Gooty and the garden in Pattikonda. This was to guard against 'the evil, direct or remote, which . . . too eager enthusiasm might produce'. He suggested that those who had provided money for the building of choultry and garden (which Graeme implied would become a shrine to Munro and be used in the manner of Hindu shrines) should build a college instead. This could be called 'Munro College', and could be located near the choultry. The previously subscribed

[11] Ibid., p. 207.

[12] Ibid., p. 210, the group of England included three former army friends, and Ravenshaw and Alexander Read.

[13] Ibid., pp. 212–13.

funds would provide for the salaries of six teachers ('professors'.) who would instruct the youth of the Ceded Districts in conformity with Munro's own ideas about education, offering tuition in languages, primarily English, Sanskrit, Marathi, Persian, Urdu, Telugu, and Kannada.[14]

Graeme's proposal, for its part, was opposed by a fellow member of the Madras Council. Lieutenant General George T. Walker, commander of the southern army at Madras, dissented on the basis of economy and injured military sensibility. An outlay of funds for Graeme's project at a time when the government demanded retrenchment was unwarranted. It was, moreover, an affront that other worthies were offered no such obsequies, not even 'old and faithful servants [such as] the late General Sir Alexander Campbell' whom Walker had replaced in Madras.[15] Graeme's proposals for a government-built choultry in Gooty and garden in Pattikonda were also opposed by the other councillor, J. H. D. Ogilvie, leaving him only the recourse of an appeal to the Court of Directors for support for his scheme. The directors, in a resolution passed on 28 November 1827, extolled Munro's great career and peevishly implied that he had been left to die in Madras by a ministry that crassly delayed replacing him long after he had sought relief from his arduous responsibilities. Still, the directors thought that to establish a college in Munro's honour was unnecessary since the Board of Public Instruction was already competent to establish colleges where these were needed.[16]

The consternation of Henry Graeme and Munro's other friends in Madras at such rebuffs was great, and possibly their surprise too. Surely it could not have been expected that the great man's memory, his acknowledged contributions to the Raj at Madras, his marvellous system of revenue and judicature that was being followed in Bombay and elsewhere in the Empire—all of this could be object of squabbling especially as he had suffered a martyr's death. When even a decorous regard for Munro's services to the Presidency and to the Empire was being denied by Madras officials and London authorities, what confidence could be placed in the promises of Munro's replacement at Madras—Stephen Rumbold Lushington? The latter arrived in Madras and took over duties from Graeme later in the year that Munro died, and immediately announced his intention to make the system of his renowned predecessor the model for his own administration. He could scarcely have done other when so many of the civilian and military luminaries of the Presidency subscribed to the sentiments uttered by Graeme in a memorial minute tabled while he was Acting Governor of Madras.

Graeme had invoked the name of Cornwallis at the outset of this minute, saying that Munro had provided valuable advice and services on civilian and on military matters during the Governor-General's campaigns against Tipu Sultan from 1790 to 1792. In recognition of these, Cornwallis had vested strong,

[14] Ibid., p. 215.
[15] Ibid.
[16] Ibid., p. 218.

independent powers in the hands of Alexander Read and his juniors, including Munro, and they had proven a bulwark against Tipu Sultan's Mysore. Graeme recalled that when his own civil career began he had received only the most kind and considerate treatment from Munro while serving under him in the Ceded Districts. Then, he returned to the magic of the Cornwallis name: 'With all of . . . [Munro's] good qualities, he united a vigour of intellect, a soundness of judgement, a firmness of purpose, a public and private integrity and a sacredness of word which have seldom been equalled. In all of these qualities of mind and heart he must be admitted to have greatly resembled the venerable Marquis Cornwallis. . . .'[17] It cannot have been long after his arrival at Madras on 18 October 1827, to replace the paragon described by Graeme, that Lushington discerned some of the cracks in the cup that was toasting his predecessor; these were to be exploited as he began the difficult task of imprinting his own personality upon the Madras government. Glimpses of what his differences would have been with Munro and Munro's programme are afforded by Lushington's career to 1827, to which brief reference has already been made.

He was born into a prosperous, professional family of Kent in 1776 and was educated at Rugby. Entering the Madras civil service in 1790, he served half of his career in various secretariat posts. These included being Persian translator to the MBOR, one of the posts that Munro had unsuccessfully sought for years, and later he was private secretary to Lieutenant General (later Lord) George Harris, who was Commander-in-Chief of Madras forces and for a time the Acting Governor of the Presidency before the arrival of Lord Clive.[18] In a biography of Harris in 1840 he made much of his own close connections with Lord Wellesley during the years of preparation for and the final war against Tipu Sultan.[19] Lushington served the Governor-General as his translator while the other was in Madras supervising the war. He also advised him about which civil officials in Madras could be depended upon to support an aggressive policy against Tipu Sultan. It is somewhat surprising that Munro was not among this elect, considering his own aggressive conception of what was to be done with Tipu Sultan, but that may have been a mark of his remoteness from the power centre of Madras. Some of Munro's military friends were in fact singled out for praise by Lushington, including Alexander Allan, Barry Close and John Malcolm, as well as friends among civil officials such as Thomas Cockburn and, after an early dissent, Josiah Webbe.[20]

In 1799 Lushington was appointed the collector of Ramnad and served

[17] MC, F/151/196, ff. 51–3; Minute by Henry S. Graeme, Acting Governor, 13 July 1827.

[18] *D. N. B.*, v. 34.

[19] S. R. Lushington, *The Life and Services of General Lord Harris, G. C. B., during his Campaigns in America, the West Indies and India* (London: J. W. Parker), pp. 512–13.

[20] Lushington, *Lord Harris*, appendix I, Governor-General Lord Wellesley to Lord Clive, 29 July 1798, naming these exceptions to the inferior quality of Madras officials as compared with those of Bengal.

for two years also as collector of Tinnevelly. Then, in 1803, he began his last service in Madras as a judge in the Sadr Adalat in Madras city, retiring from the Company in 1807. On his return to England he immediately gained a seat in Parliament, first representing Rye, from 1807 to 1812, and later Canterbury, from 1812 until he took up the governorship in Madras.

It has been noticed that Lushington sought this office in 1824 when Munro applied for relief and replacement, and he gained the prize less by his merits as a prospectively able governor of Madras (which hardly ever entered into the choice of governors in India) than by the demands he could make upon the Liverpool government for his services to the Tories and his acceptability to the directors (including John Ravenshaw) because of his previous Indian service.[21] By the time Lushington left India in 1807—the same year that Munro returned to England—he had established a reputation as a supporter of Wellesley's policy of bringing Madras under the Bengal regulations of 1793. This advocacy was presented and preserved in *The Fifth Report*, the same text that legitimated Munro's statesmanship within the Indian imperial order. In the Madras appendices of *The Fifth Report* is Lushington's account of the poligars of Ramnad, Shivaganga and Tinnevelly.[22] He reported these chiefs to be promising candidates for the permanent zamindari status that Wellesley sought to extend over Madras. Lushington's recommendations about these poligars were accepted approvingly by a commission established by the then governor, Lord Bentinck, to investigate how to establish the system of permanent zamindaris in Madras.[23] Ironically, Lushington's sympathetic report on the southern poligars in *The Fifth Report* followed the much longer report of Munro on the poligars of the Ceded Districts in which they were treated as not only inappropriate prospective landlords, but a profound danger to the Company's control over its Deccan territories.[24] Like much else in James Cumming's carefully composed Madras appendices of *The Fifth Report*, Munro's words produced the most powerful and lasting impression.

Lushington's views on the Company's judiciary differed from Munro's, but this difference was not as evident as that on the poligars because he had left the service when the judicial system was being discussed in India and in London. However, his brother, Charles May Lushington, while collector of Trichinopoly in 1817, was an outspoken critic of Munro's judicial regulations of 1816 and won Munro's admiration for his ultimate acceptance of judicial reform, even

[21] MC, F/151/197, Ravenshaw to Lady Munro, 8 October 1828, expressing his disappointment with 'my friend Lushington'; Lushington noted Ravenshaw's support in letters to George A. Robinson, an influential director and chairman in 1826, IOL, European Manuscripts, *George A. Robinson Papers*, F/142/26, letter of 1 April 1824.

[22] Report of S. R. Lushington, 'Collector of the Southern Poligar Peshcush', 30 September 1802, pp. 393–409.

[23] *The Fifth Report*, v. 3, pp. 409–22, report from the Special Commissioners to the Governor in Council, 5 April 1803.

[24] *The Fifth Report*, v. 3, pp. 350–82.

though he was opposed to them.[25] Charles Lushington became an adviser of his brother during the latter's governorship.

Given the reservations or differences with some of Munro's fundamental political, revenue and judicial principles, it is not surprising that some of Lushington's actions as governor of Madras would have seemed hostile to those who bore the Munro torch after his death.

Lushington, in fact, lost no time in attacking the Munro legacy. He accomplished this principally by removing from their high offices some of Munro's closest allies. His attack is traced in a pamphlet published in 1832, possibly the work of John Sullivan, the younger, lately returned from Coimbatore and now a major witness before the Select Committee of the House of Commons taking evidence on the 1833 Charter Act. This attack on Lushington, coming when it did, must also be seen in the light of that comprehensive review of Company policies of 1831–2, to be considered below.[26]

The 1832 pamphlet traced a set of measures undertaken by Lushington against the policies, and it was implied against the memory of Munro. He began this with a refusal to ratify Munro's last legislative proposal, the provision for criminal trials by Indian juries in Madras. This regulation was placed before Munro's council in a minute dated 3 July 1827, three days before he died. It was entitled, 'Trial of Criminal cases by Jury or Panchayat'.[27] In it Munro assembled in a single, powerful discursus, his arguments for native juries, some of which were first put years before in the Ceded Districts. Among these were the impropriety of criminal causes being examined by judges alone, and these by foreigners; the justice if not the prudence of involving Indians in some degree at all levels of administration, including those of the law; the need to reform the existing complicated and costly trial system; he added the recently proven ability of Indians to participate in the judicature, as demonstrated by the success of the 1816 regulations.

Munro's council adopted his policy for jury trials on the same day that it was presented, but Lushington set it aside shortly after assuming his place in Madras. He declared that the measure was being rushed into law without due consideration of its many provisions that Lushington said were 'replete with mischief'.[28] To this rejection Lushington added a harsh personal judgement of Munro. He charged that the trial by jury measure was 'one of the mistakes of the wise in life's last days', and implied further, to some Munro men like Graeme, that Munro in the last year or so had become 'a passive weak instrument in the hands of . . . zealots'.[29]

[25] MC, F/151/135, Munro to the Chief Secretary, 26 May 1817, ff. 219–26.

[26] *The Government of Madras under the Right Honourable Stephen Rumbold*, ibid., *Lushington* (London: H. Lindsell, 1831), p. 107. Actually published in 1832, since there are references to events of that year on p. 107.

[27] Arbuthnot, *Munro Selections*, pp. 322–6.

[28] *The Government of Madras under . . . Lushington*, p. 6.

[29] IOL, *Madras Secret Proceedings*, 1828, P/SEC/MAD/109, Lushington's minute responding to Graeme's of 22 April 1828, pp. 293–7.

Lushington's rejection of the trial by jury regulation was followed by a minute of 27 January 1828 charging Henry Graeme with irregularities while he was Acting Governor and suspending him from the Council. This evoked an infuriated response from Graeme, on his own behalf and on that of the martyred Munro's 'humane and liberal principles toward the natives of India' in his minute of 31 December 1824.[30] The first six months of 1828 saw violent verbal exchanges and minuted fustians between Graeme and Lushington in which the latter was supported by minutes from Graeme's former colleagues on the Madras Council, General George T. Walker, and the senior judge, J. H. D. Ogilvie.[31] The works of 'this master-workman', as Malcolm had called Munro in 1818, appeared somewhat fragile ten years later.[32]

This was only the beginning. Less than a month after rejecting the trial by jury regulation and humiliating Graeme, Lushington dismissed another of Munro's key allies in the Madras establishment, David Hill, the Chief Secretary. Hill was one of the most distinguished and capable public servants in Madras who followed Josiah Webbe into the chief secretaryship during the nineteenth century. His early career as an assistant collector in Tinnevelly and Malabar was followed by twenty years in the central secretariat of Madras, where he rose to be its head in 1824. Hill had earned the highest public praise from Munro during the final years of his governorship for his management of the administration during the years that Munro was occupied with the Burma war, and when Madras was making massive contributions of soldiers and material to the war.[33] Thus, when in February 1828 Lushington dismissed Hill from his high office and assigned him to a provincial judgeship in Masulipatam, 300 miles from Madras, there was deep shock among the Munro claque. Hill was accused by Lushington of being part of a cabal of officials, along with Graeme and others, to deceive him, though the specific charges were withheld from Hill for a considerable time after his dismissal. Accordingly, Hill dispatched a memorial to the Court of Directors against his demotion in rank and pay without the adjudication process open to civil servants. Lushington denounced this memorial to London when it was presented to him by Hill for transmission to London, claiming that it was an usurpation of government authority.

The directors did not respond to Hill's memorial for a year, during which time other senior colleagues of Munro were also dismissed from their posts. One was T. H. Baber, during whose thirty-two years of service in Malabar there were frequent, friendly exchanges of letters with Munro and the latter's praises for Baber's work. He was dismissed by Lushington for having mismanaged a riot in Mangalore in August 1827, and though a hearing of the case

30 *The Government of Madras under . . . Lushington*, pp. 9–10.

31 *Madras Secret Proceedings, 1828*, P/SEC/MAD/109, pp. 280–306 and 584ff.

32 Gleig, v. 1, p. 503

33 Munro's minute recording the services of Hill and Richard Clive, military secretary, 14 November 1826, IOL. *Madras Public Proceedings* P/245/79.

acquitted Baber of any blame and even applauded his bravery and decisiveness, Baber remained under suspension.[34]

The 4 February 1828 letter from the directors to Lushington on the Hill dismissal was as critical of the Governor as their deliberations had been lengthy. Their condemnation of Lushington was shaped partly by the fact that Hill had gone to London to press his case, which may also have accounted for the delay in responding to Madras. The directors referred in their letter to interviews with Hill and of receiving relevant documents from him that had been withheld from London by the Madras government. They concluded that the three months during which Hill was suspended from his office before being appointed to another, judicial, post was punishment enough for any slight procedural irregularities of which he might have been guilty, but, they continued, Hill 'stands as high in our opinion' as ever he did and that he should be restored to his post as chief secretary. Hill was re-employed in that post on his return to India in August 1829.[35]

Apart from an intention to use the trial by jury act to clear out the strongest Munro men from the centre of Madras political authority so as to place his own imprint on Madras policies, Lushington knew that there remained considerable dissent in London against Munro's judicial changes. Many directors who supported the judicial reforms urged by Munro were less moved by principle than by the potential economies, and as a result of pressure that had been exerted from the Board of Control. Others at India House had been converted neither to Munro's principles on Indian judicature nor to their promised economies. Opponents such as Lushington and Ogilvie could reasonably depend on some support from unenchanted directors, and they might have salved their wounds about the restoration of Hill as chief of the Madras secretariat with the proof of the directors' unwillingness to restore Graeme to the Council (on the grounds that he had already served the normal five years). The humiliation of having to return to a remote judicial post, as Hill had been forced to do, was spared to Graeme by the Governor-General, Lord Bentinck, who appointed him as resident to Nagpur.[36]

Others who had been close to Munro and harassed by Lushington included Colonel John Carfrae, Munro's military secretary who was with him at his death; Major-General Sir Robert Scot, who was dimissed from his post as political agent in the court of Arcot and replaced by Lushington's son, an appointment that was refused by the directors; and Colonel William Morison, whom Munro had appointed to direct supply operations of the Burma war.[37] All were charged with financial irregularities of various sorts, all were cleared by military hearings, and some were later offered new positions by Bentinck.

[34] *The Government of Madras under . . . Lushington*, p. 35.
[35] IOL, *Madras Despatches*, E/4/936, 4 February 1828, pp. 638–62.
[36] *The Government of Madras under . . . Lushington*, p. 47.
[37] Ibid., pp. 51–6.

Nor was ryotwar spared by Lushington. During his earlier career in the southern districts of Madras he had supported his patron Wellesley's policy of introducing the permanent zamindari settlement throughout the Presidency. As governor in the late 1820s he could not attack the restored ryotwar as vigorously as he attacked the reformed judiciary, but he could and did remove senior and committed ryotwar advocates from positions of authority. Graeme was head of the Board of Revenue when he was dismissed. Alexander Duncan Campbell had served on the MBOR as an appointee of Munro until 1827 when he was appointed by Munro to the strategically important district of Tanjore, a place that had long challenged the claims of universality made by ryotwar advocates.

Lushington dismissed Campbell in 1828, thereby denying one of the most troublesome districts for Munro's revenue scheme of an enthusiastic master and also denying the ryotwar establishment at Madras of one of its most able spokesmen. Campbell had proved his ability to justify ryotwar in a broadly comparative way, and he was in a few years to do this again before the Select Committee on Indian affairs of the House of Commons. Campbell is interesting in another way which connected him with Munro. He had been dismissed by Munro from his collectorate post in Bellary with considerable public criticism for failing to pursue correct practices for the restoration of ryotwar in the core of Munro's old Ceded Districts. Like other revenue officials out of employment, Campbell found a judicial post. In two years, however, he was reconciled with Munro and was appointed by him to the MBOR, and then later to Tanjore. In Munro's final year of life, he had selected Campbell as his companion on his tour of the southern Presidency, and, afterwards, wrote generously of Campbell's abilities.

Men like Graeme and Campbell were replaced on the MBOR by Charles Lushington, the governor's brother. Through him criticisms were launched against older ryotwar collectors such as Montague D. Cockburn of Salem district and John Sullivan of Coimbatore. The former was dismissed from his Salem post, to which he had been appointed by Munro in 1820 on charges of revenue irregularities which were not specified until three months after his dismissal; he was later appointed to a judgeship in Malabar.

The attack against Sullivan was launched after he had resigned his Coimbatore collectorship and had retired from the Company in 1830. None had stood higher with Munro than Sullivan. As a collaborator in the long prosecution of Kasi Setti, Sullivan gained much admiration from Munro and prestige in Madras. The publication of the compendium of revenue and judicial papers by the Court of Directors in 1820—to be discussed more fully below—included a set of papers jointly written by Munro and Sullivan on the Coimbatore abuses of Kasi Setti, and this won him some renown in London as well.[38]

Lushington levelled two accusations against the now absent Sullivan. First, charges were brought against Sullivan's long-time head of Indian officials in

[38] *SEIHR*, v. 1, pp. 710–91.

Coimbatore, the sheristadar Ramia. The charge was peculation conducted over many years amounting to Rs 20,000. This was no large amount by standards of Madras scandals, and no whisper of criticism against the sheristadar was made until after Sullivan's departure in 1830. When he learned of the action against his old subordinate Sullivan observed, reasonably, that as in the notorious case of William Garrow, his predecessor in Coimbatore and Garrow's treasurer, Kasi Setti, the charges against Ramia was simultaneously a charge against Sullivan, one that he could hardly meet in England. The charges against Ramia were brought by Sullivan's successor there, E. B. Thomas. He was probably motivated by the same desire that moved Lushington in Madras, i.e. to begin a new and important post with subordinates whom he could trust, not those left from a former regime whose closeted skeletons could haunt and ruin a successor.[39] Thomas's action was obviously seen by Lushington to fit his own purposes of taking control of a system and the staff of his predecessor.

The second attack upon Sullivan was launched in respect of the latter's properties in the Nilgiris, on the mountainous northern edge of Coimbatore and under its administration then. Sullivan had done much to improve the high plateau at Ootacmund through his construction of buildings and roads on lands taken from the indigenous pastoral people of these hills—Todas—with almost no compensation. Obliquely, the attack on Sullivan was also an assault upon the reputation of Munro, for it was with his support that the Nilgiris were chosen as a sanitorium for returning British troops from Burma. Munro's economizing solution to the provision for this facility was to lease or purchase hosues that had been privately constructed by Europeans, and Sullivan, as a major owner, was a financial beneficiary. Lushington appeared to be even more enthusiastic about the Nilgiris than Munro and directed that land be acquired to build a sanatorium and cantonment. He also suspended payments by the government to Sullivan for two houses purchased from him, charging that Sullivan had fraudulently mis-stated the condition of one of the houses and had acted improperly by making his retirement from Coimbatore conditional upon the following two things: the sale of his Nilgiris properties and the appointment of a successor of his choice to Coimbatore. These were serious charges, of course, but in themselves not without precedent for senior officials with long service in a district. Now in England, Sullivan petitioned the directors in 1831 for full payment for his houses, and he won his pleading. The directors faulted Sullivan for attempting to force a successor into his place (and thus to avert the scandal of a Ramia) and for inadequately indemnifying the Todas for their land, but they found more harshly against Lushington and the Madras government for their dealings on the Sullivan properties.[40]

[39] Thomas served in Coimbatore from January 1830 to November 1832; H. A. Nicholson, *Madras District Manuals: Coimbatore*, v. 2 (Madras: Government Press, 1898), p. 446.

[40] IOL, *Madras Despatches*, E/4/940, paper no. 5, 1831, 26 October 1831, 'Revenue Department', pp. 1135–63.

Whether Lushington's actions against these officials weakened the momentum of Munro's programme, and whether that was the intention of his actions, is not clear. An active and experienced politician (partly in India, it must be remembered), Lushington had a stake in seizing effective control of the politics in Madras. To become a cypher under the control of a cabal of officials—as he suggested Munro had become—was a condition into which he himself could have fallen, and this he was determined to avoid. And, surely, given the enormous weight of Munro's principles and precedents in Madras and his popularity with so many Madras officials and non-officials, Lushington had reason to fear becoming a cypher. Governors of Madras had before been undone by their subordinates. In the recent past this would have included Bentinck, now the Governor-General, who was made responsible for the Vellore mutiny brought on by his Commander-in-Chief's ill-conceived orders on sepoys' uniforms and privileges and by the commander's forbearance towards proselytizing junior officers. The vulnerability of reputations of Madras civil officials to the actions of subordinates—European or Indian—was widely recognized; most Company collectors feared this and therefore sought to clear their district offices of senior Indian officers whom they inherited and whom they replaced with Indians they could trust and manage, as Thomas did in Coimbatore after succeeding Sullivan there.

Apart from public humiliation, Lushington would rightly have worried about losing the splendid financial rewards of an Indian governorship or losing standing in the British politics to which he would return. When he left India in 1832, Lushington, as Munro before him, could have expected to have saved around £5,000 a year from his salary; in addition he could expect to (and did) receive an annual pension from the Company of £1,500 and to resume his place as a Privy Councillor,[41] if not with enhanced reputation, at least one not tarnished—as was Bentinck's by his Madras governorship.

There were other reasons, having to do with policy, for Lushington's opposition to the Munro men. He would have known as well as any in India of the continued resistance in London to Munro's notions about the British imperial order in India. Directors such as John Hudleston, who had vigorously resisted Munro's appointment as judicial commissioner, were active until 1826 and a letter of Huddleston to Munro in 1821 still expressed regret over 'our abandonment of the system and opinions of *Lord Cornwallis*'.[42]

CONSTRUCTING MORE COLONIAL TEXTS

An obvious source of Lushington's understanding of such sentiments would have been the four massive volumes of records published by the Court of Directors in 1820 and 1826, entitled *Selection of Papers from the Records at the East-India House Relating to the Revenue, Police, and Civil and Criminal Justice*

[41] *The Government of Madras under . . . Lushington*, p. 107.
[42] MC, F/151/73, 29 November 1821.

under the Company's Governments in India [*SEIHR*].[43] Of its nearly 4000 folio pages, over 1400 related to Madras, and of these over 1100 pages filled the first two volumes published in 1820, while Lushington was still in England. Unlike *The Fifth Report* of 1812 and the several large volumes of evidence published by Parliament in 1832, which were records of parliamentary investigations of the renewal of Company privileges, the *Selection* volumes had no obvious statutory reason for being and were not published by order of Parliament. The brief, unsigned preface of the first of these 1820 volumes stated, matter-of-factly, that the utility of *The Fifth Report* 'Appendices' having proven so great, another selection from the 'voluminous' records at India House was undertaken for 'facilitating research and rendering information more accessible to those in whom knowledge is essential to a beneficial exercise of power and an effective discharge of trust': i.e. for the Court of Directors and the Board of Control. According to the older John Sullivan, the 1820 selections were made by James Cumming at the Board, and the exertions of this compelled Cumming to retire from the Board in 1823.[44]

Selections in the first of the 1820 volumes dealt with the restoration of ryotwar in Madras and the humiliation of the MBOR under John Hodgson. Of the second volume of 1820, most of the 570 pages of Madras judicial selections consisted of papers drawn from Munro's judicial commission—the framing of the introduction of the 1816 regulations and the monitoring of their implementation by Munro up to May 1819. No reasons were given for the virtual exclusion of Bombay from the compilations of 1820, and perhaps none was required because of the recentness of Elphinstone's regime over the greatly expanded territories won in the final Maratha war. The exclusion of Bengal

[43] The four volumes of *SEIHR* were published in London for the Court of Directors; two volumes, respectively, 'Revenue' and 'Judicial' in 1820, and two further ones with the same title in 1826. Of the total of 3594 pages, 1431 pertained to Madras. The contents of the four volumes of *Selections* of 1820 and 1826 were as follows. Volumes I and III consisted of revenue papers and volumes II and IV of judicial and police papers. The first volume is about equally composed to Bengal and Madras selections, with none on Bombay. The second volume of 1820, dealing with judicial and police matters, begins with a long set of answers of Company officials who happened to be in Britain in 1813, to judicial and police queries put by the directors. Thirteen of these officials were from the Bengal service, eight from Madras (including Munro, Thackeray, and Ravenshaw), and two from Bombay. Inclusion of these 200 pages of 'Answers to Queries' was resisted by some directors because they showed the Bengal system in a bad light, but the Board of Control insisted upon their inclusion and prevailed. This fact, plus the actual content of the judicial selections of 1820, indicate the decisive role taken by the Board, and especially by James Cumming and John Sullivan Sr., in the production of the two volumes of that year.

[44] *Report of the Select Committee . . . 16 August 1832, Minutes of Evidence taken before the Select Committee, Revenue*, v. III, appendix 8, 'Observations of the Revenue Systems of India by the Right Honourable John Sullivan', dated 28 April 1832, from Sullivan's home, Richings Lodge, in Buckinghamshire.

judicial records was justified by the fact that many had been published in 1819 by order of the House of Commons in response to a motion from Joseph Hume in March 1816.[45]

The Bengal revenue selections in the first volume of 1820 deserve comment. These formed a discursive complement to the Madras revenue and judicial selections by presenting a Bengal system on the defensive. The issue around which the Bengal selections principally turned was the revenue (and judicial) system to be followed in the Gangetic territories won from the Marathas around Delhi in 1804 (the 'Upper Provinces' and the 'Ceded or Conquered Provinces' of Bengal). Reports of commissions on both tracts in 1808 began this discussion. The commissioners were Bengal officials, including two who were to exert strong influence on revenue policies for the next twenty years—Sir James Edward Colebrook and Henry St George Tucker. Their recommendations for extending the Bengal regulations to the new territories of the Company were rejected by the directors in a series of dispatches from 1811 to 1817. In that correspondence between Calcutta and London, serious attention was given to Munro's revenue methods, and in 1813 Munro's and Ravenshaw's instructions on ryotwar issued to subordinates in Madras were sent to Bengal for their instruction. To this humiliation of Bengal, Lord Hastings, the Governor-General, added another. So much uncertainty about conditions in the new territories existed and so many 'evils' could result from this ignorance that he thought a commission on internal administration, like that of Munro's of 1814–19, should be formed. He ordered his Supreme Council to obtain from the directors their orders to Munro of 4 May 1814, setting the Madras commission. Other records from Munro and from Madras provided guidance for future inquiries into the revenue and judicial administration of the new Gangetic territories. Documents from the directors of 1819 were cited to confirm Hastings' cautions about the extension of the Bengal regulations for a permanent zamindari settlement in the new territories and providing instead for a scheme of periodic settlements.[46]

Munro's papers and his letters to Sullivan and Cumming from 1808 to 1819 show that he participated in the preparation of the records and instructions that were sent to Bengal in connection with the debate over the revenue system to be followed in the new northern territories. Hence, he played a role in the double embarrassment of the 'Bengalees' at the hands of the Governor-General in Calcutta and the directors in London.

The 1820 volumes of the *Selections* record the triumph of Munro's ryotwar

[45] Great Britain, *Parliamentary Papers, Accounts and Papers*, 1819. part XIII, p. 348, paper no. 533, 'East India Affairs; Papers Relating to the Police, and Civil and Criminal Justice under the Respective Governments of Bengal, Fort St. George and Bombay, from 1810 to the Present Time; printed by order of the House of Commons, 1 July 1819'. This consisted of forty judicial selections from Bengal, dated from November 1811 to February 1819, pp. 286; twelve Madras selections from October 1813 to May 1819, 30pp.; and five Bombay selections from April 1815 to July 1818, 31pp.

[46] *SEIHR*, v. 1, pp. 314–16 and 351–66.

over his opponents in Madras. If *The Fifth Report* was Cumming's instrument for the victory of ryotwar among most directors, then the 1820 volume of revenue selections, also Cumming's work, traces how the directors' will was worked against the entrenched opponents of ryotwar in Madras and Bengal.

Almost without a hitch, this volume picks up the history from where it was left in 1812 by discussing the 1808 imposition of the decennial village-lease system in all parts of Madras then under ryotwar. This is followed by the rebuke delivered upon Hodgson's MBOR by the directors on 18 December 1811, and their more firm and humiliating instructions of a year later that ryotwar was to be introduced into all of the Presidency not under a permanent zamindari settlement. Much of this 500-page record of commands from London and resistance from Madras draws upon documents generated by Munro's commission, which, though nominally concerned with judicial questions, passed into revenue matters early, with the assent of the London authorities. Hence, by 1820, with Munro now governor, it might have been thought that the victory of his system was altogether secure. However, for many readers the 1820 record of Munro's triumphs and the humiliation of his Madras opponents must have been galling, and, worse, the later (1826) volume of revenue documents from India House continued the Munro litany, its gloria being the great 31 December 1824 minute which concluded the Madras section of revenue selections.

The 1826 selection of Madras revenue papers was more brief, and, apart from Munro's 1824 minute on the state of the country and the condition of the people, reported some of the adjustments made in ryotwar procedures to improve its operations. One of these adjustments pertained to 'putkut', which had vexed Thackeray as assistant collector in the Ceded Districts twenty years earlier. In September 1821 the matter was still vexing, and Ravenshaw, a director and an authoritative spokesman on ryotwar, asked Munro for clarification of the term and its use in revenue practice. Munro answered that 'putkut' (*pattukattu* in Telugu, *pattukadu* in Tamil) was the revenue liability of a cultivator based on the totality of the fields—his 'farm'—held under ryotwar tenure. It was, as he had long ago explained to Thackeray, an ordinary, practical way in ryotwar to assess individual revenue obligations. However, the individual 'farm' should not be regarded as a proper or permanent unit of assessment, for that was the separate surveyed field. Munro told Ravenshaw that Thackerary had never got that right, and had made misleading and incorrect statements about 'putkut'. He also advised Ravenshaw to consult a report by Henry Graeme on the whole matter, and Graeme's report of 31 March 1818 was duly added to the 1826 revenue *Selections*. Another matter dealt with in the 1826 revenue volume was the peripatetic ways of cultivators in the ryotwar areas of Madras. Munro's critics among the directors considered this a bad feature of his system. In his answer to these critics in London he defended the migration of peasants as a part of agricultural practice, and his minute on migration was included in the 1826 selections.[47]

[47] MC, F/151/92, 30 September 1821 and *SEIHR*, v. 3, pp. 523–5 and 597.

The largest massing of argumentative documentation about Madras in the four volumes of the *Selections* pertained to Munro's judicial reforms, to which over 750 pages were devoted in 1820. Throughout his governorship, Munro received letters from London friends reporting a continuing campaign against his 1816 judicial reforms in London. His enemies in the directorate remained formidable. Until 1823, when he died, Charles Grant remained opposed to the Madras reforms, and John Hudleston, a major and unrepentant opponent of Munro's changes in 1814, also continued to criticize them until he left the Court of Directors in 1826. Letters from John Sullivan, James Cumming, and John Ravenshaw during Munro's governorship frequently referred to a band of retired, senior Company officials who busily lobbied Grant, Hudleston and others to reverse the policies on the Madras judicature. They included John Hodgson, Robert Fullerton, and Edward Greenway, Madras opponents during the judicial commission period, and George Dowdeswell, Sir James Edward Colebrook, and William H. Trant from the Bengal civil service; all were now retired in England and actively involved in India House politics. Perhaps, like Hodgson, they were hoping to win a place on the directorate, as Ravenshaw suggested.

James Cumming had provided Munro with the most detailed information on these developments. A letter of his of May 1823, nearly thirty folio pages long, provided a small history of the decision-making structure at India House in relationship to the Board of Control. This was also an explanation to Munro of why Cumming decided to retire from the Board. Written in a crab-like hand, Cumming's letter suggested an ageing and ill man, which he was, but also one on such terms of intimacy with Munro that he did not need to write in that careful hand he used as a subordinate correspondent of a decade before.

The general conditions in the Direction and at the Board worried Cumming as they did the older Sullivan. Allies like Alexander Allan and Samuel Davis were now dead,[48] and George Canning, who had proved a strong supporter of Munro and his programme, had resigned the presidency of the Board. Canning was succeeded, briefly, by Charles Bathurst, and then with a long tenure by Charles W. Wynn, who was less favourably disposed to the Madras system. Sullivan had also resigned from the Board, but had arranged that Indian correspondence on revenue and the judiciary should be available to him. He told Munro that in that way he 'could co-operate with our friend Cumming in keeping things right'.[49] One of the ways in which Cumming was employed to this end was in countering the attack that was being launched by supporters of the Bengal system on the directors during Munro's governorship.

Cumming reported that Bathurst, Canning's successor in January 1821, and William M'Culloch, the influential head of the Company's revenue and judicial department from 1809, both agreed about 'the folly of . . . [the Cornwallis]

[48] MC, F/151/72, John Sullivan informed Munro to this effect, 18 February 1821.

[49] MC, F/151/72, John Sullivan to Munro 7 May 1821.

Regulations of 1793'.[50] However, Bathurst was replaced by Wynn, and M'Culloch had been given more general duties at India House. As a result, the judicial records and judicial drafts for the directors fell to Nathaniel Halhed, a man whom Cumming declared was so unfit that the directors had agreed that he, Cumming, should draft judicial dispatches in Halhed's place.[51] This unusual crossing of the jurisdictions between the Company and the Board—Cumming's employer—burdened the overworked Cumming even further, though it increased his influence. Edward Strachey's appointment to succeed Halhed not only gradually diminished Cumming's role in judicial policies, but Strachey, a retired Bengal judge, was open to the importunities of Hodgson and his friends, 'sworn advocates of the Cornwallis system', as Cumming reported.[52] The strain of years of overwork led to a breakdown of Cumming's health early in 1821 and a long recuperation in Europe. When he returned to the Board, he told Munro, he found that Edward Strachey and Charles Wynn had formed a close friendship, dining at each other's houses, and that Hodgson formed a part of their fellowship. Cumming also related how a delegation of opponents of Munro's judicial reforms had called upon him at the Board's Whitehall office, seeking support for their programme of overturning the 1816 reforms in Madras. This was spurned, and Cumming reported that he had made some progress in winning Wynn to a more neutral position on the question. In the end, however, Cumming's health drove him from the Board in 1823, thus further weakening the resistance to the Bengal counterattack against Munro's judicial policies.

Before he retired, Cumming performed one last service for the cause that he had made the centre of his administrative career at the Board of Control: he assembled a reply to the attack upon the reformed Madras judiciary by Robert Fullerton in 1820. These documents comprised the core of India House' printed Madras judicial selections of 1826.

Fullerton's minute of 7 June 1820 resembled that of John Hodgson's when he resigned from the Madras Council and retired from the Company in the same year. Fullerton's was a final argument against the Munro system in its judicial aspect, as Hodgson's had been against its revenue provisions, and it came, like Hodgson's, at the end of a long service of thirty years in Madras courts.[53] Fullerton recalled that he had previously minuted the Madras Council (in March 1816) with objections to the 1816 regulations. There, he had criticized the Court of Directors' judicial letter of 29 April 1816 authorizing Munro's

[50] MC, F/151/72, Cumming to Munro 9 May 1823, f. 64.

[51] On M'Culloch and Halhed, see Philips, pp. 17–18.

[52] MC, F/151/72, ff. 72–3. Hodgson's 'friends' included Fullerton and Greenway from Madras, and George Dowdeswell, James Edward Colebrook and William H. Trant from Bengal. The last three, along with Greenway, were resigned from their service with the Company.

[53] *SEIHR*, v. 4, pp. 46–64.

reforms.[54] He now expanded these earlier criticisms and began with the disarming observation that, contrary to his own fears of 1816, the provisions for civil justice of 1816 had proved successful and were appreciated by experienced Madras judicial officials as well as by the general public. But of the police and criminal provisions of 1816 he was more certain than ever that they would produce 'ruinous effects', and this principally 'from the union of revenue and magisterial powers in one person', the collector. He also rejected the claims of success being made for panchayats and dreaded the consequences of extending their use in criminal cases. He concluded his minute with a criticism of the directors themselves. London had failed to consult adequately with Madras officials before framing the 1816 regulations and defining the scope of the judicial commission headed by Munro: 'nothing had been left to the [Madras] Government but obedience'.[55]

Fullerton's minute was tabled three days before Munro arrived in Madras to assume the governorship, and Munro decided against responding to it; indeed, he told Ravenshaw, he did not even read it because of his certainty that it would merely reopen issues that were now settled.[56] When he learned from Ravenshaw and from John Sullivan that Fullerton's attack was being taken up by Charles Grant and John Hudleston as focus for their continuing opposition, he reacted. Two minutes were prepared against Fullerton's, one by George Stratton, now a member of his council, and the other by Munro himself.[57] These were approved by his council in March and April 1821, and between the two most of Fullerton's criticisms were disposed of along lines that Munro previously outlined in a letter to Ravenshaw for the latter's use in London. To some extent the responses prepared by Munro and Stratton recognized deficiencies in the 1816 regulations and outlined remedies which were to be proposed to the directors; otherwise, both minutes, and another by Stratton in June 1821, defended the 1816 conception and programme of judicial reforms.

James Cumming's letter of May 1823, referring to the continued opposition of the Madras reforms within India House, identified Edward Strachey as their centre. This can have been no surprise to Munro or to Cumming, for Strachey was an early opponent of Munro's reform programme and had expressed his dissent when the directors sought the views of prominent judicial officials who

[54] Fullerton had busied himself long before that, in 1815, with a long criticism of Munro's judicial ideas and his judicial commission; see *Home Miscellaneous Series*, v. 530, 'Cumming Papers', pp. 361–83, entitled 'On the Changes in Internal Administration at Madras Expected to Originate with the *Commission* Entrusted to Colonel Munro and Mr Stratton: Remarks by a Madras Covenanted Civil Servant, dated Madras, 1 March 1815'. In this Fullerton identified himself as president of the Police Committee of 1814 which Munro had criticized.

[55] *SEIHR*, v. 4, p. 64.

[56] MC, F/151/92, Munro to Ravenshaw, 30 September 1821, and Munro to Sullivan, 24 June 1821.

[57] *SEIHR*, v. 4, Stratton's minute of 12 March 1821, pp. 65–7; Munro's of 27 April 1821, pp. 70–6.

were in England before Munro's commission was formed in 1814.[58] But Munro was reassured that George Canning was not impressed with Fullerton's argument, nor by those who had found it a flag of convenience under which to mobilize to oppose Munro's reformed judicature.[59]

In the light of the fact that the selections of 1820 and 1826 present an overall justification of the Munro system—thanks to his London friends—the mystery remains why these four volumes were published by the directors. Originally, the publication project seems to have sprung from a harassing question and motion put in the House of Commons on 16 March 1819 by Joseph Hume.

Hume was a 'Radical Whig' who was regarded as an eccentric by his fellow proprietors of the Company because of his fastidious examination of and queries on the Company's finances. This made him a feared, yet clownish, figure at India House, many of whose denizens suspected that his enmity to the directors stemmed in part from having failed to be elected as one in 1813.[60] Apart from being a scourge of the directors for years, Hume was also a keen baiter of Tory ministers in Indian policy, and it was in this role that he rose in the Commons to demand the correspondence on the Indian judiciary. His reading of the Company regulations of 1814 and his concern for the welfare of the eighty or so million under Company authority led to his discovery that justice was impossible for Indians to obtain because of the high fees-costs of judicial actions and because of the backlog of cases everywhere. To his professed horror, Hume also discovered that what he and others in Parliament and among Proprietors of the Company believed was a system established by Cornwallis for all of British India was not that at all. In Bengal something like the 1793 regulations might be in force, but elsewhere 'they were altered and disfigured so that . . . there was neither uniformity of law, nor uniformity in operation . . .'[61] He insisted that Parliament should examine the whole of the judicial record of the Company's India and legislate an improvement.

Canning responded to Hume for the Tory Liverpool government as 'minister of India'. He said that there was no objection to providing information to members, but, he added chidingly, so voluminous was the documentation on the matter that the day when they could have been read and debated in the House was very far off. He therefore proposed that a selection should be made of the judicial records at India House. Hume moved this and in the debate on the motion he was supported by other Whig critics of the Company, especially of its recent costly wars and its flawed judiciary. It was ordered that important judicial dispatches of the directors to their governments in India from 1810 to

[58] Strachey's answers to these 'queries' were among the longest of any, 11 pages; they reveal a commitment to Benthamite principles as well as long judicial experience reflexively considered: *SEIHR*, v. 2, pp. 73–84.

[59] MC, F/151/72, Cumming to Munro, 9 May 1823.

[60] Philips, pp. 3 and 7. Hume was a former Company servant according to Embree, p. 282.

[61] *The Times*, Wednesday, 17 March 1819, p. 2.

the present be printed along with statements on judicial costs in Bengal and elsewhere in India.

How this possibly harassing motion in the Commons and the somewhat cynical response by Canning eventuated in the four large volumes of 1820 and 1826 is only partially illuminated by documents of the time. And why and when it was that the initial demand for judicial records was expanded to include revenue selections, or why and when the two volumes of 1820 were expanded by another two volumes in 1826—these remain unclear. Certainly afterwards, by 1832, the four volumes were not only considered as a single project but were understood to have been expressly produced by the directors for the use of the Proprietors.[62] Yet when Ravenshaw informed Munro that the two volumes of 1820 were now printed—'two huge volumes of Revenue and Judicial Selections'[63]—he did not refer to other volumes to be printed later, nor did he offer any enlightenment as to when the judicial records demanded by Hume the year before had been augmented by revenue records as well. Nor is there clarification from the correspondence between India House and the Board of Control of that time. Letters exchanged around the middle of 1819 mention only judicial records to be sent to Parliament, and on one matter there was disagreement between India House and the Board. This was whether to include the 'answers to queries' from the directors by judicial officials in Britain in 1813 in the selections for Parliament that were due to be printed in July 1819. The directors opposed inclusion of these 'answers' and the Board wanted them.[64] The directors prevailed in this disagreement, for the volume of judicial papers printed by order of Parliament did not include the 'answers'.[65] However, the Board did insist on their inclusion among selections published by the directors in 1820, where the 'answers' opened the judicial selections, occupying 200 printed pages.

In August 1819 the latter work was first mentioned when the Board transmitted a list of papers for inclusion in what appeared to be a new publication project, intended 'for the use of the Court [of Directors] and the Board', and this list included papers on the revenue of Madras and Bengal as well as judicial

[62] Testimony of Thomas Love Peacock, assistant examiner at India House before the Select Committee in 1832: *Minutes of Evidence taken before the Select Committee*, v. III, 'Revenue', 9 February 1832, p. 1, By 1836 Peacock had become Examiner at India House; Philips, p. 339.

[63] MC, F/151/73, Ravenshaw to Munro, 11 October 1820.

[64] Correspondence then between the two bodies make reference to nothing but judicial selections, and in a letter of May 1819, two months before the papers were to be turned over to Parliament for printing, there was a disagreement over whether to include the 'Answers to Queries' from judicial officers: IOL, *Letters to the Board [of Control]* 1817–21, E/2/6, from Thomas Courtenay to the Board, 13 May 1819. The papers which were published by Parliament did not include these 'Answers', however; these were included as the first part of the second volume of *SEIHR* of 1820, occupying 200 pages.

[65] *Parliamentary Papers, 1819, Accounts and Papers*, v. XIII, no. 533.

subjects.[66] It appears that at that time there was a scheme being considered for the publication by Parliament of more selections—revenue and judicial. This is suggested by a letter Munro received from Cumming, dated December 1819 (after the printing of the Bengal judicial and police selections of June 1819), referring to 'papers respecting India that may by printed by Parliament'), copies of some of which Cumming was sending to Munro in Madras.[67]

But sometime in early 1820 it was decided that selections from the burgeoning judicial and revenue records at India House should be published by the directors, and it was obviously Cumming's and John Sullivan's intentions to continue to marshall documents for a subsequent set of volumes, which were finally published by the directors in 1826. The initiative for this could have come only from the Board, and this is attested to by an 1825 letter to the Board's secretary, Thomas Courtenay, from the secretary for Indian correspondence at India House, James Dart. The latter said that he had reported to the directors the Board's view of the 'expediency of printing a further Selection of Papers in continuation of that made on the subjects of the Revenue and Judicial Systems of India', and the directors agreed entirely and would soon send a list of selections to the Board for consideration.[68]

CONTEXTUALIZING THE TEXTS

Cumming and Sullivan sought to assure everyone that the momentum gained on reforms of the internal administration of Madras should not falter and that the Bengal system should not expand into newly acquired territories. These were in Bombay and in the Gangetic plain. The colonial texts of 1820 and 1826 were intended to serve that end, but there was also a political context that required massaging to gain for the Board of Control the ascendant role that both men there, and Munro and Malcolm in India, wanted.

Bombay, from the time that Elphinstone was appointed commissioner, had committed itself to the Madras system as a result of Munro's interventions with Elphinstone during the time of his judicial commission in Madras, while he was in Dharwar supervising the acquisition of the southern Maratha tracts there, and later when he was governor. Moreover, the Munro system had a keen advocate in Bombay in the person on William Chaplin, Munro's protégé from the Ceded Districts. The Ganges tracts taken from the Marathas in 1804 were a different matter, for there the presumption of Calcutta's administrative dominance appeared unquestionable. The ability of Sullivan, who was no longer a Parliamentary commissioner, and Cumming, who was in the end a clerk, to achieve their goal of frustrating powerful Bengal was a complex outcome of many factors. One of them was George Canning.

[66] IOL, *Board of Control, Letter Book*, 1816–20, F/2/5, p. 397, dated 6 August 1819.

[67] MC, F/151/72, Cumming to Munro, 14 December 1819.

[68] IOL, *Letters to the Board [of Control] from the East India Company, 1823–25*, E/2/8, 28 July 1825.

Canning's appointment to head the Board of Control in early 1816, following the death of Lord Buckinghamshire, provided a way for Lord Liverpool to bring his old friend Canning back into government after earlier political differences between Canning and Castlereagh had resulted in the scandal of a duel between the two and Canning's resignation from the government of the Duke of Portland.[69] Though the Indian Board was considered a minor cabinet responsibility, it nevertheless brought Canning's valuable services to Lord Liverpool, as a front-bench spokesman of many issues and as an advisor on all that confronted his weak and vulnerable ministry. Moreover, Canning had served as parliamentary commissioner for India during the time of Henry Dundas, which gave him a slender claim to experience about Indian policy.[70] Finally, Cannning and others were aware that the presidency of the Board placed the talented Canning upon the ladder to high office once again.

The Board of the Parliamentary Commissioners consisted of twelve Members of Parliament of whom four, including Lord Liverpool, were pro-forma members, and the remaining eight, excepting John Sullivan, had almost no knowledge of India and no bases for framing Indian policies. It was widely understood, in fact, that the Board of Control meant its president. However, Canning's abilities, political experience and debating skills made him too valuable to Liverpool to permit any detailed concern with Indian policy. Judicial and revenue questions, even if Canning had felt competent about them, were left to others, but there was one matter for which he assumed full responsibility: the resoration of trust between the directors and the Board which Buckinghamshire had done so much to sour. This was a task for which Canning was well-suited and which he acquitted with grace and with important consequences for the Munro men in London.

When he assumed the Board in 1816, Canning was immediately faced with two matters left unresolved by his predecessor. One was the policy to be followed towards the Pindaris, who menaced much of Central India bordering on British possessions, and the linked matter of relations with the Maratha confederation; the other was the potential scope of Munro's system in the rest of British India. These were Canning's first responsibilities, and both required delicate negotiations with a directorate made resentful and suspicious by Buckinghamshire's imperious treatment.

A revision of Wellesley's policies towards the Marathas was proposed to the directors in March 1814 by the Governor-General (who, until he was honoured with the title of Marquis of Hastings in 1817, was known as Lord Moira). As this came after only five months in India, it was probably originally a proposal from Buckinghamshire. The new Governor-General proposed the total suppression of the menacing bands of unemployed horse soldiers and banditti

[69] Wendy Hinde, *George Canning* (New York: St Martin's Press, 1973), pp. 277–9; Peter Dixon, *Canning, Politician and Statesman* (London: Weidenfeld and Nicolson, 1976), pp. 181–6.

[70] *D. N. B.*, v. 3, p. 873.

known as 'Pindaris', and, even more aggressively, the supersession of the Peshwa's leadership of the Maratha confederation by British leadership. The costs and criticisms of the Nepal war against the Gurkhas from 1814 turned Buckinghamshire's early enthusiasm for the scheme to caution and finally rejection. Nothing daunted, Hastings reapplied for consideration of the plan in December 1815, seeking permission from London to act against both the Pindaris and the Marathas as conditions in India dictated, and saying that the British must ultimately act against both.

It was this resubmitted proposal that Canning found at the Board, and immediately he sought advice from others at the Board and at India House. All save John Sullivan advised against the aggressive proposal from Calcutta as too risky and costly. Sullivan supported Hastings' plan because of the disunity among the Marathas and on the grounds that Hastings' plan was not a change in Wellesley's policies but a continuation of them. He advised against instructing the Governor-General too specificially on actions that he might be required by circumstances to take. Canning adopted some of Sullivan's advice in communicating with Calcutta that London opposed a general war against the Marathas that might result from a vigorous campaign against the Pindaris, but self-defence was expected. This last was Sullivan's contribution, and it was shortly vindicated in the eyes of colleagues at the Board at India House when Pindari raids into the Northern Circars of Madras led Canning to underscore the necessity for defence of Company territories. On the strength of this the great army of 1817 was mobilized by Lord Hastings, in which Munro had sought a command.

Sullivan was even more influential on the second set of issues facing Canning at the outset of his tenure at the Board, those involving the internal administration of India. He boldly persuaded Canning to support the extension of the Madras system to all of British India not then under the permanent regulations of 1793. This directly challenged Calcutta's hegemony in the Gangetic area and the long dominance enjoyed by Bengal supporters committed to an anglicizing and christianizing programme for India. Not surprisingly, therefore, in August 1817 Grant and his followers in the Direction reacted sharply to the Board's engrossing initiative on behalf of the Madras system. They had conceded all that they would to ryotwar and to its judicial accompaniments in their commission to Munro in 1814. Determined to establish better relations with the Directors, Canning retreated before their remonstrances against the extension of ryotwar to the Ceded and Conquered provinces around Delhi, conceding the superior experience of the directors in matters of internal administration.[71]

Nevertheless, the expansion of Munro's system was now on the reform agenda of Sullivan and Cumming, and it was pressed by them for the duration of Canning's tenure at the Board. When Sullivan retired as a paid commissioner of the Board, Lord Binning, a friend of both his and Canning's could be relied on to carry the fight against Bengal, especially with Sullivan continuing to enjoy

[71] Philips, pp. 211–12.

full access to judicial and revenue papers which came to the Board from India House,[72] and with Cumming an active inside man until 1823 when he retired.

Sullivan wrote to Munro in 1821 that the appointment of the sympathetic Charles Bathurst to the Board replacing Canning might be made permanent (about which he was wrong) and that there were growing doubts among the directors about the Bengal system at India House (about which he was correct). It would only need a 'spring', he said, to force changes upon Bengal, and that Cumming was fabricating it.[73] Thus, in addition to Canning as a factor in the Board's growing relative power, there were Sullivan and Cumming.

The 'spring' to work the mechanism against the 'Bengalees' in London and Calcutta consisted of several different parts. In addition to the consistent pressure mounted by Sullivan and Cumming on revenue and judicial policies from the Board, Canning was occasionally brought into play. At a crucial juncture in the long and acrimonious confrontations between London and Calcutta on the revenue administration of the Ceded and Conquered Provinces, Canning finally intervened against the insistent Bengal revenue establishment for a permanent, zamindari settlement there. In 1817 he insisted on compliance from Bengal to the directors' demand for a settlement that permitted further investigations into tenurial patterns, in effect a periodic resettlement system. This was a compromise between the permanent settlement sought by Bengal and the annual settlement (ryotwar) favoured by Cumming and Sullivan at the Board and by an increasing number of directors.[74] By joining the debate as he did, Canning also brought support to Lord Hastings' recommendations and improved his relations with the Governor-General. The latter had resented the fact that Canning sided with the many who cautioned against the aggressive policy advocated against the Marathas and the Pindaris, and which led to war preparations in 1817.[75] To placate Hastings, Canning drew upon a note prepared

[72] MC, F/151/72, noted in Cumming to Munro, 9 May 1823, f. 77, and Sullivan to Munro, 7 May 1821. Lord Binning's connection to Canning is mentioned by Dixon, p. 185.

[73] MC, F/151/72, Sullivan to Munro, 18 February 1821.

[74] See A.D. Campbell's testimony before the Select Committee, *Report of the Select Committee*..., 16 August 1832, v. xi, p. 32.

[75] Mollification of the directors and the maintenance of good relations with Hastings in Calcutta proved extremely difficult for Canning. His relations with Hastings in Calcutta were difficult from the time that he opposed the latter's Maratha policies, and they became more difficult as a result of Hastings' private correspondence with the chairmen of the Directorate, which Canning considered a constitutional breach. Determined to maintain good relations with the directors required his restraint of Hastings, and the growing enmity between the two men became increasingly serious. The Queen Caroline divorce issue created a cabinet crisis when Canning refused to agree to move legislation for a divorce, to which Liverpool capitulated, causing Canning's resignation from the government. This he explained to Munro in late 1821 and early 1822: MC, F/151/72, 22 December 1821 and 12 January 1822. Canning later became interested in the governor-generalship, and for two years there was the tantaliz-

for him on the question of extending ryotwar to the Gangetic territories by the tireless Cumming; this thirty-six page statement had been prepared for the 1820 Selections and consisted of a set of documents from Bengal and Madras that were to be printed on the matter.[76] The partly career, partly personal, differences between Canning and Hastings, along with other matters, diverted Canning from any detailed address of revenue and judicial questions, which were left to his men at the Board, Sullivan and Cumming.

Other factors that enabled Sullivan and Cumming to 'spring' the full attack by the Board on the Bengal system paradoxically involved steps that Canning took to strengthen the Company's administration in London. The haphazard organization of India House administration of Indian affairs was recognized by many directors, but so keen were most to retain policy control from bureaucratic encroachments and keen, too, to protect their patronage over offices in India House, that they resisted changes for very long. Canning urged them to appoint a capable staff to deal with the vastly increased flow of records and correspondence between London and India, and in 1819 such brilliant men as James Mill and Thomas Peacock, and such experienced men as Edward Strachey, were introduced into India House. This was a change that the directors came to appreciate. Canning also flattered the directors by his politeness and easy consultative manner, in contrast to Buckinghamshire's bombast, and, more perhaps, by favouring the appointment of Company servants to the highest Indian offices. Thus, in August 1818 Canning wrote to James Pattison, chairman of the directors and a friend of Ravenshaw (who reported the matter to Munro), that candidates for the appointment to the vacant governorship of Bombay could include Mountstuart Elphinstone, John Malcolm, or Thomas Munro.[77] Elphinstone's greater popularity with, or support among, the directors gave him Bombay, to be followed a year later by the appointment of Munro to Madras. Such considerations won Canning much support among the directors and persuaded many directors to yield to the Board of Control a direction over Indian policy that would have been bitterly contested before by men like Charles Grant.

The death of Charles Grant at the age of seventy-three in 1823 was another factor in changing relations of power between the Board and the directors,

ing prospect that George Canning might join Munro in India. Hastings' suspicions of Canning, and his desire to return from India with the same great laurels and financial rewards as Wellesley had received, delayed his retirement so long that when he was ready to leave and Canning was about to depart for India, Castlereagh's suicide opened the foreign-ministership that Canning coveted (and Liverpool required), and he turned his back on India.

[76] Contained in v. 530 of the *H.M.S.*, pp. 253–89, in Cumming's hand, entitled 'Memo on Correspondence Out and at Home to the Introduction of Ryotwar into Ceded and Conquered Provinces', n.d., but probably 1820.

[77] Philips, pp. 211–22. Thomas Courtenay, Secretary of the Board, wrote this to Munro on 23 September 1818, and mentioned that it was so confidential that 'our friend Cumming' knew nothing of it, MC, F/151/72.

and the enhanced influence of Sullivan and Cumming. Grant's death deprived supporters of the Bengal system of a focus that never was retrieved,[78] and his passing also opened the Direction to greater influence by what was then called 'the private trade interest' over the older financial and shipping interests and the 'Indian' interest within the Company. The private trade group consisted of directors connected with the managing agencies in London and India, by whom a large part of the business with India came to be handled after the cession of the Company monopoly in 1813. Their influence waxed in the late 1820s, and by 1830 the private trade interest could claim the allegiance of fourteen of the thirty directors of the Company. One result of this was that fewer chairmen of the Company during the 1820s had any Indian experience: of seven chairmen of the Direction between 1822 and 1829, only one had resided in India. In 1831 only twelve of the thirty directors had resided in India at all. Adding to these various factors that contributed to the growing relative power of the Board of Control over the directors was the latters' failure to throttle the intransigent demand for a permanent, zamindari settlement in the Ganges territories by the Bengal revenue and judicial officialdom—even after a decade of opposition to this demand from the Board, the directors, and two governors-general (Minto and Hastings).[79]

The printed *Selections* of India House records were a symptom of the Board's growing dominance over Indian affairs as well as an instrument of it. During the 1820s, when the second set of East India House selections was being assembled by Cumming—and after his retirement by Lord Binning at the Board, and by Ravenshaw, now a director at India House—Munro maintained a steady and shaping correspondence from Madras. Several files of his papers at the IOL contain his letters and memoranda on revenue and judicial questions addressed to the governors-general, Lord Hastings and Amherst. These reinforced Sullivan's letters to Hastings, exploiting what Sullivan called 'my habits of intimacy' with him. Sullivan also passed Munro's letters to Canning and after him to Bathurst,[80] and Munro himself sent frequent letters to the less sympathetic Wynn on revenue and judicial matters after the latter succeeded to the presidency of the Board.[81] Knowing that his letters were being retailed by his friends at the Board, as well as by Ravenshaw at India House, Munro assembled arguments in defence of his system in Madras and against critics of the Bengal persuasion intent on protecting, if not enlarging, the domain of their authority. He skilfully exploited the favour that Mountstuart Elphinstone enjoyed among directors by extolling the policies that were being pursued in Bombay, which were modelled on his in Madras, and being carried out by Chaplin, with

[78] Reported by Ravenshaw, 6 November 1823, MC, F/151/78.

[79] Philips, pp. 244 and 212, referring to the abstract of the Select Committee's *Report of the Select Committee, 16 August 1832*, appended to the revenue portion of the evidence collected on revenue questions, v. XI, part 3, pp. III–V.

[80] MC, F/151/72, Sullivan to Munro, 7 May 1821, and the letter of 18 February 1821.

[81] MC, F/151/92, 'Letter Book, July 1820 to 1826', e.g. 14 June 1823 on ryotwar.

whom Munro kept in close touch. He could be confident that his approbation of Elphinstone's procedures would be passed along to others by his influential friends.[82] A point that he made in letters then was that since Bombay came under Company rule last among the great provinces of British India, it benefited from the innovations pioneered in Madras and the errors being exposed in the administration of Bengal. He also suggested that the modifications of the Madras system in Bombay provided a valuable pattern for all of British India.

Two other publications contributed to the Board's task. One of these was the work of John Malcolm, who, with Munro, was a favourite of the Board. His published writings added valuable authority and example against the whole of the 'regulation school' of Bengal, and his *The Political History of India from 1784 to 1823* was a sustained polemic for an Indian rule conceived as a process dependent upon the character of its rulers, not its rules.[83] Malcolm also lamented past practices that gave whole provinces over to men who had little knowledge of India or talent for rule, but who knew 'the right people' and had connections; and he applauded the new arrangements of 1813 which gave the Board of Control a commanding place in Indian policy formation. Under Buckinghamshire and Canning, Malcolm saw great changes, most especially the appointments of Elphinstone and Munro.[84] The wisdom of these and the Board's generally constructive role was not merely in choosing men who knew India, for that was not sufficient: 'local [Indian] experience, unless attended with other qualifications, is but a poor recommendation to status which does not so much require an acquaintance with details as that enlarged knowledge of human nature, that active energy of character, and that commanding talent for rule which has in all ages, distinguished those who have exercised power to the benefit of their country and mankind.' Moreover, 'we cannot assimilate the rules and principles of British Government with those which are essential to the maintenance of our sovereignty, as foreign conquerors. . . .'[85]

Another publication was more deliberately intended to counter the attack upon Munro's policies after his death as well as to prepare public opinion for the

[82] MC, F/151/92, Munro to Sullivan, 24 June 1821, and to Ravenshaw, 30 September 1821.

[83] Published by John Murray, London, 1826. Also, Malcolm's *A Memoir of Central India* (London: Parbury, Allen, 1832), especially his discussion of 'punchayets' in chapter XVI of v. 2. Malcolm also sought to dissuade Charles Wynn from revising Munro's system in Madras; in 1828 he reassurred Wynn that it was safe to maintain all of Munro's measures and to disregard the criticisms of Munro's opponents in London. Finally, Malcolm wrote to Lord Melville from Bombay in the same year that while Lushington was within his right to reject Munro's regulation for trials by Indian juries and under Indian judges, Malcolm disagreed with Lushington and supported Munro's regulation of 1827. These letters are found in *The Correspondence of Lord William Cavendish Bentinck*, ed. C. H. Philips (Oxford: OUP, 1977), v. 1, pp. 28 and 42.

[84] Malcolm, *Political History* v. 2, p. 74.

[85] Ibid., pp. 78–9.

coming twenty-year charter renewal of the Company; this was the biography by George Robert Gleig in 1830.

Gleig was one of the most popular and prolific writers of his day, and a very long day it was: he died at ninety-three. By then he had published forty book-length works and numerous essays in leading periodicals on such varied topics as the military, travel, religion, education and biography. Also a novelist, he frequently employed military themes drawn from his own career in the British army, from 1811 to 1816, where he served in the Peninsular campaign and in the American war of 1812.[86]

Ravenshaw initiated the biography project. Before the year of Munro's death was out, in December 1827, he wrote to Lady Munro at Cragie House in Ayr, where she lived with her father and her two sons, to suggest that there was much talk at India House about doing something to commemorate Munro's services in India, and that he was in the process of assembling Munro's papers so as to write a commemorative biography.[87] Within a month Lady Munro acted on Ravenshaw's further suggestion, which he said he had obtained from the publisher John Murray, that she invite the participation of Gleig in the biography scheme, and Lady Munro had got James Cumming's sister, Ann, to broach the matter with Gleig.[88] Gleig was reluctant merely to revise a manuscript that Ravenshaw might provide, and he proposed instead that he undertake the work of writing the 'Life', using papers supplied by Ravenshaw and others. This last was not agreed, and Ravenshaw proceeded to prepare a manuscript using the year that he was out of the Direction on rotation to complete it.[89] Among those from whom documents were sought for the biography was Stephen R. Lushington in Madras. He answered a letter from Lady Munro in 1828 with the charge that Munro's old associates were full of obstructionism and determined to advance their own policies against his in Madras, but, he added, 'I have torn the masks from their faces', and assured Munro's widow that none in Madras was more devoted to her husband's memory than he.[90] With his writing progressing, Ravenshaw asked Lady Munro to agree to a dedication of the work to the Duke of Wellington who, as an old friend of Munro and as Prime Minister, was a valuable patron for the work.[91]

[86] Sketches of Gleig's life and works are found in the *D.N.B.*, v. 7, pp. 1303–4, and in A. Austin Allibone, *A Critical Dictionary of English Literature and British and American Writers* (Philadelphia: J. B. Lippincott, 1854), v. 1, p. 672. For his periodical publications see W. F. Poole's *Index to Periodical Literature, 1802–1881* (New York: P. Smith, 1938), 2 vols, and C. E. Wall, *et al.*, *Cumulative Author Index for Poole's Index to Periodical Literature, 1802–1906* (Ann Arbor: Dierian Press, 1971), p. 167.

[87] MC, F/151/197, Ravenshaw to Lady Munro, 8 December 1827.

[88] Ibid., 6 January 1828.

[89] Ibid., 8 April 1828.

[90] Ibid., 18 May 1828.

[91] Ibid., 5 August 1828.

Ravenshaw finished in October 1828 and showed his work to Lady Munro, who sent it to Gleig for his reaction. The latter found it as 'totally and radically bad' in plan and execution as he predicted it might be, and he proposed a complete rewrite so as to make the best use of the materials Ravenshaw had gathered together. Ravenshaw duly gave his manuscript over to Gleig and promised Lady Munro that he would heed her caution not to permit Gleig 'to escape from your control'.[92] Another who seemed to require restraint was the publisher John Murray to whom Gleig had shown Ravenshaw's manuscript. Ravenshaw reported that Murray was a 'strange man' who refused to answer his letters and who, without his or Gleig's permission, announced in the *Quarterly Review*, which he owned, that his firm would 'publish "The Life of Sir Thomas Munro, K. C. B.", by G. R. Gleig'. Another publisher was accordingly found and two other matters were settled as well. One was that Ravenshaw's role in the biography should be muted, since his remarks carried the authority of a director of the Company, and the other was Gleig's remuneration for his rewrite. The latter proposed to keep any profits that might accrue from sales or, alternatively, that one of his sons might be nominated as a writer in the Company service. Ravenshaw thought the last was best and most easy to arrange.[93]

During 1829 and early 1830 Gleig's correspondence with Lady Munro revealed the scale of co-operation necessary to assemble the letters and papers used in the biography; these presently constitute the Munro Collection housed at the IOL. Many of its pages contain Ravenshaw's marginal comments and his deletions. In February 1830 the latter was busy seeing the book through the press and engaging for the reviews of it in prominent journals.

The printing of 2000 sold out quickly, and a second printing was ordered. Gleig also decided that a third volume would be useful so as to accommodate a larger part of the Wellington–Munro correspondence, and this was agreed by all involved except Alexander Munro who registered a sour view of the project. He considered that Gleig's biography of his brother was mediocre, and he regretted that the family had not insisted that Gleig should be engaged to write the 'Life' for a fee, since he estimated that Gleig now stood to earn up to £12,000 from the first edition.[94] This apparently got back to Gleig who protested that he had only £500 from the edition and offered the profits from the second edition to Lady Munro for the benefit of her youngest child, Campbell.[95]

In the preface of his *Munro*, Gleig admitted that he knew little of his subject beyond what many others, who gave some attention to Indian matters, might have known of Munro's reputation. He readily credited John Ravenshaw's contribution of documents and correspondence which had been carefully selected, edited and arranged for the purposes of the biography. There was no

[92] Ibid., 9 and 26 January 1829.

[93] Ibid., February 1829, Ravenshaw to Lady Munro.

[94] Ibid., 23 April 1830.

[95] Ibid., 3 November 1830.

deception here; Gleig's *Munro* was an *official life*, prepared by a member of the Company's management, the directorate, and intended to be useful in the 1831–2 debate where, once again, the privileges of the Company were at risk and India's internal governance would be aired.

The battle that was waged for policy hegemony in India during Munro's governorship—in which he, Malcolm, Cumming, Sullivan, Canning and others had been engaged—succeeded in denying the successors of Cornwallis in Bengal the dominance that they and their allies in London expected and felt to be their due. The struggle was by now no longer new. It had been launched in *The Fifth Report* of 1812, which was taken by the Board of Control under Buckinghamshire as a guide to a colonial policy, one that won many adherents among the directors of the Company. The struggle continued with the publication of the four volumes of India House *Selections*, which recorded how the Board, and to a lesser extent that directorate, frustrated the Bengal civil service by limiting the scope of Cornwallis's Bengal order in favour of another order, the core of which was Munro's system of Madras. Gleig's biography of 1830 opened the final phase of the struggle that now stretched from Munro's early years as a civil administrator in India to the aftermath of his death. The contribution of the biography to all of this was perceived by a journal several cuts below the prestigious *Quarterly Review* and *Edinburgh Review*,[96] where Gleig's work was reviewed, but which, for that reason, may have made its point more important. The reviewer of Gleig's *Munro* in *The Gentleman's Magazine and Historical Chronicle* remarked that, in contrast to the usual general public apathy about matters Indian, some interest was being stirred by the debate of the East India Company's charter, and that in the biography of Munro 'ample materials will be furnished for a better acquaintance of the hearings on this important question.'[97]

MUNRO AND THE 1832 CHARTER

The final episode in the short-term aftermath of Munro's death in relation to Indian colonial policy was simultaneously the final struggle against the Bengal model of Indian imperialism; this came with the debate occasioned by the

[96] *Quarterly Review*, v. 43 (May 1830), pp. 81–112. Gleig is named by John Murray, the publisher of the *Quarterly*, as co-author with John Gobson Lockhart, of the review of *Munro*, according to Walter E. Houghten, *The Wellesley Index to Victorian Periodicals* (London: Routledge and Kegan Paul, 1966), v. 1, p. 710. The review in the *Edinburgh Review* appeared in v. 51 (April 1830), pp. 247–86; its author was William Empson, according to Houghten, v. 1, p. 472. Empson was a frequent contributor to the *Edinburgh Review* on economic matters, and was a colleague of Malthus at the East India College in Haileybury.

[97] *The Gentleman's Magazine*, v. 23, part 1, p. 225. Similar reviews in the *Asiatic Journal*, n.s., v. 1 (January to April 1830), pp. 122–40, and 223–33, and *The United Service Journal and Military Magazine, 1830*, part 1, pp. 208–13, which was published by the same firm that did Gleig's *Munro*, and thus praised it extravagantly.

charter renewal of 1833. For, then, the marginalization of Bengal was confirmed, in, among other ways, by the prominent place taken in the deliberations before the Select Committee on Indian affairs of some of the very Munro men dismissed and dishonoured by Lushington. These were David Hill, Alexander D. Campbell, and the younger John Sullivan. In addition, the elder Sullivan was invited to submit a long statement for the Committee that served to anchor the continuing debate over Indian policies and against Bengal in Buckinghamshire's Board of Control of twenty years earlier.

The Right Honourable John Sullivan was three weeks beyond his ninetieth birthday when he submitted his 'Observations on the Revenue Systems of India' to the Select Committee.[98] In opening, he said that portions of it were first composed in 1817 as an appreciation for the recently deceased Lord Buckinghamshire's statesmanship and as a token of Sullivan's affection for an old friend. His 'Observations' bore on events up to 1828. Already in Buckinghamshire's time, he said, the locus of authority of the Board of Control was its president, and the late Lord found himself overwhelmed by the large and growing corpus of documentation from and to India. Only a small portion of this was printed in the volumes of 'extracts' printed in 1820 and 1826, which Sullivan said he and James Cumming prepared for Buckinghamshire's use. He paid tribute to Cumming's unstinting labours on this project and to his death as a 'martyr' to the cause of better governance in India.

According to Sullivan, Buckinghamshire's regime at the Board began 'a new epoch in Indian history', one that was framed by *The Fifth Report*, just as the Cornwallis regime in Calcutta—the previous 'new epoch'—had been defined by the regulations of 1793. By Buckinghamshire's time the Cornwallis system had come under criticism from many quarters, and most of this centred on its extension into the new tracts around Delhi. The opposition to this was recounted in detail in Sullivan's paper: from the 1808 commission report by the Calcutta officials, Cox and Tucker, to Canning's intervention in August 1817, which Sullivan interpreted as an injunction that the ryotwar system should henceforward be followed. He then traced in detail how that was achieved by following the lines first set out by Munro in the CD as amended by the later ryotwar regulations framed by his own son, John Sullivan, whose report from Coimbatore of July 1826 was quoted. The elder Sullivan agreed with his son that the only place where ryotwar had a fair trial was in Coimbatore, and also agreed that the steady increases in production and revenue from there proved Munro's ryotwar beyond any question.

The lily offered to Munro's memory by John Sullivan, the oldest Indian statesman of his time, was gilded by his son, John, now a respected and retired Indian official with twenty-two years of service in Madras. The younger Sullivan was given pride of place among witnesses by being the first called to offer substantive evidence before the Select Committee on Indian revenue. He was called on 9 February 1832, and he immediately announced: 'I consider

[98] *Report of the Select Committee, 16 August 1832*, v. 3, 'Revenue', appendix 8, pp. 49–67.

the ryotwar settlement to be the best; it is the only permanent settlement of the land revenue, all others are fluctuating assessments.'[99] The enthusiasm of this assertion would have surprised few, for Sullivan was a well-known supporter of Munro's system and enjoyed a special place among disciples in having received the approval of its master. This and other claims for ryotwar had been set before the London public in a pamphlet of the younger Sullivan in 1831, and one of the claims was that Munro had written to Sullivan before his death to say that a good account of ryotwar was needed for use by the directors and the Board and that he, Sullivan, should take up the task.[100]

But listeners might have been puzzled by the assertion that ryotwar was the only permanent settlement of the revenue. Though not queried about this startling claim, his subsequent testimony made its meaning clear. Zamindars and 'mootahdars' (village renters) had their revenue demands fixed by government, but both could demand of cultivators any rate they wanted, hence at the production base the revenue was highly variable, as Sullivan saw it. He also saw, and wished others to understand, that ryotwar meant 'the old systems under native governments'; Munro and his successors in Madras merely improved these systems. However, contrary to some of his master's accommodation to critics, Sullivan insisted that an actual survey and assessment was required under ryotwar, but he strongly agreed with Munro that this could be entrusted to Indian servants and strongly advocated 'native agency' in revenue administration. Other criticisms of ryotwar were disposed of before he predicted that under ryotwar—as demonstrated by the recent history of Coimbatore—the level of revenue would continue to increase even while the rate of revenue demand remained low (as he claimed it presently was), at around one-fifth of gross production. In his final answers to the Committee the younger Sullivan conditionally supported European colonization for the benefits that would come from greater mechanization of agricultural production and from the increase in cash cropping under European production. But he insisted that it could only succeed if there was substantial participation by Indians in administration—revenue and judicial—so as to protect their ancient rights.

The younger Sullivan was followed by Hugh Stark, a creditably loyal successor of James Cumming at the Board of Control. Stark also assumed the mantle of Samuel Davis in *The Fifth Report* by castigating both the principles of the permanent, zamindari settlement and its rigidities: 'It appears to me that a collector in Bengal never looks beyond the terms of the regulations, which only specify the zemindars as proprietors; and much of the evil that has been produced in destroying the rights of hereditary tenancy has arisen from this circumstance.'[101] In contrast, he offered the example of ryotwar that had been established in 'Booglepoor' (Bhagalpur, Bihar) in 1828 and was found to work

[99] *Report of the Select Committee, 16 August 1832*, v. 3, 'Revenue', 'Minutes of Evidence, revenue', p. 1.

[100] IOL, *Sketch of the Ryotwar System* (London: Roworth and Son), p. 1.

[101] *Report of the Select Committee, 16 August 1832*, 'Minutes of Evidence, Revenue, p. 10.

well and to the satisfaction of the people there. He asserted that ryotwar could work successfully anywhere in Bengal, except for the implacable rigidities of the regulations in that Presidency. After all, ryotwar was a success in Madras both because it maintained a satisfactory level of revenue and because it afforded the greatest welfare for the people and a profit to cultivators. In fact, Stark finally claimed, the success and superiority of ryotwar was its base in native participation: necessity had become virtue.

From the length of their printed testimony, two of the most important and respected witnesses before the Select Committee on revenue and on judicial questions were David Hill and Alexander Campbell. Hill had been restored as chief secretary in 1829 by order of the directors, after his demotion and humiliation by Lushington. When he appeared before the Committee he had resigned from the Indian service and had entered the India House administration, succeeding Edward Strachey as chief assistant examiner of judicial records. He shared responsibilities there with John Stuart Mill, also a newcomer to the Company, having replaced his father, James, in 1831.[102]

Drawing upon twenty-three years of Indian experience, Hill strongly defended the Madras system. He believed it to be suited to all of British India because it preserved ancient rights and practices and because, whatever the nominal system of revenue and judicial administration, 'the ryotwarry system must form an essential part of it'. In his answers to questions from the Committee, Hill repeatedly referred to Munro and his expressed principles, and he dismissed the criticism that successful ryotwar required collectors of unusual abilities: 'Some of our best officers have not been men of superior capacity.' However, for the system to succeed, reliance had to be placed upon Indian subordinates and Munro's judicial reforms demonstrated the workability of 'native agency'. Further:

> I conceive the improvement that is necessary in our judicial system in India is to transfer the functions of judges to natives, I conceive also that the great desideratum in the office of public functionaries of the Indian government is a knowledge of the Indian character, language and manners, and a sympathy with the people among whom they live . . . these advantages would be forfeited by [demanding of candidates for office only] high legal attainments.[103]

Alexander D. Campbell said less to the Select Committee about the judiciary than Hill, merely countering criticisms of panchayats and offering his own experience as collector of Bellary in testimony of how well 'native juries' worked and how useful they proved, especially in disputes over revenue assessments and actions of debt.[104] Modest though his judicial evidence was, there were probably few who were a part of these proceedings who missed that

[102] Philips, p. 340.

[103] *Report of the Select Committee, 16 August 1832*, 'Minutes of Evidence, Revenue', pp. 105 and 108. Hill's testimony on revenue covered 18 pages.

[104] *Report of the Select Committee, 16 August 1832*, 'Minutes of Evidence, Judicial', pp. 111–19.

Campbell's evidence was squarely opposed to that given by Lushington. The latter's sole contribution to the 1832 proceedings in London was a denunciation of the 'native juries' in a minute to his council in Madras of September 1830; this was printed in the appendices of the Select Committee's report of 1832.[105] But it was for Campbell's knowledge of revenue administration that he was called as a witness and also requested by the Select Committee to prepare a general paper on land revenue in India. This last ran to forty printed folio pages.

Campbell's career as a judicial official had consisted of two brief spells of about three years altogether out of a service career of over twenty years. Curiously, both judicial appointments resulted from conflict with a governor of Madras: one was Munro who recommended Campbell's dismissal from his position as collector of Bellary; the other was Lushington who dismissed him from the collectorate of Tanjore in 1828 and who only permitted his re-employment as registrar of the Sadr Adalat court in Madras in 1830.[106] Campbell's standing as a revenue expert was confirmed by Munro's appointment of him to the MBOR in 1826, two years after dismissing him from Bellary; Munro also asked him to attend his final tour of the southern districts of the Presidency in early 1827, and in his report of that tour Munro praised Campbell for his work in Tanjore and for his assistance in the tour.[107]

The latter's land-tenure paper of 1832 was an extended criticism of the permanent, zamindar settlement mode; this occupies two-thirds of its length. The major failures of that system were enumerated as: the violation by Bengal authorities of their pledge of 1793 to protect tenancy rights under zamindars; the official ignorance of these and other landed rights and relations because Bengal officials had cut themselves off from the agrarian base; and the indifference to accumulating criticisms of the system from the most senior Bengal officials, such as Sir James Edward Colebrook, from active and knowledgable governor-generals such as Lord Hastings, and from experienced officials such as Munro. These critics and others failed to be heeded, according to Campbell, because of the veneration with which Cornwallis continued to be held. Yet, Campbell observed, enough of the defects of the Bengal system were suspected, even at its beginning, to encourage Alexander Read, Munro and others to develop a system of annual settlements in the Baramahal. This became ryotwar and was adopted in other parts of Madras and Bombay.

Finally, a third model of settlement came into being—periodic settlements of the land revenue—as a means of dealing with the difficulties that presented themselves in the Ceded and Conquered Provinces of the western Gangetic plain. Campbell said that he and others thought it striking that permanent zamindari settlement was not immediately recommended there, but was

105 *Report of the Select Committee, 16 August 1832*, 'General Appendix', III, pp. 264–70.

106 Prinsep, *Record of Services, Madras*, pp. 21–2.

107 IOL, European Manuscripts, Carfrae Collection F/87, Box 1A, Munro to his Council, 24 February 1827.

postponed to some indeterminate future. This was from 'the Commissioners, Messrs. Cox and Tucker, themselves strenuous advocates for the [Bengal] system [and] expressly deputed to carry it there into effect'.[108] Campbell considered their reasons for hesitancy proper: land ownership was found to be a contested matter in many places around Delhi and insufficient knowledge existed for the commissioners to decide among contestants. Yet, notwithstanding the caution of Cox and Tucker, the Bengal authorities persisted on their course and only (and reluctantly) desisted when overruled by the directors and the Board of Control. Canning's 1817 decision to support the directors against Bengal was seen by Campbell to have established this third mode of revenue settlement—periodic settlement—one that permitted more information to be had before making a decision about permanence.

The solicitation by the Select Committee of Campbell's paper on modes of settlement ensured that the ryotwar view would be dominant in the 1832 revenue investigations. Together with the two Sullivans, Hugh Stark, and David Hill, Campbell hammered the Bengal men with the accusation of turpitudinous violation of the rights of cultivating groups, their ignorance, and their rigidities in working the system established in 1793. His closing remarks on ryotwar and village modes of settlement were brief. On ryotwar, he pointed to the revisions of the original system developed in the Baramahal which made that system ever more just: coercion (such as torture by revenue subordinates) and compulsory cultivation had been eliminated; private landed property was affirmed and, where this had been violated, restorations had been made; survey rates had been lowered, assuring a larger profit to cultivators; and joint liability for revenue shortfalls had ceased. Campbell even found a way to explain how his differences with and dismissal by Munro had been reversed by Munro's recognition that survey rates must be more sensitive to differences in soil fertility, as Campbell had argued in the early 1820s.[109] As for the village mode of settlement, this was dismissed by Campbell as a failure where 'every village was a petty tyranny'.[110]

Throughout the post-*Fifth Report* debate on ryotwar, policies for the Gangetic territories won from the Marathas in 1804 was an anvil on which the hammer of ryotwar was struck, and Henry St George Tucker was one of those beaten in the process. He was the chief victim of the assault mounted in the *Selections* volumes of 1820 and 1826 and again in the proceedings and published version of the 1832 hearings of the Select Committee. Tucker could not defend himself and his advocacy of the zamindari settlement from the attacks of the Munro men in the 1820s, but in 1832 he could and did. His combativeness at the time went beyond the investigations being conducted by the Select Committee,

[108] *Report of the Select Committee, 16 August 1832*, 'Minutes of Evidence, Revenue', pp. 9–48; also appendix 6, pp. 14, 15, 20 and 32.

[109] Ibid., pp. 37–48; p. 40 for this point on ryotwar.

[110] Ibid., p. 37.

for he was one of the few directors of the Company between 1830 and 1834 who sought to prevent, or limit, the dominance over Indian affairs by the Board of Control. In this he defiantly opposed another Charles Grant with great power; this was the son of the famous director.

The younger Charles Grant was raised to the Presidency of the Board in November 1830, when the ministry of the Duke of Wellington was replaced by that of Lord Gray, and Grant was given the Board, as others had been, for their political services. As head of the Board of Control and as chairman of the Select Committee of the House of Commons on East India affairs, Grant surprised nearly everyone by his hostility to the directors. The times were very different from when his father was the great force in the Direction. With his death, the older Grant's faction dissolved and major influence at India passed into the hands of directors who, unlike Tucker, were more interested in private trade between Britain and India than in India and its problems. This was a change that the older Grant would have opposed, but his son, as head of the Board, took full advantage of the decline in Indian experience among directors.[111]

The ignorance of, and indifference to, Indian policy on the part of many directors from the middle of the 1820s gave greater relative weight to the Board of Control, its president Charles Grant after 1830, and its senior staff. With Cumming's retirement in July 1823, Thomas Courtenay, who was the latter's superior as secretary of the Board from 1812, took over part of Cumming's influence and policy orientations, thereby providing stability to the Board until he, Courtenay, retired in 1828. Another of the Board's staff whose influence shot forward was Benjamin S. Jones, who became a major influence behind the new president, Charles Grant.[112] Jones had sought precisely this sort of influence from at least 1811 when he offered his services to Thomas Wallace, a member of the Board, when he campaigned for the governorship of Madras. Now Jones had attained an influential position to match that of Cumming, on whom he had modelled his career at the Board of Control; this was confirmed by his publication of a volume on Indian policy towards the Indian princely states in 1832.[113]

Even before the directors fully grasped Charles Grant's ambitions for the Board, they had attempted to reassert some of their old authority, and one arena of struggle had been the appointment of Lushington to the Madras governor-

[111] Philips, pp. 274–7.

[112] *Report of the Select Committee, 16 August 1832*, 'Minutes of Evidence', pp. 245 and 301.

[113] B. S. Jones, *Papers Relative to the Progress of the British Power in India and the subsidiary system of Alliances; Communicated to the Right Honourable Charles Grant, Chair of the Select Committee of the House of Commons of East-India Affairs* (London: J. L. Cox, 1832). Jones disagreed with Munro about 'altamgha inams', p. 116, but agreed generally about the dangers of the subsidary alliances and quoted from Munro's 12 August 1817 letter to Lord Hastings on this, pp. 95–6.

ship. Many directors saw this appointment, pressed by government and the Board, as usurpation of their appointive powers and a reversal of Canning's flattering attention to their wishes to see Company servants appointed to governorships. But, even more dangerous, the directors saw the appointment of a prominent government minister (Lushington was Secretary of the Treasury) as removing a governor from any of their rightful supervision and influence. Their failure to prevent Lushington's appointment led to other defeats. In 1830, when the failure of agency houses in Calcutta followed a trade recession in Britain during the late 1820s, the private trade interest among the directors was discredited, and India House was made even more defensive against the thrusting policies of the Board.[114]

In 1832, therefore, the Board of Control was in a strong position to press its views before the Select Committee in, among other ways, by the maintenance and advance of Indian policies the Board had advocated under Buckinghamshire and Canning. Henry St George Tucker was one of the few directors to see this strategy, and he vigorously opposed it from the time he became a director in 1826. He continued in this opposition to the Board when he became chairman of the directors in 1834, but by that time the 1833 India Act had denied the India House most of its former powers.

Tucker was elected to the Directorate in 1826 with the support of the 'Indian interest'. This was a mixed lot of men who had spent time in India either as Company servants, for example Hudleston and Ravenshaw in the Madras service, or in private business. Tucker could claim credentials for both. His Indian career began in the 1780s—about the same time as Munro's—when he disappointed his diplomat father by taking a seaman's passage to India. There an uncle was secretary to the government of Bengal and obtained for the young man a position as secretary to Sir William Jones, the famous orientalist.[115] In 1792 Tucker got a writership in the Company, and, with his interest in finance, took part in the reform of the government's Bank of Bengal. After serving as a volunteer in the war against Tipu Sultan and also as Lord Wellesley's secretary for a time in 1799, he was appointed accountant-general of Bengal, a position he held until 1811, except for two brief periods. One of these was a period as director of a managing agency in Calcutta, which established his eligibility for membership in the private trade interest later; the other was a period of imprisonment on a charge of rape, which does not seem to have damaged his career in any way, for he was voted a gift of Rs 50,000 by the directors when he returned to Britain in 1811. He was in India again shortly after with a post (Secretary to Government in the Colonial and Finance Department) created especially for him by Lord Minto, the Governor-General, to which the directors refused their assent, leaving Tucker to serve the balance of his career in Bengal as chief secretary to government.

From 1815 to 1826, when he became a director, Tucker wrote frequently

[114] Philips, p. 277.

[115] *D.N.B.*, v. 19, p. 1207; Tucker was born in 1771 and died in 1851.

on Indian questions, motivated perhaps by his ambition to become a director. Among his publications was a book ostensibly on the finances of the Company, but actually a more wide-ranging work on many aspects of internal administration. In it he observed that the Cornwallis system, while popular in Britain, found no favour in Madras, where an alternative scheme of administration—ryotwar—had developed, and this system captured the allegiance of the Board of Control and Court of Directors. That this 'change of sentiment appears unfortunately to have taken place' was never appreciated by Parliament, and its *Fifth Report*, carrying Parliamentary authority, was actually not the work of members of Parliament, but of two 'highly respected and estimable men', James Cumming and Samuel Davis.[116] Ryotwar was a 'novel doctrine' based on the 'assumption that it harmonized better with the habits and dispositions of our native subjects and . . . with usages and institutions of the country'; Munro, present governor of Madras, was the doctrine's 'able, intelligent, and zealous advocate'. Tucker protested that there were other voices in Madras which opposed Munro's innovations, and among these were Robert Fullerton and John Hodgson. He acknowledged the latter's help to him in discovering the papers of Fullerton and other writings critical of ryotwar.

Tucker's attack on ryotwar prompted a defence from John Sullivan while he was still in Coimbatore, and this was published in London under the title *Sketch of the Ryotwar System* in 1831.[117] By then a director, Tucker's objections to ryotwar, repeated and elaborated in a paper of 1827, carried additional weight.[118] Here he denounced Munro's ryotwar for violating the historical rights of intermediaries such as zamindars and talukdars. It was an innovation that destroyed the very 'native institutions' which its advocates claimed to protect. 'What is a ryot?', Tucker asked. Was this term not a lumping together of varied cultivation and land rights, and did the ryotwar doctrine not violate the freedom of cultivators to choose what lands they would cultivate? In Madras, he said, that freedom was termed 'The desertion of the Ryots'. His closing observation, perhaps suggested by Hodgson, was that the village settlements established in Madras in1808 were for the most part successful. As far as Tucker was concerned, therefore, the debate over the superiority of ryotwar was not over, and he sought to reopen it before the Select Committee.

In fact Tucker appeared thrice before the Committee considering revenue matters, more than any other witness. Yet he was unable to speak against ryotwar until his final appearance in April 1832, because he was only asked

[116] *Review of the Financial Situation of the East India Company in 1824* (London: Kingsbury *et al.*, 1824), pp. 108n, 109 and 111–34 (citing Munro's selections in *SEIHR*, v. 1), pp. 134–7, and 144n.

[117] Tamilnadu State Archives; this undated manuscript was signed by John Sullivan.

[118] Tucker's observations on the 'Settlement of the Broach Pergunnahs', in John W. Kaye, *Memorials of Indian Government. . . . A Selection from the Papers of Henry St George Tucker* (London: Richard Bentley, 1853), pp. 125–8; objections to ryotwar on monetary grounds are found on p. 132.

about the salt monopoly in Bengal. When he finally was invited to comment on land revenue, he launched a diatribe against the directors and the Board for having failed to support the Bengal government's strong wish to have the permanent zamindar settlement in the Ceded and Conquered Provinces, as he had recommended as a commissioner in 1808.[119] This was a feeble effort, and Tucker's failure to oppose the tide of ryotwar, the regnant thrust of the Board of Control's commitment to it, and the prominent place of Munro men in the deliberations of the Select Committee—all were reflected in the Report of the Select Committee.

Abstracts from that report preface the minutes of evidence on revenue presented before the Committee and summarize the victory against Bengal. Members of the House of Commons were told that 'the Zemindary System' operating in Bengal and elsewhere was a 'system arbitrarily created by ourselves... and Your Committee cannot refrain from observing that it does not appear to have answered the purposes for which it was benevolently intended by its author, Lord Cornwallis, in 1792–3.' The report continued:

> Without going into detail to show the working of the system, it may be proper to quote the opinion of Lord Hastings, as recorded in 1819, when he held the office of Governor-General of India. 'Never' says Lord Hastings, 'was there a measure conceived in purer spirit of generous humanity and disinterested justice than the plan for the Permanent Settlement in the Lower Provinces [of Bengal]. It was worthy of the soul of a Cornwallis. Yet this truely benevolent purpose, fashioned with great care and deliberation, has, to our painful knowledge, subjected almost the whole of the Lower Classes throughout these provinces to most grievious oppression; an oppression too, so guaranteed by our pledge, that we are unable to relieve the sufferers....[120]

The Committee added to this the condemnation of another senior Bengal official, Sir James Edward Colebrook, who succeeded Tucker as commissioner in the Ceded and Conquered Provinces.

Colebrook's criticisms were the more telling because he was a well-known opponent of the Madras judicial system and had, along with another senior Bengal official, William Trant, lobbied at India House against the Munro judiciary from 1824. While he was a member of Hastings' supreme council, Colebrook condemned the zamindari settlement in Bengal for having 'sacrificed... the Yeomanry, by merging all tillage rights' and for permitting the 'all-devouring recognition of the Zemindar's permanent property in the soil' to make 'any settlement with cultivators he chose'.[121]

[119] *Report of the Select Committee, 16 August 1832*, 'Minutes of Evidence, Revenue', pp. 150–7.

[120] Ibid., 'Minutes of Extract from the Report of the Select Committee', pp. III–IV.

[121] Ibid., 'Minutes of Evidence, Revenue', 'Extract from the Report of the Select Committee', p. v.

The Select Committee said in 1832 that remedies for this flawed system were to be found in the proposals made in the 'able paper' by Alexander Campbell. A more radical remedy, its Report observed, was that proposed by Lord Hastings at the end of his governor-generalship. Note was taken of how Hastings underwent a fundamental change in his view of land-revenue administration during his long stewardship in India. He began by rejecting ryotwar as an appropriate system outside Madras, but by August 1822 he had decided that ryotwar was not only practicable in much of Bengal, but was 'the system of all others calculated to secure the prosperity and comfort of the great body of the people'.[122] The Report concluded its discussion of the revenue administration of Bengal with the observation that a ryotwar settlement was actually in progress in parts of Bengal.

The Select Committee of 1832 announced itself contented with the Madras and Bombay revenue systems based on Munro's ryotwar. Both provinces were but briefly discussed in comparison with Bengal and its problems. The Report closed its discussion of revenue ironically, or with consummate rhetorical artistry, with a quotation from William Thackeray's report of 4 August 1807, the same text that Cumming had contrived to close the last volume of *The Fifth Report* of 1812.[123] The last paragraph of Thackeray's 1807 paper (and *The Fifth Report*) started with: 'I have written so long a paper on the subject [comparing ryotwar and zamindar settlements] . . . and Collector Munro had discussed it in so ample and able a way, that it seems presumptuous in me, to say anything more on the subject'.

And little more was said on this subject.

THE LONGER AFTERMATH

The interval between Munro's death and the promulgation of the 1833 Charter Act may be taken as the short-term aftermath of his career. By 1833 conditions are discernible which set the future course of imperial development in a direction that made most of what Munro had accomplished, or sought to accomplish, irrelevant, and made his vision of empire just that, a fleeting and imagined conception of an order that was destined never to materialize.

There is another aftermath to consider first, however. That has to do with how Munro's system fared in Madras from his death to the middle of the century when the so-called 'scientific survey' of ryotwar was launched and formed the basis of revenue settlements throughout the Presidency to the end of the century. This examination reveals that the purported administration of ryotwar as a technical order, rather than as a concept, was little more than a cover for highly variable political arrangements, the single purpose of which

[122] Ibid., 'Minutes of Evidence, Revenue', 'Extract from the Report of the Select Committee', p. VI.

[123] Ibid., 'Minutes of Evidence, Revenue', 'Extract from the Report of the Select Committee', p. ix; Thackeray's report of 1807 is in *The Fifth Report*, v. 3, pp. 562–95.

was the creation of a base of political economy for Munro's conception of empire in India.

Nilmani Mukherjee concluded his refreshingly agnostic study of Munro's ryotwar with an instructive summary of the state of ryotwar in Madras on the eve of the death of its creator. This was based upon the settlement documents from the southern districts as well as some of the eastern seaboard districts of the Presidency, and from Munro's report of his tours during the last year of his life.[124]

According to his findings, Tanjore remained as untamed to ryotwar as ever. No field surveys had been done on the basis of which the pattas (revenue engagements) with individuals for each cultivated field were supposed to be issued according to the theory of ryotwar. Mirasidars in Tanjore, as in Trichinopoly and Tinnevelly, opposed fixed cash assessments on fields since productivity and profitability depended on variable irrigation sources of the variable monsoons that fed all peninsular rivers. These same powerful corporate 'owners' were suspicious of any changes in revenue arrangements that might eliminate or limit whole sets of privileges gained over centuries. Trichinopoly, under Charles May Lushington, had made somewhat more progress than Tanjore by setting a money demand upon irrigated holdings, but the survey and registration of holdings was far from complete. Tinnevelly was deemed by Munro and Campbell to be without any defensible system of revenue management at all in 1827. Elsewhere, ryotwar was found to be distorted in a variety of ways. In Dindigul, revenue assessments were found to be based not upon the graded productivity and profitability of cultivated fields, but upon the crops cultivated, and here, as in neighbouring Madura district, survey records were maintained so badly as to render them useless from one crop season to the next. The ryotwar of South Arcot had been established by John Ravenshaw between 1805 and 1813 and its regulations were considered to be as authoritative a source for the adoption of ryotwar in the Gangetic plain as Munro's Ceded Districts regulations. Yet here Munro reported that certain coercive conditions existed which he and others had supposed purged from ryotwar long before. For instance, it was discovered that no crops could be cut by a cultivator without obtaining leave to do so from a local revenue official ('tahsildar') who demanded as a condition of his permission payment of revenue instalments ('kists') that had been previously contracted and recorded in a patta.

Only Coimbatore was found adequate, and this was conceded to be a tribute to John Sullivan's long stewardship of the district. Assessments here were found to be lower than elsewhere because these had been twice reduced in Sullivan's time and because lower assessments were permitted on fields used as pasture rather than as arable. This encouraged a vigorous livestock compo-

[124] Mukherejee, *Ryotwar System in Madras*, pp. 117–21. Also Munro's minutes of 1827 in Arbuthnot, *Munro Selections*, pp. 268–74; Sastri, *Munro System of Statesmanship*, pp. 155–9.

nent in Coimbatore's agriculture and supported a structure of steadily increasing revenue from 1815, when Sullivan began his tenure as collector. It was the success story of Coimbatore that received heavy attention in the evidence presented to the Select Committee in 1831–2 by both Sullivans and Alexander Campbell.

In places such as the Northern Circars, ryotwar had been superimposed over previous zamindari settlements where the failure rate of zamindari holders was high. The ryotwar introduced in many of these places was modified. Many older practices in conflict with ryotwar principles were retained in order to ease the transition to ryotwar in accordance with Munro's orders to the MBOR. He opposed as too radical, for example, the suggestion by the collector of Masulipatam that all zamindars should be pensioned off because of their record of violent exploitation of cultivators on their estates. Munro was willing for this to happen when extortion and oppression were accompanied by revenue arrears, but not otherwise, and he ordered that such measures be adopted in Rajahmundry and Guntur.

Thus, at his death and with seven years to perfect the ryotwar system in Madras as its governor, Munro left a system that was highly varied from district to district and even within districts, and one in which overassessment prevented the profitability and land sales that he had long promised. Only Coimbatore seemed a success, and there were many apparent failures. One of these was Tinnevelly, which has recently had some excellent work done by David Ludden and permits a clearer appreciation of the course of Munro's system to mid-century.[125]

One third the size of the Ceded Districts during Munro's collectorship, Tinnevelly (Tirunelveli) posed the same serious problems for the MBOR in Munro's time and after his death as Tanjore, Trichinopoly—as well as other districts where a substantial portion of the arable was under regular irrigation and where mirasidars held positions of historical dominance. These conditions confounded a system that Munro had devised, based upon the dry ecotypes of the Baramahal and the Ceded Districts. About 20 per cent of the cultivated acres of Tinnevelly between 1825 and 1837 were under irrigation, mostly in the Tambraparni river valley.[126] Here two paddy crops were taken each year: here the Brahman and Vellalar mirasidar elite was concentrated; and here, too, there were few poligar families and little of the authority of these 'little kings' who were to be found elsewhere in the district. Even in the dry portions of Tinnevelly, where poligars were found, the conditions of cultivation differed from those found by Munro in the Ceded Districts and therefore did not fit his rules from the Ceded Districts. In 1827 Munro had complained that in Tinnevelly far too much power and authority had been conceded by British collectors to village leaders—headmen and accountants. If he knew to what

[125] *Peasant History in South India* (Princeton, N.J.: Princeton University Press, 1985), especially pp. 101–30.

[126] Ludden, *Peasant History*, table 6, p. 151.

extent these concessions were the condition for attaining and maintaining an acceptable level of revenue collections he did not say. But even with his complaints, then, the domination of such village heads remained unfettered, according to Ludden's findings, until money, markets, and urban commercial groups deeply penetrated the countryside around 1850. It was only then that these village magnates could be challenged.[127]

In the wet zone of Tinnevelly, nothing resembled the conditions assumed by Munro's ryotwar. It was here, as Ludden points out, that the reliable revenue was consistently raised, and it was here that the imposition of ryotwar rules—a fixed money assessment on specific, surveyed fields—confronted historic rights and privileges reaching back to Chola times, seven or eight centuries earlier. Unable to enforce the ryotwar rules without endangering revenue collections, British collectors were compelled to negotiate with mirasidar communities in the river valley, leaving mirasi rights intact in return for an agreed level of revenue paid to the Company. Given fluctuations in price and climate and the refusal of mirasidars to accept the risks of failure in a system of fixed, money taxes, British collectors agreed that variable payments in kind, depending on the season, would be accepted from the collective mirasidars of any riverine village. Despite Munro's expressed impatience, this continued to be the mode of revenue administration after his death, with minor variations. One of the latter was the so-called 'olungu' system which assuaged mirasidars' fears of loss of their privileges by leaving these intact while establishing a system of money-tax payments. Much of the old remained thereby, and the continuing negotiations and compromise between locally dominant landed groups and the officials of the Raj proved a workable system, but one which could not be called 'ryotwar'. Another twenty years were required after Munro's criticisms for the mirasidars of Tinnevelly to accept a kind of ryotwar; and this was only because new factors had entered the field of negotiations, and persuaded the wealthy holders of wet-lands and many large holders of dry lands to accommodate to the demands of the Raj.

The factors which altered all the old relations in some degree were what Ludden distinguishes as the 'hardware' of railways and telegraph and modern public engineering works on roads, ports and irrigation, and the software of 'ideas about bureaucratic management'. These constituted 'a nineteenth century watershed' for South India in the middle decades of the century, after which came changes in agricultural prices, production, government policies, and international trade. Ludden cites the work of E. B. Thomas, collector of Tinnevelly in the 1840s (and also past collector of Coimbatore, it may be recalled, when he prosecuted John Sullivan's sheristadar, Ramia). Thomas gained permission from the MBOR to replace older, regressive assessment schedules, and to improve roads and irrigation. He also resisted the ending of certain unique provisions of Tinnevelly revenue practice that gave agriculture there more flexibility than it would otherwise have had (e.g. the *nunjah-mel-punjah* rate

[127] Ibid., pp. 108–9.

which voided irrigation rates on many fields with some potential for irrigation unless watering of fields actually occurred). Thomas also resisted the demands of the MBOR to end inams enjoyed by village officers who, as Ludden shows, were holders of the best fields in Tinnevelly as they were in the Ceded Districts and in other places.[128]

By 1850 bureaucratic controls began to penetrate even this most southern part of the Presidency. The old hegemony of revenue officials and the MBOR was ended by specialists from other centrally directed departments: public works, police, forests and registration. All contributed to the fundamental changes evident in Tinnevelly during the last quarter of the century by amplifying the transformations that were occurring in the economy where cotton production led an intensification of commercialization, doubling in production every twenty years between 1830 and 1885.[129]

These various developments of the nineteenth century have been well recognized in Indian historiography for the past fifty years at a general level.[130] Some scholars have now begun to document the beginnings of both intensified commercialization and nascent bureaucratization in South India from an earlier time, around the 1740s.[131] Some awareness of these transforming forces may be noticed in the decade of Munro's death, during the governor-generalship of Lord William Bentinck, from 1828 to 1835, as a result of the Charter renewal discussions from 1831 to 1833.

That debate and investigation turned on two primary questions: whether the Company's monopoly of the China trade was to continue and what changes should be wrought in the governance of India. The first was easily resolved, thanks in part to Bentinck's rigorous economies while in Calcutta. One effect of this was that much less of the annual surplus of earnings from the China trade had to be used to meet Indian deficits than before, and thereby weakened the claim of the directors for the continuation of the China monopoly to meet Indian costs.[132] The ease with which the China monopoly was swept aside raised anxiety among the directors about what might happen to the administrative powers of the Company. This concern was eased by the Select Committee Reports of 1831–2, stating that the Company's administration of its Indian territories was of a high standard, not likely to be improved by direct Crown administration. Moreover, there was no greater disposition by politicians in 1833 than there had been in 1785—when the Fox Bill was debated—to

[128] Ibid., p. 116.

[129] Ibid., pp. 151 and 165 ff.

[130] See, Edward J. Thompson, *Rise and Fulfilment of British Rule in India* (London: Macmillan, 1934).

[131] Washbrook, 'Law, State and Agrarian Society in Colonial India', *Modern Asian Studies*, v. 15, no. 3 (1981), pp. 649–721; Frank Perlin, 'State Formation Reconsidered', pp. 415–81, and B. Stein, 'State Formation and Economy Reconsidered', pp. 387–415, both in *Modern Asian Studies*, v. 19 (1985).

[132] Philips, pp. 287–8.

determine how the Company's patronage was to be assimilated by British political institutions.

However, the directors had to accept a diminished role in Indian policy formation and implementation. They were told in 1832 that their numbers would have to be reduced, that their powers to recall governors, governors-general, and military commanders would be subject to the veto of the King, i.e. the ruling ministry and Board of Control, and that no appeals against rulings of the Board would be permitted. When these propositions were met with grumbles, the directors were warned by Charles Grant, president of the Board, that he and his cabinet colleagues were prepared to eliminate the Directorate altogether should they refuse the new dispensation. Grant did sweeten this somewhat by offering all proprietors of East India Company stock an annual dividend of 10.5 per cent charged against Indian revenues. When the Charter Bill was debated before a House of Commons still exhausted from the Parliamentary reforms of the preceding year, and thus indifferently attentive and attending, some changes were introduced to reduce the humiliation of the directors. But neither the Commons nor the British 'public' ever grasped how completely the determination of Indian policy had shifted from India House to the Board of Control, and how much of the stability and restraint which the directors historically worked on Indian policy was lost. C. H. Philips concluded his study of the Company with a strong appreciation of the 'Home Government' of the Company, from 1784 to 1834, saying, 'it performed its best and most beneficial work in ensuring that the system of district administration, as developed not in Bengal but in Madras, should become the characteristic mode of administration in India.'[133] For Philips it was the combination of the Court of Directors *and* the Board of Control that opened the way for the Munro system to capture the heights of Indian administration. Would not the radical transformation of the old 'home government', by effectively eliminating the Directorate from it, imperil the imperial order envisaged by Munro? Not if one considers that the Board had been Munro's most constant ally in London and, whatever the changes in London then, Bentinck's governor-generalship must ensure a smooth passage for Munro's measures and the vision that sustained them.

In fact Bentinck's stewardship in Calcutta presents mixed evidence on the last question. During his regime in India changes were introduced that were to guarantee that Munro's vision never attained greater substantiality in India. Thanks to the work of John Rosselli on Bentinck, the contradictory character of the latter's policies and purposes is now more clear than these ever were before.

Rosselli joined others in denying Eric Stokes' enveloping conception of Utilitarian dominance in early-nineteenth-century India, one which haphazardly clubbed together Munro, Bentinck, and others. The doctrine is seen to have made only a modest contribution to what happened in British India, and Rosselli

[133] Ibid., pp. 304 and 290–1.

shows this with regard to the way the controversy on land policy in the Gangetic territories of the Company was settled. The settlement of 1833 for what was called 'the Western Provinces' then (and what had been called 'the Ceded and Conquered Provinces' earlier) privileged a form of village tenure ('mahalwari').[134] Bentinck had long before agreed with James Mill that ryotwar was the original tenure of India and had fully adopted Munro's land-revenue notions when governor of Madras. However, when he faced the tasks of implementing a ryotwar settlement in the Western Provinces, the oldest doubts about ryotwar rose in his mind: whether British officials could ever know enough. This doubt became a retreat into the village mode of settlement.

The debt the Bentinck owed to Munro for many of the most important views on Indian governance is acknowledged by Rosselli; even so, however, it is understated. Through his writings from 1805, Munro laid the substantive as well as the rhetorical bases for ideas that were later adopted by Bentinck. Conceptions about Indian 'nationhood' and 'national character',[135] which Bentinck espoused, were first elaborated in Munro's minute of December 1824 on the state of the country and the condition of the people. The moral and pragmatic necessity for 'native agency' which Bentinck adopted was earlier argued by Munro.[136] The conception of a single, powerful, local, executive was not, as is often assumed, the influence of Utilitarian doctrine on either Bentinck or Munro, but more likely the military experience that both had had which Munro converted to civilian ends earlier than Bentinck in his advocacy of the 'principal collector'. Finally, there was the Munro-style judicial reforms which Bentinck had resisted when he was governor but which he adopted when governor-general.[137] In Bentinck, therefore, Munro's ideas had an active, well-supported, and highly sympathetic advocate, one who could have been counted upon to nourish the Munro imperial vision, just as Bentinck seemed to have been nourished by it.

By the closing years of Bentinck's governor-generalship it became obvious that there was another set of ideas to which Bentinck lent his support—if he did not pioneer—and these ideas and the forces entailed by them were opposed to Munro's conception of empire. They therefore help us to understand that conception better than we might otherwise.

Rosselli demonstrates Bentinck's impressive contributions to the capitalist development of India.[138] His views of the existing structure of capital mobilization and investment through managing agencies were critical of how these institutions fed the chaotic economic order under the Raj, and he believed that

[134] John Rosselli, 'Theory and Practice in North India', *IESHR*, v. 8, no. 2 (1971), pp. 139–45.

[135] John Rosselli, *Lord William Bentinck, the Making of a Liberal Imperialist* (London: Chatto and Windus, 1974), pp. 249ff.

[136] Ibid., pp. 202–3.

[137] Ibid., pp. 268–69.

[138] Ibid., pp. 277–95.

the remedy for this was a system of government banks to regulate currency and finance major capital schemes. While working for this he saw that he must support failing agencies by offering government loans in defiance of directors' bans against such rescue operations. He encouraged the introduction of European capital and entrepreneurship into Indian agriculture in, among other ways, by supporting indigo planters in their exploitation of Indian cultivators. He also laid the ground for the later alienation of government 'waste' land to capitalist production under full-blown capitalist plantation enterprises, using Indian wage-labour in the 1850s. Bentinck saw transport as a vital necessity for the increasingly centralized Raj that the 1833 Act contemplated, as well as for economic growth. He therefore resisted London's insistence for economies and the doubts of his friends, Metcalfe in Calcutta and Ravenshaw in London, and found resources to construct modern roads and bridges. Starved of funds for this, he resorted to lotteries and to the sale of historical assests such as the marble bath at the Agra fort. He strongly advocated private development of the Indian infrastructure, including the private developments of steam navigation on India's rivers as well as of its oceanic links to the east and to the west. Rosselli concludes his review of Bentinck's policies for economic growth by labelling them as 'dualist', that is in positing that in economies such as that of India there were two discrete sectors: one local and subsistence oriented, the other international and wholly commercial. But, as indigo was the premier capitalist cash crop of the time and as its profitability depended on what Rosselli concedes was forced labour in its production, Bentinck's willingness to condone such coercion makes as much of a nonsense of purported 'dualism' in India as that in the Javanese 'culture system', where the notion of dual economy was first coined.

India in Bentinck's time was opened to a deepened impact of and dependency upon British capitalism, then the world's most vigorous. In his 'humane' and 'liberal' way he was as much an empire-builder as Munro and Malcolm, but with the crucial difference from these two 'founders' that the shaping thrust of Bentinck's imperial order was economic and bureaucratic whereas that of Munro and Malcolm was political. Bentinck was a man of his nineteenth century; Munro and Malcolm were caught in an earlier paradigm whose form in India had been cast by Warren Hastings.

Rosselli convincingly disposes of the false trail to understanding that Stokes had offered with his Utilitarian argument that made Munro and Bentinck manifestations of the same causes:

> Bentinck, like many others, was no doubt influenced in a general way by the Utilitarian school ['a term at once fashionable and amorphous, rather like "Socialist" in the 1890s']. But the inner springs of his career were much more clearly his need for action, his Evangelical faith, his belief, never extinguished, in 'political liberty', his pursuit of economic development through modern technology, and perhaps most important, the vision of Indian nationhood under British guidance which he first began to shape in

the battlefields of Piedmont [from 1799 to 1801].[139]

The 'inner springs' driving Munro were more experiential than doctrinal, and his experiences were necessarily different from those of Bentinck, except in that both were soldiers. Rosselli shrewdly observes that Bentinck's propensity for administrative structures with 'a clear chain of command'—seemingly Utilitarian—was really 'taken over from Munro, not from Munro's paternalist ideology but from the military experience which he and Munro shared'.[140] We may set aside Rosselli's conventional imputation of paternalism to Munro and seek to specify what of Munro's experiences were important in forming his view of the works to be done in India, and how these were different from the view of Bentinck.

VISION OF EMPIRE

Munro was not an aristocrat like Bentinck, but a bourgeois whose young world had been devasted by the threat that he and his family might fall even lower in 'the gradations of society' of eighteenth-century Glasgow. This had driven him to India as a soldier and had kept him in India for nearly the whole of his adult life. There was no wealth, standing, or parliamentary seat to be inherited, as with Bentinck; there were only the dangers of a young soldier without connection, whose intelligence and effort might, with good luck, yield a respectable career and some material security. Career and conjuncture are thus important. These led to his becoming a civil official when his prospects in the army were frustratingly poor and when the rescue offered by Alexander Read was at last seized by him after the defeat of Tipu Sultan in 1792. There was also Cornwallis's wisdom, or prejudice, in supposing that the administration of the new territories gained from Mysore in the Baramahal was best undertaken by soldiers (as Bentinck also valued his 'military officials'). Good luck augmented this conjuncture in the person of the open and nurturant Alexander Read who made possible a new career for Munro and his military colleagues, William Macleod and James G. Graham.

But luck or career cannot account for the vision of empire Munro had fashioned and sketched in the concluding paragraphs of his minute of December 1824. For this vision of some future colonial regime to have been sustained, other explanations are required. He imagined an India governed by powerful statesmen whose minds and careers had been shaped in India, but whose authority was to derive from ministers of the British Crown. Munro and Malcolm both considered that the commercial, collegial structure of the East India Company was doomed, and both had long relied on the Board of Control for support as well as for authority to carry out their programmes and advance their careers. Crown rule, then, was a first condition for achieving the future that they saw. Delegation of royal authority to viceregal officials in India—like themselves—

[139] Ibid., pp. 322 and 324–25.

[140] Ibid., p. 323.

was a second condition. Together, these constituted the first principle of a British imperium. A second principle was that direct rule over all of India should be eschewed, even if it were possible to attain. India must constitute a whole and separate political sphere, made up of a system of states under the hegemony of British India.

In this there was not so much Burkean prescriptivism or nationalism as the idea that competing, independent states in India would produce a more efficient and enduring general political order than the total dominance of any single regime, even a British one. Munro reasoned in that way about the various, and as he saw them autonomous, parts of British India, each with its distinctive approaches to problems confronting it. He envisaged the whole of the subcontinent in a similar manner: various and perhaps differently constituted regimes experimenting with government in their diverse social, economic and historic settings, and all learning from the improvements of any. Moreover, he rejected to the very end the notion that the best ways were British or European. Rather, he assumed that the state-building process of his time must continue into the future, and he seemed to think that the Indian subcontinent could become a sphere of interacting states, just as Europe had been from the seventeenth century a self-contained political world.

It is important to recognize the difference between this view and three others: his own conception about political relations in the 1790s, when he presciently compared the regimes of Tipu Sultan and the Marathas; the imperial conception of Lord Wellesley in the late 1790s; and the conceptions of Lord Bentinck shortly after Munro's death, outlined above.

Tipu Sultan's Mysore state was seen by the young soldier Munro as a profound threat to the mere survival of the Company in the South. With a clear understanding of the tenuous British hold over a few scattered territories separated from each other by the weak client regime of the Nawab of Arcot, the young Munro could well see that Tipu Sultan strove to create a centralized and militarized administration and quested for new territories to add to his power. This Munro thought had resolutely and immediately to be opposed and the Mysore state destroyed. Behind this sense of what was necessary was a notion of balance of power among the various peninsular regimes, and Munro's criticism of extant British policy was that Mysore was the wrong state to depend upon against other opponents. The chief reason for this was Munro's perception that Mysore's mercantilist regime under Tipu Sultan was the same in form and purpose as the Company's regime, hence Mysore must be considered a dangerous enemy.

Lord Wellesley's drive for empire between 1797 and 1800 obliterated the balance of power strategy: his subsidiary alliances were intended to reduce all opponents to a feeble clientage, to the absolute hegemony of the British—just as it was his conception that a single, centralized authority should reduce the three centres of Company administration to his command.[141] The mature

[141] Edward Ingram, *Commitment to Empire; Prophesies of the Great Game in Asia* (Oxford: Clarendon Press, 1981).

Munro repudiated both of Wellesley's ideas: he rejected the emasculation of all Indian states through subsidiary clientage and of the Company presidencies to a single, unified authority in Calcutta.

Behind Munro's mature conception can be glimpsed the idea of an extensive territorial domain centring on India, but reaching northwards to Central and Western Asia and southwards to South-East Asia. A zone such as this is delineated in K. N. Chaudhuri's work on the Indian Ocean.[142] Conceptually at least, it appears to have modified the views of followers of the Eurocentric 'world-system' theorist Immanuel Wallerstein about whether India was a peripheral part of a European-dominated 'world system' that he sees from the sixteenth century, or alternatively whether it might have been a 'core-state' in its own right, as some of his followers appear to believe.[143] But was such a conception as Munro seemed to imagine an attainable objective? Was the vision that he and Malcolm shared utopian? It was not, if one considers the broadly similar pasts of Europe and India during the previous two centuries.

That India and Europe could have anything in common when viewed around 1820 may seem as strange to the contemporary reader as to most historians during the present century. An obstinately held fixture of Indian historiography is that Europe meant almost nothing to India before the middle of the eighteenth century, when it suddenly came to mean nearly everything. The long relationship of Europeans with India before the conquests of the eighteenth century is still given scant attention. This is a lapse of particular importance when considering the process of state formation over the entire eighteenth century and the crucial dependence of Indian regimes upon Europe then for the modern armaments they sought; for the commercial revenues from the international trade Europeans dominated; and for some of the administrative techniques that all new states of the subcontinent adopted.

State-building in the post-Mughal era involved practices which in contemporary Europe are called 'mercantilist'. Economic policies devised by the builders of Indian states can be seen to have been as different from previous Indian states as were those of European states from both their medieval precursors and their laissez faire successors. Following the canonical analysis of mercantilism of E. F. Heckscher,[144] it is possible to see that new policies were being formulated in India, as in Europe, by the compact states that were evolving in both societies

[142] K. N. Chaudhuri, *Trade and Civilization in the Indian Ocean; An Economic History from the Rise of Islam to 1750* (Cambridge: Cambridge University Press, 1985).

[143] I. Wallerstein, *The Modern World-System*, 2 vols (London: Academic Press 1976 and 1980); also Ravi Palat, *et al.*, 'The Incorporation and Peripheralization of South Asia, 1600–1950', *Review*, vol. x (Summer, 1986), pp. 171–208.

[144] E. F. Heckscher, *Mercantilism* (translated by M. Shapiro, London: George Allen & Unwin, 1934; original Swedish publication, 1931), 2 vols. Heckscher rightly insists on the distinction between 'economic policy'—the proper concern of 'mercantilism' and 'economic development', between what people thought and debated about with respect to political economy and what economic conditions were. This distinction is important if a concept such as 'mercantalism' is to be applied to India, for it should be

to replace earlier imperial sprawls. And within both Asian and European societies, by the eighteenth century, political unification as well as the intensification of state power was a common and a compelling end. The means for achieving that was to augment the wealth available to state power.

Of course none would now claim that a debate on the economic policies best calculated to increase state power was conducted in India similar to that in Europe, for there is no textual evidence of it. But that should not be construed to mean that there were no state-building economic policies in pre-colonial India. There were, and Munro was among the few of his generation of Britons who knew something of them, as he knew something of the European debate on economic policies. Yet, notwithstanding this knowledge, and quite unlike Bentinck, Munro was unaware of the powerful forces of European capitalist development that were even then engulfing the world and creating the conditions in which separate futures for such important places as India and China were impossible. Accepting this flaw, Munro's notion of a separate development for India violated neither his pragmatic nor principled approach to India's political future.

Munro's maturation as a statesman in the Ceded Districts was partly pragmatic—the coping with conditions he found there—and partly a precocious perception of how his pragmatism might be embedded in principles. The latter were formulated during his final two years in the Ceded Districts. Throughout, career and conjuncture set the framework of his experience. His percipient writings from 1805 to 1807, subsequently elaborated in London from 1813 and 1814, arose from the desire to make a reputation worthy of some distinction. This was conferred upon him by the adoption of many of his proposals by the Board of Control—through the efforts of the equally ambitious and impecunious James Cumming—and later by the directors, searching for retrenchable expenditures and some answers to growing criticisms of the Cornwallis scheme. How different the case of Bentinck, whose name brought him great office and a seat at the head of the table where agendas were set!

Distinctions of birth and class, and therefore opportunity, account for many of the differences between the notions that each held about India, even when at times their views seemed close. In the end, however, Munro's vision of a future India can no more be reconciled with Bentinck's than with Wellesley's earlier. For Bentinck, India was an arena for enacting ideas he had gained in Britain and Italy as well as in India. Munro had no such opportunities in Europe, and, in any case, he was dependent upon India for all of the virtue that was to be his. India was not a stage where personal principles could be translated into processes for Munro as it might have been for Bentinck. India was the play itself, and it was Munro's craft that enabled him to make all that he did of it.

He had arrived on the scene too late and too poor to expect the riches of a nabob, which was not then an appropriate ambition for poor cadets in the

---

recognized that Heckscher's 1931 classic is a text about policy texts, a study of what men debated.

Company's army. A lifetime of soldiering was the lot of men like Munro and many of his friends, such as John Malcolm. They could count themselves fortunate in the end to achieve enough rank and wealth to have a decent few years of retirement in a Britain they scarcely knew. India was in some sense all that they could know, and because some, like Munro, were intelligent and courageous as well as being ambitious men, they strove to know India well. Knowing India was the basis of the careers of men like Munro and Malcolm, their credentials for illustrious achievement, if there was to be any for them.

And certainly, Munro and Malcolm believed that India itself provided all of the elements for the construction of an imperial polity of their imagining. This would be one which took an Indian civil society, if not as given, then as capable of being transformed along a trajectory defined by its own historical traditions, as they saw them. Neither Munro nor Malcolm could have accepted, nor could have been driven by Bentinck's 'inner springs', especially by the latter's admiration of bureaucratic or councilate forms of governance in India. Bentinck after all had written to Henry St George Tucker in 1834 that 'It is quite unintelligible to me how in a *settled* and *regular* government, the pure monarchical principle, the institution of so many Anglo-Indian rajas, can be deemed preferable to a collective and deliberate Council' even if composed of 'native gentlemen'.[145] As time passed Munro as well as Malcolm had become more committed to the maintenance of those 'Anglo-Indian rajas', and the younger John Sullivan devoted most of his substantial writings on India after 1833 not to ryotwar but to the protection of just these 'Anglo-Indian rajas' and their princely states.[146] As to the economic development of India by modern technology, Munro certainly showed no awareness of the profound changes occurring in Britain as a result of steam power, and had long before, in 1813, dismissed the proposition that capitalist economic development could be any sort of engine for change in India. Finally, he, as well as Malcolm, opposed any important place in India for Evangelical influence—missionaries or anglicizers—and both also opposed greater direct political participation for Indians, as made clear in their arguments against Lord Hastings' liberalization of the press.

Munro's sense of the future British Raj was of a wholly other sort. Ryotwar and a judicature founded on Indian institutions, as he understood them, and on Indian personnel, provided the foundation for a reconstituting civil society. But the play of Indian traditional forms had to be directed by men like himself,

[145] Rosselli, *Bentinck*, pp. 322–4, and note no. 14, p. 374, citing a letter of 11 August 1834.

[146] Between 1850 and 1853 Sullivan published several pamphlets on this question; these are found among the collection of IOL *Tracts*, 'Two Letters on the Native States of India' (London, 1850), *Tract* 510; 'Are We Bound by Our Treaties?' (London, 1852), 'India under Native Rulers', 'A Letter to Sir John Hobhouse on the Impolicy of Destroying the Native States of India' (London, 1852), 'Second Letter to Sir John Hobhouse on the Right of the Princes and Chiefs of India to Adopt Successors' (London, 1850), *Tract* 559; and 'Plea for the Princes of India' (London, 1853), IOL: *Tract* 566.

knowledgable and sympathetic, with great and concentrated authority. Munro was never dismayed about the variability in his ryotwar and his judicial arrangements over the large and diverse Madras Presidency. He defended this against criticism, such as that of Joseph Hume, about the lack of uniformity in the Indian judicature in British India, on the grounds that there was actually considerable variability in the agrarian and social arrangements of the peninsula. Munro always assumed that there was a time, several centuries before, in the time of the Vijayanagara kingdom, when there was uniformity and stability in South Indian government and society. Such stability could be recaptured, but only if ryotwar and native judicial institutions were there. But what converted ryotwar from the necessary to the sufficient basis for a stable, reconstructed public order in India was Munro's (and, from him, Bentinck's) notions about powerful executives within a single command structure. This was not a bureaucratic structure of divided functions, but for Munro a segmentary structure in which governors, collectors and village headmen held the same kind of executive authority, but each over a smaller domain. Bentinck's notion of bureaucracy was different, and it was his more conventional, hierarchical notion that had come to prevail in India by mid century. It was to take a considerable time for Munro to be fitted to the status of godfather of an order so perverse to his own ideas about a future imperial order.

EMBLEM OF EMPIRE

Munro's emblematic stature has steadily increased in the century and a half since his death. Almost at once with his death, some writers on Indian affairs in Britain, like Empson, took his name as a metaphor for imperial benevolence and justice. In India, however, a status of imperial benefactor and hero came more slowly, and was not manifest until the end of the nineteenth century. Then, the imperial rulers had persuaded themselves, and many of their subjects, that all was well and all was right under the Crown's rule of the subcontinent. With perhaps more than a little wonder, these rulers of India sought to explain to fellow Britons as well as to Indians how this perfection, this jewel in Victoria's magnificent imperial crown, had been achieved. By that time, such explanations were wrapped in the hubris of an inevitable world empire and attended by the doctrine, passing as explanation, of Social Darwinism. Still, agency of a more human sort was wanted, and Munro was one of those fitted to the role of agent.

But all of this was later. Even at mid century, there was no inkling among Madras officials of Munro's towering emblematic future. James Dykes, the Salem collector whose writings were considered in the discussion of the Baramahal period, was a stalwart defender of ryotwar, but he insisted in 1853 that this was an invention of Alexander Read and that Munro was a reluctant, at times churlish, collaborator with a gift for phrase-making.[147]

[147] Another of Dykes' time was J. Bourdillon, a member of the MBOR and a revenue

Shortly after Dykes' Salem district manual of 1853—the first of that series of local monographs—came J. H. Nelson's *Madura Country*. Nelson, in 1868, proved no more generous to Munro, and he even offered another administrative hero in the person of Rous Peter, collector of Madurai district from 1812 to 1828, who was renowned in Madura town and its environs as 'Peter Pandya', just as Munro was known as 'father' of the people of the Ceded Districts.[148] Dykes, Nelson and other Madras officials modulated any enthusiasm that they might occasionally have expressed for Munro by insisting that his system required fundamental reform after his time, and that much of this was achieved by the 'scientific survey' commenced in Madras during 1855 and only completed in 1895.[149]

In the twenty-two district manuals which followed those of Dykes and Nelson, Munro is given an esteemed founder's role in those districts that comprised his old Ceded Districts: Bellary (the manual of John Kelsall in 1872) Cuddapah (J. D. B. Gribble, 1875), and Kurnool (N. Gopalakristnamah Chetty, 1886). In the South Arcot manual by J. H. Garstin, 1878, John Ravenshaw is accorded a similar, if less exalted place as 'founder', and in Sir F. A. Nicholson's Coimbatore manual of 1887 it is the younger John Sullivan. Least reverential was the Chingleput manual by S. C. Crole in 1879. Premier place is accorded to Lionel Place, Munro's most serious adversary around 1800, and Munro is not even mentioned in the discussion of ryotwar there—not even when the extinction of mirasi rights are traced, without regret, by Crole.[150]

The later series of district gazetteers for Madras Presidency carry on the tradition of the district manuals in honouring founders of the local administrations of each. Most of the district gazetteers were published between 1905 and 1917, yet Munro makes no substantial hagiographic gains: where he was venerated before, as in the old Ceded Districts districts, he holds his place; where he was neglected before, he continues to be so in these early-twentieth-century works. An exception comes from Salem, where the irreverence of Dykes in 1853 yields to F. J. Richard's 1918 edition of the *Salem Gazetteer*. Here, Munro's description of the simple, poor yeoman world of the Baramahal of the 1790s is approvingly and unembarrasingly cited by Richards as no different from rural life in twentieth-century Salem. Richards relates how Munro had sought to protect eighteenth-century weavers from the exploitation of Company commercial officials, and to protect inamdars from appropriation by revenue officials. He also discusses how he had encouraged the founda-

---

secretary to government. He had harsh words for ryotwar even then, and only grudgingly acknowledged Munro's contribution to whatever excellence the ryotwar method had. See his *Remarks on the Ryotwar System of Land Revenue as it Exists in the Presidency* (Madras: Pharoah and Co., 1853), especially pp. 11–15, 22–6, 33–4.

[148] *Madura Country* (Madras: Asylum Press, 1868), part IV, p. 83.

[149] For example, B. S. Baliga, 'Early Land Revenue Systems in Madras', written in 1937 and published in his *Studies in Madras Administration* (Madras: Government Press, 1960), v. 2, pp. 94–8.

[150] C. S. Crole, *Chingleput District Manual* (Madras: Asylum Press, 1879), pp. 276–303.

tion of schools, and how he had rescued the judiciary from the errors of Whitehall.[151] Reflected in this sort of change from an irreverent Dykes to Richards is that, by the turn of the twentieth century, new sources of critical comment about Indian conditions and policies were beginning to emerge which permitted Munro to achieve greater celebrity as an imperial symbol.

In the 1890s, when the empire was in the full flood of its confidence, there were also the first murmurings of defensiveness, and Munro was invoked to attest the humanity of British rule. In the first volume of a new (and new kind of) journal dedicated to the 'science of economics', an essay by a senior Madras official, who had been collector of Bellary, gave Munro credit for having saved Madras from the full horrors of the Bengal system. While governor, Munro perfected the ryotwar system he had long before invented, thus extending its great value until the 'scientific survey' of 1855 could be undertaken.[152]

Another context in which Munro was deployed was in the remarkable volume by S. Srinivasaraghavaiyangar recording the 'progress of the Madras Presidency' in the last half of the nineteenth century.[153] This was a work intended to refute criticisms that British rule had produced poverty everywhere in India; it was one of several defensive works planned by the viceregal council in 1887. Then, Sir C. E. Buck, secretary for revenue, circulated a confidential minute to Madras and other governments requesting each to answer 'recent allegations that the people of India suffer from a daily insufficiency of food', and requesting 'any information of a positive character' on the 'condition of the poorer classes of India'.[154] The unexpected sources of these allegations were reported to be such respected officials as Sir W. W. Hunter and Sir Charles Elliot. In 1890, Srinivasaraghavaiyanagar, the Inspector-General of Registration in Madras, was ordered by the Governor, Lord Connemara to produce the response from Madras, examining whether such criticisms were 'wholly untrue or partially untrue' during the previous fifty years.[155] A 685-page apologia of British administration was duly completed and its author awarded the CIE.[156]

[151] *Salem Gazeetteer*, v. 1, part 1, p. 241 and p. 260, part 2, pp. 83 and 86.

[152] *The Economic Journal*, v. 1, no. 3 (September 1891), 'Land Revenue in Madras', H. St S. A. Goodrich.

[153] *Memorandum on the Progress of the Madras Presidency During the Last Forty Years of British Administration* (Madras: Government Press, 1893).

[154] IOL, L/E/7/185, mss. minute by C. E. Buck, dated 19 November 1888, attached to which is a printed proceeding, no. 186 of the MBOR, 27 April 1888.

[155] In this order a circular from the Viceregal Council to all governments in British India is quoted, dated 17 August 1887: IOL, L/E/7/185.

[156] Obituary in the *Madras Mail* of 10 December 1904, p. 7, states that he was born in Tanjore in 1849 and attended college in Kumbakonam and the University of Madras, where he received a BA. He found employment as a clerk in the Tanjore district office where he was spotted by David Arbuthnott and brought to serve on the MBOR. In 1889 he was appointed as Inspector-General for Registration, the statistical collections of which he used in preparation of the *Memorandum*. For the latter work, he was awarded

Munro was used in this work in two ways to defend British rule under the Crown. One was the argument that Munro's compassionate proposals for reduction of land revenue assessments were consistently thwarted by the greed of the Court of Directors of the Company who sought rather to reduce the debt in India by remittances of £1 million annually than the misery of Indian cultivators. This was a cause of famines in the Ceded Districts and elsewhere in Madras in 1811–12 and 1824. When Munro became governor and was able to reduce revenue demands, it was then too late to avert the distress and famines of the later nineteenth century. The second way that Munro was used was in the argument that his measures to ameliorate the poverty of the 'poorer classes' were cruelly ignored by the Madras administration after his death, thus exacerbating poverty until the Crown control of India, by which time it was too late to prevent the later famines.[157] This defence of the Imperial Raj against its British critics required that the Company Raj—the directors and its Indian officials—be shown as uncaring, except for individuals like Munro. When this view of the causes of poverty were challenged in newspaper reviews of his monograph, Srinivasaraghavaiyangar adroitly extended his campaign of justification—and with that Munro's fame—to the English-language press.[158]

Other voices critical of the Raj also used the emblematic Munro. These included Indian critics, among whom R. C. Dutt was the most prominent. In 1900 Dutt sent a series of letters of the Viceroy, Lord Curzon, indicting some of the same policies of the Government of India as those of retired British ICS officials. Among these charges was that the devastating famines of the past thirty years were the result of poverty created by overassessments of land revenue and that ameliorative schemes of the government—better transport, more irrigation, and emigration of India's poor to other colonial possessions—were feeble. Once again, the Viceroy ordered the provincial governments to respond, and some of these were included in a government publication of 1902 on land-revenue policy.

Dutt's charges were answered by Madras, in part by challenging the latter's assertion that Munro's early ryotwar had been violated by Madras regimes after his death and that his early ryotwar should be restored as a means of achieving a more just revenue system. In answer, Madras sought to correct Dutt's reading of Munro so as to seize his symbolic authority back to the Raj, where it belonged. But, this effort came at a cost. For example, the Madras authorities denied Dutt's assertion that Munro in 1812 and after had held that assessments under ryotwar were permanent and that therefore later revisions violated the rights and just expectations of cultivators. This assertion was met by a mix of casuistry and fact: Munro, it was claimed, did not use the terms

a CIE in 1891, after which he served as Dewan to the Baroda durbar from 1896 to 1899, before returning to serve in the Madras Revenue and Registration Departments until his death.

[157] *Memorandum*, pp. 25–33.

[158] *The Madras Mail*, 7 and 9 February 1893.

'fixed' and 'permament' to mean unalterable. It was argued that Munro had said that the level of ryotwar assessments could be increased under state needs—what Hodgson had long before ridiculed as Munro's war levy.[159] The effort of the Madras authorities in 1902 was as plain as it was pained; they had not only to maintain Munro as a morally pure founder of the Madras system, but also to resist Munro's words being used to defame the successor imperial regime.

For imperial historians at this early point in the twentieth century, Munro, along with a few others, was invoked to demonstrate the welfare concerns of some, at least, of the Company period. P. E. Roberts in 1916 extolled Bentinck's commitment to 'the welfare of the subject people [as the] . . . main, perhaps the primary, duty of the British in India' and located that commitment first in Munro. In his evaluation of the Company Raj, Roberts saw the need to acknowledge the 'blunders' and 'political crimes' of the servants of the Company, but even so there were a handful of Britons who almost balanced all evils. These included Munro, and they 'were amongst the greatest Englishmen of their day'.[160] Nevertheless, contradiction appears again; the problems of the new imperial order created under Crown rule had to be displaced upon the earlier Company era. However, as the need to maintain the moral basis of the conquests of the Company era continued, the villainies of the Company had to be offset by early heroes such as Cornwallis, Bentinck, Munro, Thomason, and Metcalfe—Roberts' pantheon.

The relationship between the era of Company rule and Crown rule was reversed by nationalist historians of post-independence India. In one of the major assessments of the Imperial Raj by Indian historians of the Nehru epoch, the Bharatiya Vidya Bhavan's *History and Culture of the Indian People*, Munro is accorded considerable honour. His governorship, from 1820 to 1827, is seen to have been chiefly involved in expanding a compassionate ryotwar, which, by reducing the level of assessments and other improvements, mitigated the worst evils of agrarian poverty. Munro's death is seen to have ended all such reforms, and what followed was an era of oppression and distress unparalleled during the century. Therefore, Munro is seen by R. C. Majumdar and his colleagues to have provided some small relief from the general condemnation of the Victorian Raj.[161] Munro offered a conception of a possibly more humane and just imperialism, and this view was picked up by, among others, those who wrote the new series of Madras gazetteers of the 1960s. In these Munro's policies are seen as the benevolent calm before the full and terrible onslaught of late-nineteenth-century imperial oppression.[162]

[159] *Land Revenue policy of the Indian Government* (Calcutta: Government Press, by order of the Governor-General in Council, 1902), pp. 2 and 159–64.

[160] Roberts, part 1, pp. 385–6.

[161] Volume 9, *British Paramountcy and Indian Renaissance*, general editor R. C. Majumdar (Bombay: 1963), part 1, p. 366.

[162] In the Cuddapah district gazetteer, new series (1967), Munro on poligars,

Epithets such as 'paternalist' or 'romantic' that have been attached to Munro are no more relevant in characterizing him and his policies than 'Utilitarian'. They are vague metaphors. Munro's paternalism' is seen as his humane and caring rule, whether in the Ceded Districts collectorship or in the Presidency governorship. More literally, of course, it was in his being called 'father' of the people of the Ceded Districts, quoted with the same pride by the gazetteers of our time as by Graeme a century and a half ago. His 'romanticism' is even more vague: a purported preference for a 'natural' as opposed to 'established' or 'ancient' state of things, or a purported idealization of simple rural life, or a liking for pretty landscapes and verse.[163]

Labels such as these are no more helpful in understanding Munro than attempts to assimilate him to more specific doctrinal affinities, Utilitarian or even Burkean. Munro was ever diligent in his public and private writings to eschew such affiliations. Though he was often content to set his purposes within an eclectic and pragmatic frame, tenuously supported by unspecified historial precedents, there was an underlying vision of empire that was hopelessly flawed by a history that had moved beyond him and his time. His vision of an empire, like that of Warren Hastings, contemplated an India so distant from Britain, and so different, that it must have its own future, one that built upon a foundation of Indian institutions, cultures and peoples under the watchful hand of architects like himself. His was a world so large as to make an Indian future necessarily different from that of Britain and Europe; he did not grasp—because he did not know Europe—that another world had already been born, one in which Europe was to be the world because it would rule all beyond.

It is difficult and unwarranted to go beyond this. We may in the end be left with little that is more profound or penetrating on the influences that shaped the life of Thomas Munro than what he said to his mother at the outset of his career in India: 'I am a great Castle Builder and can't get it out of my head that I shall do something very grand. . . .'[164] What kind of grand castle might emerge he could not know in 1782, but he seems then or only shortly after to have understood that the grains of sand and the principles of architecture for the work had to be of Indian origin, and his own intelligence, courage and effort the sole means of its construction.

---

pp. 113–14; on land revenue demands, p. 498; on judicial reforms, pp. 529–30. In that of Salem (1967), pp. 78–9; and Coimbatore (1966), p. 526.

163 Beaglehole, p. 130, and more generally pp. 130–6.

164 MC, F/151/140, Munro to his mother, dated 9 April 1782.

Bibliography

ARCHIVAL AND OFFICIAL SOURCES

British Library, London

Burney Collection.

Hardwicke Papers.

Private Correspondence of Lord Macartney.

The Hamilton-Greville Papers.

Wellesley Papers.

County of Buckingham Record Office, Aylesbury: Hobart Papers.

Great Britain, Parliamentary Papers

House of Commons, Session 1810, vols. 6 and 7.

House of Commons, Session 1812–13, v. 7.

House of Commons, Session, 1831–32; Reports from Committees, v. 2, *East India Company Affairs.*

India Office Library and Records, Commonwealth Relations Office, London

Appendixes to Court Minutes; Copies of Dissents.

Are We Bound by Our Treaties; A Plea for the Princes of India, 1853. Tracts, no. 549.

The Asiatic Journal, 1831.

Atlas of the Company's Ceded Districts under the Presidency of Fort St George, Office of the Surveyor-General, Colin Mackenzie, 1 January 1820, Map Collection, no. W-IX-2.

Blair, W. T., *A Brief Report on the Entire Operations of the Inam Commission from Its Commencement, 30 October 1869.*

Board of Control, Letter Book, 1811–1815, F/2/3.

Board [of Control]'s Collections, F/4.

Brackenbury, C. F., *Madras District Gazetteers: Cuddapah*. Madras: Government Press, 1915.

Brief Notice of the Services of Mr Cumming, Late Head of the Revenue and Judicial Departments, in the Office of the Right Honourable Board of Commissioners of the Affairs in India. July 20, 1824. London: 1824.

Carfrae Manuscripts, E/225.

Catalogue of Manuscripts of European Languages, v. 1, *Mackenzie Collection*, part II, 'General', by James Sutherland Cotton, J. Charpentier and E. H. Johnston.

Charters and Treaties, Minutes of Evidence taken before the House of Lords . . . as relates to the Charter of the East India Company. London: Directors of the E.I.C., 1813.

Cornish, W. R., *Reports of the Nature of the Food of the Inhabitants of the Madras Presidency on the Dietaries of Prisoners in Zillah Jails*, Compiled Madras: 1863.

Court [of Directors] Minutes.

The Dispatches of Field Marshall The Duke of Wellington During His Various Campaigns in India . . . 1799 to 1818, 6 vols. London: 1834–9.

Dodwell, E. and J. S. Miles, *Alphabetical List of the Honourable East India Company's Madras Civil Servants from the Year 1780 to . . . 1839 . . .* London: Longman, Orme, Brown and Co., 1839.

East India Company Charters, Minutes of Evidence taken before the House of Lords . . . as relates to the Charter of the East India Company. London: Directors of the E.I.C., 1813.

East India Registry and Directory, 1800–30.

Elphinstone, W. F., Papers, F/89.

Hobart, Lord, Governor of Madras, 1794–98, Papers. Negative Microfilm, no. 4375.

Home Miscellaneous Series.

Madras Government Gazette.

Madras Military Proceedings, P/155/.

Malcolm, John, *A Letter from an Officer at Madras ('Captain John, later Sir John') to a Friend in that Service, Now in England . . . (on) the Late . . . Insurrection in the Indian Army*. London: Murray, 3d ed, 1810.

——, *Observations on Lt. Col. Malcolm's Publication Relative to the Disturbances in the Madras Army; Containing a Refutation of the Opinions of that Officer*. London: Black, Parry and Co., Booksellers to the Honourable East India Company, 1812.

Prinsep, C. C. *Record of Services of the Honourable East India Company's Civil Servants in the Madras Presidency from 1741 to 1858*. London: 1885.

Revenue/Judicial Despatches to Madras, E/4/.

Selection of Papers from the Records at the East-India House Relating to the Revenue, Police, and Civil and Criminal Justice Under the Company's Governments in India. 4 vols. London: Court of Directors, 1820 and 1826.

Selection of Records of the Madras Government. New (Revenue) Series, Number 1, 'A Collection of Papers Relative to the Inam Settlement in the Madras Presidency'. Madras: 1906.

Sullivan, J. 'Observations Respecting the Circar of Mazulipatam in a Letter . . . to the Court of Directors of the East Indian Company, 1780'.

Symonds Collection. C240/2a.

Madras Presidency, *Selections from the Records of Bellary District*. Bellary: Collectorate Press, 1870.

Madras Presidency, *Selections from the Records of the District of Cuddapah*, No. 1. Cuddapah: Collectorate Press, 1870.

Madras Presidency. J. W. D. Dykes, *The Ryotwar Tenure: Proposed Manual General Rules Declaratory and Explanatory of the Ryotwar Tenure 1858*. Salem: District Press.

Northumberland County Record Office, Newcastle-on-Tyne: *Letters of Thomas (Baron) Wallace*.

Tamilnadu Archives, Madras

Proceedings of the Board of Revenue, 'Settlement', 'Mr Place's Report on the Jaghire,' 6 October 1795.

Sullivan, J., *Report on the Ryotwari Settlement of the Coimbatore District*. Coimbatore: District Press, 1886.

University of Manchester, John Rylands Library: Melville Papers.

University of Nottingham, Library: Bentinck Papers.

SECONDARY WORKS

Allibone, S. A., *A Critical Dictionary of English Literature and British and American Authors* . . . Philadelphia: Childs and Peterson. 1854.

Arbuthnot, A. J., *Major General Sir Thomas Munro, Bart., Governor of Madras Selections of His Minutes and other Official Writings*. London: 1881.

Baliga, B. S., *Studies in Madras Administration*, 2 vols. Madras: India Press, 1960.

Ballhatchet, K., 'The Authors of the Fifth Report of 1812', *Notes and Queries*, v. 202 (November 1957), p. 477.

Beaglehole, T. H., *Thomas Munro and the Development of Administrative Policy in Madras, 1792–1818; The Origins of the 'Munro System*. Cambridge: Cambridge University Press, 1966.

Braudel, F., *Civilization and Capitalism, 15th–18th Century*. Translated by Sian Reynolds, 3 vols. London: Fontana Books, 1985.

Briggs, A., *The Age of Improvement, 1783–1867*. London: Longman, 1978.

Brown, C. P., ed., *Three Treaties on Mirasi Right by the Late Francis W. Ellis, AD 1817*. Madras: Christian Knowledge Society Press, 1852.

Buchanan (Hamilton), F., *Journey from Madras through the Countries of Mysore, Canara and Malabar, 1800–01*, 3 vols. London: Longman, 1811.

Burke's Genealogical and Heraldic History of the Peerage, Baronetage and Knightage. London: Burke's Peerage Ltd., 9th ed., 1949.

Caldwell, R., *A Political and General History of the Origin of Tinnevelly in the Presidency of Madras*. Madras: Government Press, 1881.

Chamier, C. F., *The Land Assessment and Landed Tenures of Canara*. Mangalore: German Mission Press, 1853.

Chitnis, K. N., *Kaladi Polity*. Dharwar: Karnatak University Press, 1974.

Cobban, A., *Edmund Burke and the Revolt Against the Eighteenth Century*. London: George Allen and Unwin, Ltd., 2nd edn., 1962.

Crisp, B., *The Mysorean Regulations, Translated from the Persian*. Calcutta: 1792.

Dictionary of National Bibliography. Eds. L. Stephen and S. Lee, 22 vols. London: Oxford University Press, 1917–.

Dirks, N. B., 'Terminology and Taxonomy; Discourse and Domination: From Old Regime to Colonial Regime in South India', in *Studies of South India*. Eds. Robert E. Frykenberg and Pauline Kolenda. Madras: New Era Publications, 1985.

———, *The Hollow Crown*. Cambridge: Cambridge University Press, 1987.

Dixon, P., *Canning; Politician and Statesman*. London: Weidenfeld and Nicolson, 1976.

Ellis, F. W., *Papers on Mirasi Right; Selected from the Records of Government and Published by Permission*. Compiled by W. H. Bayley of the Madras Board of Revenue. Madras: 1862.

———, *Replies to Seventeen Questions Proposed by the Madras Government of Fort St. George Relative to the Mirasi Right, with Two Appendicies*. Madras: 1818.

———, *Three Treaties on Mirasi Right by . . . Francis W. Ellis, Lt. Colonel Blackburne, Sir Thomas Munro*. Ed. by C. P. Brown, Madras Civil Service Madras: 1852.

Felton, F., *Thomas Love Peacock*. London: George Allen and Unwin, 1913.

Frykenberg, R. E., 'The Silent Settlement in South India, 1793–1853: An Analysis of the Role of Inams in the Rise of the Indian Imperial System', in R. E. Frykenberg, ed., *Land Tenure and Peasant in South Asia*. New Delhi: Orient Longman, 1977.

———, *Guntur District, 1788–1848; A History of Local Influence and Central Authority in South India*. Oxford: Clarendon Press, 1965.

Furness, W. F., *A New Variorum Edition of Shakespeare: The Merchant of Venice*. Philadelphia: J. B. Lippincott, 13th edn., 1888.

Gleig, G. R., *Thomas Munro, Bart. and K. C. B.*, 3 vols. London: Henry Colburn and Richard Bentley, 1830.

Gopal, M. H., *The Finances of the Mysore State, 1799–1831*. Calcutta: Orient Longman, 1960.

———, *Tipu Sultan's Mysore; An Economic Study*. Bombay: Popular Prakashan, 1971.

Greville, C. B., *British India Analyzed; The Provincial and Revenue Establishments of Tippoo Sultaun and of the Mahomedan and British Conquerors in Hindustan*, 3 vols. London: R. Faulder, 1795.

Guha, R., *A Rule of Property for Bengal: An Essay on the Idea of Permanent Settlement*. Paris: Mouton, 1963.

Gururaja Bhatt, P., *Studies in Tuluva History and Culture*. Manipal: 1975.

Habib, I., *An Atlas of the Mughal Empire*. Delhi: Oxford University Press, 1982.

Hamilton, W., *The East Indian Gazeteer; Containing Particular Descriptions of the Empires, Principalities . . . of Hindostan and the Adjacent Countries . . .* London: 1815.

Hill, S. C., *Yusuf Khan, the Rebel Commandant*. London: Longmans, Green, 1914.

Houghton, W. E., *The Wellesley Index to Victorian Periodicals*. London: Routledge and Kegan Paul, 1966.

Ingram, E., *Commitment to Empire: Prophesies of the Great Game in Asia, 1797–1800*. Oxford: Clarendon Press, 1981.

Karashima, N., *South Indian History and Society; Studies from Inscriptions, AD 850–1800*. Delhi: Oxford University Press, 1984.

Karashima N. and Y. Subbarayalu, *Studies in Socio-Cultural Change in Rural Villages in Tiruchirapalli District, Tamilnadu, India*. Tokyo: Institute for the Study of the Languages and Cultures of Asia and Africa: Monograph No. 1, 1980.

Kaye, J. W., *The Life and Correspondence of Major-General Sir John Malcolm, G. C. B.* London: Smith and Elder Co., 1856.

Liscomb, G., *The History and Antiquities of the County of Buckinghamshire*. London: Robins, 1847.

Ludden, David, *Peasant History in South India*. Princeton, New Jersey: Princeton University Press, 1985.

Lumsden, H., *The Records of the Trade Houses of Glasgow, AD 1713.1777*. Glasgow: Trades Houses of Glasgow, 1934.

Maclean, C. D., *Manual of Administration of the Madras Presidency* . . . 3 vols. [vol. 3, 'Glossary'] Madras: Government Press, 1893.

Mackenzie, W. C., *Colin Mackenzie: The First Surveyor-General of India*. Edinburgh: W. and R. Chambers, 1952.

Mahalingam, T. V., *South Indian Polity*. Madras: University of Madras, 1967.

Malcolm, J., *A Memoir of Central India*. London: Parbury, Allen, 1832.

———, *The Political History of India from 1784 to 1823*, 2 vols. London: John Murray, 1826.

Marshall, P., *The Writings and Speeches of Edmund Burke*, 5 vols. Oxford: Clarendon Press, 1980.

Melville, L., ed., *The Huskisson Papers*. London: Constable, 1931.

Millar, J., *The Origin of the Distinction of Ranks* . . . Edinburgh: 1806.

Mizushima, T., *Nattar and the Socio-Economic Change in South India in the 18th–19th Centuries*. Tokyo: Institute for the Study of Languages and Cultures of Asia and Africa; Monograph No. 19, 1986.

Morris, H., *The Life of Charles Grant*. London: John Murray, 1904.

Mukherjee N. and R. E. Frykenberg, 'The Ryotwari System and Social Organization in the Madras Presidency', in R. E. Frykenberg, *Land Control and Social Structure in Indian History*. Madison: University of Wisconsin Press, 1969.

Mukherjee, N., *The Ryotwari System in Madras, 1792–1827*. Calcutta: Firma K. L. Mukhopadhyay, 1962.

Murton, B., 'Key People in the Countryside: Decision-making in Interior Tamilnadu in the Late Eighteenth Century Countryside', *The Indian Social and Economic History Review*, v. 2, no. 2 (June 1973), pp. 3–17.

———, 'Mapping the Evidence of Money: Manufacturing, Trade, Markets and Revenue Farming in Salem and the Baramahal in the Eighteenth Century', Paper presented to the Annual South Asia Meeting, University of Wisconsin, November, 1984.

———, 'Territory, Social Structure, and Settlement Dynamics in Tamil Nadu before 1800 AD', *Pacific Viewpoint*, v. 17, no. 1, 1976, pp. 3–22.

———, 'Land and Class: Cultural, Social, and Biophysical Integration in Interior Tamilnadu in the Late Eightenth Century', in R. E. Frykenberg, ed., *Land Tenure and Peasant in South Asia*. New Delhi: Orient Longman, 1977.

New Statistical Account of Scotland, v. 6, 'Lanark'. Edinburgh: W. Blackwood, 1845.

Nilakanta Sastri, K. A., *The Colas*. Madras: University of Madras, 2nd edn., 1955.

Page, W., ed., *The Victorian History of the Counties of England; Buckinghamshire*. London: St Catherine Press, 1925.

Rajayyan, K., *South Indian Rebellion*. Mysore: Rao and Raghavan, 1968.

Ramesh, K. V., *A History of South Kanara, from the Earliest Times to the Fall of Vijayanagara*. Dharwar: Karnataka University, 1970.

Rao, V. D., 'Ajnapatra', *Journal of Indian History*, v. 8, 1929, pp. 83–105, 207–33; and v. 29, 1951, pp. 63–89.

Robert, B. L., 'Agrarian Organization and Resource Distribution in South India: Bellary District, 1800–1979'. Ph.D. thesis, Department of History, University of Wisconsin, 1982.

Roberts, P. E., *A Historical Geography of the British Dependencies*, v. 7, 'Part 1, History to the End of the East India Company'. Oxford: Clarendon Press, 1916.

Rosselli, John, *Lord William Bentinck: The Making of a Liberal Imperialist 1774–1839*. Berkeley, California: University of California Press, 1974.

Srinavasa Raghavaiyangar, S., *Memorandum of the Progress of the Madras Presidency during the Last Forty Years of British Administration*. Madras: Government Press, 1893.

Sircar, D. C., *Landlordism and Tenancy in Ancient and Medieval India as Revealed by Epigraphical Records*. Lucknow: University of Lucknow, 1969.

Sivakumar, S. S., 'Transformation of the Agrarian Economy of Tondaimandalam: 1760–1900', *Social Scientist* (Indian School of Social Science, Trivandrum), no. 70, pp. 18–39.

Stein, B., 'Idiom and Ideology in Early Nineteenth Century South India', in *Rural India: Land, Power and Society under British Rule*, ed. Peter Robb. London: Curzon Press, 1983.

———, 'Notes on "Peasant Insurgency" in Colonial Mysore', *South Asia Research* (School of Oriental and African Studies, London), v. 5, May 1985, pp. 11–27.

———, *Peasant State and Society in Medieval South India*. New Delhi: Oxford University Press, 1980.

———, *Vijayanagara*. Cambridge: Cambridge University Press, forthcoming.

Stevenson, J., *Popular Disturbances in England, 1700–1870*. London: Longman, 1979.

Sturrock, J., *Madras District Manuals, South Canara*. Madras: Asylum Press, 1894.

Subrahmanyam, S., 'Trade and the Regional Economy of South India, *c.* 1550 to 1650'. Unpublished doctoral thesis, Department of Economics, Delhi School of Economics, 1986.

Sullivan, J. (Jr.), 'Sketch of the Ryotwar System...', *Edinburgh Review*, v. 55, April 1832.

Sullivan, J. (Sr.), *Tracts Upon India; Written in the Years 1779, 1780, and 1788 with Subsequent Observations*. London: 1795.

Sundaraja Iyengar, S., *Land Tenures in the Madras Presidency*. Madras: Commercial Press, 1921.

Sutherland, L. S., *The East India Company in Eighteenth Century Politics*. Oxford: Clarendon Press, 1952.

Swaminathan, K. D., *The Nayakas of Ikkeri*. Madras Varadachary, 1957.

University of Madras. *Tamil Lexicon*, 6 vols. Madras: Madras Law Journal Press, 1934.

Venkasami Row, T., *A Manual of the District of Tanjore in the Madras Presidency*. Madras: Asylum Press, 1883.

Venkatasubba Sastri, K. N., *The Munro System of British Statesmanship in India*. Mysore: University of Mysore, 1939.

Wallerstein, I., *The Modern World-System*. 2 vols. London: Academic Press, 1976.

Warren Hastings' Letters to Sir John Macpherson, ed., H. Dodwell. London: Faber and Gwyer, n.d.

Washbrook, D. A., 'Law, State and Agrarian Society in Colonial India' *Modern Asian Studies*, v. 15 (1981).

Wilkis, M., *Historical Sketches of the South of India, In an Attempt to Trace the History of Mysoor*... 2 vols. Mysore: Government Press, original edition, 1810, reprinted with notes by Murray Hammick, 1930.

Wilson, H. H., *Glossary of Judicial and Revenue Terms*... London: W. H. Allen, 1855; reprint edition Delhi: Munshiram Manoharlal, 1968.

Wilson, W. J., *History of the Madras Army*. 6 vols. Madras: Government Press, 1883.

Wink, A. 'Land and Sovereignty in India under the Eighteenth-Century Maratha Svarajya'. Doctoral thesis, University of Leiden, 1984; book based on this published by Cambridge Univesity Press, 1986.

Index